WALES

PETER DRAGICEVICH
DAVID ATKINSON

WALES

LLANDUDNO p267

Victorian seaside resort turned stylish weekend-break destination

SNOWDONIA NATIONAL PARK p210

Rugged snowcapped peaks, sparkling lakes and rivers, and charm-infused villages

PEMBROKESHIRE COAST PATH p148

Wander one of Britain's most beautiful and dramatic stretches of coast

LEGEND

- Freeway
- Primary Road
- Secondary Road
- Tertiary Road
- Railway Line
- Airport

ELEVATION

- 1000m
- 700m
- 500m
- 300m
- 200m
- 100m
- 0

0   25 miles
0   50 km

Irish Sea

Liverpool Bay

Dee Estuary

To Birmingham (25mi)

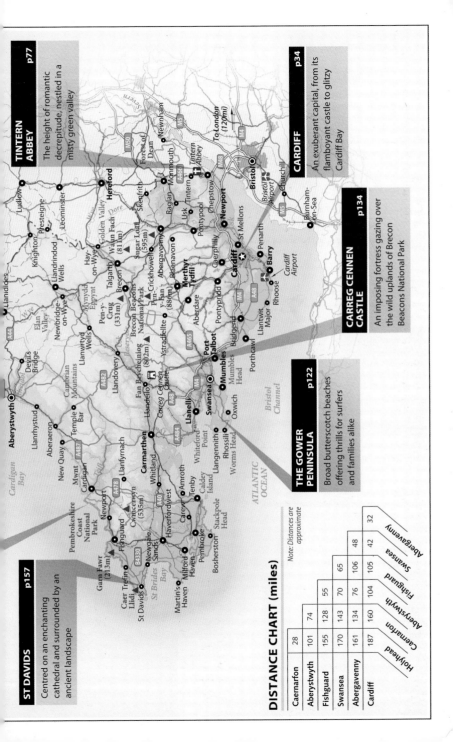

TINTERN ABBEY p77

The height of romantic decrepitude, nestled in a misty green valley

CARDIFF p34

An exuberant capital, from its flamboyant castle to glitzy Cardiff Bay

CARREG CENNEN CASTLE p134

An imposing fortress gazing over the wild uplands of Brecon Beacons National Park

ST DAVIDS p157

Centred on an enchanting cathedral and surrounded by an ancient landscape

THE GOWER PENINSULA p122

Broad butterscotch beaches offering thrills for surfers and families alike

DISTANCE CHART (miles)

Note: Distances are approximate

	Holyhead	Caernarfon	Aberystwyth	Fishguard	Swansea	Abergavenny
Caernarfon	28					
Aberystwyth	101	74				
Fishguard	155	128	55			
Swansea	170	143	70	65		
Abergavenny	161	134	76	106	48	
Cardiff	187	160	104	105	42	32

INTRODUCING
WALES

WHAT MAKES WALES SPECIAL? EASY. ITS CAPACITY FOR SELF-REINVENTION. THIS SMALL COUNTRY WITH A BIG PERSONALITY REMAINS A HOLIDAY HAVEN WHILE MOVING WITH THE TIMES.

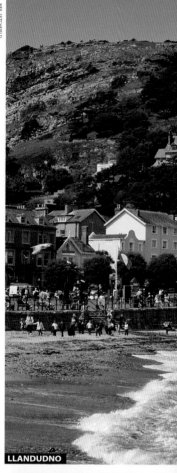

LLANDUDNO

They talk a lot in Wales about *hiraeth*. A typically Welsh word, it refers to a sense of longing for the green, green grass of home. Even if you're not from Wales, the sense of *hiraeth* will be with you from the first visit, only sated when you return. Such is the draw of this small but thrillingly diverse UK nation.

Wales has traditionally had an image problem: heavy industry, grey-slate towns, surly landladies hovering on the steps of floral B&Bs and greasy-spoon cafes with plastic tablecloths. But those stereotypes are history. Wales has been resurgent since the turn of the millennium. Devolution ensures the National (Welsh) Assembly now speaks for the nation, and Welsh culture today finds ever more forms of self-expression, cherishing its rich heritage and celebrating its contemporary voice.

That's why Wales gets under your skin, beckoning visitors with its friendly locals, fine food, remarkable landscapes, cultural draw, historic castles and green awareness. Truly the cornerstones of a country with its sights set firmly on a rosy future.

CARDIFF

TOP The wedding-cake architecture of the Llandudno waterfront (p267) **BOTTOM LEFT** Cross the drawbridge at Cardiff Castle (p42) **BOTTOM RIGHT** The butterscotch sweep of Rhossili Bay (p125) – watch out for the dragon!

THE GOWER PENINSULA

TINTERN ABBEY

SNOWDONIA NATIONAL PARK

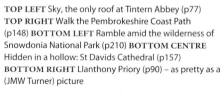

PEMBROKESHIRE COAST PATH

TOP LEFT Sky, the only roof at Tintern Abbey (p77)
TOP RIGHT Walk the Pembrokeshire Coast Path
(p148) **BOTTOM LEFT** Ramble amid the wilderness of
Snowdonia National Park (p210) **BOTTOM CENTRE**
Hidden in a hollow: St Davids Cathedral (p157)
BOTTOM RIGHT Llanthony Priory (p90) – as pretty as a
(JMW Turner) picture

ST DAVIDS

LLANTHONY PRIORY

GETTING STARTED

WHAT'S NEW?

- ★ Extensions of Snowdonia's Welsh Highland Railway (p245)

- ★ The Mawddach Way (p212), a long-distance footpath in Snowdonia

- ★ Unesco World Heritage status for Llangollen's Pontcysyllte Aqueduct (p275)

- ★ Three additional Michelin-starred restaurants (p318)

- ★ Hafod Eryri (p226), the striking visitor centre atop Snowdon

CLIMATE: CARDIFF

Average Max/Min

Temp

Rainfall

PRICE GUIDE

	BUDGET	MIDRANGE	TOP END
SLEEPING	<£60	£60-100	>£100
EATING	<£8	£8-16	>£16
ENTRANCE FEES	<£5	£5-10	>£10

TOP LEFT Italianate whimsy at Portmeirion (p246) **LEFT** Bilingual Wales (p367) **CENTRE RIGHT** Breach the walls at Caernarfon Castle (p233) **FAR RIGHT** Summit Mt Snowdon (p226), the highest peak in Wales

ACCOMMODATION

Wales has plenty of options for every budget – from funky camping yurts to cosy hideaway hotels. The mainstay of any visit, however, is the great Welsh B&B. And it's here that you will really enjoy a richer cultural experience, with family-run places offering warmth, hospitality and home-cooked food. The big new trend across Wales is the restaurant with rooms, combining boutique accommodation and locally sourced gourmet food. It highlights just how far Welsh hospitality has come in recent years. For more on accommodation, see p321.

MAIN POINTS OF ENTRY

HEATHROW AIRPORT (www.heathrowairport.com) The main international hub for Wales with a raft of global onward connections.

CARDIFF AIRPORT (www.tbicardiffairport.com) Regional air hub for the south with scheduled and charter flights across Europe.

FISHGUARD HARBOUR (Terminal Rd, Goodwick) This ferry terminal welcomes two to three car ferries a day from Rosslare in Ireland. Trains at the neighbouring station are timed to whisk arriving foot passengers on to Cardiff and beyond.

THINGS TO TAKE

★ Waterproofs for those summer showers

★ Lots of layers for climbing mountains, exploring coastal paths or city sightseeing

★ A good road map (satnav just doesn't get those country roads)

★ A taste for lamb and an appreciation of good cheese

★ An open mind to get away from tired old stereotypes

EOIN CLARKE

WEBLINKS

SEIZE THE DAYS (www.lonelyplanet.com/132days) Weekly updates on UK events.

TRAVELINE CYMRU (www.traveline-cymru.info) Essential public transport information.

VISIT WALES (www.visitwales.co.uk) Official resource for tourist information.

WALES 1000 THINGS (www.wales1000things.com) Inspiration for adventures.

WALESONLINE (www.walesonline.co.uk) News and views concerning Welsh life.

FESTIVALS & EVENTS

FEBRUARY/MARCH

SIX NATIONS CHAMPIONSHIP

CARDIFF

The highlight of the Welsh rugby calendar with the best action at Cardiff's Millennium Stadium (p51).

ST DAVID'S DAY CELEBRATIONS

March 1st honours Wales' patron saint.

MAY/JUNE

ST DAVIDS CATHEDRAL FESTIVAL

ST DAVIDS

Ten-day festival of classical music against the sublime cathedral backdrop (p157).

VICTORIAN EXTRAVAGANZA

LLANDUDNO

Victorian dress-ups over the May Day holiday weekend in the resort town (p270).

HAY FESTIVAL

HAY-ON-WYE

This ever-expanding festival of literature and the arts brings an intellectual influx to book-town Hay (p92).

JULY

INTERNATIONAL MUSICAL EISTEDDFOD

LLANGOLLEN

A week-long festival of international folk music, an eclectic fringe and big-name evening concerts at Llangollen's Royal International Pavilion (p277).

ROYAL WELSH AGRICULTURAL SHOW

BUILTH WELLS

Prize bullocks and local produce at Wales' biggest farm and livestock show at Builth's Royal Welsh Showground (p177).

CARDIFF FESTIVAL

CARDIFF

A summer-long festival taking in a food festival, cultural events and family fun at venues across the capital (p39).

AUGUST

NATIONAL EISTEDDFOD OF WALES

The largest celebration of native Welsh culture, steeped in history, pageantry and pomp (p296).

LEFT International Musical Eisteddfod at Llangollen (p277) **RIGHT** Big Weekend, part of the Cardiff Festival (p39)

BRECON JAZZ FESTIVAL

BRECON
Smoky sounds at one of Europe's leading jazz festivals (p100).

WORLD BOG SNORKELLING CHAMPIONSHIPS

LLANWRTYD WELLS
Scores of competitors converge on Britain's smallest town to submerge themselves in murky bog waters for the 110m swim and their five minutes of fame (p189).

SEPTEMBER

TENBY ARTS FESTIVAL

TENBY
A festival of autumnal music, literary and theatre events in the seaside town (p143).

ABERGAVENNY FOOD FESTIVAL

ABERGAVENNY
The mother of all food festivals and the champion of Wales' burgeoning food scene (p86). Essential stuff.

OCTOBER/NOVEMBER

DYLAN THOMAS FESTIVAL

SWANSEA
A celebration of the man's work with readings and events at Swansea's creative hub, the Dylan Thomas Centre (p119).

DECEMBER

CARDIFF WINTER WONDERLAND

CARDIFF
Festive fun for families at the heart of Cardiff's Civic Centre (p52).

CULTURE

WALES IN WORDS

SIXTEEN SHADES OF CRAZY (Rachel Trezise, 2010) Debut novel of the latest literary name to watch.

NEIGHBOURS FROM HELL (Mike Parker, 2007) Informed look at Anglo-Welsh rivalry.

SKIRRID HILL (Owen Sheers, 2005) Imagery-rich collection of poetry.

SHEEPSHAGGER (Niall Griffiths, 2002) Gritty fiction from lauded new voice.

ABERYSTWYTH MON AMOUR (Malcolm Pryce, 2001) Spoof detective story with a healthy dose of irony.

RAPE OF THE COUNTRY FAIR (Alexander Cordell, 1998) Powerful tale of family life.

WORK, SEX & RUGBY (Lewis Davies, 1993) Darkly comic take on Valleys life.

THE MABINOGION (Penguin Classics, 1976) Classic collection of folk tales.

WELSH LITERATURE

The Welsh literary movement is surprisingly rich with a clutch of standout tomes to better understand the evolving Welsh culture. An essential read, albeit by an English author, is George Borrow's *Wild Wales: Its People, Language and Scenery* (1862). The evocative and entertaining account of an 1854 walking tour of Wales makes for a fascinating historical record. Equally rich in the lyricism of its descriptions is Jan Morris' *Wales: Epic Views of a Small Country* (2000), a love letter to Wales from the celebrated globetrotter and world citizen, celebrating the origins of Welsh culture. But the best-known writer remains literary bad-boy Dylan Thomas, whose *Portrait of the Artist as a Young Dog* (1940) captures the lovely-ugly dichotomy of his Swansea home and evokes the stoic spirit of early-20th-century South Wales. For more, see p290.

TOP LEFT Llechwedd Slate Caverns (p223) **LEFT** Resting place of Wales' most famous writer (p128) **CENTRE RIGHT** Green Man Festival (p96) **FAR RIGHT** An eisteddfod: a modern take on an ancient tradition (p296)

TOP CULTURAL EVENTS

URDD NATIONAL EISTEDDFOD Europe's largest youth arts festival alternates between North and South Wales; late May/early June.

GREEN MAN Regarded as Wales' best music festival for its green policy and family-friendly site; August (p96).

CROISSANT NEUF SUMMER PARTY Child-friendly weekend festival of music and arts events; August.

DYLAN THOMAS FESTIVAL Annual celebration of literary Wales in Swansea; October/November (p119).

KATHY DEWITT / ALAMY

DON'T MISS EXPERIENCES

- ★ Opera – Catch a rousing performance at the Wales Millennium Centre, Cardiff (p49)

- ★ Fringe events – Try offbeat drama or dance at the Aberystwyth Arts Centre (p184)

- ★ Folk music – Tune up for a singalong session of traditional songs at the Ucheldre Kitchen, Holyhead (p259)

- ★ Male voice choirs – Witness the harmony of a traditional choir at the Hand Hotel, Llangollen (p278)

- ★ Drama – Avant-garde and Welsh-language productions, plus arthouse cinema, at Cardiff's edgiest arts venue, Chapter (p57)

- ★ Poetry readings – Welsh National Literature Promotion Agency Academi (www.academi. org) arranges literary evenings throughout Wales

TOP ALBUMS

MANIC STREET PREACHERS *Everything Must Go*

CATATONIA *Way Beyond Blue*

SUPER FURRY ANIMALS *Mwng*

GORKY'S ZYGOTIC MYNCI *Bwyd Time*

MAN *Endangered Species*

BUDGIE *Squawk*

THE ALARM *Strength*

Y CYRFF *Atalnod Llawn 1983-1992*

FFA COFFI *Pawb Am Byth*

Compiled by Spillers Records (p59), Cardiff

CULTURE

WALES ON FILM

THE EDGE OF LOVE (2008) The biopic of Dylan Thomas' tempestuous life focuses on a complicated love triangle.

HUMAN TRAFFIC (1999) The story of drug-fuelled hedonistic youth captured the late-Nineties zeitgeist.

TWIN TOWN (1997) Comedic exploration of urban decline set in Swansea, which launched the career of Rhys Ifans.

HOW GREEN WAS MY VALLEY (1941) John Ford's classic – a sentimental yet evocative look at the South Wales mining industry.

GALLERIES GALORE

The art gallery scene is exploding across Wales.

MOSTYN GALLERY Reopened after extensive refurbishment with galleries, events and cool photography exhibitions in the cafe (p270).

MOMA WALES Machynlleth's arts hub has one gallery for Welsh art and another for international works (p201).

ORIEL Y PARC St Davids' fantastic new tourist-office-cum-art-gallery showcases Pembrokeshire landscapes (p160).

ORIEL YNYS MÔN Home to the must-see Kyffin Williams collection (p260).

SCALA ARTS CENTRE (www.scalaprestatyn.co.uk) Prestatyn's brand new arts centre includes exhibitions to bring local history to life.

THE EISTEDDFOD

Nothing encapsulates Welsh culture like the eisteddfod – it's infused with a sense of Celtic history, drawing heavily on the Bardic tradition of verbal storytelling. The modern eisteddfod is the descendant of ancient tournaments in which poets and musicians competed for a seat of honour in the households of noblemen. The first recorded tournament dates from 1176, while the first modern-day eisteddfod was staged in Carmarthen in 1819. Today, the National Eisteddfod of Wales celebrates Welsh-language culture and is one of Europe's largest cultural events. Spin-off events are the International Musical Eisteddfod and the Urdd National Eisteddfod. For more, see p296.

LEFT The red dragon is an ancient and potent symbol of Wales (p312) RIGHT Conwy Castle (p264), one of the world's finest medieval castles

WELSH-LANGUAGE ARTS

The move to establish a stronger sense of cultural identity for Wales is attributed by many to the birth of Sianel Pedwar Cymru (S4C; Channel 4 Wales) in 1982. The dedicated Welsh-language TV station is credited with rejuvenating a threatened language, strengthening national identity and taking Wales to the world. The station is heavily subsidised and often criticised for broadcasting to a niche audience, but research shows it has done much to revive interest in the Welsh language. The long-running soap opera *Pobol y Cwm (People of the Valley)* is even transmitted with subtitles to the rest of Britain. BBC Radio Cymru also flies the flag for Welsh-language programming. For more, see p292.

TOP THEATRE VENUES

★ Catch big-name acts and Welsh productions at Venue Cymru, Llandudno (p272)

★ Soak up events, exhibitions and performances at Galeri Caernarfon (p235)

★ Don't miss the atmosphere of the converted-church venue, Cardiff's Norwegian Church Arts Centre (p51)

★ Theatre, dance, comedy and live music are all on the program at Swansea's Taliesin Arts Centre (p121)

★ For the best of local theatre, head to the recently reopened Theatr Twm o'r Nant, Denbigh (www.theatr-twm-or-nant.org.uk)

FOOD & DRINK

COOKING CLASS

COOKING WITH ANGELA GRAY (www.angelagray.co.uk) Tailored courses from the Welsh TV chef (p318) set in three fantastic period locations across North and South Wales, plus one-to-one and private group tuition.

DROVERS REST (p190) Private and group classes from dinner parties to Welsh game held at a charming Mid-Wales restaurant. Cook up then eat in.

DRYAD BUSHCRAFT (www.dryadbushcraft.co.uk) One-day Wilderness Gourmet course combines bushcraft with wild camping.

FUNGI FORAYS (www.fungiforays.co.uk) Mushroom hunting, preparation and cooking in Mid-Wales as part of weekend breaks in October.

THE CULINARY COTTAGE (www.theculinarycottage.co.uk) One-to five-day themed courses, plus the option to stay on-site near Abergavenny.

REGIONAL CUISINE

Wales has seen a food revolution in recent years, from the growth of farmers markets championing organic produce to the rise of the Welsh restaurant with rooms, and burgeoning awareness of the food-miles issue. Wales is today home to some of the most exciting young chefs in Great Britain, many embracing the idea of using only local and seasonal produce.

Of course, the country is blessed in that respect. Wales has an abundance of superb-quality regional produce and, despite the odds, has maintained an agricultural industry to handle it. Next-generation chefs are taking the basic ingredients of the Welsh larder – lamb, black beef, cheese, mussels and laver bread among others – and giving them a contemporary new spin. Wales never tasted so good.

For more, see (p316).

TOP LEFT Say cheese! Wales is famous for it (p317) **LEFT** Shane Hughes at Ynyshir Hall (p186) **CENTRE RIGHT** Laver bread (p317) – not bread at all! **FAR RIGHT** A traditional Welsh dish: *cawl* (p316)

TOP CHEFS

WALNUT TREE (www.thewalnuttreeinn.com) Shaun Hill's eatery remains the doyen of the food scene (p87).

HARDWICK (www.thehardwick.co.uk) Chef Stephen Terry has done great things for this gastropub with a twist (p87).

CROWN AT WHITEBROOK (www.crownatwhitebrook.co.uk) Head chef James Sommerin racks up the Michelin stars at this Monmouthshire restaurant with rooms (p78).

YNYSHIR HALL (www.ynyshirhall.co.uk) Shane Hughes is one of Wales' newly Michelin-starred chefs (p186).

FOODFOLIO / ALAMY

DON'T MISS EXPERIENCES

★ Farmers markets – Sniff out a local market such as Cardiff's Riverside Real Food Market for the pick of organic produce (p53)

★ Distillery tours – The return of Welsh whisky is celebrated with tours and tastings at the Penderyn Distillery (p102)

★ Real ale – Stock up on Snowdonia Ale at the Purple Moose Brewery, one of Wales' growing band of microbreweries (p247)

★ Cafe culture – Catch the sun, indulge in some people-watching and sip espresso at Cardiff's fashionable Mermaid Quay (p49)

★ Michelin stars – Wales now boasts four Michelin-starred eateries for fine-dining Welsh style; book ahead (p318)

LOCAL TREATS

★ *Bara brith* – rich, fruit tea-loaf

★ *Cawl* – hearty broth of meat and vegetables

★ Faggots – seasoned pork and liver meatballs served with peas and gravy

★ Laver bread – boiled sea-weed mixed with oatmeal and served with cockles or bacon for breakfast

★ Perl Las – the king of Welsh cheeses, blue yet with a subtle flavour

★ Sewin – wild sea trout

★ Welsh cakes – small, scone-like griddle cakes with fruit

FOOD & DRINK

FOOD BOOKS

FIRST CATCH YOUR PEACOCK (Bobby Freeman) Classic guide to Welsh food, combining proven recipes with cultural and social history.

FOOD WALES (Colin Press-dee) Encyclopaedic guide now with follow-up tome, *Food Wales A Second Helping*.

THE VERY BEST FLAVOURS OF WALES (Gilli Davies) Celebration of Welsh cookery with the qualified Cordon Bleu chef.

THE WELSH TABLE (Christine Smeeth) Simple, traditional Welsh dishes, kitchen anecdotes and words of wisdom.

REGIONAL TREATS

Our pick of the specialist food outlets in Wales.

ALBERT REES LTD (www.carmarthenham.co.uk) Delicious ham produced the farmhouse way; Carmarthen Market.

E ASHTON'S (www.ashtonfishmongers.co.uk) Fantastically fresh sea trout; Cardiff Central Market.

KIDMENOT (www.kidmenot.co.uk) Smooth and sweet goats' milk fudge made on the farm; Llandeilo.

PENARTH VINEYARD (www.penarthwines.co.uk) Fruity Welsh wines – try the Pinot Noir; Welshpool.

RHUG ESTATE FARM SHOP (www.rhug.co.uk) Slow-grown and grass-fed Welsh beef; Corwen.

TREALY FARM CHARCUTERIE (www.trealy.co.uk) Sausages made from traditional-breed pigs; Monmouthshire.

FARMERS MARKETS

The concept of farmers markets is booming in Wales with some 60 markets now working on a regular basis – more per capita than anywhere else in the UK. The leading light is Cardiff's Riverside Real Food Market, established in 2004 to bring regional food to the street markets and promote social regeneration. Ask at the local tourist office about the nearest market to visit. The National (Welsh) Assembly now even backs an initiative by local councils to let people order fresh seasonal produce online direct from producers and have it delivered to a designated collection point. See p316 for more.

TOP LEFT Take part in an old Welsh tradition: the pub (p317) **RIGHT** A foodie wave has broken on Wales, leaving behind a string of award-winning gastropubs and restaurants (p318)

CHEERS TO WALES

There's no need to go thirsty in Wales. A raft of local producers is championing microbrewery beers, ciders, wines and even whiskies. Some use traditional methods and maintain family recipes (try Upper House Farm in Monmouthshire for oak barrel–stored cider), while others are pioneering new methods and techniques (try the Penderyn Distillery near Brecon for Welsh whisky and a shiny new visitor centre). Real ale, too, is enjoying a revival with some 35 breweries now across Wales, including the Purple Moose Brewery in Porthmadog, winner of the Champion Beer of Wales. To sample the whole lot, catch the annual CAMRA Great Welsh Beer & Cider Festival held in Cardiff each July. Hic! See p317 for more.

FOOD FESTIVALS

Abergavenny is the cornerstone, but Wales' program of food festivals grows each year.

BIG CHEESE FESTIVAL Tastings and events in the shadow of Caerphilly Castle in July (p64).

CARDIFF INTERNATIONAL FOOD & DRINK FESTIVAL Showcase for Welsh produce in July (p52).

GWLEDD CONWY FEAST Traditional street market held in Conwy each October.

MOLD FOOD & DRINK FESTIVAL Food-themed activities each September.

PEMBROKESHIRE FISH WEEK Celebrates the fruits of the coast in June/July (p319).

OUTDOORS

GREEN SPACES

Wales has five Areas of Outstanding Natural Beauty (AONB).

ANGLESEY COAST Rocky coves, towering sea stacks and limestone cliffs for coastal walks make for a perfect, scenic escape from the crowds (p259).

LLŶN PENINSULA Rugged cliffs, beach coves and deserted beaches for an end-of-the-earth escape (p237).

CLWYDIAN RANGE A landscape of rolling green hills and upland moors for gentle hiking, it offers a breeding ground for the rare Black Grouse and is home to the iconic Jubilee Tower (p273).

GOWER PENINSULA Family-friendly beaches contrast with rugged coastal paths for serious hikers (p122).

WYE VALLEY A majestic riverside glen for walkers and canoeists to explore (p77).

THE WALES COAST PATH

The National (Welsh) Assembly is working on an ongoing project to link the whole of the Welsh coastline with the 850-mile Wales Coast Path. It is due for completion by 2012. The path, running from Queensferry to Chepstow, aims to improve access to the coast and when connected with the existing Offa's Dyke Path will enable ramblers to walk around the whole of the country. Large sections of the Welsh coastline already have long-distance coastal paths, notably the Isle of Anglesey Coastal Path (125 miles), the Llŷn Coastal Path (84 miles) and the Pembrokeshire Coast Path (186 miles). The newest section of coast path to open is the North Wales Coast Path (27 miles) from Prestatyn, Denbighshire, to the West Shore of Llandudno, Conwy.

TOP LEFT Sail at Abersoch (p241) **LEFT** Wales' rivers, lakes and coast are ideal for water sports (p303) **CENTRE RIGHT** Hike the Snowdon Horseshoe (p227) **FAR RIGHT** Surf the Atlantic breakers at Freshwater West (p150)

TOP WALKS

The three national trails are open to walkers, cyclists and horse riders, and are way-marked with an acorn symbol.

GLYNDŴR'S WAY (132 miles; www.nationaltrail.co.uk/glyndwrsway) Connecting sites associated with the rebellion led by Owain Glyndŵr in the early 15th century (p177).

OFFA'S DYKE PATH (177 miles; www.offas-dyke.co.uk) Skirting the Wales–England border through an astonishing range of scenery and vegetation (p195).

PEMBROKESHIRE COAST PATH (186 miles; www.pembrokeshirecoast.org.uk) Hugging the sea cliffs of the Pembrokeshire Coast National Park, this is one of the UK's most beautiful coastal walks (p148 and p158).

DON'T MISS EXPERIENCES

★ Birdwatching – Some of the best twitching in Wales can be found around South Stack in Holyhead (p258)

★ Ancient stones – The most mythology-rich are in Pembrokeshire's Preseli Hills (p170)

★ Footsteps of greatness – Explore the Taf Estuary around Laugharne (p128), the landscape that inspired Dylan Thomas

★ Industrial history – Follow the canal path from Llangollen to Trevor then take a boat trip over the Pontcysyllte Aqueduct for a World Heritage–inspired cruise (p274)

★ Wildlife encounters – Get close to grey seals, porpoises and dolphins on boat trips around Pembrokeshire's Skomer, Skokholm and Grassholm Islands (p155)

BEST BEACHES

CASWELL BAY Popular family beach for lazy days (p123).

CEMAES BAY Perfect for rock pooling and crabbing (p254).

LAUGHARNE A walkers' beach with historic connections to a literary giant (p128).

LLANDUDNO WEST SHORE Away from the crowds for pure ozone (p269).

TENBY Pembrokeshire's favourite family haunt (p139).

OUTDOORS

NATIONAL PARKS

SNOWDONIA (designated in 1951; www.eryri-npa.gov.uk) The North Wales stalwart is also home to the tallest mountain in England and Wales and is great for off-season walking (p210).

PEMBROKESHIRE COAST (designated in 1952; www.pcnpa.org. uk) Coastal walking plus boat trips to a scattering of nearby islands lends an ozone-blown frisson to a walk (p144).

BRECON BEACONS (designated in 1957; www.breconbeacons.org) A rural haven for flora and fauna amid the rugged landscape of the history-carved mountains (p88).

RESOURCES FOR WALKERS

MID-WALES & BRECON BEACONS (www. exploremidwales.com) Superb yomping country with the national park and twin national trails.

NORTH WALES BORDERLANDS (www.north walesborderlands.co.uk) Home to the Clwydian Range and trails around Llangollen.

PEMBROKESHIRE (www.visitpembrokeshire.com) Home to the must-visit coastal path and the lesser-known Preseli Hills.

SNOWDONIA MOUNTAINS & COAST (www. visitsnowdonia.gov.uk) North Wales' must-walk national park with a heritage-rich coast to boot.

WYE VALLEY & VALE OF USK (www.visitwye valley.com) Work up an appetite around food-loving Monmouthshire by walking peaceful valley trails.

CYCLING IN WALES

After walking, cycling is the most popular outdoor activity among visitors. There are 1197 miles of National Cycle Network, 331 miles of traffic-free rides and 11 cycle-hub destinations around the country, all of them chosen for their access to day-cycling routes and for their cycling infrastructure. Best of all, the variety of landscape ensures there are routes for all abilities, from easy-riding touring routes and day trips to serious mountain-biking circuits that test endurance and skill. Local cycling operators can advise on regional routes, while a handful also offer pan-Wales packages for a countryside adventure. Look out, too, for local cycling events and festivals. For more, see p302.

LEFT Wales has thousands of miles of cycling paths (p302) **RIGHT** Climb it, scramble on it, ride it, jump off it – coasteering (p163)

PLAYING GOLF IN WALES

The golf industry in Wales is booming with a slew of new facilities and infrastructure in recent years. But it was the staging of the highly prestigious Ryder Cup tournament at the Celtic Manor Resort in Newport, South Wales, in October 2010, which really cemented Wales' reputation as a golfing hub. Golf is not new to Wales, however. It may have taken 83 years to lure the Ryder Cup to the country, but the sport has been steadily attracting increasing numbers of visitors to Wales. The 200 well-crafted and scenery-rich golf courses take in snow-coated mountain valleys and wind-swept coastal stretches, while facilities at the 19th hole are increasingly open to all ages and abilities. For more, see p304.

FURTHER INFORMATION

* Blue Flag beaches (www.keepwalestidy.org) Guide to the best of Welsh beaches
* Fishing (www.fishing.visitwales.com) Essential details on the burgeoning Welsh game-fishing industry
* Golf (www.golfasitshouldbe.com) Wales boasts 200 courses and a Ryder Cup event
* Mountain biking (www.mbwales.com) Guide to Wales' biking centres and bases
* Walking (www.walking.visitwales.com) Swot up on 500 miles of National Trails
* Water sports (www.waleswatersports.co.uk) For all things wet and wild

FAMILY TRAVEL

TOP LODGINGS

ANGLESEY FARM STAYS (www.angleseyfarms.com) A group of farmstead guesthouses around the island for cosy, rural retreats.

BLUESTONE (www.bluestone wales.com) Wales' answer to Center Parcs has all the family bases covered and a greener take on short breaks.

FFYNNON (p339) Superb B&B combining child-friendly features with design-led style at the heart of Snowdonia.

VALE RESORT (www.vale-hotel. com) Voted the UK's Best Large Family Friendly Hotel at Hotel Excellence Awards 2010.

DON'T MISS EXPERIENCES

CENTRE FOR ALTERNATIVE TECHNOLOGY Educational, fun and truly green, CAT is great for curious kids (p203).

GREENWOOD FOREST PARK An all-day visit to keep kids busy with rides, activities and Wales' coolest roller coaster (p236).

ANGLESEY BEACHES From making sand-castles to licking ice creams, it's the classic family chill-out island (p254).

DOCTOR WHO UP CLOSE Don't hide behind the sofa. This exhibition charts the adventures of every family's favourite time lord (p50).

NATIONAL WATERFRONT MUSEUM For a hands-on family visit on a rainy day, Swansea's landmark museum is hard to beat (p117).

TRAVEL WITH CHILDREN

Wales is well geared towards family travel. Children are generally made to feel welcome at guesthouses and restaurants (including some of the more high-end establishments), facilities are uniformly good and there are discounts at many attractions for family tickets (typically two adults, two kids), plus under fives often go free. Public transport is easy to negotiate with buggies (strollers) and baby-changing facilities are widespread. So far so good. For parents, then, it's simply a case of some simple forward planning. Do call ahead to the B&B to ask for a child's bed in the room and don't be shy to enquire about bottle warmers. People are happy to help.

TOP RIGHT Under construction: the latest of Wales' many castles

CONTENTS

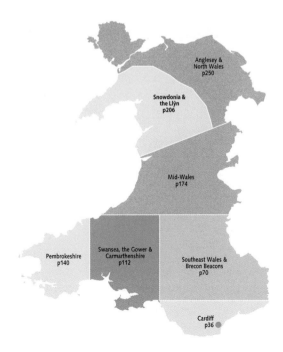

THE AUTHORS

PETER DRAGICEVICH

Coordinating Author, Itineraries, regional chapters (except Anglesey & North Wales), Accommodation, Transport

With over half a dragon in his surname, Peter has had a fascination with Wales ever since he was sent to write about Welsh castles for one of his first newspaper travel features. Since then he's coauthored 19 Lonely Planet titles, one of the most memorable of which was *Walking in Britain* where he got to trek around the entirety of the beautiful Pembrokeshire coast.

DAVID ATKINSON

Introducing Wales, Anglesey & North Wales, Background, Accommodation, Directory

Lapsed Welshman David Atkinson has been chasing the call of *hiraeth* for three editions of Lonely Planet's Wales now, focusing this time on the green, green grass of North Wales. David writes widely for newspapers and magazines, and blogs about travel around Northwest England and Wales at Hit the North (http://nowhitthenorth.wordpress.com).

LONELY PLANET AUTHORS

Why is our travel information the best in the world? It's simple: our authors are passionate, dedicated travellers. They don't take freebies in exchange for positive coverage so you can be sure the advice you're given is impartial. They travel widely to all the popular spots, and off the beaten track. They don't research using just the internet or phone. They discover new places not included in any other guidebook. They personally visit thousands of hotels, restaurants, palaces, trails, galleries, temples and more. They speak with dozens of locals every day to make sure you get the kind of insider knowledge only a local could tell you. They take pride in getting all the details right, and in telling it how it is. Think you can do it? Find out how at lonelyplanet.com.

ITINERARIES

THE FULL WELSH LOOP

TWO WEEKS // CARDIFF TO CHEPSTOW // 505 MILES

Start at modern **Cardiff** (p34) then cut through Glamorgan, Carmarthenshire and Pembrokeshire to ancient **St Davids** (p157). Continue up the coast to studenty **Aberystwyth** (p180) and then ecofriendly **Machynlleth** (p200), historic **Dolgellau** (p210) and

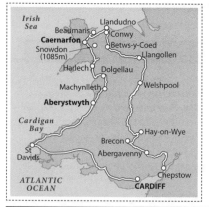

castle-dominated **Harlech** (p218). Drive alongside cloud-grazing **Snowdon** (1085m; p226) to more castles at **Caernarfon** (p232) and **Beaumaris** (p254). Proceed along the north coast to walled **Conwy** (p264) and beachy **Llandudno** (p267) before turning south to forest-dwelling **Betws-y-Coed** (p222). Head to genteel **Llangollen** (p272), stop at Powis Castle in **Welshpool** (p198), then continue on to book-loving **Hay-on-Wye** (p90). Call in at **Brecon** (p97) and food-focussed **Abergavenny** (p83), then skirt Monmouth and edge down the peaceful **Wye Valley** (p77) to **Chepstow** (p74).

SOUTH WALES CIRCUIT

10 DAYS // CARDIFF TO CHEPSTOW // 325 MILES

From rejuvenated **Cardiff** (p34) proceed through rejuvenating **Swansea** (p111) to the beach-lined **Gower Peninsula** (p122). Head back through Carmarthenshire and into Pembrokeshire, stopping at candy-striped **Tenby** (p139). Travel through **Pembroke**

(p150) and **Haverfordwest** (p153) en route to intriguing **St Davids** (p157). Continue through **Fishguard** (p165) to food-loving **Newport** (p168), then **Cardigan** (p178) and along the lush Teifi Valley. The Cambrian Mountains stand between here and lovely **Llandeilo** (p133), so cut south towards Carmarthen before heading east. Head on through **Llandovery** (p133) and on to **Brecon** (p97), then peaceful **Crickhowell** (p94) and **Abergavenny** (p83). Finish with a saunter down the Wye Valley, past romantic **Tintern Abbey** (p77), to **Chepstow** (p74).

NORTHERN EXPOSURE

10 DAYS // RUTHIN TO WELSHPOOL // 310 MILES

Start at historic **Ruthin** (p278) and cut down to charming **Llangollen** (p272). Go west to tree-shaded **Betws-y-Coed** (p222) for a taste of Snowdonia National Park before heading north to beach-loving **Llandudno** (p267). Continue through fortified **Conwy** (p264) to

Beaumaris Castle (p254) and circle the **Isle of Anglesey** (p254). Cross the Menai Strait and head up to **Snowdon** (1085m; p226) before cutting back to **Caernarfon Castle** (p233). Circle the remote **Llŷn Peninsula** (p237) and continue through **Porthmadog** (p244), **Harlech** (p218) and **Barmouth** (p216) before following the Mawddach Estuary to **Dolgellau** (p210). Head south to **Machynlleth** (p200) before rejoining the coast at buzzy **Aberystwyth** (p180). Stop at the **Devil's Bridge** (p187) waterfalls, market-centred **Newtown** (p196) and Welshpool's **Powis Castle** (p199).

STATION TO STATION

ONE TO TWO WEEKS // CHEPSTOW TO HOLYHEAD // 381 MILES

It's possible to zigzag your way through Wales by train, from its southeast to its northwest extremities. From **Chepstow** (p74) head to **Cardiff** (p34) and **Swansea** (p111). Take the Heart of Wales Line through **Llandeilo** (p133), **Llandovery** (p133),

Llanwrtyd Wells (p188), **Knighton** (p195) and on to Shrewsbury, before taking the Cambrian Line to **Welshpool** (p198), **Newtown** (p196) and **Machynlleth** (p200), then the Cambrian Coast Line to **Barmouth** (p216), **Harlech** (p218) and **Porthmadog** (p244). From here you can catch the Ffestiniog Railway to **Blaenau Ffestiniog** (p223), then continue on the Conwy Valley Line to **Betws-y-Coed** (p222) and Llandudno Junction, where the North Coast Line continues to **Conwy** (p264), **Bangor** (p261) and **Holyhead** (p256).

INDUSTRIAL HERITAGE

ONE WEEK // BLAENAVON TO LLANGOLLEN // 295 MILES

Trace the Industrial Revolution from ironworks to coal mines to slate mines, along with the railways, canals and bridges that connected them together. There's no more fitting place to start than the South Wales valleys. From **Blaenavon** (p104) head

through **Merthyr Tydfil** (p106) to the **Rhondda Heritage Park** (p108) and on to **Swansea** (p111). Stop at the **National Wool Museum** (p136) en route to **Machynlleth** (p200), where the Centre for Alternative Technology heralds a new era of green technology. Visit the slate mines at **Corris** (p204), **Blaenau Ffestiniog** (p223) and **Llanberis** (p230). Check out the famous **bridges across the Menai Strait** (p254) before heading to **Llangollen** (p272) and the World Heritage–listed **Pontcysyllte Aqueduct** (p275).

CASTLING THROUGH CYMRU

ONE WEEK // CHEPSTOW TO CONWY // 306 MILES

This itinerary only scratches the surface of Wales' preposterous preponderance of castles, yet it covers a good cross-section of styles, and the four that make up the Castles and Town Walls of King Edward in Gwynedd Unesco World Heritage Site. Start with

the oldest, **Chepstow Castle** (p74), then head to Cardiff for sturdy but beautiful **Caerphilly Castle** (p64), Disney-esque **Castell Coch** (p63) and **Cardiff Castle** (p42). Head northwest to the remote ramparts of **Carreg Cennen Castle** (p115) and then on to Welshpool for garden-draped **Powis Castle** (p199). Cross to the coast for the views from **Harlech Castle** (p218) and then north to domineering **Caernarfon Castle** (p233). Cross the Menai Strait to Anglesey for beautiful **Beaumaris Castle** (p254) and then back again for breathtaking **Conwy Castle** (p264).

WELSH CULTURAL ICONS

FIVE DAYS // ANGLESEY TO CARDIFF // 340 MILES

Start from **Anglesey** (p254), the Druids' island, and then head to the emblematic mountain of **Snowdon** (1085m; p226), with **Dinas Emrys** (p228) at its base, the mythical battleground of the red and white dragons. The Llŷn Peninsula has the **Welsh**

Language & Heritage Centre (p238); **Bardsey Island** (p240), the legendary resting place of Merlin; and **Llanystumdwy** (p243), birth and burial place of David Lloyd George. Head south to **Harlech** (p218) and **Machynlleth** (p200), both associated with Owain Glyndŵr; **Aberystwyth** (p180), seat of Welsh learning; and on to **St Davids** (p157), hometown of Wales' patron saint. Continue to **Cardiff** (p34), home of Welsh rugby, birthplace of Dame Shirley Bassey and the incubator of Welsh rock music.

CARDIFF

3 PERFECT DAYS

❦ DAY 1 // HIT THE CITY'S STREETS

Begin with the walking tour on p41. If you stop to explore Cardiff Castle (p42) and the National Museum Cardiff (p45), you'll quickly find that the day has disappeared. Enjoy lunch in Bute Park with picnic treats acquired at Cardiff Central Market (p58) or, if the weather's not cooperating, a meal at any of the reasonably priced central Cardiff eateries we've recommended (p53). Finish the day with a slap-up meal in the genteel northwestern suburbs (p54).

❦ DAY 2 // SPEND A DAY TIME-TRAVELLING

Spend the morning steeped in history at St Fagans National History Museum (p62), and if you've got wheels, continue into the countryside to delve into the prehistoric Tinkinswood and St Lythan's Burial Chambers (p62). If you're a *Gavin and Stacey* fan, continue down to Barry (p61). Head to Cardiff Bay: immerse yourself in forward-thinking architecture and get acquainted with Doctor Who Up Close (p50).

❦ DAY 3 // CATHEDRAL, CASTLE AND BAR-HOPPING

Head north to Llandaff Cathedral (p52) and discover the millennia of sacred art tucked into its medieval nooks. Continue on to Castell Coch (p63) to see what comes from having an overactive imagination and too much money. Head further north to Caerphilly Castle (p64); it may not have flamboyant interiors but it doesn't skimp on picturesque moats and battlements. For your last night in the capital, blast out the cobwebs in a live-music venue (p56).

INTRODUCING CARDIFF

☎ 029 / pop 324,800

Cool Cardiff. Contemporary Cardiff. Changing Cardiff. The Welsh capital labours under many sobriquets these days, but one thing's for sure: Cardiff feels very much alive. The capital of Wales since only 1955, the city has embraced its new role with vigour, emerging as one of Britain's leading urban centres in the 21st century. Post devolution, Cardiff has blossomed, redefining itself with a new cityscape, a creative buzz, a cultural renaissance and a vibrant nocturnal life that punches well above its weight for a city of its size.

The old Cardiff was shaped in the 19th century by the world's richest man – John Patrick Crichton-Stuart, third marquess of Bute – whose architectural legacy ranges from the colourful kitsch of Cardiff Castle to the neoclassical elegance of the Civic Centre. The 21st century has made its presence felt with the transformation of the sprawling docks that generated the Bute fortune into glitzy Cardiff Bay, centred on the futuristic flourishes of the Wales Millennium Centre.

However, it was the Romans that got the ball rolling. In AD 75 they built the fort where Cardiff Castle now stands. The name Cardiff probably derives from the Welsh Caer Tâf (Fort on the River Taff) or Caer Didi (Didius' Fort), referring to Roman general Aulus Didius. After the Romans left Britain the site remained unoccupied until the Norman Conquest. In 1093 a Norman knight named Robert Fitzhamon (conqueror of Glamorgan and later earl of Gloucester) built himself a castle here – the remains stand within the grounds of Cardiff Castle – and a small town grew up around it.

Both were damaged in a Welsh revolt in 1183 and the town was sacked in 1404 by Owain Glyndŵr during his ill-fated rebellion against English domination.

The first of the Tudor Acts of Union in 1536 put the English stamp on Cardiff and brought some stability. One of the few city-centre reminders of medieval Cardiff is St John's Church. But despite its importance as a port, market town and bishopric, only 1000 people were living here in 1801.

The city owes its present stature to iron and coal mining in the valleys to the north. Coal was first exported from Cardiff on a small scale as early as 1600. In 1794 the Bute family (see p40) – who owned much of the land from which Welsh coal was mined – built the Glamorganshire Canal for the shipment of iron from Merthyr Tydfil down to Cardiff.

In 1840 this was supplanted by the new Taff Vale Railway. A year earlier the second marquess of Bute had completed the first docks at Butetown, just south of Cardiff, getting the jump on other South Wales ports. By the time it dawned on everyone what immense reserves of coal there were in the valleys – setting off a kind of black gold-rush – the Butes were in a position to insist that it be shipped from Butetown. Cardiff was off and running.

The docklands expanded rapidly, the Butes grew staggeringly rich and the city boomed, its population mushrooming to 170,000 by the end of the 19th century and to 227,000 by 1931. A vast, multiracial workers' community known as Tiger Bay grew up in the harbourside area of Butetown. In 1905 Cardiff was officially designated a city, and a year later its elegant Civic Centre was inaugurated.

(Continued on page 40)

CARDIFF

CARDIFF

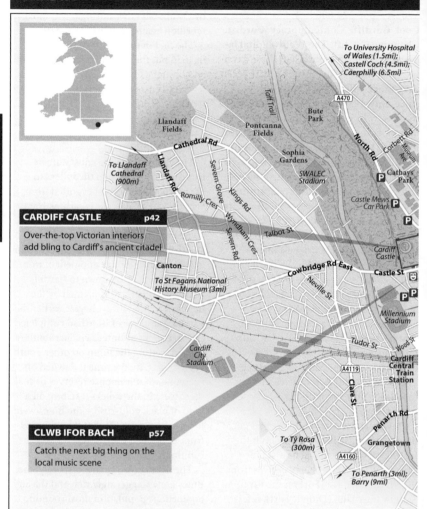

To University Hospital
of Wales (1.5mi);
Castell Coch (4.5mi);
Caerphilly (6.5mi)

A470

Taff Trail

Bute
Park

North Rd

Corbett Rd

Llandaff
Fields

Pontcanna
Fields

Cathedral Rd

Museum Ave

Sophia
Gardens

Cathays
Park

To Llandaff
Cathedral
(900m)

Llandaff Rd

SWALEC
Stadium

P

Romilly Cres

Severn Grove

Kings Rd

Castle Mews
Car Park

P

P

CARDIFF CASTLE   p42

Over-the-top Victorian interiors
add bling to Cardiff's ancient citadel

Wyndham Cres

Severn Rd

Talbot St

Cowbridge Rd East

Cardiff
Castle

Canton

To St Fagans National
History Museum (3mi)

Castle St

Neville St

P P

Millennium
Stadium

Tudor St

Wood St

Cardiff
City
Stadium

A4119

Cardiff
Central
Train
Station

Clare St

CLWB IFOR BACH   p57

Catch the next big thing on the
local music scene

To Tŷ Rosa
(300m)

Penarth Rd

Grangetown

A4160

To Penarth (3mi);
Barry (9mi)

PARKING

Cardiff shouldn't pose any particular challenges to anyone used to driving around a
reasonably large city. Apart from central Cardiff and Cardiff Bay, most street parking
is free; try Cathedral Rd for relatively handy spots. St David's has 2200 parking spaces
above the shopping centre, with an additional 550 below John Lewis. The main lot
is open 24 hours (per 2/12/24 hours £2/16/18), with free parking on Sundays and £1
overnight parking (5pm to 6am).

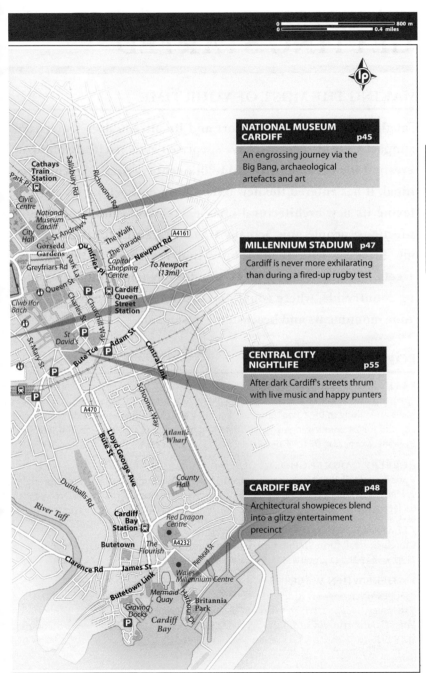

CARDIFF

NATIONAL MUSEUM CARDIFF p45

An engrossing journey via the Big Bang, archaeological artefacts and art

MILLENNIUM STADIUM p47

Cardiff is never more exhilarating than during a fired-up rugby test

CENTRAL CITY NIGHTLIFE p55

After dark Cardiff's streets thrum with live music and happy punters

CARDIFF BAY p48

Architectural showpieces blend into a glitzy entertainment precinct

CARDIFF GETTING STARTED

CARDIFF

MAKING THE MOST OF YOUR TIME

Caught between its ancient fort and its ultramodern waterfront, compact Cardiff seems to have surprised even itself with how interesting it's become. If its mid-20th-century decline seemed terminal, it has entered the new millennium pumped up on steroids, flexing its new architectural muscles. Its newfound confidence is infectious; people now actually travel *to* Cardiff for a good night out, bringing with them a buzz that reverberates through the streets. The city makes a great base for day trips to the surrounding countryside, where you'll find castles, Roman ruins, Neolithic stone monuments and beachside amusements.

TOP TOURS

CITY SIGHTSEEING
Open-top bus tours of the city, departing every 30 to 60 minutes from outside Cardiff Castle and taking in the Civic Centre, Cardiff Bay and the Millennium Stadium. Tickets are valid for 24 hours, and you can hop on and off at any of the stops. (☎ 2047 3432; www .city-sightseeing.com; adult/child £9/4; ☻ daily Feb-Oct, Sat & Sun only Nov-Jan)

CREEPY CARDIFF GHOST TOUR
A one-hour walking tour, departing from National Museum Cardiff, promising frights and laughs in equal doses. (☎ 07980 975135; www.creepycardiff.com; adult/child £5/4, minimum £40 if less than 10 bookings)

LLANDAFF GHOST TOUR
A torch-lit stroll through the ruins, lanes and graveyards of old Llandaff. (☎ 07538 878609; www.cardiffhistory.co.uk; tours £5; ☻ 7.30pm Thu & Sat)

WHERE WHEN WALES
Operates seven one-day itineraries, heading as far afield as Pembrokeshire and the Wye Valley. *Valleys Heritage* takes in Castell Coch, Caerphilly and Big Pit, while *Wales Capital* cruises Cardiff Bay, explores St Fagans and tours Millennium Stadium. (☎ 01633-869700; www.wherewhenwales.com; adult/child £45/40)

GETTING AWAY FROM IT ALL

* **Taff Trail** Following canal towpaths, country lanes and disused railway routes, the 55-mile Taff Trail walking and cycling route connects Cardiff's Mermaid Quay with Brecon, passing Castell Coch and Merthyr Tydfil on the way. Pick up a free map from the visitor centre. Starting from Brecon will ensure more downhill runs.

* **Castell Coch** These dreamy turrets peer out from a secluded wooded hillside (p63).

* **Bute Park** Back to nature in the middle of the city in this large, leafy park (p45).

* **Tinkinswood & St Lythan's Burial Chambers** Explore fairy castles secluded in the Glamorgan countryside (p62).

ADVANCE PLANNING

* **Six Nations** (www.rbs6nations.com) The city gets booked out for Wales' matches in the premier European rugby championship, every February and March.

* **Cardiff Festival** (www.cardiff-festival.com) Runs throughout summer, from July to early September. Includes Welsh Proms (two weeks of classical concerts at St David's Hall); Big Weekend (funfair, bands and the Lord Mayor's parade); Cardiff Comedy Festival; Cardiff International Food & Drink Festival; Grand Medieval Melee; lesbian and gay Mardi Gras; National Classic Car & Motor Boat Rally; Everyman Summer Theatre Festival; and lots of crazy one-offs (p51).

* **Great British Cheese Festival** Brush shoulders with the big cheeses in Cardiff Castle, late September (p52).

TOP EATS

* **WOODS BAR & BRASSERIE**
Excellent food, stylish surrounds and a great position on Cardiff Bay (p54).

* **LE GALLOIS**
Wales meets France off the rugby field and they get on very well (p55).

* **CAMEO CLUB & BISTRO**
Artsy and exclusive, but relaxed at the same time (p54).

* **GARÇON!**
A traditional French brasserie beamed directly into Cardiff Bay (p53).

* **BRAVA**
Our favourite brunch spot: good coffee, tasty food and a buzzy atmosphere (p54).

RESOURCES

* **Visit Cardiff** (www.visitcardiff.com) Cardiff's official tourism website.

* **Visit Caerphilly** (www.visitcaerphilly.com) Caerphilly's version of the above.

* **Visit the Vale** (www.visitthevale.com) Ditto, for the Vale of Glamorgan.

* **Cardiff Council** (www.cardiff.gov.uk) Has useful information for cyclists and public transport users, as well as events.

* **Newport City Council** (www.newport.gov.uk/tourism) Lots of visitor information.

(Continued from page 35)

The city's wealth and its hold on the coal trade persuaded Captain Robert Scott to launch his ill-fated expedition to the South Pole from here in 1910. In 1913 Cardiff became the world's top coal port, exporting some 13 million tonnes of the stuff.

But the post-WWI slump in the coal trade and the Great Depression of the 1930s slowed this expansion. The city was badly damaged by WWII bombing, which claimed over 350 lives. Shortly afterwards the coal industry was nationalised, which led to the Butes packing their bags and leaving town in 1947, donating the castle and all their land to the city.

Wales had no official capital and the need for one was seen as an important focus for Welsh nationhood. Cardiff had the advantage of being Wales' biggest city and boasting the architectural riches of the Civic Centre. It was proclaimed the first ever capital of Wales in 1955, chosen via a ballot of the members of the Welsh authorities. Cardiff received 36 votes to Caernarfon's 11 and Aberystwyth's four.

ESSENTIAL INFORMATION

EMERGENCIES // Police (☎ 2022 2111; King Edward VII Ave) **University Hospital of Wales** (☎ 2074 7747; Heath Park) Two miles north of the Civic Centre, with an accident and emergency department.
TOURIST OFFICES // Cardiff Bay Visitor Centre (Map p48; ☎ 2087 7927; The Tube, Harbour Dr; 🕙 10am-6pm) **Cardiff tourist office** (Map p44; ☎ 2087 3573; www.visitcardiff.com; Old Library, The Hayes; 🕙 9.30am-5.30pm Mon-Sat, 10am-4pm Sun)

ORIENTATION

Cardiff city centre is a compact area on the east bank of the River Taff, stretching

THE BEAUT BUTES

The Butes, an aristocratic Scottish family related to the Stuart monarchy, arrived in Cardiff in 1766 in the shape of John, Lord Mountstuart, who had served briefly as prime minister under King George I. He married a local heiress, Charlotte Jane Windsor, acquiring vast estates and mineral rights in South Wales in the process.

Their grandson, the second marquess of Bute, grew fabulously wealthy from coal mining and then in 1839 gambled his fortune to create the first docks at Cardiff. The gamble paid off. The coal-export business boomed, and his son, John Patrick Crichton-Stuart, the third marquess of Bute, became one of the richest people on the planet. He was not your conventional Victorian aristocrat; an intense, scholarly man with a passion for history, architecture, ritual and religion (Catholic), he neither hunted nor fished but instead supported the antivivisection movement and campaigned for a woman's right to a university education.

The Butes had interests all over Britain and never spent more than about six weeks at a time in Cardiff. By the end of WWII they had sold or given away all their Cardiff assets, the fifth marquess gifting Cardiff Castle and Bute Park to the city in 1947. The present marquess, the seventh, lives in the family seat at Mount Stuart House on the Isle of Bute in Scotland's Firth of Clyde; another maverick, he's better known as Johnny Dumfries, the former Formula One racing driver.

CARDIFF ACCOMMODATION

Being the capital, Cardiff has Wales' broadest range of accommodation, including luxury hotels, personable guesthouses and the country's best hostels. If you get stuck, the tourist office can help you find a room for a small fee.

The central city has the best of the budget and the upmarket accommodation, and it's the perfect locale if you're planning a few nights on the tiles. Long, leafy Cathedral Rd is lined with midrange accommodation, nearly all of it in restored Victorian town houses. Parking is usually good and it's only a 15- to 20-minute walk from the centre, or a £6 taxi ride from the train or bus station.

Hostels have slightly higher rates on the weekends while business-oriented hotels tend to drop theirs, but it totally depends on what's occurring. It can be almost impossible to find a bed anywhere near the city on big sporting weekends, especially rugby internationals, so keep an eye on the fixtures and choose another date or book well in advance. It's sometimes so bad that hotels as far away as Swansea get swamped with the overflow.

A Space in the City (☎ 0845 260 7050; www.aspaceinthecity.co.uk) is an agency that lets out luxury, short-stay apartments in the city centre and at Cardiff Bay; rates begin at around £90 a night for a one-bedroom flat and there's a minimum two-night stay.

These are our top accommodation picks:

* **NosDa Budget Hotel** (p324) Upmarket hostel right by the river.

* **Park Plaza** (p324) Cardiff's best top-end hotel.

* **Parc Hotel** (p324) Central hotel with midrange rates.

* **Jolyons Boutique Hotel** (p324) Stylish and personable, in Cardiff Bay.

* **Tŷ Rosa** (p325) Well-run, hospitable, gay-friendly B&B.

south from Cardiff Castle for 500m to Cardiff Central train station and bus station, and from the vast Millennium Stadium east to Cardiff Queen Street station. The tourist office is bang in the centre on the Hayes.

Bute Park stretches north from the castle. To its east lie the government and university buildings of Civic Centre and the student suburb of Cathays. To its west, along Cathedral Rd, are the leafy upmarket suburbs of Pontcanna and Canton, filled with good-value guesthouses and B&Bs.

The redeveloped dockland area of Cardiff Bay lies a mile south of the city centre, through Butetown.

WALKING TOUR

Distance: 1.5 miles
Duration: one hour

Start from **Cardiff Bridge (1)** on Castle St, head east towards Cardiff Castle on the north side of the street, and take a look at the creatures perched on top of the **Animal Wall (2; p45)**. Originally by the castle's south gate, the animals were moved here after WWI. Turn right on Womanby St, which is lined with warehouses. 'Womanby' has Viking roots and possibly means 'the strangers' quarter' or 'quarter of the keeper of the hounds'. As you head down the street the **Millennium Stadium (3; p47)** will come into view on your right.

CARDIFF

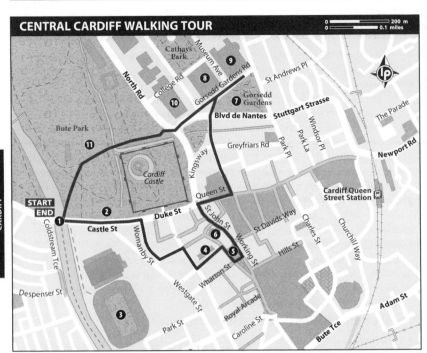

CENTRAL CARDIFF WALKING TOUR

Take a left on Quay St, then right on High St and left again to enter **Cardiff Central Market** (**4**, p58) – this cast-iron market hall has been selling fresh produce and hardware since 1891. There's an old market office and a clock tower in the centre. Exit on the far side on Trinity St; across the street to your right is the Old Library, which houses the tourist office and the **Cardiff Story** (**5**; p47). The south facade features figures representing calligraphy, literature, printing, rhetoric and study.

Go left around the Old Library and then north on Working St towards the castle, past **St John's Church** (**6**; p47). When you reach the junction with Queen St turn right, then left into the Friary. Continue under Blvd de Nantes (named after one of Cardiff's twin towns) to leafy **Gorsedd Gardens** (**7**).

Looming over the gardens are the grand **City Hall (8)**, **National Museum Cardiff (9**; p45) and the **Law Courts (10)**. Take the underpass under busy North Rd to enter **Bute Park (11**; p45), where you can circle behind the castle to your starting point.

EXPLORING CARDIFF

CENTRAL CARDIFF

❧ **CARDIFF CASTLE //**
A MESMERISING MISHMASH OF HISTORY AND WHIMSICAL FANTASY
The grafting of Victorian mock-Gothic extravagance onto Cardiff's most important historical relics makes **Cardiff Castle** (Map p44; ☎ 2087 8100; www.cardiffcastle. com; Castle St; adult/child £8.95/6.35, incl guided tour £11.95/8.50; ☼ 9am-6pm Mar-Oct, 9am-5pm Nov-Feb), quite rightly, the city's leading attraction.

Until it was donated to the city in 1947, this was the private domain of the Butes, the family who transformed Cardiff from a small town into the world's biggest coal port.

It's far from a traditional Welsh castle, more a collection of disparate castles scattered around a central green, encompassing practically the whole history of Cardiff. The most conventional castle-y bits are the 12th-century motte-and-bailey **Norman keep** at its centre and the 13th-century **Black Tower** that forms the entrance gate.

A house was built here in the 1420s by the earl of Warwick and was extended in the 17th century by the Herbert family (the earls of Pembroke), but by the time the Butes acquired it a century later it had fallen into disrepair. The first marquess of Bute hired architect Henry Holland and Holland's father-in-law, the famous landscape-architect Lancelot 'Capability' Brown, to get the house and grounds into shape.

It was only in the 19th century that it was discovered that the Normans had built their fortifications on top of the original 1st century Roman fort. The high walls that surround the castle now are largely a Victorian reproduction of the 3rd-century 3m-thick Roman walls. A line of red bricks, clearly visible from the city frontage, marks the point where the original Roman section ends and the reconstruction commences.

Also from the 19th century are the towers and turrets on the west side, dominated by the colourful 40m **clock tower**. This faux-Gothic extravaganza was dreamed up by the mind-bendingly rich third marquess of Bute and his architect William Burges, a passionate eccentric who used to dress in medieval costume and was often seen with a parrot on his shoulder. Both were obsessed with Gothic architecture, religious symbolism and astrology, influences that were incorporated into the designs both here and at the Butes' second home at Castell Coch.

A 50-minute guided tour takes you through the interiors of this flamboyant fantasy world, from the **winter smoking room**, with decor reflecting the seasons of the year (and a fright for anyone who dares listen at the door – look up as you pass through the doorway), through the elaborate Moorish decoration of the **Arab room** (marble, sandalwood, parrots and acres of gold leaf), to the mahogany-and-mirrors narcissism of **Lord Bute's bedroom**, with a gilded statue of St John the Evangelist (the marquess' name saint) and 189 bevelled mirrors on the ceiling, which reflect the name 'John' in Greek.

The **banqueting hall** boasts a fantastically over-the-top fireplace and is overlooked by that medieval must-have, a minstrels' gallery. The **nursery** – perhaps the most sympathetic room in the castle – is decorated with fairy-tale characters and the **small dining room** has an ingenious table, designed so that a living vine could be slotted through it, allowing diners to pluck fresh grapes as they ate. The **roof garden** seems to underline how much of a fantasy all this really was – designed with southern Italy in mind, rather than Wales.

Some but not all of these rooms can be accessed with a regular castle entry, which includes an excellent audioguide (available in a children's edition and in a range of languages).

Housed below the **Interpretation Centre** to the right of the entrance is the **Welch Regiment Museum** (Wed-Mon), which records the military achievements of South Wales' infantry regiment.

CARDIFF

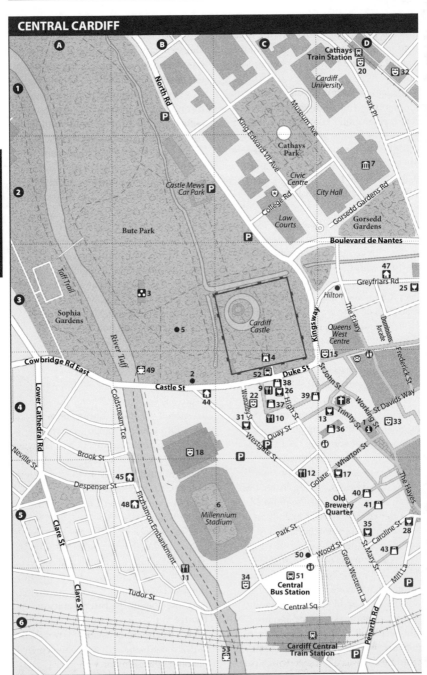

CENTRAL CARDIFF

Cathays Train Station 20 · 32

Cardiff University

North Rd

Cathays Park

Cardiff University

King Edward VII Ave

Museum Ave

Park Pl

Castle Mews Car Park

Civic Centre

College Rd

City Hall

Gorsedd Gardens Rd

Law Courts

Gorsedd Gardens

Bute Park

Boulevard de Nantes

47

Greyfriars Rd 25

Hilton

Toff Trail

3

Sophia Gardens

5

Cardiff Castle

Kingsway

The Friary

Queens West Centre

Dominions Arcade

River Taff

15

Frederick St

Cowbridge Rd East

49

4

52

Duke St

St John St

Working St Davids Way

Lower Cathedral Rd

Castle St

2

44

38 26

9

22 37

Womanby St

31 10

High St

39

8

13

Trinity St

1

33

36

Neville St

Brook St

Coldstream Tce

18

Westgate St

Quay St

Wharton St

45

Despenser St

P

12

Golate

17

48

Fitzhamon Embankment

6
Millennium Stadium

Park St

Old Brewery Quarter

40

41

The Hayes

35

Caroline St

28

Clare St

50

Wood St

St Mary St

43

Mill La

11

34

51

Central Bus Station

Central Sq

Tudor St

Clare St

Penarth Rd

53

Cardiff Central Train Station

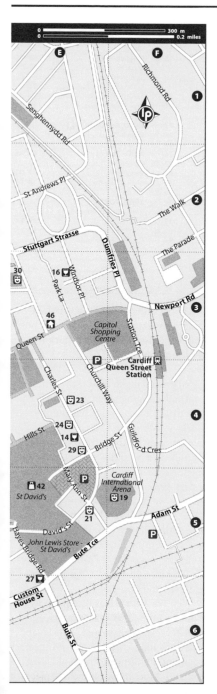

♥ BUTE PARK // THE CITY'S LEAFY BREATHING SPACE

Flanked by the castle and the River Taff, Bute Park was donated to the city along with the castle in 1947. With Sophia Gardens, Pontcanna Fields and Llandaff Fields, it forms a green corridor that stretches northwest for 1½ miles to Llandaff. All were once part of the Bute's vast holdings.

Forming the park's southern edge, the **Animal Wall** is topped with stone figures of lions, seals, bears and other creatures. It was designed by castle architect William Burges but only completed in 1892 after his death, with more animals added in the 1920s. In the 1930s they were the subject of a newspaper cartoon strip and many Cardiff kids grew up thinking the animals came alive at night.

In Cooper's Field, the part of the park just west of the castle, is a stone circle – not Neolithic but fin de siècle – erected in 1899 when Cardiff hosted the Royal National Eisteddfod (see p296). Such so-called **gorsedd stones** are found all over Wales where eisteddfodau (gatherings or sessions) have been held.

Nearby are the foundations of the 13th-century **Blackfriars Priory**, which was destroyed in 1404 when Owain Glyndŵr attacked Cardiff, and later rebuilt, only to be finally vacated in 1538 when the monasteries were dissolved.

♥ NATIONAL MUSEUM CARDIFF // THE STORY OF WALES

Northeast of Cardiff Castle is the Civic Centre, an early 20th-century complex of neo-baroque buildings in gleaming white Portland stone, set around the green lawns and colourful flowerbeds of Alexandra Gardens. It houses the City Hall, police headquarters, law courts, crown offices and Cardiff University.

In the southeast corner is the excellent **National Museum Cardiff** (Map p44; ☎ 2039 7951; www.museumwales.ac.uk; Gorsedd Gardens Rd; admission free; ☺ 10am-5pm Tue-Sun), which is one of Britain's best museums, covering natural history, archaeology and art.

The *Evolution of Wales* exhibit whizzes onlookers through 4600 million years of geological history, with a rollicking multimedia display that places Wales into a global context. Spectacular films of volcanic eruptions and aerial footage of the country's stunning landscape demonstrate how its scenery was formed, while model dinosaurs and woolly mammoths help keep the little ones interested.

The natural-history displays range from brightly coloured insects to the awesome 9m-long skeleton of a humpback whale that washed up near Aberthaw in 1982. The world's largest turtle (2.88m by 2.74m), which was found on Harlech beach, is also here, suspended on wires from the ceiling.

The art gallery houses an excellent collection. Many impressionist and post-Impressionist pieces were bequeathed to the museum in 1952 and 1963 by the Davies sisters, Gwendoline and Margaret, granddaughters of 19th-century coal and shipping magnate David Davies (see p197). Treasures include luminous works by Monet and Pissaro, Sisley's *The Cliff at Penarth* (the artist was married in Cardiff) and portraits by Renoir, including the shimmering *La Parisienne*. The sisters' favourite was Cézanne, but there are also works by Matisse and the anguished *Rain: Auvers* by Van Gogh, who killed himself just a few days after finishing the painting. The Pre-Raphaelites are well represented, as is Rodin, with a cast of *The Kiss*. Older works include those by El Greco and Poussin.

Welsh artists such as Richard Wilson, Thomas Jones, David Jones and Ceri Richards are all here, as well as Gwen and Augustus John – a highlight is Augustus' beguilingly angelic portrayal of Dylan Thomas. Modern works include pieces by Francis Bacon, David Hockney and Rachel Whiteread.

You'll need at least three hours to see the museum properly – and it could easily take up a whole day. The museum hosts regular classical and jazz concerts – call or check the website for information.

❦ MILLENNIUM STADIUM // MODERN CARDIFF INCARNATE

The spectacular **Millennium Stadium** (Map p44; ☎ 2082 2228; www.millenniumstadium.com; Westgate St; tours adult/child £6.50/4; ☙ 10am-5pm Mon-Sat, 10am-4pm Sun) squats like a stranded spaceship on the River Taff's east bank. Attendance at international rugby and football matches has increased dramatically since this 72,500-seat, three-tiered stadium with sliding roof was completed in time to host the 1999 Rugby World Cup. The famous **Cardiff Arms Park**, its predecessor, lies literally in its shadow.

Not everyone is happy with it: one critic called it 'an absurdly overexcited structure…that rears over the surrounding streets like a sumo wrestler'. The stadium cost £110 million to build and big matches paralyse the city centre, but when the crowd begins to sing, the whole city resonates and all is forgiven.

It's well worth taking a tour – you get to walk through the players' tunnel and sit in the VIP box. The entrance for guided tours is at Gate 3 on Westgate St.

Rugby is the national game; to watch a test here is to catch a glimpse of the Welsh psyche, especially when the Six Nations tournament (contested annually in February and March between Wales, England, Scotland, Ireland, France and Italy) is in full swing. Tickets for international fixtures are difficult for mere mortals to get hold of; other matches are easier.

❦ ST JOHN THE BAPTIST CHURCH // A CALM RETREAT FROM THE SHOPPING STRIP

A graceful Gothic lantern tower rises from the 15th-century **church of St John the Baptist** (Map p44; Working St), its delicate stonework almost like filigree. A church has stood on this site since at least 1180. Inside are simple, elegant arches. Regular lunchtime organ concerts are held here.

❦ CARDIFF STORY // LIKE IT SAYS ON THE WRAPPER, WE PRESUME

We can't say too much about this **museum** (Map p44; ☎ 2078 8334; www.cardiffstory.com; Old Library, The Hayes; ☙ 10am-5pm Mon-Sat, 10am-4pm Sun), as it hadn't quite opened when we were researching this book. Yet the concept is appealingly simple: tell the story of Cardiff's transformation from a small market town into the world's biggest coal port and then into the capital city you see before you today. It's housed in the beautiful Old Library building, which is also home to the tourist office.

TOP FIVE

CASTLES

★ **Cardiff Castle** (p42) As camp as any military edifice could ever wish to be.

★ **Caerphilly Castle** (p64) Ask any kid, this is what a castle should look like.

★ **Carreg Cennen Castle** (p115) Dramatic, isolated and supremely mysterious.

★ **Powis Castle** (p199) Sumptuous and palatial – the only one you'd seriously consider living in.

★ **Caernarfon Castle** (p233) Imposing, foreboding and surprisingly beautiful.

CARDIFF BAY

❧ CARDIFF BAY WATERFRONT // FROM STINKING MUDFLATS TO A NATION'S SHOWCASE

Lined with important national institutions such as Y Senedd (the National Assembly) and the Millennium Centre, Cardiff Bay is where the modern Welsh nation is put on display in an architect's playground of interesting buildings, large open spaces and public art.

It wasn't always this way. By 1913 more than 13 million tonnes of coal were being shipped from Cardiff docks. Following the post-WWII slump the docklands deteriorated into a wasteland of empty basins, cut off from the city by the railway embankment. The bay outside the docks, which has one of the highest tidal ranges in the world (more than 12m between high and low water), was ringed for up to 14 hours a day by smelly, sewage-contaminated mudflats. The nearby residential area of Butetown became a neglected slum.

Since 1987 the area has been completely redeveloped. The turning point

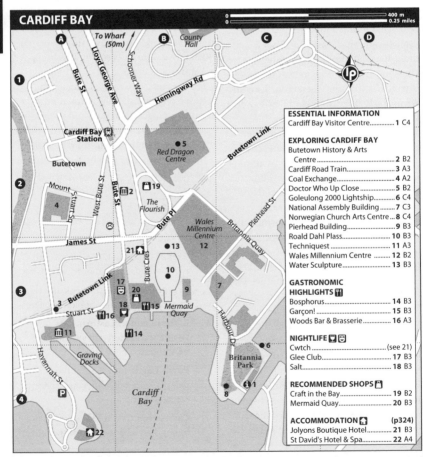

came with the erection of a state-of-the-art tidal barrage, completed in 1999, which transformed the stinking mudflats into a freshwater lake by containing the waters at the mouth of the Rivers Taff and Ely. It was a controversial project, as its construction flooded 200 hectares of intertidal mudflats which, despite their unpleasant aspects, were an important habitat for waterfowl. The barrage includes sluice gates to control the water flow, three lock gates to allow passage for boats, and a fish pass that lets migrating salmon and sea trout pass between the river and the sea.

Cardiff Bay Visitor Centre (Map p48; ☎ 2087 7927; Harbour Dr; ☺ 10am-6pm), housed in an oval tubular structure on the eastern side of the harbour, expands on the area's history with a short film, information panels and a large scale model of Cardiff.

The main commercial centre at Cardiff Bay is **Mermaid Quay**, packed with bars, restaurants and shops. To its east is **Roald Dahl Plass**, a large public space (it used to be a dock basin), named after the Cardiff-born writer, that serves as an open-air performance area, overseen by a soaring, stainless-steel **water sculpture**.

**❦ WALES MILLENNIUM CENTRE //
INSPIRATIONAL ARCHITECTURE AT
ITS BEST**
The centrepiece and symbol of Cardiff Bay's regeneration is the superb **Wales Millennium Centre** (Map p48; ☎ 2063 6464; www.wmc.org.uk; Bute Pl; admission free), an architectural masterpiece of stacked Welsh slate in shades of purple, green and grey topped with an overarching bronzed steel shell. Designed by Welsh architect Jonathan Adams, it opened in 2004 as Wales' premier arts complex.

The roof above the main entrance is pierced by 2m-high, letter-shaped windows, spectacularly backlit at night, that spell out phrases from poet Gwyneth Lewis: '*Creu Gwir fel Gwydr o Ffwrnais Awen*' (Creating truth like glass from inspiration's furnace) and 'In these stones horizons sing'.

The centre is home to several major cultural organisations, including the Welsh National Opera, National Dance Company, National Orchestra, Academi (Welsh National Literature Promotion Agency), HiJinx Theatre and Ty Cerdd (Music Centre of Wales). You can wander through the public areas at will, or go on an official **guided tour** (adult/child £5.50/4.50; ☺ 9am-5pm) that will take you behind the giant letters, onto the main stage and into the dressing rooms, depending on what shows are on.

**❦ SENEDD (NATIONAL ASSEMBLY
BUILDING) // A DESIGN FOR A
GREEN NATION**
Designed by Lord Richard Rogers (the architect behind London's Lloyd's Building and Millennium Dome and Paris' Pompidou Centre), the **Senedd** (Map p48; ☎ 0845 010 5500; www.assemblywales.org/sen-home; admission free; ☺ 10.30am-4.30pm, extended during plenary sessions) is a striking structure of concrete, slate, glass and steel with an undulating canopy roof lined with red cedar.

The building has won awards for its environmentally friendly design, which includes a huge rotating cowl on the roof for power-free ventilation and a gutter system that collects rainwater for flushing the toilets. The lobby and surrounding area is littered with public artworks, including the 'meeting place', a curved bench made of 3-tonne slate blocks from Blaenau Ffestiniog, thoughtfully provided as a place for protesters to rest their legs.

The National (Welsh) Assembly usually meets in a plenary session from 1.30pm on Tuesday and Wednesday, and seats in the public gallery may be pre-booked, although you can always take your chances on the day.

❧ PIERHEAD // AN OLD SURVIVOR LOOKING TO THE FUTURE

One of the area's few Victorian remnants, **Pierhead** (Map p48; ☎ 0845 010 5500; www.pierhead.org; admission free; ☺ 10.30am-4.30pm Mon-Fri & most weekends) is a red-brick French-Gothic Renaissance confection – nicknamed Wales' Big Ben – built with Bute family money for the Cardiff Municipal Railway Co to impress the maritime traffic. It's now part of the National Assembly complex and at the time of research was about to open as an interactive museum 'highlighting issues that matter in Wales'.

❧ DOCTOR WHO UP CLOSE // CLOSE ENCOUNTERS OF THE BBC KIND

The huge success of the reinvented classic TV series *Doctor Who,* produced by BBC Wales, has brought Cardiff to the attention of sci-fi fans worldwide. City locations have featured in many episodes and the spin-off series *Torchwood* is set in Cardiff Bay, the hidden lift to their headquarters emerging beneath the water sculpture in Roald Dahl Plass. Capitalising on Timelord tourism, this permanent **exhibition** (Map p48; ☎ 2048 9257; www.doctorwhoexhibitions.com; Red Dragon Centre; adult/child £6.50/5; ☺ 10am-6.30pm) has opened in the Red Dragon Centre, with props and costumes from both shows displayed alongside video clips from the episodes they feature in. It's great fun – especially when you come face to face with full-size Daleks in full 'ex-ter-min-ate' mode. Super fans can pick up a locations guide (30p) from the nerdalicious shop.

The Red Dragon Centre also has an IMAX cinema, a casino and restaurants.

❧ TECHNIQUEST // UNLEASH YOUR INNER MAD SCIENTIST

For engrossing, fun, hands-on exhibits aimed at introducing kids to science, visit **Techniquest** (Map p48; ☎ 2047 5475; www.techniquest.org; Stuart St; adult/child £7/5; ☺ 10am-4.30pm). You can explore whirlwinds, race bubbles, play a harp with no strings and more – equally enjoyable for under-fives and inquisitive adults. There's also a planetarium, which stages night-sky demonstrations and science shows.

❧ BUTETOWN // WHEN COAL DUST TURNED TO GOLD DUST

Victorian Butetown, spanning out from Mount Stuart Sq, just northwest of the waterfront, was the heart of Cardiff's coal trade – a multiethnic community that propelled the city to world fame. The old **Coal Exchange** (Map p48; ☎ 2049 4917; www.coalexchange.co.uk; Mount Stuart Sq) was the place where international coal prices were set. It was here in March 1908 that a coal merchant wrote the world's first-ever £1 million cheque. It now houses an arts and performance venue.

The **Butetown History & Arts Centre** (Map p48; ☎ 2025 6757; www.bhac.org; 4-5 Dock Chambers, Bute St; admission free; ☺ 10am-5pm Tue-Fri, 11am-4.30pm Sat & Sun) is devoted to preserving oral histories, documents and images of the docklands. Its exhibits put the area into both a historical and present-day context.

❧ CARDIFF ROAD TRAIN // EXPLORE THE BARRAGE ON YOUR BUTT

Providing the only public access through the working port on the east side of Cardiff Bay to the barrage, this toy-town trackless **train** (Map p48; ☎ 2052 2729; www.cardiffroadtrain.com; adult/child return £4/3; ☺ hourly noon-4pm Sat, Sun & school holidays), with live commentary, runs from Stuart St (opposite Techniquest).

🦢 NORWEGIAN CHURCH ARTS CENTRE // MINISTERING TO THE ARTISTIC SPIRIT

Looking like it's popped out of the pages of a story book and settled on the eastern edge of the harbour, the **Norwegian Church** (Map p48; ☎ 2087 7959; www.norwegianchurchcardiff.com; Harbour Dr; admission free; ⊙ 9am-4pm) is a white-slatted wooden building with a black witch's-hat spire, modelled on a traditional Norse village church. It was built in 1868 to minister to Norwegian sailors and remained a place of worship until 1974; Roald Dahl was christened here, and served as president of the preservation trust that restored and renovated the church. It has now been reincarnated as an arts centre with a cafe, interesting exhibitions, concerts and arts courses.

🦢 GOLEULONG 2000 LIGHTSHIP // A RED LIGHT ZONE OF A DIFFERENT SORT

Bright red and with a lighthouse grafted onto it, this **Lightship** (Map p48; ☎ 2048 7609; www.lightship2000.co.uk; admission free; ⊙ 10am-5pm Mon-Sat, 2-5pm Sun) was last stationed off Rhossili, warning sailors away from the Helwick Swatch, a treacherous sandbank. It now houses a Christian centre but you can check out the neat little cabins and climb to the top of the light tower for the view. It's staffed by volunteers, so the hours can be erratic.

CATHEDRAL ROAD AREA

🦢 CARDIFF CITY STADIUM // WHERE BLUEBIRDS DO BATTLE

Map p36; ☎ 0845 345 1400; www.cardiffcitystadium.co.uk; Leckwith Rd, Canton

Greedy Cardiff couldn't stop with one new stadium – this 26,800-seater opened in 2009. It's home to both the **Cardiff Blues** (www.cardiffblues.com), Wales' most star-studded professional rugby union club, and **Cardiff City Football Club** (www.cardiffcityfc.co.uk). Local football fans still hark back to 1927 when the Bluebirds took the English FA Cup out of England for the first (and only) time – Welsh football's equivalent of Owain Glyndŵr's rebellion. They now play in the Championship League.

🦢 SWALEC STADIUM // TAKING ON THE ENGLISH AT THEIR OWN GAME

Map p54; ☎ 2041 9311; www.swalecstadium.co.uk; Sophia Gardens

This is the home to the **Glamorgan Cricket Club** (www.glamorgancricket.com), the only Welsh club belonging to the England and Wales Cricket Board. Not to be outdone, they also have a fancy, redeveloped stadium.

FESTIVALS & EVENTS

Six Nations Championship (www.rbs6nations.com) The premier European rugby championship, held every February and March, with Wales taking on England, Scotland, Ireland, Italy and France. Cardiff normally hosts two home games – the atmosphere is supercharged.

Cardiff Festival (www.cardiff-festival.com) Runs throughout summer, from July to early September, and acts as an umbrella over many of the festivals listed below. Includes the Big Weekend (funfair, bands and the Lord Mayor's parade) and lots of crazy one-offs such as 2010's Elvis World Cup.

Everyman Summer Theatre Festival (www.everymanfestival.co.uk) Three weeks of theatre, from early July.

Welsh Proms (www.stdavidshallcardiff.co.uk) Two weeks of classical concerts at St David's Hall, starting mid-July.

Cardiff Comedy Festival (www.stdavidshall cardiff.co.uk) Also over two weeks, at St David's Hall and starting in mid-July.

Cardiff International Food & Drink Festival (www.cardiff-festival.com; Roald Dahl Plass; admission free) Over a long weekend (Friday to Sunday) in mid-July.

Grand Medieval Melee (www.cardiffcastle. com; Cardiff Castle) Armoured knights engaging in drills, swordplay, mass battles and general medieval mayhem; staged over a weekend in mid-August.

National Classic Car & Motor Boat Rally (Cardiff Harbour) A mid-August Saturday convergence of old cars and racy boats.

Mardi Gras (www.cardiffmardigras.co.uk; Coopers Field) Cardiff's lesbian, gay, bisexual and transgender pride festival, held in late August or early September.

Great British Cheese Festival (www.great britishcheesefestival.co.uk) Brush shoulders with the big cheeses in Cardiff Castle in late September.

Cardiff Winter Wonderland (www.cardiffs winterwonderland.com; Civic Centre) Makes the most

of the cold weather with an outdoor ice-skating rink, Santa's grotto and family-friendly activities, preceded by the switching on of the Christmas lights and the John Lewis Eye (a smaller version of the London Eye).

GASTRONOMIC HIGHLIGHTS

As Cardiff has become more glossy, cosmopolitan and multicultural, so has its food scene. A diverse array of restaurants is scattered around the city, with a particularly ritzy batch lining Cardiff Bay. Burger joints, curry houses and kebab shops cater to the central city's throngs of young drinkers, well into the small hours. While there are cafes everywhere, the UK has been slow to wake up to the joys of a well-made coffee – but Cardiff, unlike the rest of Wales, does now have a few exemplars of the art. A good cuppa tea is much easier to find.

∼ WORTH A TRIP ∼

Llandaff is a peaceful suburb 2 miles north of the centre – a village clustered around a green that has been swallowed up by the expanding city. Set in a hollow on the west bank of the River Taff is beautiful **Llandaff Cathedral** (☎ 2056 4554; www.llandaffcathedral. org.uk; Cathedral Rd; ☻ 10am-4pm), built on the site of a 6th-century monastery founded by St Teilo. His tomb is on the south side of the sanctuary and an ancient stone Celtic cross stands nearby.

The present cathedral was begun in 1120 – it crumbled throughout the Middle Ages, and during the Reformation and Civil War it was used as an alehouse and then an animal shelter. Derelict by the 18th century, it was largely rebuilt in the 19th century and extensively restored after being damaged by a German bomb in 1941. The towers at the western end epitomise the cathedral's fragmented history – one was built in the 15th century, the other in the 19th.

Inside, clear glass windows provide a striking clarity of light. A giant arch supports Sir Jacob Epstein's huge, aluminium sculpture *Majestas* – its modern style a bold contrast in this gracious, vaulted space. Pre-Raphaelite fans will appreciate the Burne-Jones reredos (screens) in St Dyfrig's chapel and the stained glass by Rossetti and William Morris' company.

Buses 24, 25, 33, 33A and 62 (15 minutes, every 10 to 15 minutes) run along Cathedral Rd to Llandaff.

CENTRAL CARDIFF

☙ CAFE MINUET £

Map p44; ☎ 2034 1794; 42 Castle Arcade, High St; mains £6-10; ☺ 10am-5pm Mon-Sat

It may look a bit greasy spoon from the outside, but this unassuming eatery produces excellent cheap and cheerful Italian food. The menu includes good vegetarian dishes, including lots of pasta options. Get in early at lunchtime or expect to wait for a table.

☙ GOAT MAJOR £

Map p44; ☎ 2033 7161; 33 High St; mains £7-8; ☺ food noon-6pm Mon-Sat, noon-4pm Sun

A solidly traditional pub with armchairs, a fireplace and lip-smacking Brains Dark real ale on tap, the Goat Major's gastronomic contribution comes in the form of its selection of homemade pies. Its Wye Valley pie (a mixture of buttered chicken, leek, asparagus and Tintern Abbey cheese) was named Britain's best in 2010.

☙ MADAME FROMAGE £

Map p44; ☎ 2064 4888; www.madamefromage.co.uk; 18 Castle Arcade, High St; mains £3-6; ☺ 10am-5.30pm Mon-Sat, noon-5pm Sun

One of Cardiff's finest delicatessens, with a wide range of charcuterie and French and Welsh cheeses. The Madame also has a cafe with tables spilling into the arcade, where you can read French newspapers and eat a mixture of Breton dishes and Welsh caffi food: rarebit, lamb *cawl* and *bara brith*.

☙ PLAN £

Map p44; ☎ 2039 8464; 28 Morgan Arcade; mains £5-8; ☺ 9am-5pm; V

Serving quite possibly Wales' best coffee, this satisfying cafe specialises in healthy, organic, locally sourced food, including vegan options. Grab a window seat and a copy of the *Guardian* newspaper and caffeinate to your (racing) heart's content.

☙ RIVERSIDE REAL FOOD MARKET £

Map p44; Fitzhamon Embankment; ☺ 10am-2pm Sun

What it lacks in size it makes up for in sheer yumminess. This riverside market has stalls heaving with cooked meals, cakes, cheese, organic meat, charcuterie, apple juice and real ale. There are lots of options for vegetarians and the Welsh cakes hot off the griddle are exceptional.

☙ ZERODEGREES £

Map p44; ☎ 2022 9494; 27 Westgate St; mains £7-13

Within a big factory-like space this microbrewery-cum-restaurant combines all-day food with lip-smacking artisan-crafted beers – try the Black Lager, with hints of caramel and coffee. The excellent dining options include a UN of pizza toppings (Thai, Mexican, Indian, Portuguese), pasta, risotto and kilo pots of mussels, the house speciality.

CARDIFF BAY

☙ BOSPHORUS ££

Map p48; ☎ 2048 7477; 31 Mermaid Quay; mains £10-14; V

While the food is good, it's the setting that really distinguishes this upmarket Turkish restaurant. Jutting out over the water on its own private pier, Bosphorus enjoys wonderful views all round; the best of all are from the outdoor tables at the end. Early eaters can take advantage of the pre-7pm offer: two courses plus a drink for £13.

☙ GARÇON! ££

Map p48; ☎ 2049 0990; Mermaid Quay; mains £11-18; ☺ closed Mon Oct-Feb

The name may conjure up the worst Brits-do-French stereotypes but this place is the real deal. Seemingly beamed in directly from Normandy, the ambience and menu are perfectly authentic, even down to

CARDIFF

offering reasonable prix fixe deals (two-/three-courses £13/16, served before 6pm).

♨ WOODS BAR & BRASSERIE ££

Map p48; ☎ 2049 2400; Stuart St; mains £11-18; ⌚ closed Sun dinner

The historic Pilotage Building has been given a modern makeover – zany wallpaper, exposed stone walls and a floor-to-ceiling glass extension – to accommodate Cardiff Bay's best restaurant. The cuisine is modern European, light and flavoursome, with an emphasis on local ingredients.

CATHEDRAL ROAD AREA

♨ BRAVA ££

Map p54; ☎ 2037 1929; 71 Pontcanna St; brunch £3-7, dinner £9-15

With local art on the walls and an informal vibe, this cool cafe is our favourite brunch spot on the strength of its eggs

Benedict, silky white coffee and attentive service. Tables spill out onto the pavement in summer and in the evening it morphs into a licensed bistro. Brava indeed.

♨ CAMEO CLUB & BISTRO ££

Map p54; ☎ 2037 1929; 3 Pontcanna St; mains £13-21; ⌚ breakfast & lunch daily, dinner Mon-Sat; ⌘

Once a notorious after-hours drinking den, this private members' club is much more respectable these days, but it's still the hub for Cardiff's arts and media scene. Anyone can now partake in the delicious food offered in its effortlessly hip bistro, lined with black-and-white photos of Welsh entertainers, but the bar is members-only after 5pm.

♨ CINNAMON TREE £

Map p54; ☎ 2037 4433; www.thecinnamontree.co.uk; 173 Kings Rd; mains £6-11

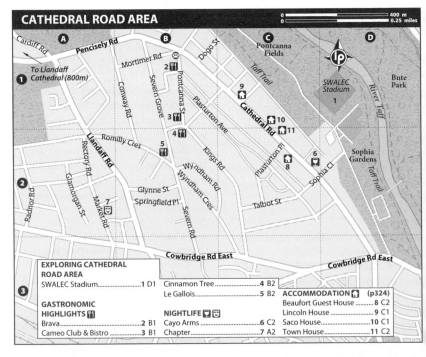

CATHEDRAL ROAD AREA

0 ――――― 400 m
0 ――――― 0.25 miles

A cut above your usual curry house, the Cinnamon Tree has modern decor and a menu of specialities that includes unusual dishes such as *tharav sofyani* (duck seasoned with chilli, coriander and fenugreek in a thick, spicy sauce) and *hiran champan* (venison cooked with roast garlic cloves, onion and coriander seeds).

☘ LE GALLOIS £££

Map p54; ☎ 2034 1264; 6-10 Romilly Cres; lunch 2-/3-courses £20/25, dinner £25/30; ⊗ Tue-Sat

One of Cardiff's finest, Le Gallois (the Welshman) majors in an inspirational blend of Welsh produce and French cuisine. The decorous dining room of grey walls, walnut-veneer tables and starched-linen napkins makes sure the focus is on the seasonal menu of half-a-dozen starters and half-a-dozen main courses.

NIGHTLIFE

Pick up a copy of *Buzz*, a free monthly magazine with up-to-date entertainment listings in the city, available from the tourist office and entertainment venues. The staff at tourist offices can also help out with recommendations.

BARS & PUBS

Cardiff is a prodigious boozing town – Friday and Saturday nights see the city centre invaded by hordes of generally good-humoured, beered-up lads and ladettes tottering from bar to club to kebab shop, whatever the weather (someone fetch that young woman a coat). Wednesdays are student nights, with cheap drink promos prompting a wave of midweek overindulgence. It's not all as tacky as it sounds – a lively alternative scene, some swish bars and a swathe of old-fashioned pubs keep things interesting.

Don't forget to try the local Brains SA (meaning Special Ale, Same Again or Skull Attack depending on how many you've had), brewed by the same family concern since 1882.

☘ 10 FEET TALL

Map p44; ☎ 2022 8883; www.thisis10feettall.co.uk; 11-12 Church St

The newer sister property to Buffalo Bar, this hip venue over three floors merges a cafe, cocktail and tapas bar, and live-music venue. Chic bar-keeps swish together two-for-one cocktails between 5pm and 8pm, weekdays and all day Sundays.

☘ BUFFALO BAR

Map p44; ☎ 2031 0312; www.myspace.com/weare buffalobar; 11 Windsor Pl

A haven for cool kids about town, the laid-back Buffalo features retro furniture, tasty daytime food, life-affirming cocktails and cool tunes with DJ sets. Upstairs a roster of cutting-edge indie bands take to the stage.

☘ CAYO ARMS

Map p54; ☎ 2039 1910; 36 Cathedral Rd

This is a real-ale pub with a warm atmosphere and a loyal band of regulars. It serves a fine range of Tomos Watkins real ales and is filled to bursting on match days.

☘ CWTCH

Map p48; ☎ 2048 8775; 5 Bute Cres

A *'cwtch'* is either a warm, safe place or a cuddle. This little bar, below Jolyons Hotel, is certainly the former and it imparts a cosy feeling that's almost as good as the latter. Lethal two-for-one cocktail deals add to the merriment, as do occasional open-mike nights. Sink into a sofa and slip into Cwtch's warm embrace.

❦ FAT CAT CAFE BAR

Map p44; ☎ 2022 8378; www.fatcatcafebars.co.uk; Greyfriars Rd; mains £6-14

This chain of bar/restaurants started in Wales, and the Cardiff outpost is one of the smarter ones, with boudoir-style decor and comfy sofas to nurse a hangover in. Food is served until 10pm (4pm Sunday) and there's a two-for-one cocktail deal offered nightly from Sunday through to Thursday.

❦ PICA PICA

Map p44; ☎ 2034 5703; 15-23 Westgate St

Housed in a series of low-ceiling brick vaults, this cool bar serves tapas, meze and two-for-one cocktails before 8pm.

❦ SALT

Map p48; ☎ 2049 4375; Mermaid Quay, Cardiff Bay

A large, modern, nautical-themed bar (ocean-liner decor, blue-and-white drapes, bits of driftwood, pictures of the Welsh coast) with plenty of sofas and armchairs for lounging around and, best of all, a 1st-floor open-air terrace with a view of the yachts out in the bay.

❦ TAFARN TÂF

Map p44; ☎ 2037 8866; 53-59 Despenser St

A cool little bar attached to an upmarket backpacker hostel, Tafarn Tâf has outdoor tables on a riverside terrace, a big screen for watching all the rugby action and an all-day menu of tasty Welsh snacks.

❦ WHARF

off Map p48; ☎ 2040 5092; 121 Schooner Way, Cardiff Bay

A glass-and-brick building with a Victorian-industrial look, the Wharf is a big family-friendly pub with a children's area and picnic tables overlooking the water. It offers live music on Fridays and Saturdays, and big screens showing major sports matches.

❦ YARD

Map p44; ☎ 2022 7577; 42-43 St Mary St

Occupying the site of an 18th-century brewery, Yard sports an industrial-chic decor of stainless steel, polished copper pipes and zinc ducting, with a trad-looking bar in front and clubby sofas out back. Outdoor tables, good food and a child-friendly policy (until 7pm) pull in families, while on the weekends its cocktails and DJs that bring the crowds.

LIVE MUSIC

Major concerts are staged at the **Cardiff International Arena** (Map p44; ☎ 2022 4488; Mary Ann St) or, if they're really huge, at Millennium Stadium (see p47). If you're after a more intimate experience, try one of the many bars hosting live bands, such as Buffalo Bar, 10 Feet Tall and the Wharf.

Most classical companies are now based at the Wales Millennium Centre (p49) but **St David's Hall** (Map p44; ☎ 2087 8444; www.stdavidshallcardiff.co.uk; The Hayes), the national concert hall, hosts the Welsh Proms in July and a full program of performances. Occasional classical music concerts are held in Cardiff Castle, Llandaff Cathedral and St John's Church.

❦ BARFLY

Map p44; ☎ 0844 847 2424; www.barflyclub.com; Kingsway

Part of a UK-wide chain of music clubs, the Cardiff Barfly is a major live-music venue with gigs six nights a week, providing a stage for local talent as well as major bands on tour, and alternative and electronica club nights.

❦ CAFE JAZZ

Map p44; ☎ 2038 7026; www.cafejazzcardiff.com; Sandringham Hotel, 21 St Mary St

It's not exactly your traditional smoky jazz basement, but this cafe-bar is the

GAY & LESBIAN CARDIFF

Cardiff has a relaxed and thriving gay and lesbian scene, with a cluster of venues on Charles St (for listings and general information check www.gaycardiff.co.uk). The big event is the annual **Mardi Gras** (www.cardiffmardigras.co.uk), held as part of the Cardiff Festival in late August or early September (see p39).

Bar Icon (Map p44; www.bariconcardiff.co.uk; 60 Charles St) Cocktail bar with comfy sofas that attracts a mixed crowd.

Edge Bar Club X (Map p44; www.edgebar-clubx.com; 35 Charles St; admission £4-10; ⏰ 10pm-3am Wed, 10pm-6am Fri, 10pm-6am Sat) Cardiff's biggest gay club has two dance floors, with a chill-out bar and covered beer garden upstairs. Wednesday night is student night, with cheap drinks, but Saturday is the big one, with chart hits out front and funk/electro in the back room.

Exit Club (Map p44; www.exitclubcardiff.com; 48 Charles St) A long-standing, attitude-free bar, with disco and pop filling the two dance floors until the early hours.

Golden Cross (Map p44; 283 Hayes Bridge Rd) One of the oldest pubs in the city and a long-standing gay venue, this Victorian bar retains its handsome stained glass, polished wood and ceramic tiles. It hosts drag, cabaret, quiz and karaoke nights.

Kings Cross (Map p44; 25 Caroline St) Prominently positioned in the shopping district, KX (as its known) is a stalwart of the gay scene, with DJs, cabaret, karaoke and quiz nights.

Locker Room (Map p44; www.lockerroomcardiff.co.uk; 50 Charles St; admission £12; ⏰ noon-11pm Mon-Fri, nonstop noon Sat-10pm Sun) Gay men's sauna.

CARDIFF

city's main jazz venue, with live jazz kicking off at 9pm Monday to Thursday, and blues from 10pm Friday (Saturdays are disco nights). Monday-night jam sessions give new talent a chance to sit in with the house band.

❧ CARDIFF UNIVERSITY STUDENTS' UNION

Map p44; ☎ 2078 1400; www.cardiffstudents.com; Park Pl, Cathays

The students' union hosts regular live gigs by big-name bands, usually of an alternative bent, in its three venues, and also hosts club nights. You'll find the box office on the 2nd floor of the union building.

❧ CLWB IFOR BACH

Map p44; ☎ 2023 2199; www.clwb.net; 11 Womanby St

Truly an independent music great, Y Clwb has broken many a Welsh band since the early 1980s. It started as a venue for Welsh-language music in Anglophone Cardiff and has survived the Cool Cymru backlash with its reputation as Cardiff's most eclectic and important venue. It now hosts bands performing in many tongues and it's the best place to catch gigs by up-and-coming new acts as well as by more established artists.

THEATRE, COMEDY & CINEMA

Other companies are based at the Wales Millennium Centre (p49).

❧ CHAPTER

Map p54; ☎ 2030 4400; www.chapter.org; Market Rd, Canton

The city's edgiest arts venue, the Chapter has a varied program of contemporary drama, as well as art exhibitions, arthouse cinema, workshops, alternative theatre and dance performances. There's also a good cafe-bar, with Cardiff's biggest range of European beers.

❦ GLEE CLUB

Map p48; ☎ 0871 472 0400; www.glee.co.uk; Mermaid Quay, Cardiff Bay

The Glee Club is a busy comedy hangout with a well-regarded program of comedy nights featuring touring comics and local unknowns.

❦ NEW THEATRE

Map p44; ☎ 2087 8889; www.newtheatrecardiff. co.uk; Park Pl

This restored Edwardian playhouse – Anna Pavlova and Sarah Bernhardt are among those who have trod the boards here – hosts various touring productions, including big West End and Broadway shows, musicals and pantomime.

❦ SHERMAN CYMRU

Map p44; ☎ 2064 6900; www.shermancymru.co.uk; Senghennydd Rd, Cathays

The Sherman is South Wales' leading theatre company and stages a wide range of material from classics and children's theatre to works by new playwrights.

Also recommended:

Vue (Map p44; ☎ 08712 240 240, calls per min 10p; www.myvue.com; Millennium Plaza, Wood St) Huge 13-screen multiplex.

Cineworld (Map p44; ☎ 0871 200 2000, per min 10p; www.cineworld.co.uk; Mary Ann St) An even huger 15-screen multiplex.

RECOMMENDED SHOPS

If you thought Cardiff's 21st-century makeover was all about political edifices, arts centres and sports stadia, think again. One of the most dramatic developments in the central city is the transformation of the Hayes shopping strip, with the giant, glitzy extension of the St David's shopping centre now eating up its entire eastern flank. Costing £675 million, St David's is one of the UK's largest. Balancing this ultramodern mall is a historic network of Victorian and Edwardian arcades spreading their dainty tentacles either side of St Mary St.

❦ CARDIFF CENTRAL MARKET

Map p44; www.cardiff-market.co.uk; btwn St Mary & Trinity Sts; ☒ 8am-5.30pm Mon-Sat

For an age-old shopping experience, head to this Victorian covered market, which is packed with stalls selling everything from fresh fish to mobile phones. Stock up here for a picnic in Bute Park with goodies such as fresh bread, cheese, cold meats, barbecued chicken, cakes and pastries.

❦ CASTLE ARCADE

Map p44; btwn Castle & High Sts

The most decorative of the city's arcades, it houses Troutmark Books (secondhand and Welsh-language books), Madame Fromage (p53; cafe, deli and cheese shop) and Cafe Minuet (p53).

❦ CASTLE WELSH CRAFTS

Map p44; ☎ 2034 3038; www.castlewelshcrafts. co.uk; 1 Castle St

If you're after stuffed dragons, lovespoons, Cardiff T-shirts or a suit of armour (£1600 and wearable, if you're interested), this is the city's biggest souvenir shop, conveniently located across the street from the castle.

❦ CRAFT IN THE BAY

Map p48; ☎ 2048 4611; Lloyd George Ave, Cardiff Bay; ☒ 10.30am-5.30pm

This retail gallery showcases work by contemporary Welsh artists and crafts people, with a wide range of ceramics, textiles, woodwork, jewellery, glassware, canvases and ironwork.

CARDIFF

♥ HIGH ST ARCADE

Map p44; btwn High & St John Sts

Divergent points on the music spectrum come together in this arcade: traditional music specialist Telynau Vining Harps (sheet music and instruments) and dance-music gurus Catapult 100% Vinyl (DJ equipment and records). Pussy Galore stocks funky women's fashion and sparkly accessories, while Hobo's is great for secondhand 1960s and '70s clothing.

♥ ROYAL & MORGAN ARCADES

Map p44; www.royalandmorganarcades.co.uk; btwn St Mary St & The Hayes

Cardiff's oldest arcade (1858), the Royal Arcade is home to the excellent, large Wally's Delicatessen and Melin Tregwynt (Welsh woven fabric designs – cushions, blankets, lampshades, scarves, coats, hats). It connects to Morgan Arcade, where you can stop for a coffee break at the Plan (p53) and visit Spillers Records.

♥ SPILLERS RECORDS

Map p44; ☎ 2022 4905; www.spillersrecords.com; Morgan Arcade

The world's oldest record shop, founded in 1894 (when it sold wax phonograph cylinders), Spillers is a national treasure. It stocks a large range of CDs and vinyl, prides itself on catering to the non-mainstream end of the market (it's especially good on punk), and promotes local talent through in-store gigs.

♥ ST DAVID'S

Map p44; www.stdavidscardiff.com; The Hayes; 9.30am-8pm Mon-Fri, 9.30am-6pm Sat, 10.30am-5pm Sun

Immense is the best way to describe this shiny new shopping centre. All of the High St chains you could name have a home here, along with a smorgasbord of eateries, a cinema multiplex and a large branch of the John Lewis department store, which dominates its south end.

♥ WYNDHAM ARCADE

Map p44; btwn St Mary St & Mill Lane

Yet another historic arcade, this one has the gloriously old-fashioned Bear Shop – a specialist tobacconist from a bygone era.

TRANSPORT

TO/FROM THE AIRPORT

Cardiff Airport (☎ 01446-711111; www.tbi cardiffairport.com) is 12 miles southwest of Cardiff, past Barry. A shuttle bus (free with a train ticket) links the airport terminal to nearby Rhoose Cardiff Airport train station, which has regular trains into the city (£3.30, 35 minutes); they run hourly Monday to Saturday and every two hours on Sunday. The X91 bus (£3.40, 35 minutes, every two hours) runs from the airport to the central bus station (stand F1). A taxi from the airport to the city centre takes 20 to 30 minutes, depending on traffic, and costs about £26.

GETTING AROUND

BIKE // Cyclists rejoice: Cardiff is one of Britain's flattest cities. The city council has a dedicated cycling officer and its website (www.cardiff.gov.uk) has lots of information including lists of bike shops and route maps; click on Environment, then Cycling.

BOAT // The most appealing way to reach Cardiff Bay is on the **Cardiff Aquabus** (Map p44; ☎ 2047 2004; www.cardiffaquabus.com), which stops at jetties from Bute Park to Mermaid Quay along the River Taff (£3 one way, 25 minutes); there are departures hourly, from 10.30am to 4.30pm, from Mermaid Quay and half an hour later from the city. The boats also stop at Penarth.

BUS – LOCAL // Local buses are operated by **Cardiff Bus** (Map p44; ☎ 2066 6444; www.cardiffbus. com; trip/day-pass £1.50/3); buy your ticket from the driver (no change given). Free route maps and timetables are available from its Wood St office. The baycar (bus 6) runs to Cardiff Bay from the city centre (every 10 to 15 minutes), with stops outside the Hilton Hotel (on North Rd, east of the castle), St Mary St and Penarth Rd

CARDIFF

(just south of Cardiff Central train station). **Free B** (www.cardiff.gov.uk/freeb; travel free; ☺ 8am-8pm Mon-Fri, 8am-6pm Sat, 9am-6pm Sun) buses loop around the inner city, departing every 10 minutes.

BUS – REGIONAL // Intercity services depart from the central bus station on Wood St. The **First** (www. firstgroup.com) Shuttle100 service heads regularly between Cardiff and Swansea (peak/off-peak £6.50/5 return, one hour). Other buses head to Caerphilly, Merth-yr Tydfil, Abergavenny, Carmarthen and Aberystwyth, among others. See also Beacons Buses (p89).

COACH // **National Express** (www.nationalex press.com) coach destinations include Swansea (£7.30, one hour), Brecon (£4.10, 1¼ hours), Newport (£3.50, 30 minutes), Monmouth (£9.70, 1¼ hours), Chepstow (£5.20, one hour) and London (£22, 3¼ hours).

CAR & MOTORCYCLE // Depending on where you're coming from, Cardiff is reached from any of exits 29 to 33 from the M4 (which runs from London to north-west of Swansea). Cardiff has branches of all the major rental-car companies.

PARKING // St David's (p59) has 2200 parking spaces above the shopping centre, with an additional 550 below John Lewis. The main car park is open 24 hours (per two/12/24 hours £2/16/18), with free parking on Sun-days and £1 overnight parking (5pm to 6am). In Cardiff Bay, there's a car park on Havannah St (per hour/day 50p/£5). If you're prepared to walk, it's often possible to find free street parking in the surrounding suburbs.

TAXI // Official black cabs can be hailed in the street, ordered by phone, or picked up at taxi ranks outside the train station, in Duke St opposite the castle, and at the corner of Greyfriars Rd and Park Pl. Reliable companies include **Capital Cabs** (☎ 2077 7777) and **Drag-on Taxis** (☎ 2033 3333).

TRAIN // Trains from major UK cities arrive at Cardiff Central station, on the southern edge of the city centre. **Arriva Trains Wales** (www.arrivatrainswales. co.uk) operate all train services in Wales. Direct services from Cardiff include London Paddington (£43, 2¾ hours), Swansea (£7.80, one hour), Carmarthen (£15, 1¾ hours), Fishguard Harbour (£20, 2¼ hours), Abergavenny (£11, 40 minutes) and Bangor (£40, 4¼ hours). Frequent trains run from Cardiff Queen St station to Cardiff Bay station (£1, four minutes), which is 500m from the harbour.

From Cathays or Central stations you have to change at Queen St.

AROUND CARDIFF

· · · · · ·

GLAMORGAN

If you're basing yourself in Cardiff there's a diverting selection of day trips to choose from in the historic county of Glamorgan – from the peculiar time-warped traditions of the British seaside, on display at Penarth and Barry, to the hills and valleys of the hinterland, rich with industrial heritage and castles straight out of childhood dreams.

☙ PENARTH // TRAVEL BACK 50 YEARS, DOCTOR WHO–STYLE, TO CARDIFF'S BEACH

Penarth (population 24,300) is an old-fashioned seaside resort – stuck some-where between the 19th and 21st centu-ries – with a tatty, turquoise, Victorian pier staggering out to sea, a trim seafront lined with Victorian terraces, and a ma-ture population wielding thermos flasks. It's connected to Cardiff Bay by the freshwater lake formed by the construc-tion of the barrage and it now sports a busy marina on the lakefront.

A block east of the train station, the red-brick **Turner House Gallery** (☎ 2070 8870; www.ffotogallery.org; Plymouth Rd; admission free; ☺ 11am-5pm Tue-Sat) has changing pho-tographic exhibitions, and runs summer workshops where kids can do stuff like print-making and pinhole photography. From the town centre, it's a five-minute walk through pretty topiary-filled **Alex-andra Gardens** down to the esplanade.

From June to September, **Waverley Excursions** (☎ 0845 130 4647; www.waver leyexcursions.co.uk) runs cruises on either the *Waverley,* the world's last seagoing paddle steamer, or its sister ship the *Balmoral,* departing from Penarth pier for a trip across the Bristol Channel to Holm Island, Clevedon, Minehead or Ilfracombe.

Cardiff buses 89, 92, 93 and 94 (20 minutes, half-hourly Monday to Saturday, hourly Sunday) run to Penarth, and there are frequent trains from Cardiff Central (£2.10, 20 minutes). There's also a **Waterbus** (☎ 0794 014 2409; www.cardiffcats. com), with departures from Penarth (near the barrage) every 45 minutes from 10am to 4pm daily, and Cardiff Bay (Pierhead Pontoons) half an hour later (single/ return £2/4, 20 minutes). See also the Aquabus service (p59).

♥ **BARRY // OH. WHAT'S OCCURRING. IN STACEY'S HOMETOWN.**
The massive popularity of the BBC Wales comedy *Gavin and Stacey* has put Barry Island back on the map. Like Penarth, it's a faded seaside resort but with a better beach and a waterfront lined with amusement arcades and fun parks. Fans of the BAFTA (British Academy of Film and

CARDIFF

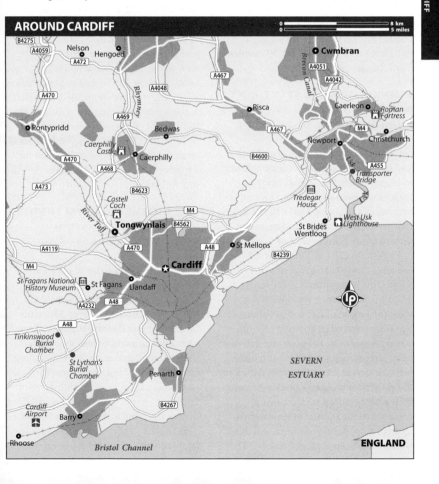

AROUND CARDIFF

Television Arts) award–winning show won't have trouble picking many of the locations used. The staff at Island Leisure (on the Promenade) are used to pilgrims stopping to pay homage at the booth where Nessa worked (played in the show by co-writer Ruth Jones). Other sites include Trinity St, where Stacey's mum and Uncle Bryn live, and the Colcot Arms pub (Colcot Rd).

Barry (population 47,900) is 8 miles southwest of Cardiff, and Barry Island is well signposted at the south end of the town. It stopped being a real island in the 1880s when it was joined to the mainland with a causeway. There are frequent Cardiff Bus services (route 95, £2.10, one hour) and trains (£2.60, 30 minutes) from the city centre.

❧ TINKINSWOOD & ST LYTHAN'S BURIAL CHAMBERS // ANCIENT STONE MEGALITHS JUST OUTSIDE THE MODERN CITY

Neolithic standing stones, stone circles and burial chambers are a dime a dozen in Wales – so much so that many of them don't even make it into tourist brochures and maps. That's the case with this mysterious duo, both standing in forlorn fields, 7 miles west of Cardiff.

The 6000-year-old Tinkinswood chamber consists of a wall of stones supporting a mammoth 7.4m-long, 36-tonne limestone capstone, thought to be the largest of its kind in Britain. It was once covered in an earth mound, but excavations in 1914 left one half of it open after removing pottery and bones belonging to at least 40 people, dating to the early Bronze Age. A brick pillar was then added to prop up the capstone. The entrance to the mound is approached by a curving avenue of stones and other stones have been arranged nearby. The

site was once known as Castell Carreg – the fairy castle.

Dating from a similar age, the St Lythan's cromlech is considerably smaller, consisting of three supporting stones capped with a large, flat stone, forming a chamber nearly 2m high. It too was probably once covered with a mound that is now long gone. As with many such pre-Christian, pre-Celtic sites, St Lythan's has many local legends attached to it. It was once thought to be a Druid's altar and on midsummer's eve the capstone supposedly spins around three times. The field it stands in is known as the Accursed Field.

You'll need your own car to get here and preferably a detailed road map. Head west of the city to Culverhouse Cross and continue west on the A48 to St Nicholas, where the sites are signposted. Turn left at the lights and look for a parking area to the right of the road where you can walk across the field to the Tinkinswood chamber. Continue down this road for a further mile and turn left at the end to find St Lythan's.

❧ ST FAGANS NATIONAL HISTORY MUSEUM // A FASCINATING RETIREMENT VILLAGE FOR AGING EDIFICES

Historic buildings from all over the country have been dismantled and re-erected in a beautiful rural setting at **St Fagans National History Museum** (☎ 2057 3500; www.museumwales.ac.uk/en/stfagans; admission free, car park £3; ☺ 10am-5pm). More than 40 buildings are on show, including farmhouses of timber and stone, barns, a watermill, a school and an 18th-century Unitarian chapel, with native breeds of livestock grazing in the surrounding fields.

St Fagans Castle is no Johnny-come-lately construction; this medieval fortress with a 16th-century manor house at its heart was donated by the earl of Plymouth in 1948, along with its extensive formal gardens, forming the basis of the museum. You'll need at least half a day to do the whole complex justice and you could easily spend longer, picnicking in the grounds.

Highlights include a farmhouse dating from 1508, redolent with the smells of old timber, beeswax and wood smoke, and a row of six miners' cottages from Merthyr Tydfil, each one restored and furnished to represent different periods in the town's history, from the austere minimalism of 1805 to all the mod cons of 1985. It took 20 years to move St Teilo's church here (built 1100 to 1520), stone by stone. It's been restored to its original look, before Protestant whitewash covered the vividly painted interior.

Not original but equally fascinating is the reproduction of three circular Celtic houses based on the archaeological remains of actual buildings.

You can see craftspeople at work in many of the buildings, showing how blankets, clogs, barrels, tools and cider were once made, and the woollen mill sells its own handmade blankets. It's a great place for kids, with special events in the summer.

The indoor galleries hold plenty of interest also, exploring the nature of Welshness through traditional costume, farming implements and the accounts of immigrants. Look for the 'Welsh Not', wooden signs that children were forced to wear as punishment if they had the temerity to speak their native tongue at school.

St Fagans is 5 miles west of central Cardiff; take bus 32 or 320 (25 minutes, hourly) from the bus station. By car, head west on Castle Rd (A4161) and continue to the end; turn right on Western Ave (A48) and left on St Fagans Rd.

🍴 CASTELL COCH // A FAIRY-TALE CASTLE, DESPITE THE NAME

Perched atop a thickly wooded crag on the northern fringes of the city is Cardiff Castle's little brother. Fanciful **Castell Coch** (☎ 2081 0101; www.cadw.wales.gov.uk; Tongwynlais; adult/child £3.60/3.20; 🕙 9am-5pm Apr-Oct, 9.30am-4pm Mon-Sat & 11am-4pm Sun Nov-Mar), run by Cadw (the Welsh historic monuments agency), was the summer retreat of the third marquess of Bute. Like Cardiff Castle it was designed by William Burges in gaudy Victorian Gothic style complete with working drawbridge and portcullis.

Raised on the ruins of Gilbert de Clare's 13th-century Castell Coch (Red Castle), the Butes' Disneyesque holiday home is a monument to high camp. Lady Bute's huge, circular bedroom is pure fantasy – her bed, with crystal globes on the bedposts, sits in the middle beneath an extravagantly decorated and mirrored cupola, with 28 painted panels around the walls depicting monkeys (fashionable at the time, apparently; just plain weird now). The corbels are carved with images of birds nesting or feeding their young, and the washbasin is framed between two castle towers.

Lord Bute's bedroom is small and plain in comparison but the octagonal drawing room is another hallucinogenic tour de force, the walls painted with scenes from Aesop's fables, the domed ceiling a flurry of birds and stars, and the fireplace topped with figures depicting the three ages of men and women. The tower to the right of the entrance houses exhibits explaining the castle's history.

Stagecoach buses 26 and 132 (30 minutes) stop at Tongwynlais, from where it's a 10-minute walk to the castle. Bus 26

CARDIFF

CARDIFF

continues to Caerphilly Castle, and the two can be combined in a day trip. Bus 26A (four daily Monday to Friday) stops right at the castle gates.

It's also an easy cycle from Cardiff to Castell Coch along the Taff Trail.

🐾 CAERPHILLY (CAERFFILI) // I'LL HAVE CHEESE WITH MY CASTLE, THANKS

The town of Caerphilly (population 31,000) – now almost a suburb of Cardiff – guards the entrance to the Rhymney Valley to the north of the capital. Its name is synonymous with a popular variety of hard, slightly crumbly white cheese (similar to cheddar, but saltier) that originated in the surrounding area.

You could be forgiven for thinking that **Caerphilly Castle** (Cadw; ☎ 2088 3143; www.cadw.wales.gov.uk; adult/child £3.60/3.20; ⏰ 9am-5pm Apr-Oct, 9.30am-4pm Mon-Sat & 11am-4pm Sun Nov-Mar) – with its profusion of towers and crenellations reflected in a duck-filled lake – was a film set rather than an ancient monument. Indeed, it often *is* used as a film set and makes a spectacular backdrop for the annual Big Cheese festival. But it is also one of Britain's finest examples of a 13th-century fortress with water defences.

Unusually, Caerphilly was never a royal castle. Most of the construction was completed between 1268 and 1271 by the powerful English baron Gilbert de Clare (1243–95), Lord Marcher of Glamorgan, in response to the threat of Prince Llewellyn ap Gruffydd, prince of Gwynedd (and the last Welsh Prince of Wales). In the 13th century Caerphilly was state-of-the-art, being one of the earliest castles to use lakes, bridges and a series of concentric fortifications for defence; to reach the inner court you had to overcome no fewer than three drawbridges, six portcullises and five sets of double gates.

Edward I's subsequent campaign against the Welsh princes put an end to Llewellyn's ambitions and Caerphilly's short-lived spell on the front line came to an end without ever tasting battle; the famous leaning tower at the southeast corner is a result of subsidence rather than sabotage. In the early 14th century it was remodelled as a grand residence and the magnificent great hall was adapted for entertaining, but from the mid-14th century onward the castle began to fall into ruin.

Much of what you see today is the result of restoration from 1928 to 1939 by

THE BIG CHEESE

Any festival that includes a Cheese Olympics and a Tommy Cooper Tent has got to be worth a look. Each year, at the end of July, Caerphilly welcomes more than 70,000 people to the **Big Cheese** (www.caerphilly.gov.uk/bigcheese; admission free), three days of family-oriented fun and games that offers everything from fireworks to falconry, comedy acts to cheese-tasting, along with medieval battle re-enactments, food and craft stalls, archery demonstrations, live music and a traditional funfair.

The Cheese Olympics are held Friday evening, and include cheese-throwing, -rolling and -stacking events. The Tommy Cooper Tent – named after the much-loved British comedian, who was born in Caerphilly and died in 1984 – stages comedy acts, including a Tommy Cooper tribute act. A statue to Cooper, in his trademark fez and with a rabbit at his feet, overlooks the castle near the tourist office.

the fourth marquess of Bute; work continued after the state bought the castle in 1950. The great hall was given a magnificent wooden ceiling in the 19th century and the Gothic windows were restored in the 1960s; it is now used to host special events. On the south dam platform you can see reconstructions of medieval siege weapons; they are working models and lob stone projectiles into the lake during battle re-enactments.

You can buy Caerphilly cheese from the **tourist office** (☎ 2088 0011; www.visitcaer philly.com; Twyn Sq; ☺ 10am-5.30pm), just east of the castle, itself clearly visible 500m north of Caerphilly train station (along Cardiff Rd).

The easiest way to reach Caerphilly from Cardiff is by train (£3.30, 19 minutes). Stagecoach buses 26, A and B (45 minutes) go from Cardiff bus station to Castle St near the tourist office; this is the same bus that goes to Castell Coch, and the two castles make a good day trip.

NEWPORT (CASNEWYDD)

☎ 01633 / pop 140,000

Hello. My name is Newport, and I'm a bit of a dump. Ah well – they say the first step on the road to recovery is admitting you have a problem, and poor old Newport has been saddled for too long with a reputation for a grim appearance and an alcoholic, binge-fuelled nightlife. Since the turn of the millennium it has made concerted efforts to clean up its act. Yet first-time visitors will ponder the car tyres and shopping carts lodged in the muddy riverbanks and wonder what's changed.

Newly crowned with city status in 2002, some of the more obvious attempts at rejuvenation are the angular Riverfront Theatre & Art Centre (opened in 2004) and the striking Usk Footbridge (opened in 2006). The city centre has some quirky pieces of modern sculpture. Northeast of the bus station, by the river, is the huge red circle of *Steel Wave* (1990) by Peter Fink, now almost a civic trademark. *Stand and Stare*, a ghostly shrouded figure on Commercial St, is dedicated to local writer WH Davies, author of *The Autobiography of a Super-Tramp*. There are several other sculptures, which are described in a leaflet available from the tourist office.

Newport takes its name from the fact that it was built after the 'old port' at Caerleon, further upstream, following the construction of Newport Castle in Norman times. Like many harbour towns in South Wales, it grew rich on the back of the iron and coal industries in the 19th and early 20th centuries.

In the second half of the 20th century, Newport's shipbuilding industry disappeared, and the docks declined in importance as coal exports shifted to Barry and iron-ore imports to Port Talbot. In 2001 the huge Llanwern steelworks closed down. Today, the city is busy trying to reinvent itself as a centre for the service sector and technology industries.

But the most famous event in Newport's history – perhaps fittingly, considering its present-day nightlife – was a street riot. Chartism, a parliamentary reform movement that arose during the early years of Queen Victoria's reign, was particularly strong in Wales. On 4 November 1839 some 5000 men from the Usk, Ebbw and Rhymney Valleys converged on Newport, intent on taking control of the town and sparking off a national uprising. They tried to storm the Westgate Hotel, where several Chartists were being held; police and infantrymen inside fired into the crowd, killing at least 20 people. Five men were

THE NEWPORT SHIP

In 2002 construction work for the new Riverfront Art Centre uncovered the remains of the most complete medieval ship ever found. Buried in the mud on the west bank of the River Usk, the 25m-long **Newport Ship** (www.thenewportship. com) dates from around 1465 and was probably built in France (archaeologists discovered a French silver coin that had been placed in one of the ship's timbers by the boat builder). Some 1700 individual timbers have been recovered, and are currently undergoing conservation so that the ship's remains can be reassembled and put on display in a purpose-built facility beneath the new arts centre. In the meantime, the ship can be viewed on monthly open days; enquire at the tourist office or check its website for details.

subsequently imprisoned and three – including John Frost, who was a major organiser – were deported to Australia.

The event is celebrated in several plaques and monuments around town, notably the Westgate Hotel on Commercial St, where the entrance pillars are still bullet-scarred. Outside, among the hurrying shoppers, is an ensemble of angry bronze figures memorialising the Chartist riot.

ESSENTIAL INFORMATION

TOURIST OFFICES // Tourist office
(☎ 842962; www.newport.gov.uk/tourism; John Frost Sq; ☾ 9am-6pm Mon-Fri, 9am-4pm Sat)

ORIENTATION

The city centre lies on the west bank of the River Usk, stretching south from the train station along pedestrianised High

St and Commercial St to the shopping plaza of John Frost Square. The entrance to the bus station is at the northern end of this square; the tourist office is at the south end.

EXPLORING NEWPORT

❧ **MEDIEVAL REMAINS //**
IT WOULDN'T BE WALES WITHOUT
A CASTLE
Not much remains of Newport's pre-industrial past, apart from the litter-strewn ruins of **Newport Castle** close to the train station – the three towers, now squeezed between traffic-clogged Kingsway and the river, were largely rebuilt after being trashed by Owain Glyndŵr in 1402 – and **St Woolos Cathedral** (www.newportcathedral.com; Stowhill), a steep 10-minute walk west of the city centre. A church was built here in 500 on the burial site of St Gwynllyw but the oldest part of the current cathedral dates from the 9th century; unfortunately it's often locked. After the Chartist riots, the bodies of 10 rioters were surreptitiously recovered and buried in the churchyard in unmarked graves.

❧ **MUSEUM & ARTS CENTRE //**
WHERE HIGH CULTURE STAKES ITS
CLAIM
In the same building as the tourist office, **Newport Museum** (☎ 656656; www.newport.gov.uk.museum; John Frost Sq; admission free; ☾ 9.30am-5pm Mon-Thu, 9am-4.30pm Fri, 9.30am-4pm Sat) covers the town's history from the Romans at Caerleon to the rise of the coal and iron industries. The nearby **Riverfront Theatre & Arts Centre** (☎ 656757; www.newport.gov.uk/riverfront; Bristol Packet Wharf; ☾ 11am-7pm Mon-Fri, 11am-5pm Sun) is the city's swish new cultural centre. Temporary exhibitions are held in its gallery and it also stages theatre, opera, clas-

sical music and dance, as well as cinema, comedy and pantomime.

⚘ TRANSPORTER BRIDGE // ONE FOR THE ENGINEERING ENTHUSIASTS

About a mile south of the city centre along Commercial St and Commercial Rd (A4042) rise the elegant spidery towers of the 1906 **Transporter Bridge** (www.newport.gov.uk/transporterbridge). A remarkable piece of Edwardian engineering, it can carry up to six cars across the river in a gondola suspended beneath the high-level track, while still allowing high-masted ships to pass beneath. It's the largest of eight such bridges remaining in the world. It operated until 1985, reopened following a £3-million refurbishment in 1995 and then closed again in 2008. By the time you're reading this, all things going to plan, it will once again be charging a nominal rate to ferry cars and pedestrians across the river.

TRANSPORT

BUS // Cardiff Bus, Newport Bus (both route 30, £1.50, 50 minutes) and **National Express** (www.nation alexpress.com; £3.50, 30 minutes) have services from Cardiff to Newport. Local bus routes and timetables are available online at www.newporttransport.co.uk.

For one week in early June and from mid-July to late August, **City Sightseeing** (☎ 263600; www.city-sightseeing.com) operates hop-on hop-off, open-top bus tours (£6, four a day) that link the bus station to all the main sights, including Caerleon, the Transporter Bridge, Tredegar House and St Woolos Cathedral.

TRAIN // The fastest and easiest connection with Cardiff is by train (£3.60, 13 minutes, six per hour). Direct trains also head to London (£39, 2½ hours).

AROUND NEWPORT

⚘ TREDEGAR HOUSE // THE STATELY HOME OF AN ECCENTRIC CLAN

The seat of the Morgan family for more than 500 years, **Tredegar House** (☎ 01633-815880; www.newport.gov.uk/tredegarhouse; park admission free, house adult/child £6.25/4.65; ⊗ park 9am-dusk year-round, house 11am-4pm Wed-Sun Easter-Sep) is a stone garland-bedecked, red-brick 17th-century country house set amid gorgeous gardens and is one of the finest examples of a Restoration mansion in Britain. The Morgans, once one of the richest families in Wales, were an interesting lot – Godfrey, second Lord Tredegar, survived the Charge of the Light Brigade; Viscount Evan kept a boxing kangaroo; and Sir Henry was a 17th-century pirate (Captain Morgan's Rum is named after him) – and the house (guided tours hourly) is a monument to their wealth and taste.

Tredegar House is 2 miles west of Newport city centre. Buses 30 and 36 stop nearby.

⚘ CAERLEON ROMAN FORTRESS // THEY CAME, SAW, CONQUERED AND BATHED

After the Romans invaded Britain in AD 43, they controlled their new territory

---

THE LEGENDARY TJ'S

No account of Newport would be complete without a mention of **TJ's** (☎ 216608; www.tjsnewport.com; 14-18 Clarence Pl). This notorious dive has been nurturing local talent since the 1970s, and still boasts a packed program of live indie and alternative music from both local and international bands. The sticky floors and poster-plastered walls have heard it all, from the Buzzcocks and Echo & the Bunnymen to Oasis, Catatonia and Green Day, and legend claims that it was here that Kurt Cobain proposed to Courtney Love.

CARDIFF

through a network of forts and military garrisons. The top tier of military organisation was the legionary fort, of which there were only three in Britain – at Eboracum (York), Deva (Chester) and Isca (Caerleon).

Caerleon (meaning 'fort of the legion') was the headquarters of the elite 2nd Augustan Legion (they fought against the Picts in Scotland and helped build Hadrian's Wall) for more than 200 years, from AD 75 until the end of the 3rd century. It wasn't just a military camp but a purpose-built township some 9 miles in circumference, complete with a 6000-seat amphitheatre and a state-of-the-art Roman baths complex. Today it is one of the largest and most important Roman settlements in Britain. The Cadw guidebook *Caerleon Roman Fortress* (£3.50) is worth buying for its maps, sketches and aerial views, which help to visualise the settlement among the distractions of the modern town.

Begin with a visit to the excellent **National Roman Legion Museum** (☎ 01633-423134; www.museumwales.ac.uk/en/roman/; High St; admission free; ☺ 10am-5pm Mon-Sat, 2-5pm Sun), which displays a host of intriguing Roman artefacts, from jewellery to armour,

teeth to tombstones, and shows what life was like for Roman soldiers in one of the remotest corners of empire.

Head next for the **Roman Baths** (Cadw; ☎ 01633-422518; www.cadw.wales.gov.uk; High St; admission free; ☺ 9.30am-5pm Apr-Oct, 9.30am-5pm Mon-Sat, 11am-4pm Sun Nov-Mar; ℗) a block to the southeast. Caerleon's baths were once as huge and splendid as the baths at Cluny in France, and remained standing until the 12th century. Parts of the outdoor swimming pool, apodyterium (changing room) and frigidarium (cold room) are on show under a protective roof, and give some idea of the scale of the place.

Broadway, the side street opposite the museum, leads to a park on the left, where you'll find the turf-covered terraces of the **Roman Amphitheatre** (admission free; ☺ 9.30am-5pm). The oval structure is the only fully excavated Roman amphitheatre in Britain; it lay just outside the old Roman city walls. Follow the signs on the other side of the road to see the foundations of the **barracks**.

Caerleon is 4 miles northeast of Newport. Buses 27D, 28A-E, 28X, 29 and 29B (15 minutes, four per hour) run from Newport bus station to Caerleon High St.

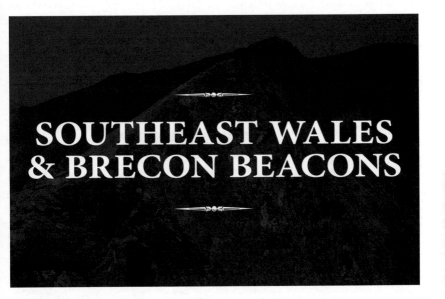

SOUTHEAST WALES & BRECON BEACONS

3 PERFECT DAYS

❧ DAY 1 // FOLLOW THE RIVERS

Spend the first part of the day exploring the lower Wye Valley, starting at the impressive castle at Chepstow (p74). Head upstream to the ghostly remains of Tintern Abbey (p77) and then continue through the wooded gorge, crossing in and out of England, until you reach Monmouth (p78). Have a quick look around but don't stop just yet. Instead, follow the River Monnow to either Skenfrith (p82) or Grosmont (p83): they're both wonderfully isolated hamlets, each with an ancient church, castle, good place to sleep and, of course, a village pub.

❧ DAY 2 // SPLENDID ISOLATION

Continuing on roads less travelled, take the A465 to Llanfihangel Crucorney (p90) and journey through the heart of the Black Mountains on the lonely road traversing the Vale of Ewyas (p90). Llanthony Priory's photogenic ruins are worth a visit. Continue over Gospel Pass, soaking up the moody moorland vistas. Drop anchor in charming Hay-on-Wye (p90), spending the afternoon rummaging through secondhand bookshops and antiques shops. Have dinner at one of the excellent pubs then check out whatever's happening at the Globe.

❧ DAY 3 // FOOD FIRST

Have a quick wander around Brecon (p97) in the morning then continue towards Abergavenny (p83). Some of Wales' best eateries lurk in country lanes along this route, so book for lunch and dinner. You can spend the afternoon walking off the calories, but if that sounds too physical, head to World Heritage–rated Blaenavon (p104). Consider Crickhowell (p94) as a place to spend the night.

SOUTHEAST WALES & BRECON BEACONS

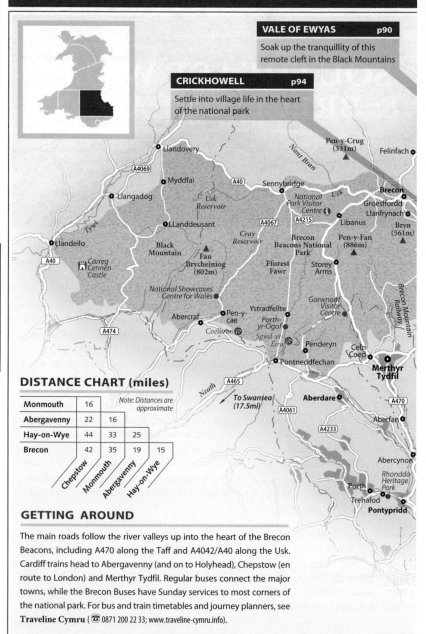

VALE OF EWYAS **p90**

Soak up the tranquillity of this remote cleft in the Black Mountains

CRICKHOWELL **p94**

Settle into village life in the heart of the national park

DISTANCE CHART (miles)

Note: Distances are approximate

Monmouth	16			
Abergavenny	22	16		
Hay-on-Wye	44	33	25	
Brecon	42	35	19	15
	Chepstow	Monmouth	Abergavenny	Hay-on-Wye

GETTING AROUND

The main roads follow the river valleys up into the heart of the Brecon Beacons, including A470 along the Taff and A4042/A40 along the Usk. Cardiff trains head to Abergavenny (and on to Holyhead), Chepstow (en route to London) and Merthyr Tydfil. Regular buses connect the major towns, while the Brecon Buses have Sunday services to most corners of the national park. For bus and train timetables and journey planners, see **Traveline Cymru** (☎ 0871 200 22 33; www.traveline-cymru.info).

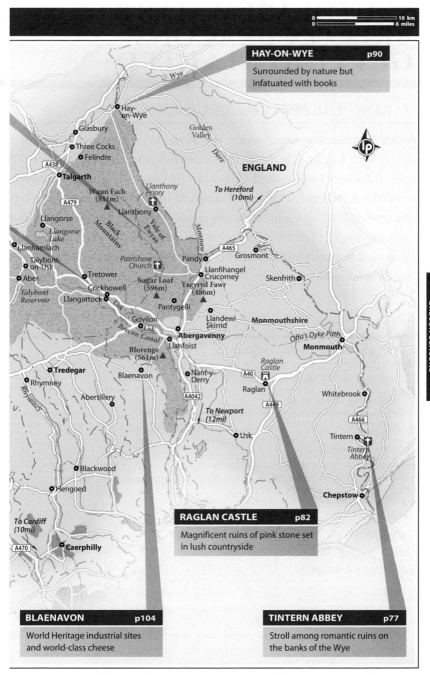

HAY-ON-WYE   p90

Surrounded by nature but infatuated with books

RAGLAN CASTLE   p82

Magnificent ruins of pink stone set in lush countryside

BLAENAVON   p104

World Heritage industrial sites and world-class cheese

TINTERN ABBEY   p77

Stroll among romantic ruins on the banks of the Wye

SOUTHEAST WALES & BRECON BEACONS

SOUTHEAST WALES & BRECON BEACONS GETTING STARTED

MAKING THE MOST OF YOUR TIME

Wales' southeast corner, where the River Wye meanders along the border with England, is the birthplace of British tourism. For over 200 years travellers have visited this tranquil waterway and its winding, wooded vale, where the ruins of Tintern Abbey have long inspired poets and artists. But there's more to the region than the market towns and rural byways of the Lower Wye. To the west the serried South Wales valleys tell the story of the industrial revolution through heritage sites and close-knit communities. Move north and the landscape changes to the magnificent upland scenery of Brecon Beacons NP.

TOP TOURS & COURSES

❧ BLACK MOUNTAIN ACTIVITIES
Try your hand white-water kayaking, rafting, climbing, abseiling, caving or mountain biking (☎ 01497-847897; www.blackmountain.co.uk; Three Cocks).

❧ CULINARY COTTAGE
Extend the gastronomic offerings of the Abergavenny countryside with themed cooking courses (☎ 01873-890125; www.theculinarycottage.co.uk; Rose Cottage, Pandy).

❧ DROVER HOLIDAYS
Tackle a long-distance cycling or walking route anywhere in Wales and this crowd will take care of the logistics (transfers, bags, bikes and accommodation); see p94.

❧ LLANTHONY RIDING & TREKKING
Explore the Black Mountains on horseback (p90).

❧ MONMOUTH CANOE & ACTIVITY CENTRE
Re-enact the Wye Tour in a Canadian canoe or kayak, with or without a guide (p81).

❧ PADDLES & PEDALS
Take to the Wye waters at Hay and get collected further downstream (☎ 01497-820604; www.canoehire.co.uk; 15 Castle St).

❧ PARAVENTURE AIRSPORTS
Learn how to paraglide (two-/four-/eight-day course £300/600/1200) or take a tandem flight off the Blorenge (£85, 20 to 30 minutes) and enjoy a red kite's perspective of the Brecon Beacons (☎ 07775-865095; www.paraventure.co.uk).

GETTING AWAY FROM IT ALL

★ **Wye Valley Walk** (www.wyevalleywalk.org) A 136-mile riverside trail running from the river's source on the slopes of Plynlimon Fawr to Chepstow. The section downstream from Monmouth, past Tintern, is particularly beautiful.

★ **Beacons Way** (www.breconbeaconsparksociety.org) A 100-mile, eight-day trail that wends its way across the national park from Abergavenny to Llangadog, knocking off all the highest summits.

★ **The Gap** (www.mtbbreconbeacons.co.uk/hubs/brecon/the-gap) Brecon Beacons' classic off-road mountain-biking route, following a 24-mile loop from Brecon that takes in a high pass close to Pen-y-Fan and an easy return along the canal.

ADVANCE PLANNING

Accommodation is hard to find during these wonderful, high-profile festivals:

★ **Abergavenny Food Festival** The most important gastronomic event in Wales, held on the third weekend in September (p86).

★ **Brecon Jazz Festival** On the second weekend in August Brecon hosts one of Europe's leading jazz events (p100).

★ **Green Man** An indie music festival with a strong green ethos, Crickhowell's August three-dayer is a highlight of the UK's summer circuit (p96).

★ **Hay Festival** Britain's leading festival of literature and the arts, held over 10 days starting late May (p92).

TOP RESTAURANTS

❦ **CROWN AT WHITEBROOK**
One of Wales' finest, hidden away in the Wye Valley (p78).

❦ **KING'S ARMS**
Abergavenny's best gastropub, serving hearty rustic fare (p86).

❦ **WALNUT TREE**
The most famous restaurant in Wales' culinary capital (p87).

❦ **HARDWICK**
Sophisticated country cooking in a thoroughly rural setting (p87).

❦ **OLD BLACK LION**
Though cosy and pub-like, this Hay-on-Wye veteran raises the culinary bar (p92).

❦ **FELIN FACH GRIFFIN**
Relaxed village inn with a formidable gastronomic reputation (p101).

RESOURCES

★ **Brecon Beacons National Park** (www.breconbeacons.org) The national park's online home.

★ **Fforest Fawr Geopark** (www.fforestfawrgeopark.org.uk) Information on the 'great forest' in the western half of the Beacons.

★ **Monmouthshire County Council** (www.monmouthshire.gov.uk) Information on events and council-run museums.

★ **Wye Valley & Vale of Usk** (www.visitwyevalley.com) In-depth tourist information.

MONMOUTH-SHIRE (SIR FYNWY)

· · · · · ·

You need only ponder the preponderance of castles to realise that this pleasantly rural county was once a wild frontier. The Norman Marcher lords kept stonemasons extremely busy, erecting mighty fortifications to keep the unruly Welsh at bay. Despite this stone line marking out a very clear border along the Rivers Monnow and Wye, the 1543 second Act of Union left Monmouthshire in a kind of jurisdictional limbo between England and Wales. This legal ambiguity wasn't put to rest until 1974 when Monmouthshire was definitively confirmed as part of Wales.

The River Wye, Britain's fifth-longest, flows from the mountains of Mid-Wales, tootles its way into England and then returns to the middle ground – forming the border of the two countries – before emptying into the River Severn below Chepstow. Much of it is designated an area of outstanding natural beauty (www.wyevalleyaonb.org.uk), famous for

its limestone gorges and dense broadleaved woodland. The most beautiful stretch lies between Monmouth and Chepstow, along the border between Monmouthshire and Gloucestershire.

CHEPSTOW (CAS-GWENT)

☎ 01291 / pop 14,200

Chepstow is an attractive market town nestled in a great S-bend in the River Wye, with a splendid Norman castle perched dramatically on a cliff above the water. The town is also home to one of Britain's best known racecourses.

Chepstow was first developed as a base for the Norman conquest of southeast Wales, later prospering as a port for the timber and wine trades. As river-borne commerce gave way to the railways, Chepstow's importance diminished to reflect its name, which means 'market place' in Old English.

ESSENTIAL INFORMATION

TOURIST OFFICES // Tourist office
(☎ 623772; castle car park, Bridge St; ⏰ 9.30am-5.30pm Apr-Oct, 9.30am-3.30pm Nov-Mar)

ORIENTATION

Chepstow sits on the west bank of the River Wye, at the north end of the old Severn Road Bridge. The train station is 250m southeast of the compact town centre (follow Station Rd); the bus station is 250m west. There are convenient car parks off Welsh St and next to the castle.

EXPLORING CHEPSTOW

❧ **CHEPSTOW CASTLE //**
BATTLEMENTS ON THE BORDERLINE
Run by Cadw (the Welsh historic monuments agency), magnificent **Chepstow**

WHAT'S IN A NAME?

Probably the greatest insult you can give the Welsh is to refer to their country as 'England'. It may seem an obvious point but it's important to get it right. England dominates the UK to such an extent that not only the English but most of the world tends to say 'England' when they mean the UK. When you cross the border into Wales, it pays to remember you're in another country. England, Scotland and Wales make up Great Britain; add in Northern Ireland and you've got the UK: the United Kingdom of Great Britain and Northern Ireland.

Castle (☎ 624065; www.cadw.wales.gov.uk; Bridge St; adult/child £3.60/3.20; ☺ 9am-5pm Apr-Oct, 9.30am-4pm Mon-Sat & 11am-4pm Sun Nov-Mar) perches atop a limestone cliff overhanging the river, guarding the main river crossing from England into South Wales (the best view is from the far bank – cross the 1816 Old Wye Bridge and turn left). It is one of the oldest castles in Britain – building began in 1067, less than a year after William the Conqueror invaded England – and the impressive Great Tower retains its original Norman architecture.

The castle's history is explained in an exhibition in the Lower Bailey, where you can see the oldest surviving castle door in Europe, a massive wooden barrier dated to before 1190. Nearby, beside the stairs down to the wine cellar, take a peek into the latrine and imagine baring your backside over this draughty stone box with a giddy drop straight down to the river. Kids will enjoy the castle grounds – there are plenty of staircases, battlements and wall walks to explore and lots of green space.

A cave in the cliff below the castle is one of many places where legend says King Arthur and his knights are napping until the day they're needed to save Britain.

Once the entire town was enclosed in fortifications, fastening it to the castle. Parts of the 13th-century **Port Wall** edge the west side of the town centre. You can see it from the Welsh St car park and near the train station. Chepstow's main street, High St, passes through the **Gate House**, the original city gate, which was restored in the 16th century.

SOUTHEAST WALES & BRECON BEACONS

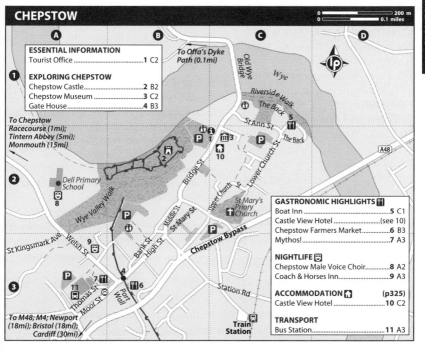

CHEPSTOW

To Offa's Dyke Path (0.1mi)

Old Wye Bridge

Wye

Riverside Walk

The Back

St Ann St

The Back

To Chepstow Racecourse (1mi); Tintern Abbey (5mi); Monmouth (15mi)

Bridge St

Lower Church St

A48

Dell Primary School

Wye Valley Walk

St Mary's Priory Church

Upper Church St

Middle St

St Mary St

Chepstow Bypass

St Kingsmark Ave

Welsh St

Bank St

High St

Station Rd

Thomas St

Moor St

Port Wall

To M48; M4; Newport (18mi); Bristol (18mi); Cardiff (30mi)

Train Station

0   200 m
0   0.1 miles

SOUTHEAST WALES & BRECON BEACONS

❦ CHEPSTOW MUSEUM // FREE LOCAL MUSEUM – WORTH A QUICK GANDER

Housed in an 18th-century town house just across the road from the castle, this small, child-friendly **museum** (☎ 625981; Bridge St; admission free; ⏰ 11am-5pm Mon-Sat & 2-5pm Sun) covers Chepstow's industrial and social history. Upstairs are depictions of Chepstow Castle as well as some intriguing hair-styling devices.

❦ CHEPSTOW RACECOURSE // PARTAKE OF THE SPORT OF KINGS

Set in rolling parkland alongside the River Wye, north of the town centre, **Chepstow Racecourse** (☎ 622260; www. chepstow-racecourse.co.uk) is one of Britain's most famous horse-racing venues. It's home to Wales' most prestigious race meeting, the Welsh National – a roughly 3-mile steeplechase held between Christmas and New Year.

❦ TINTERN AND RETURN // IN POETRY-MAD WALES EVEN THE WALKS RHYME

This classic walk begins at the tourist office and heads upriver along the Wye Valley path to Tintern Abbey, returning via Offa's Dyke Path on the eastern bank. The total distance is around 13 miles; allow a full day, with lunch at Tintern. The tourist office sells various guides, but Ordnance Survey (OS) Explorer Map OL14 is recommended. You can cut the walk short at Tintern and return to Chepstow (or continue to Monmouth) by bus.

FESTIVALS & EVENTS

Chepstow Farmers Market Held on the morning of the 2nd and 4th Saturdays of the month.
Chepstow Festival (www.chepstowfestival. co.uk) Month-long festival held in July in even-numbered years, with medieval pageantry, drama and music, outdoor art exhibits, comedy, street entertainment and Shakespeare in the castle.

Two Rivers Folk Festival (www.tworivers folkfestival.com) Three days of traditional music, morris dancers and concerts held in the castle in early July, which happily coincides with a beer and cider festival at the Coach & Horses Inn.

Chepstow Show (www.chepstowshow.co.uk) An agricultural one-dayer in August, with the usual array of livestock, craft and kennel club competitions.

GASTRONOMIC HIGHLIGHTS

❦ BOAT INN £

☎ 628192; The Back; mains £3-6

A great riverside pub strewn with nautical knick-knacks and a particularly snug 'snug', the Boat dishes up better-than-average pub grub and a good menu of daily specials. The three best tables are upstairs, beside the windows overlooking the river.

❦ CASTLE VIEW HOTEL ££

☎ 620349; 16 Bridge St; mains £9-17

Serving up solid, meaty, country fare (much of it sozzled in vodka or wine-based sauces), this historic, castle-gazing gastropub isn't short on atmosphere. It's heightened in the evening when candles flicker in moody corners and the young owner is in host-with-the-most mode.

❦ MYTHOS! ££

☎ 627222; Welsh St; mains £11-16; ⏰ noon-2am Mon-Sat, 5pm-midnight Sun

Exposed beams, stone walls and dramatic lighting make this lively Greek bar and restaurant memorable, but it's the authentic, delicious food that justifies that pretentious exclamation mark in the name: tzatziki, grilled haloumi, spanakopita (spinach-filled pastries), lamb and chicken souvlaki, moussaka – served as meze or main-sized portions.

NIGHTLIFE

♥ CHEPSTOW MALE VOICE CHOIR

☎ 641675; www.chepstowmvc.co.uk; Dell Primary School, Welsh St

Chepstow's equivalent of the cast of *Glee* (albeit a considerably older, exclusively male, much more Welsh version) rehearses every Monday and Thursday from 7.30pm to 9.15pm at a local primary school. All fans of booming Welsh manhood are welcome.

♥ COACH & HORSES INN

☎ 622626; www.sabrain.com/coach-and-horses; Welsh St

The owners of this welcoming pub, housed in a 15th-century coaching inn, are from South Africa, so they understand the Welsh passion for rugby. It gets packed to the rafters during games. Sunday night is quiz night.

TRANSPORT

BIKE // Lôn Las Cymru, the Welsh National Cycle Route (Sustrans route 8; see p302), starts at Chepstow, heading north to Abergavenny.

BUS // Bus route 69 links Chepstow with Monmouth (40 minutes) via Tintern (15 minutes), while route 74 heads to Newport (55 minutes).

COACH // National Express (www.national express.com) destinations include London (£22, three hours), Cardiff (£5.20, one hour), Swansea (£12, two hours), Carmarthen (£19, 2¼ hours), Tenby (£24, three hours) and Pembroke (£22, 3¼ hours).

PARKING // Short-term pay-and-display parking is available in large lots by the castle, off Welsh St, off Lower Church St and off Upper Church St (per hour £2, free 5pm to 9am and on Sundays). All except the latter offer long-stay rates (per day £3.50).

TRAIN // There are direct **Arriva Trains Wales** (www.arrivatrainswales.co.uk) services to Chepstow from Cardiff (£7.30, 40 minutes) via Newport (£5.50, 23 minutes), and from Gloucester (£7.40, one hour).

CHEPSTOW TO MONMOUTH

The A466 road follows the snaking, steep-sided valley of the River Wye from Monmouth all the way to Chepstow, passing through the straggling village of Tintern and its famous abbey. This is a beautiful drive, rendered particularly mysterious when a twilight mist rises from the river and shrouds the illuminated ruins.

♥ TINTERN ABBEY // BRITAIN'S MOST ROMANTIC RUINS? QUITE POSSIBLY

The spectral ruins of **Tintern Abbey** (Cadw; ☎ 01291-689251; www.cadw.wales.gov.uk; adult/child £3.60/3.20; ⏰ 9am-5pm Apr-Oct, 9.30am-4pm Mon-Sat & 11am-4pm Sun Nov-Mar; Ⓟ) sit by the River Wye, the worn stone scabbed with lichen and mottled grey, purple, pink and gold. Founded in 1131 by the Cistercian order, this sprawling monastic complex is one of the most intact medieval abbeys in Britain, its soaring Gothic arches and ornate tracery a testament to Cistercian wealth and power.

The haunting ruins and their riverside setting have inspired poets and artists through the centuries, including William Wordsworth, who penned *Lines Composed a Few Miles Above Tintern Abbey* during a visit in 1798, and JMW Turner, who made many paintings and drawings of the ruins.

The huge abbey church was built between 1269 and 1301, and the stone shell remains surprisingly intact; the finest feature is tracery that once contained the magnificent west windows. Spreading to the north are the remains of the cloisters, the infirmary, the chapter house, the refectory, the latrines and a complex system of drains and sewers.

SOUTHEAST WALES & BRECON BEACONS

SOUTHEAST WALES & BRECON BEACONS

SOUTHEAST WALES & BRECON BEACONS ACCOMMODATION

While the post-industrial valleys are well worth visiting, most travellers prefer staying in the lush Monmouthshire countryside or within the national park itself. Villages such as Crickhowell, Skenfrith and Grosmont may not have an awful lot of sights per se, but they make for peaceful retreats. If you're a bit booky, arty, or a closet *Antiques Roadshow* watcher, then Hay-on-Wye may be for you. For full accommodation reviews, see p325. Small, personable B&Bs top our picks for the region:

* ★ **Gentle Jane** (p326) Characterful rooms in the sleepy village of Grosmont.
* ★ **Highfield House** (p326) Victorian town house in a quiet Abergavenny street.
* ★ **Start** (p327) Eighteenth-century ambience on the edge of Hay-on-Wye.
* ★ **Gwyn Deri** (p327) Hospitable hosts and modern rooms in Crickhowell.
* ★ **Cantre Selyf** (p329) Atmospheric 17th-century town house in Brecon.

The site is clearly visible from the road, but if you want to explore it properly you'll need at least two hours to do it justice. It's best visited towards the end of the day after the coach-tour crowds have dispersed.

There are plenty of options for riverside walks around Tintern. One of the best begins at the old railway bridge just upstream from the abbey, and leads up to the Devil's Pulpit, a limestone crag on the east side of the river with a spectacular view over the abbey (2.5 miles round trip).

Bus 69 stops here, en route between Chepstow (15 minutes) and Monmouth (30 minutes).

❦ OLD STATION TINTERN // STOP FOR A PICNIC AND A STROLL

Just over 1 mile upstream from the abbey is **Old Station Tintern** (☎ 01291-689566; www.monmouthshire.gov.uk/oldstationtintern; admission free, parking per 3/5 hr 50p/£1; ☯ 10am-5.30pm Apr-Oct), a Victorian train station with old railway coaches that house a tourist information desk, temporary exhibitions and a cafe. There's a large grassy play area for kids, picnic spots and easy riverside walks.

❦ CROWN AT WHITEBROOK // A RESTAURANT THAT'S A DESTINATION IN ITSELF

Sometimes dining at the very best restaurants requires a commitment, which is certainly true of the **Crown** (☎ 01600-860254; www.crownatwhitebrook.co.uk; Whitebrook; 2-/3-course lunch £25/28, 3-/6-/9-course dinner £48/55/70; ☯ closed Sun dinner). It's reached by a narrow country lane following the west bank of the Wye, 1 mile north of the turnoff where the A466 crosses the river into England; look for the rarefied light of the Michelin star that's hung over it since 2007. The elegant dining room and the riverside setting may conspire to ignite romance in the hardest of hearts, while the fine cuisine (combining fusion flavours with game meats) may melt them completely. If you don't fancy driving afterwards, or the romantic ambience has worked its magic, get a room (doubles £125 to £150).

MONMOUTH (TREFYNWY)

☎ 01600 / pop 9500

Against a background of pastel-painted Georgian prosperity, the compact market town of Monmouth bustles and thrives.

It sits at the confluence of the Rivers Wye and Monnow, and has hopped in and out of Wales over the centuries as the border shifted back and forth. Today, it feels more English than Welsh.

The town is famous as the birthplace of King Henry V, victor at the Battle of Agincourt in 1415 and immortalised by Shakespeare. Other locals who have passed into history include the 12th-century historian Geoffrey of Monmouth (p313) and Charles Stewart Rolls, co-founder of Rolls-Royce.

In modern times Monmouth's main claim to fame is the Rockfield recording studio, a few miles to the northwest. Established in the 1960s, the studio has produced a string of hit albums, including Queen's *A Night at the Opera,* Oasis' *(What's the Story) Morning Glory?* and Super Furry Animals' *Rings Around the World,* and has been used by artists from Iggy Pop to Coldplay. It's not unknown for rock stars to be spotted in Monmouth's pubs and restaurants.

ESSENTIAL INFORMATION

TOURIST OFFICES // Tourist office
(☎ 713899; www.visitwyevalley.com; Priory St;
⏱ 9.30am-1pm & 2-3.30pm Mon-Sat)

EXPLORING MONMOUTH

❧ MONNOW STREET // A RICH HISTORY LURKS BEHIND THE CHAIN STORES

Monmouth's main drag, such that it is, starts at car-free **Monnow Bridge**, the UK's only complete example of a medieval fortified bridge. It was built in 1270, although much of what you see now was restored in 1705. Before you cross into town, it's worth poking your head into **St Thomas the Martyr's Church**. Parts of it date from around

1180 – there's an impressive Norman Romanesque arch, and pews and a gallery fashioned out of dark wood.

When Catholicism was banned in Britain, Monmouthshire was a pocket of resistance. In the 16th-century, secret Masses were held at the **Robin Hood Inn** (☎ 715423; 124 Monnow St), which still stands at the foot of Morrow St; apart from its historic connections, it's a great place for a pint or pub meal, with a big beer garden. In 1679 a Catholic priest, Fr (later St) David Lewis, was discovered, tried in Monmouth and hung, drawn and quartered in nearby Usk. In 1793, after the Catholic suppression ended, the first new Catholic church in Wales was built in Monmouth. Even then, **St Mary's Church** (St Mary's St) needed to be discreet and was hidden behind a line of cottages; they're now removed, explaining why it's set back from the road.

At the top end of Monnow St is Agincourt Sq, dominated by the arcade of the 1724 **Shire Hall** and a statue of former Monmouth resident Charles Stewart Rolls (1877–1910). One half of the team that founded Rolls-Royce, Rolls was not only a pioneering motorist and aviator, he was the first British citizen to die in an air accident (his statue is clutching a model of the Wright biplane in which he died).

❧ NELSON MUSEUM & LOCAL HISTORY CENTRE // PROVING INFATUATED FANS AREN'T A MODERN PHENOMENON

Admiral Horatio Nelson visited Monmouth twice in 1802, officially en route to inspect Pembrokeshire forests for ship timber (though it may have had more to do with his affair with local heiress Lady Emma Hamilton). Despite this tenuous connection, Lady Llangattock, local aristocrat and mother of Charles Stewart Rolls, became an obsessive collector of 'Nelsoniana', and the results of her obsession can be seen in this endearing **museum** (☎ 710630; www.visitwyevalley. com/nelsonmuseum.html; Priory St; admission free; ☷ 10am-1pm & 2-5pm Mon-Sat, 2-5pm Sun). It's fascinating to see how fanatical Nelsonworship was in 19th-century Britain, with forged items, such as locks of his hair, displayed alongside banal relics of the great man himself (his first attempt at left-handed writing being a

case in point). Monmouth history is also covered, including a display on Rolls, naturally, and some interesting old photographs.

⚑ MONMOUTH CASTLE & REGIMENTAL MUSEUM // SHAKESPEARE MADE IT SOUND GRANDER

The meagre remains of **Monmouth Castle** (Castle Hill), where in 1397 Henry V was born, are set back from Monnow St. Except for the great tower (no public access), it was dismantled in the 17th cen-

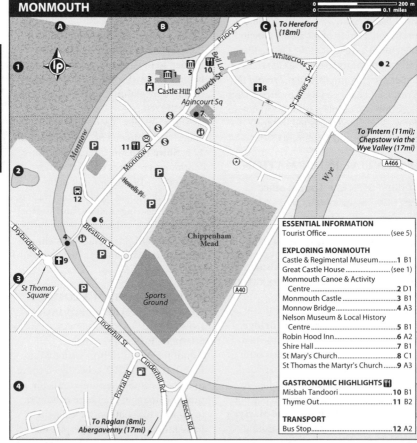

MONMOUTH

0 .... 200 m
0 .... 0.1 miles

To Hereford (18mi)

To Tintern (11mi); Chepstow via the Wye Valley (17mi)

To Raglan (8mi); Abergavenny (17mi)

ESSENTIAL INFORMATION
Tourist Office .... (see 5)

EXPLORING MONMOUTH
Castle & Regimental Museum..........**1** B1
Great Castle House .... (see 1)
Monmouth Canoe & Activity
  Centre **2** D1
Monmouth Castle **3** B1
Monnow Bridge..................................**4** A3
Nelson Museum & Local History
  Centre **5** B1
Robin Hood Inn..................................**6** A2
Shire Hall...**7** B1
St Mary's Church................................**8** C1
St Thomas the Martyr's Church **9** A3

GASTRONOMIC HIGHLIGHTS 🍴
Misbah Tandoori **10** B1
Thyme Out..**11** B2

TRANSPORT
Bus Stop..**12** A2

SOUTHEAST WALES & BRECON BEACONS

tury and the stone used to build **Great Castle House** next door, now headquarters of the Royal Monmouthshire Regiment. Inside is the volunteer-run **Castle & Regimental Museum** (☎ 772175; www .monmouthcastlemuseum.org.uk; admission free; ⦿ 2-5pm Easter-Oct), a labour of love squeezed into a cupboard-sized space, tracing the regiment's history from the 16th century.

❧ RIVER PADDLES // FOLLOW IN THE WAKE OF BRITAIN'S FIRST TOURISTS

If you're keen to do your own version of the Wye Tour you can hire a two-person Canadian canoe (half-day/day/five days £26/35/135), single kayak (£20/25/115) or double kayak (£26/35/165) from the **Monmouth Canoe & Activity Centre** (☎ 713461; www. monmouthcanoe.co.uk; Castle Yard, Old Dixton Rd); transport and guides/instructors cost extra (guided trips £45 to £95). You'll need a guide to navigate the tidal section of the river downstream from Bigsweir Bridge, near Tintern. Beginners can opt for a half-day trip through the gorge at Symonds Yat (near the Welsh-English border), or an evening's leisurely paddle from Monmouth down to Redbrook.

FESTIVALS & EVENTS

Wye Valley Chamber Music Festival (www.wyevalleyfestival.com) A week of warming chamber music, held in early January at Treowen Manor (when it's not cut off by the snow, as it was in 2010).
Monmouth Women's Festival (www. monmouthwomensfestival.org.uk) Interesting speakers, films and exhibitions, held over two weeks in early March.
Monmouth Festival (www.monmouthfestival. co.uk) Nine days of free music held in late July. It's a

mixed bag of mainly obscure acts with the occasional nearly-there or past-their-prime performer.
Monmouth Show (www.monmouthshow.co.uk) A one-day agricultural show, held in late August, with entertainment, livestock competitions and skurry (horse and carriage) races.

GASTRONOMIC HIGHLIGHTS

❧ MISBAH TANDOORI ££
☎ 714940; 9 Priory St; mains £6-14
One of Wales' top curry houses (check out the Welsh Curry House of the Year Awards 2010, if you don't believe us), the Misbah is an authentic Bangladeshi family restaurant with a large, loyal and sometimes famous following. Paul Weller, REM, Oasis and Arthur Scargill have all dined here.

❧ THYME OUT £
☎ 719339; 31-33 Monnow St; mains £4-7; ⦿ 9am-5pm Mon-Sat
An excellent little place for breakfasts (croissants, eggs or a fry-up) and snack lunches (soup, quiche, baked potatoes, salads and wraps), this little gem has a sunny patio and an equally sunny disposition. It's located upstairs from the Salt & Pepper kitchenware shop, and the neighbouring clothes boutique is part of the same group.

TRANSPORT

BUS // Bus route 69 runs along the Wye Valley from Monmouth to Chepstow (40 minutes) via Tintern (35 minutes); route 83 heads to Abergavenny (45 minutes) via Raglan (20 minutes); and route 60 heads to Newport (55 minutes) via Raglan.
COACH // National Express (www.national express.com) coaches head from Monmouth to Birmingham (£20, 1½ hours), Newport (£7.60, 35 minutes) and Cardiff (£9.70, 1¼ hours).
PARKING // There's free parking on Cinderhill St, near St Thomas the Martyr's Church.

SOUTHEAST WALES & BRECON BEACONS

THE WYE TOUR

The Wye Valley has a valid claim to be the birthplace of British tourism. Boat trips along the River Wye began commercially in 1760, but a best-selling book – in fact, one of the first ever travel guidebooks – William Gilpin's *Observations on the River Wye and Several Parts of South Wales* (1771), inspired hundreds of people to take the boat trip down the river from Ross-on-Wye (in England) to Chepstow, visiting the various beauty spots and historical sites en route. Early tourists included many famous figures, from poets William Wordsworth and Samuel Taylor Coleridge and painter JMW Turner to celebrities such as Admiral Lord Nelson, who made the tour in 1802. Doing the Wye Tour soon became de rigueur among English high society.

Local people made good money providing crewed rowing boats for hire, which were equipped with canopies and comfortable chairs and tables where their clients could paint or write, while inns and taverns cashed in on the trade by providing food, drink and accommodation. It was normally a two-day trip, with an overnight stay in Monmouth and stops at Tintern Abbey and Chepstow Castle, among others. In the second half of the 19th century, with the arrival of the railways, the hundreds increased to thousands, and the tour became so commercialised that it was no longer fashionable.

You can still do the Wye Tour, but these days it's a less glamorous, more DIY affair; see p81 for details of canoe hire.

AROUND MONMOUTH

❦ RAGLAN CASTLE // THE FINEST OF MONMOUTHSHIRE'S MANY CASTLES

The last great medieval castle to be built in Wales was the magnificent **Raglan Castle** (Cadw; ☎ 01291-690228; www.cadw.wales. gov.uk; adult/child £3/2.60; ☒ 9am-5pm Apr-Oct, 9.30am-4pm Mon-Sat & 11am-4pm Sun Nov-Mar; ℗). Designed more as a swaggering declaration of wealth and power than a defensive fortress, it was built in the 15th and 16th centuries by Sir William ap Thomas and his son, the earl of Pembroke.

A sprawling complex built of dusky pink sandstone, its centrepiece is the lavish Great Tower, a hexagonal keep ringed by a moat. It bears a savage wound from the civil wars of the 1640s, when it was besieged by Cromwell's soldiers – after its surrender the tower was undermined, until eventually two of the six walls collapsed.

The impressive courtyards beyond the Great Tower display the transition from fortress to grandiose palace, with ornate windows and fireplaces, gargoyle-studded crenellations and heraldic carvings.

Raglan is 8 miles southwest of Monmouth and 9 miles southeast of Abergavenny. Bus 83 from Monmouth (20 minutes) and Abergavenny (25 minutes), and bus 60 from Monmouth and Newport (36 minutes) stop here; it's a five-minute walk to the castle.

❦ SKENFRITH // RIVER, CASTLE, CHURCH AND PUB IN PERFECT HARMONY

A chocolate-box village of stone buildings set around a hefty castle and ancient church and skirted by the River Monnow, Skenfrith encapsulates the essence of the Monmouthshire countryside.

Skenfrith Castle (admission free; ☾ 24hr) was built around 1228 by Hubert de Burgh on the site of earlier Norman fortifications. Its keep and walls remain reasonably intact and there are no barriers to prevent you entering and picnicking on the central lawn. Nearby, a squat tower announces 750-year-old **St Bridget's Church**, accessed by a low wooden door with a foot-high step.

The riverside village pub, the Bell (p326), has had a gastro makeover and is now an esteemed restaurant serving upmarket country fare (mains £15 to £19). It produces its own walk pamphlets (50p) – one route leads over the English border to **Garway Church**, which is adorned with swastikas and mason's mark from its Knights Templar past.

Skenfrith is 8 miles northwest of Monmouth via the B4233, B4347 and B4521. There's no public transport to these parts.

❧ **GROSMONT // COMBINING THE SAME ELEMENTS TO THE SAME EFFECT**

Pressed from a similar mould to Skenfrith, although its contours are a little more rugged, Grosmont is another charming and character-filled village set amid the classically beautiful Monmouthshire countryside. Its **castle** (admission free) has the same history as Skenfrith's, although de Burgh completed this one 24 years earlier. The ruins are very picturesque, set behind a deep moat with an elegant 14th-century chimney jutting out.

Two protected species of bats live in the belfry of ancient **St Nicholas Church**. Its churchyard is well worth an idle wander, while the **Angel Inn** is the centrepiece of the village and is never

short of good beer and friendly locals. If you feel like stopping, there are excellent rooms above Gentle Jane tearooms (p326).

Grosmont is 5 miles northwest of Skenfrith along the B4347.

ABERGAVENNY (Y-FENNI)

☎ 01873 / pop 14,000

Bustling, workaday Abergavenny is set amid shapely, tree-fringed hills in the northwest corner of Monmouthshire, on the eastern edge of Brecon Beacons National Park. While not the most immediately attractive town, it's well worth getting under its skin.

Abergavenny was traditionally best known as a place for outdoor pursuits (it makes a fine base for walks, cycling and paragliding in the surrounding hills), but it's as the capital of a burgeoning food scene that the town has really come into its own. Its position at the heart of Wales' new cuisine, which celebrates the best in fresh, local and organic produce, is generating international interest in both its food festival and its acclaimed eateries, the best of which are actually just out of town in the surrounding countryside.

Its ancient name, Y-Fenni (uh-*ven*-ni; Welsh for 'place of the smiths'), was given to a stream that empties into the River Usk here, and later anglicised to Gavenny (Abergavenny means 'mouth of the Gavenny'). The Romans established Gobannium Fort here, exactly a day's march from their garrison at Caerleon (p67), which they maintained from AD 57 to 400. In around 1100 a Marcher lord, Hamelin de Ballon, built the castle and the town's regional importance grew.

SOUTHEAST WALES & BRECON BEACONS

ESSENTIAL INFORMATION

EMERGENCIES // Nevill Hall Hospital
(☎ 732732; Brecon Rd; ☼ 24hr) Emergency service.
Police station (☎ 852273; Tudor St)
TOURIST OFFICES // Tourist office
(☎ 853254; www.visitabergavenny.co.uk; Swan
Meadow, Cross St; ☼ 10am-5pm Apr-Oct, 10am-4pm
Nov-Mar) Merged with the Brecon Beacons National Park
visitor centre.

ORIENTATION

The tourist office is next to the bus station, a few minutes' walk southeast of the
town centre; the train station is a further
half-mile walk along Monmouth Rd and
Station Rd.

EXPLORING ABERGAVENNY

♥ ST MARY'S PRIORY CHURCH // WELSH HISTORY'S CELEBS, FROZEN IN STONE

The relatively modest-looking **St Mary's
Priory Church** (www.stmarys-priory.org; Monk
St; ☼ 10am-4pm) has been described as the
'Westminster Abbey of South Wales' be-
cause of the remarkable treasury of aris-
tocratic tombs that lies within. During

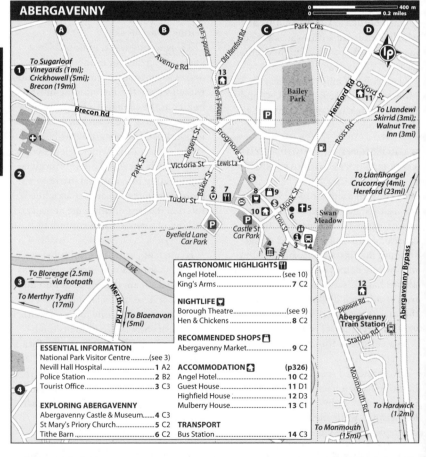

ABERGAVENNY

0 _____ 400 m
0 _____ 0.2 miles

To Sugarloaf Vineyards (1mi); Crickhowell (5mi); Brecon (19mi)

To Llandewi Skirrid (3mi); Walnut Tree Inn (3mi)

To Llanfihangel Crucorney (4mi); Hereford (23mi)

To Blorenge (2.5mi) via footpath

To Merthyr Tydfil (17mi)

To Blaenavon (5mi)

To Hardwick (1.2mi)

To Monmouth (15mi)

the official opening hours there's usually a volunteer warden around to answer questions; outside of these times, ask at the neighbouring Tithe Barn to have the doors unlocked.

St Mary's was founded at the same time as the castle (1087) as part of a Benedictine priory, but the present building dates mainly from the 14th century, with 15th- and 19th-century additions and alterations. A graceful, worn, carved-oak effigy (1325) in the north transept commemorates Sir John de Hastings, who was responsible for the church's 14th-century transformation. It survived Henry VIII's dissolution of the monasteries by being converted into a parish church, making it an interesting counterpoint to the ruins of nearby Tintern and Llanthony abbeys.

The oldest memorial (1256) is the stone figure near the sanctuary of Eva de Braose, Lady Abergavenny, portrayed holding a shield. Her husband William was hanged after being found in the bedchamber of Prince Llywelyn the Great's wife, daughter of England's King John; the family tradition of royal adultery and execution continued with their direct descendant, Anne Boleyn.

In the northern transept is one of the most important medieval carvings in Europe – a monumental 15th-century wooden representation of the biblical figure of Jesse. It was the base of what must have been a mighty altarpiece showing the lineage of Jesus and the only such figure to survive the Reformation.

The Herbert Chapel is packed with recumbent effigies. Most depict members of the Herbert family, starting with Sir William ap Thomas, founder of Raglan Castle (p82), and his wife Gwladys – Sir William's feet rest on a lion that looks like it was modelled on a sheep. The oak choir stalls were carved in the 15th century (note the lively misericords and the little dragons at the ends).

❦ TITHE BARN // FEED YOUR MIND AND YOUR BELLY

The large blocky building next to the church is the former abbey's 13th-century **tithe barn** (☎ 858787; www.stmarys-priory.org; Monk St; admission free; ☘ 9am-5pm), the place where people brought their obligatory contributions to the church, usually 10% of whatever they produced. This particular one has had a chequered history (it was a 17th-century theatre and a 20th-century disco, among other things) but has recently been fully restored and converted into an excellent heritage centre and a food hall focussing on locally sourced Welsh products.

Pride of place goes to the **Abergavenny Tapestry**, produced by 60 local volunteers over six years to mark the new millennium. Within its 8m width it depicts the history of the town; look for faint messages from the stitchers in the borders. Elsewhere on this floor a combination of artefacts and touch-screen monitors tell the story of the town and the abbey in an excellent interactive display.

❦ ABERGAVENNY CASTLE & MUSEUM // TREACHERY, SADDLERY AND GROCERY IN THE RUINS

Not much remains of **Abergavenny Castle** except for an impressive stretch of curtain wall on either side of the gatehouse on the northwest side. It was the site of a notorious event in 1175 when the Norman lord invited his Welsh rivals for a Christmas dinner and had them massacred. Frequently besieged but never taken, the castle was wrecked by royalist forces in 1645 during the Civil War in order to keep it out of parliamentary hands.

SOUTHEAST WALES & BRECON BEACONS

The castle keep, converted into a hunting lodge by the Victorians, now houses the small **Abergavenny Museum** (☎ 854282; www.abergavennymuseum.co.uk; Castle St; admission free; ⏰ 11am-1pm & 2-5pm Mon-Sat, 2-5pm Sun Mar-Oct, 11am-1pm & 2-4pm Mon-Sat Nov-Feb). It tells the history of the castle and the town, and includes re-creations of a Victorian Welsh farmhouse kitchen, a saddlery workshop, and Basil Jones' grocery shop. The latter was transferred when it closed in the 1980s and makes a fascinating display, with many items dating back to the 1930s and '40s.

☙ WALKS // CLIMB EVERY MOUNTAIN OR WALK ALONG THE STREAM

Abergavenny sits between three impressive protrusions: Blorenge (p94) to the southwest, Ysgyryd Fawr (p89) to the northeast and Sugar Loaf (p89) to the northwest. Each has rewarding walks and fine views of the Usk Valley and the Black Mountains, of which the last two form the southernmost summits.

For more leisurely walks, you can follow easy paths along the banks of the River Usk or explore the towpath of the Monmouthshire and Brecon Canal, which passes 1 mile southwest of the town.

You can buy national park walk cards from the tourist office.

FESTIVALS & EVENTS

South Wales Three Peaks Trial (www.threepeakstrial.co.uk) An annual walking challenge held in March to test your endurance and map-reading skills.
Abergavenny Festival of Cycling (www.abergavennyfestivalofcycling.co.uk) A mid-July lycra-enthusiasts' meet incorporating the Iron Mountain Sportif, a participatory event with 25-mile, 50-mile and 100-mile courses.
Abergavenny Food Festival (www.abergavennyfoodfestival.co.uk) The most important gas-tronomic event in Wales, held on the third weekend in September, with demonstrations, debates, competitions, courses, stalls and the odd celebrity. But the real draw-card is that this is an enthusiastically local festival, run by volunteers, and not some big-budget food producer's showcase. Kooky things can and do happen.

GASTRONOMIC HIGHLIGHTS

☙ ANGEL HOTEL ££
☎ 857121; 15 Cross St; mains £7-21
The Angel offers a choice of eating options, from an informal meal in front of the log fire in the bar to the sophisticated restaurant with its crisp, white linen and attentive service, to a romantic dinner in the candle-lit courtyard. The menu makes the most of local produce – the roast lamb is tender and succulent – and there's an excellent wine list.

☙ KING'S ARMS ££
☎ 855074; 29 Nevill St; mains £10-17
Cosy and atmospheric, the King's Arms is a great old tavern (at least 14th-century) where you can down a pint accompanied with a quality steak-and-ale pie or bangers and mash. The restaurant menu (Brecon venison, Swansea Bay sea bass) takes things to the next level of sophistication, while still keeping a rustic edge.

NIGHTLIFE

☙ BOROUGH THEATRE
☎ 850805; www.boroughtheatreabergavenny.co.uk; Cross St
It's strange now to think that the Beatles played this small theatre in Abergavenny Town Hall in 1963. It stages a varied program of drama, opera, dance, comedy and music.

☙ HEN & CHICKENS
☎ 853613; 7 Flannel St; 🖥
A traditional real-ale pub tucked down a pedestrianised alley, the Hen & Chick-

ens hosts live jazz sessions on Sunday afternoons (outside when it's sunny) and occasional folk music sessions. The pub grub's good too.

RECOMMENDED SHOPS

⚘ ABERGAVENNY MARKET

☎ 735811; www.abergavennymarket.co.uk; Cross St
The 19th-century **Market Hall** is a lively place, hosting a general market (food, drink, clothes, household goods) on Tuesday, Friday and Saturday, a flea market (bric-a-brac, collectables, secondhand goods) on Wednesday, regular weekend craft and antiques fairs, and a farmers market on the fourth Thursday of each month.

⚘ SUGARLOAF VINEYARDS

☎ 853066; www.sugarloafvineyard.co.uk; ☺ 10.30am-5pm Tue-Sat & noon-5pm Sun Easter-Oct, 11am-5pm Tue-Sat Nov-24 Dec
Established in 1992, these **vineyards** on the western edge of town produce a variety of wines, including an award-winning sparkling. You can take a self-guided tour before sampling the goods at the cafe and gift shop.

TRANSPORT

BIKE // Lôn Las Cymru (p302) passes through Abergavenny, heading north to Builth Wells and south to Chepstow.
BUS // Bus routes include 83 to Monmouth (45 minutes) via Raglan (20 minutes); X3 to Cardiff (1½ hours); X4 to Merthyr Tydfil (1½ hours); and X43 to Brecon (50 minutes) via Crickhowell (15 minutes). See p89 for details about the Beacons Buses.
COACH // National Express (www.national express.com) coaches head to Birmingham (£12, three hours) and Merthyr Tydfil (£8, 50 minutes).
PARKING // There's free parking at a large lot on Byefield Lane, every day except Tuesday. Otherwise the Bailey Park and Castle St lots are cheap (per two hours/day 80p/£3.50, free Sunday and from 5pm to 9am).

TAXI // Local companies include **Taxis Abergavenny** (☎ 750006; www.abergavennytaxi.co.uk).
TRAIN // There are direct trains from Cardiff (£11, 40 minutes), Newport (£6.80, 25 minutes), Shrewsbury (£22, 1¼ hours), Wrexham (£21, two hours), Bangor (£35, 3½ hours) and Holyhead (£37, 4¼ hours).

AROUND ABERGAVENNY

⚘ WALNUT TREE // THE MOST FAMOUS RESTAURANT IN WALES' CUISINE CAPITAL

Established in 1963, the legendary **Walnut Tree** (☎ 852797; www.thewalnuttreeinn. com; Llandewi Skirrid; mains £12-20, 2-/3-course lunch £18/23; ☺ Tue-Sat) remains one of Wales' finest restaurants despite a change of ownership, with a Michelin star to prove it. Fresh, local produce dominates, and with wood pigeon and hare on the menu last time we visited, we wouldn't be all that surprised if some of it was once scurrying around the back yard. The Walnut Tree is 3 miles northeast of Abergavenny on the B4521.

⚘ HARDWICK // COUNTRY COOKING AT ITS BEST

The **Hardwick** (☎ 854220; www.thehardwick. co.uk; Old Raglan Rd; mains £14-20, 2-/3-course lunch £19/24; ☺ Tue-Sat) is a traditional pub-style restaurant with an old stone fireplace, low ceiling beams and terracotta floor tiles. Ex–Walnut Tree alumnus Stephen Terry has created a gloriously unpretentious menu that celebrates the best of country cooking; save room for the homemade ice cream. The Hardwick is 2 miles south of Abergavenny on the B4598.

⚘ FOXHUNTER // ANOTHER RUSTIC RESTAURANT IN BEAUTIFUL SURROUNDS

A Victorian stationmaster's house with flagstone floors and wood-burning stoves

SOUTHEAST WALES & BRECON BEACONS

that's had an elegant contemporary makeover, the **Foxhunter** (☎ 881101; www.thefoxhunter.com; Nant-y-Derry; mains £17-22; ☺ lunch Tue-Sun, dinner Tue-Sat) brings an adventurous approach to fresh, seasonal produce, which might include slow-roasted goose leg or wild elvers (baby eels from the River Wye). The Foxhunter is 7 miles south of Abergavenny, just east of the A4042.

BRECON BEACONS NATIONAL PARK

· · · · · ·

Rippling dramatically for 45 miles from Llandeilo in the west all the way to the English border, Brecon Beacons National Park (Parc Cenedlaethol Bannau Brycheiniog) encompasses some of the finest scenery in South Wales. High mountain plateaus of grass and heather, their northern rims scalloped with glacier-scoured hollows, rise above wooded, waterfall-splashed valleys and green, rural landscapes. It couldn't be more different than rock-strewn Snowdonia to the north, but it offers comparable thrills.

There are four distinct regions within the park, neatly bounded by main roads: the wild, lonely **Black Mountain** (Mynydd Du) in the west, with its high moors and glacial lakes; **Fforest Fawr** (Great Forest), which lies between the A4067 and A470, whose rushing streams and spectacular waterfalls form the headwaters of the Rivers Tawe and Neath; the **Brecon Beacons** (Bannau Brycheiniog) proper, a group of very distinctive, flat-topped hills that includes Pen-y-Fan (886m), the park's (and southern Britain's) highest peak; and, from the A40 northeast to the English border, the rolling heathland ridges of the **Black Mountains** (Y Mynyddoedd Duon) – don't

confuse them with the Black Mountain (singular) in the west.

In 2005 the western half of the national park was given geopark recognition by Unesco. The **Fforest Fawr Geopark** (www.fforestfawrgeopark.org.uk) stretches from Black Mountain in the west to Pen-y-Fan in the east, and it takes in important landscape features such as the ice-sculpted northern faces of the Brecon Beacons, the gorges and waterfalls around Ystradfellte, and the caves and limestone pavements of the southern Black Mountain.

There are hundreds of walking routes in the park, ranging from gentle strolls to strenuous climbs. The park's staff organise guided walks and other active events throughout the summer. A set of six Walk Cards (£1 each) is available from the town tourist offices in and around the park, as well as the main park visitor centre near Libanus (p101).

Likewise, there are many excellent off-road mountain-biking routes, including a series of 14 graded and waymarked trails detailed in a map and guidebook pack (£7.50); see also www.mtbbreconbeacons.co.uk.

Ordnance Survey (OS) Landranger maps 160 and 161 cover most of the park, and have walking and cycling trails marked.

BLACK MOUNTAINS (Y MYNYDDOEDD DUON)

The hills that stretch northward from Abergavenny to Hay-on-Wye, bordered by the A479 road to the west and the English border to the east, are known as the Black Mountains (not to be confused with the Black Mountain, singular, at the western end of the national park). The hills are bleak, wild and largely uninhabited, making them a popular walking area; the highest summit is Waun Fach

BEACONS BUSES

The **Beacons Buses** (☎ 01873-853254; www.travelbreconbeacons.info) only run on Sundays and bank holidays from April to September, but during that time they successfully shunt visitors both into and around the national park. With a day ticket (£8, buy it on the first bus you board) and a careful analysis of the online timetable you can plan a full day of sightseeing and activities. On the B16 and B17 circular routes you can get on and off at any point (adult/child £5/3.50). Some services allow bikes to be transported. Useful routes include the following:

B1 Cardiff, Merthyr Tydfil, Storey Arms, Libanus, Brecon

B2 Storey Arms, Libanus, Brecon

B3 Penderyn, Storey Arms, Libanus, Brecon

B4 Newport, Abergavenny, Crickhowell, Tretower, Brecon

B5 Cardiff, Caerphilly, Merthyr Tydfil, Libanus, Brecon

B6 Swansea, National Showcaves Centre, Brecon

B10 Carmarthen, National Botanic Garden, Llandeilo, Llandovery, Brecon

B11 Brecon, National Park Visitor Centre

B12 Brecon, Llangorse Lake, Hay-on-Wye

B13 (Geopark Circular) Brecon, National Park Visitor Centre, Storey Arms, National Showcaves Centre, Penderyn

B15 Brecon, Tretower, Crickhowell, Big Pit, Blaenavon

B16 (Taff Trail Roundabout) Brecon, National Park Visitor Centre, Storey Arms, Brecon Mountain Railway, Llanfrynach

B17 (Offa's Dyke Flyer) Hay-on-Wye, Llanthony Priory, Llanfihangel Crucorney, Pandy

(811m). The Offa's Dyke Path runs along the easternmost ridge between Pandy and Hay-on-Wye (see p195).

❧ SUGAR LOAF // A BLACK MOUNTAIN WITH A SWEET NAME

The cone-shaped pinnacle of Sugar Loaf (596m) is a 9-mile return trip from the centre of Abergavenny via heath, woodland and the superb viewpoint of Mynydd Llanwenarth. You can cheat by driving to a car park about halfway up on Mynydd Llanwenarth; from here it's a 4-mile round trip. Head west on the A40, and at the edge of town turn right for Sugarloaf Vineyards, then go left at the next two junctions.

❧ YSGYRYD FAWR (SKIRRID) // ASCEND SOUTH WALES' HOLY MOUNTAIN

Of the glacially sculpted hills that surround Abergavenny, Skirrid (486m) is

the most dramatic looking and has a history to match. A cleft in the rock near the top was believed to have split open at the exact time of Christ's death and a chapel was built here on what was considered a particularly holy place (a couple of upright stones remain). During the Catholic persecutions, as many as 100 people at a time would attend illegal Masses at this remote spot.

Begin your trek from Abergavenny, or take the B4521 to the car park at the base of the hill. It's a steep climb from here through the woods on a track that can be muddy; wear sensible shoes. Once you clear the tree line the walk is less steep, with a final climb right at the end to the summit where you're rewarded with extravagant views. From here you can return the way you came or continue down the other side to Llanfihangel Crucorney.

❧ LLANFIHANGEL CRUCORNEY // A PEACEFUL HAMLET WITH A VIOLENT PAST

The name of this little village, 4.5 miles north of Abergavenny, means 'Church of St Michael at the Corner of the Rock'. It's famous as the home of the Skirrid Inn (p326), said to be the oldest pub in Wales and thoroughly haunted by the many people who were hanged here (it doubled as an assizes court). It serves decent pub grub and it makes a good base camp or finishing point for an ascent of Ysgyryd Fawr; it's a 4-mile round trip from pub to summit.

❧ PARTRISHOW CHURCH // REMOTE, BEAUTIFUL AND A LITTLE CREEPY

Halfway up a hillside on a narrow country lane, 5 miles northwest of Llanfihangel Crucorney, is this tiny part-Norman and part-medieval church. It contains a remarkable, finely carved wooden rood screen and loft, dating from around 1500. On the walls are medieval frescoes of biblical texts, coats of arms, and a red-ochre skeleton (once believed to have been painted with human blood) bearing hourglass and scythe – the figure of Death. The church is usually open; leave a donation in the box.

❧ VALE OF EWYAS // AN EXTREMELY BEAUTIFUL ROAD LESS TRAVELLED

The scenic and secluded valley of the River Honddu runs through the heart of the Black Mountains from Llanfihangel Crucorney to the 542m-high Gospel Pass, which leads down to Hay-on-Wye. It's a magical place, with only a very narrow, single-track road running along it, best explored on foot, bike or horseback.

Halfway along the valley lie the atmospheric ruins of the 13th-century **Llanthony Priory**, set among grasslands and wooded hills by the River Honddu. Though not as grand as Tintern Abbey, the setting is even more romantic; JMW Turner painted the scene in 1794. **Llanthony Riding and Trekking** (☎ 01873-890359; www.llanthony.co.uk; Court Farm; half-/full day beginners £28/50, experienced £35/60), next door to Llanthony Priory and the Abbey Hotel, has horses available for pony trekking and hacking. Half-day rides begin at 10am and 2pm. It also offers basic campsites (per person £3) and rents self-catering cottages.

There are lots of walking possibilities. From Llanthony, several paths lead up to the top of the Hatterall ridge to the east; it's a stiff climb, but straightforward (2 to 3 miles round trip). For a more ambitious hike, follow the ridge north for 4 miles then descend to Vision Farm, then walk back along the valley road to Llanthony (9 miles round trip).

TRANSPORT

BUS // There is no public transport other than the Beacons Buses (p89).

HAY-ON-WYE (Y GELLI GANDRYLL)

☎ 01497 / pop 1500

Hay-on-Wye, a pretty little town on the banks of the River Wye, just inside the Welsh border, has developed a reputation disproportionate to its size. First came the explosion in secondhand bookshops, a charge led by the charismatic and forthright local maverick Richard Booth. Booth opened his eponymous bookshop in the 1960s, stocking it with cast-off libraries from various national institutions and country houses. He went on to proclaim himself the King of Hay, among other elaborate publicity stunts, while campaigning for an international network of book towns to support failing rural economies.

With Hay becoming the world's secondhand book capital, a festival of literature and culture was established in 1988, growing in stature each year to take in all aspects of the creative arts. Today the Hay Festival is a major attraction in its own right, famously endorsed by former US president Bill Clinton, a high-profile guest in 2001, as 'the Woodstock of the mind'.

But Hay is not all about book browsing and celebrity spotting – it also makes an excellent base for active pursuits, with the Black Mountains, River Wye and Offa's Dyke Path all within easy access of the town's superb facilities.

The small town centre is made up of narrow sloping lanes, peppered by interesting shops and peopled by the differing types that such individuality and so many books tend to attract. Even outside of festival time, it has a vaguely alternative ambience.

Hay has had a tempestuous history, due to its borderlands position. In fact, at the time of the Norman Conquest it was administered separately as English Hay (the town proper) and Welsh Hay (the countryside to the south and west).

Around 1200 William de Braose II, one of the Norman barons (marcher lords), built a castle here on the site of an earlier one (Richard Booth became king of this castle, buying the dilapidated remains in 1961). For the next three-and-a-half centuries Hay changed hands many times. Following the Tudor Acts of Union it settled down as a market town, and by the 18th century it had become a centre of the flannel trade.

ESSENTIAL INFORMATION

TOURIST OFFICES // Tourist office
(☎ 820144; www.hay-on-wye.co.uk; Oxford Rd; ☻ 10am-5pm Apr-Oct, 11am-4pm Nov-Mar; ▣)

EXPLORING HAY-ON-WYE

☙ **BOOKSHOPS & ANTIQUES // MUSTY, DUSTY STORES PACKED WITH TREASURES**
There are 26 secondhand and antiquarian bookshops in Hay, with hundreds of thousands of tomes stacked floor to ceiling across town – 500,000 in Booth's alone. Each shop is profiled on a free map, available from the tourist office and from venues around town. However, Hay's shopping potential doesn't stop with books. There are also excellent stores selling antiques, craft, art and historic maps.

Here are some picks:

Addyman Books (☎ 821136; www.hay-on-wye books.com; 39 Lion St) Stocks books on all sorts of subjects, has a sitting room upstairs and a sci-fi room.

Booth Books (☎ 820322; www.boothbooks. co.uk; 44 Lion St) The most famous, and still the best; has a sizeable Anglo-Welsh literature section, and a Wales travel section.

Hay Castle Books (☎ 820503; Hay Castle, Oxford Rd) Booth's primary domain these days, with a suitably eclectic stock and an honesty bookshop (50p per book) in the castle grounds.

Hay Cinema Bookshop (☎ 820071; www.hay cinemabookshop.co.uk; Castle St) Huge collection of books about filmmaking and cinema, in a converted cinema.

Mostly Maps (☎ 820539; www.mostlymaps. com; 2 Castle St) Exquisite antiquarian maps, many hand-coloured.

Murder & Mayhem (☎ 821613; 5 Lion St) Filled to the brim with detective fiction, true crime and horror.

Rose's Books (☎ 820013; www.rosesbooks.com; 14 Broad St) Rare children's and illustrated books.

Tom's Record Shop (☎ 821590; 13 Castle St) Some books alongside new and secondhand records and CDs.

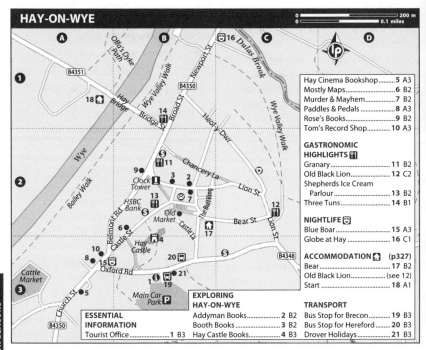

🌿 HAY FESTIVAL // 'THE WOODSTOCK OF THE MIND'

The 10-day **Hay Festival** (☎ 822629; www .hayfestival.com) has become Britain's leading festival of literature and the arts – a kind of bookworms' Glastonbury or, according to a former American president, 'the Woodstock of the mind'. Like those legendary music festivals, it pulls more than its fair share of the leading exponents of its genre. As well as Bill Clinton, past speakers have included famous writers (Ian McEwan, Zadie Smith, Stephen Fry, Bill Bryson), priests (Rowan Williams, Desmond Tutu) and politicians (Rhodri Morgan, Gordon Brown, Al Gore). It's proved such a popular formula that there are now Hay Festivals in Segovia, Alhambra, Cartagena, Zacatecas and Nairobi.

As well as readings, workshops, book signings, concerts and club nights, there's also a very successful children's festival called Hay Fever. There are shuttle buses from Hay-on-Wye and surrounding towns to the site, in fields on Hay's southwest fringe.

GASTRONOMIC HIGHLIGHTS

🌿 GRANARY ££
☎ 820790; Broad St; mains £6-11;
🕙 9am-5.30pm; 🛜

Popular and welcoming, this bustling country-kitchen cafe is a reliable choice for breakfasts and snack lunches. Vegetarians and families are well catered for, with menus for all, and you can check your email over a coffee on the free wi-fi.

🌿 OLD BLACK LION ££
☎ 820841; Lion St; mains £12-18

Walkers, book browsers and the literary glitterati all flock to this creaky, part-13th-century inn, with heavy black beams and warm red walls. The atmosphere is as cosy as you'd hope such a pub would be, but the food is many leagues beyond pub grub: think stuffed guinea fowl, or pork loin with black pudding.

🌶 SHEPHERDS ICE CREAM PARLOUR £

☎ 821898; 9 High Town; single scoop £1.50; 🕒 9.30am-6pm Mon-Sat, 10.30am-5pm Sun

Nobody should leave Hay without trying the homemade ice cream from Shepherds. It's made from sheep's milk for a lighter, smoother taste.

🌶 THREE TUNS ££

☎ 821855; Broad St; mains £12-19; 🕒 Wed-Sun

Rebuilt and expanded after a fire partially destroyed the 16th-century building, this smart gastropub is a welcoming place. It has a large garden area for alfresco food and a fancier restaurant upstairs. The international menu follows that increasingly common mantra: local, organic and sustainable.

NIGHTLIFE

🌶 BLUE BOAR

☎ 820884; Castle St

This cosy, traditional pub serves Timothy Taylor's ale and hearty pub food.

🌶 GLOBE AT HAY

☎ 821762; www.globeathay.co.uk; Newport St

Finally, there's something to do in Hay at night other than reading all those books. Converted from a Methodist chapel and filled with mismatched chairs and sofas, this very cool venue is part cafe, part bar, part club, part theatre and all-round community hub – hosting DJs, live music, comedy, theatre, film, kids' events, chess clubs and political talks.

RICHARD BOOTH, KING OF HAY

Richard Booth is a larger-than-life character and the dynamic force behind Hay's metamorphosis from declining border town into eminent book capital. A provocative character, he's been called a monarchist, anarchist, socialist and separatist. All of which have some element of truth, and he's definitely a superb self-publicist. After graduating from Oxford he bought Hay's old fire station and turned it into a secondhand bookshop. He bought whole libraries from all over the world and sold in bulk to new universities. He's had setbacks, becoming bankrupt in 1984, but never lost his instinct for a good story. He first hit the headlines when he offered books for burning at £1.50 a car-boot load.

Booth established the world's largest bookshop in the old cinema before opening Booth Books and Hay Castle Books. His success attracted other booksellers and nowadays there are over two dozen bookshops in tiny Hay-on-Wye.

The idea for a separate state blossomed during a liquid lunch in 1976. Booth announced that Hay would declare independence on 1 April (April Fools' Day). Breconshire Council fiercely dismissed the idea as a Booth publicity stunt, which only fuelled the media hype. On declaration day, three TV stations, eight national newspapers and the world's press covered the event. Booth was crowned king (King Richard, Coeur de Livre) and the Hay navy sent a gunboat (a rowing boat) up the Wye, firing blanks from a drainpipe. Many of the king's drinking pals gained cabinet posts.

All this comedy has a serious undercurrent, and Booth continues to campaign against the causes of rural decline – with particular contempt reserved for rural development boards, supermarkets and factory farming.

TRANSPORT

BIKE // Drover Holidays (☎ 821134; www.
droverholidays.co.uk; St Johns Place; per half-day/day/
week £18/25/70) rents mountain and touring bikes.

BUS // Bus 39 heads to Brecon (41 minutes). See also
Beacons Buses B12 and B17 (p89).

PARKING // There's a large car park on Oxford Rd (per
hour 50p, over four hours £2.50, free 6pm to 8am).

DRIVING TOUR

Distance: 49 miles
Duration: full day
This slow-paced drive takes you
through a remote section of the Black
Mountains on the narrowest of back
roads, and returns you via a much easier
route. Start at **Hay-on-Wye** (**1**; p90),
heading south on the B4350 but turning sharp left onto Forest Rd at the edge
of town. The road narrows to a single
lane (you'll need to pull over if you encounter another car) and quickly leads
up onto desolate moors as it crosses
the **Gospel Pass** (**2**). The country gets
greener as you head down the other side
into the Vale of Ewyas, where you'll find
the ruins of **Llanthony Priory** (**3**, p90).
Stop at the Skirrid Inn in **Llanfihangel
Crucorney** (**4**, p90) and then turn right
onto the A465, the main road into **Abergavenny** (**5**, p83), where you can stop
for lunch and to check out the sights.
Take the A40 west out of town and stop
to have a look around **Crickhowell** (**6**,
p94). Continue along the A40 and turn
right at **Nantyffin Cider Mill** (**7**, p96)
onto the A479. After a short while you'll
come to **Tretower Court & Castle** (**8**,
p96), your last stop of the day. Head
back onto the A479 and turn right at
the edge of the national park onto the
A438 and then the B4350 and take it
back to Hay-on-Wye.

ABERGAVENNY TO BRECON

☙ BLORENGE // CLIMB UP AND FLY
BACK DOWN
Of the three mountains encircling Abergavenny, the summit of the **Blorenge**
(561m) is the closest to town – the
round trip is only 5 miles – but it is a
steep and strenuous outing, and good
walking boots are recommended. Cross
the bridge over the Usk on Merthyr Rd
and immediately turn right and follow
the lane past the cemetery and under
the main road. Cross the B4246 road
in Llanfoist and follow the lane beside
the church until it bends left; continue
through a tunnel under the canal and
then follow a steep path straight uphill (a
former tram-road that carried coal down
to the canal). When you emerge from the
woods, there is a final steep climb up an
obvious path to the summit.

This is one of Britain's finest paragliding and hang-gliding sites. In fact, it is so
good that the **South East Wales Hang
Gliding and Paragliding Club** (www.
sewhgpgc.co.uk) purchased the mountain in
1998. Several records have been set from
here, and the mountain regularly hosts
competition events.

☙ CRICKHOWELL (CRUGHYWEL) //
A VILLAGE AS PRETTY AS A PICTURE
This prosperous, picturesque, flower-
bedecked village on the Abergavenny–
Brecon road is named after the distinctive
flat-topped **Crug Hywel** (Hywel's Rock;
451m), better known as Table Mountain,
which rises to the north. You can hike to
the remains of an Iron Age fort at the top
(3 miles round trip); the **tourist office**
(☎ 01873-812105; www.crickhowellinfo.org.uk; Beaufort St) has a leaflet showing the route.

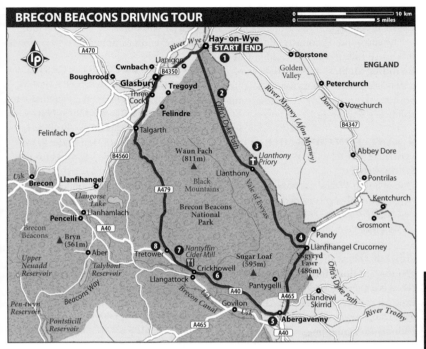

There's not a lot to see in Crickhowell itself, but it's a pleasant place for an overnight stop. Every Friday and Saturday there's an arts and craft market held in the **old market hall** (High St).

The town grew up around the Norman motte (mound) and bailey castle and the nearby ford on the River Usk. All that remains of the **castle** is a few tumbledown towers, and the ford was superseded by an elegant 17th-century **stone bridge**, leading to the neighbouring village of Llangattock; it's famous for having 12 arches on one side, and 13 on the other. Try counting them from the riverside beer garden at the **Bridge End Inn** (☎ 810338; Bridge St). The inn serves a range of real ales, including Hancocks and Speckled Hen, and inside it's all timber beams and angling paraphernalia.

The best of several eateries in the town centre is the **Bear Hotel** (☎ 01873-810408; www.bearhotel.co.uk; Beaufort St; mains £7-16), a fine old coaching inn with low-ceilinged rooms, stone fireplaces, blackened timber beams and antique furniture. The menu ranges from hearty, meaty country fare (roast venison; slow-roasted pork belly) to more exotic dishes (Moroccan lemon chicken; salmon marinated in chilli, lime and coriander).

❦ LLANGATTOCK (LLANGATWG) // CRICKHOWELL'S EQUALLY PRETTY NEIGHBOUR

Across the oddly arched bridge from Crickhowell, Llangattock's old stone houses are clustered around a castle-like 12th-century church. A late-afternoon stroll is rewarded by views back to Crug Hywel bathed in golden light, its fort looking like one of the magical fairy circles of Welsh myth.

The surrounding countryside is perfect horse-riding country. **Golden Castle Riding Stables** (☎ 01873-812649; www. golden-castle.co.uk; per 1½hr/day from £35/55) offers pony trekking, hacking, trail riding and children's activity days.

❧ NANTYFFIN CIDER MILL // FINE LOCAL FOOD IN ATMOSPHERIC SURROUNDS

One of South Wales' gastronomic pioneers, this 16th-century **drovers' inn** (☎ 01873-810775; mains £13-19; ☽ closed Sun dinner Oct-Mar & Mon) takes great pride in using local produce, creating simple, unfussy dishes that allow the quality of the ingredients to shine through. The dining room is a stylish blend of bare stone, exposed roof beams, designer chairs and white table linen, set around the original 19th-century cider press. The Nantyffin is 1 mile northwest of Crickhowell on the A40.

❧ GREEN MAN FESTIVAL // RED-HOT BANDS WRAPPED UP IN BIODEGRADABLE PACKAGING

Staged in late August in Glanusk Park, 2 miles west of Crickhowell via the B4558, **Green Man** (www.greenman.net; adult/child £120/50) sits proudly at the forefront of Britain's summer music festival circuit as an event with a strong green ethos that caters well for children and people with disabilities. Yet that would all count for naught if the line-up wasn't any good, and here's where Green Man excels. Despite its relatively small size (around 10,000 people) it consistently attracts the current 'it' bands of the alternative music firmament – acts like Animal Collective, Joanna Newsom, Flaming Lips and Wilco, and dead-set legends such as Jarvis

Cocker and Robert Plant. Unsurprisingly, it sells out early. Tickets include the weekend's camping.

❧ TRETOWER COURT & CASTLE // FROM CASTLE TO COUNTRY HOUSE

Originally the home of the Vaughan family, **Tretower** (Cadw; ☎ 01874-730279; www. cadw.wales.gov.uk; admission £3; ☽ 10am-5pm Apr-Oct, 9.30am-4pm Fri & Sat & 11am-4pm Sun Nov-Mar) gives you two historic buildings for the price of one – the sturdy circular tower of a Norman motte-and-bailey castle, and a 15th-century manor house with a fine medieval garden. Together they illustrate the transition from military stronghold to country house that took place in late medieval times.

Tretower is 3 miles northwest of Crickhowell on the A479.

❧ LLANGORSE LAKE // NATURAL LAKE TRUMPS ARTIFICIAL CLIFFS AND CAVES

Reed-fringed Llangorse Lake (Llyn Syfaddan), to the east of Brecon, may be Wales' second-largest natural lake (after Llyn Tegid), but it's barely more than a mile long and half a mile wide. Close to the northern shore is a **crannog**, a lake dwelling built on an artificial island. Such dwellings or refuges were used from the late Bronze Age until early medieval times. Tree-ring dating shows that this one (of which only the base remains) was built around AD 900, probably by the royal house of Brycheiniog. Among the artefacts found here was a dugout canoe, now on display in Brecon's Brecknock Museum; other finds can be seen at the National Museum Cardiff (p45). There's a reconstruction of a crannog house on the shore.

The lake is the national park's main water sports location, used for sailing, windsurfing, canoeing and water-skiing. **Lakeside Caravan Park** (☎ 01874-658226; www.llangorselake.co.uk), on the north shore, rents rowing boats (per hour/day £12/30), Canadian canoes (per hour/day £12/36) and Wayfarer sailing dinghies (per hour £25; you'll need to know how to rig them yourself).

Set on a hillside above the eastern end of Llangorse Lake is the **Llangorse Multi Activity Centre** (☎ 01874-658272; www.activityuk.com; Gilfach Farm; 9am-10pm Mon-Sat, 9am-5pm Sun). It offers a range of adventure activities, including an outdoor aerial assault course that involves clambering up cargo nets, balancing along logs, swinging on tyres and zipping through the air on a 100m-long ropeway (£17 for two hours). There's also an indoor facility with artificial rock-climbing walls, a log climb, an abseil area, a rope bridge and even an artificial caving area. A one-hour climbing 'taster' session costs £14.

❤ PETERSTONE COURT // DINE IN STATELY SURROUNDS

The genteel environment of a Georgian manor house is a very good starting point for a memorable dining experience. **Peterstone** (☎ 01874-665387; www.peterstone-court.com; A40, Llanhamlach; mains £13-19) has the added advantage of serving produce from its own farm, turned out by a Ritz-trained chef who won the Welsh International Culinary Championships in 2010.

❤ WHITE SWAN // ANOTHER MEMORABLE COUNTRY INN SERVING FIRST-RATE FOOD

A traditional village **inn** (☎ 01874-665276; www.the-white-swan.com; Llanfrynach; mains £14-16; Tue-Sun) that offers a candle-lit dining room with old wooden floors, a bar with comfortably worn leather sofas and arm-chairs, and a beautiful garden terrace. The White Swan is a great place to relax after a walk along the canal or a hike in the Brecon Beacons. The menu emphasises Welsh lamb, beef and venison, with daily fish and vegetarian specials. Llanfrynach is 3.5 miles southeast of Brecon off the B4558.

TRANSPORT

BUS // Bus X43 connects Crickhowell with Abergavenny (17 minutes), Brecon (26 minutes), Merthyr Tydfil (1½ hours) and Cardiff (2¼ hours). See p89 for Beacons Buses.

BRECON (ABERHONDDU)

☎ 01874 / pop 7900

The handsome stone market town of Brecon stands at the meeting of the River Usk and the River Honddu. For centuries the town thrived as a centre of wool production and weaving; today it's the main hub of the national park and a natural base for exploring the surrounding countryside.

An Iron Age hill fort on Pen-y-Crug (331m), northwest of town, and the remains of a Roman camp at Y Gaer, to the west, testify to the site's antiquity. After the Romans, the area was ruled by the Irish-born king Brychan, who married into a Welsh royal house in the 5th century. The town takes its name from him, and his kingdom, Brycheiniog (anglicised to Brecknock), gave its name to the old county of Brecknockshire. Merthyr Tydfil was named for Brychan's daughter, St Tudful.

It was not until Norman times that Brecon began to burgeon. The local Welsh prince, Rhys ap Tewdwr, was defeated in 1093 by Bernard de Neufmarché, a Norman lord, who then built the town's castle and church (which is now a cathedral). The scant remains of the castle have been incorporated into the Castle of Brecon Hotel (p329). Across the road from the hotel is the original Norman motte, capped by the ivy-clad **Ely Tower** (not open to the public).

ESSENTIAL INFORMATION

EMERGENCIES // Brecon War Memorial Hospital (☎ 622443; Cerrigcochion Rd) **Police station** (☎ 0845 330 2000; Lion St)
TOURIST OFFICES // Tourist office (☎ 622485; market car park; ⏲ 9.30am-5.30pm Mon-Sat, 10am-4pm Sun)

EXPLORING BRECON

❦ BRECON CATHEDRAL // THE CASTLE'S BETTER-PRESERVED PIOUS SISTER

Perched on a hill above the River Honddu, **Brecon Cathedral** (☎ 623857; www. breconcathedral.org.uk; Cathedral Close) was founded as part of a Benedictine monastery in 1093, though little remains of the Norman structure except the carved font and parts of the nave. It's a lovely church and very visitor-friendly; seven information points provide information about key features.

At the western end of the nave, just inside the door, is a stone cresset (an ancient lighting device), the only one in Wales; the 30 cups were filled with oil and lit to illuminate dark corners or steps. To the north is the Harvard Chapel, the regimental chapel of the South Wales Borderers, draped with banners from the Zulu wars.

In the cathedral grounds is a **Heritage Centre** (☎ 625222; admission free; ⏲ 10am-4.30pm Mon-Sat year-round, 12.15-4.15pm Sun Apr-Oct), cafe and gift shop housed in a

restored 15th-century tithe barn. The cathedral hosts regular choral concerts.

❦ BRECKNOCK MUSEUM & ART GALLERY // AN INTERESTING RAINY-DAY DIVERSION

Behind the stolid neoclassical exterior of the former shire hall is the town's **museum** (☎ 624121; www.powys.gov.uk; Captain's Walk; adult/child £1/50p; ⏲ 10am-5pm Mon-Fri, 10am-1pm & 2-5pm Sat year-round, noon-5pm Sun Apr-Sep). Exhibits include a 1200-year-old dugout canoe found at Llangorse Lake, a Victorian assize court complete with a stilted recording of court pronouncements, and that favourite of Welsh museums, a recreated Welsh kitchen. Also featured are the archaeology, history and natural history of the Brecon area, and an art gallery with changing exhibits.

❦ SOUTH WALES BORDERERS MUSEUM // MEDALS, GUNS AND MEMORIES

This **regimental museum** (☎ 613310; www.rrw.org.uk; The Barracks; adult/child £3/free; ⏲ 10am-5pm Mon-Fri year-round, 10am-4pm Sat Easter-Sep) commemorates the history of the Royal Regiment of Wales, which is based in Brecon. Many of the soldiers are Gurkhas, often to be seen in their civvies around the town. The highlight is the Zulu War Room – the regiment's predecessor fought in the 1879 Anglo-Zulu war in South Africa, inspiration for the 1964 film *Zulu* starring Michael Caine. The collection of artefacts recalls the defence of Rorke's Drift, when 150 Welsh soldiers held out against 4000 Zulu warriors.

❦ MONMOUTHSHIRE & BRECON CANAL // FLOAT THROUGH THE HEART OF THE NATIONAL PARK

Brecon is the northern terminus of this canal, built between 1799 and 1812 for

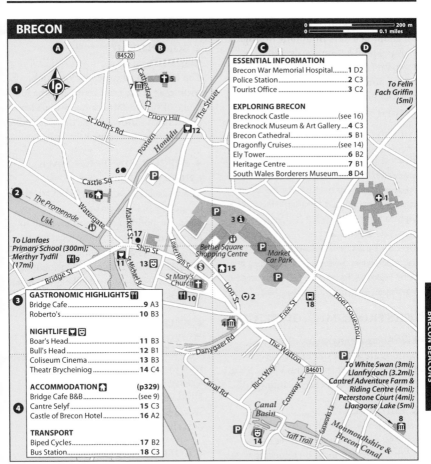

BRECON

0 ————— 200 m
0 ————— 0.1 miles

ESSENTIAL INFORMATION
Brecon War Memorial Hospital........**1** D2
Police Station................................**2** C3
Tourist Office **3** C2

EXPLORING BRECON
Brecknock Castle...........................(see 16)
Brecknock Museum & Art Gallery **4** C3
Brecon Cathedral..........................**5** B1
Dragonfly Cruises.........................(see 14)
Ely Tower.....................................**6** B2
Heritage Centre **7** B1
South Wales Borderers Museum......**8** D4

GASTRONOMIC HIGHLIGHTS
Bridge Cafe...................................**9** A3
Roberto's......................................**10** B3

NIGHTLIFE
Boar's Head...................................**11** B3
Bull's Head...................................**12** B1
Coliseum Cinema **13** B3
Theatr Brycheiniog **14** C4

ACCOMMODATION (p329)
Bridge Cafe B&B............................(see 9)
Cantre Selyf..................................**15** C3
Castle of Brecon Hotel **16** A2

TRANSPORT
Biped Cycles.................................**17** B2
Bus Station...................................**18** C3

To Felin Fach Griffin (5mi)

To Llanfaes Primary School (300m); Merthyr Tydfil (17mi)

To White Swan (3mi); Llanfrynach (3.2mi); Cantref Adventure Farm & Riding Centre (4mi); Peterstone Court (4mi); Llangorse Lake (5mi)

SOUTHEAST WALES & BRECON BEACONS

the movement of coal, iron ore, limestone and agricultural goods. The 33 miles from Brecon to Pontypool is back in business, transporting a generally less grimy cargo of holidaymakers and river dwellers. The busiest section is around Brecon, with craft departing from the canal basin, 400m south of the town centre.

You can take to the water with **Beacon Park Boats** (☎ 01873-858277; www.beacon parkboats.com; ☺ 10am-5pm Mar-Oct), which rents out four- or six-seater electric-powered boats (per hour/half-day/day from £16/35/50; up to six people) and three-seater Canadian canoes (per hour/half-day/day from £10/20/30). It also has a fleet of luxury narrowboats for longer live-in voyages, as does **Cambrian Cruisers** (☎ 665315; www.cambriancruisers.co.uk; Ty Newydd, Pencelli). **Backwaters Adventure Equipment Ltd** (☎ 01873-831 825; www.back watershire.co.uk; per day kayak/canoe £28/40) also rents kayaks and canoes, including buoyancy aids and waterproof barrels.

Dragonfly Cruises (☎ 685222; www. dragonfly-cruises.co.uk; adult/child £7/4.50; ☺ Mar-Oct) runs 2½-hour narrowboat trips; there are departures once or twice daily on

Wednesday, Saturday and Sunday, and on additional days from June to August.

A peaceful 8.5-mile walk along the towpath leads to the picturesque village of Talybont-on-Usk. You can return on the X43 bus or, on summer Sundays, the Beacons Bus B4 or B16.

FESTIVALS & EVENTS

Brecon Jazz Festival (www.breconjazz.co.uk) Organised by the team behind the Hay Festival, one of Europe's leading jazz events is held in Brecon in the second weekend in August. Emerging British talent and big-name internationals, such as 2010 headliners the Buena Vista Social Club, perform.

Brecon Beast (www.breconbeast.co.uk) A gruelling mountain-bike challenge over 44 or 68 miles, held in mid-September. The entry fee (£28) covers camping, refreshments on the route, a 'pasta party' and a T-shirt.

GASTRONOMIC HIGHLIGHTS

Like Abergavenny, many of the best options are a little out of town, such as Peterstone Court (p97), the White Swan (p97) and the Felin Fach Griffin (p101).

✤ BRIDGE CAFE ££
☎ 622024; www.bridgecafe.co.uk; 7 Bridge St; mains £8; ☽ breakfast Sun, dinner Thu-Sat; ☞
With a particular focus on refuelling weary walkers and mountain bikers, Bridge Cafe offers home-cooked meals such as hearty casseroles in cosy surrounds. Local, organic ingredients are used wherever possible.

✤ ROBERTO'S ££
☎ 611880; St Mary St; mains £9-20; ☽ dinner daily, closed Sun winter; Ⓥ
They may be plastic vines hanging from the trellis on the ceiling, but everything else about Roberto's is authentically Italian, from the relaxed atmosphere to the free olives and crostini, to the *puttanesca* sauce. Though, of course, that's Welsh beef lurking underneath the gorgonzola.

NIGHTLIFE

✤ BOAR'S HEAD
☎ 622856; Ship St
The Boar's Head is a lively local pub, with sofas in the back room and the full range of Breconshire Brewery real ales on tap. It has a sunny beer garden overlooking the river, and regular live music.

✤ BRECON & DISTRICT MALE CHOIR
www.breconchoir.co.uk; Llanfaes Primary School, Orchard St; ☽ 7.30-9.30pm Fri
For a few booming harmonies, head to the practice sessions of the local men's choir; visitors are welcome. Since its formation in 1937 it has performed at London's Royal Albert Hall eight times and has even released its own CD.

✤ BULL'S HEAD
☎ 623900; 86 The Struet
Arguably the best real-ale pub in town, with Evan Evans beer from Llandeilo and a range of guest ales, the riverside Bull's Head is cosy, quiet and friendly. It also serves good pub grub and occasionally hosts live music.

✤ COLISEUM CINEMA
☎ 622501; www.coliseumbrecon.co.uk; Wheat St; tickets £6
The Coliseum is a refreshingly old-fashioned family cinema with two screens. As well as mainstream films, the local film society shows art-house films on Monday evenings.

✤ THEATR BRYCHEINIOG
☎ 611622; www.theatrbrycheiniog.co.uk; Canal Rd
This attractive canalside theatre complex is the town's main venue for drama, dance, comedy and music. It's worth checking the program, as it sometimes hosts surprisingly big-name touring acts.

TRANSPORT

BIKE // **Biped Cycles** (☎ 622296; www.biped cycles.co.uk; 10 Ship St; per half-/full day £16/20) rents bikes and can arrange guided rides. The Taff Trail (p39) heads south from here to Cardiff. This forms part of Lôn Las Cymru (p302), which also heads north to Builth Wells.

BUS // Bus X43 heads to Abergavenny (50 minutes), Crickhowell (26 minutes), Merthyr Tydfil (37 minutes) and Cardiff (1½ hours); X63 to Swansea (two hours); 39 to Hay-on-Wye (41 minutes); and 704 to Newtown (two hours) via Builth Wells (40 minutes) and Llandrindod Wells (55 minutes). Most Beacons Buses routes (p89) converge on Brecon.

COACH // **National Express** (www.nation alexpress.com) coaches head to Birmingham (£27, 4¼ hours), Cardiff (£4.10, 1¼ hours) and Merthyr Tydfil (£2.60, 30 minutes).

PARKING // The Market car park offers short-stay pay-and-display parking (per two hours £2). There are long-stay lots on Hoel Gouesnou and near the canal basin (per hour/day 50p/£2.50 8am to 6pm, free after hours).

TAXI // **Ride & Hike** (☎ 07971-527660; www. rideandhike.com) offers regular taxi services as well as a walkers' shuttle. Indicative fares: National Park Visitor Centre (£12), Merthyr Tydfil (£30), Cardiff (£60).

AROUND BRECON

❧ PEN-Y-CRUG // RISE TO HISTORICAL HEIGHTS

The conical hill of Pen-y-Crug (331m), capped by an Iron Age hill fort, rises to the northwest of the town, and makes a good objective for a short hike (2.5 miles round trip). There's a superb view of the Brecon Beacons from the summit. The tourist office sells national-park walking cards.

❧ FELIN FACH GRIFFIN // VILLAGE INN WITH A GASTRONOMIC REPUTATION

With a string of awards as long as its extensive wine list, the **Griffin** (☎ 01874-620111; www.felinfachgriffin.co.uk; Felinfach; mains £17-19, 1-/2-/3-course £15/22/26; ☾ closed Mon lunch) offers gourmet dining in a relaxed and unpretentious setting. Open fires, leather sofas and timber beams create a comfortable atmosphere, while the kitchen follows a 'simple things done well' mantra, making the most of local fish, meat and game. The Griffin is 5 miles northeast of Brecon on the A470.

❧ CANTREF ADVENTURE FARM & RIDING CENTRE // BRING ON THE DANCING HORSES

In the countryside south of Brecon, **Cantref** (☎ 665223; www.cantref.com; Upper Cantref Farm, Llanfrynach; adult/child £7.50/6.50; ☾ 10.30am-5.30pm Easter-Nov, weekends & school holidays only Dec-Easter) operates a child-focused fun farm, complete with pig races, lamb feeding and unfortunates dressed as horses, dancing for the little troops. More interesting for adults are the pony trekking and hacking (per hour/half-/full day £18/27/50), heading out into the Brecon Beacons.

It's reached by a set of narrow country lanes; follow the horseshoe signs from the A40, southeast of town. Bunkhouse accommodation (from £14) and basic camping is available.

❧ NATIONAL PARK VISITOR CENTRE // STOCK UP ON INFORMATION AND RESOURCES

Set high on a ridge with fine views of Pen-y-Fan and Corn Du is the park's main **visitor centre** (☎ 01874-623366; www. breconbeacons.org; Libanus; admission free, parking 2hr/day £1/2.50; ☾ 9.30am-5pm Mar-Jun, Sep & Oct, 9.30am-6pm Jul & Aug, 9.30am-4.30pm Nov-Feb), with full details of walks, hiking and biking trails, outdoor activities, wildlife and geology. It has easy wheelchair access, as well as a book and gift shop, a tearoom and picnic tables. During school holidays there are kids' activities, organised farm visits, guided walks and themed minibus tours.

The centre is off the A470 road, 5 miles southwest of Brecon and 15 miles north of Merthyr Tydfil. Some of the Beacons Buses (p89) stop here; otherwise, any of the buses on the Merthyr Tydfil–Brecon route stop at Libanus village, a 1.25-mile walk away.

FFOREST FAWR & BLACK MOUNTAIN

West of the A470, this entire half of the national park is sparsely inhabited, without any towns of note. **Fforest Fawr** (Great Forest), once a Norman hunting ground, is now a Unesco geopark famous for its varied landscapes, ranging from bleak moorland to flower-flecked limestone pavement and lush wooded ravines choked with moss and greenery. **Carreg Cennen Castle**, in the far southwestern corner of the national park, is best approached from Llandeilo; see p102.

♣ GARWNANT VISITOR CENTRE // EASY WALKS AND A ROPE COURSE
The Forestry Commission's **Garwnant Visitor Centre** (☎ 01685-723060; www.forestry.gov.uk; admission free), at the head of Llwyn Onn Reservoir (5 miles north of Merthyr on the A470), is the starting point for a couple of easy forest walks and a cycle trail, and also has a cafe, an adventure play area and a rope-swing 'assault course' for kids.

♣ WATERFALL COUNTRY // WANDER THE WOOD OF THE WATERFALLS
Between the villages of **Pontneddfechan** and **Ystradfellte** is a series of dramatic waterfalls, where the Rivers Mellte, Hepste and Pyrddin pass through steep forested gorges. The finest is **Sgwd-yr-Eira** (Waterfall of the Snow), where you can actually walk behind the torrent. At one point the River Mellte disappears into **Porth-yr-Ogof** (Door to the Cave), the biggest cave entrance in Britain (3m high and 20m wide), only to reappear 100m further south.

Walks in the area are outlined on the national park's Wood of the Waterfalls walk card (£1), which is available from visitor centres, including the **Waterfalls Centre** (☎ 01639-721795; Pontneathvaughan Rd, Pontneddfechan; ⊗ 9.30am-5pm Apr-Oct, 9.30am-3pm Sat & Sun Nov-Mar). Take special care – the footpaths can be slippery, and there are several steep, stony sections.

♣ PENDERYN DISTILLERY // A WELSH ON THE ROCKS, ANYONE?
Before the ascendency of the chapels in the 19th century, the Welsh were as fond of their whisky as their Gaelic cousins in Scotland and Ireland. **Penderyn Distillery** (☎ 01685-813300; www.welsh-whisky.co.uk; adult/child £5/2; ⊗ 9.30am-5pm) marks the resurgence of Welsh whisky-making after an absence of more than 100 years (the Frongoch Distillery in Bala closed in the late 1800s).

This boutique, independently owned distillery released its first malt whisky in 2004. It's distilled with fresh spring water drawn from directly beneath the distillery, then matured in bourbon casks and finished in rich Madeira wine casks to create a golden-hued drop of liquid fire. It also produces Brecon Gin, Brecon Five Vodka and Merlyn Cream Liqueur.

From the imposing black visitors centre you can watch the spirits being made and adult tickets include tastings of two products. If the weather's a bit cold and wet, it's a great way to warm up. Enthusiasts can take a 2½-hour Master

CLIMBING PEN-Y-FAN

One of the most popular hikes in the national park is the ascent of Pen-y-Fan (886m), the highest peak in the Brecon Beacons (around 120,000 people each year make the climb, giving it the nickname 'the motorway'). The shortest route to the summit begins at the Pont ar Daf car park on the A470, 10 miles southwest of Brecon. It's a steep but straightforward slog up a deeply eroded path (now paved with natural stone) to the summit of Corn Du (873m), followed by a short dip and final ascent to Pen-y-Fan (4.5 miles round trip; allow three hours). A slightly longer (5.5 miles round trip) but just as crowded path starts at the Storey Arms outdoor centre, 1 mile to the north. The X43 and various Beacons Buses stop at the Storey Arms. (Note: the Storey Arms is not a pub!)

You can avoid the crowds by choosing one of the longer routes on the north side of the mountain, which also have the advantage of more interesting views on the way up. The best starting point is the Cwm Gwdi car park, at the end of a minor road 3.5 miles southwest of Brecon. From here, you follow a path along the crest of the Cefn Cwm Llwch ridge, with great views of the neighbouring peaks, with a final steep scramble up to the summit. The round trip from the car park is 7 miles; allow three to four hours. Starting and finishing in Brecon, the total distance is 14 miles.

Remember that Pen-y-Fan is a serious mountain – the weather can change rapidly and people have to be rescued here every year. Wear hiking boots and take warm clothes, waterproofs and a map and compass. You can get advice and weather forecasts at the National Park Visitor Centre or from the **Met Office** (☎ 0870 900 0100; www.metoffice.gov.uk).

Class (per person £45, bookings essential), which includes a guided tour and tastings.

❧ **FFOREST FAWR CAVES //
FROM SERIOUS SQUEEZES TO KID-
FRIENDLY CHAMBERS**

The limestone plateau of the southern Fforest Fawr, around the upper reaches of the River Tawe, is riddled with some of the largest and most complex cave systems in Britain. Most can only be visited by experienced cavers, but the **National Showcaves Centre for Wales** (☎ 01639-730284; www.showcaves.co.uk; adult/child £13/7; ☺ 10am-4pm Apr-Oct, last entry to caves 3pm) is a set of three caves that are well-lit, spacious and easily accessible, even to children.

The highlight of the 1.5-mile self-guided tour is the **Cathedral Cave**, a high-domed chamber with a lake fed by two waterfalls that pour from openings in the rock. Nearby is the **Bone Cave**, where 42 Bronze Age skeletons were discovered. **Dan-yr-Ogof Cave**, part of a 10-mile complex, has interesting limestone formations.

The admission fee also gives entry to various other attractions on site, including a museum, a reconstructed Iron Age farm, a prehistoric theme park filled with life-sized fibreglass dinosaurs, a shire-horse centre and a children's playground. The complex is just off the A4067 north of Abercraf.

Beneath the hillside to the east lies the twisting maze of subterranean chambers known as **Ogof Ffynnon Ddu** (Cave of the Black Spring), the deepest and third-longest cave system in the UK (308m deep, with 30 miles of passages). This one is for expert potholers only, but you can explore it virtually at www.ogof.net.

♣ BLACK MOUNTAIN // A PLACE TO LOSE YOURSELF, HOPEFULLY NOT LITERALLY

Black Mountain (Mynydd Du), the western section of the national park, contains the wildest, loneliest and least-visited walking country. Its finest feature is the sweeping escarpment of **Fan Brycheiniog** (802m), which rises steeply above the scenic glacial lakes of Llyn y Fan Fach and Llyn y Fan Fawr. It can be climbed from Llanddeusant; the round trip is 12 miles.

TRANSPORT

BUS // Bus 63 between Swansea and Brecon stops at the National Showcaves Centre. See also the Beacons Buses boxed text (p89).

SOUTH WALES VALLEYS

· · · · · ·

The valleys fanning northwards from Cardiff and Newport were once the heart of industrial Wales. Although the coal, iron and steel industries have withered, the valley names – Rhondda, Cynon, Rhymney, Ebbw – still evoke a world of tight-knit working-class communities, male voice choirs and rows of neat terraced houses set amid a scarred, coal-blackened landscape. Today, the region is fighting back against its decline by creating a tourist industry based on industrial heritage – places such as the Rhondda Heritage Park, Big Pit and Blaenavon Ironworks are among Wales' most impressive tourist attractions.

The valleys' industrial economy emerged in the 18th century, based on the exploitation of the region's rich deposits of coal, limestone and iron ore. At first the iron trade dictated the need for coal, but by the 1830s coal was finding its own worldwide markets and people poured in from the countryside looking for work. The harsh and dangerous working conditions provided fertile ground for political radicalism – Merthyr Tydfil elected Britain's first ever Labour Party MP in 1900, and many locals went to fight in the Spanish Civil War in the 1930s.

BLAENAVON (BLAENAFON)

☎ 01495 / pop 6000

Of all the valley towns that were decimated by the demise of heavy industry, the one-time coal and iron town of Blaenavon shows the greenest shoots of regrowth. This rejuvenation is helped to a large part by the awarding of Unesco World Heritage status in 2000 to its unique conglomeration of industrial sites. Its proximity to Brecon Beacons National Park and Abergavenny doesn't do it any harm either.

Blaenavon is an interesting town to visit, but not necessarily to stay in; the nearest recommended accommodation is in Abergavenny.

ORIENTATION

Blaenavon sits at the head of the Llwyd Valley, 16 miles north of Newport. Most buses stop in High St, in the centre of town. Broad St, with its bookshops, is a block to the east. Blaenavon Ironworks is 400m west of High St: walk uphill to the top of High St, turn left on Upper Waun St, then left again on North St. Big Pit: National Coal Museum is another mile west of the ironworks.

THE ABERFAN DISASTER

On 21 October 1966 Wales experienced one of its worst disasters. On that day, heavy rain loosened an already dangerously unstable spoil heap above Aberfan, 4 miles south of Merthyr Tydfil, and sent a 500,000-tonne mudslide of liquefied coal slurry down onto the village. It wiped out a row of terraced houses and ploughed into Pantglas primary school, killing 144 people, most of them children.

Today, the A470 Cardiff–Merthyr Tydfil road cuts right through the spot where the spoil heap once stood. The site of the school has been turned into a memorial garden, while the village cemetery contains a long, double row of matching headstones, a mute and moving memorial to those who died.

EXPLORING BLAENAVON

☙ BLAENAVON WORLD HERITAGE CENTRE // THE BEST STARTING POINT TO ANY VISIT

Housed in an artfully converted old school, this **centre** (☎ 742333; www.world-heritage-blaenavon.org.uk; Church Rd; admission free; ⏰ 9am-5pm Tue-Sun Apr-Oct, until 4pm Nov-Mar) houses a cafe, tourist office, gallery, gift shop and, more importantly, excellent interactive, audiovisual displays that explore the industrial heritage of the region.

☙ BIG PIT: NATIONAL COAL MUSEUM // EXPERIENCE A REAL MINE WITH REAL MINERS

The atmospheric **Big Pit** (☎ 790311; www.museumwales.ac.uk; admission free; ⏰ 9.30am-5pm, guided tours 10am-3.30pm) provides an opportunity to explore a real coal mine and get a taste of what life was like for the miners who worked here up until 1980. Visitors descend 90m into the mine and explore the tunnels and coalfaces in the company of an ex-miner guide. It's sobering to experience something of the dark, dank working conditions, particularly considering that children once worked here by candlelight.

Above ground, you can see the pithead baths, blacksmith's workshop and other colliery buildings, filled with displays on the industry and the evocative reminiscences of ex-miners.

You'll be decked out in hard hat, power pack and other safety gear weighing some 5kg, and won't be allowed to take matches or anything electrical (including photo equipment and watches) down with you. It's cold underground, so take extra layers and wear sturdy shoes. Children must be at least 1m tall. Disabled visitors can arrange tours in advance.

☙ BLAENAVON IRONWORKS // A TESTIMONY TO WALES' ERSTWHILE INDUSTRIAL PROWESS

When it was completed in 1788, **Blaenavon Ironworks** (Cadw; ☎ 792615; www.cadw.wales.gov.uk; North St; admission free; ⏰ 10am-5pm Apr-Oct, 9.30am-4pm Fri & Sat, 11am-4pm Sun Nov-Mar) was one of the most advanced in the world. Its three huge coal-fired blast furnaces were provided with air powered by a steam engine, making them much more powerful than older, smaller furnaces fired with charcoal and blasted with air from a waterwheel-powered bellows. Within a few years it was the world's second-biggest ironworks, after Cyfarthfa at Merthyr Tydfil. Innovation and development continued here until 1904, when the last furnace was finally shut down.

**SOUTHEAST WALES &
BRECON BEACONS**

TOP FIVE

INDUSTRIAL HERITAGE SIGHTS

- ★ Big Pit: National Coal Museum (p105)
- ★ Blaenavon Ironworks (p105)
- ★ National Wool Museum (p136)
- ★ Llechwedd Slate Caverns (p223)
- ★ National Slate Museum (p230)

Today the site is one of the best-preserved of all the Industrial Revolution ironworks. You can follow the whole process of production, from the charging of the furnaces to the casting of molten iron in the casting sheds. Also on display are the ironworkers' tiny terraced cottages. The surrounding hillsides are pitted with old tramlines, mines, tunnels and 'scouring' sites, where water was released from holding ponds to wash away topsoil and expose ore seams.

☙ PONTYPOOL & BLAENAVON RAILWAY // ANOTHER INDUSTRIAL RELIC BACK IN BUSINESS

Built to haul coal and passengers up and down the valley, this **railway** (☎ 792263; www.pontypool-and-blaenavon.co.uk; adult/child £4.50/2.25; ⊙ check online) stopped taking passengers in 1941, and coal haulage ceased when the Big Pit was closed. Since then a section has been restored by local volunteers, allowing you to catch a steam train from the town centre to Big Pit and on to Whistle Halt, the highest train station in England and Wales (396m). The Whistle Inn Pub, beside the station, has a huge collection of miners' lamps.

☙ CHEESE, WALKS & BIKES // LOAD UP ON WELSH VICTUALS

On the main drag, **Blaenavon Cheddar Company** (☎ 793123; www.chunkofcheese.

co.uk; 80 Broad St; ⊙ 10am-5pm Mon-Sat) is both a champion for the town and evidence of its gradual resurgence. The shop stocks the company's range of handmade cheese, some of which are matured down in the Big Pit mine shaft. The Pwll Mawr is particularly good, winning a bronze in the British cheese awards, but for extra kick try the chilli- and ale-laced Dragon's Breath. It also stocks a range of Welsh speciality ales, wines and whisky.

The same crew arranges guided walking and mountain-biking tours for all abilities (walks per person from £2.50) and hires bikes (half-/full-day £8/15).

TRANSPORT

BIKE // A branch of Lôn Las Cymru (p302) connects to Abergavenny, before heading north to Builth Wells and south to Chepstow.

BUS // Buses X24 and 30 head here from Newport (50 minutes). See also Beacons Bus B15 (p89).

MERTHYR TYDFIL

☎ 01685 / pop 55,000

Merthyr Tydfil (*mur*-thir *tid*-vil) occupies a spectacular site, sprawled across a bowl at the head of the Taff Valley, ringed and pocked with quarries and spoil heaps. It was even more spectacular 200 years ago when the town was at the heart of the Industrial Revolution, and this bowl was a crucible filled with the fire and smoke of the world's biggest ironworks.

Today, all the industry has gone and unemployment (11.7% in 2010) runs at 27% more than the national average. But the town is endeavouring to turn itself around, redeveloping former industrial sites and turning its past into a tourist attraction.

Perhaps unusually for such an industrial town, Merthyr Tydfil has produced two internationally famous fashion designers – Laura Ashley (famed for her flowery, feminine designs in the 1970s) and Julien Macdonald (he of the shimmery, figure-hugging dresses favoured by Kylie and Britney).

Merthyr Tydfil means 'the place of Tydfil's martyrdom' – the town was named in honour of a Welsh princess who, according to legend, was murdered for her Christian beliefs in the 5th century. St Tydfil's Church is said to mark the spot where she died.

Merthyr remained a minor village until the late 18th century, when its proximity to iron ore, limestone, water and wood led to it becoming a centre of iron production. The subsequent discovery of rich coal reserves upped the ante, and by 1801 a string of settlements, each growing around its own ironworks – Cyfarthfa, Penydarren, Dowlais, Pentrebach and others – had merged together to become the biggest town in Wales (population 10,000, eight times the size of Cardiff at that time). Immigrants flooded in from all over Europe, and the town's population peaked at 81,000 in the mid-19th century.

By 1803, Cyfarthfa was the world's biggest ironworks. Ever more efficient ways to make iron were pioneered, on the backs of overworked labourers (including, until 1842, women and children as young as six) who lived in appalling, disease-ridden conditions. By the 19th century Merthyr was a centre of political radicalism. The Merthyr Rising of 1831 was the most violent uprising in Britain's history – 10,000 ironworkers, angry over pay cuts and lack of representation, faced off against a handful of armed soldiers, and rioting continued for a month.

As demand for iron and steel dwindled in the early 20th century, one by one the ironworks closed down. Unemployment soared, reaching as high as 60% in 1935. In 1939 a Royal Commission even suggested that the whole town should be abandoned. But community ties were strong and people stayed on.

The Taff Trail (p39) runs along the river on the western edge of town, crossing the handsome railway viaducts of Cefn Coed (the third biggest in Wales) and Pontsarn, both completed in 1866, as it heads up to Pontsticill Reservoir.

ESSENTIAL INFORMATION

TOURIST OFFICES // Tourist office
(☎ 727474; www.merthyr.gov.uk; 14 Glebeland St; ☒ 9.30am-4pm Mon-Sat) Near the bus station.

ORIENTATION

Merthyr sprawls across the head of the Taff Valley, and you'll need to do a bit of walking or cycling to see all the sights. The train and bus stations are close together at the south end of town; Cyfarthfa Castle is 1 mile to the north.

EXPLORING MERTHYR TYDFIL

☙ CYFARTHFA CASTLE //
OSTENTATIOUSLY HOUSED
ARTEFACTS, OLD AND NEWISH
For a measure of the wealth that accumulated at the top of the industrial pile, check out this **castle** (☎ 723112; www.merthyr.gov.uk/museum; Brecon Rd; admission free; ☒ 10am-5.30pm Apr-Sep, 10am-4pm Tue-Fri, noon-4pm Sat & Sun Oct-Mar; ℗), built in 1824 by William Crawshay II, overlooking his ironworks. Set into the hillside across the river from the castle are the Cyfarthfa Blast Furnaces, all that remains of them. The house is now jam-packed with interesting stuff, from ancient Egyptian and Roman artefacts

to a George Best tie rack. The basement houses an excellent exhibition on Merthyr's gritty history.

❦ JOSEPH PARRY'S COTTAGE // A GIANT OF WELSH SONG, PREDATING TOM JONES

A half-mile to the south of the castle, a row of pint-sized 19th-century iron-workers' houses, built by the Crawshays, stands in bald contrast to Cyfarthfa Castle. At No 4 is **Joseph Parry's Cottage** (☎ 723112; 4 Chapel Row; admission free; ⏲ 2-5pm Thu-Sun Apr-Sep), furnished in 1840s style. It was the birthplace of Welsh composer and songwriter Joseph Parry (1841–1903).

❦ INDUSTRIAL RELICS // GAINFUL STOPS FOR ENGINEERING BUFFS

Across the river from the bus station is **Ynysfach Engine House**, a distinctive landmark that once housed the huge beam engines that created the blast of hot air for the iron furnaces.

Trainspotters will relish **Trevithick's Tunnel**, site of the first test of Richard Trevithick's steam-powered locomotive. In 1804 it was the first in the world to haul a load on rails – it lugged 10 tonnes of iron for 9.5 miles, at a speed of 4mph. It's off the A470 in Pentrebach, 1.25 miles south of Merthyr.

❦ BRECON MOUNTAIN RAILWAY // PUFF YOUR WAY INTO THE NATIONAL PARK

Between 1859 and 1964 this narrow-gauge **railway** (☎ 722988; www.breconmountain railway.co.uk; adult/child £9.50/4.75) hauled coal and passengers between Merthyr and Brecon. A 5.5-mile section of track, between Pant Station and Torpantau at the head of Pontsticill Reservoir, has been

---

∼ WORTH A TRIP ∼

Northwest of Cardiff, the **Rhondda Valley** – the most famous of the South Wales valleys – was once synonymous with coal mining. The closure of the last pit in 1990 left the valley bereft, but since then Rhondda has succeeded in converting an abandoned colliery into an interesting exploration of the region's industrial heritage.

Rhondda Heritage Park (☎ 01443-682036; www.rhonddaheritagepark.com; Trehafod; admission free; ⏲ 9am-4.30pm, closed Mon Oct-Easter) brings new life to the old colliery buildings of the Lewis Merthyr coal mine (which closed in 1983). The displays are fascinating, if a little depressing: one sign is headed 'A whole society was crucified', and the display on the Tynewydd Colliery Disaster makes for sobering reading.

The highlight is the 90-minute **Black Gold Tour** (adult/child £5.60/4.30; ⏲ 10am, noon & 2pm, bookings advised), where you don a miner's helmet and lamp and, accompanied by a guide (all are ex-miners), experience a simulated descent to the coalface. The compelling commentary vividly re-creates the experience of mine workers in the 1950s, and hammers home the social impact of the coal industry. Back at the surface, a multimedia show explores the story of coal mining in South Wales, including daily life for miners' families.

The park is 13 miles northwest of Cardiff, between Pontypridd and Porth; take the A470 and then the A4058. There are frequent trains from Cardiff Central station to Trehafod (£3.30, 35 minutes, every half-hour); the station's a 10-minute walk from the heritage park.

restored and operates steam locomotive trips. Most days from April to October there are five departures, and the trip takes 65 minutes with a 20-minute stop at Pontsticill (you can stay longer if you like and return on a later train). The timetable varies widely in other months; enquire at the tourist office or check online.

Pant Station is 3.5 miles north of Merthyr bus station; take bus 35 (20 minutes, four per hour Monday to Saturday) to the Pant Cemetery stop, from where it's a five-minute walk.

TRANSPORT

BIKE // The Taff Trail (p39) heads south from here to Cardiff and north to Brecon.

BUS // Bus X43 connects Merthyr Tydfil with Cardiff (45 minutes), Brecon (37 minutes), Crickhowell (1½ hours) and Abergavenny (1½ hours). X4 also heads to Abergavenny (1½ hours) and Cardiff (55 minutes). See also the Beacons Buses boxed text (p89).

COACH // National Express (www.nationalexpress.com) coaches head to London (£24, 4¼ hours), Cardiff (£1.70, 50 minutes), Newport (£7.30, 1¾ hours), Brecon (£2.60, 30 minutes) and Abergavenny (£8, 50 minutes).

TRAIN // Regular trains head to/from Cardiff (£4.50, one hour).

SWANSEA, THE GOWER & CARMARTHENSHIRE

3 PERFECT DAYS

🐦 DAY 1 // SWAN AROUND SWANSEA

Potter around Swansea's Maritime Quarter in the morning, splitting your time between the Dylan Thomas Centre (p117) and the National Waterfront Museum (p117). Devote your afternoon to exploring the Gower (p122): scoot down to Three Cliffs Bay (p123), hike up to Arthur's Stone (p126) and wander along Rhossili Bay (p125). Cap it off with a pint at the Joiners Arms (p127) before heading back to Mumbles (p118). Slip into your smart-casuals for an evening stroll along the promenade, dinner, and a nightcap at Jones (p120).

🐦 DAY 2 // COUNTRY ROADS

Take a long, leisurely drive into the Carmarthenshire countryside. Choose between birds, bastions and botany for your first stop: take a gander at a Canadian goose at the National Wetland Centre (p128), storm Kidwelly Castle (p128) or get green-fingered at the National Botanic Garden of Wales (p132). Call into Carmarthen Market (p130) for some ham, then follow the A484 as it meanders along the River Gwili and then the Teifi as far as pretty little Cenarth (p136). If you've got time, call into the National Wool Museum (p136) on your way back, before pressing on to Llandeilo (p133) for the night.

🐦 DAY 3 // CASTLES AND GARDENS

After yesterday's solid driving, spend today within a few miles' radius of Llandeilo. Carreg Cennen Castle (p134) is a highlight of any Carmarthenshire trip. Spend the morning among the lonely battlements before heading back to Llandeilo for lunch (p133). Divide your afternoon between Dinefwr Park & Castle (p132) and Aberglasney Gardens (p132) or, if you didn't make it there yesterday, the National Botanic Garden.

SWANSEA (ABERTAWE)

· · · · · ·

☎ 01792 / pop 229,100

Dylan Thomas called Swansea an 'ugly, lovely town', and that remains a fair description today. Wales' second-largest city sprawls along the 5-mile sweep of Swansea Bay, ending to the southwest in the smart seaside suburb of Mumbles at the foot of the Gower Peninsula. It's currently in the grip of a Cardiff-esque bout of regeneration, slowly transforming the drab, post-war city centre into something worthy of its natural assets. A new marina, a national museum, a water park, an architecturally tricksy footbridge and a transport centre have already opened and plans are afoot to bulldoze and rebuild the central shopping precinct and create a fitting seaside boulevard out of shabby Oystermouth Rd.

Swansea makes up for its visual short-comings with a visceral charm. A hefty student population takes to the city's bars with enthusiasm and a newly minted restaurant scene has emerged from among all the Chinese and Indian takeaways.

Swansea's Welsh name, Abertawe, describes its location at the mouth of the Tawe, where the river empties into Swansea Bay. The Vikings named the area Sveins Ey (Swein's Island), probably referring to the sandbank in the river mouth.

The Normans built a castle here, but Swansea didn't really get into its stride until the Industrial Revolution, when it developed into an important copper-smelting centre. Ore was first shipped in from Cornwall, across the Bristol Channel, but by the 19th century it was arriving from Chile, Cuba and the USA, in return for Welsh coal.

By the 20th century the city's industrial base had declined, although Swansea's oil refinery and smaller factories were still judged a worthy target by the Luftwaffe, which devastated the city centre in 1941. It was rebuilt as a rather soulless retail development in the 1960s, '70s and '80s, and now has another date with destruction, courtesy of a wrecking ball.

A small pocket around Wind St and Castle Sq escaped the wartime bombing and retains a remnant of Georgian and Victorian Swansea as well as the ruins of 14th-century **Swansea Castle** (closed to the public). The castle was mostly destroyed by Cromwell in 1647, but had a brief lease of life as a prison in the 19th century.

ESSENTIAL INFORMATION

EMERGENCIES // Morriston Hospital (☎ 702222; Heol Maes Eglwys, Morriston) Accident and emergency department, 5 miles north of the city centre. **Police station** (☎ 456999; Grove Pl)

TOURIST OFFICES // Mumbles (☎ 361302; www.mumblestic.co.uk; Methodist Church, Mumbles Rd; ◷ 10am-5pm Mon-Sat, noon-5pm Sun Jul & Aug, 10am-4pm Mon-Sat Sep-Jun) **Swansea** (☎ 468321; www.visitswanseabay.com; Plymouth St; ◷ 9.30am-5.30pm Mon-Sat year-round, 10am-4pm Sun Jun-Sep)

ORIENTATION

The compact city centre clusters around Castle Sq and pedestrianised Oxford St on the west bank of the River Tawe. To its south and east are the redeveloped docklands of the Maritime Quarter, linked to the new SA1 district on the Tawe's east bank by the graceful Sail Bridge (2003). The bus station and tourist office are on the western edge of the city centre, by the Quadrant shopping

(Continued on page 117)

SWANSEA, THE GOWER & CARMARTHENSHIRE

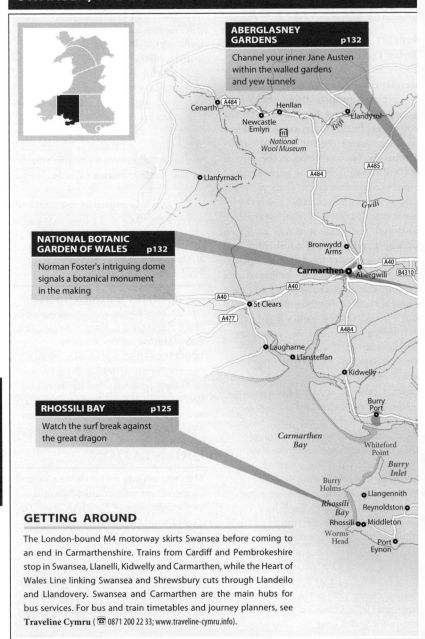

ABERGLASNEY GARDENS p132

Channel your inner Jane Austen within the walled gardens and yew tunnels

NATIONAL BOTANIC GARDEN OF WALES p132

Norman Foster's intriguing dome signals a botanical monument in the making

RHOSSILI BAY p125

Watch the surf break against the great dragon

Cenarth
Henllan
Newcastle Emlyn
Llandysul
National Wool Museum
Llanfyrnach
Bronwydd Arms
Carmarthen
Abergwili
St Clears
Laugharne
Llansteffan
Kidwelly
Burry Port
Carmarthen Bay
Whiteford Point
Burry Inlet
Burry Holms
Llangennith
Reynoldston
Rhossili Bay
Rhossili Middleton
Worms Head
Port Eynon

GETTING AROUND

The London-bound M4 motorway skirts Swansea before coming to an end in Carmarthenshire. Trains from Cardiff and Pembrokeshire stop in Swansea, Llanelli, Kidwelly and Carmarthen, while the Heart of Wales Line linking Swansea and Shrewsbury cuts through Llandeilo and Llandovery. Swansea and Carmarthen are the main hubs for bus services. For bus and train timetables and journey planners, see **Traveline Cymru** (☎ 0871 200 22 33; www.traveline-cymru.info).

SWANSEA, THE GOWER & CARMARTHENSHIRE

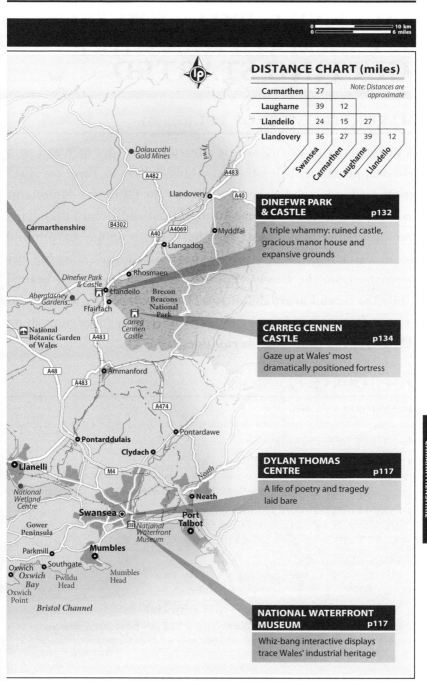

| 0 | | | 10 km |
| 0 | | | 6 miles |

DISTANCE CHART (miles)

	Swansea	Carmarthen	Laugharne	Llandeilo
Carmarthen	27	*Note: Distances are approximate*		
Laugharne	39	12		
Llandeilo	24	15	27	
Llandovery	36	27	39	12

DINEFWR PARK & CASTLE   p132

A triple whammy: ruined castle, gracious manor house and expansive grounds

CARREG CENNEN CASTLE   p134

Gaze up at Wales' most dramatically positioned fortress

DYLAN THOMAS CENTRE   p117

A life of poetry and tragedy laid bare

NATIONAL WATERFRONT MUSEUM   p117

Whiz-bang interactive displays trace Wales' industrial heritage

SWANSEA, THE GOWER & CARMARTHENSHIRE

SWANSEA, THE GOWER & CARMARTHENSHIRE GETTING STARTED

MAKING THE MOST OF YOUR TIME

A hodgepodge of experiences is offered in this slice of Wales with physical proximity being the only thing linking its three constituent ingredients, sandwiched together by the Cambrian Mountains to the north, the Brecon Beacons to the east and attention-hogging Pembrokeshire to the west. Each has its own unique flavour and set of attractions: Swansea offers something approaching big-city sophistication, the Gower Peninsula revels in its coastal beauty, while the fecund heartland of rural Carmarthenshire offers country comfort in abundance. Try a taste of each or gorge yourself on whichever you think sounds yummiest.

TOP TOURS & COURSES

❦ EUPHORIA SAILING
Try your hand water-skiing, wake-boarding (both £45 per 30 minutes) or dinghy sailing (one-day intro course £90). (☎ 01792-234502; www.euphoriasailing.co.uk; Oxwich Bay)

❦ GOWER COAST ADVENTURES
Speedboat trips to Worms Head from Port Eynon (adult/child £30/20) or Mumbles (adult/child £38/24). (☎ 07866-250440; www.gowercoastadventures.co.uk)

❦ PARC-LE-BREOS PONY TREKKING
The rural byways and bridleways of Gower are ideal territory for exploring on horseback. (☎ 01792-371636; www.parc-le-breos.co.uk; Parkmill; half-/full day £30/43)

❦ SAM'S SURF SHACK
Learn to surf at the Gower's most beautiful beach. (☎ 01792-390519; www.samssurfshack.com; Rhossili; per hr $20)

❦ WELSH SURFING FEDERATION SURF SCHOOL
The governing body for surfing in Wales offers initial two-hour surfing lessons for £25 and subsequent lessons for £20. (☎ 01792-386426; www.wsfsurfschool.co.uk; Llangennith)

GETTING AWAY FROM IT ALL

* **Arthur's Stone** Set atop Cefn Bryn, the rugged moor at the heart of the Gower, this ancient dolmen is a suitably moody landmark (p126).
* **Carreg Cennen Castle** You may well find yourself king or queen of this remote castle, set on a limestone crag on the edge of the Beacons. Look for the two sets of twinned bumps on the facing ridge – they're Bronze Age burial cairns (p115).
* **Llyn y Fan Fach** Seek out the lady of the lake, on the little-travelled slopes of the Black Mountain (p136).

ADVANCE PLANNING

Swansea restaurants It can be surprisingly hard to get a table at the better restaurants without forward bookings during any of the traditional feeding frenzies, such as the weeks of Valentine's Day and Mother's Day.

Six Nations (www.rbs6nations.com) Even though the home matches are played in Cardiff, it can be hard to get accommodation in Swansea during the big rugby fixtures.

Laugharne Weekend (http://s233406860.websitehome.co.uk/index.html) Literate musos and music-loving scribes descend on Dylan Thomas' favourite town for an edgy little festival in April.

Swansea Bay Summer Festival An umbrella festival encompassing a broad spectrum of summer events (p119).

TOP CULINARY TREATS

❦ JOE'S ICE CREAM
The taste of Swansea's summers since 1922 (p120).

❦ PENCLAWDD COCKLES
Harvested on the edge of the Gower since at least Roman times, and a key ingredient in the iconic Welsh breakfast, laver bread.

❦ SALT-MARSH LAMB
Distinctively flavoured meat, grazed on the Gower.

❦ CARMARTHEN HAM
Wales' indigenous version of Parma ham.

❦ ANGEL VAULTS
Carmarthenshire's top restaurant (p131).

❦ HEAVENLY
Handcrafted chocolates, artisanal ice cream, enticing pastries and cakes (p133).

RESOURCES

* **Swansea Bay, Mumbles & Gower** (www.visitswanseabay.com) Official tourism site.
* **Mumbles Tourist Information Centre** (www.visitmumbles.co.uk) In-depth tourist information.
* **Coast & Countryside in Carmarthenshire** (www.discovercarmarthenshire.com) Official tourist website.
* **Llandovery** (www.llandovery.org.uk) Community portal with information on history, sights, accommodation and eateries.

SWANSEA, THE GOWER & CARMARTHENSHIRE

SWANSEA

SWANSEA, THE GOWER & CARMARTHENSHIRE

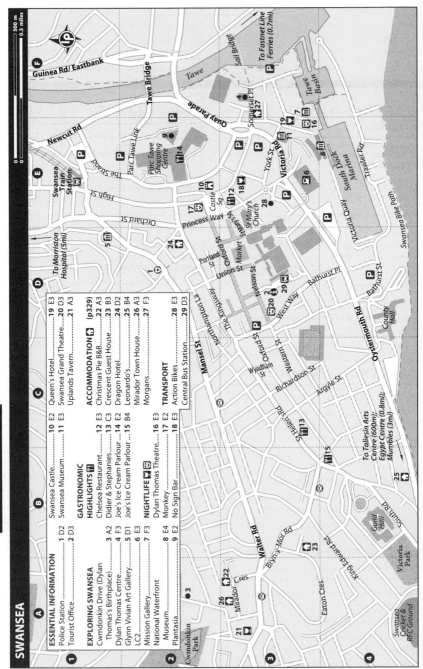

ESSENTIAL INFORMATION
Police Station...................1 D2
Tourist Office...................2 D3

EXPLORING SWANSEA
Cwmdonkin Drive (Dylan
  Thomas's Birthplace)......3 A2
Dylan Thomas Centre........4 F3
Glynn Vivian Art Gallery....5 D1
LC2................................6 E3
Mission Gallery................7 F3
National Waterfront
  Museum.......................8 E4
Plantasia........................9 E2

Swansea Castle................10 E2
Swansea Museum.............11 E3

GASTRONOMIC
HIGHLIGHTS
Chelsea Restaurant..........12 E3
Didier & Stephanies..........13 C3
Joe's Ice Cream Parlour....14 E2
Joe's Ice Cream Parlour....15 D1

NIGHTLIFE
Dylan Thomas Theatre......16 E3
Monkey..........................17 E2
No Sign Bar.....................18 E3

Queen's Hotel..................19 E3
Swansea Grand Theatre....20 D3
Uplands Tavern................21 A3

ACCOMMODATION (p329)
Christmas Pie B&B............22 A3
Crescent Guest House.......23 B3
Dragon Hotel...................24 D2
Leonardo's......................25 B4
Mirador Town House.........26 A3
Morgans.........................27 F3

TRANSPORT
Action Bikes....................28 E3
Central Bus Station...........29 D3

(Continued from page 111)

centre. The train station is 600m north of Castle Sq along Castle St and High St.

Uplands, where many of the city's guesthouses are found, is 1 mile west of the city centre, along Mansel St and Walter Rd. From the southern edge of the city centre, Oystermouth Rd runs for 5 miles west and then south along Swansea Bay, becoming Mumbles Rd.

EXPLORING SWANSEA

❧ NATIONAL WATERFRONT MUSEUM // A REVOLUTIONARY INDUSTRIAL MUSEUM

The Maritime Quarter's flagship attraction is the **National Waterfront Museum** (☎ 638950; www.waterfrontmuseum.co.uk; South Dock Marina; admission free; ☒ 10am-5pm), housed in a 1901 dockside warehouse with a striking glass and slate extension. The 15 hands-on galleries explore Wales' industrial history and the impact of industrialisation on its people, from 1750 to the present day, making much use of interactive computer screens and audiovisual presentations. The effect can be a bit overwhelming but there is enough interesting stuff here to occupy several hours.

❧ SWANSEA MUSEUM // THE TRADITIONAL MUSEUM EXPERIENCE

It would be hard to find a more complete contrast to the Waterfront Museum than the gloriously old-fashioned Swansea Museum (☎ 653763; www.swanseaheritage.net; Victoria Rd; admission free; ☒ 10am-5pm Tue-Sun) – Dylan Thomas referred to it as 'the museum which should have *been* in a museum'. Founded in 1834, it remains charmingly low-tech, from the eccentric Cabinet of Curiosities to the glass cases of archaeological finds from Gower caves. Pride of place goes to the Mummy of Hor, which has been here since 1887 – a video in the display room explains the process of its repair and conservation.

❧ DYLAN THOMAS CENTRE // A TRIBUTE TO SWANSEA'S FAVOURITE SON

Housed in the former guildhall, the **Dylan Thomas Centre** (☎ 463980; www.swansea.gov.uk/dtc; Somerset Pl; admission free; ☒ 10am-4.30pm) contains an absorbing exhibition on the poet's life and work. Entitled *Man and Myth,* it pulls no punches in examining the propensity of 'the most quoted author after Shakespeare' for puffing up his own myth. Aside from the collection of memorabilia, what really brings his work to life is a series of recordings, including the booming baritone of Richard Burton performing *Under Milk Wood* and Thomas himself reading *Do Not Go Gentle into That Good Night,* the celebrated paean to his dying father.

❧ LC2 // HIGH-TECH, WET AND WILD

The Marine Quarter's new £32-million **leisure centre** (☎ 466500; www.thelcswansea.com; Oystermouth Rd; water park adult/child £7/3; ☒ 6.30am-10pm Mon-Fri, 8am-9pm Sat & Sun, water park 4-9pm Mon-Fri, 9am-8pm Sat & Sun) includes a gym and a 10m indoor climbing wall, but best of all is the water park, complete with a wave pool, water slides and the world's first indoor surfing ride.

❧ MISSION GALLERY // MODERN ART ON A MISSION

Set in a converted 19th-century seamen's chapel, the **Mission Gallery** (☎ 652016; www.missiongallery.co.uk; Gloucester Pl; admission free; ☒ 11am-5pm) stages some of Swansea's most striking exhibitions of contemporary art. It is also sells glassware, ceramics, jewellery and art magazines.

❦ GLYNN VIVIAN ART GALLERY // LOCALS HOLDING THEIR OWN ALONGSIDE ARTISTIC HEAVYWEIGHTS

Housed in an elegant Italianate building, the city's main **art gallery** (☎ 516900; www.swansea.gov.uk/glynnvivian; Alexandra Rd; admission free; ☺ 10am-5pm Tue-Sun) displays a wide range of Welsh art (Richard Wilson, Gwen John, Ceri Richards, Shani Rhys James) alongside works by Claude Monet and Lucien Freud and a large ceramics collection.

❦ PLANTASIA // EXOTIC PLANTS AND CRITTERS BUT NO DANCING HIPPOS

The name may conjure up images of Disney's hippos in tutus but it's smaller critters that feature in this glass pyramid, parked between the Parc Tawe Shopping Centre and the river. **Plantasia** (☎ 474555; www.plantasia.org; Parc Tawe Link; adult/child £3.80/2.80; ☺ 10am-5pm) contains hundreds of species of exotic plants, plus attendant insects, reptiles, snakes, tropical fish (including piranhas), birds and tamarin monkeys. A coffee shop and range of kids' activities make it a popular rainy-day retreat.

❦ EGYPT CENTRE // COME TO WALES AND VISIT ANCIENT EGYPT

Swansea University is in the suburb of Sketty, halfway between the city centre and the Mumble. The university possesses the UK's biggest collection of Egyptian antiquities outside the British Museum. Opened to the public in 1998, the volunteer-run **Egypt Centre** (☎ 295960; www.swan.ac.uk/egypt; Taliesin Arts Centre, Singleton Park, Mumbles Rd; admission free; ☺ 10am-4pm Tue-Sat) displays a fascinating collection of everyday ancient Egyptian artefacts, ranging from a 4000-year-old razor and cosmetic trays to a mummified crocodile.

❦ MUMBLES (Y MWMBWLS) // SWANSEA'S MOST EXCLUSIVE SUBURB

Strung out along the shoreline at the southern end of Swansea Bay, Mumbles has been Swansea's seaside retreat since 1807, when the Oystermouth Railway was opened. Built for transporting coal, the horse-drawn carriages were soon converted for paying customers, and the now defunct Mumbles train became the first passenger railway service in the world.

THE DYLAN THOMAS TRAIL

The legacy of Dylan Thomas (see p129) is inescapable in this part of Wales. Whether you're a fan, or whether you're just interested to know what all the fuss is about, you'll find plenty of sites in Swansea to stalk the shade of the maverick poet and writer. When you've exhausted them all, you can always head on to Laugharne (p128).

Start at the Dylan Thomas Centre (p117) and then check out his statue gazing across the marina outside the Dylan Thomas Theatre (p121). In Uplands, a plaque marks his **birthplace** (5 Cwmdonkin Dr), an unassuming terraced house where he wrote two-thirds of his poetry.

Perhaps the places where you're most likely to feel his presence are his beloved drinking haunts, which include No Sign Bar (p120), Queen's Hotel (p120), Uplands Tavern (p121) and Mermaid Brasserie (p120).

Once again fashionable, with gourmet restaurants vying for trade along the promenade, Mumbles got a boost to its reputation when its most famous daughter, Hollywood actress Catherine Zeta-Jones, built a £2 million luxury mansion at Limeslade, on the south side of the peninsula. Singer Bonnie Tyler also has a home here.

At the end of its mile-long strip of pastel-painted houses, pubs and restaurants is a rocky headland abutted by a Victorian pier with a sandy beach below. Built in 1898, **Mumbles Pier** (☎ 365220; www.mumbles-pier.co.uk; Mumbles Rd) houses the usual amusement arcade and a once-grand cafe, festooned with chandeliers.

It wouldn't be Wales without a castle, hence the trendy shops and bars of Newton Rd are guarded by the majestic ruin of **Oystermouth Castle** (www.oystermouth castle.wordpress.com; Castle Ave; adult/child £1/80p; ☙ 11am-5pm Apr-Sep). Once the stronghold of the Norman lords of Gower it's now the focus of summer Shakespeare performances. There's a fine view over Swansea Bay from the battlements.

The origin of Mumbles' unusual name is uncertain, although one theory is that it's a legacy of French seamen who nicknamed the twin rounded rocks at the tip of the headland *Les Mamelles* – 'the breasts'.

FESTIVALS & EVENTS

Swansea Bay Summer Festival (www.swan seabayfestival.com) From May to September, the waterfront from the city round to the Mumbles is taken over by a smorgasbord of shows, fun fairs, carnivals, music, exhibitions, children's events and smaller festivals.
Swansea Bay Film Festival (www.swansea filmfestival.com) Held over a week in May, under the umbrella of the Summer Festival, it includes workshops and free screenings at the Dylan Thomas Centre.
Escape into the Park (www.escapefestival.com) Wales' biggest outdoor dance-music festival, a one-day event featuring lots of different tents with big-name DJs enthusing the crowd. It takes place in mid-June at Singleton Park (next to Swansea University campus).
Swansea Festival of Music & the Arts (www.swanseafestival.org) Concerts, drama, lectures and exhibitions, staged in five city venues during the first three weeks of October.
Dylan Thomas Festival (www.dylanthomas. com) Celebrates Swansea's most famous son with poetry readings, talks, films and performances, and is held from 27 October (his birthday) to 9 November (the date he died).

GASTRONOMIC HIGHLIGHTS

The main eat streets are Wind St and St Helen St in the centre and Newton and Mumbles Rds in Mumbles, with a range of pubs, cafes and restaurants to cater to all budgets and appetites.

❧ CHELSEA RESTAURANT // CITY CENTRE ££

☎ 464068; 17 St Mary's St; mains £12-19, 2-/3-course lunch £13/17; ☙ Mon-Sat
Perfect for a romantic liaison, this elegant little dining room is discreetly tucked away behind the frenzy of Wind St. Seafood's the focus and blackboard specials are chalked up daily. While the name sounds flash, the prices aren't too bad; a £20 three-course set dinner is offered from Monday to Thursday.

❧ DIDIER & STEPHANIE // UPLANDS £££

☎ 655603; 56 St Helen's Rd; mains £16-19; ☙ Tue-Sat
Swansea's top restaurant is an intimate and relaxed place, run by the Gallic duo with their names on the door. It's well regarded for its French cooking, refined setting and attentive service and it offers good-value set menus at lunch (two/three courses £14/17).

❤ JOE'S ICE CREAM PARLOUR //
UPLANDS £

☎ 653880; 85 St Helen's Rd; 🕙 11am-8pm Mon-Fri, noon-7.30pm Sat & Sun

For an ice-cream sundae or a cone, locals love Joe's – a Swansea institution founded in 1922 by Joe Cascarini, son of immigrants from Italy's Abruzzi mountains. There are also branches at **Parc Tawe Shopping Centre** (☎ 460370; Park Tawe Link; 🕙 10.30am-6pm) and **Mumbles** (☎ 368212; 524 Mumbles Rd; 🕙 11am-5.30pm Sun & Mon, 9.30am-5.30pm Tue-Sat).

❤ MERMAID BRASSERIE //
MUMBLES ££

☎ 367744; 686 Mumbles Rd; 2-course lunch £13, 3-course dinner £25; 🕙 Tue-Sun

Fresh-from-the-bay mains and local organic produce are the cornerstones of this sleek, sea-facing eatery, divided between a lounge area for tapas and the main restaurant. In a former incarnation it was a favourite haunt of Dylan Thomas and a quote from a poem referencing the Mermaid is painted on a wall.

NIGHTLIFE

BARS, CLUBS & LIVE MUSIC

In a city synonymous with Dylan Thomas you'd expect some hard drinking to take place…and you'd be right. Swansea's main boozing strip is Wind St (pronounced to rhyme with 'blind', as in drunk), and on weekends it can be a bit of a zoo, full of generally good-natured alcopop-fuelled teens teetering around on high heels.

The famous Mumbles Mile – a pub crawl along Mumbles Rd – is not what it once was; many of the old faithful inns have succumbed to the gastropub bug. Newton Rd does have some rather nice wine bars, though, which aren't too bad for a spot of celebrity spotting.

Buzz magazine (free from the tourist office and bars around town) has its finger on the pulse of the local scene.

❤ JONES

☎ 361764; www.jonesbar.co.uk; 61 Newton Rd, Mumbles

The best of the Newton Rd wine bars, Jones buzzes with 40-somethings giving the chandeliers a run for their money in the bling stakes. There's no chance Dylan Thomas ever did, or would, hang out here, but there's a good wine list and a friendly vibe.

❤ MONKEY

☎ 480822; www.monkeycafe.co.uk; 13 Castle St

An organic, vegie-friendly cafe-bar by day, with chunky tables, big sofas, modern art and cool tunes, this funky little venue transforms after dark into Swansea's best alternative club, hosting DJs, live musicians, burlesque and salsa upstairs.

❤ NO SIGN BAR

☎ 456110; 56 Wind St

Once frequented by Dylan Thomas (it appears as the Wine Vaults in his story *The Followers*), the No Sign stands out as the only vaguely traditional bar left on Wind St. It's a long, narrow haven of dark-wood panelling, friendly staff, good pub grub and decent beer and on weekends there's live music downstairs in the Vault. The window seats, looking out over the hectares of goose-bumped flesh on the street outside, offer a frisson of *schadenfreude*.

❤ QUEEN'S HOTEL

☎ 521531; Gloucester Pl

An old-fashioned corner pub with polished mahogany and brass bar, Victorian tiles and a range of cask-conditioned beers on tap, including Theakston's Old

Peculier. Thomas propped up the bar here when he was a cub reporter around the corner at the *South Wales Evening Post*.

☙ UPLANDS TAVERN
☎ 458242; www.myspace.com/uplandstavern; 42 Uplands Cres

Yet another Thomas hang-out, Uplands still serves a quiet daytime pint in the Dylan Thomas snug. Come nightfall, it turns into a different beast altogether as the hub of the city's live-music scene. It's big and brassy with reasonably priced beer (Greene King Abbott real ale), pool tables and bands playing most nights to a mixed crowd of students and locals.

PERFORMING ARTS

☙ DYLAN THOMAS THEATRE
☎ 473238; www.dylanthomastheatre.org.uk; Gloucester Pl

Home to Swansea Little Theatre, an amateur dramatic group of which DT was once a member. The company stages a wide repertoire of plays, including regular performances of your man's *Under Milk Wood*.

☙ SWANSEA GRAND THEATRE
☎ 475715; www.swanseagrand.co.uk; Singleton St

The city's largest theatre stages a mixed program of ballet, opera, musicals, theatre, pantomimes and a regular comedy club.

☙ TALIESIN ARTS CENTRE
☎ 602060; www.taliesinartscentre.co.uk; Singleton Park, Mumbles Rd

Part of the University of Wales, Swansea, this vibrant arts centre has a program of live music, theatre, dance and film.

TRANSPORT

BIKE // Part of the Celtic Trail (Sustrans National Route 4) hugs the bay from downtown Swansea to Mumbles; **Action Bikes** (☎ 464640; 5 St David's Sq) rents bicycles.

BOAT // **Fastnet Line** (☎ 0844 576 8831; www.fastnetline.com; King's Dock) sails to Cork (Ireland) three to four times per week; the 10-hour trip costs £85 to £149 for a standard car plus one passenger. The ferry terminal is 1 mile east of the centre, on the east side of the river mouth. At the time of writing **Severn Link** (www.severnlink.com), a new ferry service from Swansea to Ilfracombe in Devon, was awaiting official approval.

SWANSEA, THE GOWER & CARMARTHENSHIRE ACCOMMODATION

If you've got business to do in Swansea, or if you have ambitions to booze it up with the locals, you'll find some good hotels in the city centre and personable B&Bs a little further out, in suburbs like Uplands and Mumbles. For a more tranquil base, you can't beat the Carmarthenshire countryside. Avoid Carmarthen and head straight to the smaller towns such as Laugharne, Llandeilo and Llandovery. The Gower Peninsula is also supremely restful in the off season, but come summer it's the first choice of battalions of beach lovers. For accommodation reviews, see p329. All of our top-five picks have a modern, boutique sensibility:

* **Morgans** (p329) Classy conversion of historic ports building in Swansea.
* **Tides Reach Guest House** (p330) Smart waterfront B&B in Mumbles.
* **King's Head** (p331) Modern rooms behind pub in Llangennith.
* **Fronlas** (p332) Chic town-house B&B in Llandeilo.
* **New White Lion** (p332) Stylish boutique hotel in Llandovery.

SWANSEA, THE GOWER & CARMARTHENSHIRE

BUS – LOCAL // First Cymru (www.firstgroup.com) runs local services; buses 2, 3 and 37 head to Newton Rd in Mumbles (20 minutes), departing from Oxford St. A Swansea Bay Day Ticket offers all-day bus travel in the Swansea and Mumbles area for £4.25; buy tickets from the driver.

BUS – REGIONAL // Bus X63 links Swansea with Brecon (two hours); X40 with Carmarthen (45 minutes) and Aberystwyth (3¼ hours); and X13 with Llandeilo (1½ hours). See also the Cardiff–Swansea Shuttle 100 (p60) and Beacons Bus B15 (p89).

COACH // National Express (www.nationalexpress.com) destinations include London (£26, five hours), Chepstow (£12, two hours), Cardiff (£7.30, one hour), Carmarthen (£6, 45 minutes), Tenby (£8, 1½ hours) and Pembroke (£8, 1¾ hours).

PARKING // Outside of the main commercial strips you should be able to find free street parking; check signs carefully. In the centre, the car park near the intersection of Princess Way and Oystermouth Rd offers two hours free between 10am and 5pm, Monday to Saturday; unlimited at other times.

ROAD TRAIN // On weekends from May to August the **Swansea Bay Rider** (☎ 635142; adult/child £2.20/1.60), a toy-town road train, runs along the promenade between Swansea and the Mumbles.

TAXI // Yellow Cabs (☎ 644446)

TRAIN // Arriva Trains Wales (www.arrivatrainswales.co.uk) has direct services to Swansea from London Paddington (£28, three hours), Cardiff (£7.80, one hour), Carmarthen (£7, 45 minutes), Tenby (£12, 1½ hours), Llandeilo (£5.60, 57 minutes) and Llandrindod Wells (£9.70, 2¼ hours).

GOWER PENINSULA (Y GŴYR)

· · · · · ·

☎ 01792

With its broad butterscotch beaches, pounding surf, precipitous clifftop walks and rugged, untamed uplands, the Gower Peninsula feels a million miles away from Swansea's urban bustle – yet it's just on the doorstep. This 15-mile-long thumb of land stretching west from Mumbles was designated the UK's first official Area of Outstanding Natural Beauty (AONB) in 1956. The National Trust (NT) owns about three-quarters of the coast and though there is no continuously waymarked path, you can hike almost the entire length of the coastline. The peninsula also has the best surfing in Wales outside Pembrokeshire.

The main family beaches, patrolled by lifeguards during the summer, are

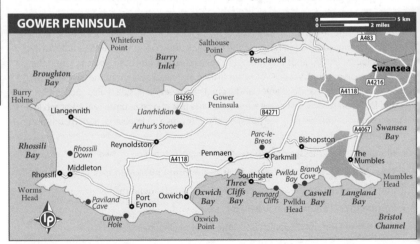

GOWER PENINSULA

Langland Bay, Caswell Bay and Port Eynon. The most impressive, and most popular with surfers, is the magnificent 3-mile sweep of Rhossili Bay at the far end of the peninsula. Much of Gower's northern coast is salt marsh that faces the Burry Inlet, an important area for wading birds and wildfowl.

ESSENTIAL INFORMATION

TOURIST OFFICES // Rhossili Visitor Centre (☎ 390707; www.nationaltrust.org.uk; Coastguard Cottages, Rhossili; ☺ 10.30am-5pm Apr-Oct, 11am-4pm Fri-Sun Nov-Mar) The National Trust's centre has information on local walks and wildlife, and an audiovisual display upstairs.

DRIVING TOUR

Distance: 40 miles
Duration: half-day
Take the A4118 west from **Swansea** (**1**, p111) and turn right onto the B4271, the secondary road running through the centre of the Gower Peninsula. Turn left on the back road signposted to Reynoldston, stopping to walk to **Arthur's Stone** (**2**, p126). Continue down to the beach

at **Rhossili** (**3**, p125). Backtrack to **Oxwich** (**4**, p124) and visit the castle. Turn off at Parkmill to visit the Long Cairn at **Parc-le-Breos** (**5**, p124) and then walk down to **Three Cliffs Bay** (**6**, p124). Stop at the **Joiners Arms** (**7**, p127) for a pint and then meander along the **Mumbles** (**8**, p118).

EXPLORING GOWER PENINSULA

🦢 **MUMBLES HEAD TO THREE CLIFFS BAY //** SOME OF BRITAIN'S BEST BEACHES
Going west from Mumbles Head there are two small bays, **Langland Bay** and **Caswell Bay**, shingly at high tide but exposing hectares of golden sand at low water. Both are easily reached from Swansea and are popular with families and surfers. About 500m west of Caswell, along the coast path, is beautiful **Brandy Cove**, a tiny secluded beach away from the crowds. West again is **Pwlldu Bay**, a shingle beach backed by a wooded ravine known as Bishopston Valley; you can walk there from Bishopston village (1.5 miles).

SWANSEA, THE GOWER & CARMARTHENSHIRE

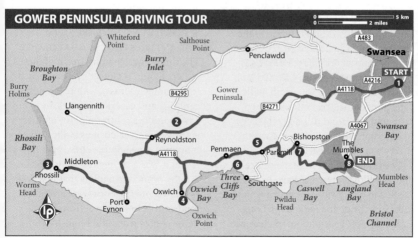

GOWER PENINSULA DRIVING TOUR

From Pwlldu Head the limestone **Pennard Cliffs**, honeycombed with caves, stretch westwards for 2 miles to Three Cliffs Bay. Halfway along is the National Trust's Pennard Cliffs car park (a little confusingly, it's in the village of **Southgate**, not Pennard; the Pennard Cliffs bus stop is also here). The car park is the starting point for scenic coastal walks east to Pwlldu (1.5 miles) and west to Three Cliffs Bay (1 mile).

Three Cliffs Bay is named for the triple-pointed crag, pierced by a natural arch, that guards its eastern point. It is regularly voted one of the most beautiful beaches in Britain, even though the sand disappears completely at high tide.

The only way to get there is on foot. The most scenic approach is along the Pennard Cliffs, but you can also walk in from Parkmill village (1 mile), either along the valley of Pennard Pill, or along the edge of the golf course to the east via the ruins of Pennard Castle.

It is dangerous to swim here at high tide, because of river currents, but safe at low water. The triple-pointed crag is a popular rock-climbing site.

☙ PARKMILL // THE TRULY ANCIENT AND THE SIMPLY OLD

The village of Parkmill is home to the **Gower Heritage Centre** (☎ 371206; www.gowerheritagecentre.co.uk; adult/child £5.50/4.50; ☙ 10am-5.30pm Apr-Sep, 10am-4.30pm Oct-Mar), housed in a restored watermill, with a cafe, puppet theatre, craft workshop, farm and fish pond. It's a good place to entertain the kids when the weather drives you off the beaches.

Continue past the heritage centre and you'll reach bucolic **Parc-le-Breos**, nestled in a tiny valley between wooded hills. Just inside the park is the **Long Cairn**, a 5500-year-old burial chamber

consisting of a stone entryway, a passageway and two chambers. It once contained numerous bones but these were removed, along with its protective earth mound, after it was dug out in 1869. Further into the park you'll find a limekiln, used until a century ago for the production of quicklime fertiliser.

☙ OXWICH BAY // MAKE SAND CASTLES THEN VISIT THE REAL THING

Oxwich Bay is a windy, 2.5-mile-long curve of sand backed by dunes. Road access and a large car park (£2) make it popular with families and water-sports enthusiasts (no lifeguard, though). Behind the beach lies **Oxwich Nature Reserve**, an area of salt and freshwater marshes, oak and ash woodlands and dunes; it is home to a variety of bird life and dune plants.

Set on a hillside above the beach, the stately grey ruin of **Oxwich Castle** (☎ 390359; www.cadw.wales.gov.uk; Oxwich Castle Farm; adult/child £2.60/2.25; ☙ 10am-5pm Apr-Sep), run by Cadw (the Welsh historic monuments agency), is less a castle and more a sumptuous 16th-century, mock-military Tudor mansion.

☙ PORT EYNON // SAFE SWIMMING AND INTERESTING ARCHAEOLOGY

The three-quarter-mile stretch of dunes at Port Eynon is Gower's busiest beach (in summer, at least), with half a dozen camping and caravan sites nearby.

Around the southern point of the bay is **Culver Hole**, a curious stone structure built into a gash in the cliff. Legend has it that it was a smugglers' hiding place, but the mundane truth is that it served as a dovecote (pigeons were a valuable food source in medieval times; the name comes from Old English *culufre*, meaning 'dove'). It's quite tricky to find – the easiest route is signposted from the youth hostel – and is only accessible for three hours either side of low tide; make sure you don't get caught out by the rising waters.

The coastal walk west from Port Eynon to Rhossili (7 miles) is along the wildest and most dramatic part of the Gower coast, and is fairly rough going. Halfway along is **Paviland Cave** (see below).

🌑 **RHOSSILI // GOLDEN SANDS GUARDED BY A DRAGON**
Saving the best to last, the Gower Peninsula ends spectacularly with the 3 miles of golden sand that edges **Rhossili Bay**. Facing nearly due west towards the very bottom of Ireland, this is one of Wales' best and most popular surfing beaches. Access to the beach is via a path next to the Worms Head Hotel, across from the NT car park in Rhossili village. When the surf's up, swimming can be dangerous.

The beach is backed by the steep slopes of **Rhossili Down** (193m), a humpbacked, heather-covered ridge whose updraughts create perfect soaring conditions for hang-gliders and paraglid-ers. On the summit are numerous Iron Age earthworks, a burial chamber called Sweyne's Howe and the remains of a WWII radar station. At its foot, behind the beach, is the Warren, the sand-buried remains of an old village. At low tide the stark, ghostly ribs of the *Helvetica*, a Norwegian barque wrecked in a storm in 1887, protrude from the sand in the middle of the beach.

The southern extremity of the bay is guarded by **Worms Head** (from the Old English *wurm*, meaning 'dragon' – the rocks present a snaking, Loch Ness–monster profile). There is a four-hour window of opportunity (two hours either side of low tide) when you can walk out across a causeway and along the narrow crest of the Outer Head to the furthest point of land. There are seals around the rocks, and the cliffs are thick with razorbills, guillemots, kittiwakes, fulmars and puffins during nesting season (April to July).

Pay close attention to the tides – tide tables are posted at the Rhossili Visitor Centre – as people are regularly rescued after being cut off by the rising waters. Among those who have spent a cold, nervous half-night trapped there was

THE RED LADY OF PAVILAND

Halfway along the Gower coast between Port Eynon and Rhossili is Paviland Cave, where in 1823 the Reverend William Buckland discovered a Stone Age human skeleton dyed with red ochre. As he also found jewellery buried along with the bones, the good Reverend assumed the deceased must be a woman. Being a devout Christian, he believed she must date from the Roman era, as she could not be older than the biblical flood. The 'Red Lady', as the skeleton became known, was therefore a Roman prostitute or witch, according to Buckland.

Modern analysis shows that the Red Lady was actually a man – possibly a tribal chief – who died, aged around 21, some 29,000 years ago. Dating before Britain was abandoned in the last Ice Age, his are the oldest human remains found in the UK, accorded the oldest known ritual burial in Western Europe. The Red Lady's peaceful seaside slumber is no more – he's now on display in the National Museum Cardiff (p45).

TOP FIVE

SURFING BEACHES

★ Rhossili (p125)

★ Porth Neigwl (p241)

★ Freshwater West (p150)

★ Newgale Sands (p156)

★ Whitesands Bay (p162)

the young Dylan Thomas, as he relates in the story 'Who Do You Wish Was With Us?', from *Portrait of the Artist as a Young Dog*. If you do get stuck, do not try to wade or swim back. The currents are fierce and the rocks treacherous.

South of the village is the Viel (pronounced 'vile'), a rare surviving example of a patchwork of strip-fields first laid out in medieval times.

♣ LLANGENNITH // THE HUB OF THE SURFIE SOCIAL SCENE

Surfers head to this pretty village at the northern end of Rhossili Bay where there's a good local pub and a large camping ground right by the beach. **PJ's Surf Shop** (☎ 386669; www.pjsurfshop. co.uk), owned by Pete Jones, the former European surf champion, stocks all the gear you'll need (wetsuits/surfboards/bodyboards per day £10/10/5). It also operates a 24-hour **surfline** (☎ 0901 603 1603; calls per min 60p). There's a similar (but free) service online at www.gowerlive. co.uk.

♣ ARTHUR'S STONE // AN ANCIENT BURIAL CHAMBER WEIGHED DOWN WITH LEGENDS

At the heart of peninsula is Cefn Bryn, a ruggedly beautiful expanse of moorland that rises to a height of 186m. On a fittingly desolate ridge stands a mysterious Neolithic burial chamber capped by the 25-tonne quartz boulder known as Arthur's Stone (Coeten Arthur). In legend it's a pebble that Arthur removed from his boot; the deep cut in the rock was either made by Arthur's Excalibur or by St David; and the muddy spring beneath the stone grants wishes. Local lore also says that a woman who crawls around the stone at midnight during the full moon will be joined by her lover – if he is faithful.

The view from here is fantastic – you can see out to the edges of the Gower in every direction, and on a clear day you can see south to Lundy Island and the Devon and Somerset coast. It's a great spot to watch the sunset.

To find it, turn right on the road leaving the King Arthur Hotel in Reynoldston and look out for a rough parking area on your left. Looking north, you can see the stone on the horizon.

GASTRONOMIC HIGHLIGHTS

The peninsula's north coast produces two of the region's most famous foodstuffs: Gower lamb, with its diet of salt-marsh vegetation imparting a distinct and delicious flavour; and Penclawdd cockles, harvested from the mudflats at the eastern end of the inlet.

♣ BAY BISTRO & COFFEE HOUSE // RHOSSILI £

☎ 390519; mains £5-8; Ⓨ 10am-5.30pm daily summer, weekends & sunny days only in winter; Ⓥ A buzzy beach cafe with a sunny terrace, good surfy vibrations and the kind of drop-your-panini views that would make anything taste good – although the roster of burgers, sandwiches, cakes and coffee stands up well regardless. Summer night are given over to alfresco meals (mains £10 to £14).

❦ FAIRYHILL // REYNOLDSTON £££

☎ 390139; www.fairyhill.net; 2-/3-course lunch £16/20, 2-/3-course dinner £35/45; Ⓟ

Hidden (as any proper fairy place should be) down a narrow lane north of Reynoldston, Fairyhill draws on local produce, including organic home-grown goodies from its kitchen garden. The Georgian country house setting is suitably magical, and the menu is pleasantly Welsh – laver-bread tart, and sea bass with a laver-bread sauce both featured when we visited.

❦ MAES-YR-HAF // PARKMILL ££

☎ 371000; www.maes-yr-haf.com; mains £12-18; ☽ lunch Tue-Sun, dinner Tue-Sat; Ⓟ

The refined, dark-wood part of this restaurant with rooms (see p330) has a focus on locally farmed meat, game and seafood, with just a hint of a Greek influence courtesy of head chef Christos Georgakis.

NIGHTLIFE

❦ JOINERS ARMS

☎ 232658; 50 Bishopston Rd, Bishopston

No visit to the Gower is complete without popping into the Joiners for a pint from the pub's own on-site microbrewery. A drop of the Three Cliffs Gold Ale is *the* one to try.

❦ KING ARTHUR HOTEL

☎ 390775; www.kingarthurhotel.co.uk; Higher Green, Reynoldston; Ⓟ

As traditional as swords in stone and ladies of the lake, this King Arthur serves real ales in a cosy wood-panelled bar and a lengthy menu in the neighbouring dining room (mains £6 to £17).

❦ KING'S HEAD

☎ 386212; www.kingsheadgower.co.uk; Llangennith

The centre of Llangennith's social life is the King's Head, which serves real ales and home-cooked bar meals (mains £6 to £12), including a good range of vegetarian dishes.

TRANSPORT

BUS // Swansea's First Cymru buses head as far as Limeslade, Langland, Bishopston and Pennard Cliffs, and in summer to Caswell Bay, Parkmill, Oxwich Bay, Port Eynon and Rhossili. The Gower Explorer (day ticket adult/child £4/2.20) has year-round services looping the peninsula: 115 Llangennith–Reynoldston–Port Eynon; 117 Port Eynon–Oxwich–Parkmill; 118 Rhossili–Port Eynon–Reynoldston–Swansea.

PARKING // Carry coins if you're hoping to park anywhere near a beach. For Three Cliffs Bay, the Gower Heritage Centre charges £3, whereas the NT car park at Southgate only charges at weekends and in summer. At Port Eynon they charge between April and September (per hour/day £1.10/4). The NT car park at Rhossili is £2.50 all year, or you can park a five-minute walk up the road at the church (donation requested). Hillend Campsite at Llangennith charges a hefty £3 year-round to park near this part of Rhossili Bay.

CARMARTHEN-SHIRE (SIR GAERFYRDDIN)

· · · · · ·

Castle-dotted Carmarthenshire has gentle valleys, deep-green woods and a small, partly sandy coast. Caught between dramatic neighbours – Pembrokeshire to the west and the Brecon Beacons to the east – it remains much quieter and less explored. Yet the appeal of its tranquil countryside hasn't gone entirely unnoticed and charming places like Llandeilo are starting to sprout upmarket eateries, galleries and shops. If your interests stretch to gardens, stately homes and all things green, add this quiet county to your itinerary.

SWANSEA, THE GOWER & CARMARTHENSHIRE

CARMARTHENSHIRE COAST

❦ NATIONAL WETLAND CENTRE // BIRDS OF MANY FEATHERS, FLOCKING TOGETHER

Covering 97 hectares on the northern shore of the Burry Inlet, across from the Gower Peninsula, the **National Wetland Centre** (☎ 01554-741087; www.wwt.org.uk/llanelli; Llanelli; adult/child £7.05/3.86; ☺ 9.30am-5pm Apr-Sep, 9.30am-4.30pm Oct-Mar; ℗) is one of Wales' most important habitats for waders and waterfowl. The big attraction for birdwatchers is the resident population of little egret, whose numbers have increased from a solitary pair in 1995 to around 400. Winter is the most spectacular season, when up to 60,000 birds converge on the salt marsh and mudflats; species include oystercatchers, greylag geese, gadwalls, widgeons, teals and black-tailed godwits. Flashiest of all are the resident flock of nearly fluorescent pink Caribbean flamingos.

There's always plenty on for the littl'uns during the school holidays. Late spring's Duckling Days are filled with downy cuteness, while in the summer months there are canoes and bikes to borrow. There are plenty of hides and observation points, and you can hire binoculars (£5) if you don't have your own.

Approaching from the southeast, take the A484 and turn left onto the B4304. Trains head to Llanelli from Carmarthen (£6.40, 25 minutes) and Swansea (£4.20, 15 minutes); the centre's a 2.5-mile walk from the station.

❦ KIDWELLY CASTLE // AN ARCHETYPAL, WELL-PRESERVED, MEDIEVAL CASTLE

The small town of Kidwelly, at the mouth of the River Gwendraeth Fach, is dominated by the impressive pigeon-inhabited remains of **Kidwelly Castle** (Cadw; ☎ 01554-890104; www.cadw.wales.gov.uk; Castle St; adult/child £3/2.60; ☺ 9am-5pm Apr-Oct, 9.30am-4pm Mon-Sat & 11am-4pm Sun Nov-Mar), a forbidding grey eminence that rises above a narrow waterway dotted with gliding swans. It was founded by the Normans in 1106, but most of the system of towers and curtain walls was built in the 13th century in reaction to Welsh uprisings. If it looks at all familiar, that may be because it featured in the opening scene of *Monty Python and the Holy Grail*.

Trains head to Kidwelly from Carmarthen (£3.60, 16 minutes) and Swansea (£6.60, 34 minutes).

LAUGHARNE (TALACHARN)

☎ 01994 / pop 2940

Sleepy little Laugharne (pronounced 'larn') sits above the tide-washed shores of the Taf Estuary, overlooked by a Norman castle. Dylan Thomas, one of Wales' greatest writers, spent the last four years of his life here, during which he produced some of his most inspired work, including *Under Milk Wood*; the town is one of the inspirations for the play's fictional village of Llareggub (spell it backwards and you will get the gist).

On Thomas' first visit to Laugharne he described it as the 'strangest town in Wales', but returned repeatedly throughout his restless life. Many Thomas fans make a pilgrimage here to see the Boathouse where he lived, the shed where he wrote, Brown's Hotel where he drank (he used to give the pub telephone number as his contact number; sadly it's now closed) and the churchyard where he's buried.

DYLAN THOMAS

Dylan Thomas is a towering figure in Welsh literature, one of those poets who seemed to embody what a poet should be – chaotic, dramatic, drunk, tragic and comic. His work, although written in English, is of the bardic tradition – written to be read aloud, thunderous, often humorous, with a lyrical sense that echoes the sound of the Welsh voice.

Born in Swansea in 1914 (see p118), he lived an itinerant life, shifting from town to town in search of cheap accommodation and to escape debt. He married Caitlin Macnamara (a former dancer, and lover of Augustus John) in 1936 but had numerous, infamous affairs. Margaret Thomas, who was married to the historian AJP Taylor, was one of his admirers and paid his Boathouse rent (mysteriously enough, AJP detested him). His dramatic inclinations sometimes spilt over into real life: during a stay in New Quay he was shot at by a jealous local captain.

Thomas was also a promiscuous pub-goer, honing the habit that eventually killed him in an astonishing number of taverns. By 1946 he had become an immense commercial success, making regular book tours to America, but his marriage was suffering. In December 1952 his father died – his failing health had inspired one of Thomas' most resonant poems *Do Not Go Gentle into That Good Night*. Less than a year later, a period of depression while in New York ended in a heavy drinking spell, and he died shortly after his 39th birthday.

EXPLORING LAUGHARNE

❦ DYLAN THOMAS BOATHOUSE //
THE ULTIMATE PILGRIMAGE FOR
DYLAN DEVOTEES

Except at high tide, you can follow a path along the shoreline below the castle, then up some stairs to a lane that leads to the **boathouse** (☎ 427420; www.dylanthomasboat house.com; Dylan's Walk; adult/child £3.50/1.75; ☙ 10am-5.30pm May-Oct, 10.30am-3.30pm Nov-Apr) where the poet lived from 1949 to 1953 with his wife Caitlin and their three children. It's a beautiful setting, looking out over the estuary with its 'heron-priested shore', silent except for the long, liquid call of the curlew and the urgent 'pleep pleep pleep' of the oystercatcher, birds that appear in Thomas' poetry of that time.

The parlour of the Boathouse has been restored to its 1950s appearance, with the desk that once belonged to Thomas' schoolmaster father and recordings of the poet reading his own works. Upstairs are photographs, manuscripts, a short video about his life, and his death mask, which once belonged to Richard Burton, while downstairs is a coffee shop.

Along the lane from the Boathouse is the old shed where Thomas did most of his writing. It looks as if he has just popped out, with screwed-up pieces of paper littered around, a curiously prominent copy of *Lives of the Great Poisoners* and, facing out to sea, the table where he wrote *Under Milk Wood* and poems such as *Over Sir John's Hill* (which describes the view).

Dylan and Caitlin Thomas are buried in a grave marked by a simple white, wooden cross in the churchyard of **St Martin's Church**, on the northern edge of the town. **Dylan's Walk** is a scenic 2-mile loop that continues north along the shore beyond the Boathouse, then turns inland past a 17th-century farm and back via St Martin's Church. It's clearly signposted.

SWANSEA, THE GOWER &
CARMARTHENSHIRE

❧ LAUGHARNE CASTLE // IT'S NOT ALL ABOUT DYLAN THOMAS, AFTER ALL

Built in the 13th century, **Laugharne Castle** (Cadw; ☎ 427906; www.cadw.wales.gov.uk; adult/child £3/2.60; ☼ 10am-5pm Apr-Oct) was converted into a mansion in the 16th century for John Perrot, thought to be the illegitimate son of Henry VIII. It was landscaped with lawns and gardens in Victorian times, and the adjoining Castle House was leased by Richard Hughes, author of *High Wind in Jamaica*. Hughes was a friend of Dylan Thomas, who sometimes wrote in the little gazebo looking out over the estuary.

❧ GREEN ROOM // MAN CANNOT LIVE ON POETRY ALONE

Laugharne doesn't exactly abound with gastronomic options, making the **Green Room** (☎ 427870; www.thegreenroomcafe.co.uk; 6 The Grist; lunch £7-10, dinner £13-17; ☼ Thu-Mon) a welcome find. It serves lighter dishes (salads, quiches, pasta) by day and hearty home-cooked bistro meals after dark. Comfy sofas for coffee, delicious desserts and views of the castle add a cosy, welcoming ambience.

TRANSPORT

BUS // Bus 222 runs from Carmarthen to Laugharne (30 minutes).

CARMARTHEN (CAERFYRDDIN)

☎ 01267 / pop 14,600

Carmarthenshire's county town is a place of legend and ancient provenance, but it's not the kind of place you'll feel inclined to linger in. It's a handy transport and shopping hub, but there's not a lot to see. The Romans built a town here, complete with a fort and amphi-theatre. A couple of solid walls and a few crumbling towers are all that remains of Carmarthen's Norman castle, which was largely destroyed in the Civil War.

Most intriguingly, Carmarthen is reputed to be the birthplace of the most famous wizard of them all (no, not Harry Potter) – Myrddin of the Arthurian legends, better known in English as Merlin. An oak tree planted in 1660 for Charles II's coronation came to be called 'Merlin's Tree' and was linked to a prophecy that its death would mean curtains for the town. The tree died in the 1970s and the town, while a little down at heel, is still standing. Pieces of the tree are kept under glass at the Carmarthenshire County Museum.

ESSENTIAL INFORMATION

TOURIST OFFICES // Tourist office (☎ 231557; www.discovercarmarthenshire.com; 113 Lammas St; ☼ 10am-5pm Apr-Sep, 10am-4pm Mon-Sat Oct-Mar)

EXPLORING CARMARTHEN

❧ CARMARTHEN MARKET // SHOP IN A TIME-HONOURED MANNER

There's been a market here since Roman times and in 1180 it was given a royal charter. The main indoor **market** (www.carmarthenmarket.co.uk; Market Way; ☼ 9am-5pm Mon-Sat) has an edgy modern home and sells a bit of everything, from produce to antiques. On Wednesday and Saturday the general market spills out onto Red St, while on Friday there's a farmers market.

❧ GALLERIES // ART TO ADMIRE AND TO ACQUIRE

Housed in a former art college, **Oriel Myrddin** (Merlin Gallery; ☎ 222775; www.orielmyrddingallery.co.uk; Church Lane; admission free;

10am-5pm Mon-Sat) stages changing exhibitions of contemporary art. Opposite is the **King Street Gallery** (☎ 220121; www.kingstreetgallery.co.uk; King St; 10am-4pm Mon-Sat), selling interesting works by a cooperative of 29 local painters, sculptors, ceramicists and printmakers.

GASTRONOMIC HIGHLIGHTS

Carmarthen's contribution to Welsh gastronomy is a salt-cured, air-dried ham. Local legend has it that the Romans liked the recipe so much that they took it back to Italy with them. Look for it at the market.

☙ ANGEL VAULTS £££

☎ 238305; 3 Nott Sq; mains £14-22; lunch Mon-Sat, dinner Tue-Sat

For a swanky night out, locals head to Angel Vaults for heavenly food and then finish off across the square at Diablo's for devilish cocktails. The decor marries the modern and ancient, with a beautiful 15th-century limestone window linking the two halves of the upstairs dining room. A locally focussed menu features Pembrokeshire salmon and scallops, Gower salt marsh lamb, and Welsh beef and cheeses.

☙ CAFE AT NO 4 QUEEN ST £

☎ 220461; 4 Queen St; mains £4-8; 9am-5pm Mon-Sat

This chic little corner cafe right in the middle of Carmarthen brews the best coffee in town and serves fantastic homemade cakes and scones as well as soups, salads, sandwiches and daily specials.

TRANSPORT

BUS // The main bus stop is on Blue St. Bus X40 links Carmarthen with Cardiff (two hours), Swansea (45 minutes) and Aberystwyth (2¼ hours); 280 and 281 head to Llandeilo (40 minutes) and Llandovery (1½ hours); 322

to Haverfordwest (one hour); and 460 to Cardigan (1½ hours). See also Beacons Bus B10 (p89).

COACH // National Express (www.nationalexpress.com) destinations include London (£26, 5¾ hours), Chepstow (£19, 2¼ hours), Swansea (£6, 45 minutes), Tenby (£5.10, 40 minutes), Pembroke (£5.10, one hour) and Haverfordwest (£6.70, 1½ hours).

TRAIN // The station is 300m south of town across the river. There are direct trains to Cardiff (£15, 1¾ hours), Swansea (£7, 45 minutes), Fishguard Harbour (£7.10, 49 minutes), Tenby (£7.20, 41 minutes) and Pembroke (£7.20, 1¼ hours).

CARMARTHEN TO LLANDEILO

☙ GWILI STEAM RAILWAY // CHUG BACK IN TIME

The standard-gauge **Gwili Steam Railway** (☎ 01267-238213; www.gwili-railway.co.uk; adult/child £5.50/3) runs along the lovely Gwili valley, departing from Bronwydd Arms, 3.5 miles north of Carmarthen on the A484. It runs nearly daily in August; check the website or Carmarthen tourist office for a full timetable.

Bus 460 between Carmarthen (16 minutes) and Cardigan (one hour and 10 minutes) stops at Bronwydd Arms.

☙ CARMARTHENSHIRE COUNTY MUSEUM // FREE ACCESS TO 700-YEAR-OLD PALACE

Located in the country-house setting of a 13th-century bishop's palace, this **museum** (☎ 01267-228696; www.carmarthenmuseum.org.uk; Abergwili; admission free; 10am-4.30pm Mon-Sat) is a musty emporium of archaeology, Egyptology, pottery and paintings, with re-creations of a Victorian schoolroom and a collection of prehistoric standing stones.

The museum is 2 miles east of Carmarthen on the A40; take the 280 or 281 bus (11 minutes).

🌱 NATIONAL BOTANIC GARDEN OF WALES // A BOTANICAL MONUMENT IN THE MAKING

Concealed in the rolling Tywi valley countryside, the lavish **National Botanic Garden of Wales** (☎ 01558-667148; www.gardenofwales.org.uk; Llanarthne; adult/child £8.50/4; ⏲ 10am-6pm Apr-Oct, 10am-4.30pm Nov-Mar) is twice the size of London's Kew Gardens, though it isn't as mature. Opened in 2000, the garden is still a work in progress, with new features being added every year.

Formerly an aristocratic estate, the garden has a broad range of plant habitats, from lakes and bogs to woodland and heath, and has lots of decorative areas too – for instance, a walled garden, a Japanese garden and an apothecaries' garden – and educational exhibits on plant medicine and organic farming. The centrepiece is the Norman Foster–designed **Great Glasshouse**, an arresting glass dome that's sunk into the earth, which houses endangered plants from Mediterranean climes all over the world.

The garden is east of Carmarthen; take the A48 out of town (signposted Swansea and the M4) and after 8 miles take the B4310 on the left (signposted Nantgaredig), then follow the signs to the garden.

🌱 ABERGLASNEY GARDENS // ANOTHER ESSENTIAL STOP FOR GARDEN ENTHUSIASTS

Wandering through the formal walled gardens of **Aberglasney House** (☎ 01558-668998; www.aberglasney.org; Llangathen; adult/child £6.36/3.63; ⏲ 10am-6pm Apr-Sep, 10.30am-4pm Oct-Mar) feels a bit like walking into a Jane Austen novel. They date back to the 17th century and contain a unique cloister built solely as a garden decoration. You'll also find a pool garden, a 250-year-old

yew tunnel and a 'wild' garden in the bluebell woods to the west. Several derelict rooms in the central courtyard of the house have been converted into a glass-roofed atrium garden full of subtropical plants such as orchids, palms and cycads.

Aberglasney is in the village of Llangathen, just off the A40, 4 miles west of Llandeilo. Bus 280 between Carmarthen and Llandeilo stops on the A40, 500m north of the gardens.

🌱 DINEFWR PARK & CASTLE // A HISTORIC TREBLE: PARK, CASTLE AND MANOR

National Trust–run **Dinefwr** (☎ 01558-824512; www.nationaltrust.org.uk; adult/child £6.09/3.04; ⏲ 11am-5pm mid-Feb–Oct, 11am-4pm Fri-Sun Nov–mid-Dec) is a large, landscaped estate to the west of Llandeilo, home to fallow deer and a herd of rare White Park cattle. Recent archaeological digs uncovered remains of a roman fort here. At the estate's heart is a wonderful 17th-century manor, **Newton House**, made over with a Victorian facade in the 19th century. It's presented as it was in Edwardian times, focussing particularly on the experience of servants in their downstairs domain; recordings start as you enter each room. Other rooms recall Newton's WWII incarnation as a hospital.

Striking 13th-century **Dinefwr Castle** is set on a hilltop in the southern corner of the estate and has fantastic views across the Tywi to the foothills of the Black Mountain. In the 17th century it suffered the indignity of being converted into a picturesque garden feature. There are several marked walking routes around the grounds, some of which are accessible to disabled visitors.

Bus 280 between Carmarthen and Llandeilo stops here.

LLANDEILO

☎ 01558 / pop 3000

Set on a hill encircled by the greenest of fields, Llandeilo is little more than a handful of narrow streets lined with grand Georgian and Victorian buildings and centred on a picturesque church and graveyard. The surrounding region was once dominated by large country estates, and though they have long gone, the deer, parkland trees and agricultural character of the landscape are their legacy. The genteel appeal of such a place can't be denied, so it's small wonder that Llandeilo's little high street is studded with fashionable shops and eateries.

GASTRONOMIC HIGHLIGHTS

❦ HEAVENLY £

☎ 822800; 60 Rhosmaen St; ⏰ 9.30am-5pm Mon-Sat

Believe the name and enter an Aladdin's cave stacked with handcrafted chocolates, artisanal ice cream and enticing pastries and cakes. Grab something yummy and head to the benches by the churchyard for a taste of sweet paradise.

❦ Y CAPEL BACH BISTRO AT THE ANGEL ££

☎ 822765; 62 Rhosmaen St; lunch £5-10; ⏰ closed Sun

A lively blackboard menu, hung between an unusual display of historical wedding photos, announces fresh daily specials at this popular gastropub. Thursday nights are devoted to ethnically themed buffets (£10), while a set-price menu is offered otherwise (two/three courses £10/12, add £2 on Saturdays).

RECOMMENDED SHOPS

❦ FOUNTAIN FINE ART

☎ 824244; www.fountainfineart.com; 115 Rhosmaen St; ⏰ 10am-5pm Mon-Sat

This fountain overflows with excellent local art, including many recognisable landmarks and landscapes – making for excellent, if rather pricey, holiday mementoes.

TRANSPORT

BUS // Buses 280 and 281 between Carmarthen (40 minutes) and Llandovery (37 minutes) stop here, along with X13 from Swansea (1½ hours). See also Beacons Bus B10 (p89).

TRAIN // Llandeilo is on the Heart of Wales Line, with direct services to Swansea (£5.60, 57 minutes), Llandovery (£2.50, 19 minutes), Llanwrtyd Wells (£3.90, 45 minutes), Llandrindod Wells (£6.10, 1¼ hours), Knighton (£8.60, two hours) and Shrewsbury (£11, three hours).

LLANDOVERY (LLANYMDDYFRI)

☎ 01550 / pop 2870

Sleepy Llandovery is an attractive market town that makes a good base for exploring the western fringes of the Brecon Beacons National Park (p88). The name means 'the church among the waters', and the town is indeed surrounded by rivers, sitting at the meeting place of three valleys: the Tywi, the Bran and the Gwydderig.

It was once an important assembly point for drovers taking their cattle towards the English markets. The Bank of the Black Ox – one of the first independent Welsh banks – was established here by a wealthy cattle merchant.

EXPLORING LLANDOVERY

❦ HERITAGE CENTRE // ENLIVENING HISTORY WITH SOME NIFTY TRICKS

Doubling as the tourist office, this **centre** (☎ 720693; www.llandovery.org.uk; Kings Rd; admission free; ⏰ 10am-5pm Easter-Oct, 10am-4pm Mon-Sat, 11am-1pm Sun Nov-Easter) has displays about the drovers, the Black Ox bank,

∾ WORTH A TRIP ∾

Perched atop a steep limestone crag high above the River Cennen, **Carreg Cennen Castle** (☎ 01558-822291; www.carregcennencastle.com; adult/child £3.60/3.25; ☺ 9.30am-6.30pm Apr-Oct, 9.30am-4pm Nov-Mar) is Wales' ultimate romantic ruined castle, visible for miles in every direction.

There was a stronghold here in the time of Rhys ap Gruffydd, ruler of Deheubarth, who in the 12th century reversed many of the territorial gains of the Normans. This castle, and others at Lord Rhys' royal seat of Dinefwr and at Dryslwyn, faced down the Tywi valley towards the Norman castle at Carmarthen. What you see today, however, was built at the end of the 13th century in the course of Edward I's conquest of Wales. It was dismantled in 1462 during the Wars of the Roses to prevent it being used by Lancastrians.

The steep uphill walk from the car park to the castle is rewarded with inspirational views over waves of rippling green hills. The inner ward, defended by two drawbridges and three gate towers, is lined with the remains of water cisterns, kitchens and a great hall. The most unusual feature is a stone-vaulted passage running along the top of the sheer southern cliff, which leads down to a long, narrow, natural cave; bring a torch, or hire one from the ticket office (£1.50).

Take the A483 south from Llandeilo and turn left in the village of Ffairrach, then fork right after you pass under the railway; 3 miles further on, turn left just before the bridge over the Cennen.

---

local legends and the Heart of Wales railway. Cleverly, faces are projected onto life-sized statues of important identities to bring to life the history of the town. The helpful staff can sort you out with information on walks in Brecon Beacons National Park, to the south, and the moorlands and valleys of Mynydd Epynt, to the east.

❦ LLANDOVERY CASTLE // ONE TO GAZE UPON, NOT VISIT

Across the car park from the heritage centre rises the shattered stump of the motte-and-bailey Llandovery Castle, which was built in 1116. The castle changed hands many times between the Normans and the Welsh, and between one Welsh prince and another, taking a severe beating in the process; it was finally left to decay after Owain Glyndŵr

had a go at it in 1403. It's fronted by an eerie disembodied stainless-steel statue commemorating Llewellyn ap Gruffydd Fychan, who was gruesomely hung, drawn and quartered by Henry IV for refusing to lead him to Owain Glyndŵr's base.

❦ DINEFWR CRAFT CENTRE // WHEN A FORK JUST WON'T DO THE TRICK

The town's Victorian market hall now has a cafe and a couple of shops selling local handicrafts of varying descriptions, including lovespoons (p135).

GASTRONOMIC HIGHLIGHTS

❦ KINGS HEAD // FAMILY-FRIENDLY PUB WITH GREAT GRUB

The best place to eat in Llandovery, this ancient coaching **inn** (☎ 720393; 1 Market

LOVESPOONS

All over Wales, craft shops turn out wooden spoons with contorted handles in a variety of different designs, at a speed that would have left their original makers – village lads with their eyes on a lady – gawking in astonishment. The carving of these spoons seems to date back to the 17th century, when they were made by men to give to women to mark the start of a courtship. If you want to see carving in progress, the St Fagans National History Museum (see p62) can usually oblige. Any number of shops will be happy to sell you the finished product.

Various symbols were carved; the meanings of a few of them are as follows:

Anchor I'm home to stay; you can count on me.

Balls in a cage, links in a chain Captured love, together forever; the number of balls or links may correspond to the number of children desired, or the number of years already spent together.

Bell Marriage.

Celtic cross Faith; marriage.

Double spoon Side by side forever.

Flowers Love and affection; courtship.

Horseshoe Good luck; happiness.

Key, lock, little house My house is yours.

One heart My heart is yours.

Two hearts We feel the same way about one another.

Vines, trees, leaves Our love is growing.

Wheel I will work for you.

Sq; bar £8-14, restaurant £13-18) has blazing log fires in winter and sagging oak-beamed ceilings. The restaurant serves the likes of Brecon venison and Swansea Bay sea bass while the bar turns out alcohol-absorbing comfort food like steak-and-ale pies and pork-and-leek sausages. Wash it all down with an Old Speckled Hen real ale.

TRANSPORT

BUS // Buses 280 and 281 head to Llandeilo (37 minutes) and Carmarthen (one hour 23 minutes), and 64 heads to Brecon (45 minutes). See also Beacons Bus B10 (p89).

TRAIN // Llandovery is on the Heart of Wales Line, with direct services to Swansea (£6.60, one hour 34 minutes), Llandeilo (£2.50, 19 minutes), Llanwrtyd Wells (£2.30, 23 minutes), Llandrindod Wells (£4.70, 58 minutes) and Knighton (£7, one hour 36 minutes).

NORTH CARMARTHENSHIRE

❦ DOLAUCOTHI GOLD MINES // A CELEBRATION OF 1900 GOLDEN YEARS

Set in a beautiful wooded estate, the **Dolaucothi Gold Mines** (☎ 01558-650177; www.nationaltrust.org.uk; Pumsaint; adult/child £3.60/1.80; ⏰ 11am-5pm mid-Mar–Oct) are on the site of the only known Roman gold mine in the UK. The Romans left around AD 120, but the locals carried on for a couple of hundred more years. Mining recommenced with the Victorians and by the time the mine was finally closed down in 1938 the works employed more than 200 men.

The exhibition and the mining machinery above ground are interesting,

THE PHYSICIANS OF MYDDFAI

About 8 miles southeast of Llandovery, nestled beneath the high escarpment of the Black Mountain, is a tiny lake called **Llyn y Fan Fach** (Lake of the Little Peak). In the mid-13th century, a young man grazing his cattle beside the lake saw a woman, the loveliest he had ever seen, sitting on the surface of the water, combing her hair. He fell madly in love with her, coaxed her to shore with some bread and begged her to marry him. Her fairy father agreed, on the condition that if the young man struck her three times she would return to the fairy world. As dowry she brought a herd of magic cows and for years the couple lived happily near Myddfai, raising three healthy sons.

Naturally the three-strikes-and-you're-out story ends badly. After three abusive incidents, she and her cattle returned forever to the lake. Her sons often visited the lake and one day their mother appeared. She handed the eldest, Rhiwallon, a leather bag containing the secrets of the lake's medicinal plants, and informed him that he should heal the sick.

From this point, legend merges with fact. Historical records confirm that Rhiwallon was a well-known 13th-century physician, and his descendants continued the tradition until the 18th century.

The Pant-y-Meddygon, or 'Physicians' Valley', on Mynydd Myddfai is still rich in bog plants, herbs and lichens, and is well worth visiting for the scenery alone; ask at Llandovery tourist office for details of walks.

but the main attraction is the chance to go underground on a guided tour of the old mine workings (adult/child extra £3.80/1.90). Back at the surface, there's a sediment-filled water trough where you can try your hand at panning for gold.

The mines are 10 miles northwest of Llandovery, off the A482.

❦ NATIONAL WOOL MUSEUM // SPINNING A YARN ABOUT THE WOOL INDUSTRY

The Cambrian Mills factory, world famous for its high-quality woollen products, closed in 1984 and this interesting **museum** (☎ 01559-370929; www.museumwales .ac.uk; Dre-fach Felindre; admission free; ☉ daily Apr-Sep, 10am-5pm Tue-Sat Oct-Mar) has taken its place. Former mill workers are often on hand to get the machines clickety-clacking but there's also a working commercial mill next door where you can watch the operations from a viewing platform. A cafe

is on site, as is a gift shop selling snugly woollen blankets.

The museum is positioned in verdant countryside, 14 miles north of Carmarthen and 14 miles southeast of Cardigan, signposted from the A484.

❦ TEIFI VALLEY RAILWAY // PUFF THROUGH THE VALLEY

Pocket-sized steam locomotives puff their way along the wonderful little **Teifi Valley Railway** (☎ 01559-371077; www.teifivalleyrail way.com; adult/child £6/4; ☉ Apr-Oct), a 2-mile stretch of narrow-gauge line at Henllan (14 miles southeast of Cardigan). They run to a complicated timetable, so check on the website or with the Cardigan tourist office before making the trip.

❦ CENARTH // NAVIGABLE BASKETS AND HOLY WELLS

The village of Cenarth occupies a picturesque spot by an old stone bridge over the River Teifi, at the foot of a stretch of rapids. It's home to the **National Coracle Centre** (☎ 01239-710980; www.coracle-centre. co.uk; adult/child £3/1; ⊙ 10.30am-5.30pm Easter-Oct), which comprises a 17th-century flour mill and a collection of coracles (small boats made of hide and wicker) from all over the world, along with exhibits and demonstrations showing how these fragile craft were made and used. If you're wondering what one looks like but don't fancy paying the admission, there's one attached to the wall of the 16th-century White Hart Tavern across the road.

Near the south side of the bridge is **Ffynnon Llawddog**, a holy well linked to an early Celtic saint. It's one of many such sites throughout Wales, popular during medieval times for their supposedly curative powers, although many have ancient pre-Christian origins.

Cenarth is 8 miles southeast of Cardigan and can be reached by bus 460, which runs between Cardigan (14 minutes) and Carmarthen (one hour 12 minutes). A car park on the north side of the bridge charges £2 but there are some free parks by the river on the south side.

SWANSEA, THE GOWER &
CARMARTHENSHIRE

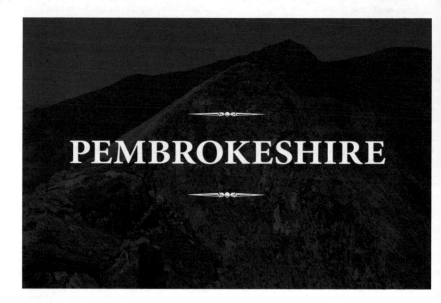

PEMBROKESHIRE

3 PERFECT DAYS

❧ DAY 1 // LOOP THE LIP

Spend the day looping around Pembrokeshire's southern lip, stopping to hang out at the beach if the weather's agreeable. Start at Tenby (p139), carry on to Manorbier (p147), stop for a cuppa at Ye Olde Worlde Cafe (p149), pop down to St Govan's Chapel (p150) and the Green Bridge of Wales (p150), watch the waves crashing at Freshwater West (p150), then loop back to Pembroke (p150). Of the five castles in the immediate vicinity, Pembroke Castle is the most impressive, so allocate at least an hour to explore.

❧ DAY 2 // ST DAVIDS DAY

Head straight for St Davids (p157), checking out the pretty harbour at Lower Solva (p161) on the way. Spend the day soaking up the charms of this tiny city, including St Davids Cathedral (p157) and landscape gallery Oriel Y Parc (p160). Stroll down to St Non's Bay (p161) to visit the holy well and ruined chapel and watch the surf pummelling the cliffs. Drive down to Whitesands Bay (p162) and take a walk around St Davids Head (p163).

❧ DAY 3 // ANCIENT STONES, GOOD FOOD

Aim to reach Newport (p168) by lunch, factoring in a few stops on the way such as Porthgain (p164), Carreg Sampson (p164), Pwll Deri (p164) and Strumble Head (p165). Check into your accommodation (p335) and book for dinner (p169); for a small town, Newport has excellent sleeping and eating options. Little Carreg Coetan (p169) is a good teaser for the mysterious sites nearby. Visit its big sister Pentre Ifan (p170), Iron Age fort Castell Henllys (p171) and Nevern's bleeding yew and Celtic crosses (p170).

SOUTH PEMBROKESHIRE

· · · · · ·

South Pembrokeshire boasts some of Wales' best sandy beaches and most spectacular limestone formations and makes an impressive starting point for the Pembrokeshire Coast Path. Once known as Little England Beyond Wales, it was divided from the north by the Landsker Line – a physical and then a linguistic barrier roughly following the old Norman frontier. The divide is less pronounced now, but there's a noticeable English feel to places like Tenby, especially in summer, when the masses descend with their buckets and spades, building miniature replicas of the castles their ancestors once used to keep the Welsh at bay. Those sturdy fortifications are still visible in Tenby, Manorbier, Carew and Haverfordwest, reaching their apotheosis at Pembroke Castle.

TENBY (DINBYCH Y PYSGOD)

☎ 01834 / pop 4900

Perched on a headland with sandy beaches either side, Tenby is a postcard-maker's dream. Houses are painted from the pastel palette of a classic fishing village, interspersed with the white elegance of Georgian mansions. The main part of town is still constrained by its Norman-built walls, funnelling holidaymakers through medieval streets lined with pubs, ice-creameries and gift shops. In the off-season, without the tackiness of the promenade-and-pier beach towns, it tastefully returns to being a sleepy little place. In the summer months it has a boisterous, boozy holiday-resort feel, with packed pubs seemingly all blasting out Status Quo simultaneously.

Tenby flourished in the 15th century as a centre for the textile trade, exporting cloth in exchange for salt and wine. Clothmaking declined in the 18th century, but the town soon reinvented itself as a fashionable watering place. The arrival of the railway in the 19th century sealed its future as a resort, and William Paxton (owner of the Middleton estate in Carmarthenshire, now home to the National Botanic Garden of Wales; p132) developed a saltwater spa here. Anxiety over a possible French invasion of the Milford Haven waterway led to the construction in 1869 of a fort on St Catherine's Island.

Among those who have taken inspiration or rest here are Horatio Nelson, Jane Austen, George Eliot, JMW Turner, Beatrix Potter and Roald Dahl. The artist Augustus John was born here, and he and his sister Gwen lived here during their early life.

ESSENTIAL INFORMATION

EMERGENCIES // Police station (☎ 0845 330 2000; Warren St)

TOURIST OFFICES // National park centre (☎ 845040; South Pde; ☺ 9.30am-5pm daily Apr-Sep, 10am-4.30pm Mon-Sat Oct-Mar) Tourist office (☎ 842402; Upper Park Rd; ☺ 9.30am-5pm Mon-Fri, 10am-4pm Sat & Sun Easter-Oct, 10am-4pm Mon-Sat Nov-Easter)

ORIENTATION

The town's main landmark is the prominent headland of Castle Hill, site of the Norman stronghold. Tenby Harbour lies to its west, with the old town rising steeply above it. The old town is bounded to the west by the city walls, which run north–south along South Pde and St Florence Pde.

PEMBROKESHIRE

(Continued on page 144)

PEMBROKESHIRE

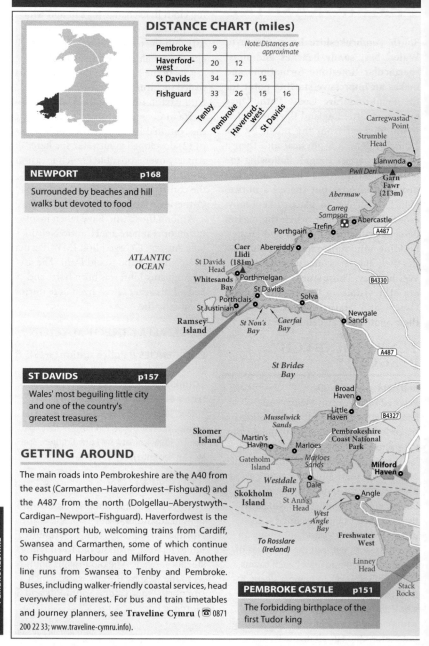

DISTANCE CHART (miles)

Pembroke	9	Note: Distances are approximate	
Haverfordwest	20	12	
St Davids	34	27	15
Fishguard	33	26	15	16

Tenby Pembroke Haverfordwest St Davids

NEWPORT   p168

Surrounded by beaches and hill walks but devoted to food

ATLANTIC OCEAN

Carregwastad Point
Strumble Head
Llanwnda
Pwll Deri
Garn Fawr (213m)
Abermaw
Carreg Sampson
Porthgain Trefin Abercastle
A487
Caer Llidi (181m)
Abereiddy
St Davids Head
Porthmelgan
Whitesands Bay
St Davids
Porthclais
St Justinian Solva
B4330
Ramsey Island
St Non's Bay
Caerfai Bay
Newgale Sands
A487
St Brides Bay

ST DAVIDS   p157

Wales' most beguiling little city and one of the country's greatest treasures

Broad Haven
Little Haven
B4327
Musselwick Sands
Pembrokeshire Coast National Park
Skomer Island
Martin's Haven
Marloes
Gateholm Island
Marloes Sands
Milford Haven

GETTING AROUND

The main roads into Pembrokeshire are the A40 from the east (Carmarthen–Haverfordwest–Fishguard) and the A487 from the north (Dolgellau–Aberystwyth–Cardigan–Newport–Fishguard). Haverfordwest is the main transport hub, welcoming trains from Cardiff, Swansea and Carmarthen, some of which continue to Fishguard Harbour and Milford Haven. Another line runs from Swansea to Tenby and Pembroke. Buses, including walker-friendly coastal services, head everywhere of interest. For bus and train timetables and journey planners, see **Traveline Cymru** (☎ 0871 200 22 33; www.traveline-cymru.info).

Westdale Bay
Skokholm Island
St Ann's Head
Dale
Angle
West Angle Bay
To Rosslare (Ireland)
Freshwater West
Linney Head

PEMBROKE CASTLE   p151

The forbidding birthplace of the first Tudor king

Stack Rocks

PEMBROKESHIRE

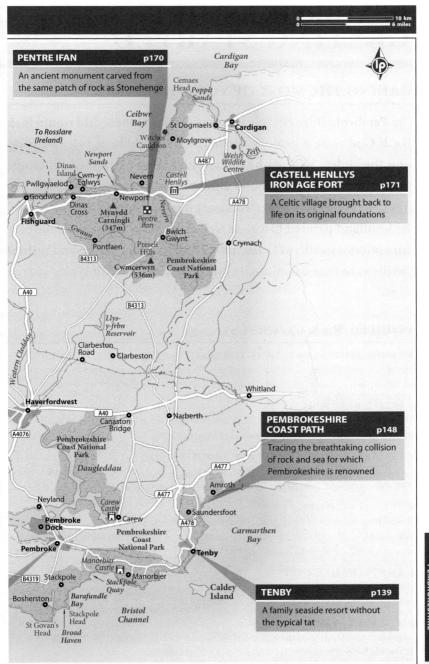

0 _____ 10 km
0 _____ 6 miles

PENTRE IFAN p170

An ancient monument carved from the same patch of rock as Stonehenge

Cardigan Bay

Cemaes Head *Poppit Sands*

Ceibwr Bay

St Dogmaels ● **Cardigan**

To Rosslare (Ireland)

Witches Cauldron ● Moylgrove

Newport Sands   Nevern

Dinas Island   Cwm-yr- Eglwys

Pwllgwaelod

● Goodwick   ● Newport

Fishguard   Dinas Cross

Gwaun   Mynydd Carningli (347m)   ▲

Pontfaen   Preseli Hills

B4313   Cwmcerwyn (536m) ▲

A40

Llys-y-frbn Reservoir

Clarbeston Road   ● Clarbeston

Haverfordwest

A4076   A40   Canaston Bridge   ● Narberth

Pembrokeshire Coast National Park

Daugleddau

Neyland   *Carew Castle*

Pembroke Dock   ● Carew

Pembroke ●   Pembrokeshire Coast National Park

B4319   Stackpole   *Manorbier Castle*   ● Manorbier

Bosherston   *Stackpole Quay*

Barafundle Bay

St Govan's Head   Stackpole Head   *Broad Haven*

Bristol Channel

A487   *Teifi*

Welsh Wildlife Centre

Castell Henllys 血

CASTELL HENLLYS IRON AGE FORT p171

A Celtic village brought back to life on its original foundations

A478

Pentre Ifan ✿

Bwlch Gwynt

● Crymach

Pembrokeshire Coast National Park

Nevern

Whitland

A477

PEMBROKESHIRE COAST PATH p148

Tracing the breathtaking collision of rock and sea for which Pembrokeshire is renowned

A477   Amroth ●

A478   ● Saundersfoot

Carmarthen Bay

● **Tenby**

Caldey Island

TENBY p139

A family seaside resort without the typical tat

Western Cleddau

PEMBROKESHIRE

PEMBROKESHIRE GETTING STARTED

MAKING THE MOST OF YOUR TIME

The Pembrokeshire coast is what you imagine the world would look like if God were a geology teacher: knobbly hills of volcanic rock, long thin inlets scoured by glacial meltwaters, stratified limestone eroded into arches, blowholes and sea stacks, and towering red and grey cliffs giving way to perfect sandy beaches, only to resume around the headland painted black. As well as its natural assets, Pembrokeshire offers a wealth of Celtic and pre-Celtic sites, castles and little St Davids – the magical mini-city forever associated with Wales' patron saint.

TOP TOURS & COURSES

❦ LEGENDARY WELSH ADVENTURE CO
Based in Pembrokeshire but heading all over Wales; offers an eclectic range of active, adrenalin-infused and cultural tours. (☎ 07861-679205; www.legendarywelshadventure.com)

❦ OUTER REEF SURF SCHOOL
Learn to surf at Newgale Sands or Manorbier before hitting the big breaks at Freshwater West. (☎ 01646-680070; www.outerreefsurfschool.com)

❦ PEMBROKESHIRE COAST PATH GUIDED WALK
Expert national park rangers lead treks of varying lengths; arrange your accommodation and carry your own bags. (☎ 0845 345 7275; www.pcnpa.org.uk; full 14 days £186)

❦ PRESELI VENTURE
Has its own lodge near Abermawr, on the coast between St Davids and Fishguard. Activities include coasteering (see p163), sea kayaking, mountain biking, surfing and coastal hiking. (☎ 01348-837709; www.preseliventure.com)

❦ TOWN TRAILS TENBY
Guided walks of Tenby's historical sites with themes such as ghosts or pirates. (☎ 01834-845841; www.guidedtourswales.co.uk; adult/child £4.50/3.50; ☻ Mon-Sat mid-Jun–mid-Sep)

❦ TYF ADVENTURE
Organises coasteering, surfing, sea-kayaking and rock-climbing trips from its St Davids base. (Map p159; ☎ 01437-721611; www.tyf.com; 1 High St)

GETTING AWAY FROM IT ALL

Despite Pembrokeshire's popularity, it's not too difficult to escape human company, particularly on remote stretches of the Pembrokeshire Coast Path.

★ **St Ann's Head** Forming the north head of the great harbour of Milford Haven, the landscape of St Ann's Head owes more to the Iron Age than the heavy industry on the horizon (p155).

★ **St Davids Head** Wild ponies usually outnumber people on this lost-in-time promontory (p163).

★ **Celtic Trail** (www.routes2ride.org.uk/wales/routes2ride/celtic_trail/) Escape the worst of the traffic on this 377-mile cycling route, starting from Fishguard and passing through the best bits of Pembrokeshire on its way to Chepstow.

ADVANCE PLANNING

★ **St David's Day** The first day of March is a big deal in Wales and a good day to be in the saint's own city.

★ **Fishguard Folk Festival** (www.pembrokeshire-folk-music.co.uk) Held over the Spring Bank Holiday weekend at the end of May.

★ **Fishguard Music Festival** (www.fishguardmusicfestival.co.uk) Takes place in the last week of July, with classical concerts and choirs whooping it up around town.

★ **Tenby Arts Festival** (www.tenbyartsfest.co.uk) Runs for a week in late September, with street performers, poetry, classical-music concerts, comedy, sand-sculpture competitions, choirs and dancing.

TOP EATS

❦ **OLD KING'S ARMS HOTEL**
Hefty serves of local meat and seafood in a country kitchen atmosphere (p152).

❦ **CWTCH**
Stone walls and wooden beams mark this as St Davids' most upmarket eatery (p160).

❦ **CHAPEL CHOCOLATES**
More than 100 varieties of handmade Welsh chocolates and truffles (p161).

❦ **SHED**
One of Wales' finest seafood restaurants, showcasing Porthgain crab and lobster (p164).

❦ **LLYS MEDDYG**
Stylish surrounds and an ever-changing menu reflecting the best of seasonal local produce (p169).

RESOURCES

★ **Pembrokeshire Coast National Park Authority** (www.pcnpa.org.uk) Includes a downloadable version of the national park's annual *Coast to Coast* publication.

★ **Pembrokeshire Information Centres** (www.pembrokeshireinformationcentres.co.uk) Details of the seven county-run information centres scattered around Pembrokeshire.

★ **Pembrokeshire County Council** (www.pembrokeshire.gov.uk) Bus and train route maps and timetables.

★ **National Trust** (NT; www.nationaltrust.org.uk) Information on the 50 miles of trust-owned coast.

PEMBROKESHIRE

(Continued from page 139)

EXPLORING TENBY

❦ ST MARY'S CHURCH // LOOK TO THE HEAVENS AND GAWP AT THE ROOF

The graceful arched roof of 13th-century **St Mary's Church** (High St) is studded with fascinating wooden bosses, mainly dating from the 15th century and carved into flowers, cheeky faces, mythical beasts, fish and even a mermaid holding a comb and mirror. There's a memorial here to Robert Recorde, the 16th-century writer and mathematician who invented the 'equals' sign, along with a confronting cadaver-topped tomb intended to remind the viewer of their own mortality.

The young Henry Tudor was hidden here before fleeing to Brittany. It's thought he left via a tunnel into the cellars under Mayor Thomas White's house across the road (where Boots is now).

❦ CASTLE HILL // VIEWS, ART AND LOCAL HISTORY

William Paxton built his saltwater baths above the harbour in what is now **Laston House** (1 Castle Sq). The Greek writing on the pediment translates as the optimistic 'The sea will wash away all the evils of man'. Beyond here, a path leads out past the old and new Royal National Lifeboat Institution (RNLI) lifeboat stations and around the Castle Hill headland.

On top of the hill are the ruins of the Norman **castle**, a **memorial to Prince Albert**, a fine view over the coast and the **Tenby Museum & Art Gallery** (☎ 842809; www.tenbymuseum.org.uk; adult/child £4/2; ☺ 10am-5pm Mon-Fri Nov-Easter, 10am-5pm daily Easter-Oct). Displays cover the town's development from a fishing village into a 19th-century seaside resort bigger than Blackpool, with interesting exhibits ranging from delicate Roman vases to a Victorian antiquarian's study. There's also a recreated pirate's cell and a gallery including paintings by Augustus and Gwen John.

❦ ST CATHERINE'S ISLAND // INDULGE YOUR FAMOUS FIVE FANTASIES

At low tide you can walk across the sand from Castle Beach to this little island but it's a long, cold wait if you get trapped by the tide; check tide tables in *Coast to Coast* or ask at the tourist office. The Victorian **fort** is closed to the public.

PEMBROKESHIRE COAST NATIONAL PARK

Established in 1952, the Pembrokeshire Coast National Park (Parc Cenedlaethol Arfordir Sir Benfro) takes in almost the entire coast and its offshore islands, as well as the moorland hills of Mynydd Preseli in the north. Pembrokeshire's sea cliffs and islands support huge breeding populations of sea birds, while seals, dolphins, porpoises and whales are frequently spotted in coastal waters.

There are three national park information centres (in Tenby, St Davids and Newport) and the local tourist offices scattered across Pembrokeshire are well stocked with park paraphernalia. The free annual publication *Coast to Coast* (online at www.pcnpa.org.uk) has lots of information on park attractions, a calendar of events and details of park-organised activities, including guided walks, themed tours, cycling trips, pony treks, island cruises, canoe trips and minibus tours. It's worth picking it up for the tide tables alone – they're a necessity for many legs of the coast path.

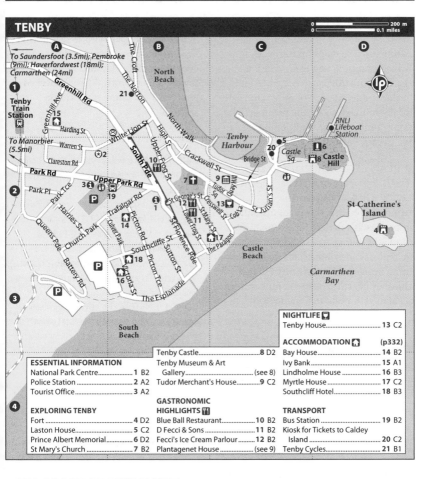

TENBY

0 — 200 m
0 — 0.1 miles

To Saundersfoot (3.5mi); Pembroke (9mi); Haverfordwest (18mi); Carmarthen (24mi)

Tenby Train Station

To Manorbier (5.5mi)

North Beach

Tenby Harbour

RNLI Lifeboat Station

Castle Sq

Castle Hill

St Catherine's Island

Carmarthen Bay

Castle Beach

South Beach

The Esplanade

Greenhill Rd · Greenhill Ave · Harding St · Warren St · Clareston Rd · Park Rd · Park Pl · Park Tce · Queens Pde · Harries St · Church Park · Culver Park · Battery Rd · Victoria St · Picton Tce · Sutton St · St Florence Pde · Picton Rd · Lower Frog St · St Mary's St · Cresswell St · Crackwell St · St Julian's St · The Paragon · Southcliffe St · Trafalgar Rd · Upper Park Rd · South Pde · High St · North Walk · White Lion St · The Norton · The Croft · St George's St · Cob La · Bridge St · Tudor Sq · Upper Frog St

ESSENTIAL INFORMATION	
National Park Centre	1 B2
Police Station	2 A2
Tourist Office	3 A2

EXPLORING TENBY	
Fort	4 D2
Laston House	5 C2
Prince Albert Memorial	6 D2
St Mary's Church	7 B2
Tenby Castle	8 D2
Tenby Museum & Art Gallery	(see 8)
Tudor Merchant's House	9 C2

GASTRONOMIC HIGHLIGHTS	
Blue Ball Restaurant	10 B2
D Fecci & Sons	11 B2
Fecci's Ice Cream Parlour	12 B2
Plantagenet House	(see 9)

NIGHTLIFE	
Tenby House	13 C2

ACCOMMODATION	(p332)
Bay House	14 B2
Ivy Bank	15 A1
Lindholme House	16 B3
Myrtle House	17 C2
Southcliff Hotel	18 B3

TRANSPORT	
Bus Station	19 B2
Kiosk for Tickets to Caldey Island	20 C2
Tenby Cycles	21 B1

♥ TUDOR MERCHANT'S HOUSE
// ENTER THE WORLD OF TENBY'S TUDOR BOURGEOISIE

Tenby's oldest buildings are found on steep Quay Hill. You can visit the handsomely restored **town house** (NT; ☎ 842279; www.nationaltrust.org.uk; Quay Hill; adult/child £3/1.50; ☉ 11am-5pm Sun-Fri Easter-Oct). It was once the dwelling of a late-15th-century merchant, and has period furnishings and the remains of early frescoes on the interior walls.

GASTRONOMIC HIGHLIGHTS

♥ BLUE BALL RESTAURANT ££

☎ 843038; www.theblueballrestaurant.co.uk; Upper Frog St; mains £9-22; ☉ dinner daily summer, Thu-Sun low season

Polished wood, old timber beams and exposed brickwork create a cosy, rustic atmosphere in what is probably Tenby's best restaurant. The menu makes good use of local produce, notably seafood. Pork Wellington is the signature dish.

PEMBROKESHIRE

❤ D FECCI & SONS £

☎ 842484; Lower Frog St; mains £2-4

Eating fish and chips on the beach is a British tradition, and D Fecci & Sons is a Tenby institution, having been in business since 1935. Not only is the fish locally sourced, so are the potatoes. The same family run the traditional **Fecci's Ice Cream Parlour** on St George's St.

❤ PLANTAGENET HOUSE £££

☎ 842350; Quay Hill; mains £14-22; ⏰ lunch Sat & Sun, dinner Fri & Sat, daily summer

Atmosphere-wise, this place instantly impresses; it's perfect for a romantic, candle-lit dinner. Tucked down an alley in Tenby's oldest house, it's dominated by an immense 12th-century Flemish chimney hearth. The menu ranges from acclaimed seafood to organic beef.

NIGHTLIFE

There are about two dozen pubs crammed into the area around Tudor Sq, and the place can get pretty riotous on summer nights with big groups of lads and ladettes heading between them.

❤ TENBY HOUSE

☎ 842000; www.tenbyhousehotel.com; Tudor Sq

Tenby House is a lively hotel bar with cool tunes on Friday and Saturday nights, and a sunny, flower-bedecked courtyard for summer afternoon sessions.

TRANSPORT

BIKE // Tenby Cycles (☎ 845573; The Norton; ⏰ 9.30am-5pm Mon-Sat Easter-Sep) Rents bikes for £12 a day.

BUS // The bus station is next to the tourist office on Upper Park Rd. Routes include 333 to Carmarthen (one hour); 349 to Manorbier (18 minutes), Pembroke (43 minutes) and Pembroke Dock (53 minutes); 350/351 to Saundersfoot (eight minutes) and Amroth (22 minutes); 360 to Carew (17 minutes); and 381 to Haverfordwest (one hour).

COACH // National Express (www.national express.com) coach destinations include London (£30, 6½ hours), Chepstow (£24, three hours), Swansea (£8, 1½ hours), Carmarthen (£5.10, 40 minutes), Pembroke (£2.60, 20 minutes) and Haverfordwest (£4.40, 50 minutes).

PARKING // If you're coming in high season, expect to pay for parking. There are short-term parks in the

PEMBROKESHIRE ACCOMMODATION

In summer you'll need to book well ahead, especially at the beach towns. Our three favourite places to stay are Tenby (for family beach holidays and reasonably priced B&Bs), Newport (for the winning combo of beaching and eating) and, especially, St Davids, an atmospheric little city with beaches and wild walks nearby. See p332 for recommended accommodation; we've included options for Pembrokeshire Coast Path (PCP) walkers, but you'll need to flesh out your itinerary from the hostel list (p328).

These are our top Pembrokeshire picks:

★ **Canaston Oaks** (p332) B&B set amid Narbeth farmland.

★ **St Brides Spa Hotel** (p332) Luxurious beach retreat in Saundersfoot.

★ **Tregenna** (p334) Modern, well-equipped B&B rooms in Pembroke.

★ **Ramsey House** (p334) Stylish B&B rooms on a quiet St Davids street.

★ **Llys Meddyg** (p336) Upmarket Newport restaurant with rooms that have a boutique sensibility.

PEMBROKESHIRE

multilevel building next to the tourist office on Upper Park Rd (30/40p per one/two hours). The car park near the train station, on the corner of Lower Park and Marsh Rds, charges £1.50 per day from April to September. The large lot at the end of Southcliffe St charges £2.50 per day (9am to 9pm) and £1 overnight.

TRAIN // Arriva Trains Wales (www.arriva trainswales.co.uk) has direct services to Tenby from Swansea (£12, 1½ hours), Llanelli (£12, 1¼ hours), Carmarthen (£7.20, 41 minutes), Manorbier (£2.50, 10 minutes) and Pembroke (£4.20, 34 minutes).

TENBY TO ANGLE

☙ CALDEY ISLAND // MONKS CARRYING ON AN ANCIENT TRADITION

Boat trips run from Tenby Harbour to **Caldey Island** (☎ 01834-844453; www.caldey -island.co.uk; adult/child £11/6; ☙ Mon-Sat Apr-Oct), home to lots of grey seals and sea birds, and a red-topped, whitewashed monastery that houses a community of around 15 Cistercian monks. The monks live an austere life but make various luxurious products for sale, including perfume (based on the island's wildflowers), shortbread and chocolate, and do so well that they now employ people from the mainland.

There are guided tours of the monastery and great walks around the island, with good views from the lighthouse. Make sure you visit the old priory and St Illtyd's Church, with its oddly shaped steeple. Inside is a stone with inscriptions in ogham (an ancient Celtic script).

Boats to Caldey Island depart half-hourly from about 10.30am, from the harbour at high tide and from Castle Beach at low tide. Tickets are sold from a kiosk at the harbour slipway.

Little **St Margaret's Island** at the western tip of Caldey is a nature reserve (landings are prohibited); it's home to grey seals and Wales' biggest colony of cormorants.

☙ MANORBIER // SAND MEETS CASTLE

Manorbier (pronounced man-er-beer) is a little village of leafy, twisting lanes nestled above a lovely sandy beach. It's home to craggy, lichen-spotted **Manorbier Castle** (☎ 01834-871394; www.manorbiercastle .co.uk; adult/child £3.50/1.50; ☙ 10am-6pm Easter-Sep), the birthplace of Giraldus Cambrensis (Gerald of Wales, 1146–1223), one of the country's greatest scholars and patriots. 'In all the broad lands of Wales, Manorbier is the best place by far,' he wrote.

The 12th- to 19th-century castle buildings are grouped around a pretty garden. Medieval music plays in the Great Hall and there's a murky dungeon, a smuggler's secret passage and a tableaux of wax figures in period costume – apparently rejects from Madame Tussaud's in London. Look out for the figure that was originally Prince Philip, now sporting a coat of chain mail. The castle starred in the 2003 film *I Capture the Castle*.

Head down to the beach and turn left onto the Coast Path and before you round the headland you'll come to **King's Quoit**, a simple Neolithic dolmen (burial chamber) fashioned from slabs of rock.

Castle Inn (☎ 01834-871268; mains £7-11) is a classic village pub with a rhododendron-shaded beer garden, a jukebox and live music on Saturday nights.

Manorbier is 5.5 miles southwest of Tenby. It's served by bus 349 to Tenby (18 minutes), Pembroke (25 minutes), Pembroke Dock (35 minutes) and Haverfordwest (70 minutes). There's also a train station, a mile north of the village, with direct services to Swansea (£11.50,

PEMBROKESHIRE COAST PATH (PCP)

Straddling the line where Pembrokeshire drops suddenly into the sea, the PCP is one of the most spectacular long-distance routes in Britain. Traversing the entire coast, it's the best way to experience Pembrokeshire Coast National Park. If you don't have the time or the stamina for the full route, it can easily be split into smaller chunks, especially in summer when public transport is at its peak.

We've suggested a south-to-north route, allowing an easy start in highly populated areas and building up to longer, more isolated stretches. We've also omitted the two whole days taken up by the industrial landscape of the Milford Haven waterway, suggesting skipping from Angle to Dale by ferry or buses.

Some distances look deceptively short but you must remember the endless steep ascents and descents where the trail crosses harbours and beaches. Take a tide table (found in *Coast to Coast*; see p144) and wet-weather gear – it can be quite changeable, even at the height of summer.

WHEN TO WALK

In spring and early summer, wildflowers transform the route and migratory birds are likely to be seen. Late summer will tend to be dryer and you might spot migrating whales, flocks of butterflies and wild blackberries to snack on. In autumn, seals come ashore to give birth to their pups. Winter is generally more problematic, as many hostels and campsites close from October until Easter, and buses are less frequent. Needless to say, walking around precipitous cliffs in the wind, rain and chill may not be the most enjoyable (or safest) experience.

SOUTH PEMBROKESHIRE LEGS

★ **Amroth to Tenby** (three to four hours, 7 miles) Starting at a wide sandy beach, this short section is the perfect teaser for what's to come.

★ **Tenby to Manorbier** (3½ to 4½ hours, 8.5 miles) Another brilliant day with breathtaking clifftop views. There are steep climbs, but the distance is mercifully short.

★ **Manorbier to Bosherston** (5½ to seven hours, 15 miles) A longer day, continually alternating between sheer cliffs and sandy beaches.

★ **Bosherston to Angle** (5½ to seven hours, 15 miles) There are patches of wonderful coastal scenery, but prepare for some tedious road walking, courtesy of the British Army. Either stay overnight in Angle and catch the ferry the following day to Dale, or catch the Coastal Cruiser bus to Pembroke.

★ **Dale to Marloes Sands** (three hours, 5 miles) A short leg, but if you're travelling from Pembroke you'll need to catch the bus to Milford Haven and then pick up the Puffin Shuttle to Dale. The walk takes in St Ann's Head's rugged cliffs.

★ **Marloes Sands to Broad Haven** (4½ to six hours, 13 miles) A wonderful walk along dramatic clifftops, ending in an impressive beach.

For the northern section, see p158.

1¾ hours), Carmarthen (£7.20, 54 minutes), Tenby (£2.50, 10 minutes) and
Pembroke (£3.30, 19 minutes).

❦ STACKPOLE ESTATE // BEACHES, WOODLANDS AND WATER LILIES

Run by the NT, **Stackpole Estate**
(☎ 01646-661359; www.nationaltrust.org.uk;
admission free; ☽ dawn-dusk) takes in 8 miles
of coast, including two fine beaches, a
wooded valley and a system of artificial
ponds famous for their spectacular display of water lilies. Stackpole was the
seat of the Campbells, earls of Cawdor,
a family with local roots dating back
to medieval times; in the 12th-century
Stackpole Elidor Church are effigies
of Elidor de Stackpole and his wife,
and Lord Cawdor, who featured in the
French invasion of Fishguard (see p166).

The tiny harbour of **Stackpole Quay**
marks the point where pink and purple
sandstone gives way to the massive grey
limestone that dominates the South
Pembrokeshire coast from here to Freshwater West. There's an NT car park
with information leaflets, and a good
tearoom.

A 10-minute walk south along the
coast path from Stackpole Quay leads to
Barafundle Bay, regularly voted one of
Britain's most beautiful beaches. Scenic
it certainly is, but its reputation has put
paid to seclusion – on summer weekends
it can get pretty crowded. Go on a weekday in spring, though, and you might
have the place to yourself.

A car park in Bosherston village gives
access to the famous **Bosherston Lily
Ponds** (at their best in June), criss-
crossed by a network of footpaths and
wooden bridges; parts are wheelchair
accessible. The ponds are home to otters, herons and more than 20 species of
dragonfly, while the ruins of the manor

house are inhabited by the greater horseshoe bat.

A mile southeast of Bosherston village
is the beautiful golden beach of **Broad
Haven**, framed by grey limestone cliffs
and pointed sea stacks.

Bosherston is 5 miles south of Pembroke. The Coastal Cruiser (p152) stops
at Stackpole Quay, Stackpole, Bosherston
and Broad Haven.

❦ YE OLDE WORLDE CAFE // TEA AND A SLICE OF EDWARDIAN CHARM

Better known as Auntie Vi's, this appeal-
ing **cafe** (☎ 01646-661216; Bosherston; snacks £2-5;
☽ 9am-6.30pm, to 9pm Jul & Aug), housed in the
front room of an old, ivy-covered coastguard cottage, has been serving tea and
cake since 1921. Its octogenarian guardian, who took over the business from her
parents, was made an MBE (Member of
the British Empire) in 2009 to acknowledge her decades of service to the
stomachs of coast path walkers. A recent
recipient of her olde worlde charm was
one Russell Crowe, who called in while
filming *Robin Hood* at nearby Freshwater
West in 2009.

❦ ST GOVAN'S HEAD & STACK ROCKS // COASTAL SCENERY AT ITS MOST DRAMATIC

The southern coast of Pembrokeshire
around St Govan's Head boasts some of
the most harshly beautiful coastline in
the country, with sheer cliffs dropping
50m into churning, thrashing surf. Unfortunately, much of this coastline lies
within the army's Castlemartin firing
range and is off limits to the public. Two
minor roads run south to the coast at St
Govan's Head and Stack Rocks; when
the range is in use these roads are closed.
You can check whether the roads, and
the section of coast path that links them,

are open by calling ☎ 01646-662367, or by checking the notices posted in Bosherston.

From the car park at the end of the St Govan's Head road, steps hacked into the rock lead down to tiny **St Govan's Chapel**, wedged into a slot in the cliffs just out of reach of the sea. The chapel dates from the 5th or 6th century, and is named for an itinerant 6th-century Irish preacher. The story goes that one day, when he was set upon by thieves, the cliff conveniently opened and enfolded him, protecting him from his attackers; in gratitude he built this chapel on the spot. The waters from St Govan's Well (now dried out), just below the chapel, were reputed to cure skin and eye complaints.

A 10-minute walk along the coast path to the west leads to a spectacular gash in the cliffs known as **Huntsman's Leap**, its vertical walls often dotted with rock climbers.

The car park at **Stack Rocks**, 3 miles to the west, gives access to even more spectacular cliff scenery, including the **Green Bridge of Wales**, the biggest natural arch in the country.

The Coastal Cruiser (p152) stops at both car parks.

❧ FRESHWATER WEST // WILD, DANGEROUS AND READY FOR ITS CLOSE-UP

Wild and windblown Freshwater West, a 2-mile strand of golden sand and silver shingle backed by acres of dunes, is Wales' best surf beach, sitting wide open to the Atlantic rollers. But beware – although it's great for surfing, big waves, powerful rips and quicksand make it dangerous for swimming; several people have drowned here and the beach has year-round red-flag status.

In 2009 scenes from Ridley Scott's *Robin Hood* and *Harry Potter and the Deathly Hallows* were filmed here.

The Coastal Cruiser (p152) stops at the car park.

❧ ANGLE // THE POINTY END OF SOUTH PEMBROKESHIRE

At the southern head of the Milford Haven waterway, the village of Angle feels a long way off the beaten track. The main attraction is the tiny beach in **West Angle Bay**, which has great views across the mouth of Milford Haven to St Ann's Head, and offers good coastal walks with lots of rock pools to explore. Old Point House (p333) is an atmospheric spot to rub shoulders with the locals over a pint.

If you're walking the coast path, consider catching the **Havenlink** (☎ 01646-600288; www.ruddersboatyard.co.uk; about £5; ☺ Fri-Sun Jun-Sep) ferry from Angle to Dale and skip two grim days passing the giant oil refineries lining Milford Haven. The Coastal Cruiser (p152) is another option; it stops in the village and at the beach.

PEMBROKE (PENFRO)

☎ 01646 / pop 7200

Pembroke is not much more than a single street of neat Georgian and Victorian houses sitting beneath a whopping great castle – the oldest in West Wales and birthplace of Henry VII, the first Tudor king.

In 1154 local traders scored a coup when a Royal Act of Incorporation made it illegal to land goods anywhere in the Milford Haven waterway except at Pembroke (now Pembroke Dock). In 1648, during the English Civil War, the castle was besieged for 48 days before it fell, after which Cromwell had the town walls demolished.

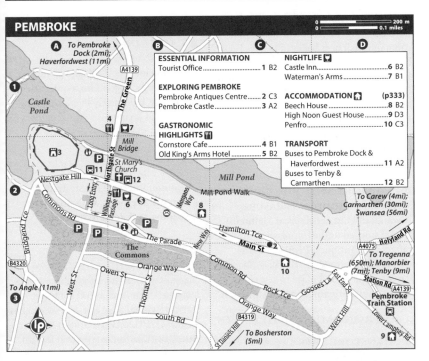

PEMBROKE

0 ____ 200 m
0 ____ 0.1 miles

ESSENTIAL INFORMATION
Tourist Office..................................1 B2

EXPLORING PEMBROKE
Pembroke Antiques Centre........2 C3
Pembroke Castle...........................3 A2

GASTRONOMIC HIGHLIGHTS
Cornstore Cafe...............................4 B1
Old King's Arms Hotel 5 B2

NIGHTLIFE
Castle Inn..6 B2
Waterman's Arms...........................7 B1

ACCOMMODATION   (p333)
Beech House 8 B2
High Noon Guest House 9 D3
Penfro..10 C3

TRANSPORT
Buses to Pembroke Dock &
    Haverfordwest 11 A2
Buses to Tenby &
    Carmarthen 12 B2

ESSENTIAL INFORMATION

TOURIST OFFICES // Tourist office
(☎ 01437-776499; Commons Rd; ✆ 10am-4pm Mon-Fri, 10am-1pm Sat Apr-Oct, 10am-1pm Tue-Sat Nov-Mar; ▭)

ORIENTATION

The 700m-long Main St stretches east along a ridge from the prominent castle, with a drop down to the Mill Pond to the north and to the Commons, a strip of low-lying parkland, to the south. Pembroke Dock is a separate town, 2 miles to the northwest.

EXPLORING PEMBROKE

❤ **PEMBROKE CASTLE // WALK ALL ALONG THE WATCHTOWERS**
Spectacular and forbidding **Pembroke Castle** (☎ 681510; www.pembrokecastle.co.uk;

Main St; adult/child £4.50/3.50; ✆ 9.30am-6pm Apr-Sep, 10am-5pm Mar & Oct, 10am-4pm Nov-Feb) was the home of the earls of Pembroke for over 300 years. A fort was established here in 1093 by Arnulph de Montgomery, but most of the present buildings date from the 12th and 13th centuries. The sinister, looming **keep**, built in 1200, is the oldest part. One hundred steps lead to the top, where there are great views over the town.

Next to the keep is the **Dungeon Tower**, where you can peer into the dank, dark prison cell. Nearby, with access through the Northern Hall, are steps to the creepy **Wogan Cavern**, a large natural cave that was partially walled in by the Normans and probably used as a store and boathouse.

The castle is a great place for kids to explore – wall walks and passages run from

PEMBROKESHIRE

tower to tower, and there are vivid exhibitions detailing the castle's history. In the room in which he is believed to have been born, in 1456, a tableau commemorates Henry Tudor (Harri Tudur), who defeated Richard III at the Battle of Bosworth Field in 1485 to become King Henry VII.

Guided tours are available from May to August (£1; phone for times). Falconry displays and costumed re-enactments are held in summer.

☙ **PEMBROKE ANTIQUES CENTRE //
SEARCH FOR HIDDEN TREASURE**
A wonderful old neoclassical Methodist chapel stocked to the impressively high rafters with antiques, **Pembroke Antiques Centre** (☎ 687017; Main St; 🕙 10am-5pm Mon-Sat; 🅿) is a good place to search for a quirky souvenir with a bit of history to it.

GASTRONOMIC HIGHLIGHTS

☙ **CORNSTORE CAFE £**
☎ 684290; The Green; mains £4-6; 🕙 10am-5pm Mon-Sat
Housed in an 18th-century granary on the Mill Pond, this cafe conjures up delicious lunches – daily specials include homemade soups and simple hot meals. Choose from the extensive range of speciality teas for the perfect cuppa to accompany one of the homemade cakes. It's worth checking out the homeware shop upstairs for interesting souvenirs.

☙ **OLD KING'S ARMS HOTEL £££**
☎ 683611; Main St; mains £15-22
Dark timber beams, ochre walls and polished copperware lend a country kitchen atmosphere to the restaurant here. The locally sourced protein (black beef, Carmarthen ham, daily seafood specials) comes accompanied with enough potatoes and vegetables to fill even a Tudor king.

NIGHTLIFE

☙ **CASTLE INN**
☎ 682883; 17 Main St
This snug local pub, all bare stone and horse brasses, is good for a quiet afternoon pint, but it fairly livens up in the evenings as a youngish crowd gathers for a night on the town.

☙ **WATERMAN'S ARMS**
☎ 682718; 2 The Green
The outdoor terrace is a suntrap on a summer afternoon, with fine views across the Mill Pond to the castle.

TRANSPORT

BOAT // Irish Ferries (☎ 08717-300 500; www .irishferries.co.uk) have two sailings a day on the four-hour route between Pembroke Dock and Rosslare in the southeast of Ireland (car and driver from £89, additional adult/child £23/13; foot passenger from £26).

BUS // Most buses heading to Pembroke Dock and Haverfordwest depart near the castle entrance; those bound for the coast leave further along Main St outside the Co-op supermarket. Bus 349 heads to Tenby (43 minutes), Manorbier (25 minutes), Pembroke Dock (10 minutes) and Haverfordwest (45 minutes); and bus 356 to Pembroke Dock (12 minutes) and Milford Haven (50 minutes). The Coastal Cruiser (daily May to September; Monday, Thursday and Saturday October to April) loops in both directions between Pembroke, Angle, Freshwater West, Bosherston and Stackpole, terminating at Pembroke Dock. From Pembroke you'll catch the 387 and return on the 388, although for the last destinations on this list it may be quicker to head to Pembroke Dock and catch the 388 in the opposite direction.

COACH // National Express (www.national express.com) destinations include London (£30, seven hours), Chepstow (£22, 3¼ hours), Swansea (£8, 1¾ hours), Carmarthen (£5.10, one hour), Tenby (£2.60, 20 minutes) and Haverfordwest (£4.40, 30 minutes).

PARKING // Parking is free down by the Commons from October to March and £1 otherwise. Below the castle, by Mill Bridge, it's 40p for two hours or 50p for four hours. If you don't fancy the steep walk, there's parking just behind Main St (enter from the Parade) at 30p per hour or 50p for four hours. Note: Main St is one-way, heading east.

TRAIN // There are direct trains to Swansea (£12, 2¼ hours), Llanelli (£12, 1¾ hours), Carmarthen (£7.20, 1¼ hours), Manorbier (£3.30, 19 minutes) and Tenby (£4.20, 34 minutes).

AROUND PEMBROKE

☙ PEMBROKE DOCK // GRIM PORT WITH A DASH OF HISTORY

Between 1814 and 1926 more than 260 Royal Navy ships were built at Pembroke Dock, which was then a Royal Dockyard. It also served as a Royal Air Force (RAF) base for flying boats during WWII and after. Today it's a sprawling expanse of suburbia with a ferry terminal and commercial port, but some of its history survives in the **Gun Tower Museum** (☎ 01646-622246; www.guntowermuseum.org.uk; adult/child £2.50/1.50; ☽ 10am-4pm Easter-Oct), housed in a 19th-century Martello tower that was built to defend the harbour from possible attack by French invaders. There was rather an unfair distribution of space here – 33 men slept in hammocks in one room, while the officer got the other room all to himself. A walkway now runs from the shore but when the tower was in use the men had to lower a rope ladder for supplies.

There are frequent bus services between Pembroke and Pembroke Dock.

☙ CAREW // ROMANTIC RUINS AND CELTIC CROSS

Looming romantically over the River Carew with its gaping windows reflected in the glassy water, craggy **Carew Castle** (☎ 01646-651782; www.carewcastle.com; adult/child £4.50/3; ☽ 10am-5pm Apr-Oct) is an impressive sight. These rambling limestone ruins range from functional 12th-century

fortification (built by Gerald de Windsor, Henry I's constable of Pembroke) to Elizabethan country house.

Abandoned in 1690, the castle is now inhabited by a large number of bats, including the protected greater horseshoe bat. A summer program of events includes battle re-enactments and open-air theatre. The castle ticket also gives you admission to **Carew Tidal Mill**, the only intact tidal mill in Wales.

Near the castle entrance is the 11th-century **Carew Cross**, one of the grandest of its kind – around 4m tall and covered in psychedelic Celtic squiggles. Directly across the road, **Carew Inn** (☎ 01646-651267; mains £8-18; Ⓥ) serves lunch and dinner, and has a beer garden overlooking the castle.

Carew is 4 miles northeast of Pembroke and 6 miles northwest of Tenby. Bus 360 heads here from Tenby (17 minutes).

HAVERFORDWEST (HWLFFORDD)

☎01437 / pop 13,400

A workaday town rather than a tourist hot spot, Haverfordwest is Pembrokeshire's main transport and shopping hub. Though it retains some fine Georgian buildings, it lacks the prettiness and historic atmosphere of many of its neighbours. It grew up around a shallow spot on the Western Cleddau River where it was possible to ford the stream, and probably takes its name from the Old English term *haefer* (billy goat) – this was the western *haefer* ford, the place where drovers crossed the river with their goats.

Founded as a fortified Flemish settlement by the Norman lord Gilbert de Clare in about 1110, its castle became the nucleus for a thriving market and its port remained important until the railway arrived in the mid-19th century.

Today the Riverside Shopping Centre is the main focus of activity and home to an excellent farmers market with organic and local produce stalls every other Friday.

ESSENTIAL INFORMATION

EMERGENCIES // **Police station** (☎ 0845 330 2000; Merlin's Hill) **Withybush General Hospital** (☎ 764545; Fishguard Rd)
TOURIST OFFICES // **Tourist office** (☎ 763110; Old Bridge St; ☼ 9.30am-5pm Mon-Sat Apr-Oct, 10am-4pm Mon-Sat Nov-Mar)

ORIENTATION

The old town centre is a compact maze of narrow streets and alleys between the two main road bridges over the river, with Castle Hill on the west bank. A one-way system runs clockwise around the centre, on High St, Dew St, Barn St and Cartlett Rd. The bus station and tourist office are on the east side of the river, close to the pedestrianised Old Bridge at the north end of the Riverside Shopping Centre. The train station is 400m east of the town centre, just off the A4067/A40 Narberth Rd.

EXPLORING HAVERFORDWEST

❤ **HAVERFORDWEST CASTLE & TOWN MUSEUM // WORTH A QUICK LOOK IF YOU'RE PASSING THROUGH**
The meagre ruins of **Haverfordwest Castle** (Castle St) consist of little more than three walls. The castle survived an on-slaught by Owain Glyndŵr in 1405, but according to one local story it was abandoned by its Royalist garrison during the English Civil War, when its soldiers mistook a herd of cows for Roundheads.

The **museum** (☎ 763087; www.haverfordwest-town-museum.org.uk; adult/child £1/free; ☼ 10am-4pm Mon-Sat Apr-Oct) is housed in the

residence of the governor of the prison, which once stood in the castle's outer ward – it was here that the unsuccessful French invasion force was incarcerated in 1797 (see p166). It covers the town's history, complete with a boil-ridden plague victim and an interesting section on local nicknames – a study has recorded 700 evocative endearments, such as Arse and Pockets, Drips and Stinko.

GASTRONOMIC HIGHLIGHTS

❤ **GEORGES ££**
☎ 766683; 24 Market St; mains £10-18; ☼ 10am-5.30pm Tue-Thu, 10am-11pm Fri & Sat; Ⓥ
Gargoyles on leashes guard the door of this trippy, hippy gift shop that doubles as an offbeat cafe. The Georges has cosy nooks of stained glass and candlelight, lanterns and fairy lights, along with a simple menu of home-cooked food ranging from steak to pasta to curry.

❤ **MOON & SIXPENCE £**
☎ 767851; www.moonsixpence.co.uk; Swan Sq; mains £4-6; ☼ 9am-4.30pm Mon-Sat
Floral wallpaper and twinkling chandeliers set the scene for this popular local cafe, tucked away in the top floor of a gift shop. It serves good cakes, pastries, salads, paninis and wraps with a large range of fillings.

TRANSPORT

BUS // Routes include 322 to Carmarthen (one hour); 349 to Pembroke Dock (40 minutes), Pembroke (45 minutes), Manorbier (1¼ hours) and Tenby (1½ hours); 411 to Newgale Sands (18 minutes), Solva (29 minutes) and St Davids (40 minutes); 412 to Fishguard (37 minutes), Dinas Cross (46 minutes), Newport (52 minutes), Castell Henllys (one hour) and Cardigan (1¼ hours); and the Puffin Shuttle (p155).
COACH // **National Express** (www.national express.com) destinations include Chepstow (£24, four

hours), Swansea (£8.50, 2½ hours), Carmarthen (£6.70, 1½ hours), Tenby (£4.40, 50 minutes) and Pembroke (£4.40, 30 minutes).

TRAIN // There are direct trains to Newport (£23, 2¾ hours), Cardiff (£20, 2½ hours), Swansea (£12, 1½ hours), Llanelli (£11.30, one hour) and Carmarthen (£7.10, 35 minutes).

DALE TO NEWGALE SANDS

♥ AROUND DALE // BEAUTIFUL BEACHES AND HEADLANDS IN QUICK SUCCESSION

The fishing village of **Dale** sits on a rugged and remote peninsula, forming the northern head of the Milford Haven waterway. As you round beautiful **St Ann's Head**, all vestiges of heavy industry and, indeed, human habitation disappear from view. Little **Westdale Bay** follows and then the impressive sweep of **Marloes Sands**, with views over **Gateholm Island** – a major Iron Age Celtic settlement where the remains of 130 hut circles have been found.

Around Wooltack Point is **Martin's Haven**, the tiny harbour that is the jumping-off point for boat trips to Skomer and Skokholm Islands. An unstaffed information room here has displays on the marine environment, including touch-screen displays of wildlife activity around Skomer. Look for a 7th-century **Celtic cross** set into the wall outside.

Further around the headland the cliffs change from red to black and **Musselwick Sands** comes in to view: a large, sandy beach with plenty of craggy inlets to explore.

The Puffin Shuttle stops at Dale, Marloes and Martin's Haven.

♥ SKOMER, SKOKHOLM & GRASSHOLM ISLANDS // WHERE THE WILD THINGS ARE

The rocky islands that lie in the turbulent, tide-ripped waters at the south end of St Brides Bay are one of the richest wildlife environments in Britain. In the nesting season, Skomer and Skokholm Islands are home to more than half a million sea birds, including guillemots, razorbills, puffins, storm petrels, and a significant colony of Manx shearwaters. These unusual birds nest in burrows and after a day spent feeding at sea return to their nests under the cover of darkness. Grey seals are also plentiful on Skomer, especially in the pupping season (September).

Skomer and Skokholm Islands are nature reserves run by the **Wildlife Trust of South and West Wales** (www.welshwildlife.org), while the surrounding waters are protected by a marine nature reserve. **Dale Sailing Company** (☎ 01646-603123; www.pembrokeshire-islands.co.uk; adult/child £10/7; ☼ 10am, 11am & noon Tue-Sun Apr-Oct) runs boats to Skomer on a first-come, first-served basis, departing from Martin's Haven. If you go ashore, there's an additional landing fee of £7 for adults (children under 16 are free).

Other cruises include one-hour round-the-island trips (adult/child £10/7) with commentary, and an evening

---

PUFFIN SHUTTLE

Between May and September walkers can make use of the Puffin Shuttle (315/400; fares less than £4), which crawls around the coast three times daily in each direction from Haverfordwest to St Davids. Stops include Milford Haven, Dale, Marloes, Martin's Haven, Little Haven, Broad Haven, Newgale Sands and Solva. For the rest of the year the route is split, with 315 heading from Haverfordwest to Marloes (no Sunday service) and 400 heading from St Davids to Marloes (Monday, Thursday and Saturday only).

PEMBROKESHIRE

cruise (£13/8) that offers the opportunity to see (and hear – the noise can be deafening) the huge flocks of Manx shearwaters returning to their nests. Some boats depart from Dale.

Eleven miles offshore, Grassholm Island has one of the largest gannet colonies in the northern hemisphere, with 39,000 breeding pairs. Grassholm is owned by the **Royal Society for the Protection of Birds** (RSPB; www.rspb.org.uk) and landing is not permitted, but Dale Sailing Company runs three-hour, round-the-island trips (£30) departing Martin's Haven at 1pm on Mondays from April to mid-August. Seals, porpoises and dolphins are often spotted en route; book ahead.

For avid birdwatchers, there is bunkhouse accommodation on Skomer (dorms/singles from £25/38); book well ahead through www.welshwildlife.org. The Puffin Shuttle heads to Martin's Haven (p155).

❧ LITTLE & BROAD HAVENS // CONJOINED BUCKET-AND-SPADE BEACHES

Tucked into the southern corner of St Brides Bay, these two bays are joined at low tide but separated by a rocky headland otherwise. Little Haven is the upmarket neighbour, with a tiny shingle beach and a village vibe formed by a cluster of pastel-painted holiday cottages and some nice pubs. The slipway is much used by local dive boats; the **West Wales Dive Centre** (☎ 01437-781457; www .westwalesdivers.co.uk) offers a one-day Discover Scuba Diving course (£125) and boat dives for certified divers (two dives for two people £160).

Nest Bistro (☎ 01437-781728; 12 Grove Pl; mains £14-19; ☽ dinner Thu-Sat, extended in summer) is an informal little restaurant that specialises in locally caught seafood,

including lobster, crab, sea bass, turbot and plaice.

The beach is both bigger and better at Broad Haven, backed by tearooms, gift shops, and places selling rubber rings, water wings and boogie boards. **Haven Sports** (☎ 01437-781354; www.havensports.co.uk; Marine Rd), at the south end of the prom behind the Galleon Inn, rents wetsuits (per day £15), body boards (£15), surfboards (£20) and kayaks (£30).

The Puffin Shuttle (p155) and the 311 to Haverfordwest (20 minutes) both stop here.

❧ NEWGALE SANDS // GROOMING GROUND FOR GROMMETS

As you pass over the bridge by the pub near the north end of Newgale, you're officially crossing the Landsker Line into North Pembrokeshire (see p284). Newgale is the biggest beach in St Brides Bay, stretching for 2.5 miles. It's one of the best beaches in South Wales for beginning surfers; you can hire surfboards (£4/13 per hour/day), body boards (£3/9) and wetsuits (£3.50/10) from **Newsurf Hire Centre** (☎ 01437-721398; www.newsurf .co.uk), which also offers surfing and kitesurfing lessons.

Both the Puffin Shuttle (p155) and bus 411 between Haverfordwest and St Davids stop here.

NORTH PEMBROKESHIRE
· · · · · ·

The Welsh language may not be as ubiquitous in North Pembrokeshire as it once was but there's no escaping the essential Welshness of the region. It's a land of Iron Age hill forts, holy wells and Celtic saints – including the nation's patron, Dewi Sant (St David). Predating even the ancient Celts are the remnants

of an older people, who left behind them dolmens and stone circles – the same people who may have transported their sacred bluestones all the way from the Preseli Hills to form the giant edifice at Stonehenge. Much of the coastline from St Davids onwards is inaccessible by car. If you're only going to walk part of the Pembrokeshire Coast Path (PCP), this is an excellent section to tackle.

ST DAVIDS (TYDDEWI)

☎ 01437 / pop 1800

Charismatic St Davids (yes, it has dropped the apostrophe from its name) is Britain's smallest 'city', its status ensured by the magnificent 12th-century cathedral that marks Wales' holiest site. The birth and burial place of the nation's patron saint, St Davids has been a place of pilgrimage for more than 1500 years.

The setting itself has a mystical presence. The sea is just beyond the horizon on three sides, so you're constantly surprised by glimpses of it at the ends of streets. Then there are those strangely shaped hills in the distance, which seem to sprout from a particularly ancient landscape.

Dewi Sant (St David; see p283) founded a monastic community here in the 6th century, only a short walk from where he was born at St Non's Bay. In 1124, Pope Callistus II declared that two pilgrimages to St Davids were the equivalent of one to Rome, and three were equal to one to Jerusalem. The cathedral has seen a constant stream of visitors ever since.

Today, St Davids attracts hordes of non-religious pilgrims too, drawn by the town's laid-back vibe and the excellent hiking, surfing and wildlife-watching in the surrounding area.

ESSENTIAL INFORMATION

TOURIST OFFICES // National park visitor centre & tourist office (☎ 720392; www .orielyparc.co.uk; High St; ⊗ 9.30am-5.30pm Easter-Oct, 10am-4.30pm Nov-Easter) See Oriel y Parc, p160. **National Trust Visitor Centre** (☎ 720385; High St; ⊗ 10am-5.30pm Mon-Sat, 10am-4pm Sun mid-Mar–Dec, 10am-4pm Mon-Sat Jan–mid-Mar) Sells local-interest books and guides to NT properties in Pembrokeshire.

EXPLORING ST DAVIDS

♥ ST DAVIDS CATHEDRAL //
MAGNIFICENT AND ANCIENT, YET
SURPRISINGLY RETIRING

Hidden in a hollow and behind high walls, **St Davids Cathedral** (www.stdavids cathedral.org.uk; suggested donation £4; ⊗ 8.30am-5.30pm Mon-Sat, 12.45-5.30pm Sun) is intentionally unassuming. The valley site was chosen in the vain hope that the church would be overlooked by Viking raiders, but it was ransacked at least seven times. Yet once you pass through the gatehouse separating it from the town and its stone walls come into view, it's as imposing as any of its contemporaries.

Built on the site of a 6th-century chapel, the building dates mainly from the 12th to the 14th centuries. Extensive works were carried out in the 19th century by Sir George Gilbert Scott (architect of the Albert Memorial and St Pancras in London) to stabilise the building and repair damage caused by an earthquake in 1248 and the sloping, boggy ground on which it sits. The distinctive **west front**, with its four pointed towers of purple stone, dates from this period.

The atmosphere inside is one of great antiquity. As you enter the **nave**, the oldest surviving part of the cathedral, the first things you notice are the sloping floor and the outward lean of the massive,

PEMBROKESHIRE

purplish-grey pillars linked by semicircular Norman Romanesque arches, a result of subsidence. Above is a richly carved 16th-century oak ceiling, adorned with pendants and bosses.

At the far end of the nave is a delicately carved 14th-century Gothic **pulpitum** (the screen wall between nave and choir), which bears a statue of St David dressed as a medieval bishop, and contains the tomb of Bishop Henry de Gower (died 1347), for whom the Bishop's Palace (p160) was built.

Beyond the pulpitum is the magnificent **choir**; check out the mischievous carved figures on the 16th-century mis-

PEMBROKESHIRE COAST PATH (PCP) CONTINUED

Picking up the PCP from Broad Haven, the first day's walk crosses the Landsker Line into North Pembrokeshire. See p148 for the southern section.

★ **Broad Haven to Solva** (four to 5½ hours, 11 miles) Don't be fooled by the distance: today's no easy stroll. There are several steep climbs, but thankfully the scenery remains superb. Ancient fortifications are even more evident today.

★ **Solva to Whitesands Bay** (five to seven hours, 13 miles) The spectacular coastline takes a spiritual turn as you follow in the footsteps of Wales' patron saint. From St Non's Bay, cut inland and follow the marked path through the fields to St Davids for lunch.

★ **Whitesands Bay to Trefin** (4½ to six hours, 12 miles) Wild St Davids Head offers a rugged new landscape at the beginning of a beautiful but taxing walk.

★ **Trefin to Pwll Deri** (3½ to 4½ hours, 10 miles) Today's walk is yet another wonderful experience, with cliffs, rock buttresses, pinnacles, islets, bays and beaches. It's tempered by a distinct paucity of eating and accommodation options.

★ **Pwll Deri to Fishguard** (3½ to 4½ hours, 10 miles) There's excellent cliff scenery and reasonably easy walking on this deserted section, but come prepared or you may be very hungry by the time you reach Goodwick.

★ **Fishguard to Newport** (five to six hours, 12.5 miles) Leaving Fishguard the trail heads through the picturesque Lower Town and then along the clifftops once again. It's possible to take a shortcut through the valley that almost divides Dinas Island from the mainland, but don't be tempted – you might spot seals and dolphins from the main trail. From Cwm-yr-Eglwys it's only 3 miles to the Parrog, the old port of Newport. Follow the PCP through a small wooded section; turn right at the fingerpost to the youth hostel and you'll hit the centre of Newport.

★ **Newport to St Dogmaels** (six to eight hours, 15.5 miles) We've saved the longest, steepest day till last – when those newly formed rocklike thighs and buns of steel can best handle it. Pack a lunch and head for the finish line, enjoying some of the best walking on the whole route. East of Newport Sands, the coast is wild and uninhabited, with numerous rock formations and caves. You may see Atlantic grey seals on the rocks nearby. Onwards from Ceibwr Bay is quite tough, but it's a wonderful roller-coaster finale, past sheer cliffs reaching a height of 175m – the highest of the trail. At Cemaes Head, stop and take stock. The end of the trail is nigh but aesthetically this headland is the finish. So, turning your back on the cliffs, follow the lane towards St Dogmaels.

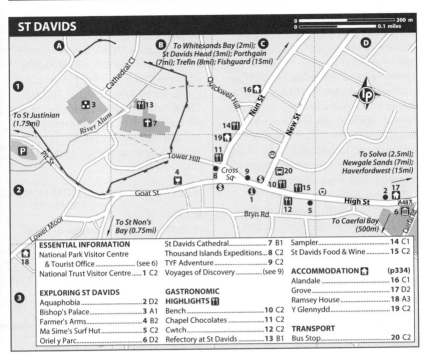

ericords (under the seats), one of which depicts pilgrims being seasick over the side of a boat. Don't forget to look up at the colourfully painted lantern tower above (those steel tie rods around the walls were installed in the 19th century to hold the structure together).

In a recess in the **Holy Trinity Chapel** at the east end of the cathedral is the object of all those religious pilgrimages: a simple oak casket that contains the bones of St David and St Justinian. The chapel ceiling is distinguished by superb fan vaulting dating from the early 16th century.

Accessed from the north wall of the nave the **Treasury** (admission free) displays vestments and religious paraphernalia crafted from precious metals and stones. Just as valuable are the treasures in the neighbouring **Library** (admission £1; ☺ 2-4pm Mon), the oldest of which dates to 1505.

Lord Rhys ap Gruffydd, the greatest of the princes of South Wales, and his son Rhys Gryg are known to be buried in the cathedral, although their effigies in the south choir aisle date only from the 14th century. Gerald of Wales, an early rector of the cathedral, has a gravestone here, but scholars suggest he is actually buried at Lincolnshire Cathedral.

In August there are hour-long **guided tours** (☎ 720204; suggested donation £5) at 11.30am Monday and 2.30pm Friday; at other times, tours can be arranged in advance.

The **St Davids Cathedral Festival** is 10 days of classical-music performances, starting on the Spring Bank Holiday weekend at the end of May. Many other concerts are performed at the cathedral throughout the year.

PEMBROKESHIRE

❦ BISHOP'S PALACE // THE MEDIEVAL CHURCH'S WEALTH AND POWER ON DISPLAY

Across the river from the cathedral, this atmospheric ruined **palace** (☎ 720517; www .cadw.wales.gov.uk; adult/child £3/2.60; ⏲ 9am-5pm daily Apr-Oct, 9.30am-4pm Mon-Sat, 11am-4pm Sun Nov-Mar), run by Cadw (the Welsh historic monuments agency), was begun at the same time as the cathedral, but its final, imposing form owes most to Henry de Gower, bishop from 1327 to 1347.

Its most distinctive feature is the arcaded parapet that runs around the courtyard, decorated with a chequerboard pattern of purple and yellow stone blocks. The corbels that support the arches are richly adorned with a menagerie of carved figures – lions, monkeys, dogs and birds, as well as grotesque mythical creatures and human heads. The distinctive purple sandstone, also used in the cathedral, comes from Caerbwdy Bay, a mile southeast of St Davids.

The palace courtyard provides a spectacular setting for open-air plays in summer.

❦ ORIEL Y PARC // ENJOY THE SCENERY, EVEN ON A RAINY DAY

Occupying a bold, semicircular, environmentally friendly building on the edge of town, **Oriel y Parc** (Landscape Gallery; ☎ 720392; www.orielyparc.co.uk; admission free; High St; ⏲ 9.30am-5.30pm Easter-Oct, 10am-4.30pm Nov-Easter) is a winning collaboration between the Pembrokeshire Coast National Park Authority and the National Museum Wales. Not only does it function as a tourist office and national park visitor centre, it houses changing exhibitions from the museum's art collection. The focus is on landscapes, particularly Pembrokeshire scenes.

❦ FARMER'S ARMS // A VILLAGE PUB IN THE 'CITY'

Even though St Davids is a bit of a tourist trap, you'd be hard-pressed finding a more authentic country pub than the **Farmer's Arms** (☎ 721666; 14 Goat St). There's real ale and Guinness on tap and it's the place to be when the rugby's playing. The beer garden out back is a pleasant place to watch the sun go down on a summer's evening.

GASTRONOMIC HIGHLIGHTS

❦ CWTCH £££

☎ 720491; www.cwtchrestaurant.co.uk; 22 High St; 3-course dinner £29; ⏲ dinner Wed-Sun, daily summer

Stone walls and wooden beams mark this out as a sense-of-occasion place, yet there's a snugness that lives up to its name (*cwtch* means 'a cosy place' or 'a cuddle'). There's an emphasis on local produce, so expect plenty of fresh seafood on the menu.

❦ REFECTORY AT ST DAVIDS £

☎ 721760; St Davids Cathedral; mains £5-9; ⏲ 10am-5pm; 🖨

Part of the ongoing restoration of the cathedral cloister, the new refectory may not be the cheapest place to eat (simple sandwiches cost £5.75) but it's a triumph of design. Medieval St Mary's Hall has been given an ultramodern facelift, with blonde wood contrasting with the exposed stone walls and a shiny mezzanine supported on slanted legs. Take a seat upstairs for better views. On Sundays there's a traditional carvery.

❦ SAMPLER £

☎ 720757; 17 Nun St; mains $5-6; ⏲ 10am-5.30pm Mon-Thu, extended in summer

Named after the embroidery samples blanketing the walls, this may be the perfect exemplar of the traditional Welsh tearoom. Pembrokeshire Clotted Cream Tea comes served with freshly baked scones and *bara brith* (a rich, fruit tea-loaf), and there are Welsh cheese platters, jacket potatoes, soups and sandwiches.

Also recommended:

Bench (☎ 721778; www.bench-bar.co.uk: 11 High St; mains £5-17; 9am-late;) A bustling rabbit warren of a bar-bistro with a strong Mediterranean motif, the Bench serves up all-day snacks and lip-smacking ice creams. Internet access costs £3 per hour.

Chapel Chocolates (☎ 720528; www.chapel chocolates.com; The Pebbles) Dieters beware – the shelves in this shop are stacked floor to ceiling with more than 100 varieties of handmade Welsh chocolates, truffles and other confectionery.

St Davids Food & Wine (☎ 721948; High St; 8.30am-5pm Mon-Sat) Stock up on picnic supplies at this delicatessen, which specialises in local organic produce.

TRANSPORT

BIKE // The Celtic Way cycling route passes through St Davids. There's pleasant cycling on minor roads around the peninsula but no off-road action (the coast path is for walkers only).

BUS // Routes include the 411 to Solva (nine minutes), Newgale Sands (20 minutes) and Haverfordwest (40 minutes) and the 413 to Trefin (20 minutes), Goodwick (45 minutes) and Fishguard (50 minutes). The **Strumble Shuttle** (404; Tue, Thu & Sat Oct-Apr, daily May-Sep) follows the coast between St Davids and Fishguard, calling at Porthgain, Trefin, Strumble Head and Goodwick. The **Celtic Coaster** (403; return/day ticket £1/2; Apr-Sep) circles between St Davids, St Non's Bay, St Justinian and Whitesands Bay. See also the Puffin Shuttle (p155). The main bus stops are in New St and the Oriel y Parc car park.

PARKING // The main car park is next to Oriel y Parc and there's a smaller one just off Nun St on Quickwell Hill; both cost 60p/£3 per hour/day.

TAXI // **Tony's Taxis** (☎ 720931; www.tonystax is.net) provides a luggage transfer service for PCP walkers, covering the area from Little Haven to Fishguard.

AROUND ST DAVIDS

❧ **LOWER SOLVA //** **GENTEEL VILLAGE ON A PICTURESQUE INLET**
Lower Solva sits at the head of a peculiar L-shaped harbour, where the water drains away completely at low tide leaving its flotilla of yachts tilted onto the sand. Its single street is lined with brightly painted, flower-laden cottages housing little galleries, pubs and tearooms.

If sailing takes your fancy, you can enjoy a three-hour/full-day cruise aboard a 24ft yacht for £70/120 (up to three passengers) with **Solva Sailboats** (☎ 01437-720972; www.solva.net/solvasailboats; 1 Maes-y-Forwen). It also rents sailing dinghies (£22 per hour) and runs official Royal Yachting Association sailing courses.

The **Old Pharmacy** (☎ 01437-720005; 5 Main St; mains £13-19; 5.30-10pm) is the village's gastronomic highlight, with a cosy cottage atmosphere, outdoor tables in a riverside garden, and a bistro-style menu that includes Solva lobster (£25 for half) and crab, Pembrokeshire rabbit and Welsh black beef.

Both the Puffin Shuttle (p155) and bus 411 between Haverfordwest and St Davids stop here.

❧ **ST NON'S BAY //** **A MAGICAL LOCATION FOR A SAINTLY BIRTH**
Immediately south of St Davids is this ruggedly beautiful spot, named after St David's mother and traditionally accepted as his birthplace (see p283). A path leads down to the 13th-century ruins of **St Non's Chapel**. Only the base of the walls remains, along with a stone marked with a cross within a circle, believed to date from the 7th century. Standing stones in the surrounding field suggest that the chapel may have been built within an ancient pagan stone circle.

PEMBROKESHIRE

On the approach to the chapel is a pretty little **holy well**. The sacred spring is said to have emerged at the moment of the saint's birth and the water is believed to have curative powers. Although pilgrimages were officially banned following the suppression of Catholicism in the 16th century, people continued to make furtive visits.

The site has now come full circle. In 1935 a local Catholic, Cecil Morgan-Griffiths, built the **Chapel of Our Lady and St Non** out of the stones of ruined religious buildings that once stood nearby. Its dimensions echo those of the original chapel. The Catholic Church repaired the stone vaulting over the well in 1951, and Morgan-Griffith's house is now used by the Passionist Fathers as a retreat centre.

❦ RAMSEY ISLAND // A SITE FOR NATURE PILGRIMS

Ramsey Island lies off the headland to the west of St Davids, ringed by dramatic sea cliffs and an offshore armada of rocky islets and reefs. The island is an RSPB reserve famous for its large breeding population of choughs – members of the crow family, with glossy black feathers and distinctive red bills and legs – and for its grey seals. If you're here between late August and mid-November, you will also see seal pups.

You can reach the island by boat from the tiny harbour at St Justinian, 2 miles west of St Davids. Longer boat trips run up to 20 miles offshore, to the edge of the Celtic Deep, to spot whales, porpoises and dolphins. What you'll see depends on the weather and the time of year; July to September are the best months. Porpoises are seen on most trips, dolphins on four out of five, and there's a 40% chance of seeing whales. The most

common species is the minke, but pilot whales, fin whales and orcas have also been spotted.

Thousand Islands Expeditions (Map p159; ☎ 01437-721721; www.ramseyisland.com; Cross Sq, St Davids) is the only operator permitted by RSPB to land day-trippers on the island (adult/child £15/7.50); bookings advised. It has a range of other boat trips, including hour-long blasts in a high-speed inflatable boat (£24/12), 2½-hour whale- and dolphin-spotting cruises around Grassholm Island (£55/30), and one-hour jet-boat trips (£24/12).

Voyages of Discovery (Map p159; ☎ 01437-721911; www.ramseyisland.co.uk; 1 High St, St Davids) and **Aquaphobia** (Map p159; ☎ 01437-720471; www.aquaphobia-ramseyisland .co.uk; Grove Hotel, High St, St Davids) offer a similar selection of cruises.

The Celtic Coaster (p161) heads to St Justinian from St Davids.

❦ WHITESANDS BAY // A WONDERFUL BEACH AT ST DAVIDS' DOORSTEP

The mile-long strand of Whitesands Bay (Porth Mawr) is another popular surfing spot. At extremely low tide you can see the wreck of a paddle tugboat that went aground here in 1882, and the fossil remains of a prehistoric forest. If Whitesands is really busy – and it often is – you can escape the worst of the crowds by walking north along the coastal path for 10 to 15 minutes to the smaller, more secluded beach at **Porthmelgan**.

Whitesands Surf School (www.white sandssurfschool.co.uk) runs surfing lessons; a 2½-hour beginner's session costs £30, including equipment. You can book at **Ma Sime's Surf Hut** (Map p159; ☎ 01437-720433; www.masimes.co.uk; 28 High St) in St Davids; it also rents wetsuits, surfboards and body boards.

PEMBROKESHIRE

ST DAVIDS WALKING TOUR

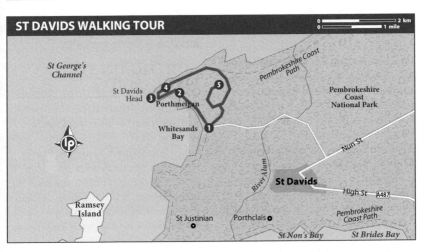

WALKING TOUR

Distance: 4 miles
Duration: two hours
Start the walk at **Whitesands Bay (1)** and follow the coast path to **Porthmelgan (2)** and then on to **St Davids Head (3)**. Keep an eye out for the remains of an Iron Age fort and the **Coetan Arthur burial chamber (4)**. Continue around the headland and then turn right at the path heading around and then up **Carn Llidi (5)**. Backtrack slightly before returning on the road through Porthmawr Farm.

Expect to pay about £2 for parking, more in summer. The Celtic Coaster (p161) heads here from St Davids.

♥ ST DAVIDS HEAD // PLACE OF THE ANCIENTS

This atmospheric heather-wreathed promontory was fortified by the ancient Celts. The jumbled stones and ditch of an Iron Age rampart are still visible, as are rock circles, which once formed the foundations of huts. The tip of the headland is a series of rock and turf ledges, a great place for a picnic or wildlife-spotting – in summer you can see gannets diving into the sea and choughs soaring on the breeze. Adding to the ancient ambience, wild ponies can often be spotted.

Further along the grassy path through the heather, an even older structure stands. The simple burial chamber known as **Coetan Arthur** (Arthur's Quoit) consists of a capstone supported by a rock at one end and dates to about 3500 BC.

The rocky summit of **Carn Llidi** (181m) rises behind, offering panoramic views that take in Whitesands Bay, Ramsey and Skomer Islands and, on a clear day, the coast of Ireland on the horizon.

COASTEERING

If you fancy a spot of rock climbing, gully scrambling, cave exploration, wave riding and cliff jumping, all rolled together, then try coasteering. More or less conceived on the Pembrokeshire coast, this demanding activity is the mainstay of the local adventure-sports scene. It's also risky, so take guidance from an instructor and don't be tempted to take flight from the nearest precipice.

PEMBROKESHIRE

PORTHGAIN

☎ 01348

For centuries the tiny harbour of Porthgain consisted of little more than a few sturdy cottages wedged into a rocky cove. In the mid-19th century it began to prosper as the port for shipping out slate quarried just down the coast at Abereiddy, and by the 1870s its own deposits of granite and fine clay had put it on the map as a source of building stone. The post-WWI slump burst the bubble, and the sturdy stone quays and overgrown brick storage 'bins' are all that remain.

Despite having been an industrial harbour, Porthgain is surprisingly picturesque and today it is home to a couple of art galleries and restaurants.

GASTRONOMIC HIGHLIGHTS

♥ SHED ££

☎ 831518; www.theshedporthgain.co.uk; lunch £9-17, dinner £19-26; ⏱ lunch Fri-Sun, dinner Mon, Fri & Sat, lunch & dinner daily summer

Housed in a beautifully converted machine shop right by the little harbour, the Shed has grown into one of Pembrokeshire's finest seafood restaurants; the menu lists Porthgain crab and lobster, and locally caught sea bass, gurnard, mullet and squid.

♥ SLOOP INN ££

☎ 831449; www.sloop.co.uk; mains £10-17

With wooden tables worn smooth by many a bended elbow, old photos of Porthgain in its industrial heyday, and interesting nautical clutter all over the place, the Sloop is a cosy and deservedly popular pub. It dishes up breakfast (to 11am) and hearty, home-cooked meals to hungry walkers.

TRANSPORT

BUS // See the Strumble Shuttle, p161.

PORTHGAIN TO FISHGUARD

♥ CARREG SAMPSON // PREHISTORIC BURIAL CHAMBER WITH A VIEW

Sitting in a farmer's field, with terrific views of Strumble Head, this dolmen is quite remarkable. The massive capstone seems to be only just touching the stones that it is balanced on. It's signposted off the minor road between Trefin and Abercastle.

♥ PWLL DERI // TINY ROADS OFFER PRECIPITOUS CLIFFTOP VIEWS

The approach to the little cove of Pwll Deri follows cliffs that reach 137m in height and offer expansive views over the sometimes turbulent Irish Sea. The cove is a good place for seal-watching. The rocky summit of **Garn Fawr** (213m), topped by an Iron Age fort, rises above Pwll Deri.

TOP FIVE

DOLMENS, STANDING STONES & STONE CIRCLES

For those with a yen for mystery and mysticism, Wales' ancient shaped stones offer plenty to ponder.

* ★ Tinkinswood & St Lythan's Burial Chambers (p62)
* ★ Arthur's Stone (p126)
* ★ Carreg Sampson (p164)
* ★ Pentre Ifan (p170)
* ★ Ysbyty Cynfyn (p187)

❦ STRUMBLE HEAD // TRAFFIC LIGHTS FOR A SEAL, DOLPHIN AND FERRY HIGHWAY

At wild and rocky Strumble Head, the nearest point to Ireland, a lighthouse beams out its signal of four flashes every 15 seconds as the huge, high-speed ferries thunder past on their way from Fishguard to Rosslare. The headland makes a good vantage point for spotting dolphins, seals, sharks and sunfish; below the parking area is a WWII lookout that now serves as a shelter for observing wildlife.

For public transport, see the Strumble Shuttle, p161.

❦ LLANWNDA // CELTIC CARVINGS FROM THE AGE OF SAINTS

The tiny village of Llanwnda has at its heart St Gwyndaf's Church. Its antiquity is highlighted by the carved stones, inscribed with crosses and Celtic designs, set into the outside walls. Inside, look up at the timber roof beams; at the far end of the third beam from the west (door) end, facing the altar, is a 15th-century carving of a tonsured monk's head.

Across the lane from the church, a wooden gate with a yellow waymark indicates the start of the mile-long track to **Carregwastad Point**, the site of the infamous 1797 invasion (see p166).

FISHGUARD (ABERGWAUN)

☎ 01348 / pop 3200

Perched on a headland between its modern ferry port and former fishing harbour, Fishguard is often overlooked by travellers, most of them passing through on their way to or from Ireland. It doesn't have any sights as such, but it's an appealing little town with some good eating and drinking options.

The Lower Town (Y Cwm), next to the old fishing harbour, was used as a setting for the 1971 film version of *Under Milk Wood* with Richard Burton, Peter O'Toole and Elizabeth Taylor. It also featured (for all of two minutes) in the classic *Moby Dick,* starring Gregory Peck.

Around the other side of the headland, Goodwick (Wdig; pronounced oo-dick) was the site of the 1078 battle between northern and southern Celtic lords (as if they didn't have enough to worry about from the encroaching Normans), culminating in a bloody massacre of the southerners. Fishguard also has the quirky distinction of being the setting for the last foreign invasion of Britain (see p166).

The Marine Walk, which follows the coast from the car park on the Parrog around to the Lower Town, offers great views over the old harbour and along the coast to Dinas Head.

ESSENTIAL INFORMATION

TOURIST OFFICES // Fishguard (☎ 01437-776636; Town Hall, Market Sq; ⏰ 9.30am-5pm Mon-Fri, 9.30am-4pm Sat Easter-Sep, 10am-4pm Mon-Sat Oct-Easter; 🖳) Goodwick (☎ 874737; Ocean Lab; ⏰ 9.30am-5pm Easter-Oct, 10am-4pm Nov-Easter; 🖳) Houses an exhibition on marine life and the environment aimed mainly at kids.

ORIENTATION

Fishguard is split into three distinct areas. The main town sits on top of a raised headland west of the river mouth, and is centred on Market Sq, where the buses stop; to the east is the picturesque harbour of the Lower Town. The train station and ferry terminal lie a mile to the northwest of the town centre in Goodwick.

THE LAST INVASION OF BRITAIN

While Hastings in 1066 may get all the press, the last invasion of Britain was actually at Carregwastad Point, northwest of Fishguard, on 22 February 1797. The ragtag collection of 1400 French mercenaries and bailed convicts, led by an Irish-American named Colonel Tate, had intended to land at Bristol and march to Liverpool, keeping English troops occupied while France mounted an invasion of Ireland. But bad weather blew them ashore at Carregwastad where, after scrambling up a steep cliff, they set about looting the Pencaer peninsula for food and drink.

The invaders had hoped that the Welsh peasants would rise up to join them in revolutionary fervour but, not surprisingly, their drunken pillaging didn't endear them to the locals. The French were quickly seen off by volunteer 'yeoman' soldiers, with help from the people of Fishguard including, most famously, one Jemima Nicholas who single-handedly captured 12 mercenaries armed with nothing more than a pitchfork.

The beleaguered Tate surrendered and a mere two days after their arrival the invaders laid down their weapons at Goodwick and were sent off to the jail at Haverfordwest.

EXPLORING FISHGUARD

❦ FISHGUARD TOWN HALL // MARKETS AND FANCY STITCHING

Much that goes on in Fishguard happens in this central building on Market Sq. The tourist office is here, as is the library (handy for free internet access) and the **market hall**. It hosts a country market on Tuesday, a town market on Thursday and a farmers market on Saturday.

Upstairs is the **Last Invasion Gallery** (☎ 776122; admission free; ☼ 9.30am-5pm Mon-Sat Apr-Sep, until 1pm Sat Oct-Mar), which displays the Fishguard Tapestry. Inspired by the Bayeux Tapestry, which recorded the 1066 Norman invasion at Hastings, it was commissioned in 1997 to commemorate the bicentenary of the failed Fishguard invasion. It uses a similar cartoonish style as Bayeux' (albeit with less rude bits) and tells the story in the course of 37 frames and 30m of cloth. A film about its making demonstrates what a huge undertaking it was.

❦ WATER SPORTS // KEEP THOSE FISH EN GARDE

Celtic Diving (☎ 871938; www.celticdiving .co.uk; The Parrog, Goodwick) runs half-day scuba-diving taster sessions in its own practise pool (£65), as well as PADI-certificated diving courses. Dive sites include several wrecks.

Mike Mayberry Kayaking (☎ 874699; www.mikemayberrykayaking.co.uk) offers instruction courses (one-/two-day £87/147) and guided kayaking tours for more experienced paddlers.

❦ ROYAL OAK INN // HISTORY, GOOD GRUB AND LIVE MUSIC

Suffused with character, this old **inn** (☎ 872514; Market Sq; mains £5-15) was the site of the French surrender in 1797 and the table on which it was signed takes pride of place at the back of the dining room. The pub has turned into something of an invasion museum, filled with memorabilia. Not only does the Royal Oak have an important place in Fishguard's history, it also serves the best pub food in town and hosts a popular live folk night on Tuesdays, when musicians are welcome to join in.

☙ BAR FIVE // A BUZZY BAR-BISTRO WITH HARBOUR VIEWS

For a completely different ambience, **Bar Five** (☎ 875050; www.barfive.com; 5 Main St; mains £13-16; 🕑 lunch Fri & Sun, dinner Thu-Sun, extended in summer) is a hip, upmarket bar and restaurant in a cleverly renovated Georgian town house with a terrace overlooking the harbour. The bistro menu focuses on fresh local produce, especially crab and lobster hauled in from the restaurant's own boat.

☙ SHIP INN // A TIMELESS TASTE OF LOWER FISHGUARD

This is a lovely little **pub** (☎ 874033; Old Newport Rd, Lower Town) with an open fire in winter and lots of memorabilia on the walls, including photos of Richard Burton filming *Under Milk Wood* outside

(the street and nearby quay have not changed a bit).

TRANSPORT

BOAT // Stena Line (☎ 08447 70 70 70; www.stenaline.co.uk) has two regular ferries a day, year-round (car and driver from £69, additional adult/child £23/13; foot passenger £25; bike £5), and a 'Fastcraft' most days in July and August (car and driver from £94; other fares the same), between Rosslare in the southeast of Ireland and Fishguard Harbour.

BUS // Buses include the 412 to Haverfordwest (37 minutes), Dinas Cross (13 minutes), Newport (19 minutes), Castell Henllys (28 minutes) and Cardigan (41 minutes), and the 413 to Goodwick (two minutes), Trefin (18 minutes) and St Davids (50 minutes). See also the Strumble Shuttle (p161), Poppit Rocket (p170) and Green Dragon Bus (p171).

TRAIN // There's a daily direct train to Fishguard Harbour from Cardiff (£20, 2¼ hours) via Llanelli (£12, 1¼ hours) and Carmarthen (£7.10, 49 minutes). On Sunday there's a slower service via Swansea (£11.60, two hours).

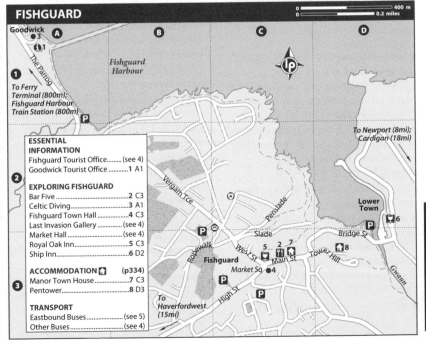

FISHGUARD

PEMBROKESHIRE

FISHGUARD TO NEWPORT

❧ CWM GWAUN // THE VALLEY THAT TIME FORGOT

Running inland to the southeast of Fishguard is **Cwm Gwaun** (pronounced coom gwine), the valley of the River Gwaun. This narrow, wooded cleft, best explored on foot or bicycle, feels strangely remote and mysterious. Famously, the inhabitants retain a soft spot for the Julian calendar (abandoned by the rest of Britain in 1752), which means that they celebrate New Year on 13 January.

Stop for a pint at the **Dyffryn Arms** (☎ 01348-881305; Pontfaen), better known as Bessie's, a rare old-fashioned pub in the front room of the octogenarian land-lady's house. Beer is served from jugs filled straight from the barrel; no hand pumps here!

The Green Dragon Bus has seasonal services through the valley from Fishguard to the Preseli Hills (see p170).

❧ DINAS ISLAND // A FAUX ISLAND WITH REAL SEALS

The great wedge-shaped profile of Dinas Island juts out from the coast between Fishguard and Newport. It's not really an island as it's attached to the mainland by a neck of land, framed on either side by picturesque coves – the sandy strand of **Pwllgwaelod** to the west, and the rocky inlet of **Cwm-yr-Eglwys** to the east, where you can see the ruin of 12th-century St Brynach's Church, destroyed by the great storm of 1859.

The circuit of the headland (3 miles) makes an excellent walk, with the chance of spotting seals and dolphins from the 142m-high cliffs at Dinas Head, the northernmost point; a path across the neck between Pwllgwaelod and Cwm-yr-Eglwys allows you to return to your starting point.

Bus 412 (Haverfordwest–Fishguard–Cardigan) stops at Dinas Cross, just over a mile from Pwllgwaelod. See also the Poppit Rocket (p170).

NEWPORT (TREFDRAETH)

☎ 01239 / pop 1120

In stark contrast to the industrial city of Newport in Gwent, the Pembrokeshire Newport is a pretty cluster of flower-bedecked cottages huddled beneath a small Norman castle. It sits at the foot of Mynydd Carningli, a large bump on the seaward side of the Preseli Hills, and in recent years has gained a reputation for the quality of its restaurants and guesthouses.

Newport makes a pleasant base for walks along the coastal path or south into the Preseli Hills, but it does get crowded in summer. At the northwest corner of the town is little Parrog Beach, dwarfed by Newport Sands (Traeth Mawr) across the river.

Newport Castle (now a private residence) was founded by a Norman nobleman called William FitzMartin – who was married to a daughter of Lord Rhys ap Gruffydd – after his father-in-law drove him out of nearby Nevern in 1191. Newport grew up around the castle, initially as a garrison town.

ESSENTIAL INFORMATION

TOURIST OFFICES // National park information centre & tourist office (☎ 820912; Long St; ☺ 10am-6pm Mon-Sat Easter-Oct, 10.30am-3pm Mon & Fri, 10.30am-1pm Tue-Thu & Sat Nov-Easter)

EXPLORING NEWPORT

♥ CARREG COETAN // NEOLITHIC BURIAL CHAMBER IN PERFECT BALANCE

There's a little dolmen right in town, well signposted from the main road just past the Golden Lion. At first glance it looks like the capstone is securely supported by the four standing stones. A closer inspection suggests that some old magic has held it together all these thousands of years, as it's balanced on only two of them.

♥ NEVERN ESTUARY // SPOTTING BIRDS BY THE BEACH

If you keep walking past Carreg Coetan, you come to an iron bridge over the **Nevern Estuary**, a haven for birdlife, especially in winter. Cross the bridge and turn left for an easy walk along the shoreline to the sandy beach of **Newport Sands**.

♥ MYNYDD CARNINGLI // THE MOUNT OF ANGELS

It's said that in the 6th century St Brynach of Nevern used to head up Mynydd Carningli (347m) to commune with angels, which is the likely derivation of the name. You can climb to the summit from town (a 3.5-mile round trip) via Market St then Church St, keeping the castle on your right. At a fork in the lane called College Sq, go right (uphill), following narrow tracks past a couple of farms and houses to reach a gate leading onto the open hillside. Work your way up on grassy paths to the summit, the site of an Iron Age hill fort, with great views of Newport Bay and Dinas Head. On a fine day you might spot Ireland.

GASTRONOMIC HIGHLIGHTS

♥ CANTEEN £

☎ 820131; www.thecanteen.org; Market St; lunch £4-9, dinner £10-14; ☺ lunch Mon-Sat, dinner Fri & Sat

The name, reasonable prices and stark decor suggest a no-nonsense approach, echoed by a menu focusing on crowd-pleasers such as fish and chips, chicken Caesar salad and mushrooms on toast. Yet there's no skimping on quality. A good selection of wine is offered by the glass and meals are kicked off with complimentary bread and olive oil.

♥ CNAPAN £££

☎ 820575; East St; 2-/3-course dinner £24/30; ☺ Wed-Mon

The somewhat formal dining room offers candlelight and crisp white linen table-cloths, but the service is friendly and relaxed. Local seafood (Penclawdd mussels and the fresh catch of the day) features on the set menu, alongside Welsh black beef and a tempting array of desserts.

♥ LLYS MEDDYG £££

☎ 820008; www.llysmeddyg.com; East St; mains £17-34

From the slate floor and leather armchairs in the bar to the modern art in the elegant dining room, this place oozes style. The food is superb – the seasonal menu reflects the best of local produce, combined with an international palate of flavours.

Also recommended:

Golden Lion Hotel (☎ 820321; www.goldenlionpembrokeshire.co.uk; East St; mains £10-20; ℗ ☎) Good pub grub in a cosy environment.

Wholefoods of Newport (☎ 820773; www.wholefoodsofnewport.co.uk; East St) Stock up on planet-friendly provisions.

PEMBROKESHIRE

TRANSPORT

BIKE // The back roads around the Preseli Hills and Cwm Gwaun offer some of the best on-road cycling in southwest Wales. You can rent a bike from **Newport Bike Hire** (☎ 820773; www.newportbikehire.com; East St; per half-/full day £10/15), based in Wholefoods of Newport. It also stocks cycling guides and books on outdoor pursuits.

BUS // Buses include the 412 to Haverfordwest (52 minutes), Dinas Cross (six minutes), Fishguard (19 minutes), Castell Henllys (nine minutes) and Cardigan (26 minutes), and the Poppit Rocket.

NEWPORT TO CARDIGAN

❦ NEVERN (NANHYFER) // CARVED CELTIC STONES AND A BLEEDING TREE

With its overgrown castle and atmospheric church, this little village 2 miles east of Newport makes a good objective for an easy walk. You approach the **Church of St Brynach** along a supremely gloomy alley of yew trees, estimated to be six to seven centuries old; second on the right as you enter is the so-called **bleeding yew,** named after the curious reddish-brown sap that oozes from it. The beautifully melancholy churchyard dates from around the 6th century, predating the church.

Among the gravestones is a tall **Celtic cross,** one of the finest in Wales, decorated with interlace patterns and dating from the 10th or 11th century. According to tradition, the first cuckoo that sings each year in Pembrokeshire does so from atop this cross on St Brynach's Day (7 April).

Inside the church, the **Maglocunus Stone,** thought to date from the 5th century, forms a windowsill in the south transept. It is one of the few carved stones that bears an inscription in both

---

POPPIT ROCKET

Between May and September, the Poppit Rocket (405) heads three times daily in each direction from Fishguard to Cardigan. Stops include Pwllgwaelod, Newport, Moylgrove, Poppit Sands and St Dogmaels. For the rest of the year it only covers the stops between Newport and Cardigan (Monday, Thursday and Saturday only).

Latin and ogham, and was instrumental in deciphering the meaning of ogham, an ancient Celtic script.

❦ PENTRE IFAN // THE MOTHER OF ALL DOLMENS

The largest dolmen in Wales, Pentre Ifan is a 4500-year-old Neolithic burial chamber set on a remote hillside with superb views across the Preseli Hills and out to sea. The huge, 5m-long capstone, weighing more than 16 tonnes, is delicately poised on three tall, pointed, upright stones, made of the same bluestone that was used for the menhirs at Stonehenge.

The site is about 3 miles southeast of Newport, on a minor road south of the A487; it's signposted.

❦ PRESELI HILLS // A SETTING AS MYSTERIOUS AS STONEHENGE ITSELF

The only upland area in the Pembrokeshire Coast National Park is the Preseli Hills (Mynydd Preseli), rising to 536m at Foel Cwmcerwyn. These hills are at the centre of a fascinating prehistoric landscape, scattered with hill forts, standing stones and burial chambers, and are famous as the source of the mysterious bluestones of Stonehenge.

An ancient track called the **Golden Road,** once part of a 5000-year-old trade route between Wessex and Ireland, runs along the crest of the hills, passing

MYSTERY OF THE BLUESTONES

There are 31 bluestone monoliths (plus 12 'stumps') at the centre of Stonehenge, each weighing around four tonnes. Geochemical analysis shows that the Stonehenge bluestones originated from outcrops around Carnmenyn and Carn Goedog at the eastern end of the Preseli Hills (Mynydd Preseli). Stonehenge scholars have long been of the opinion that Preseli and the bluestones held some religious significance for the builders of Stonehenge, and that they laboriously dragged these monoliths down to the River Cleddau, then carried them by barge from Milford Haven, along the Bristol Channel and up the River Avon, then overland again to Salisbury Plain – a distance of 240 miles.

In 2000 a group of volunteers tried to re-enact this journey, using primitive technology to transport a single, three-tonne bluestone from Preseli to Stonehenge. They failed – having already resorted to the use of a lorry, a crane and modern roads, the stone slipped from its raft and sank just a few miles into the sea journey.

An alternative theory is that the bluestones were actually transported by Ice Age glaciers, and dumped around 40 miles to the west of the Stonehenge site some 12,000 years ago.

prehistoric cairns and the stone circle of **Bedd Arthur**.

The 430 bus from Cardigan heads to Crymych (30 minutes; no service Sunday), at the eastern end of hills. From here you can hike along the Golden Road to the car park at Bwlch Gwynt on the B4329 (7.5 miles). You can return to Crymych (34 minutes) or continue through the Gwaun Valley to Fishguard (50 minutes) on the 15-seater **Green Dragon Bus** (☎ 0845 686 0242; www.green dragonbus.co.uk; membership £5; Tue, Thu & Sat Jul-Sep). It's a members-only service; pay £5 on top of your fare to the driver the first time you use it.

 CASTELL HENLLYS // SEE, TOUCH AND SMELL IRON AGE LIVING
From about 600 BC and right through the Roman occupation there was a thriving Celtic settlement at what's now called Castell Henllys (Castle of the Prince's Court). Students from the University of York archaeology department have been digging and sifting at the site every summer since 1981, and

have learned enough to build a remarkable re-creation of the settlement on its original foundations, complete with educated guesses about the clothing, tools, ceremonies and agricultural life of that time.

A visit to **Castell Henllys Iron Age Fort** (☎ 01239-891319; www.castellhenllys.com; Felindre Farchog; adult/child £4/3; 10am-5pm Easter-Oct, 11am-3pm Nov-Easter) is like travelling back in time. There are reconstructions of the settlement's buildings – four thatched roundhouses, animal pens, a smithy and a grain store – which you can enter and touch. Costumed staff, craft demonstrations, Celtic festivals and other events bring the settlement to life. There are even Iron Age breeds of cattle and reconstructions of Celtic gardens.

Castell Henllys is 4 miles east of Newport. Bus 412 from Cardigan (15 minutes) to Haverfordwest (1¼ hours), via Newport (nine minutes) and Fishguard (25 minutes), stops at Castell Henllys junction hourly.

PEMBROKESHIRE

❦ CEIBWR BAY // HANG OUT WITH THE SEALS

Most of the 15 miles of coast between Newport and Cardigan is accessible only on foot. The one spot where a car or bike can get close is at the scenic, seal-haunted inlet of **Ceibwr Bay**, near the tiny hamlet of Moylgrove, reached via a maze of very narrow roads. A grassy platform near the road end, carpeted with sea pinks in summer, makes a great picnic spot.

The coastal scenery here is spectacular, with contorted cliffs to the north and a couple of sea stacks to the south. A half-mile walk south along the coast path leads to the **Witches' Cauldron**, a large cliff-ringed, sea-filled hole caused by a cavern collapse.

The Poppit Rocket (p170) stops at Moylgrove.

❦ ST DOGMAELS // STOCK UP ON PRODUCE AND PRACTISE YOUR OGHAM

Just across the River Teifi from Cardigan, this large village marks the end of the Pembrokeshire Coast Path. From as early as the 5th or 6th century there was a Celtic monastic community here, which the Normans replaced with French Tironian monks in 1115. **St Dogmaels Abbey** was dissolved along with all of Britain's monasteries by Henry VIII in 1536. Chickens now scratch around the artful ruins and a **produce market** (9am-2pm Tue) is held here. At the time of research a new visitor centre was being built.

The neighbouring **parish church of St Thomas the Martyr** houses several ancient stones relating to the first monastery, including the Sagranus Stone, inscribed in Latin and ogham. The church's altar was originally from the abbey and is one of the oldest in Britain.

Y Felin (☎ 01239-613999; www.yfelin.co.uk; tours adult/child £2/1; 10am-5.30pm Mon-Sat, 2-5.30pm Sun) is a working watermill dating from the 1640s. It's still used to make flour, which you can purchase, along with bread, at the mill door.

The Poppit Rocket (p170) stops here, as does the 407 (Poppit Sands–Cardigan; no Sunday service).

❦ WELSH WILDLIFE CENTRE // WATCHING THE WILDLIFE

Bordering the River Teifi just southeast of Cardigan, the Teifi Marshes Nature Reserve is a haven for birds, otters, badgers and butterflies. You can find out more about the surrounding river, marsh and woodland habitats at this **interpretation centre** (☎ 01239-621600; www.welshwildlife.org; admission free, parking £3; 10.30am-5pm Easter-Christmas).

There are several short waymarked trails, most of them wheelchair-accessible. The centre has live feeds from remote cameras on the reserve and also on Skomer Island (p155) so that you can watch nesting birds without causing disturbance. There's also a shop and cafe.

The centre is about a mile from Cardigan along a riverside path, or 4 miles by road.

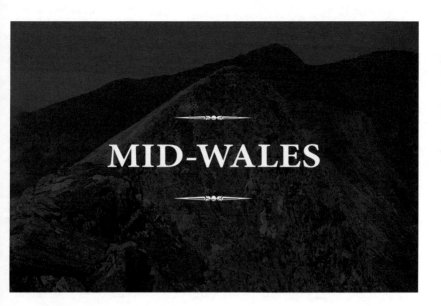

MID-WALES

3 PERFECT DAYS

❦ DAY 1 // ABSOLUTELY ABERYSTWYTH

Start by checking the timetable of the Vale of Rheidol Railway (p183) and locking in a few hours for the trip to Devil's Bridge (p187). Spend the rest of the day hanging around Aberystwyth (Abba, as the cool kids call it). Have coffee at Blue Creek Cafe (p184), stroll along the promenade (p181), climb Constitution Hill (p183), have lunch at Ultracomida (p184), visit Ceredigion Museum (p183) and delve into the National Library of Wales (p183). Grab dinner at the Orangery (p184) and then hit the bars (p184).

❦ DAY 2 // THE FUTURE, THE PRESENT AND THE PAST

Visit the Centre for Alternative Technology (p203) before heading down to Machynlleth (p200) for lunch. Quickly visit MOMA Wales (p201) before pressing on to palatial Powis Castle (p199), just outside of Welshpool (p198). Stay in Welshpool for the night or continue on to Newtown (p196), which offers a few more choices.

❦ DAY 3 // WELLS, WELLS, WELLS

In Newtown, discover the story of Robert Owen (p196) before heading to Radnorshire (p193). Take a leisurely drive to Presteigne (p194), visit the church and holy well at Pilleth (p194) and aim to get to Gigrin Farm (p194), near Rhayader, for the 2pm (3pm in summer) red-kite feeding. The area south of here is known for its spa towns, or Wells. You can pass fairly quickly through Llandrindod Wells (p190) and Builth Wells (p190) before settling into quirky little Llanwrtyd Wells (p188) for the night.

MID-WALES

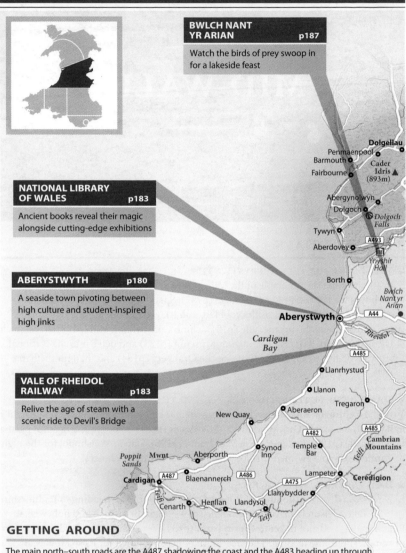

BWLCH NANT YR ARIAN   p187

Watch the birds of prey swoop in for a lakeside feast

NATIONAL LIBRARY OF WALES   p183

Ancient books reveal their magic alongside cutting-edge exhibitions

ABERYSTWYTH   p180

A seaside town pivoting between high culture and student-inspired high jinks

VALE OF RHEIDOL RAILWAY   p183

Relive the age of steam with a scenic ride to Devil's Bridge

Dolgellau
Penmaenpool
Barmouth
Fairbourne
Cader Idris (893m)
Abergynolwyn
Dolgoch
Dolgoch Falls
Tywyn
A493
Aberdovey
Ynyshir Hall
Borth
Bwlch Nant yr Arian
Aberystwyth
A44
Rheidol
Cardigan Bay
A485
Llanrhystud
Llanon
Tregaron
Aberaeron
New Quay
A482
A485
Cambrian Mountains
Teifi
Temple Bar
Synod Inn
Mwnt
Aberporth
Poppit Sands
A487
Blaenannerch
A486
Lampeter
Ceredigion
Cardigan
Teifi
A475
Llanybydder
Cenarth
Henllan
Llandysul
Teifi

GETTING AROUND

The main north–south roads are the A487 shadowing the coast and the A483 heading up through Powys. Separating the two, to the south, are the Cambrian Mountains. Buses mainly follow these routes. The Heart of Wales Line (Swansea to Shrewsbury) passes through Llanwrtyd Wells, Llandrindod Wells and Knighton, while the Cambrian Line (Aberystwyth to Birmingham) stops in Machynlleth, Newtown and Welshpool. For bus and train timetables and journey planners, see **Traveline Cymru** (☎ 0871 200 22 33; www.traveline-cymru.info).

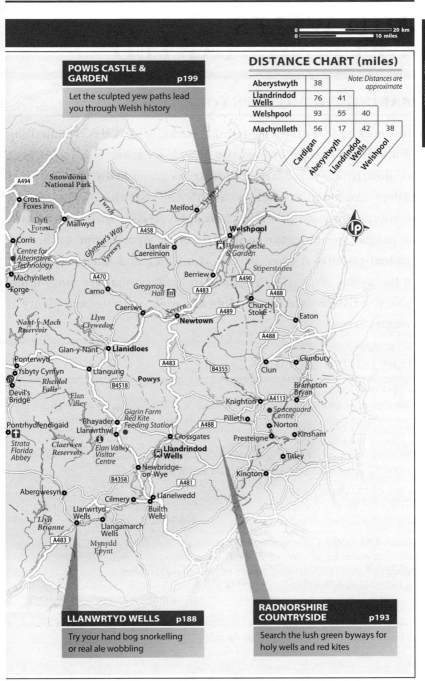

MID-WALES

DISTANCE CHART (miles)

	Cardigan	Aberystwyth	Llandrindod Wells	Welshpool
Aberystwyth	38		*Note: Distances are approximate*	
Llandrindod Wells	76	41		
Welshpool	93	55	40	
Machynlleth	56	17	42	38

POWIS CASTLE & GARDEN   p199

Let the sculpted yew paths lead you through Welsh history

LLANWRTYD WELLS   p188

Try your hand bog snorkelling or real ale wobbling

RADNORSHIRE COUNTRYSIDE   p193

Search the lush green byways for holy wells and red kites

MID-WALES GETTING STARTED

MAKING THE MOST OF YOUR TIME

Bordered by three famous national parks, Mid-Wales is something of a well-kept secret but worthy of a closer look. This is Wales at its most rural – a landscape of lustrous green fields, wooded river valleys and small market towns; it's the part that the Industrial Revolution missed. It's also thoroughly Welsh, with around 40% of people speaking the mother tongue. Apart from exuberant, student-populated Aberystwyth, you won't find much excitement in the urban areas. It's the places in between that are more interesting – criss-crossed with cycling and walking routes and plenty of country lanes.

TOP TOURS & COURSES

☙ FFOREST OUTDOOR
Take a guided canoe or kayak trip on the River Teifi through Cilgerran Gorge or try your hand climbing, sea kayaking, coasteering, surfing or white-water rafting (p180).

☙ DIRTY WEEKENDS
Get down and dirty on an off-road mountain-biking tour in the Elan Valley with the folks at Clive Powell Mountain Bike Centre in Rhayader (p193).

☙ SPACEGUARD CENTRE
Try out the telescopes and camera obscura and take in a planetarium show at this hilltop observatory, devoted to research into asteroids and comets (p194).

☙ CENTRE FOR ALTERNATIVE TECHNOLOGY
Offers an extensive program of residential courses on topics such as biomass, solar power and photovoltaics, wind power, environmental building, organic gardening and environmental campaigning (p203).

☙ CORRIS MINE EXPLORERS
Guides lead you through the dark, cramped depths of an old slate mine. You'll need to be reasonably fit and willing to get dirty (p204).

GETTING AWAY FROM IT ALL

★ **Ceredigion Coast Path** Take the coastal path less travelled, either as a continuous six-day trek or broken into bite-sized chunks (p177).

★ **Elan Valley** Lose yourself within the 70 sq miles of the Elan Valley Estate, a peaceful enclave of wooded hills and large water reservoirs (p193).

★ **Glyndŵr's Way National Trail** Of all the off-road routes that traverse the region, this one offers the most remote stretches – you'll need a compass and a detailed map (p177).

ADVANCE PLANNING

★ **Offa's Dyke Trail & Glyndŵr's Way** Stock up with maps, a compass, wet-weather gear and book accommodation well ahead if you're tackling these long-distance walking routes.

★ **Royal Welsh Agricultural Show** (www.rwas.co.uk) Builth Wells fills to bursting at the beginning of July, when 230,000 people descend for the show (founded in 1904), which involves everything from livestock judging to lumberjack competitions.

★ **Victorian Festival** (☎ 01597-823441; www.victorianfestival.co.uk) In the middle of August Llandrindod Wells indulges in nine days of 19th-century costumes and shenanigans.

★ **Cardigan River & Food Festival** (☎ 01239-615554) A one-dayer in the middle of August, with 100 food stalls, cooking demonstrations and boat races.

TOP EATS

❦ **ORANGERY**
The smartest restaurant in Aberystwyth focuses on Welsh staples, especially lamb (p184).

❦ **ULTRACOMIDA**
With its blend of Spanish, French and Welsh produce, this deli-cafe is foodie heaven (p184).

❦ **YNYSHIR HALL**
A grand manor house restaurant that's one of Wales' four Michelin-star holders (p186).

❦ **SPENCER'S BAR & BRASSERIE**
A menu of classics sits confidently within the grand Victorian surrounds (p192).

❦ **WYNNSTAY HOTEL**
In this 1780 coaching inn the country grub is matched by a country pub ambience (p202).

RESOURCES

★ **Ceredigion** (www.tourism.ceredigion.gov.uk) Ceredigion's official tourism site

★ **Explore Mid-Wales** (www.exploremidwales.com) The official Powys tourism site

★ **Powys Trails** (www.powystrails.org.uk) Fast track to information on Powys' 10 most famous walking trails

★ **Leaping Stiles** (www.leapingstiles.co.uk) Another site devoted to Mid-Wales walking

★ **Taste of Powys** (www.tasteofpowys.org.uk) Devoted to sustainable food producers; includes a list of farmers markets

CEREDIGION

· · · · · ·

Ceredigion (pronounced with a *dig* not a *didge*) re-emerged from the pages of history in 1974 when it became a district and it was only in 1996 that it replaced Cardiganshire as the name for the county. The name dates back to a 5th to 7th century Welsh kingdom founded by a chieftain called Ceredig; Cardigan was the anglicised version. The Welsh language is stronger in Ceredigion than any other part of Wales except Gwynedd and Anglesea. It's been kept alive in rural communities that escaped the massive population influxes of the coal-mining valleys of the south and the slate-mining towns of the north.

That lack of heavy industry has left Ceredigion with some of Britain's cleanest beaches and with no train access south of Aberystwyth, they tend to be less crowded. Adding to the isolation is the natural barrier known as the Desert of Wales, consisting of the barren uplands of the Cambrian Mountains, which separate Ceredigion from Powys. If any area could be described as off-the-beaten-track in Wales, this is it.

CARDIGAN (ABERTEIFI)

☎ 01239 / pop 4100

Refusing to be typecast by the town's name, the folk of Cardigan are much more likely to be found ambling along the main street in hoodies and trainers than in any grandfatherly knitwear. Yet this is the sort of town where taking up knitting might just help the time pass faster – there's not a lot to do or see here. In fact, all of the most interesting places to visit (the Welsh Wildlife Centre [WWC], St Dogmaels and Poppit Sands) are just across the river in Pembrokeshire.

It is, however, the closest town to the end of the Pembrokeshire Coast Path (PCP) and the first town at the beginning of the new Ceredigion Coast Path (CCP), so it sees plenty of hikers coming and going.

Aberteifi, the Welsh name for Cardigan, refers to its location at the mouth of the River Teifi. In Elizabethan times this was Wales' second most important port and, by the 18th century, one of Britain's busiest seafaring centres. By the late 19th century, however, the railway was displacing sea transport, and the river began silting up.

ESSENTIAL INFORMATION

EMERGENCIES // Cardigan Hospital (☎ 612214; Pont-y-Cleifion) Police station (☎ 101; Priory St)

TOURIST OFFICES // Tourist office (☎ 613230; www.tourism.ceredigion.gov.uk; Bath House Rd; ⏰ 10am-6pm Mon-Sat Jun-Aug, 10am-5pm Mon-Sat Sep-Jun) In the lobby of the Theatr Mwldan.

ORIENTATION

The town centre lies on the northern bank of the River Teifi. From the main bus stop on Finch Sq, it's a 200m walk up Priory St to High St/Pendre, the town's main drag – turn right and then take the first left to find the tourist office.

EXPLORING CARDIGAN

♣ **HISTORIC TOWN CENTRE //** **ECHOES OF THE GLORY DAYS**
The shored-up and overgrown walls of **Cardigan Castle** (www.cardigancastle. com; Bridge St) make for a sorry sight – a contrasting vision of ragged stone, rampant ivy, plastic tarpaulin and metal stanchions. Long neglected by its private owner, the crumbling castle was purchased by Ceredigion Council in 2003. Plans are underway to restore it and it's

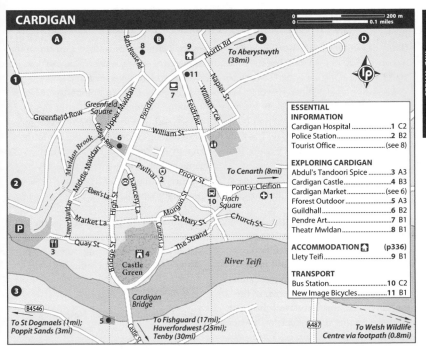

occasionally used for special events. It holds an important place in Welsh culture, having been the venue for the first competitive National Eisteddfod (see p296), held in 1176 under the aegis of Lord Rhys ap Gruffydd.

The neo-Gothic **Guildhall** (High St) dates from 1860 and is now home to **Cardigan Market**. A country market is held here every Friday. The field cannon outside commemorates the Charge of the Light Brigade in 1854, which was led by Lord Cardigan (after whom the button-up woollen sweater was named).

☙ PENDRE ART // SUPPORT LOCAL ARTISTS, EAT WELL AND GET CONNECTED

Not only a great place to buy local art, **Pendre** (☎ 615151; www.pendreart.com; 35 Pendre; ☉ 10am-5pm Mon-Sat; ☎) has an excellent coffee shop serving sandwiches, wraps,

baguettes and home-baked scones. Bring your laptop to take advantage of the free wireless connection.

☙ ABDUL'S TANDOORI SPICE // SPICE UP YOUR LIFE

A cut above your usual curry house, **Abdul's** (☎ 621416; 2 Royal Oak, Quay St; mains £4-16; ☉ dinner; Ⓥ) has gained a loyal local following with its consistently tasty tandoori dishes and excellent service. Serves are substantial, so resist the urge to over order. No alcohol is available.

☙ THEATR MWLDAN // SOMETHING TO DO ON THOSE QUIET EVENINGS

Located in the former slaughterhouse, **Theatr Mwldan** (☎ 621200; www.mwldan.co.uk; Bath House Rd) stages comedy, drama, dance, music, films and has an art gallery and a good cafe. In summer there are open-air productions.

CEREDIGION COAST PATH

Not to be outdone by its showy neighbour across the Teifi in Pembrokeshire, Ceredigion has opened up its own shoreline to the relentless march of coastal walkers. You can now walk 63 miles along a waymarked path between mouths of the Rivers Teifi and Dovey.

A sensible six-day itinerary would see you stopping overnight in Aberporth (12 miles from Cardigan), New Quay (14 miles), Aberaeron (6.5 miles), Llanrhystud (7.5 miles), Aberystwyth (11 miles) and Borth (12 miles); each has its own sandy beach to relax on at the end of the day. The truly hardcore enthusiast could tack this on to the end of the 13- to 15-day PCP (see p148) – a total of 249 continuous coastal miles.

For more information, visit www.walkcardiganbay.co.uk. The number 600 **Cardi Bach bus** (Thu-Tue Jul-Sep) covers the coast between Cardigan and New Quay in summer, making it easy to split this stretch into day-long walks.

❧ WALKS // TACKLE A CHUNK OF COAST OR SOMETHING SMALLER

For a challenging but spectacular day's walk, head to St Dogmaels and tackle the last leg of the PCP in reverse, catching the bus back from Newport. In the other direction, the first day of the CCP is shorter, ending up in Aberporth where you can catch the 550 bus back.

If you don't fancy a full-day's trek, you can walk or cycle from Cardigan through the Teifi Marshes to the WWC (see p172). Start from Finch Sq then head east along Pont-y-Cleifion to the roundabout and turn right, cross the bridge and descend the stairs on the right, then follow the trail east under the bridge (1 mile).

The tourist office stocks the *Walking the Teifi Estuary* brochure, outlining five other graded walks in the area.

❧ FFOREST OUTDOOR // KEEP AN EYE OUT FOR THE OTTERS

Cardigan's main outdoor-activity company has a cafe and shop by the south end of the bridge and a flash set of camping options near the WWC. If you fancy splashing along the River Teifi, **Fforest** (613961; www.fforestoutdoor.co.uk) offers guided canoe or kayak trips through Cilgerran Gorge (adult/child £30/20),

leaving from the slate cottage by the WWC. They can also arrange climbing, sea kayaking, coasteering, surfing and white-water rafting expeditions.

TRANSPORT

BIKE // You can hire bikes from **New Image Bicycles** (621275; www.newimagebicycles.co.uk; 29-30 Pendre; per half-day/day £12/18).

BUS // The main bus station is on Finch Sq. Routes include X50 to Aberystwyth (1½ hours); 407 to St Dogmaels (five minutes) and Poppit Sands (15 minutes); 412 to Castell Henllys (15 minutes), Newport (24 minutes), Dinas (30 minutes), Fishguard (40 minutes) and Haverfordwest (1¼ hours); 460 to Cenarth (14 minutes) and Carmarthen (90 minutes) and the Poppit Rocket (p170).

PARKING // The main car park is off Feidrfair (per day £1.70).

ABERYSTWYTH

 01970 / pop 16,000

Thanks to its status as one of the liveliest university towns in Wales and to an admirable range of options for eating out, drinking and partaking in Welsh culture, Aberystwyth is an essential stop along the Ceredigion coast. Welsh is widely spoken here and locals are proud of their heritage. It's a particularly buzzy town during term time and retains a cosmopolitan feel year-round.

When pub culture and student life get too much for you, though, the quintessential Aberystwyth experience remains soaking up the sunset over Cardigan Bay. Here the trappings of a stately Georgian seaside resort remain, with an impressive promenade skirted by a sweep of pastel-coloured buildings.

Like many other towns in Wales, Aberystwyth is a product of Edward I's mania for castle-building. The now mainly ruined castle was erected in 1277; like many other castles in Wales it was captured by Owain Glyndŵr at the start of the 15th century and wrecked by Oliver Cromwell's forces during the Civil War. By the beginning of the 19th century, the town's walls and gates had completely disappeared.

The town developed a fishing industry, and silver and lead mining were also important here. With the arrival of the railway in 1864, it reinvented itself as a fashionable seaside destination. In 1872 Aberystwyth was chosen as the site of the first college of the University of Wales (Aberystwyth University now has over 12,000 students) and in 1907 it became home to the National Library of Wales.

ESSENTIAL INFORMATION

EMERGENCIES // **Bronglais Hospital** (☎ 623131; Caradoc Rd) **Police station** (☎ 101; Blvd St Brieuc)
TOURIST OFFICES // Tourist office (☎ 612125; www.tourism.ceredigion.gov.uk; cnr Terrace Rd & Bath St; ☉ 10am-5pm Mon-Sat Sep-May, daily Jun-Aug) Below the Ceredigion Museum, this office stocks maps and books on local history; the helpful staff can arrange accommodation.

ORIENTATION

Aberystwyth sits where the River Rheidol and the smaller River Ystwyth empty into Cardigan Bay, at the end of the train line that crosses Mid-Wales. Beaches make up the town's entire western side. The train station is at the southeastern end of town at the bottom of Terrace Rd, a thoroughfare that bissects the town and leads directly to the seafront by means of a brisk 10-minute stroll. Regional buses and National Express coaches stop in the vicinity of the train station.

EXPLORING ABERYSTWYTH

❦ THE WATERFRONT // FANCY A STROLL, MY DEAR?

Marine Tce, stretched along North Beach, harks back to the town's halcyon days as a fashionable resort. When you reach the bottom of the 1½-mile prom, it's customary to kick the white bar, although the locals can't seem to explain the rationale behind this ritual.

North Beach is lined by somewhat shabby Georgian hotels, albeit with a couple of notable exceptions. Since the 1980s it's been decorated with the flags of minority nations – places like Alsace, Brittany, the Isle of Man, South Tyrol and, of course, Wales that are subsumed into a greater whole.

The top-heavy **Royal Pier** lumbers out to sea under the weight of its cheerfully tacky amusement arcade, offering a stark contrast to the grand **Old College** building a little further along. The enigmatic, sparse ruins of the **castle** sit looking out to sea from the southern end of the beach, offering views along the Llŷn Peninsula all the way to Bardsey Island. A stone circle planted in the centre of the castle is a relic of a 1915 eisteddfod, while the large war memorial in front of it features a surprisingly raunchy nude.

The prom pivots before leading along **South Beach** – a more desolate but still attractive seafront. Many locals prefer the stony but emptier **Tanybwlch Beach,**

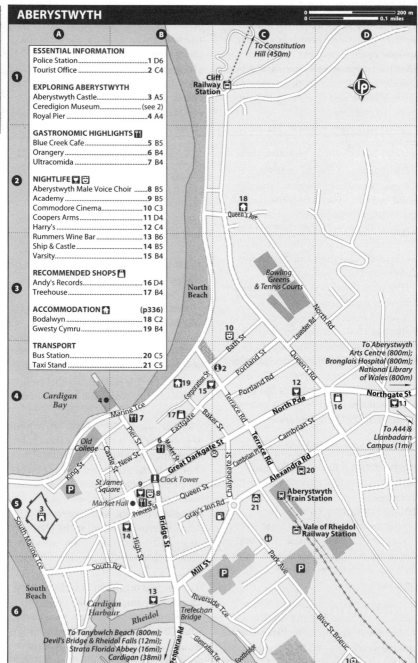

ABERYSTWYTH

0   200 m
0   0.1 miles

ESSENTIAL INFORMATION
Police Station.........................1 D6
Tourist Office..........................2 C4

EXPLORING ABERYSTWYTH
Aberystwyth Castle..................3 A5
Ceredigion Museum.............(see 2)
Royal Pier...............................4 A4

GASTRONOMIC HIGHLIGHTS 🍴
Blue Creek Cafe.......................5 B5
Orangery.................................6 B4
Ultracomida............................7 B4

NIGHTLIFE 🖥️ 🎭
Aberystwyth Male Voice Choir.......8 B5
Academy..................................9 B5
Commodore Cinema...............10 C3
Coopers Arms........................11 D4
Harry's...................................12 C4
Rummers Wine Bar.................13 B6
Ship & Castle.........................14 B5
Varsity...................................15 B4

RECOMMENDED SHOPS 🛍️
Andy's Records.......................16 D4
Treehouse..............................17 B4

ACCOMMODATION 🏠   (p336)
Bodalwyn..............................18 C2
Gwesty Cymru.......................19 B4

TRANSPORT
Bus Station............................20 C5
Taxi Stand.............................21 C5

To Constitution Hill (450m)

Cliff Railway Station

Queen's Ave

Bowling Greens & Tennis Courts

North Road

North Beach

To Aberystwyth Arts Centre (800m);
Bronglais Hospital (800m);
National Library of Wales (800m)

Bath St

Portland St

Queen's Rd

Loveden Rd

Portland Rd

North Pde

Cardigan Bay

Marine Tce

Corporation St

Terrace Rd

Cambrian St

Northgate St

To A44 & Llanbadarn Campus (1mi)

Pier St

Eastgate

Baker St

Old College

Castle St

New St

Market St

Great Darkgate St

Chalybeate St

Cambrian Rd

Terrace Rd

Alexandra Rd

King St

St James Square

Clock Tower

Queen St

Gray's Inn Rd

Aberystwyth Train Station

Market Hall

Princess St

Bridge St

Vale of Rheidol Railway Station

High St

South Marine Tce

South Rd

Mill St

Park Ave

South Beach

Cardigan Harbour

Rheidol

Riverside Tce

Trefechan Bridge

Blvd St Brieuc

To Tanybwlch Beach (800m);
Devil's Bridge & Rheidol Falls (12mi);
Strata Florida Abbey (16mi);
Cardigan (38mi)

Penparcau Rd

Glenofran Tce

Footbridge

just south of the harbour where the Rivers Rheidol and Ystwyth meet. It's a great spot for a stroll and some terrific ozone-fuelled views.

♥ CONSTITUTION HILL // VIEWS AND VICTORIANA

If your constitution's not up to the climb of Constitution Hill (135m), at the northern end of North Beach, you can catch a lift on the trundling little **Cliff Railway** (☎ 617642; www.aberystwythcliffrailway.co.uk; adult/child £3.50/2.50; ☉ 10am-5pm daily Apr-Oct, Wed-Sun mid-Feb–Mar), the UK's longest electric funicular (1896) and possibly the slowest too at a G-force-busting 4mph.

From the wind-blown balding hilltop there are tremendous, long coastal views – 60 miles from the Llŷn to Strumble Head – and you can spot 26 mountain peaks including Snowdon. The site has been redeveloped in recent years with new children's attractions, while the erstwhile Victorian tearooms have been rebuilt.

One relic of the Victorian era is a **camera obscura** (admission £1), an immense pinhole camera or projecting telescope that allows you to see practically into the windows of the houses below.

♥ VALE OF RHEIDOL RAILWAY // RATTLE UP THE VALLEY

One of Aberystwyth's most popular attractions is the one-hour ride (each way) on this **narrow-gauge railway** (☎ 625819; www.rheidolrailway.co.uk; Park Ave; adult/child return £14/3.50; ☉ Apr-Oct, check online timetable). Old steam locomotives (built between 1923 and 1938) have been lovingly restored by volunteers and chug for almost 12 miles up the valley of the River Rheidol to Devil's Bridge. The line opened in 1902 to bring lead and timber out of the valley.

♥ NATIONAL LIBRARY OF WALES // A THOROUGHLY ENGAGING REPOSITORY OF KNOWLEDGE AND ART

Sitting proudly on a hilltop half a mile east of town, the **National Library** (☎ 632800; www.llgc.org.uk; admission free; ☉ 9.30am-5pm Mon-Sat) is a cultural powerhouse. Founded in 1911, it holds millions of books in many languages – it's a copyright library so it has copies of every book published in the UK.

The **Hengwrt Room** is where they display all of the really important stuff, such as the 12th-century Black Book of Carmarthen (the oldest existing Welsh text), the 13th-century Tintern Abbey Bible, 15th-century Albert Dürer engravings, a first edition of Milton's *Paradise Lost* from 1668 and early editions by Shakespeare and Newton. Other galleries display an ever-stimulating set of changing exhibitions.

The entrance to the library is off Penglais Rd; take a right just past the hospital.

♥ CEREDIGION MUSEUM // ECLECTIC AND ENTERTAINING LOCAL EXHIBITS

This **museum** (☎ 633088; http://museum.ceredigion.gov.uk; Terrace Rd; admission free; ☉ 10am-5pm Mon-Sat Apr-Sep, noon-4.30pm Oct-Mar) is in the Coliseum, which opened in 1905 as a theatre and served as a cinema from 1932 onwards. The elegant interior still has its stage and has acquired an audience of cardboard cut-outs sitting in the circle (see if you can spot Nick Cave). The museum houses entertaining exhibitions on Aberystwyth's history – everything from old chemist furnishings and hand-knitted woollen knickers to a wall devoted to the *Little Britain* TV series.

🕈 RHEIDOL CYCLE TRAIL // RIDE THE RIVER VALLEY

Sticking mainly to designated cycle paths and quiet country lanes, this 18-mile trail heads from Aberystwyth Harbour to Devil's Bridge (p187) through the beautiful Rheidol Valley. Along the way it passes the Woodland Trust's Coed Geufron, and side routes lead to Bwlch Nant yr Arian (p187), Rheidol Power Station and Rheidol Mines.

🕈 YSTWYTH TRAIL // CUT ACROSS CEREDIGION, MAINLY OFF-ROAD

Suitable for cyclists and walkers, this 20-mile waymarked route mainly follows an old train line from Aberystwyth southeast to Tregaron, at the foot of the Cambrian Mountains. For the first 12 miles it shadows the River Ystwyth, while at the end it enters the Teifi Valley. At the Aberystwyth end you can pick up the trail from the footbridge on Riverside Tce, although you'll get more downhills if you start from Tregaron.

GASTRONOMIC HIGHLIGHTS

🕈 BLUE CREEK CAFE £

11 Princess St; ⏱ 10am-6pm Mon-Fri, 10am-5pm Sat; 🛜

In a country littered with cafes, it's harder than you might expect to find a half-decent coffee. You won't have any worries here – this is easily the best cafe we've found outside of Cardiff. It actually makes a flat white without bubbling the milk, stocks a good selection of homemade cakes and snacks, and offers newspapers to read and free wireless internet.

🕈 ORANGERY ££

☎ 617606; www.theorangerybistro.co.uk; Market St; mains £13-15

The smartest place in town brings a sense of contemporary style to the

erstwhile Talbot Inn, an 1830 coaching house, dividing the space between the restaurant and a cocktail bar. The menu focuses on Welsh staples, especially lamb, with the odd pasta and risotto dish thrown into the mix.

🕈 ULTRACOMIDA ££

☎ 630686; www.ultracomida.co.uk; 31 Pier St; tapas £4, 1-/2-/3-course dinner £12/16/19; ⏱ lunch daily, dinner Fri & Sat

With its blend of Spanish, French and Welsh produce, this is a foodie's idea of Nirvana: a delicatessen out front with a cheese counter to die for and communal tables out the back for tapas and wine. The deli platters are excellent, coming in a choice of meat, mixed fish or cheese (£8.95).

NIGHTLIFE

Thanks to its large student population, during term time Aberystwyth has a livelier nightlife than anywhere else in the northern half of the country, so if you're going to go out bar-hopping anywhere, make it here. Wednesday nights can be a surreal experience when the various university clubs hit the town in costume: one minute you might be sitting in an empty pub and the next minute the whole place may fill up with Kiss impersonators, cross-dressers or school girls.

🕈 ABERYSTWYTH ARTS CENTRE

☎ 623232; www.aberystwythartscentre.co.uk; Penglais Rd

One of the largest arts centres in Wales, it stages excellent opera, drama, dance and concerts, plus it has a bookshop, an art gallery, a bar and a cafe. The cinema shows a good range of world and foreign-language movies. The centre is on the Penglais campus of the university, half a mile east of the town.

❦ ACADEMY
☎ 636852; New Darkgate St

An incongruous setting for a booze palace, perhaps, but an incredibly beautiful one. This former chapel has Victorian tiles on the floor, a mezzanine supported by slender cast-iron columns, red lights illuminating a wooden staircase leading to an eagle-fronted pulpit and organ pipes behind the bar. The whole effect is upmarket, sophisticated and, well, heavenly.

❦ HARRY'S
☎ 612647; www.harrysaberystwyth.com; 40-46 North Pde; mains £5-15

Although it describes it itself as an Irish bar, Harry's is far more sophisticated than that epithet suggests. For one thing, the candlelit bistro section serves up an imaginative menu of tasty, well-presented meals, including local wild boar. Elsewhere, a series of rooms wraps itself around the central bar, ranging from a large sports bar to a small clubby lounge.

❦ SHIP & CASTLE
☎ 612334; www.shipandcastle.co.uk; 1 High St

A sympathetic renovation has left this 1830 pub as cosy and welcoming as ever, while adding big screens to watch the rugger on. It is the place to come for real ales, with a large selection on tap, along with a few ciders.

❦ VARSITY
☎ 615234; www.varsitybars.com; Portland St; 🖳

Spacious, simple and student-friendly, Varsity has huge pipes running around the ceiling and big windows for watching activity on the street. It's packed on weekend nights and relaxing during the daytime when you can make the most of the free wi-fi.

Also recommended:

Aberystwyth Male Voice Choir (www.aberchoir.co.uk; Bridge St; admission free) Rehearses at the RAFA Club from 7pm to 8.30pm most Thursdays.
Commodore Cinema (☎ 612421; www.commodorecinema.co.uk; Bath St) Shows current mainstream releases and there's a bar here for a pre-flick beer.
Coopers Arms (☎ 624050; Northgate St) Popular, friendly pub with regular live music.
Rummers Wine Bar (☎ 625177; Bridge St) Right by the river, this popular place has seats outside for summer nights, a friendly vibe and some live bands.

RECOMMENDED SHOPS

❦ ANDY'S RECORDS
☎ 624581; 16 Northgate St

A handy indie record shop that also sells gig tickets for bands at the university.

❦ TREEHOUSE
☎ 625116; www.treehousewales.co.uk; 3 Eastgate St; 🕙 9.30am-5.30pm Mon-Sat

The sister property to the Treehouse deli and restaurant across the road, this little boutique specialises in organic and fairtrade homewares, cosmetics and baby goods.

TRANSPORT

BUS // Routes include X18 to Rhayader (1¼ hours), Llandrindod Wells (1½ hours) and Builth Wells (1¾ hours); 28 to Machynlleth (45 minutes) and Fairbourne (two hours); X32 to Corris (one hour), Dolgellau (1¼ hours), Porthmadog (2¼ hours), Caernarfon (three hours) and Bangor (3½ hours); X40 to Carmarthen (2¼ hours), Swansea (3¼ hours) and Cardiff (4¼ hours); and X50 to Cardigan (1½ hours).

COACH // A daily National Express (www.nationalexpress.com) coach heads to/from Newtown (£9.40, 80 minutes), Welshpool (£11, 1¾ hours), Shrewsbury (£14, 2¼ hours), Birmingham (£27, four hours) and London (£33, seven hours).

CAR // A complicated one-way system operates in the central streets.

MID-WALES

PARKING // If you're prepared to prowl the fringes and hunt for a park, there is some free street parking. Otherwise, there's a big car park behind Park Ave and Mill St (per hour/four hours £1/2.90).

TRAIN // Aberystwyth is the terminus of the **Arriva Trains Wales** (www.arrivatrainswales.co.uk) Cambrian Line, which crosses Mid-Wales every two hours en route to Birmingham (£17, three hours) via Machynlleth (£4.90, 33 minutes), Newtown (£9.80, 1¼ hours), Welshpool (£11, 1½ hours) and Shrewsbury (£15, two hours).

DRIVING TOUR

Distance: 28 miles
Duration: two hours
Head south from **Aberystwyth** (**1**; p180) on the A487, turning left at Southgate and following the A4120 to **Devil's Bridge** (**2**; p187). Stop to check out the bridge and waterfalls and then continue on, looking out for **Ysbyty Cynfyn** (**3**; p187) on your left. There's not much to it – just a church beside a farm – but see if you can make out the remains of the stone circle embedded within the churchyard fence. Continue on the A4120 until it reaches the A44 and turn left. Stop at **Bwlch Nant yr Arian** (**4**; p187) to watch the red kites before heading back to Aberystwyth.

CEREDIGION COUNTRYSIDE

☙ YNYSHIR HALL // FEAST LIKE A QUEEN

Tucked away to the south of the River Dovey (Afon Dyfi) estuary, just off the main Aberystwyth–Machynlleth road (A487), this grand manor house was once kept as a hunting lodge by Queen Victoria. It's now a wonderful boutique hotel and its **restaurant** (☎ 01654-781209; www.ynyshirhall.co.uk; 3-course lunch/dinner £22/70; Ⓟ) is one of Wales' finest; part of a very small club of Welsh Michelin-star holders. The house's Victorian purpose is reflected in a menu that includes game birds such as quail, partridge and pheasant, all faultlessly executed. The friendly (rather than fawning) staff are never less than professional.

A little ironically, given the fowl-bothering menu, immediately behind the house is the 550-hectare **Ynys-hir Royal Society for the Protection of Birds Reserve** (☎ 01654-700222;www.rspb.org.uk; adult/child £3/1; Ⓨ reserve 9am-9pm; Ⓟ), complete with hides and a small visitor centre.

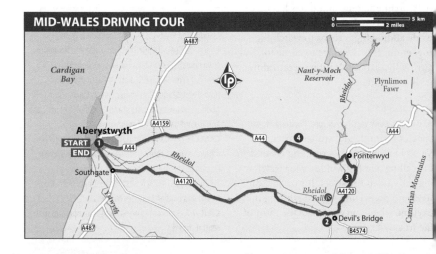

MID-WALES DRIVING TOUR

LÔN TEIFI & LÔN CAMBRIA

Two long-distance cycling routes that are part of the **Sustrans** (☎ 0845 113 0065; www.sustrans.org.uk) National Cycle Network cut clear through Mid-Wales. The Lôn Teifi (route 82) heads 98 miles from Fishguard through Cardigan, Lampeter and Tregaron to Aberystwyth. From here the 113-mile Lôn Cambria (route 81) kicks in, passing through Rhayader, Newtown and Welshpool en route to Shrewsbury. Sustrans is a charity devoted to promoting sustainable transport modes. You can buy maps of the routes through its website.

❤ BWLCH NANT YR ARIAN // RAVENOUS RED KITES AND LAKESIDE TRAILS

Part of a forestry commission block, **Bwlch Nant yr Arian** (☎ 01970-890453; www.forestry.gov.uk/bwlchnantyrarian; ☺ summer 10am-5pm, winter 11am-dusk) is a picturesque piece of woodland set around a lake, ringed with mountain-biking and walking tracks. The main drawcard, however, is the red-kite feeding, which takes place at 2pm daily (3pm daylight-saving time). Even outside mealtime you'll quite often see the majestic birds of prey circling around. You can watch all the action from the terrace of the attractive turf-roofed visitor centre and cafe.

It's 9 miles east of Aberystwyth on the A44.

❤ YSBYTY CYNFYN // WHOSE SHRINE IS IT ANYWAY?

Just 2 miles up the A4120 from Devil's Bridge, Ysbyty Cynfyn is a fascinating example of the grafting of the Christian onto the pagan, which is evident in many ancient religious sites throughout Wales. Here the remains of a stone circle are clearly visible within the churchyard walls. The church once belonged to the Knights Hospitaller, the precursor of the Order of St John, which runs the St John Ambulance service. The order ran a pilgrims' hospice here to care for invalids making their way to St Davids.

❤ DEVIL'S BRIDGE & RHEIDOL FALLS // DIABOLICAL STORY IN HEAVENLY GORGE

This dramatic **bridge** (☎ 01970-890233; www.devilsbridgefalls.co.uk; adult/child £3.50/1.50; ☺ 9.45am-5pm Apr-Oct, other times access via turnstile £2) spans the Rheidol Valley on the lush western slopes of 752m Plynlimon (Pumlumon Fawr), source of the Rivers Wye and Severn. Here the Rivers Mynach and Rheidol tumble together in a narrow gorge.

The Mynach is spanned by three famous stone bridges, stacked on top of each other. The lowest and oldest is believed to have been built by the monks of Strata Florida Abbey before 1188. It's one of many bridges associated with an arcane legend that involves the devil building the bridge on the condition that he gets the first thing to cross it. An old lady then outwits the devil by throwing some food over, which her dog chases and everybody's happy – except the devil and, presumably, the dog.

However, it's not the bridges that are the real attraction here. Just above the confluence, the Rheidol drops 90m in a series of spectacular waterfalls. Access to the waterfalls and the old bridges is from beside the top-most bridge. There are two possible walks: one, just to view the three bridges, takes only 10 minutes (£1); the other, a half-hour walk, descends 100 steps (Jacob's Ladder), crosses the Mynach and ascends the other side, passing what is said to have been a robbers' cave.

MID-WALES

It's a beautiful walk but it's very steep and can be muddy.

The Vale of Rheidol Railway (p183) heads to Devil's Bridge from Aberystwyth, as does the Rheidol Cycle Trail (p184).

☙ STRATA FLORIDA ABBEY // RUINS SET AMID BUCOLIC FARMLAND

On an isolated, peaceful site southeast of Aberystwyth lies this ruined Cistercian **abbey** (☎ 01974-831261; www.cadw.wales. gov.uk; adult/child £3/2.60; ⏱ 10am-5pm Apr-Sep, unattended & free in other months) run by Cadw (the Welsh historic monuments agency). The best preserved remnant is a simple, complete arched doorway, with lines like thick rope. At the rear of the site a roof has been added to protect two chapels, which still have some of their 14th-century tiling, including one depicting a man admiring himself in a mirror.

The Cistercians were a monastic order with roots in France and the community at Strata Florida (Ystrad Fflur or 'Valley of the Flowers') was founded in 1164 by a Norman lord named Robert Fitz-Stephen. After Welsh resurgence in the southwest, however, the independent, self-sufficient Cistercians won the support of the Welsh princes. Their abbeys also became a focus for literary activity and influence. The present site was established under Lord Rhys ap Gruffydd, and a number of princes of Deheubarth, as well as the great 14th-century poet Dafydd ap Gwilym, are buried here.

The site is a mile down a rural road from the village of Pontrhydfendigaid on the B4343; the village is 15 miles from Aberystwyth or 9 miles south of Devil's Bridge. Bus T21 has limited services from Monday to Saturday from Aberystwyth (35 minutes).

POWYS
· · · · · ·

By far Wales' biggest county, Powys took the name of an ancient Welsh kingdom when it was formed in 1974 from the historic counties of Montgomeryshire, Radnorshire and Brecknockshire. Overwhelmingly rural, the majority of its 132,000 inhabitants live in villages and small towns. Newtown is easily the largest town, yet even it only just scrapes above the 10,000-person mark. This county isn't just green in a literal sense – Machynlleth has become a focal point for the nation's environmentally friendly aspirations and all over the county, efforts to restore the threatened red kite have been met with outstanding success. The bird is now the very symbol of Powys, the county at Wales' green heart.

LLANWRTYD WELLS (LLANWRTUD)

☎ 01591 / pop 600

Llanwrtyd (khlan-*oor*-tid) Wells is an odd little town: mostly deserted except during one of its oddball festivals when it's packed to the rafters with an influx of crazy contestants and their merrymaking supporters. According to the *Guinness Book of Records,* it is the UK's smallest town – some local residents even claim that to cling onto this status there's a periodic cull.

Apart from its newfound status as the capital of wacky Wales, Llanwrtyd Wells is surrounded by beautiful walking, cycling and riding country, with the Cambrian Mountains to the northwest and the Mynydd Epynt to the southeast.

Theophilus Evans, the local vicar, first discovered the healing properties of the Ffynon Droellwyd (Stinking

Well) in 1732 when he found it cured his scurvy. The popularity of the waters grew and Llanwrtyd became a spa town. Nowadays, however, its wells have been capped and, outside of the festivals, it's hard to find much by way of vital signs.

ESSENTIAL INFORMATION

TOURIST OFFICES // In the Pink (☎ 610666; Irfon Tce; ✆ variable) As kooky as you'd hope in such a place, the tourist office operates out of this little cafe/ gift shop, where you can stock up on hiking and camping accessories and check your email (per 20 minutes £1).

ORIENTATION

The town centre is Y Sgwar (The Square), the five-way intersection by the old bridge on which the A483 crosses the River Irfon. Virtually nothing in town is much more than a stone's throw away from here, including the tourist office, post office, police station and Barclays Bank. The train station is half a mile to the southeast.

EXPLORING LLANWRTYD WELLS

❤ NEUADD ARMS HOTEL // WHERE CRAZY SCHEMES ARE HATCHED
Like any good village pub should be, the Neuadd Arms (☎ 610236; www.neuaddarms hotel.co.uk; Y Sgwar) is a focal point for the community. It was here that former landlord Gordon Green and his punters cooked up many of the kooky events that have put Llanwrtyd Wells on the tourist trail. If you want to find out anything about mountain biking, pony trekking or hiking in the area, it's the place to come. During winter you might join one of the farmers' dogs on the couch in front of the fire.

There's also a surprisingly interesting menu (mains around £7), which when we visited included an excellent goat's cheese, pear and walnut tart; rabbit and beef pie; and some hefty-looking desserts. The pub even brews its own beer!

LLANWRTYD'S TWISTED EVENTS

While mulling over how to encourage tourism in Llanwrtyd in the dark winter months, some citizens started an inspired roll call of unconventionality. There's something on each month (see www.green-events.co.uk for more details) but these are some of the wackiest.
Saturnalia Beer Festival & Mountain Bike Chariot Racing Roman-themed festival in mid-January including a 'best dressed Roman' competition, the devouring of stuffed bulls' testicles and the chariot race.
Man vs Horse Marathon The event that kicked all the craziness off, it's been held every year since 1980 and has resulted in some tense finishes. Two-legged runners have won only twice, the first in 2004. Held mid-June.
World Bog Snorkelling Championships The most famous event of all, held every August bank holiday. Competitors are allowed wetsuits, snorkels and flippers to traverse a trench cut out of a peat bog, using no recognisable swimming stroke and surfacing only to navigate. Spin-off events include Mountain Bike Bog snorkelling ('like trying to ride through treacle') and the Bog snorkelling Triathlon; both held in July.
Real Ale Wobble & Ramble In conjunction with the Mid-Wales Beer Festival, every November cyclists and walkers follow waymarked routes (10, 15 or 25 miles, or 35 miles for the wobblers), supping real ales at the 'pint-stops' along the way.
Mari Llwyd A revival of the ancient practice of parading a horse's skull from house to house on New Year's Eve while reciting Welsh poetry.

♥ **DROVERS REST //** **EAT LIKE A HORSE BEFORE RACING ONE**

A well-regarded restaurant-with-rooms, the **Drovers** (☎ 610264; www.food-food-food. co.uk; Y Sgwar; lunch £6-11, dinner £14-18) has a snug little restaurant serving up the best of local produce and lots of fresh fish mains. The Sunday roasts are excellent (£13). The owners also run regular cooking classes, including a Welsh cooking day (£185).

TRANSPORT

BIKE // Lôn Las Cymru, the Welsh National Cycle Route (Sustrans route 8; see p302), passes through Llanwrtyd Wells, heading north to Machynlleth and east to Builth Wells. There's excellent mountain biking in the surrounding hills; enquire at the Drovers Rest or In the Pink.

BUS // Bus 48 heads to Builth Wells (23 minutes).

TRAIN // Llanwrtyd is on the Heart of Wales Line, with direct services to Swansea (£8.40, two hours), Llandeilo (£3.90, 45 minutes), Llandovery (£2.30, 23 minutes), Llandrindod Wells (£3.20, 30 minutes) and Shrewsbury (£11, two hours).

BUILTH WELLS & AROUND

♥ **CILMERY //** **A SHRINE FOR WELSH NATIONALISTS**

Two miles before Builth Wells on the A483 is the place where Llewellyn ap Gruffydd, the last Welsh Prince of Wales, was killed in a chance encounter with a lone English soldier in 1282. The spot is marked with a sad obelisk of Caernarfon granite. The site is often strewn with nationalist banners and pamphlets.

♥ **BUILTH WELLS (LLANFAIR-YM-MUALLT) //** **BUSTLING TOWN BY THE WYE**

Builth (pronounced bilth) Wells is by far the liveliest of the former spa towns, with a bustling, workaday feel. Once the playground of the Welsh working classes, it has a pretty location on the River Wye. While there are no attractions per se, it's a handy base for walkers or cyclists tackling any of the long-distance paths that pass through.

The thriving **Wyeside Arts Centre** (☎ 01982-552555; www.wyeside.co.uk; Castle St) is a great little venue with a bar, exhibition space, cinema and live shows. You can catch a rehearsal of the **Builth Male Voice Choir** (www.builthmalechoir.org.uk) from 8pm on Monday nights in the upper room of the **Greyhound Hotel** (☎ 01982-553255; www.thegreyhoundhotel.co.uk; 3 Garth Rd), which is also the best of the town's pubs. The choir formed in 1968 as a rugby choir and now sing internationally.

There's no tourist office anymore but maps and brochures are available from **Curio & Welsh Craft** (☎ 01982-552253; www.visitbuilthwells.co.uk; 24 High St; ☺ 9am-6pm Mon-Sat). **Cosy Corner** (☎ 01982-551700; 55 High St; mains £3-7; ☺ 10am-4pm Mon-Sat) is an atmospheric and, yes, cosy tearoom, offering homemade cakes, sandwiches and jacket potatoes in an 18th-century building.

Buses stopping here include X18 from Llandrindod Wells (17 minutes), Rhayader (45 minutes) and Aberystwyth (1¾ hours); 48 from Llanwrtyd Wells (23 minutes); and 704 from Brecon (40 minutes) and Newtown (1½ hours).

LLANDRINDOD WELLS

☎ 01597 / **pop 5100**

This spa town struck gold in Victorian times by touting its waters to the well-to-do gentry who rolled in for rest and recuperation. The grand architecture of the era remains, but now it's the town that's sleepy – you'd need to prod it with a sharp stick to rouse it on a Wednesday afternoon, when most of the shops close.

Roman remains at nearby Castell Collen show that it wasn't the Victorians who first discovered the healthy effects of the local spring waters, but it was the arrival of the Central Wales railway (now the Heart of Wales Line) in 1865 that brought visitors en masse.

ESSENTIAL INFORMATION

EMERGENCIES // **Llandrindod Wells Memorial Hospital** (☎ 822951; Temple St) **Police station** (☎ 101; High St)
TOURIST OFFICES // **Tourist office** (☎ 822600; Temple St; ⊗ 10am-1pm Mon-Sat Oct-Mar, to 4pm Apr-Sep)

ORIENTATION

The town sits on the eastern bank of the River Ithon with the A483 (as Temple St) and the train line plunging right through the town centre. Between the two is the main shopping zone, Middleton St. Most

regional buses stop outside the train station on Station Cres.

EXPLORING LLANDRINDOD WELLS

⚑ NATIONAL CYCLE COLLECTION // POWER TO THE PEDAL!

Housed in the art nouveau Automobile Palace, the **National Cycle Collection** (☎ 825531; www.cyclemuseum.org.uk; Temple St; adult/child £3.50/1.50; ⊗ 10am-4pm daily Mar-Oct, Tue, Thu & Sun Nov-Feb) comprises over 250 bikes. The exhibits show the progression from clunky boneshakers and circus-reminiscent penny-farthings to bamboo bikes from the 1890s and the vertiginous 'Eiffel Tower' of 1899 (used to display billboards), as well as slicker, modern-day versions. Great effort has been made to put the bikes in context, with recreated Victorian and Edwardian cycle shops,

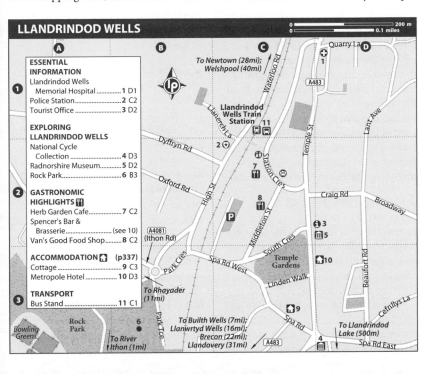

LLANDRINDOD WELLS

ESSENTIAL INFORMATION
Llandrindod Wells
  Memorial Hospital 1 D1
Police Station............................2 C2
Tourist Office 3 D2

EXPLORING LLANDRINDOD WELLS
National Cycle
  Collection 4 D3
Radnorshire Museum............5 D2
Rock Park...................................6 B3

GASTRONOMIC HIGHLIGHTS
Herb Garden Cafe....................7 C2
Spencer's Bar &
  Brasserie...........................(see 10)
Van's Good Food Shop..........8 C2

ACCOMMODATION (p337)
Cottage..9 C3
Metropole Hotel 10 D3

TRANSPORT
Bus Stand 11 C1

photos and signboards – it's run with infectious enthusiasm. The building was constructed by Tom Norton, a local entrepreneur who started as a bicycle dealer and became the main Austin distributor. The trike on which Norton used to ride to work is here, with a picture of him on it.

❧ ROCK PARK // SUP RUSTY WATER FROM A FOREST GLADE

In 1670 the local spring was given the name the 'Well of the Blacksmith's Dingle', but it was not till the mid-18th century that its therapeutic qualities were discovered. An eminent German doctor had a variety of diseases, drank the waters and was cured; hence the spa became enormously popular. However, the allure of stinky water gradually diminished and it closed in 1972.

You can still soothe your nerves beside Arlais Brook as it tinkles through serene, forested Rock Park. This is the site of the earliest spa development and there's still a small **complementary health centre** (☎ 822997; www.actionteam.org.uk) offering therapies such as massage, chiropractic and acupuncture. You can still sup from the rusty looking and tasting Chalybeate Spring (donated to the public by the Lord of the Manor in 1879) beside the brook – apparently the water is good for treating gout, rheumatism, anaemia and more (chalybeate refers to its iron salts).

❧ LLANDRINDOD LAKE // DON'T FEED THE DRAGON

Just southeast of the centre is a sedately pretty, tree-encircled lake, built at the end of the 19th century to allow Victorians to take their exercise without appearing to do so. The original boathouse is now a private residence, but you can still rent a boat, fish for carp or take lunch at the cafe. The centrepiece of the lake is a sculpture of a Welsh dragon.

❧ RADNORSHIRE MUSEUM // A BRIEF DIVERSION FOR A RAINY DAY

Small and low-key, rather like the town itself, this **museum** (☎ 824513; www.powys. gov.uk/radnorshiremuseum; Temple St; adult/child £1/50p; ☸ 10am-4pm Tue-Fri, 10am-1pm Sat) offers a taste of local social history, archaeology and palaeontology. Radnorshire was a historic county, which was incorporated into Powys in 1974.

GASTRONOMIC HIGHLIGHTS

❧ HERB GARDEN CAFE £

☎ 823082; www.herbgardencafe.co.uk; 5 Spa Centre, Station Cres; mains £3-7; ☸ 9.30am-5pm Mon-Sat; 🖳 🛜 Ⓥ

Tucked down an alley by the Co-op supermarket, the Herb Garden Cafe serves tasty light meals made from organic and wholefood produce. While not strictly vegetarian the cafe makes an effort to cater for various dietary requirements. It gets busy at lunchtime, so book ahead.

❧ SPENCER'S BAR & BRASSERIE ££

☎ 823700; Temple St; mains £11-18

Echoes of Victorian grandeur linger in the Metropole Hotel, not least in Spencer's with its elegant veranda and waiters bedecked in bow ties. The formal dining area is tucked in the back and here too there's a touch of the classic (Welsh beef and lamb, and a perfect coq au vin) alongside Thai and Italian dishes.

❧ VAN'S GOOD FOOD SHOP £

☎ 823074; Middleton St; ☸ 9am-5.30pm Mon-Sat; Ⓥ

This excellent vegetarian deli features the best of local produce, including organic fruit, cheese and wine, plus ecofriendly cleaning products and other ethically selected goods.

TRANSPORT

BUS // Bus routes include X18 to Builth Wells (17 minutes), Rhayader (17 minutes) and Aberystwyth (1½ hours) and 704 to Newtown (one hour) and Brecon (55 minutes).

TAXI // Procabs (☎ 822877)

TRAIN // Llandrindod is on the Heart of Wales Line, with direct services to Swansea (£9.70, 2¼ hours), Llandeilo (£6.10, 80 minutes), Llanwrtyd Wells (£3.20, 30 minutes), Knighton (£3.50, 34 minutes) and Shrewsbury (£11, 1½ hours).

RADNORSHIRE

❧ ELAN VALLEY // AN IDYLLIC FOCUS FOR WELSH RESENTMENT

The Elan Valley is filled with strikingly beautiful countryside, split by impressive Edwardian impositions of grey stone on the landscape. In the early 19th century, dams were built on the River Elan (pronounced ellen), west of Rhayader, mainly to provide a reliable water supply for the English city of Birmingham. Around 100 people had to move, but only landowners received compensation. In 1952 a fourth, large dam was inaugurated on the tributary River Claerwen. Together their reservoirs now provide over 70 million gallons of water daily for Birmingham and parts of South and Mid-Wales.

Though not a project to warm Welsh hearts, the need to protect the 70-sq-mile watershed (called the Elan Valley Estate) has turned it and adjacent areas into an important wildlife conservation area. The dams and associated projects also produce some 4.2 megawatts of hydro-electric power.

Just downstream of the lowest dam, 3 miles from Rhayader on the B4518, is Welsh Water's **Elan Valley Visitor Centre** (☎ 01597-810880; www.elanvalley.org.uk; admission free; ☺ 10am-5.30pm Mar-Oct) with interesting exhibits on the water scheme, complete with photos of houses being swallowed up by the waters, native wildlife and local history. It also provides leaflets on the estate's 80 miles of nature trails and footpaths. Check the website for details of the frequent guided walks and bird-watching trips, which are mostly free.

The **Elan Valley Trail** is an 8-mile traffic-free walking, horse-riding and cycling path that mostly follows the line of the long-gone Birmingham Corporation Railway alongside the River Elan and its reservoirs. It starts just west of Rhayader at Cwmdauddwr.

❧ RHAYADER (RHAEADR GWY) // A DIRTY WEEKEND DESTINATION OF A DIFFERENT SORT

Rhayader is a small and fairly uneventful livestock-market town (population 2100) revolving around a central crossroads marked by a war-memorial clock. It's a place that appeals to walkers visiting the nearby Elan Valley and tackling the 136-mile Wye Valley Walk. Rhayader is deserted on Thursdays when businesses trade for only half a day, but market day on Wednesdays attracts a crowd.

The **Clive Powell Mountain Bike Centre** (☎ 01597-811343; www.clivepowellmountainbikes.co.uk; West St) is run by a former cycling champion and coach. You can hire a mountain/off-road bike here (£20/15 per day, including helmet and puncture kit), and Powell runs a regular program of 'Dirty Weekends', all-inclusive mountain-biking weekends hitting trails around the Elan Valley (£176 to £299).

The tiny 16th-century **Triangle Inn** (☎ 01597-810537; www.thetriangleinn.co.uk; mains £7-13), just over the bridge from the town centre, is the pick of the local places to eat and drink for its unique sense of character and history. It's so small that the toilets are across the road and the ceiling is so low that there's a trapdoor in the floor so that darts players can stand in a hole to throw their arrows.

Bus X18 from Builth Wells (45 minutes) to Aberystwyth (1¼ hours) via Llandrindod Wells (17 minutes) passes through here.

♥ GIGRIN FARM RED KITE FEEDING STATION // WITNESS A RAPTOR FEEDING FRENZY

There's been a dramatic Mid-Wales resurgence in the UK's threatened population of red kites (see p308). A feeding program continues at the **Gigrin Farm Red Kite Feeding Station** (☎ 810243; www.gigrin.co.uk; adult/child £4/1.50), a working farm on the A470 half a mile south of Rhayader town centre (or 1 mile from the Wye Valley Walk). At 2pm (3pm during summer daylight-saving time) meat scraps from local butchers and a local abattoir are spread on a field. Altogether anywhere from 12 to 500 kites may partake, though usually less than 20 at any one time. First come crows, then ravens, then the acrobatically swooping kites – often mugging the crows to get the meat – and later ravens and buzzards. You can watch from a wheelchair-accessible hide.

There's an interpretive centre with information on red kites and other local wildlife, recorded night-time footage of badgers, a camera overlooking the feeding site and marked nature trails.

♥ PRESTEIGNE (LLANANDRAS) // STEP INTO A VICTORIAN WORLD

At the far west of the vanished country of Radnorshire, pressed right up against the English border, is **Presteigne** (www.presteigne.org.uk) – its former county town. It's a quaint little place, lined with attractive old buildings and surrounded by beautiful countryside.

The **Judge's Lodging** (☎ 01544-260650; www.judgeslodging.org.uk; adult/child £5.95/3.95; ❧ 10am-5pm Tue-Sun Mar-Oct, 10am-4pm Sat & Sun Nov-Dec) offers an intriguing glimpse into Victorian times through an audio-guided wander through the town's 19th-century courthouse, lock-up and judge's apartments. The commentary does tend to ramble on but the displays are fascinating. The local tourist office is based here.

Bus 41 heads to Knighton (20 minutes).

♥ PILLETH // BLISSFUL COUNTRYSIDE WITH HIDDEN SECRETS

You could spend a very pleasant few days driving or cycling around the Radnorshire countryside. At tiny Pilleth, 5 miles northwest of Presteigne, a whitewashed church on a hill overlooks the peaceful valley where 800 men were killed in the 1402 victory by Owain Glyndŵr over Edmund Mortimer (Mortimer was captured, switched sides and married Glyndŵr's daughter). Most of them were buried in mass graves in the churchyard.

While the current church dates from the 13th century, it's built on the site of an outpost of St Cynllo (died 460) and its idyllic location speaks of the close relationship of the early Celtic church to nature. Behind the church, steps lead into a well-preserved holy well, which was believed to have had healing powers, particularly for eye complaints. It's now home to a rowdy family of far-sighted frogs.

♥ SPACEGUARD CENTRE // SEARCHING FOR A BRUCE WILLIS–LESS SOLUTION TO COMET IMPACT

Two miles southeast of town, the hilltop **Spaceguard Centre** (☎ 520247; www.spaceguarduk.com; adult/child £5/2.50; ❧ Wed-Sun, 1½-hr tours 2pm & 4pm Nov-Apr, plus 10.30am May-Oct), in the former Powys Observatory, is a centre for research into asteroids and comets. Tours take in the telescopes, camera obscura and planetarium shows.

🌳 KNIGHTON (TREF-Y-CLAWDD) // A HUB FOR WALKERS AND WIFE-SELLERS

Hilly Knighton (population 2800, www.visitknighton.co.uk) is so close to the border that its train station is actually in England. It sits midway along the Offa's Dyke Path National Trail and at one end of the Glyndŵr's Way National Trail. The two-in-one **tourist office & Offa's Dyke Centre** (☎ 01547-528753; www.offasdyke.demon.co.uk; West St; ☀ 10am-5pm Apr-Oct, 10am-4pm Mon-Sat Nov-Mar) is full of information for walkers and interactive displays about the dyke, a section of which runs behind the centre.

The town's two Norman castles haven't fared as well as 11th-century **St Edward's Church** (Church St), although the later has had an unusual, stumpy 18th-century bell tower grafted onto it. The coming of the railway in 1861 and the growth of livestock farming saw Knighton's fortunes rise, but they fell again with the decline in population post WWII and failed attempts to turn it into a spa town. One disturbing piece of local folklore suggests that it was possible for a man to obtain a divorce by 'selling' his wife at the square where the 1872 clock tower now stands. Husbands would bring their spouse to the square at the end of a rope; the last wife was sold in 1842.

The town's best refuelling option is the **Horse & Jockey Inn** (☎ 01547-520062; www.thehorseandjockeyinn.co.uk; Station Rd; mains bar £4-7, restaurant £6-14), a former 14th-century coaching inn. You can eat in the bar or sit down to a more substantial meal in the restaurant; they do an excellent Sunday lunch.

OFFA'S DYKE PATH *BECKY OHLSEN*

They say that good fences make good neighbours, but King Offa may have taken the idea a bit far. The 8th-century Mercian king built Offa's Dyke, Britain's longest archaeological monument, to mark the boundary between his kingdom and that of the Welsh princes, and even today, though only 80 miles of the dyke remains, the modern Wales–England border roughly follows the line it defined.

The Offa's Dyke Path National Trail criss-crosses that border around 30 times in its journey from the Severn Estuary near Chepstow, through the beautiful Wye Valley and Shropshire Hills, to the coast at Prestatyn in North Wales. The dyke itself usually takes the form of a bank next to a ditch, although it's overgrown in some places and built over in others. The trail often strays from the dyke, covering an astonishing range of scenery and vegetation, including river valleys, hill country, oak forests, heathland and bracken, conifer forest, green fields, high moors and the mountainous terrain of the Clwydian Ranges in the north.

While it can be walked in either direction, it's best done south to north, with the wind and sun mainly on your back. Most people take 12 days to complete the 177-mile walk, though it's wise to allow at least two rest days, bringing your adventure to an even two weeks.

The Offa's Dyke Centre (p195) is the best source of information about the route, stocking maps, guidebooks and pamphlets.

Knighton is one of the stops on the lovely Heart of Wales Line; destinations include Swansea (£25, 3¼ hours), Llandeilo (£8.60, two hours), Llanwrtyd Wells (£3.20, 30 minutes), Llandrindod Wells (£3.50, 34 minutes) and Shrewsbury (£7.50, 52 minutes). Bus 41 heads to Presteigne (20 minutes).

NEWTOWN (Y DRENEWYDD)

☎ 01686 / pop 10,400

Newtown's a former mill town with lots of history but, as a destination, it's also a sleepy place these days – absolutely soporific on a Sunday, but waking up for the Tuesday and Saturday markets. Its big claim to fame is that Robert Owen, the factory reformer, founder of the co-operative movement and 'father of Socialism', was born here in 1771, though he left at the age of 10 and only returned just before his death in 1858. Monuments to his esteemed memory abound in the town centre.

Newtown was also once the home of Welsh flannel and a major UK textile centre. When competition began driving wages down, Wales' first Chartist meeting was held here in October 1838. Pryce Jones, the world's first-ever mail-order firm, got its start here, on the back of the textile trade. By the end of the 19th century Newtown's boom days were over – and they've never been back. There are several small museums devoted to those long-gone salad days.

Newtown is almost the home of Laura Ashley (she opened her first shop in Carno, 10 miles west of the centre).

ORIENTATION

Newtown nestles in a bend of the River Severn (Afon Hafren) north of the Welshpool–Aberystwyth road (A489).

TOP FIVE

LONG-DISTANCE WALKING PATHS

- ★ Wye Valley Walk (p73)
- ★ Beacons Way (p73)
- ★ Pembrokeshire Coast Path (p148)
- ★ Offa's Dyke Path (p195)
- ★ Glyndŵr's Way (p177)

The centre is The Cross, at the intersection of Broad, High, Severn and Shortbridge Sts. The post office and most of the banks are on Broad St, which at its northern end traverses the river. From the train station to the centre, it is a walk of approximately 600m via Old Kerry Rd, Shortbridge St and Wesley St. If you get stuck at any point, there are information boards with maps scattered around town.

EXPLORING NEWTOWN

❦ ROBERT OWEN MEMORIALS // CELEBRATING A LIFE WELL LIVED
If you're not aware of Robert Owen's legacy, you're best to start at the tiny **Robert Owen Museum** (☎ 626345; www.robert-owen-museum.org.uk; The Cross; admission free; ◷ 9.30am-noon & 2-3.30pm Mon-Fri, 9.30-11.30am Sat), in the town-council building (which also serves at the de facto tourist office and has free internet access). The displays are broken up with mementos and pictures; it's quite text-heavy but it makes fascinating reading.

Owen was the son of a saddler who became a successful cotton-mill owner. His then-radical reforms included reducing working hours from 14 to 16 hours per day to 10 to 12, setting a minimum working age of 10 and funding schools for his employees' children, which included music and dancing alongside academic instruction. He's considered a founding father of the co-operative and the trade union movements. At the corner of Gas and Short Bridge Sts a **statue and garden** herald him as a 'pioneer, social reformer and philanthropist'.

Owen's well-tended **grave** is in the grounds of **St Mary's Old Parish Church** (Old Church St). Dating from at least 1253, the church was allowed to fall into ruin after a bigger church was built in 1856 and it's now a public garden, thanks to the local co-operative union. There's also a memorial here to Thomas Powell, a disciple of Owen who became a Chartist leader, part of the movement demanding a vote for all men, not just the rich.

❧ THE PARK // CASTLE, STONE CIRCLE, ART AND GOOD FOOD

A block west of Broad St is a leafy riverside park that contains a mound that is all that remains of Newtown's 13th-century **castle** and a gorsedd stone circle dating from the Royal National Eisteddfod of 1965. Where the park meets Back Lane is the **Oriel Davies** (☎ 625041; www .orieldavies.org; The Park; admission free; 🕑 10am–5pm Mon-Sat), one of Wales' leading contemporary spaces hosting often edgy exhibitions. The **cafe** (☎ 622288; mains £5-7) in the sunny, glassed-in corner of the gallery is best place in Newtown for a light meal, such as homemade soup, quiche or baked potatoes.

❧ OTHER MUSEUMS & GALLERIES // MORE LOCAL HISTORY ON DISPLAY

In former weavers' cottages and workshops, just north of the river, the **Textile Museum** (☎ 622024; www.powys.gov.uk; 5-7 Commercial St; admission free; 🕑 2-5pm Mon, Tue & Thu-Sat May-Sep) has impressively re-created rooms to show what living conditions

were like in the 1820s. Above the cottages are the workshops with depictions of the workers, both adults and children.

The **WH Smith bookshop** (☎ 626280; 24 High St; 🕑 9am-5.30pm Mon-Sat) has been restored to its original 1929 look, complete with wooden furniture and skylights. Upstairs is a little free company **museum**.

TRANSPORT

BUS // Bus routes include X75 to Welshpool (25 minutes) and Shrewsbury (1¼ hours); X85 to Machynlleth (54 minutes) and 704 to Llandrindod Wells (one hour), Builth Wells (1½ hours) and Brecon (two hours).

COACH // The daily **National Express** (www. nationalexpress.com) coach from Aberystwyth (£9.40, 80 minutes) to London (£30, 5½ hours), via Welshpool (£4.30, 25 minutes), Shrewsbury (£7.50, 55 minutes) and Birmingham (£10, 2½ hours) stops here.

TRAIN // Newtown is on the Cambrian Line, which crosses from Aberystwyth (£9.80, 1¼ hours) to Birmingham (£13, 1¾ hours) every two hours, via Machynlleth (£7.40, 42 minutes), Welshpool (£3.90, 15 minutes) and Shrewsbury (£5.60, 39 minutes).

NEWTOWN TO WELSHPOOL

❧ GREGYNOG HALL // WONDERFUL GARDENS ENCIRCLING A GRAND MANSION

Dating from the 19th-century in its current mock-Tudor incarnation, **Gregynog Hall** (☎ 01686-650224; www.gregynog.wales.ac.uk; Tregynon) has been here in some form for 800 years. From 1924 it was the home of the Davies sisters, Gwendoline and Margaret, who are known for the extraordinary collection of paintings they bequeathed to the National Museum (see p45). Their grandfather was David Davies (a sawyer turned miner) who, when prevented by the Bute family from exporting his coal from Cardiff, built his own docks at Barry and made a fortune.

MID-WALES

The sisters intended to make the house an arts centre, founding a fine-arts press in the stables and holding an annual Festival of Music and Poetry. In the 1960s the estate was given to the University of Wales, which uses it as a conference centre. Successor to the sisters' festival is the week-long **Gwyl Gregynog Festival** (☎ 01686-207100; www.gwylgregynogfestival.org) held annually in mid-June, with operatic, choral, orchestral and instrumental music performed in the grounds of the house. The house, its interior largely unchanged since Margaret's death in 1963, opens for group tours by appointment and you'll find a cafe and shop (open daily).

However, the main drawcard is the 300 hectares of Grade 1–listed **garden**, which are estimated to date from at least the 16th century. There are avenues of sculpted yews, impressive rhododendrons and azaleas, 300-year-old oaks and bird-filled beech woodlands, all accessible on a series of walking tracks. Admission to the grounds is unrestricted, although there is a small charge for parking.

Gregynog Hall is situated 5 miles north of Newtown, signposted from the B4389.

❧ BERRIEW // AS PRETTY A VILLAGE AS ANY IN MID-WALES

Shortly before the River Rhiw empties into the Severn it gurgles through this postcard-perfect village of black and white houses, grouped around an ancient oval churchyard.

It's the unlikely location for the supremely flouncy and fascinating **Andrew Logan Museum of Sculpture** (☎ 01686-640689; www.andrewlogan.com; adult/child £3/1.50; ☽ noon-4pm Sat & Sun Jun-Sep). The building is actually a former squash court but it has played host to a very different display of physical prowess

since Logan took it over in 1991. Today, it's a glorious celebration of sequins and camp, with beautiful, frivolous, humorous artworks, including a huge cosmic egg made of fibreglass and a larger-than-life portrayal of fashion designer Zandra Rhodes. Logan has been running the *Alternative Miss World* contest since 1972 ('a parade of freaks, fops, show-offs and drag queens') and the museum contains many relics of the shows.

In the eight months of the year when the museum is closed, it's still worth stopping at Berriew for a stroll and lunch at **Lychgate Cottage** (☎ 01686-640750; mains £4-6). This little tearoom and delicatessen serves delicious Welsh cheese and pate platters, Ludlow olives, sandwiches, baguettes and cakes.

Berriew is 6 miles south of Welshpool, just off the A483; take bus 75 from Newtown (18 minutes) or Welshpool (14 minutes).

WELSHPOOL (Y TRALLWNG)

☎ 01938 / pop 6300

The English originally called this place Pool, after the 'pills' – boggy, marshy ground (long since drained) along the nearby River Severn. It was changed in 1835 to Welshpool, so nobody would get confused with Poole in Dorset. It's a workaday place with few distractions in the town centre proper and few inspiring options for people seeking to stay overnight. More compelling, however, are the peripheral sights such as glorious Powis Castle and the narrow-gauge Welshpool and Llanfair Light Railway.

ESSENTIAL INFORMATION

EMERGENCIES // Police station (☎ 101; Severn St) **Victoria Memorial Hospital** (☎ 553133; Salop Rd)

TOURIST OFFICES // Tourist office
(☎ 552043; Vicarage Gardens, Church St; ◷ 9.30am-5pm Mon-Sat, 10am-4pm Sun)

ORIENTATION

The centre of town is The Cross, a four-way intersection where Severn Rd, Church St, Broad St and Berriew Rd meet. Severn Rd leads into Broad St, which rapidly changes name to High St, Mount St and then Raven St – this is the main shopping strip.

EXPLORING WELSHPOOL

❦ POWIS CASTLE & GARDEN // A CASTLE FIT FOR A KING

Surrounded by magnificent gardens, the red-brick **Powis Castle** (☎ 551920; www.nationaltrust.org.uk; adult/child castle & gardens £10.40/5.10, garden only £7.70/3.85; ◷ castle 1-5pm Thu-Mon Mar-Oct, garden 11am-5.30pm Thu-Mon Mar-Oct, 11am-3.30pm Sat & Sun Nov) rises up from its terraces as if floating on a fantastical cloud of massive, manicured yew trees. It was originally constructed in the 13th-century by Gruffydd ap Gwenwynwyn, prince of Powys, and was subsequently enriched by generations of the Herbert and Clive families.

The extravagant mural-covered, wood-panelled interior contains one of Wales' finest collections of furniture and paintings, including works by Gainsborough and Rubens and curios such as Mary, Queen of Scot's rosary beads.

The **Clive Museum**, in the former ballroom, holds a fascinating and exquisite cache of jade, ivory, armour, textiles and other treasures brought back from India by Baron Clive (British conqueror of Bengal at the Battle of Plassey in 1757), allowing a rare insight into the lifestyle of early colonialists.

The baroque garden is peerless, dotted with ornamental lead statues and an orangery, formal gardens, wilderness, terraces and orchards.

The castle is just over a mile south of The Cross, off Berriew Rd.

❦ WELSHPOOL & LLANFAIR LIGHT RAILWAY // WORK UP A HEAD OF STEAM

This sturdy **narrow-gauge railway** (☎ 810441; www.wllr.org.uk; Raven Sq; adult/child £11.80/5.90; ◷ Apr-Oct, check times online) was completed in 1902 to help people bring their sheep and cattle to market. It runs up steep inclines and through the pretty Banwy Valley. The line was closed in 1956 but reopened seven years later by enthusiastic volunteers.

Trains make the 8-mile journey from Raven Square Station to Llanfair Caereinion in 50 minutes and according to a complex timetable. There are also courses on offer to learn how to drive your very own steam engine.

❦ POWYSLAND MUSEUM & MONTGOMERY CANAL // WATERSIDE SETTING FOR LOCAL HISTORY

The Montgomery Canal originally ran for 35 miles starting at Newtown and ending at Frankton Junction in Shropshire, where it joined the Llangollen Canal. After sections of its banks burst in 1936 it lay abandoned until a group of volunteers and the British Waterways Board began repairing it in 1969.

Beside the canal wharf is the **Powysland Museum** (☎ 554656; www.powys.gov.uk; Severn Rd; adult/child £1/free; ◷ 11am-5pm Thu-Tue May-Sep, 11am-5pm Mon-Tue & Thu-Fri, 11am-2pm Sat Oct-Apr), marked outside by a big blue handbag (an Andy Hancock sculpture to commemorate the Queen's Jubilee) and pillars painted by local schoolchildren and topped by carved birds. Inside, the museum tells the story of the county, with great details – such as the Roman recipe for stuffed dormouse.

FESTIVALS & EVENTS

Country & Western Music Festival

(☎ 552563; www.countrywestern.org.uk; adult/child £10/1; ⏱ 10am-7pm) On the third Sunday in July, the county showground near Powis Castle becomes the unlikely venue for a one-day hoedown with spit roasts and line dancing; proceeds benefit disabled children through the Heulwen Trust.

TRANSPORT

BUS // Bus routes include X2 to Bala (1¾ hours) and Llandudno (3½ hours) and X75 to Newtown (25 minutes) and Shrewsbury (45 minutes).

COACH // The daily National Express (www. nationalexpress.com) coach from Aberystwyth (£11, 1¾ hours) to London (£30, five hours), via Newport (£4.30, 25 minutes), Shrewsbury (£4.60, 30 minutes) and Birmingham (£9.40, 2¼ hours) stops in front of the tourist office.

PARKING // There's a large car park near the tourist office at Vicarage Gardens, just off Church St (per hour 50p, over four hours £2.50, free from 6pm to 8am).

TRAIN // Welshpool is on the Cambrian Line, which crosses from Aberystwyth (£11, 1½ hours) to Birmingham (£13, 1½ hours) every two hours, via Machynlleth (£9.50, 57 minutes), Newtown (£3.90, 15 minutes) and Shrewsbury (£4.70, 24 minutes).

MACHYNLLETH

☎ 01654 / pop 2200

Little Machynlleth (ma-*hun*-khleth) punches well above its weight. The town is saturated in historical significance, as it was here that nationalist hero Owain Glyndŵr established the country's first parliament in 1404. But even that legacy is close to being trumped by Machynlleth's recent reinvention as the green capital of Wales – thanks primarily to the Centre for Alternative Technology (CAT), 3 miles north of town.

The centre has given Machynlleth a green cache that attracts alternative lifestylers from far and wide. If you want to get your runes read, take up yoga or explore holistic dancing, Machynlleth is the ideal place for you – and you won't

GLYNDŴR'S WAY NATIONAL TRAIL   BECKY OHLSEN

Named after the renowned Welsh leader, Glyndŵr's Way cuts an arc through Powys, taking in many sites connected with him. The persistence of a strong Welsh identity, clear at every stop along the trail, is one of the unique pleasures of walking it.

The landscape is predominantly low moorland and farmland, with lakes, gentle hills and beautiful valleys. A particular highlight is the impressive range of bird life, including buzzards, kingfishers, woodpeckers, red kites, peregrine falcons, flycatchers and wrens.

Most people take nine days to complete the 132-mile walk. Starting from Knighton, we'd suggest making Felindre (15 miles) your first stop, followed by Abbey-cwm-hir (14 miles), Llandiloes (15.5 miles), Dylife (16 miles), Machynlleth (14.5 miles), Llanbrynmair (14 miles), Llanwddyn (17.5 miles), Pontrobert (12 miles) and Welshpool (13.5 miles). Accommodation is scarce along the route, so book ahead. On some of the more remote sections you'll need to pack a lunch and carry enough water for the day.

The hilly terrain and difficulty of route-finding, due to a multitude of paths crossing the trail, can make for pretty slow going, so it's wise to allow a little more time than you would for more established trails. It's essential to carry a compass and a good set of maps. Your best bet is to pick up the *Glyndŵr's Way* official National Trail Guide by David Perrott, which includes extracts from the relevant Ordnance Survey 1:25,000 Explorer maps.

have any problem finding vegetarian and organic food. Better still, it's surrounded by serene countryside, particularly suited to mountain biking.

ESSENTIAL INFORMATION

EMERGENCIES // **Police station** (☎ 101; Doll St)

TOURIST OFFICES // **Dyfi Craft & Clothing** (☎ 703369; Owain Glyndŵr Centre, Maengwyn St; ☺ 10am-4pm Mon-Sat) Following the demise of the official tourist office, this little store stocks brochures, maps and accommodation information.

ORIENTATION

The town pivots around the overwrought Castlereagh Clock Tower, at the intersection where the A489 (Maengwyn St) meets the A487 (Penrallt and Pentrehedyn Sts). Buses stop near here, while the train station is half a mile north, via Penrallt and then Doll St.

EXPLORING MACHYNLLETH

♥ MOMA WALES // **IT'S HARDLY NEW YORK BUT IT'S PRETTY GOOD** Housed partly in the Tabernacle, a neoclassical former Methodist chapel (1880), the **Museum of Modern Art** (☎ 703355; www.momawales.org.uk; Penrallt St; admission free; ☺ 10am-4pm Mon-Sat) exhibits work by contemporary Welsh artists as well as an annual international competition (mid-July to early September). The small permanent collection is supplemented by a continuous roster of temporary exhibitions. The chapel itself has the feel of a courtroom but the acoustics are good – it's used for concerts, theatre and talks.

♥ OWAIN GLYNDŴR CENTRE // **A MEDIEVAL IMPOSTOR TELLING A GENUINE WELSH STORY** Housed in a rare example of a latemedieval Welsh town house, the **Owain**

Glyndŵr Centre (☎ 702932; www.canol fanglyndwr.org; Maengwyn St; adult/child £2/free; ☺ 10am-4pm Tue-Sat Easter-Sep) has somewhat dry displays but nevertheless tells a riproaring story of the Welsh hero's fight for independence. Although it's called the Old Parliament Building it was probably built around 1460, some 50 years after Glyndŵr instituted his parliament on this site, but it's believed to closely resemble the former venue.

♥ MOUNTAIN BIKING // **HEAD TOWARDS A MUDDY CLI-MACHX** Maintaining three waymarked mountainbike routes from Machynlleth, **Dyfi Mountain Biking** (www.dyfimountainbiking. org.uk) offers the Mach 1 (10 miles), 2 (14 miles) and 3 (19 miles), each more challenging than the one before. The Mach 3's certainly not for beginners. In the Dyfi Forest, near Corris, is the custombuilt, 9-mile, Cli-machx loop trail. In May the same crew run the **Dyfi Enduro**, a non-competitive, long-distance, mountain-bike challenge, limited to 650 riders.

There is, in addition, a walking and cycling trail that leads off the A487 (just north of the train station) and follows a countryside path, crossing the Millennium Bridge, and leading you towards the CAT by the greenest possible forms of transport.

Holey Trail (☎ 700411; 31 Maengwyn St; ☺ 10am-6pm Mon-Sat) hires mountain bikes (per day £25), performs repairs and offers bunkhouse accommodation. It is also a mine of information on the local trails.

FESTIVALS & EVENTS

Machynlleth Comedy Festival (www. machcomedyfest.co.uk) A long weekend of laughs in late April.

MID-WALES

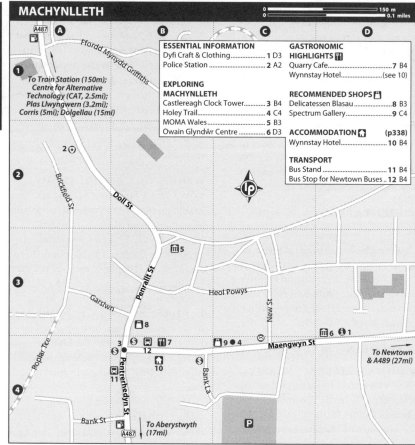

MACHYNLLETH

To Train Station (150m); Centre for Alternative Technology (CAT, 2.5mi); Plas Llwyngwern (3.2mi); Corris (5mi); Dolgellau (15mi)

Ffordd Mynydd Griffiths

Brickfield St

Doll St

Penrallt St

Garsiwn

Heol Powys

New St

Poplar Tce

Maengwyn St

To Newton & A489 (27mi)

Pentrerhedyn St

Bank La

Bank St

To Aberystwyth (17mi)

ESSENTIAL INFORMATION		
Dyfi Craft & Clothing	1	D3
Police Station	2	A2

EXPLORING MACHYNLLETH		
Castlereagh Clock Tower	3	B4
Holey Trail	4	C4
MOMA Wales	5	B3
Owain Glyndŵr Centre	6	D3

GASTRONOMIC HIGHLIGHTS		
Quarry Cafe	7	B4
Wynnstay Hotel	(see 10)	

RECOMMENDED SHOPS		
Delicatessen Blasau	8	B3
Spectrum Gallery	9	C4

ACCOMMODATION	(p338)	
Wynnstay Hotel	10	B4

TRANSPORT		
Bus Stand	11	B4
Bus Stop for Newtown Buses	12	B4

Gŵyl Machynlleth (Machynlleth Festival; www. momawales.org.uk) Takes place during the third week of August at the Tabernacle (see MOMA p201), with music ranging from kids' stuff to cabaret, plus a lively fringe festival.

GASTRONOMIC HIGHLIGHTS

The town's Wednesday **farmers market** (Maengwyn St) has been going on for over seven centuries and remains a lively affair.

☎ QUARRY CAFE £

☎ 702624; Maengwyn St; mains £3-7; ⓧ breakfast & lunch Mon-Sat; � 🛜 Ⓥ

Run by the same people as the CAT, this popular place dishes up delicious, wholesome, vegetarian lunch specials, using mostly organic ingredients. It's also very baby friendly with organic baby food on the menu, and changing facilities available.

☎ WYNNSTAY HOTEL ££

☎ 702941; www.wynnstay-hotel.com; Maengwyn St; mains £11-17

Flying in the face of Machynlleth's vegie-warrior image, the Wynnstay's menu revels in gaminess – offering dishes like a trio of rabbit and confit duck. In this 1780 coaching inn the country grub is matched by a country pub feel, with roaring fires in winter and dining areas scattered around the ground floor.

RECOMMENDED SHOPS

Machynlleth has a proud tradition of keeping local, independent shops alive with the main suspects found along Maengwyn St.

❦ DELICATESSEN BLASAU

☎ 700410; Penrallt Rd; ⏰ 10am-5pm Mon-Sat

A superb little deli selling take-away sandwiches, organic produce and fairtrade supplies. Specialising in local produce, it has a good selection of fruit wines, mead, liqueurs and chocolate – all of which would make excellent gifts for the cat-sitter back home.

❦ SPECTRUM GALLERY

☎ 702877; www.spectrumgallery.co.uk; Maengwyn St; ⏰ 10am-5pm Mon-Sat Mar-Dec, closed Mon & Thu Jan & Feb

A particularly interesting little place with a range of paintings, arty crafts and design-led gifts. Look for the all-seeing eye that glares over the street from the shop's facade.

TRANSPORT

BIKE // Lôn Las Cymru passes through Machynlleth, heading north to Corris, south to Llanwrtyd Wells and southeast to Rhayader.

BUS // Routes include 28 to Aberystwyth (45 minutes) and Fairbourne (1¼ hours); X32 to Corris (13 minutes), Dolgellau (35 minutes), Porthmadog (1½ hours), Caernarfon (2¼ hours) and Bangor (2¾ hours); and X85 to Newtown (54 minutes).

PARKING // The main car park is south of Maengwyn St, off Bank Lane (per hour 50p, over four hours £2.50, free 6pm to 8pm).

TRAIN // Machynlleth is on the Cambrian and Cambrian Coast Lines. Destinations include Aberystwyth (£4.90, 33 minutes), Porthmadog (£11, 1¾ hours), Pwllheli (£13, 2¼ hours), Newtown (£7.40, 42 minutes) and Birmingham (£15, 2¼ hours).

AROUND MACHYNLLETH

❦ CENTRE FOR ALTERNATIVE TECHNOLOGY // INFORMATIVE, THOUGHT-PROVOKING, INSPIRING AND FUN

A small but dedicated band of enthusiasts have spent over 30 years practising sustainability at the thought-provoking CAT (☎ 705950; www.cat.org.uk; adult/child £8.50/4; ⏰ 10am-5.30pm), set in a beautiful wooded valley 3 miles north of Machynlleth.

Founded in 1974 (well ahead of its time), CAT is a virtually self-sufficient workers' cooperative that acts as an ecologically driven laboratory and information source for alternative technologies. There are now more than three hectares of displays dealing with topics such as composting, organic gardening, environmentally friendly construction, renewable energy sources and sewage treatment and recycling. It has about 130 on-site workers and 15 full-time residents. To explore the whole site takes about two hours – take rainwear as it's primarily outdoors. Kids love the interactive displays and adventure playground and there's a great organic wholefood restaurant.

The visit starts with a 60m ride up the side of an old quarry in an ingenious water-balanced cable car (closed in winter to save water). A drum beneath the top car fills with stored rainwater and is then drawn down while the bottom car is hauled up. At the top you disembark by a small lake with great views across the Dyfi Valley.

MID-WALES ACCOMMODATION

Aberystwyth is by the far the liveliest place to base yourself but much of the charm of this region is in its secluded valleys and green fringes. Llanwrtyd Wells fits the bill but still keeps things interesting with a healthy dose of crazy. The other Wells (Builth and Llandrindod) are more sedate and could get dull after a day. Active sorts, eco-warriors and hippies should follow the green brick road to Machynlleth. For accommodation reviews, see p336. These are our top picks:

★ **Bodalwyn** (p336) Homely Edwardian B&B in Aberystwyth.

★ **Ynyshir Hall** (p336) Stately manor in Eglwysfach with a Michelin-starred restaurant.

★ **Ardwyn House** (p336) Grand old house on the edge of Llanwrtyd Wells.

★ **Cottage** (p337) Welcoming B&B in the centre of Llandrindod Wells.

★ **Horse & Jockey Inn** (p337) Smartly renovated pub accommodation in Knighton.

There are workshops and games for children during the main school holidays and an extensive program of residential courses for adults throughout the year (day courses start from around £45). Volunteer helpers willing to commit to a six-month stint are welcome, but you'll need to apply.

To get to the CAT from Machynlleth (six minutes) you can take the 32, X32 or 34 bus. Arriving by bus or bicycle gets you a discount of £1.

❦ CORRIS // FANTASY AND GRIMY REALITY BENEATH THE GROUND

Set within a commercial pine forest on the edge of Snowdonia National Park, Corris is a peaceful former slate village, 5 miles north of Machynlleth and 2 miles past the CAT. Built in the 1850s to transport slate, the narrow-gauge **Corris Railway** (☎ 761303; www.corris.co.uk; adult/child £5/2.50; ☺ Apr-Sep, see website for timetable) now offers 50-minute trips, which include a guided tour of the sheds.

On the A487, just outside of the village is the **Corris Craft Centre** (☎ 761244; www.corriscraftcentre.co.uk; ☺ 10am-5.30pm Apr-Oct), a virtual hive of interconnected hexagonal workshops for potters, glass-blowers, leatherworkers, wood turners, candle-makers and quilters, along with a cafe to keep everyone productive.

Below here is the old slate mine, which is used for two subterranean tours. Child-focused **King Arthur's Labyrinth** (☎ 761584; www.kingarthurslabyrinth.com; adult/child £7.50/5; ☺ 10am-5pm Easter-Oct) includes an underground boat ride and tour through tunnels where a sound-and-light show, manikins and a hooded guide bring the old tales to life.

Corris Mine Explorers (☎ 761244; www.corrismineexplorers.co.uk; 90min/half-day £15/30), on the other hand, requires a reasonable level of fitness, a willingness to get wet and dirty and the nerve to last at least 90 minutes exploring the dark, cramped, abandoned depths of the old mine; minimum age 13 years, bookings essential.

The X32 bus between Machynlleth (11 minutes) and Dolgellau (22 minutes) and the 30 and 34 from Machynlleth all stop here.

SNOWDONIA & THE LLŶN

3 PERFECT DAYS

❧ DAY 1 // CONQUER THE MOUNTAIN

Check the weather forecast before making an assault on Snowdon (p226). If you're fit, catch the Snowdon Sherpa bus to Pen-y-Pass and take the Pyg Track (p227). Time your descent via the Rhyd Ddu Path to catch the Welsh Highland Railway (p244) back to Caernarfon. If you're not up for climbing, head to Llanberis and take the Snowdon Mountain Railway (p227). You'll be up and down the mountain in 2½ hours, leaving plenty of time to check out the National Slate Museum (p230) and Dolbadarn Castle (p231) before stocking up on mead at Snowdon Honey Farm (p231). Head to Caernarfon and watch the sunset over the Menai Strait from beside the city walls before dining at the Black Boy Inn (p235).

❧ DAY 2 // BE A PILGRIM

Spend the morning exploring Caernarfon Castle (p233) before heading for the Llŷn Peninsula. Ideally you'll have prebooked a boat to Bardsey but if they're not running, make do with gazing at the island from Braich-y-Pwll (p239). Abersoch (p241), Criccieth (p243) and Porthmadog (p244) are good places to stop for the night, but Harlech (p218) has the best restaurants – along with another World Heritage castle.

❧ DAY 3 // A SCENIC OVERLOAD

Wherever you ended up, take the scenic A498 through the Pass of Aberglaslyn and back into the national park. Spend the day pottering along the route between Beddgelert (p228) and Betws-y-Coed (p222), stopping at the lakes, lookouts and falls. Betws makes a wonderfully atmospheric coda to a Snowdonia stay.

SNOWDONIA & THE LLŶN

CAERNARFON CASTLE p233

A Byzantine show of strength beside the Menai Strait

SNOWDON p226

Wales rises to a crescendo at this beautiful, surprisingly accessible, peak

WELSH HIGHLAND RAILWAY p245

A (nearly) coast-to-coast alpine train journey you'll never forget

BRAICH-Y-PWLL p239

The Llŷn gazes towards the holy island from this magical land's end

GETTING AROUND

Driving through this region involves zigzagging around mountains on well-kept, exceedingly scenic, minor roads. A network of regular and heritage lines makes a rail-based itinerary appealing. The Cambrian Coast Line connects Machynlleth to Pwllheli, via Porthmadog, where the Ffestiniog & Welsh Highland Railways head to Blaenau Ffestiniog and (by the time you're reading this) Caernarfon. From Blaenau the Conwy Valley Line heads through Betws-y-Coed to Llandudno. Pwllheli is the hub for Llŷn buses, while Snowdon Sherpa services zip around Snowdonia.

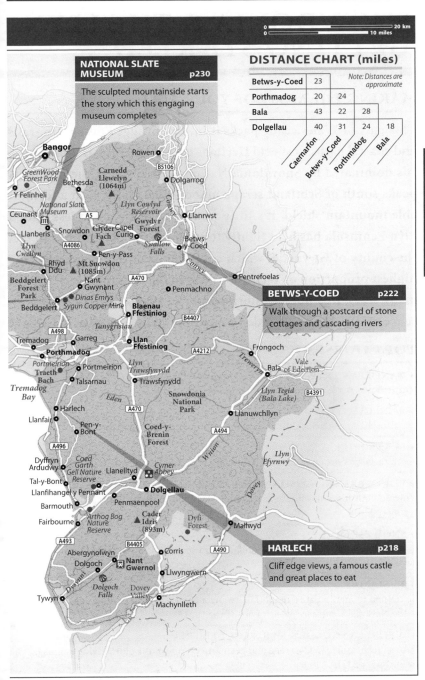

NATIONAL SLATE MUSEUM   p230

The sculpted mountainside starts the story which this engaging museum completes

DISTANCE CHART (miles)

	Betws-y-Coed	Porthmadog	Bala
Betws-y-Coed	23	Note: Distances are approximate	
Porthmadog	20	24	
Bala	43	22	28
Dolgellau	40	31	24	18

Caernarfon   Betws-y-Coed   Porthmadog   Bala

BETWS-Y-COED   p222

Walk through a postcard of stone cottages and cascading rivers

HARLECH   p218

Cliff edge views, a famous castle and great places to eat

0 ——— 20 km
0 ——— 10 miles

Bangor
Rowen
GreenWood Forest Park
Bethesda
Carnedd Llewelyn (1064m)
Dolgarrog
B5106
Y Felinheli
National Slate Museum
Llyn Cowlyd Reservoir
Gwydyr Forest
Llanrwst
Ceunant
A5
Llanberis
Snowdon
Glyder Fach
Capel Curig
Betws-y-Coed
Swallow Falls
Llyn Cwellyn
A4086
Pen-y-Pass
Rhyd Ddu
Mt Snowdon (1085m)
Nant Gwynant
A470
Pentrefoelas
Beddgelert Forest Park
Dinas Emrys
Sygun Copper Mine
Penmachno
Beddgelert
Blaenau Ffestiniog
Tanygrisiau
B4407
Tremadog
A498
Garreg
Llan Ffestiniog
Frongoch
Treweryn
Vale of Edeirnion
Porthmadog
Portmeirion
Portmeirion
A4212
Llyn Trawsfynydd
Bala
Traeth Bach
Talsarnau
Trawsfynydd
Tremadog Bay
Eden
Snowdonia National Park
Llyn Tegid (Bala Lake)
B4391
Harlech
A470
Llanuwchllyn
Llanfair
Pen-y-Bont
Coed-y-Brenin Forest
A494
Whion
A496
Llyn Efyrnwy
Dyffryn Ardudwy
Coed Garth Gell Nature Reserve
Llanelltyd
Cymer Abbey
Tal-y-Bont
Llanfihangel y Pennant
Dolgellau
Dovey
Barmouth
Penmaenpool
Arthog Bog Nature Reserve
Cader Idris (893m)
Dyfi Forest
Mallwyd
Fairbourne
A493
B4405
Abergynolwyn
Corris
A490
Dolgoch
Nant Gwernol
Llwyngwern
Dysynni
Dolgoch Falls
Dovey Valley
Tywyn
Machynlleth

SNOWDONIA & THE LLŶN GETTING STARTED

SNOWDONIA & THE LLŶN

MAKING THE MOST OF YOUR TIME

This part of Wales really packs it in, from rugged mountain trails and coastal paths to World Heritage castles and historic train lines. It's dominated by Snowdonia National Park, where the mightiest peaks south of Scotland scrape moody skies. With such a formidable mountain shield, it's little wonder that the much less visited Llŷn Peninsula has held tightly to its language and culture. In fact the county of Gwynedd, which covers most of this region, has the highest proportion of Welsh speakers in the country – over 76%. In many ways, this northwestern corner of Wales distils the very essence of Welshness – just don't mention that to the folks in Cardiff!

TOP COURSES

❦ **CANOLFAN TRYWERYN NATIONAL WHITEWATER CENTRE**
Hurtle down the River Tryweryn in a rubber raft (p220).

❦ **PARC GLYNLLIFON**
Try slate shaping, blacksmithing, appliqué or wood carving at a Craft Taster Day (p237).

❦ **PLAS MENAI**
Learn to sail, kayak or windsurf on the calm waters of the Menai Strait (p236).

❦ **PLAS Y BRENIN NATIONAL MOUNTAIN CENTRE**
Unleash your inner mountain goat, with instruction in rock climbing and mountaineering (p226).

❦ **SNOWBIKERS**
Learn to mountain bike or take a guided tour (☎ 430628; www.snowbikers.com; per day £60).

❦ **TŶ SIAMAS**
Be trained to manipulate a mandolin, twang a *telyn* (harp) or twiddle a *ffidl* (violin) at the National Centre for Welsh Folk Music (p212).

❦ **WELSH LANGUAGE & HERITAGE CENTRE**
Take a crash course in Cymraeg and get a grip on one of the oldest living languages in Europe (p237).

GETTING AWAY FROM IT ALL

* **Mawddach Estuary** Wetlands and woodlands edge the river and although you're never far from the road, it's a peaceful place to stretch your legs (p215).

* **Gwydyr Forest** Walking and mountain-biking paths criss-cross the forest surrounding Betws-y-Coed (p225).

* **Snowdon's Southern Approaches** While the summit and the tracks leading from Llanberis and Pen-y-Pass can get log-jammed in summer, the other half of the mountain is much quieter (p227).

* **Llŷn Peninsula** It's much less visited than Snowdonia National Park; wander its forgotten corners on the Llŷn Coastal Path and the Edge of Wales Walk (p241).

ADVANCE PLANNING

* **Snowdon Mountain Railway** With the new visitor centre now open at the summit, it's best to book well ahead to secure your place on the train (p227).

* **Prisoner Convention** (www.netreach .net/~sixofone/) One to either pencil in or avoid, the annual gathering of fans of the cult TV show converge on Portmeirion for a weekend in April.

* **Abersoch Jazz Festival** (www.abersoch jazzfestival.com) Hep cats join the surf rats at Abersoch for a weekend of smooth sounds in mid-June.

* **Bala Triathlons** (www.wrecsamtri.org.uk) Bala gets booked up during the middle distance triathlon in mid-June and the standard version in mid-September.

TOP RESTAURANTS

❦ **CASTLE RESTAURANT & ARMOURY BAR**
Big Caribbean flavours come to little old Harlech (p219).

❦ **CASTLE COTTAGE**
French technique brought to bear on Welsh classics (p219).

❦ **TYDDYN LLAN**
Highly rated country restaurant offering a palpable sense of occasion (p222).

❦ **BISTRO BETWS-Y-COED**
A bastion for Welsh cooking, traditional and modern (p224).

❦ **POACHERS RESTAURANT**
Traditional Welsh dishes married with exotic flavours (p243).

RESOURCES

* **Abersoch & Llŷn Tourism** (www.aber sochandllyn.co.uk) In-depth tourism information for the Llŷn Peninsula

* **Gwynedd Council** (www.gwynedd.gov.uk) Public transport and event information for the county

* **Met Office** (www.metoffice.gov.uk/ loutdoor/mountainsafety) Up-to-date weather conditions and forecasts

* **Snowdonia Mountains & Coast** (www .visitsnowdonia.info) Things to do, places to visit and where to stay

* **Snowdonia National Park** (www.eryri-npa. gov.uk) The national park's online home

SNOWDONIA NATIONAL PARK

· · · · · ·

Snowdonia National Park (Parc Cenedlaethol Eryri) was founded in 1951 (making it Wales' first national park), primarily to keep the area from being loved to death. This is, after all, Wales' best-known and most heavily used slice of nature, with the busiest part around Snowdon (1085m). Around 750,000 people climb, walk or take the train to the summit each year, and all those sturdy shoes make trail maintenance a never-ending task for park staff. Yet the park is so much more than just Snowdon, stretching some 35 miles east to west and over 50 miles north to south and incorporating coastal areas, rivers and Wales' biggest natural lake.

The Welsh name for Snowdonia, is Eryri (eh-*ruh*-ree) meaning highlands. The Welsh call Snowdon Yr Wyddfa (uhr-*with*-vuh), meaning Great Tomb – according to legend a giant called Rita Gawr was slain here by King Arthur and is buried at the summit.

Like Wales' other national parks, this one is very lived-in, with sizeable towns at Dolgellau, Bala, Harlech and Betws-y-Coed. Two-thirds of the park is privately owned, with over three-quarters used for raising sheep and cattle. While the most popular reason for visiting the park is to walk, you can also go climbing, whitewater rafting, kayaking and pony trekking, even windsurfing.

The park is the only home to two endangered species, an alpine plant called the Snowdon lily as well as the rainbow-coloured Snowdon beetle. The *gwyniad* is a species of whitefish found only in Llyn Tegid (Bala Lake), which also has probably the UK's only colony of glutinous snails.

The park authority publishes a free annual visitor newspaper, which includes information on getting around, park-organised walks and other activities. The Met Office keeps the weather conditions constantly updated on its website (www.metoffice.gov.uk/loutdoor/mountainsafety).

In the alpine reaches you'll need to be prepared to deal with hostile conditions at any time of the year; the sudden appearance of low cloud and mist is common, even on days that start out clear and sunny. Never head into isolated reaches without food, drink, warm clothing and waterproofs, whatever the weather. Carry *and* know how to read the appropriate large-scale Ordnance Survey (OS) map for the area, and carry a compass at all times. Also be aware that even some walks described as easy may follow paths that go near very steep slopes and over loose scree – the Pyg Track up Snowdon, for example.

DOLGELLAU

☎ 01341 / pop 2400

Dolgellau is a little place steeped in history with a palpable olde worlde feel. More than 200 of its stern stone buildings are listed for preservation – the highest concentration in Wales. It's thought the Welsh hero Owain Glyndŵr met with fellow rebels here, although the likely venue (on Bridge St) is now derelict and forgotten.

The Dolgellau area also has historical links with the Society of Friends (the Quakers). After George Fox visited in 1657, preaching its philosophy of direct communication with God, free from creeds, rites and clergy, a Quaker community was founded here. Converts, from simple farmers to local gentry, were

SNOWDONIA & THE LLŶN ACCOMMODATION

You can't really go wrong basing yourself in any of this region's charismatic towns and villages. Try Dolgellau for excellent boutique accommodation, Harlech for a genteel ambience and restaurants, Bala for outdoor activities and Welsh-language immersion, Betws-y-Coed or Beddgelert for alpine prettiness, Llanberis for interesting sights, Caernarfon for its medievalness, Aberdaron for isolation and Abersoch, Criccieth or Porthmadog for beaches. What Snowdonia's YHAs may lack in creature comforts, they more than make up for in stunning locations (see p328) and they are essential pit stops for walkers and cyclists. However, it's once again B&Bs that have topped our picks for the region:

* **Ffynnon** (p339) Boutique Dolgellau guesthouse with a contemporary design.

* **Maelgwyn House** (p339) Friendly hosts and homely rooms in Harlech.

* **Victoria House** (p341) Exceptional guesthouse within Caernarfon's old town walls.

* **Venetia** (p342) Slick designer rooms above an Italian restaurant in Abersoch.

* **Yr Hen Fecws** (p342) Characterful slate cottage in Porthmadog.

persecuted with vigour because their refusal to swear oaths – in particular to the king – was considered treasonous. Many eventually emigrated to William Penn's Quaker community in America.

Dolgellau was a regional centre for Wales' prosperous wool industry in the 18th and early 19th centuries. Many of the town's finest buildings, sturdy and unornamented, were built at that time and the town centre hasn't changed all that much since. Local mills failed to keep pace with mass mechanisation however, and decline set in after about 1800. The region bounced back when the Romantic Revival made Wales' wild landscapes popular with genteel travellers. There was also, surprisingly, a minor gold rush here in the 19th century. The wedding rings of Queen Elizabeth II and Diana, Princess of Wales were made from Dolgellau gold, and there are plans to reopen the mine.

Today however, this grey-slate, charmingly gruff little market town relies on tourism. One of Snowdonia's premier peaks, bulky Cader Idris, rises to the south, the lovely Mawddach Estuary lies to the west and, to the north, the Coed y Brenin Forest Park offers glorious mountain-biking country. In recent years some plush boutique accommodation options have sprung up, making it an appealing base from which to explore the national park.

ESSENTIAL INFORMATION

TOURIST OFFICES // Tourist office & national park information centre (☎ 422888; Eldon Sq; ☯ 9.30am-4.30pm) Sells an excellent range of maps, local history books and leaflets charting the trails for a climbing excursion to Cader Idris. Upstairs there's a permanent exhibition on the region's Quaker heritage in a suitably dour wood-panelled room.

ORIENTATION

Dolgellau sits at the confluence of the River Wnion (a tributary of the Mawddach) and the smaller River Arran. The A470 passes just north of the Wnion, while the town centre is to its south, reached by Bont Fawr (Big Bridge; built 1638).

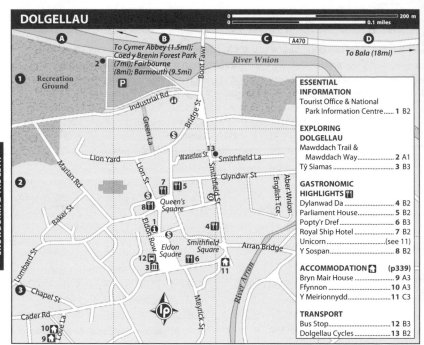

DOLGELLAU

To Cymer Abbey (1.5mi);
Coed y Brenin Forest Park
(7mi); Fairbourne
(8mi); Barmouth (9.5mi)

To Bala (18mi)

River Wnion

Recreation Ground

Industrial Rd

Green La

Bridge St

Bont Fawr

Marian Rd

Lion Yard

Lion St

Waterloo St

Smithfield La

Smithfield St

Glyndwr St

Aber-Wnion

English Tce

Baker St

Queen's Square

Eldon Row

Eldon Square

Smithfield Square

Arran Bridge

Lombard St

Chapel St

Cader Rd

Meyrick St

River Arran

EXPLORING DOLGELLAU

❧ TŶ SIAMAS // CELEBRATING A TRADITION EVEN OLDER THAN TOM JONES

Dolgellau has been an important hub for Welsh folk music ever since it held the first Welsh folk festival in 1952. In recognition of that, the town's former market hall has been transformed into the **National Centre for Welsh Folk Music** (☎ 421800; www.tysiamas.com; Eldon Sq; adult/child £4/2; ☷ 10am-5pm Mar-Oct, 10am-4pm Tue-Sat Nov-Feb), which opened in 2007. It's named after Elis Sîon Siamas, a harpist from Dolgellau who was the royal harpist to Queen Anne between 1702 and 1714. He was one of the first people to introduce the triple harp to Wales. The permanent exhibition includes audiovisual clips, musical instruments and interesting displays about Welsh folk traditions. Yet it's not

just a museum; it has a recording studio, stages workshops and performances, and offers lessons on traditional instruments.

❧ MAWDDACH TRAIL // PICTURESQUE PEDALLING OR STROLLING

The 9.5-mile **Mawddach Trail** (www .mawddachtrail.co.uk) is a flat (and in places wheelchair-accessible) path that follows an old train line through woods and past wetlands on the southern side of the Mawddach Estuary, before crossing over the train viaduct to Barmouth (where you can catch the bus back). The trail starts in the car park beside the bridge.

❧ MAWDDACH WAY // A MORE CHALLENGING MAWDDACH TRACK

While the Mawddach Trail follows the estuary's southern edge, **Mawddach Way** (www.mawddachway.co.uk) is a 30-mile, two- to

SNOWDONIA & THE LLŶN

three-day track looping through the hills on either side. Although the highest point is 346m, by the end of the undulating path you'll have climbed 2226m. The official guide splits the route into three legs: Barmouth–Taicynhaeaf (10 miles, five to six hours), Taicynhaeaf–Penmaenpool (9 miles, four to five hours) and Penmaenpool–Barmouth (11 miles, six to seven hours). Fit walkers should be able to do it in two days, with pit stops at Barmouth and Dolgellau.

An A5 booklet can be ordered or downloaded online (booklet/download £10/5); GPS route data can be downloaded for free.

❦ PUBS // CAP OFF A HARD DAY'S HOLIDAYING

For a straightforward pint with the locals, try the **Unicorn** (☎ 422742; Smithfield Sq) or the ivy-covered **Royal Ship Hotel** (☎ 422209; www.royalshiphotel.co.uk; Queen's Sq).

GASTRONOMIC HIGHLIGHTS

❦ DYLANWAD DA ££

☎ 422870; www.dylanwad.co.uk; 2 Smithfield St; mains £13-19; ⏰ Thu-Sat Apr-Sep

Informal cafe, wine and tapas bar by day, contemporary restaurant by night, this well-run, low-lit eatery has been serving up high-quality food for over 20 years. A long-standing favourite on the Snowdonia scene, it has a healthy wine list and an imaginative menu.

❦ PARLIAMENT HOUSE £

☎ 421938; Glyndŵr St; mains £4-6; ⏰ 9.30am-5.30pm Mon-Sat; 📶

With a fantastic period setting in a Grade II-listed former ironmonger's shop, still with its original fittings, this atmospheric coffee shop has light meals (soup, Welsh rarebit, sandwiches, ciabatta, baguettes), newspapers to browse, free internet access for patrons and a huge range of speciality teas.

❦ POPTY'R DREF £

☎ 422507; Smithfield St; honey buns 65p

Hello honey buns! We're not being rude – they're the house speciality at this fantastic deli, one of the few left with the original bakery out the back. Get in quick; they're usually sold out by 11am.

❦ Y SOSPAN ££

☎ 423174; Queen's Sq; breakfast & lunch £3-7, dinner £10-17; ⏰ breakfast & lunch daily, dinner Wed-Sun

In a book-lined and woody 1606 building that once served as a prison, this relaxed eatery serves fry-up breakfasts, sandwiches, jacket potatoes and light cooked meals during the day. At night, it switches to a heavier bistro menu, where lamb plays a starring role and most of the desserts have been on the booze, including an excellent bread-and-butter pudding.

TRANSPORT

BIKE // **Dolgellau Cycles** (☎ 423332; Smithfield St) Rents bikes, performs repairs and offers advice on local cycle routes. Lôn Las Cymru, the Welsh National Cycle Route (Sustrans route 8; see p302), passes through Dolgellau, heading north to Porthmadog and south to Machynlleth.

BUS // Buses stop on Eldon Sq in the heart of town. Routes include 28 to Penmaenpool (five minutes) and Fairbourne (20 minutes); X32 to Aberystwyth (1¼ hours), Machynlleth (35 minutes), Porthmadog (50 minutes), Caernarfon (1½ hours) and Bangor (two hours); 35 to Coed y Brenin (15 minutes) and Blaenau Ffestiniog (54 minutes); and X94 to Barmouth (24 minutes), Bala (35 minutes), Llangollen (1½ hours) and Wrexham (two hours).

PARKING // There's a car park just south of the River Wnion, next to Bont Fawr (50p per hour, over four hours £5.30, free 6pm to 8am).

AROUND DOLGELLAU

❦ TALYLLYN RAILWAY AND TALYLLYN LAKE // THOMAS THE TANK ENGINE'S REAL-LIFE INSPIRATION

Famous as the inspiration behind Rev W Awdry's *Thomas the Tank Engine* stories, the narrow-gauge **Talyllyn Railway** (☎ 01654-710472; www.talyllyn.co.uk; Wharf Station, Tywyn; adult/child £13/6.25; ⏰ check online timetable) was opened in 1865 to carry slate from the Bryn Eglwys quarries near Abergynolwyn. In 1950 the line was saved from closure by the world's first railway preservation society. It's one of Wales' most enchanting little railways and puffs for 7⅓ scenic, steam-powered miles up the Fathew Valley to Abergynolwyn. There are five stations along the way, each with waymarked walking trails (and waterfalls at Dolgoch and Nant Gwernol); leaflets on these are available at the stations. Your ticket entitles you to all-day travel.

At Tywyn's Wharf Station, the **Narrow Gauge Railway Museum** (www.ngrm. org.uk; admission free; ⏰ 10am-4.30pm May-Sep, 10am-2pm Oct) is one for the history buffs, with shiny narrow-gauge steam locomotives and the story of the volunteers who preserved the railway.

About 2 miles northeast of Abergynolwyn along the B4405 is **Talyllyn Lake**, a substantial and tranquil body of water edged by fields and hills and overlooked by Cader Idris. It's stocked with trout and popular with anglers.

Tywyn is on the Cambrian Coast Line, with direct trains to Machynlleth (£4.50, 26 minutes), Fairbourne (£3, 17 minutes), Barmouth (£4.50, 25 minutes), Porthmadog (£8.50, 1½ hours) and Pwllheli (£9.90, two hours). Bus 28 from Aberystwyth (1¼ hours) to Dolgellau (55 minutes) via Machynlleth (35 minutes) and Fairbourne (35 minutes) stops here.

❦ CADER IDRIS // LESS TAXING THAN SNOWDON BUT A LEGENDARY CLIMB

Cader Idris (893m), or the 'Seat of Idris' (a legendary giant), is a hulking, menacing-looking mountain with an appropriate mythology attached. It's said that hounds of the underworld fly around its peaks, and strange light effects are often sighted in the area. It's also said that anyone who spends the night on the summit will awake either mad or a poet – although perhaps you'd have to be a little mad or romantic to attempt it in the first place. Regardless of its repute, it's popular with walkers and it's the park's favourite locale for rock climbers.

The usual route to the summit is the 'Dolgellau' or **Tŷ Nant Path**, southeast from Tŷ Nant Farm on the A493. The farm is 3 miles west of Dolgellau, just beyond Penmaenpool. It's a rocky but safe, straightforward route, taking about five hours there and back.

The easiest but longest route (5 miles each way, six hours return) is the 'Tywyn' or **Llanfihangel y Pennant Path**, a gentle pony track that heads northeast from the hamlet of Llanfihangel y Pennant, joining the Tŷ Nant Path at the latter's midpoint. Llanfihangel is 1.5 miles from the terminus of the Talyllyn Railway (p214) at Abergynolwyn.

The shortest (3 miles each way) but steepest route is the **Minffordd Path**, running northwest from the Dol Idris car park, a few hundred metres down the B4405 from Minffordd, itself 6.5 miles from Dolgellau on the A487 Machynlleth road. This route, taking around five hours there and back, requires the most caution, especially on the way back down.

Whichever route you choose, wear stout shoes, carry protective clothing and check the weather conditions, either online (www.metoffice.gov.uk/loutdoor/mountainsafety) or at the Dolgellau tourist office (p211). It also stocks pamphlets on each route (40p).

✿ FAIRBOURNE // WHERE THOMAS GOES ON HIS HOLIDAYS, PERHAPS

Fairbourne has a lovely, long beach but little else to offer except the steam-hauled **Fairbourne Railway** (☎ 01341-250362; www.fairbournerailway.com; Beach Rd; adult/child £7.80/4.20; ☺ check online timetable), Wales' only seaside narrow-gauge railway. It was built in 1895 to move materials for the construction of the village. The line heads north along the coast for 2.5 miles to Penrhyn Point, where there are ferries across the mouth of the Mawddach to Barmouth, timed to meet the trains.

There's a restaurant at Penrhyn Point, while Fairbourne station has a cafe and the take-it-or-leave-it **Rowen Indoor Nature Centre** (admission free; ☺ 10.30am-4.30pm), showcasing an odd mix of ferrets, lizards and a model railway.

Fairbourne is on the Cambrian Coast Line, with direct trains to Machynlleth (£4.50, 26 minutes), Tywyn (£3, 17 minutes), Barmouth (£2, seven minutes), Porthmadog (£6.20, 58 minutes) and Pwllheli (£8.70, 1¼ hours). Bus 28 from Aberystwyth (two hours) to Dolgellau (20 minutes) via Machynlleth (1¼ hours) and Tywyn (35 minutes) stops here.

✿ MAWDDACH ESTUARY // TREASURED BY WALKERS AND WARBLERS

The glorious Mawddach Estuary is a striking sight: a mass of water flanked by woodlands, wetlands and the romantic mountains of southern Snowdonia. There are two Royal Society for the Pro-tection of Birds (RSPB) **nature reserves** (www.rspb.org.uk; admission free) in the estuary valley. On the south side, **Arthog Bog** is a small wetland reserve favoured by cuckoos, grasshopper warblers, lesser redpolls, reed buntings and siskins. Set in oak woodlands along the northern side, **Coed Garth Gell** has two circular walking trails; one 1.25 miles, the other 1.5 miles. Spring visitors include redstarts, wood warblers and pied flycatchers, while in summer you might spot dippers and in winter, woodcocks.

The estuary is easily reached on foot or by bike from Dolgellau or Barmouth via the Mawddach Trail (p212). Arthog Bog is 8 miles west of Dolgellau on the access road to Morfa Mawddach station, off the A493, while Coed Garth Gell is 2 miles west of Dolgellau on the A496.

✿ MAWDDACH RESTAURANT & BAR // FOOD WITH A VIEW

Two miles west of Dolgellau on the A496, **Mawddach** (☎ 01341-424020; www.mawddach.com; Llanelltyd; mains £10-17; ☺ lunch Wed-Sun, dinner Wed-Sat) brings a touch of urban style to what was once a barn. Black slate floors, brown leather seats and panoramic views across to Cader Idris set the scene. The food is equally impressive: meat straight from nearby farms, fresh local fish specials and traditional Sunday roasts (two/three courses £13/17).

✿ CYMER ABBEY // A PICTURESQUE PICNIC SPOT

This Cistercian abbey, founded in 1198, wasn't especially grand but the ruined walls and arches are still picturesque, especially when the daffodils are in bloom. There are walks in the vicinity and nice picnic spots near the river. It's 2 miles northwest of Dolgellau, signposted from the A470.

❦ COED Y BRENIN FOREST PARK // MOUNTAIN BIKING AND MONKEY BUSINESS

Covering 3640 hectares, this woodland park is the premier location for mountain biking in Wales. It's laced with 70 miles of purpose-built cycle trails, divided into seven graded routes to suit beginners or guns, and impressively presented by way of old-fashioned waterproof trail cards or downloadable geocaches and MP3 audio files.

The park's impressive environmentally friendly **visitor centre** (☎ 01341-440747; www.forestry.gov.uk/wales; ⏰ 9.30am-4.30pm daily) is 8 miles north of Dolgellau off the A470. You can buy the aforementioned trail cards here, as well as a set covering 10 tracks for walkers and runners. There's also a cafe, toilets and a children's play area, while downstairs you can hire bikes from **Beics Brenin** (☎ 01341-440728; www.beicsbrenin.co.uk; per day £25-50).

At the time of research a new high-wires course called **Go Ape** (☎ 0845 643 9215; www.goape.co.uk; adult/child from £30/20; ⏰ Easter-Oct) was about to open.

BARMOUTH (ABERMAW)

☎ 01341 / pop 2300

Despite a Blue Flag beach and the beautiful Mawddach Estuary on its doorstep, the seaside resort of Barmouth has a faded feel to it. In the summer months it becomes a typical kiss-me-quick seaside resort – all chip shops and dodgem cars – catering to the trainloads arriving in their thousands from England's West Midlands. Outside of the brash neon of high summer it's considerably mellower but it still has its rough edges.

Wales' only surviving wooden rail viaduct spans the estuary and has a handy pedestrian walkway across it. Behind the town rises rocky Dinas Oleu, the first property ever bequeathed to the National Trust (NT; in 1895) and an irresistible temptation for walkers.

ESSENTIAL INFORMATION

TOURIST OFFICES // Tourist office (☎ 280787; train station, Station Rd; ⏰ 10am-5pm Apr-Oct, 9.30am-3pm Mon-Fri Nov-Mar) Sells leaflets on local walks and train tickets for mainline connections, and offers an accommodation service.

ORIENTATION

The main commercial strip is spread out along the A496; as it passes through town it's known as Church St, High St and King Edward's St.

EXPLORING BARMOUTH

❦ WALKS // SOME CRACKING CALF-MUSCLE WORKOUTS

Apart from the Mawddach Trail (p212), you can scramble up any one of several alleys running off Church St, where you'll find the town gets more and more vertical, with better and better views, until the old houses are nearly on top of

---

> **TOP FIVE**
>
> **BIRDWATCHING**
>
> Whether you're chuffed by choughs or pleased by puffins, Wales offers plenty to get twitchy about.
>
> ★ National Wetland Centre (p128)
>
> ★ Bwlch Nant yr Arian (p187)
>
> ★ Gigrin Farm Red Kite Feeding Station (p194)
>
> ★ Mawddach Estuary (p215)
>
> ★ Ellin's Tower RSPB Nature Reserve (p258)

one another. Carry on up to a network of trails crossing 258m **Dinas Oleu**. Bear eastwards around the headland – on one of these paths or from the far end of Church St – to the popular **Panorama Walk**, which has the best of the estuary views. For more details, ask at the tourist office.

If you'd prefer some companions on the journey, the **Barmouth Festival of Walking** (www.barmouthwalkingfestival .co.uk) takes place over eight days in September.

❧ QUAYSIDE // BARMOUTH'S HISTORIC QUARTER

The oldest part of Barmouth is around Church St and the quay to its south. The unusual round building, **Tŷ Crwn**, was once a jail where drunk and disorderly sailors could cool off until morning. Nearby, in **Tŷ Gwyn**, supporters of Henry Tudor once met to plot his ascension to the throne. The ferry for Penrhyn Point (p215) departs from here.

❧ LAST INN // COSY, ATMOSPHERIC AND JUST PLAIN NICE

The best place to eat, drink and hang out in Barmouth is this old **inn** (☎ 280530; www .lastinn-barmouth.co.uk; Church St; mains £9-13), the last one before you hit the estuary. Dating from the 15th century, it's full of old ship timber, inglenook fireplaces and there's a mural portraying the town's history. Most unusually, the mountain forms the rear wall, with a spring emerging right inside the pub. Kids are welcome and the menu's full of pub crowd-pleasers, including a traditional Sunday roast. There's also live music from time to time.

Other decent pubs include the **Tal y Don** (☎ 280508; www.tal-y-don.co.uk; High St) and the **Royal Hotel** (☎ 281682; www.royal hotelsnowdonia.co.uk; King Edward St).

❧ THREE PEAKS YACHT RACE // STORMING THE HEIGHTS OF THREE COUNTRIES

Held in late June, this arduous **challenge** (www.threepeaksyachtrace.co.uk) has been attracting international crews for more than 30 years. Contestants sail to Caernarfon where two crew members run to the summit of Snowdon. They then sail to Whitehaven in England and run up Scafell Pike; and finally to Fort William in Scotland for an ascent of Ben Nevis – in all, 389 nautical miles of sailing and 72 miles of fell running. The record time for the race thus far is an astonishing two days, 14 hours and four minutes, achieved in 2002.

❧ DRAGON THEATRE // TREADING THE BARMOUTH BOARDS

The cultural life of the town is centred on the former Victorian chapel, which is now the **Dragon Theatre** (Theatr y Ddraig; ☎ 281697; www.dragontheatre.co.uk; Jubilee Rd) and its occasional program of live performances and cinema (including a kids' film club). Things really heat up in September when the Dragon hosts most of the events in the weeklong **Barmouth Arts Festival** (www .barmouthartsfestival.co.uk).

TRANSPORT

BIKE // Lôn Las Cymru passes through Barmouth, heading north to Harlech and south to Dolgellau.

BUS // Buses stop on Jubilee Rd, across Beach Rd from the train station. Routes include 38 to Harlech (34 minutes); and X94 to Dolgellau (24 minutes), Bala (1½ hours), Llangollen (2½ hours) and Wrexham (three hours).

TRAIN // Barmouth is on the Cambrian Coast Line, with direct trains to Machynlleth (£7, 57 minutes), Fairbourne (£2, seven minutes), Harlech (£3.70, 24 minutes), Porthmadog (£5.40, 48 minutes) and Pwllheli (£8.70, 1¼ hours).

HARLECH

SNOWDONIA & THE LLŶN

☎ 01766 / pop 2000

Hilly Harlech is best known for the mighty, grey stone towers of its castle, framed by gleaming Tremadog Bay and with the mountains of Snowdonia as a backdrop. Some sort of fortified structure has probably surmounted the rock since Iron Age times, but Edward I removed all traces when he commissioned the construction of the castle. Finished in 1289, Harlech Castle is the southernmost of four fortifications included in the Castles and Town Walls of King Edward in Gwynedd Unesco World Heritage Site.

Harlech is such a thoroughly pleasant place that it has become one of the more gentrified destinations in Snowdonia – every other shop seems to sell antiques or tea and there are some sophisticated places to eat at and sleep in. While it's bustling in summer, it can be deliciously sleepy otherwise. It makes a great base for a beach holiday or for day trips into the national park – and those views never get boring.

ESSENTIAL INFORMATION

TOURIST OFFICES // Tourist office
(☎ 780658; High St; ☽ 9.30am-5.30pm Apr-Oct)

ORIENTATION

The sea used to lap at the base of the rocks below the castle but now this flat piece of land is where you'll find the train station, a petrol station and a newer clump of houses; it's a strenuous 20-minute climb on one of several stepped tracks up to High St, or about half a mile by road.

EXPLORING HARLECH

♨ HARLECH CASTLE // THE CASTLE OF LOST CAUSES

Run by Cadw (the Welsh historic monuments agency), **Harlech Castle** (☎ 780552;

www.cadw.wales.gov.uk; adult/child £3.60/3.20; ☽ 9am-5pm Apr-Oct, 9.30am-4pm Mon-Sat, 11am-4pm Sun Nov-Mar) is an intimidating yet spectacular building. Edward I finished it in 1289, the southernmost of his 'iron ring' of fortresses designed to keep the Welsh firmly beneath his boot.

Despite its might, the story-book fortress has been called the 'Castle of Lost Causes' because it has been lucklessly defended so many times. Owain Glyndŵr captured it after a long siege in 1404. He is said to have been crowned Prince of Wales in the presence of envoys from Scotland, France and Spain during one of his parliaments in the town. He was, in turn, besieged here by the future Henry V.

During the Wars of the Roses the castle is said to have held out against a siege for seven years and was the last Lancastrian stronghold to fall. The siege inspired the popular Welsh hymn 'Men of Harlech', which is still played today in regimental marches and sung with patriotic gusto at rugby matches. The castle was also the last to fall in the English Civil War, finally giving in to Cromwell's forces in 1647.

The grey sandstone castle's massive, twin-towered gatehouse and outer walls are still intact and give the illusion of impregnability even now. Enter through the ticket office/gift shop and cross the drawbridge through the gatehouse into the compact inner ward. Four gloomy round towers guard the corners and you can climb onto the ramparts for views in all directions. Some are closed off and partly ruined, but you still get a good feel for what it was once like. The fortress' great natural defence is the seaward cliff face. When it was built, ships could sail supplies right to the base.

The finest exterior view (with Snowdon as a backdrop) is a craggy outcrop on Ffordd Isaf, opposite Maelgwyn House.

❧ THEATR HARLECH // FOCAL POINT FOR THESPIANS AND FILM-LOVERS

Quite an impressive theatre for a town of this population, **Theatr Harlech** (☎ 760557; www.theatrharlech.com; Ffordd Newydd) is a lively local arts centre that stages dance, theatre and music, and screens a well-considered assortment of Hollywood blockbusters and artier, higher-brow films.

GASTRONOMIC HIGHLIGHTS

❧ CASTLE COTTAGE £££

☎ 780479; www.castlecottageharlech.co.uk; Ffordd Pen Llech; 3-course dinner £37

Within arrow's reach of the castle, this fine dining restaurant serves a deliciously patriotic menu – revelling in local produce (Welsh lamb, beef and cod, Ruthin chicken, Menai mussels, wild duck, woodcock, cheeses) and traditional dishes such as *bara brith* (rich fruit tea loaf) and rarebit. Yet the execution is in the classical French style.

❧ CASTLE RESTAURANT & ARMOURY BAR ££

☎ 780416; Castle Sq; mains £12-15; ⏱ lunch & dinner Tue-Sun

If this place were transported to London it would have queues out the door, so one has to admire the gumption of opening such a wonderful Caribbean restaurant in Wales, let alone sleepy Harlech. Upstairs is the coolest cocktail bar in North Wales – red curtains, bauble chandeliers and a smooth soundtrack of Trojan reggae. Downstairs, the locals are switching on to the spicy delights of goat curry, jerk chicken and blackened salmon.

❧ CEMLYN TEA SHOP £

☎ 780425; www.cemlyntea.co.uk; High St; snacks around £5; ⏱ 10.30am-5pm Wed-Sun

The Coles (Jan and Geoff) may be merry old souls but it's tea that's king here. There are over 30 varieties on offer, along with a simple range of snacks to accompany them and a slew of Tea Guild Awards of Excellence on the walls. Best of all are the views from the terrace.

❧ PLAS RESTAURANT £££

☎ 780204; www.theplas.co.uk; High St; lunch £6-10, dinner £16-25

Boasting the finest view of any restaurant in town – over the castle and across to the Llŷn Peninsula – the Plas has a charmingly old-fashioned formal dining room and a sunny terrace. Lunch takes the form of baguettes and lighter cooked meals, with heavier fare served at dinner: Welsh beef and lamb, roast duckling, local seafood etc.

Also recommended:

Blue Lion (Y Llew Glas; 3 Plas y Goits; mains around £5) Deli-eatery with good-quality local produce, set in a small courtyard.

Castle Creamery (Hufenfar Castell; Castle Sq) Espresso and homemade ice cream.

Weary Walker (☎ 780751; High St; mains £3-8; ⏱ Sat-Wed winter, extended summer) Bacon butties and mugs of coffee are the go at this friendly place.

TRANSPORT

BIKE // Lôn Las Cymru passes through Harlech, heading north to Porthmadog and south to Barmouth.

BUS // Bus 38 to Barmouth (34 minutes) stops on High St.

PARKING // The car park by the castle charges £2 for two hours or £4 for 24 hours.

TRAIN // Harlech is on the Cambrian Coast Line, with direct trains to Machynlleth (£9.20, 1½ hours), Fairbourne (£4.50, 46 minutes), Barmouth (£3.70, 24 minutes), Porthmadog (£3, 22 minutes) and Pwllheli (£6.30, 45 minutes).

BALA (Y BALA) & AROUND

☎ 01678 / pop 2000

The town of Bala is synonymous with beautiful **Llyn Tegid** (Bala Lake), which sits at the northeastern end of town and was formed during the last Ice Age when glaciers blocked up the valley of the River Dee (Afon Dyfrdwy) with debris. This is Wales' largest freshwater lake – 4 miles long, three-quarters of a mile wide and, in places, over 140ft deep. The town, 18 miles northeast of Dolgellau, sits where the River Dee flows out of the lake and is joined by the River Tryweryn.

Bala is big on folk tales (see the boxed text, p221). One such tale, an alternative to the glacial version of events, says the valley was once the home of a cruel and dissolute prince named Tegid Foel. One night the harpist, at a banquet thrown by the prince, kept hearing a small bird urging him to flee the palace. He finally did so, fell asleep on a hilltop, and awoke at dawn to find the palace and principality drowned beneath the lake.

Bala was a centre for the Welsh wool industry during the 18th century but today it's better known as a gateway town to Snowdonia National Park. It has also recently built a reputation as a centre for water sports. The tiny main street is often bustling with visitors in summer and increasingly dotted with adventure sports and outdoors shops. The proximity to the lake and availability of top-notch adventures makes it a very lively little place.

The Romans had a camp here, the remains of which have been found on private land near the river. Just behind the high street is a Norman motte (castle mound) that would once have supported a wooden castle. Today Bala is staunchly Welsh and a predominantly Welsh-speaking town – about 80%. Local hero and MP

Thomas Edward Ellis, the Liberal Member of Parliament elected in 1886, was a prominent contemporary of Lloyd George in the movement towards an independent Wales at the end of the 19th century. One of Ellis' friends was Michael D Jones, founder of the Welsh colony in Patagonia.

ESSENTIAL INFORMATION

TOURIST OFFICES // Tourist office
(☎ 521021; Pensarn Rd; ☼ 10am-5pm Apr-Oct, 9.30am-3pm Fri-Mon Nov-Mar) Southwest of the centre, next to the leisure centre.

ORIENTATION

The town is essentially one long street (the A494), called Pensarn Rd at the southwestern end, High St (Stryd Fawr) through the centre and Station Rd (Heol Yr Orsaf) on the other side.

EXPLORING BALA & AROUND

❧ BALA LAKE RAILWAY // STEAM ALONG THE LAKESHORE

The genteel narrow-gauge **Bala Lake Railway** (☎ 540666; www.bala-lake-railway.co.uk; adult/child return £9/3; ☼ Apr-Oct) was opened in 1868 to link mainline stations at Bala and Dolgellau. In 1965 the entire route from Barmouth to Llangollen was shut down and Bala station was closed. Volunteers reopened the 4.5-mile stretch from Bala to Llanuwchllyn in 1971, with vintage locomotives departing from a little station at Penybont, half a mile from Bala town centre, off the B4391. There are now up to four daily services skirting the lake for a scenic 90-minute return journey.

❧ WHITE-WATER RAFTING // YEAR-ROUND THRILLS ON THE TRYWERYN

Due to the damming of the River Tryweryn in the 1960s, this and the River

THE LEGEND OF TEGGIE

Sightings of the beast of Llyn Tegid (Bala Lake) have been reported since at least the 1920s and it has been variously likened to a crocodile or a small dinosaur. Affectionately known as Teggie, this Welsh answer to the Loch Ness monster prompted a three-day search by a Japanese film crew in 1995, but their mini-submarine failed to find any sign of the elusive beast.

One man who claims to have seen the beastie from the deep, however, is local farmer Rhodri Jones, whose sheep farm extends to the lake's foreshore. 'One night in the summer of 2006 I was heading home from the fields when I saw something making concentric ripples. The lake was very still, pretty spooky in the dusk and the water was very calm. That's when I saw the top of a creature about the size of a crocodile moving through the water.'

Since then Jones has spoken to other local farmers and found that many of them have stories of mysterious sightings and evidence they have collected dating back over 60 years.

'Bala is a landlocked, volcanic lake and there are species of fish living there that are only to be found in the lake,' says Jones. 'I think there's something special about the waters, but we live in a narrow-minded world where people are afraid of the unexplained. Still, humanity always needs a mystery.'

Dee are among the few Welsh rivers with fairly reliable white water all year round. The **Canolfan Tryweryn National Whitewater Centre** (☎ 521083; www.ukrafting.co.uk; Frongoch; 1/2hr trip £32/60; 9am-4.30pm Mon-Fri, 8.30am-6pm Sat & Sun Dec–mid-Oct) runs rafting trips on a 1.5-mile stretch of the Tryweryn that is almost continuous class-III white water with class IV sections.

The centre is 3.5 miles northwest of Bala on the A4212. Bookings are best made at least two days in advance and are subject to cancellation in the event of insufficient releases from the dam – call to check the day before.

The Adventure Breaks program marries rafting with another activity, such as rock climbing, mountain biking, pony trekking, high ropes, bushcraft, 4x4 off-road driving, canyoning, clay-pigeon shooting or quad biking; prices start at £135 and include accommodation.

❦ **BALA ADVENTURE & WATERSPORTS CENTRE // HEAD OUT IN SEARCH OF TEGGIE**
This one-stop activity and hire **centre** (☎ 521059; www.balawatersports.com; Pensarn Rd), behind the tourist office by the lakeshore, offers windsurfing, sailing, canoeing, kayaking, white-water rafting, mountain-biking, rock-climbing and abseiling courses (prices start from £35/60 per half-/full day). Rental gear includes kayaks (£10), canoes (£20), rowing boats (£24), pedaloes (£15), windsurfers (£16) and wayfarers (£30); all prices are per hour.

GASTRONOMIC HIGHLIGHTS

❦ **EAGLES INN ££**
☎ 540278; www.theeagleinn-bala.co.uk; Llanuwchllyn; mains £7-15; lunch Fri-Sun, dinner daily
Right down the other end of the lake, Tafarn Yr Eryod (as its mainly Welsh-speaking clientele know it) is a consummate North Welsh village pub – a friendly community boozer with a popular

dartboard. The food, however, is a step above. Most of the vegies and some of the meat comes from their own garden, and for dessert there's a delicious array of homemade pies and puddings.

❦ PLAS-YN-DRE ££

☎ 521256; 23 High St; lunch £5-11, dinner £12-16
The decor in this smart eatery is a tasteful take on country-kitchen chic, finished with soft-leather chairs. The hearty dinner menu has lots of interesting Welsh dishes, including fresh Menai mussels.

❦ SIOP Y GORNEL £

☎ 520423; www.siop-y-gornel.co.uk; 21 Tegid St;
🕑 8.30am-4.30pm Mon-Sat, to 2pm Wed
It takes 24 hours to make sourdough this good and that's just one of the homemade, organic delights on sale at this wonderful little delicatessen-bakery-cafe. Staff also concoct delicious baguettes, croissants, cakes, slices and pies. Stop in to fill up your picnic hamper or settle in with a newspaper and coffee.

❦ TYDDYN LLAN £££

☎ 01490-440264; www.tyddynllan.co.uk; Llandrillo;
2-/3-course lunch £24/30, dinner £39/48;
🕑 lunch Fri-Sun, dinner daily
The glowing reputation of this country restaurant with rooms was given a boost in 2010 by some Michelin starlight. On our last visit some dishes were extraordinary and some merely good, but overall it was a memorable experience. Proceedings kick off with complementary canapés served in the sitting room before progressing into the elegant dining area. It's 7.5 miles east of Bala on the B4401.

TRANSPORT

BIKE // Roberts Cycles (☎ 520252; www.rhroberts-cycles.co.uk; High St; per day £13) Rents out mountain bikes. The tourist office stocks a *Bike Routes Around Bala* pamphlet.

BUS // X94 from Dolgellau (35 minutes), Barmouth (1½ hours), Llangollen (one hour) and Wrexham (1½ hours) stops on the High St.

BETWS-Y-COED

☎ 01690 / pop 950
If you're looking for a base with an Alpine feel from which to explore Snowdonia National Park, the bustling little stone village of Betws-y-Coed *(bet-us-ee-koyd)* stands out as a natural option. It boasts a postcard-perfect setting above an inky river, engulfed in the verdant leafiness of the Gwydyr Forest and near the junction of three river valleys: the Llugwy, the Conwy and the Lledr.

The town has blossomed as Wales' most popular inland resort since Victorian days when a group of countryside painters founded an artistic community to record the diversity of the landscape. The arrival of the railway in 1868 cemented its popularity and today Betws-y-Coed is as busy with families and coach parties as it is with walkers.

Activities are its stock-in-trade, however, with outdoor-activity shops strung out along the A5 (known locally as the Holyhead Rd), which forms the main thoroughfare. The Rivers Conwy and Llugwy are rich with salmon in autumn while water sports and skiing are best organised through the nearby Plas y Brenin National Mountain Centre (p226). For specialist references for walkers, climbers and cyclists, call into **Ultimate Outdoors** (☎ 710888; www.ultimateoutdoors.co.uk; Holyhead Rd), an adventure shop with a huge range of equipment.

ESSENTIAL INFORMATION

TOURIST OFFICES // National park information centre (☎ 710426; www.betws-y-coed.co.uk; Royal Oak Stables; 🕑 9.30am-5.30pm Apr-Oct, 9.30am-4.30pm Nov-Mar) Stocks a comprehensive array of books and maps. The adjoining free exhibition on Snowdonia National Park includes a virtual-reality helicopter ride over Snowdon.

EXPLORING BETWS-Y-COED

♥ BRIDGES AND RIVERSIDE WALKS // MANY RIVERS TO CROSS
One of the joys of Betws is wandering along its riverbanks and criss-crossing over its historic bridges. Behind the information centre a pleasant path leads around the tongue of land framed by the convergence of the Conwy and Llugwy Rivers, alongside a golf course and back past St Michael's Church.

Nearby, **Sapper's Bridge** is a white suspension footbridge (1930), leading to a path through the fields up to the A470. If you turn right, the road leads to **Waterloo Bridge** (1815). Known locally as 'iron bridge', it spans 32m and bears a large inscription celebrating its construction in the year the battle was fought.

At the other end of the village, the 15th-century stone **Pont-y-Pair**, the 'Bridge of the Cauldron', crosses a set of rapids on the Llugwy. A riverside path leads to the **Miners' Bridge**, about a mile downstream, so called as this was the route miners took on their way to work in nearby lead mines. This is a modern replacement of the oldest crossing of the Llugwy.

♥ ST MICHAEL'S CHURCH // CHILD OF THE ORIGINAL BETWS
The name Betws is thought to be derived from 'bead house', meaning a place of prayer (*y coed* – in the woods). It's likely that 14th-century **St Michael's Church** (www.stmichaelsbyc.org.uk; Old Church Rd; ◷ 10am-5pm Easter-Oct) stands on the site of that early sanctuary. In 1873 it was replaced as the parish church by the much larger **St Mary's Church** (Holyhead Rd) but it's still used on St Michael's Day (29 September) and for the occasional funeral. The main item of interest inside is a stone effigy of

---

∼ WORTH A TRIP ∼

Most of the slate used to roof 19th-century Britain came from Wales, and much of that came from the mines of **Blaenau Ffestiniog**. However, only about 10% of mined slate is usable, so for every ton that goes to the factory, nine tons are left as rubble. Despite being in the very centre of Snowdonia National Park, the grey mountains of mine waste that surround Blaenau (*blay*-nye) prevented it from being officially included in the park – a slap in the face for this close-knit but impoverished town in the days before Wales' industrial sites were recognised as part of its heritage.

Blaenau's main attraction, the **Llechwedd Slate Caverns** (☎ 01766-830306; www.llechwedd-slate-caverns.co.uk; either ride adult/child £9.45/7.15, both rides £15.20/11.60; ◷ from 10am daily, last tour 5.15pm Apr-Sep, 4.15pm Oct-Mar) offer a chance to descend into a real slate mine. Of the two tours offered, the more evocative Deep Mine tour includes a descent on the UK's steepest passenger railway and recreates the harsh working conditions of the 19th-century miners – be prepared to duck and scramble around dark tunnels. If you can't manage a lot of steps, go for the Miner's Tramway Tour, a ride through the huge 1846 network of tunnels and caverns.

Today, although slate mining continues on a small scale, Blaenau has a mournful feel to it, not helped by famously miserable weather. It's an interesting place to stop but it's unlikely you'll be tempted to stay.

SNOWDONIA & THE LLŶN

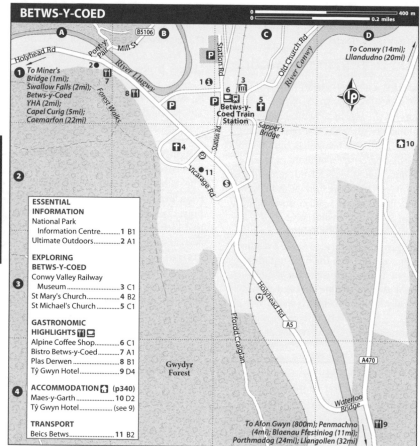

BETWS-Y-COED

0 — 400 m
0 — 0.2 miles

Holyhead Rd
Pont-y-Pair
Mill St
B5106
River Llugwy
Forest Walks
Station Rd
Old Church Rd
River Conwy
To Conwy (14mi);
Lllandudno (20mi)

To Miner's
Bridge (1mi);
Swallow Falls (2mi);
Betws-y-Coed
YHA (2mi);
Capel Curig (5mi);
Caemarfon (22mi)

Betws-y-
Coed Train
Station

Sapper's
Bridge

Vicarage Rd

Holyhead Rd
A5

Ffordd Craiglan

Gwydyr
Forest

A470

Waterloo
Bridge

To Afon Gwyn (800m); Penmachno
(4mi); Blaenau Ffestiniog (11mi);
Porthmadog (24mi); Llangollen (32mi)

**ESSENTIAL
INFORMATION**
National Park
    Information Centre..........1 B1
Ultimate Outdoors..............2 A1

**EXPLORING
BETWS-Y-COED**
Conwy Valley Railway
    Museum 3 C1
St Mary's Church.............. 4 B2
St Michael's Church 5 C1

**GASTRONOMIC
HIGHLIGHTS**
Alpine Coffee Shop.............6 C1
Bistro Betws-y-Coed............7 A1
Plas Derwen 8 B1
Tŷ Gwyn Hotel.....................9 D4

ACCOMMODATION (p340)
Maes-y-Garth 10 D2
Tŷ Gwyn Hotel................... (see 9)

TRANSPORT
Beics Betws...........................11 B2

Gruffydd ap Dafydd Goch, the grand-nephew of Llewelyn ap Gruffydd, the last native Prince of Wales.

❧ CONWY VALLEY RAILWAY MUSEUM // ONE FOR THE KIDS, EVEN THE GROWN-UP ONES

If you're the sort who's fascinated by dioramas and model train sets, this tiny museum (☎ 710568; www.conwyrailwaymuseum .co.uk; adult/child 1.50/0.80; ⏱ 10am-5pm) is for you. In which case the model shop you have to pass through in order to enter might pose an unfair temptation. The big attraction for kids is the miniature steam train rides (the 1-mile round trip costs £1.50) and there's a cafe in a full-sized carriage.

GASTRONOMIC HIGHLIGHTS

❧ BISTRO BETWS-Y-COED ££

☎ 710328; www.bistrobetws-y-coed.com; Holyhead Rd; lunch £6-9, dinner £12-17; ⏱ Wed-Sun, daily summer

This cottage-style eatery's statement of intent is 'modern and traditional Welsh'. Expect the likes of locally made sausages, rarebit and haddock-and-chips – battered with Llandudno Orme real ale, naturally. Reservations are recommended at weekends during peak season.

❤ TŶ GWYN HOTEL ££

☎ 01690-710383; www.tygwynhotel.co.uk; mains £13-18

This historic coaching inn (it dates from 1636) oozes character from every one of its numerous exposed beams. The menu focuses on hearty, meaty mains but vegetarian choices and lighter bar-style meals are also available. It's on the A5, just across Waterloo Bridge. You'll need to book ahead on the weekend, throughout the year.

Also recommended:

Alpine Coffee Shop (☎ 710747; www.alpine coffeeshop.net; Old Station Buildings; mains £6-8; ☺ 8.30am-5.30pm) Serves toasted sandwiches, snacks and 25 varieties of tea, including the world's rarest, Jun Shan Silver Needles (£8.80 per pot).

Plas Derwen (☎ 710388; www.plasderwen.com; Holyhead Rd; mains £8-14) A few tables overlook the main street for an al fresco morning coffee. The dinner menu meanders from Tex-Mex to Moroccan but lingers mainly in Wales: local pork sausages, leek and Caerphilly cheese pie etc.

TRANSPORT

BIKE // Beics Betws (☎ 710766; www.bikewales .co.uk; Vicarage Rd; ☺ 9am-5pm) Advises on local cycling trails, performs repairs and hires mountain bikes from £25 per day.

BUS // Snowdon Sherpa (www.snowdonia greenkey.co.uk) Buses S2 and S6 stop outside the train station, with services to Llanrwst (15 minutes), Swallow Falls (five minutes), Capel Curig (10 minutes), Pen-y-Pass (25 minutes) and Llanberis (33 minutes).

PARKING // There's a free parking area opposite the station. If you miss out, there are pay car parks on Holyhead Rd and just over Pont-y-Pair.

TRAIN // Betws-y-Coed is on the **Conwy Valley Line** (www.conwyvalleyrailway.co.uk), with six daily services (three on Sundays) to Llandudno (£4.70, 52 minutes) and Blaenau Ffestiniog (£3.80, 32 minutes).

AROUND BETWS-Y-COED

❤ GWYDYR FOREST // HIT THE TRACKS ON FOOT, BIKE OR HORSEBACK

The 28-sq-mile Gwydyr Forest, planted since the 1920s with oak, beech and larch, encircles Betws-y-Coed. It's an ideal setting for a day's walking close to town, though it gets very muddy in wet weather. There are over a dozen marked tracks, many of which are outlined in *The Gwydyr Forest Guide* (£2) and *Walks Around Betws-y-Coyd* (£5), both available from the national park information centre.

The **Marin Trail** is a challenging 15.5-mile mountain-biking loop, starting immediately southwest of Llanrwst, 3.5 miles north of Betws. In the southern part of the park is the similarly difficult 13.5-mile **Penmachno Trail**; take the A5 and then the B4406 to Penmachno, 5 miles south of Betws.

Also in Penmachno, **Gwydir Stables** (☎ 760248; www.horse-riding-wales.co.uk; per hr/half-day/day £19/34/53) arranges rides through the forest for novice and regular riders alike. It also offers a pub ride for £40, lasting around four hours and stopping off for a pint at a couple of local pubs along the way.

❤ SWALLOW FALLS // PRETTY AND POPULAR – A PREDICTABLE COMBINATION

Betws-y-Coed's main natural tourist trap is 2 miles west of town along the Llugwy. It's a beautiful spot, with the torrent weaving through the rocks into a green pool below. Bring a £1 coin for the turnstile. The entry is from the A5 and there's a pub and car park across the road.

SNOWDONIA & THE LLŶN

♥ UGLY HOUSE // A RUSTIC COTTAGE WITH A BENEVOLENT PURPOSE

A bit like Ugly Betty, the **Ugly House** (☎ 720287; www.snowdonia-society.org.uk; admission by donation; ⏰ 9.30am-5.30pm Easter-Oct) isn't actually ugly at all. This unusual cottage is constructed from huge boulders and is home to the Snowdonia Society, a charity working to protect and enhance Snowdonia National Park. Visitors can wander through the grounds and visit the small shop on the ground floor.

The origins of the house make for great local folklore. One yarn suggests it was built in 1475 by two local bandits as their hideout; according to another, there was a Welsh law in the Middle Ages that allowed any man who built on common land after sunset and had smoke coming out of the chimney by daybreak to stake a claim for the freehold as far as he could throw an axe around the property. The Snowdonia Society rescued the property from dereliction and turned it into their headquarters in 1988 following painstaking renovations by a team of dedicated volunteers.

It's half a mile past Swallow Falls on the A5.

♥ CAPEL CURIG // A MAGNET FOR OUTDOORSY TYPES

Tiny Capel Curig (population 190), 5 miles west of Betws-y-Coed, is one of Snowdonia's oldest hill stations, and has long been a magnet for walkers, climbers and other outdoor junkies. The village spreads out along the A5 but the main clump of activity is at the intersection of the A4086. It's a heady setting, ringed by looming mountains.

The **Plas y Brenin National Mountain Centre** (☎ 720214; www.pyb.co.uk), at the western edge of the village, is a multi-activity centre with excellent facilities and a huge array of residential, year-round courses, ranging from basic rock climbing to summer and winter mountaineering, and professional development and teaching qualifications. Kayaking and canoeing courses are also offered. Advance bookings are required. There's a communal bar area to meet other students and regular talks cover related topics on Monday, Tuesday and Saturday evenings at 8pm. Taster days run throughout the school holidays with an introduction to three activities for £35.

Snowdon Sherpa buses S2 and S6 stop here.

SNOWDON & AROUND

♥ SNOWDON (YR WYDDFA) // THE COUNTRY'S LITERAL HIGH POINT

No Snowdonia experience is complete without coming face-to-face with Snowdon (1085m), one of Britain's most awe-inspiring mountains and the highest summit in Wales (it's actually the 61st highest in Britain, with the higher 60 all in Scotland). On a clear day the views stretch to Ireland and the Isle of Man, over Snowdon's fine jagged ridges, which drop away in great swoops to sheltered *cwms* (valleys) and deep lakes. Even on a gloomy day you could find yourself above the clouds. Thanks to the Snowdon Mountain Railway it's extremely accessible – the summit and some of the tracks can get frustratingly crowded.

Just below the cairn that marks the summit is **Hafod Eryri**, a striking piece of architecture that opened in 2009 to replace the dilapidated 1930s visitor centre, which Prince Charles famously labelled 'the highest slum in Europe'. Clad in granite and curved to blend into the mountain, it's a wonderful building, housing a cafe that serves snacks and light lunches, toilets and ambient interpretative elements built into the structure itself. A wall of picture-windows gazes down towards the west, while a small row faces the cairn. The centre (including the toilets) closes in winter or if the weather's terrible; it's open whenever the train is running.

❦ SNOWDON TRAILS // BEAT A PATH TO THE PEAK

Six paths of varying length and difficulty lead to the summit. Simplest (and dullest) is the **Llanberis Path** (10 miles, six hours return) running beside the train line. The **Snowdon Ranger Path** (7 miles, five hours) starts at the Snowdon Ranger YHA near Beddgelert; this is the shortest and also the safest in winter.

The two options that start from Pen-y-Pass require the least amount of ascent: the **Miner's Track** (7 miles, six hours) starts out gently but ends steeply; the **Pyg Track** (7 miles, six hours) is more interesting and meets the Miner's Track where it steepens. The classic **Snowdon Horseshoe** route (7.5 miles, six to seven hours) combines the Pyg Track to the summit (or via the precipitous ridge of Crib Goch if you're very experienced) with a descent over the peak of Llewedd and a final section down the Miner's Track.

The straightforward **Rhyd Ddu Path** (8 miles, six hours) is the least-used route; the trailhead is on the Caernarfon–Beddgelert road (A4085). The most challenging route is the **Watkin Path** (8 miles, six hours), involving an ascent of more than 1000m on its southerly approach from Nantgwynant.

For some fine variants on the trails, see the Snowdonia chapter of Lonely Planet's *Walking in Britain*. Make sure you're well prepared with warm and waterproof clothing and sturdy footwear. Check the weather forecast at www.metoffice.gov.uk/loutdoor/mountainsafety before setting out.

The Welsh Highland Railway (p244) stops at the trailheads of the Snowdon Ranger and Rhyd Ddu paths, while the Snowdon Sherpa buses stop at all of them. Even if you've got your own car, it's worth considering this option as the Pen-y-Pass car park, in particular, can fill up quickly. Another option is to take the Snowdon Mountain Railway to the top and walk back down. It's more difficult to do this the other way around as the train will only take on new passengers at the top if there are gaps.

❦ SNOWDON MOUNTAIN RAILWAY // CHUG TO THE TOP

If you're not physically able to climb a mountain, short on time or just plain lazy, those industrious, railway-obsessed Victorians have gifted you an alternative. Opened in 1896, the **Snowdon Mountain Railway** (☎ 0844 493 8120; www.snowdonrailway.co.uk; adult/child return £25/18; ⏲ 9am-5pm Mar-Oct) is the UK's highest and only public rack-and-pinion railway. Vintage steam and modern diesel locomotives haul carriages from Llanberis up to Snowdon's very summit in an hour. Return trips involve a scant half-hour at the top before heading back down again. Single tickets can only be booked for the journey up (adult/child £18/15).

In the first season after the opening of Hafod Eryri, the trains carried 159,000 people to the summit, so make sure you book well in advance or you may miss out. Departures are weather dependent and the railway is completely closed from November to mid-March. Until May, the trains can only head as far Clogwyn Station (adult/child £18/14) – an altitude of 762m.

❦ DINAS EMRYS // HERE BE DRAGONS

A mile east of Beddgelert, near the southern end of Llyn Dinas, is **Dinas Emrys**, the hill where the legendary King Vortigern – son-in-law of Britain's last Roman ruler, Magnus Maximus – tried to build a castle. According to folklore, the young wizard Merlin liberated two dragons in a cavern under the hill, a white one representing the Saxons and a red one representing the Britons, and prophesied that they'd fight until the red dragon was triumphant. The act was the spiritual birth of the Welsh nation and the two dragons have been at each other's throats ever since.

❦ SYGUN COPPER MINE // A RICH SEAM OF HISTORY

Across the road from Dinas Emrys, this **copper mine** (☎ 01766-890595; www.sygun coppermine.co.uk; adult/child £8.75/6.75; ☼ 9.30am-5pm Mar-Oct) dates from Roman times, although extraction was stepped up in the 19th century. Abandoned in 1903, it has since been converted into a museum, with an audiovisual underground tour that evokes the life of Victorian miners. You can also try your hand at archery (£3) or panning for gold (£2).

❦ BEDDGELERT // CHARACTER-FILLED HOME OF A SHADY SHAGGY DOG'S TALE

At the heart of the national park, charming little Beddgelert (population 500) is a conservation village of rough greystone buildings, overlooking the trickling River Glaslyn with its ivy-covered bridge. Flowers festoon the village in spring and the surrounding hills are covered in a purple blaze of heather in summer, reminiscent of a Scottish glen. Scenes from Mark Robson's 1958 film,

The Inn of the Sixth Happiness, set in China and starring Ingrid Bergman, were shot here.

Beddgelert, meaning 'Gelert's Grave', is said to refer to a folk tale concerning 13th-century Welsh prince, Llewellyn. Believing that his dog Gelert had savaged his baby son, Llewellyn slaughtered the dog, only to discover that Gelert had fought off the wolf that had attacked the baby. More likely, the name Beddgelert is derived from a 5th-century Irish preacher, Celert, who is believed to have founded a church here. Regardless, the 'grave' of Gelert the dog is a popular attraction, reached by a pretty riverside trail. It was probably constructed by an unscrupulous 19th-century hotelier in an attempt to boost business.

There's a helpful **tourist office and national park information centre** (☎ 01766-890615; Canolfan Hebog; ☼ 9.30am-5.30pm daily Easter-Oct, 9.30am-4.30pm Fri-Sun Nov-Mar; ▣) at the southern end of the village, close to the car park (per day £4).

In summer, **Glaslyn Ices & Cafe Glandwr** (☎ 01766-890339; www.glaslynices .co.uk; mains £4-14) is the busiest place in the village. This excellent ice-cream parlour serves a huge array of homemade flavours and is attached to a family restaurant offering simple meals, especially pizza.

Lyn's Cafe (☎ 890374; meals £3-12; ☼ 10am-5.30pm winter, plus dinner summer) is a family-friendly all-rounder (with a separate children's menu), split between a restaurant serving big breakfasts and Sunday roasts, and a tearoom around the back with seats by the river for simple snacks.

Beside the bridge, **Beddgelert Bistro & Antique Shop** (☎ 890543; www .beddgelert-bistro.co.uk/index2.html; mains £6-16) is a tearoom-style place divided between several small rooms with exposed flagstone walls. It offers knick-knacks and snacks and – rather incongruously – a range of fondues.

Beddgelert is a stop on the historic Welsh Highland Railway (p244), which currently runs from Caernarfon (£22 return, 1½ hours) and will connect to Porthmadog in 2011. Snowdon Sherpa bus S4 heads from here to Caernarfon (30 minutes) and Pen-y-Pass (15 minutes), while S97 heads to Porthmadog (25 minutes).

❤ BEDDGELERT FOREST // BIKE THE BYR THEN HIT THE HIR

Within this forestry commission block, 2 miles north of Beddgelert along the A4805, is a popular campsite and two mountain-bike trails: the 6-mile Hir Trail and the easier 2.5-mile Byr Trail. **Beics**

Beddgelert (☎ 01766-890434; www.beddgelert bikes.co.uk; 2/4/8hr £12/18/25), rents out mountain bikes, tandems and child seats.

DRIVING TOUR

Distance: 34.5 miles
Duration: two hours

The roads circumnavigating Snowdon make for a memorable drive. From **Caernarfon (1**, p232), the A4086 heads through **Llanberis (2**, p230) before making a spectacular ascent to **Pen-y-Pass (3)** and dropping again to the junction of the A498. Turn right for a particularly picturesque stretch leading to Beddgelert, passing a wonderful viewpoint at **Gueastadanas (4)** and the lakes **Llyn Gwynant (5)** and **Llyn Dinas (6)**. At **Beddgelert (7)** turn right and take the A4085 back to Caernarfon.

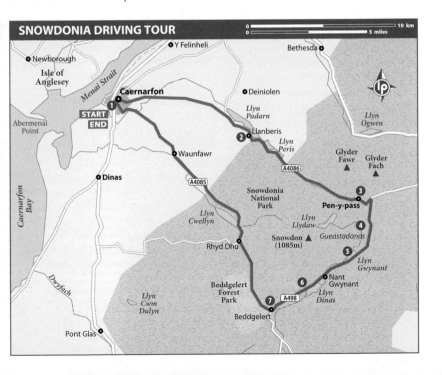

LLANBERIS

☎ 01286 / pop 1900

While not the most instantly attractive town in the area, Llanberis is a mecca for walkers and climbers, hosting a steady flow of rugged, polar fleece-wearers year-round but especially in July and August when accommodation is at a premium. It's actually positioned just outside the national park but functions as a hub for many, partly because the Snowdon Mountain Railway (p227) leaves from here.

The town was originally built to house workers in the Dinorwig slate quarry, whose massive waste tips are hard to miss as you approach from the east. While tourism is the cornerstone of Llanberis life these days, the town wears its industrial heritage on its sleeve with pride. Indeed, Dinorwig, which once boasted the largest artificial cavern in the world, has now become part of Europe's biggest pumped-storage power station. Some of the old quarry workshops have been reincarnated as a museum of the slate industry, and the narrow-gauge railway that once hauled slate to the coast now tootles along Llyn Padarn.

ESSENTIAL INFORMATION

TOURIST OFFICES // Tourist office (☎ 870765; 41 High St; ⏱ 9.30am-4.30pm Apr-Oct, 9.30am-3pm Fri-Mon Nov-Mar)

ORIENTATION

Llanberis straddles the A4086 with nearly all the points of interest spread out along the High St, which runs parallel to it. Across the A4086 are the village's two lakes, Llyn Padarn and Llyn Peris. The Snowdon Mountain Railway has its base at the southern end of town.

EXPLORING LLANBERIS

☙ **NATIONAL SLATE MUSEUM //** **THERE'S NO DARK TUNNELS AT THIS INDUSTRIAL MUSEUM**

Even if you're not all that fussed by industrial museums, this one's well worth checking out. At Llanberis, much of the slate was carved out of the open mountainside – leaving behind a jagged, sculptural cliff-face that's fascinating if not quite beautiful. The **museum** (☎ 870630; www.museumwales.ac.uk/en/slate; admission free; ⏱ 10am-5pm Apr-Oct, 10am-4pm Sun-Fri Nov-Apr), occupies the Victorian workshops beside Llyn Padarn, featuring video clips, a huge working water wheel, reconstructed workers' cottages (furnished as they would have been between 1860 and 1969 when the quarries closed) and demonstrations on elements of the tile-making process.

The turn-off is along the A4086 between the Electric Mountain exhibition centre and the Snowdon Mountain Railway station.

☙ **ELECTRIC MOUNTAIN //** **A SPARKY NAME FOR A POWER STATION**

The Dinorwig pumped-storage power station is the largest scheme of its kind in Europe. Located deep below Elidir mountain, its construction required one million tonnes of concrete, 200,000 tonnes of cement and 4500 tonnes of steel. The power station uses surplus energy to pump water from Llyn Peris up to Marchlyn Reservoir. When half the population switches on their kettles for tea during a TV ad break, the water is released to fall through underground turbines. Dinorwig's reversible turbine pumps are capable of reaching maximum generation in less than 16 seconds.

Electric Mountain (☎ 870636; www .electricmountain.co.uk; ☼ 10am-4.30pm Sep-May, 9.30am-5.30pm Jun-Aug), the power station's visitor centre, has free interactive exhibits on the history of hydro-power. An interesting **guided tour** (adult/child £7.50/3.75; bookings required) into the underground power station starts from here. You'll also find a cafe and a children's playground.

The centre is by the lakeside on the A4086, near the south end of High St.

☙ DOLBADARN CASTLE // FORGOTTEN FORTRESS OF THE WELSH PRINCES

Wales is so spoilt for castles that this one gets little attention. Built before 1230 by the Princes of Gwyneth, the keep rises like a perfect chessboard rook from a green hilltop between the two lakes. It's an easy stroll from the town, rewarded by wonderful views of the lakes, quarries and Snowdon itself.

☙ SNOWDON HONEY FARM & WINERY // BUZZ IN FOR A SWEET BEVERAGE

All manner of honey-related goodies are sold here, including a range of mead, graded Roman, Celtic or medieval, depending on sweetness. There are also homemade fudges, preserves and fruit wine, and if you ask nicely the engaging owner may let you sip before you commit. It also functions as a **cafe** (☎ 870218; www.snowdonhoneyfarmandwinery.co.uk; High St; snacks £4-5), serving ice cream, cream tea, cakes and sandwiches.

☙ LLANBERIS LAKE RAILWAY // A CHILD-PLACATING ALTERNATIVE IF THE SNOWDON TRAIN'S FULL

This little **steam train** (☎ 870549; www .lake-railway.co.uk; adult/child £7.20/6.70; ☼ see online timetable) departs on a 5-mile return jaunt beside Llyn Padarn, part of the

route (though not the same track) used from 1843 to 1961 to haul slate to the port on the Menai Strait. It's a tame but scenic one-hour return trip past the slate museum and through Padarn Country Park to the terminus at Penllyn; there's a wheelchair-adapted carriage.

The terminus station is across the A4086 from the Snowdon Mountain Railway station.

☙ HIKER & CLIMBER HANG-OUTS // TRADE TIPS WITH FELLOW TRAVELLERS

Pete's Eats (☎ 870117; www.petes-eats.co.uk; 40 High St; meals £4-6; ☐ ☜) is a local institution, a busy, bright cafe where hikers and climbers swap tips over monster portions in a hostel-like environment. There's bunkhouse accommodation upstairs, a huge noticeboard full of travellers information, a book exchange, a map and guidebook room, and computers for internet access.

Joe Brown (☎ 870327; www.joebrownonline .co.uk; 63 High St; ☼ 9am-5.30pm), a climbing shop selling all things outdoors, has a notice board that includes gear for sale, accommodation, five-day forecasts and lots of information and advice for walkers.

Another reliable place to gather reconnaissance is **Swigod a Sebon** (☎ 870088; 54 High St), the walker-friendly laundry on the main street.

☙ LAKE CRUISES // DRIFT BENEATH THE CARVED CLIFFS

The running times are a little sporadic, especially in the off season, but it's worth calling ahead for the departure times of the **Snowdon Star** (☎ 07974-716418; www .snowdonstar.co.uk; adult/child £5/3.50; ☼ 11am-5pm May-Oct), which runs scenic 45-minute boat trips on Llyn Padarn. The boat sails from the Padarn Country Park jetty near the National Slate Museum car park.

🌱 BOULDER ADVENTURES //
FAMILY BONDING WITH ADDED
ADRENALIN

If you are interested in outdoor activities such as coasteering, kayaking, canoeing, climbing, abseiling and gorge scrambling, contact **Boulder Adventures** (☎ 870556; www.boulderadventures.co.uk; Bryn Du Mountain Centre, Ty Du Rd; half-/full-day courses £35/55). Small groups and families can devise their own adventure, plus hostel-style accommodation is available within the spacious Victorian property.

GASTRONOMIC HIGHLIGHTS

🌱 DOLAFON TEA ROOM £

☎ 870993; www.dolafon.com; High St; sandwiches £4-7, high tea £13; ⏰ 10am-4.30pm

After taking that frightfully delightful little train up Snowdon, one does rather work up an appetite for tea and sandwiches. This *dahling* little place offers 30 different teas, served with finger sandwiches, *bara brith* and scones with jam and cream.

🌱 PEAK RESTAURANT ££

☎ 872777; 86 High St; mains £12-15; ⏰ dinner Wed-Sun

Charming owners and adventurer-sized portions underpin this restaurant's popularity and longevity. It continues to serve the best hearty, Welsh-style dinners in town.

🌱 SAFFRON £

☎ 871777; www.llanberisorganics.co.uk; 48 High St; Ⓥ

This organic deli and health-food shop sells takeaway foodstuffs, including soups and sandwiches, as well as natural medicines and environmentally friendly products.

TRANSPORT

BUS // Snowdon Sherpa buses stop on the High St. S1 heads to Pen-y-Pass (15 minutes) while S2 continues on to Capel Curig (23 minutes), Swallow Falls (28 minutes), Betws-y-Coed (33 minutes) and Llanrwst (50 minutes). Buses 85 and 86 head directly to Bangor (44 minutes) while 87 and 88 head first to Caernarfon (30 minutes).

PARKING // There are several large car parks scattered along the lakefront, charging about £4 per day.

WEST OF SNOWDONIA
· · · · · ·

Just because it doesn't have national park status doesn't mean that the western extremity of Gwynedd is lacking in any way. It may not have the mountains but it certainly has the sea – lapping peacefully alongside Caernarfon's historic walls, battering the rocks at Braich-y-Pwll, producing surfer-friendly swells at Porth Neigwl and cooling off the kids at Criccieth. You're never far from it – you can dip your toes in it while enjoying a pint at Porth Dinllaen's Tŷ Coch Inn or catch glimpses of it between the Italianate colonnades of Portmeirion village. And all those bracing sea breezes seem to have blown any shreds of stuffiness or British reserve from the local populace.

CAERNARFON

☎ 01286 / pop 9600

Wedged between the gleaming Menai Strait and the deep-purple mountains of Snowdonia, Caernarfon's main claim to fame is its fantastical castle. Given the town's crucial historical importance, its proximity to the national park and its reputation as a centre of Welsh culture (it has the highest percentage of Welsh-speakers of anywhere), parts of the town centre are surprisingly down-at-heel. Still, there's a lot of charm and a tangible sense of history in the streets around the castle. Within the cobbled lanes of the old walled town are some fine Georgian buildings, while the waterfront area has started on the inevitable march towards gentrification.

The castle was built by Edward I as the last link in his 'iron ring' and it's now part of the Castles and Town Walls of King Edward in Gwynedd Unesco World Heritage Site.

In an attempt by the then–prime minister, David Lloyd George (himself a Welshman), to bring the royals closer to their Welsh constituency, the castle was designated as the venue for the 1911 investiture of the Prince of Wales. In retrospect, linking the modern royals to such a powerful symbol of Welsh subjugation may not have been the best idea. At the crowning of Prince Charles in 1969 the nationalist sentiment climaxed with an attempt to blow up his train.

ESSENTIAL INFORMATION

EMERGENCIES // Police station (☎ 673333; Maesincla Lane) Half a mile east of the town centre.
TOURIST OFFICES // Tourist office (☎ 672232; Castle Ditch; ⏰ 9.30am-4.30pm Apr-Oct, 10am-3.30pm Mon-Sat Nov-Mar) Opposite the castle's main entrance; incorporates the Pendeitsh Gallery.

ORIENTATION

The historical heart of Caernarfon is enclosed within stout 14th-century walls, just to the north of the castle, beside the River Seiont (where it empties into the Menai Strait). The centre of modern Caernarfon is just east of the castle, at Castle Sq (Y Maes). The main shopping area is pedestrianised Pool St, running east from Castle Sq.

EXPLORING CAERNARFON

❧ CAERNARFON CASTLE // ONE OF THE WORLD'S GREATEST MEDIEVAL CASTLES

Majestic **Caernarfon Castle** (Cadw; ☎ 677617; www.cadw.wales.gov.uk; adult/child/family £4.95/4.60/15; ⏰ 9am-5pm Apr-Oct, 9.30am-4pm Mon-Sat & 11am-4pm Sun Nov-Mar) was built between 1283 and 1330 as a military stronghold, a seat of government and a royal palace. Like the other royal strongholds of the time, it was designed and mainly supervised by Master James of St George, from Savoy, but the brief and scale were extraordinary. Inspired by the dream of Macsen Wledig recounted in the *Mabinogion,* Caernarfon echoes the 5th-century walls of Constantinople, with colour-banded masonry and polygonal towers, instead of the traditional round towers and turrets.

Despite its fairy-tale aspect it is thoroughly fortified with a series of murder holes and a sophisticated arrangement of multiple arrow slits. It repelled Owain Glyndŵr's army in 1404 with a garrison of only 28 men, and resisted three sieges during the English Civil War before surrender to Cromwell's army in 1646.

A year after construction of the building was begun, Edward I's second son was born here, becoming heir to the throne four months later when his elder brother died. To consolidate Edward's power he was made Prince of Wales in 1301, and his much-eroded statue is over the **King's Gate**. He came to a very nasty end via a red-hot poker, but this did not destroy the title. However, the first investiture that took place here, rather than in London, wasn't until 1911 – of the rather less ill-fated Edward VIII. Although initiated by the Prime Minister, Welshman David

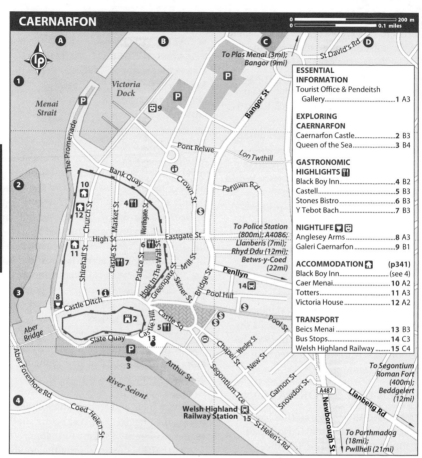

CAERNARFON

Lloyd George, it incensed the largely Nationalist local population.

Caernarfon Castle is a large, relatively intact structure. You can walk on and through the interconnected walls and towers gathered around the central green, most of which are well preserved but empty.

Start at the **Eagle Tower**, the one with the flagpoles to the right of the entrance. On the turrets you can spot the weathered eagle from which it gets its name, alongside stone helmeted figures intended to swell the garrison's numbers

(they're easier to spot from the quay). Inside there are displays on Edward I and the construction of the castle as well as a short film *The Eagle & The Dragon*, which screens on the half-hour.

There is an exhibition plus cinematic glimpse of the 1969 investiture of today's Prince of Wales, HRH Prince Charles, in the **North East Tower**. In the **Queen's Tower** (named after Edward I's wife Eleanor) is the **Regimental Museum of the Royal Welsh Fusiliers**; poets Robert Graves and Siegfried Sassoon both served in the brigade.

☙ SEGONTIUM // WHEN IN WALES, BUILD A FORT

Just east of the centre, the excavated foundations of the **Segontium Roman Fort** (☎ 675625; www.segontium.org.uk; Ffordd Cwstenin; admission free; ☽ 12.30pm-4.30pm Tue-Sun) represent the westernmost Roman legionary fort of the Roman Empire. Overlooking the Menai Strait, the fort dates back to AD 77, when General Gnaeus Julius Agricola completed the Roman conquest of Wales by capturing the Isle of Anglesey. It was designed to accommodate a force of up to 1000 infantrymen, and coins recovered from the site indicate that it was an active garrison until AD 394 – a reflection of the crucial strategic position.

The on-site museum explains the background to complement the stark remains, although it's not always open, as it's staffed by volunteers. The site is about half a mile along the A4085 (to Beddgelert), which crosses through the middle of it.

☙ CRUISES // MEANDER ALONG THE MENAI

The 1937 ferry **Queen of the Sea** (☎ 672772; adult/child £5.50/3.50; ☽ May-Oct) offers 40-minute cruises, with a full commentary, to the southwest entrance of the Menai Strait and two-hour cruises in the other direction as far as the Menai Suspension Bridge. They leave from Slate Quay, beside the castle.

GASTRONOMIC HIGHLIGHTS

☙ BLACK BOY INN ££

☎ 673604; www.black-boy-inn.com; Northgate St; mains £7-16; ☽

Packed with original 16th-century features, this cosy pub is divided into a series of snug rooms and although the wine might come out of a box, they serve real ale and excellent hearty meals such

as cassoulet and game pie. If you're after something a little lighter, try the daily seafood specials.

☙ CASTELL ££

☎ 669539; 33 Castle Sq; mains £8-9

Caernarfon's chicest bar looks on to Castle Sq from behind its grand facade. Inside it's all black furniture and pink trim – which isn't anywhere near as much of a 1980s nightmare as it sounds. Drop in for soup or a sandwich at lunchtime (about £4) or a more substantial evening meal.

☙ STONES BISTRO ££

☎ 671152; 4 Hole in the Wall St; mains £11-16; ☽ dinner Tue-Sat, lunch Sun

Housed in what was a 17th-century temperance house, this dark but cosy French-style bistro is open for dinner and Sunday lunch, with speciality roast lamb and some decent options for vegetarians.

☙ Y TEBOT BACH £

☎ 678444; 13 Castle St; sandwiches £5; ☽ 10.30am-5pm Tue-Sat

The nicest of the many tearooms around the castle, this tiny place for a light bite has a cosy, living-room feel and offers homemade cakes and sandwiches.

NIGHTLIFE

☙ ANGLESEY ARMS

☎ 672158; The Promenade; ☞

For a pint, the Anglesey Arms, down by the water, is your best bet, especially with outside seating in summer offering a great harbour view for a sundowner.

☙ GALERI CAERNARFON

☎ 685222; www.galericaernarfon.com; Victoria Dock

This excellent multipurpose arts centre hosts exhibitions, theatre, films and events; check the program online for details. The stylish in-house DOC Cafe Bar serves all-day snacks and pre-event suppers.

TRANSPORT

BIKE // Beics Menai (☎ 676804; www.beics menai.co.uk; 1 Slate Quay; per 2/4/6/8hr £13/15/17/20; ☻ 9.30am-4pm Tue-Sat) Hires bikes (including tandems, children's bikes and child seats) and can advise on local cycle routes. A brochure on Gwynedd recreational cycle routes includes the 12.5-mile Lôn Eifion (starting near the Welsh Highland Railway station and running south to Bryncir) and the 4.5-mile Lôn Las Menai (following the Menai Strait to the village of Y Felinheli). Lôn Las Cymru passes through Caernarfon, heading northeast to Bangor and south to Criccieth.

BUS // Buses stop at stands along Penllyn, two blocks north of Pool St. Snowdon Sherpa bus S4 heads to Beddgelert (30 minutes) via the Snowdon Ranger (20 minutes) and Rhyd Ddu (24 minutes) trailheads. Buses include 1/1A to Bangor (25 minutes), Plas Menai (five minutes), Criccieth (35 minutes), Tremadog (37 minutes) and Porthmadog (45 minutes); X5 to Conwy (1¼ hours) and Llandudno (1½ hours); 12 to Parc Glynllifon (12 minutes) and Pwllheli (45 minutes) and 87/88 to Llanberis (30 minutes).

COACH // A National Express (www.national express.com) coach heads between Pwllheli (£6.80, one hour) and London (£31, 10½ hours) daily, via Bangor (£6, 25 minutes), Llandudno (£7.30, one hour) and Birmingham (£24, six hours).

PARKING // Free street parking is at a premium but you might snatch a park in the walled town and there are highly contested free parks by the water on the south embankment of Victoria Dock. Otherwise, there's pay-and-display parking by Slate Quay and on Balaclava Rd near Galeri Caernarfon (50p per hour, free from 8pm to 8am).

TRAIN // Caernarfon is the northern terminus of the Welsh Highland Railway tourist train (p244), which currently runs to just past Beddgelert (£22 return, 1½ hours) and will connect to Porthmadog in 2011. The station is near the river on St Helen's Rd.

AROUND CAERNARFON

☙ BEACON CLIMBING CENTRE // START INDOORS BEFORE TAKING IT OUTSIDE

This large **indoor climbing centre** (☎ 0845 450 8222; www.beaconclimbing.com; Ceunant) has over 100 climbs to learn and the chance to hone your skills; it's situated near the village of Ceunant, halfway between Caernarfon and Llanberis, off the A4086. There are also 1½-hour taster sessions for beginners for £55 per person. Registered climbers pay £6.50 per session.

☙ PLAS MENAI // LEARN NEW TRICKS ON THE WATER

The excellent **National Watersports Centre** (☎ 01248-670964; www.plasmenai.co.uk), 3 miles out along the A487 towards Bangor, offers a year-round range of water-based courses for all interests and ability levels (sailing, power-boating, kayaking, windsurfing) plus multi-activity courses suitable for families and youth groups. Advance reservations are necessary. The centre also offers on-site accommodation with en suite B&B (singles/doubles £45/70) and a bunkhouse (dorms £25). Bus 1A (Caernarfon to Bangor) stops here.

☙ GREENWOOD FOREST PARK // GREEN FUN FOR ALL THE FAMILY

A 7-hectare adventure park underpinned by a strong green ethos, **GreenWood** (☎ 01248-670076; www.greenwoodforestpark .co.uk; Y Felinheli; adult/child £11/9.90; ☻ 11am-5pm mid-Mar–Oct) has a slew of rides and activities. Grab a ride on the Green Dragon, the world's first people-powered roller coaster.

It's signposted from the A487 near Y Felinheli, 4 miles northeast of Caernarfon.

☙ INIGO JONES SLATEWORKS //
WIPE THE SLATE CLEAN THEN TAKE
IT HOME

Since 1861 slate has been shaped and shipped from here, but it's a safe bet they made less garden ornaments, placemats and picture frames back then. Before you get laden down with what's perhaps the ultimate North Welsh souvenir (dragon scales being hard to get hold of these days), you can take a self-guided tour of the **slateworks** (☎ 01286-830242; www .inigojones.co.uk; Groeslon; tour per adult/child £4.50/4; ☺ 9am-5pm). The on-site Welsh Rock Cafe makes great Welsh cakes.

It's on the A487, 5 miles south of Caernarfon.

☙ PARC GLYNLLIFON // A LEAFY
ESCAPE FOR CRAFTY INDIVIDUALS

Strewn with rare plants, follies, sculptures and fountains, these historic **gardens** (☎ 01286-830222; www.gwynedd.gov.uk/parc glynllifon; adult/child £4/1.50; ☺ 10am-5pm) once belonged to the estate of the Lords Newborough. The grand neoclassical manor house has been sold off separately and is only sporadically open to the public. The heart and soul of the Parc is a craft centre where nine resident artisans rent units and sell their wares in the shop. They also run monthly Craft Taster Days where they teach the likes of slate shaping, blacksmithing, appliqué and wood carving (from £20; call ahead for details).

Parc Glynllifon is 6 miles south of Caernarfon on the A499.

LLŶN PENINSULA

Jutting out into the Irish Sea from the mountains of Snowdonia, the Llŷn Peninsula is a green finger of land, some 25 miles long and averaging 8 miles in width. It's a peaceful and largely undeveloped region with isolated walking and cycling routes, some excellent beaches, a scattering of small fishing villages and 70 miles of wildlife-rich coastline (much of it in the hands of the NT, and almost 80% of it designated an Area of Outstanding Natural Beauty). Over the centuries the heaviest footfalls have been those of pilgrims on their way to Bardsey Island.

Welsh is the language of everyday life here. Indeed, this is about as Welsh as it gets. The Llŷn (pronounced khlee'en) and the Isle of Anglesey were the last places on the Roman and Norman itineraries, and both have maintained a separate identity, the Llŷn especially so. Isolated physically and culturally from the rest of Wales, the Llŷn remained sympathetic to Catholicism long after it was suppressed by Henry VIII and in later centuries it's been an incubator of Welsh activism. It was the birthplace of David Lloyd George, the first Welsh prime minister of the UK, and of Plaid Cymru (the Party of Wales), which was founded in Pwllheli in 1925 and is now the main opposition party in the National (Welsh) Assembly.

ESSENTIAL INFORMATION

TOURIST OFFICES // Abersoch (☎ 01758-712929; www.abersochandllyn.co.uk; High St; ☺ 10.30am-4.30pm daily in summer) Independently run and very helpful, it also offers internet access (£2.50 per 30 minutes). **Pwllheli** (☎ 01758-613000; Station Sq; ☺ 10.30am-3pm Mon-Wed, Fri & Sat Nov-Mar, 9am-5pm Apr-Oct)

EXPLORING THE LLŶN PENINSULA
NANT GWRTHEYRN // A GHOST
VILLAGE RESURRECTED BY A LIVING
LANGUAGE

According to tradition it is here that the semi-mythical Celtic King Vortigern is buried. Today's village was built for quarry-workers in the 19th century, when granite was dug out of the surrounding mountains and shipped to Liverpool, Manchester and elsewhere to be used in building roads. The quarries closed after WWII and the village was gradually abandoned. In 1978 it was given a new lease of life when it was bought and restored as the home of the **Welsh Language & Heritage Centre** (☎ 01758-750334; www .nantgwrtheyrn.org; admission free; ❧ call ahead for times). Even if you don't take a course, it's a magical place – eerily quiet and ideal for a tranquil walk along world's-end cliffs.

The heritage centre has a small but compelling exhibition on the history of the Welsh language, but its main focus is offering residential Welsh language and literature courses to suit all levels of ability (from £280 for three days full-board), including B&B accommodation in homely little grey-stone cottages and meals at the on-site restaurant.

The centre is reached from the village of Llithfaen (on the B4417) by following a path down a steep valley. If you're driving take it very slowly and be extremely careful.

❧ ST BEUNO'S CHURCH // WHERE LLŶN VISITORS HAVE STOPPED FOR CENTURIES

One of the main pit-stops on the Bardsey pilgrimage, this ancient hospice church sits peacefully in the middle of its oval churchyard below the village of Pistyll. St Beuno (died 640) was to North Wales what St David was to the south of the country (another St Beuno church is further up the coast at Clynnog Fawr, where his religious community was based).

This tiny stone church's slate roof would originally have been thatched, but original features include a Celtic carved font and a window beside the altar that allowed lepers standing outside to watch Mass being celebrated. On the interior face of this wall there are rare remnants of pre-Reformation frescoes. St Beuno's is at its most atmospheric during the Christmas, Easter and harvest seasons, when the floors are covered in reeds and fragrant herbs – unless, of course, you're a hay-fever sufferer.

East of Pistyll are the 100m sea cliffs of **Carreg y Llam**, a major North Wales seabird site, with huge colonies of razorbills, guillemots and kittiwakes.

❧ MORFA NEFYN // POSSIBLY WALES' BEST POSITIONED PUB

The diminutive village of Morfa Nefyn sits above a pretty crescent of sand at **Porth Dinllaen**. It's hard to believe that this was once a busy cargo, shipbuilding and herring port, the only safe haven on the peninsula's north coast. Indeed, it was eyed up by slate magnate William Madocks as a possible home for ferries to Ireland, but in 1839 the House of Commons gave that job to Holyhead. Today, it's owned in its entirety by the NT, which maintains a small information kiosk in its car park (£3 in summer, free to NT members).

At the western end of the beach is an isolated cluster of buildings, which include the legendary **Tŷ Coch Inn** (☎ 01758-720498; www.tycoch.co.uk; ❧ noon-4pm Sat & Sun, daily summer). It was famous for its views and toes-in-the-water pints even before Demi Moore shot key scenes from the 2006 movie *Half Light* here.

For pub grub try **Cliffs Inn** (☎ 01758-720356; mains £9-15), with views from the conservatory eating area and generous Sunday roasts. If you're looking for a post office or a supermarket, the larger but less attractive settlement of Nefyn lies slightly to the east.

WELSH LANGUAGE WOES

Although support for the Welsh language has strengthened in recent years and other minority cultures look to Wales as a shining example, in reality the threat to the language is acute.

Economic hardship in rural areas, particularly Welsh-speaking communities, has resulted in migration to urban centres. Meanwhile, large numbers of non-Welsh speakers have been moving in, changing the cultural dynamic of rural Wales in a very short time. Historically, few of these migrants have learnt the Welsh language or become involved in local traditions, and their presence inflates house prices and forces local people out.

During the rise of nationalism from the 1960s to 1980s, opposition to the English 'invaders' rose steadily and anti-English slogans and graffiti were common. Slogans such as '*Dal dy dir*' (Hold your ground) and '*Ildiwch*' (Surrender) were emblazoned on mountain sides and rural walls. A radical underground organisation, the Sons of Glyndŵr, went even further, firebombing English-owned holiday homes and, in doing so, causing much harm to the nationalists' cause.

Today, peaceful 'No Colonisation' campaigns, such as those run by pressure group Cymuned, target estate agents in England who are selling Welsh properties to outsiders. For more information visit www.wales4sale.com.

These days more people are learning Welsh as a second language and all schoolchildren are required to study Welsh up to the age of 16, but pressure on Welsh as a living first language remains.

❦ WHISTLING SANDS // SECLUDED BEACH WITH SQUEAKY SAND

Just north of Aberdaron is this crescent-shaped beach where the sand squeaks when you walk on it. From here it's a 2-mile coastal walk west via the twin headlands of Dinas Bach and Dinas Fawr to the cove of Porth Orion.

❦ BRAICH-Y-PWLL // NEXT STOP, BARDSEY

While the boats for Bardsey now leave from Porth Meudwy, this rugged NT property on the very tip of the Llŷn Peninsula is where the medieval pilgrims set off from – and one glimpse of the surf-pounded rocks will reinforce what a terrifying final voyage that must have been. It's an incredibly dramatic, ancient-looking landscape, with Bardsey rising out of the slate-grey sea like the mystical Avalon. A path leads down past the earthworks, which are all that remain of St Mary's Abbey, to a Neolithic standing stone known as Maen Melyn, bent like a finger towards the island and suggesting this was a holy place long before the Celts or their saints arrived.

Beneath the stone, a natural freshwater spring issues from a cleft in the rock below the high tide mark; called St Mary's Well (Ffynnon Fair), it was held to be holy and pilgrims would sip from here before setting out. There are sheer drops to the sea and high surf, and we don't recommend you attempt it.

Inland are strip fields that preserve many of the patterns of ancient land-use. Keep an eye out for choughs, a cheeky red-legged relation of the crow, and the rare spotted rock rose – this is the only place on the British mainland where this yellow bloom is found.

🌿 ABERDARON // SEASIDE VILLAGE WITH SURPLUS PERSONALITY AND HISTORY

Aberdaron (population 1000) is an ends-of-the-earth kind of place with white-washed, windswept houses contemplating Aberdaron Bay. It was traditionally the last resting spot before pilgrims made the treacherous crossing to Bardsey.

Lingering from this time is **St Hywyn's Church** (🕙 10am-5pm Apr-Oct, to 4pm Nov-Mar), stoically positioned above the pebbly beach. The left half of the church dates from 1100 while the right half was added 400 years later, to cope with the volume of pilgrims. Welsh poet RS Thomas was the minister here from 1967 to 1978 and it seems an appropriate setting for his bleak, impassioned work (see p291). The church was restored in 2006 and today has lots of information about local history as well as two 6th-century memorial stones and a medieval font and holy-water stoup.

With their spiritual needs sorted, the Bardsey-bound saints could then claim a meal at **Y Gegin Fawr** (The Big Kitchen; ☎ 01758-760359; 🕘 9am-6pm), a little thick-walled building with tiny windows, just over the bridge in the centre of the village. Dating from 1300, it still dishes up meals to hungry visitors. Other reliable eating options are Tŷ Newydd and the Ship Hotel (p341). There's little else in the centre of the village apart from a store and a Spar supermarket with a post office attached.

The little **Gwylan Islands** in the bay are North Wales' most important puffin-breeding site.

Parking is a problem in the village but there is a small private car park just before the bridge (£2 per two hours) and the NT is looking at buying some land to use for this purpose.

🌿 BARDSEY ISLAND (YNYS ENLLI) // MYTHS, MAGICIANS, MONKS AND MANY, MANY BONES

This mysterious island, 2 miles long and 2 miles off the tip of the Llŷn, is a magical place, its otherworldliness emphasised by its most poetic epithet: the Isle of 20,000 Saints. In the 6th or 7th century the obscure St Cadfan founded a monastery here, giving shelter to Celts fleeing the Saxon invaders, and medieval pilgrims followed in their wake.

A Celtic cross amidst the abbey ruins commemorates the 20,000 pilgrims who came here to die – the 20,000 saints who give the island its ancient name. Their bones still periodically emerge from unmarked graves; it's said that in the 1850s they were used as fencing, there were so many of them.

To add to its mythical status, it is one of many candidates for the Isle of Avalon, where King Arthur was taken after the Battle of Camlann. Other legends say the wizard Merlin is asleep in a glass castle on the island along with the magical Thirteen Precious Curiosities of Britain.

The island's Welsh name means 'Isle of the Currents', a reference to the treacherous tidal surges in Bardsey Sound, which doubtless convinced medieval visitors that their lives were indeed in God's hands.

Most modern pilgrims to Bardsey are seabird-watchers (the island is home to an important colony of Manx shearwaters), although there are also some 6th-century **carved stones** and the remains of a 13th-century **abbey tower** – along with a candy-striped lighthouse.

The **Bardsey Island Trust** (☎ 0845 811 2233; www.bardsey.org) is the custodian of the island and can arrange holiday lets in cottages there. In the summer months both **Bardsey Boat Trips** (☎ 07971-769895; www.bardseyboattrips.com) and **Enlli Charters**

THE BARDSEY PILGRIMAGE

At a time when journeys from Britain to Italy were long, perilous and beyond the means of most people, the Pope decreed that three pilgrimages to the holy island of Bardsey would have the same spiritual value as one to Rome. Tens of thousands of penitents took advantage of this get-out-of-purgatory-free (or at least quickly) card and many came here to die. In the 16th century, Henry VIII's dissolution of the monasteries and ban on pilgrimages put pay to the practice – although a steady trickle of modern-day pilgrims still walk the route today.

The traditional pilgrimage route stops at ancient churches and holy wells along the way. It's broken into nine legs on the **Edge of Wales Walk** (☎ 01758-760652; www.edge ofwaleswalk.co.uk) website, run by a cooperative of local residents. They can help to arrange a 47-mile, self-guided walking tour, including five nights' accommodation and baggage transfers (around £56 per night). A similar service is also offered for the 84-mile **Llŷn Coastal Path**, which circumnavigates the peninsula.

(☎ 0845 811 3655; www.enllicharter.co.uk) takes boats to the island from Porth Meudwy (adult/child £30/15), while Enlli Charters also departs from Pwllheli (adult/child £35/20); call ahead for details.

✿ PLAS-YN-RHIW // GARDENS AND VIEWS FROM A HISTORIC HOUSE

A 16th-century Welsh manor house restored by three sisters in the 1930s and '40s, **Plas-yn-Rhiw** (☎ 01758-780219; www .nationaltrust.org.uk; adult/child £5/2.50; ⏲ noon-5pm Thu-Sun Apr & Oct, Wed-Mon May-Aug, Thu-Mon Sep) features ornamental gardens that are a sharp contrast to the surrounding moorland and wonderful views over Cardigan Bay. It's on the heights near the hamlet of Rhiw, 4 miles east of Aberdaron.

✿ ABERSOCH // SOCKING IT TO SURFERS AND SAILORS

Abersoch (population 1000) comes alive in summer with a 30,000-person influx of boaties, surfers and beach bums. Packed in high season, it's a virtual ghost town in winter. Edged by gentle blue-green hills, the town's main attraction is its beaches and today it's the Llŷn's premier water-sports centre. Surfers head for the Atlantic swell at **Porth Neigwl**

(Hell's Mouth) and Porth Ceiriad, while sailors, windsurfers and boaters prefer the gentle waters of Abersoch Bay.

West Coast Surf Shop (☎ 713067; www .westcoastsurf.co.uk; Lôn Pen Cei; ⏲ 9.30am-5pm) hires out boards and wetsuits all year around. Its website features a live surf-cam and daily surf reports. **Offaxis** (☎ 713407; www.offaxis.co.uk; Lôn Engan; lessons incl equipment from £30) is another outdoors-cum-surf shop, which specialises in wakeboarding, windsurfing and surfing lessons.

Abersoch Sailing School (☎ 712963; www.abersochsailingschool.co.uk) offers sailings lessons (from £45), joy rides (£25 per person) and hires laser fun boats (one/two/three hours £30/45/60), catamarans (one/two/three hours £40/60/80), sea kayaks (single/double per hour £10/20) and skippered day racers and keelboats (£75 per hour, minimum two hours).

Abersoch's smartest boutique hotel is also its best restaurant. **Venetia** (☎ 01758-713354; www.venetiawales.com; Lôn Sarn Bach; mains £9-20; ⏲ Thu-Sun winter, daily summer; Ⓟ) specialises in the traditional tastes of Venice, particularly fish and pasta dishes and serves them under twinkling modern chandeliers in a grand Edwardian house.

The ultimate surfer's hang-out, whether for a beer or a hearty dinner, **Fresh** (☎ 01758-710033; www.fresh-abersoch.co.uk; Stryd Fawr; mains £8-20; ☽ lunch Sat & Sun, dinner Mon-Sat) has beanbags, a TV area and a regular clientele of surfer dudes. Head to **Abersoch Cafe** (☎ 01758-713433; Stryd Fawr; mains £5-7; ☽ 9am-5pm) for cheap and cheerful snacks, such as cooked breakfasts, wraps, burgers and jacket potatoes.

For a pint try the **Vaynol Arms** (☎ 712776; Stryd Fawr; ☎), which has real ales, simple bar snacks and wi-fi access. There's a convenience store, post office and various banks on the high street (*stryd fawr*).

♥ LLANBEDROG // ATTENTION-SEEKING MANSION AND TOP-NOTCH ART

Only part of the attraction of the excellent **Oriel Plas Glyn-y-Weddw** (☎ 01758-740763; www.oriel.org.uk; admission free; ☽ 10am-5pm Wed-Mon, daily summer) is the lively collection of work by contemporary Welsh artists, all of which is available for purchase. The gallery is worth visiting just to gape at the flamboyant Victorian Gothic mansion it's housed in, with its flashy exposed beams and stained glass. There's also a nice little cafe and paths through the wooded grounds, which roll down to NT-owned Llandbedrog beach.

Up on the main road (the A499), the **Ship Inn** (☎ 01758-741111; www.theshipinn.org.uk; mains £6-14) is a popular, family-friendly pub offering hearty bar meals with lots of daily specials.

Llanbedrog is 3 miles from Abersoch and 4 miles west of Pwllheli.

♥ PLAS BODEGROES // CLASSIC COOKING IN AN ELEGANT SETTING

Set in a stately Georgian manor house strewn with modern art, a mile inland from Pwllheli along the A497, this slick **restaurant with rooms** (☎ 01758-612363; www.bodegroes.co.uk; 3-course dinner £43; ☽ lunch Sun, dinner Tue-Sat; ℗) has an elegant dining room but ups the Welshness by serving its dishes on slabs of slate. Local, organic and sustainable produce features heavily on the menu.

♥ PWLLHELI // A TRANSPORT HUB AND LITTLE ELSE

With a population of 3900, Pwllheli (poolth-*heh*-lee; meaning 'salt-water pool') is the largest town on the Llŷn. While it's staunchly Welsh and has a long sandy beach, it's not a particularly interesting or attractive town to linger in. It is, however, the peninsula's public transport hub.

Enlli Charters has boats departing from here for Bardsey Island (p240). The harbour, tourist office, train station, bus stands, post office and supermarket are all within a block of one another just south of Y Maes, the main square.

Stylish yet relaxed, **Taro Deg** (☎ 01758-701271; Lôn Dywod; mains £4-6; ☽ 9am-4.30pm Mon-Sat; ☎) is a central cafe offering newspapers to browse and a tasty selection of sandwiches and cakes. Another good lunch option is friendly **Pili Palas** (☎ 01758-612248; 2-4 Stryd Moch; mains £4-5; ☽ 10am-4.30pm Mon-Sat), which serves light bites, such as hot ciabatta.

♥ PENARTH FAWR MEDIEVAL HOUSE // STEP INTO THE MIDDLE AGES

Surrounded by stone farm buildings that time forgot, Penarth Fawr is a privately owned 1416 house that has somehow survived into the 21st century. It's basically one large hall with a big open hearth, and there are no set opening hours or admission charges – just turn up and see if it's open. The affable owners are more than happy for you to potter about; keep a third eye open for the resident ghost. The hall sometimes doubles as an arts and craft gallery.

It's signposted from the A497, 3.5 miles east of Pwllheli.

🐾 LLANYSTUMDWY // BIRTHPLACE OF A WARTIME LEADER

The village of Llanystumdwy is the boyhood home and final resting place of David Lloyd George, one of Wales' finest ever political statesmen, and the British prime minister from 1916 to 1922 (see p287). There's a small **Lloyd George Museum** (☎ 01766-522071; adult/child £4/3; 🕙 10.30am-5pm Mon-Fri Apr & May, Mon-Sat Jun, daily Jul-Sep, 11am-4pm Mon-Fri Oct), which gives an impression of the man and to some extent illustrates the tension between his nationality and position, through photos, posters and personal effects. Highgate, the house he grew up in, is 50m away, and his grave is about 150m away on the other side of the car park. The memorial is designed by Clough Williams-Ellis, the creator of Portmeirion (p246).

The turn-off to the village is 1.5 miles west of Criccieth on the A497.

🐾 CRICCIETH // CASTLE ABOVE THE SAND

This genteel slow-moving seaside town (population 1800) sits above a sweep of sand-and-stone beach about 5 miles west of Porthmadog. Its main claim to fame is ruined **Criccieth Castle** (Cadw; ☎ 01766-522227; www.cadw.wales.gov.uk; adult/child £3/2.60; 🕙 10am-5pm Apr-Oct, 9.30am-4pm Fri & Sat, 11am-4pm Sun Nov-Mar) perched up on the clifftop and offering views stretching along the southern coast and across Tremadog Bay to Harlech. Constructed by Welsh prince Llewellyn the Great in 1239, it was overrun in 1283 by Edward I's forces and recaptured for the Welsh in 1404 by Owain Glyndŵr, who promptly burnt it.

Today there is a small but informative exhibition centre at the ticket office.

The town's focal point is Y Maes, a wide square on the High St (Stryd Fawr), the A497 Porthmadog–Pwllheli road. The seaside road running parallel to High St is Castle St (Ffordd Castell). There's parking on the opposite side of High St behind the Lion Hotel and the train station is about two blocks west down the A497. **Roots** (☎ 01766-523564; 46 High St; 🕙 10am-5pm), a Christian bookshop, acts as the de-facto tourist office. It has OS maps and offers internet access (£3 per hour). Also on High St is a small supermarket, a post office and a bank with an ATM.

The best place to eat in town is **Poachers Restaurant** (☎ 01766-522512; www.poachers restaurant.co.uk; 66 High St; mains £11-19; 🕙 lunch Sun, dinner Wed-Sat). Look past the paper serviettes and limited wine choice and you'll find tasty Welsh dishes married with some flavours of Asia. Try the good-value three-course set menu (£17). The liveliest pub in town is the **Prince of Wales** (☎ 01766-522556; www.princeofwales-criccieth.co.uk; Y Maes; lunch £4-5, mains £7-15; 🕙 noon-11pm), with local ales and decent bar meals.

TRANSPORT

BIKE // Lôn Las Cymru passes through Criccieth, heading north to Caernarfon and east to Porthmadog.

BUS // Bus 1 (Porthmadog–Caernarfon–Bangor) stops in Criccieth. All of the peninsula's other bus services originate or terminate at Pwllheli, including bus 3 to Llanystumdwy (20 minutes), Criccieth (24 minutes), Tremadog (37 minutes) and Porthmadog (41 minutes); 8 to Morfa Nefyn (20 minutes); 8B to Llanbedrog (10 minutes), Rhiw (35 minutes) and Whistling Sands (one hour); 12 to Caernarfon (45 minutes); 17/17B to Llanbedrog (10 minutes), Aberdaron (45 minutes) and Rhiw (one hour); 18 to Llanbedrog (12 minutes) and Abersoch (25 minutes) and 27 to Llithfaen (25 minutes) and Pistyll (30 minutes).

COACH // A **National Express** (www.national express.com) coach heads between Pwllheli and London (£31, 10½ hours) daily, via Criccieth (£5.20, 17 minutes), Caernarfon (£6.80, one hour), Bangor (£7.30, 1½ hours) and Birmingham (£24, seven hours).

TRAIN // Pwllheli is the terminus of the Cambrian Coast Line, with direct trains to Criccieth (£2.70, 13 minutes), Porthmadog (£3.90, 22 minutes), Harlech (£6.30, 45 minutes), Barmouth (£8.70, 1¼ hours), Fairbourne (£8.70, 1¼ hours) and Machynlleth (£13, 2¼ hours).

PORTHMADOG & AROUND

☎ **01766 / pop 4200**

Given its abundance of transport connections and its position straddling the Llŷn Peninsula and Snowdonia National Park, busy little Porthmadog (port-*mad*-uk) makes an excellent place to base yourself for a few days. While the town centre is nothing to look at, its estuarine setting offers some nice views and walks.

Despite a few rough edges, Porthmadog has a considerable amount of charm and a conspicuously friendly populace. It's also overwhelmingly Welsh-speaking.

The town was founded by an 1821 Act of Parliament granting permission to slate magnate William Alexander Madocks (after whom the town is named) to reclaim estuary land and create a new harbour. Madocks began by laying a mile-long causeway called The Cob across Traeth Mawr, the estuary at the mouth of the River Glaslyn. Some 400 hectares of wetland habitat behind The Cob was drained and turned into farmland. The resulting causeway provided the route Madocks needed to transport slate on the new Ffestiniog Railway down to the new port.

In the 1870s it was estimated that over a thousand vessels per year departed from the harbour and, at the peak in 1873, over 116,000 tons of Blaenau Ffestiniog slate left Porthmadog for ports around the world.

Today Porthmadog is the southern terminus for two of Wales' finest narrow-gauge train journeys, the Ffestiniog & Welsh Highland Railways. On its doorstep is the village of Portmeirion, a fantasy-style pocket of *la dolce vita* Italy in North Wales.

ESSENTIAL INFORMATION

EMERGENCIES // Police station (☎ 512226; High St)

TOURIST OFFICES // Tourist office (☎ 512981; High St; ☺ 9.30am-5pm Easter-Oct, 10am-3.30pm Mon-Sat Nov-Easter)

ORIENTATION

The Cob is the only direct road to Porthmadog from the southeast and as such it's subject to major traffic congestion in summer.

EXPLORING PORTHMADOG & AROUND

♥ FFESTINIOG & WELSH HIGHLAND RAILWAYS // ROMANTIC RAIL ROUTES THROUGH THE MOUNTAINS

There are 'little trains' all over Wales, a legacy of Victorian industry, but Porthmadog is doubly blessed. The two lines of the **Ffestiniog & Welsh Highland Railways** (☎ 516024; www.festrail.co.uk) top and tail the town, with a station at each end of the High St. They're run by the oldest independent railway company in the world, established by an Act of Parliament in 1832.

Departing from the south end, near the Cob, the **Ffestiniog Railway** (adult/child return £18/17) is a fantastic, twisting and precipitous narrow-gauge railway

IS AMERICA REALLY WELSH?

Porthmadog may be named after William Alexander Madocks, but there's another legendary namesake associated with the area. The story goes that in 1170 Madog ab Owain Gwynedd, a local prince, set off from here and 'discovered' America. The tale was dusted off during Elizabeth I's reign to justify the English crown's claim on the continent over Spain's; the land's indigenous occupants had no say in the matter. It gained further traction during Wales' 18th-century Romantic renaissance when it was deployed to give the Welsh a sense of pride in their past.

Madog and his followers were said to have intermarried with Native Americans and formed their own Welsh-speaking tribe. After America's 're-discovery', explorers returned with stories of meeting Welsh-speaking clans in Virginia and Kentucky. In 1796 John Evans, the leader of a party that helped map the Missouri River, sought and failed to find any evidence of them. Given that many small Native American tribes disappeared soon after colonisation, the Madog story still has some traction amongst hardcore Welsh patriots.

that was built between 1832 and 1836 to haul slate down to Porthmadog from the mines at Blaenau Ffestiniog. Horse-drawn wagons were replaced in the 1860s by steam locomotives and the line became a passenger service. Saved after years of neglect, it is one of Wales' most spectacular and beautiful narrow-gauge journeys. Because it links the Cambrian Coast and Conwy Valley main lines, it also serves as a serious public transport link. Nearly all services are steam-hauled.

The 13.5-mile (one-hour) journey heads through fern-fringed valleys and tree-line passes before entering the soot-saturated darkness of the Moelwyn Tunnel. It then hugs the fringe of Tan-y-Grisiau Reservoir and progresses into a landscape of mist-shrouded mountains and slate-grey cottages.

Exciting things are afoot with its sibling, the **Welsh Highland Railway** (Caernarfon–Pont Croesor adult/child return £28/26). An amalgamation of several late 19th-century slate railways, the line opened for passenger traffic in 1923 but closed just 14 years later. It reopened as a tourist attraction in 1997 and until recently was offering only short trips from Porthmadog and rather longer ones from Caernarfon as far as the trailheads of the Snowdon Ranger and Rhyd Ddu tracks on the slopes of Snowdon. In 2010 the line was extended to Beddgelert and through the outrageously beautiful Aberglaslyn Pass to Pont Croesor, 2 miles from Porthmadog. By the time you're reading this, the last small gap should have been plugged, connecting Caernarfon with Porthmadog, with a final leg along the main street to a new terminus near the Ffestiniog Railway.

☙ **TREMADOG // LAWRENCE OF ARABIA AND THE GOLDEN FLEECE**
Less than a mile north of central Porthmadog, Tremadog seems like an outlying suburb but it's actually a separate village, grouped around a handsome town square. TE Lawrence (Lawrence of Arabia) was born here on 16 August 1888, although the Lawrence family moved to Oxford 12 years later. At the time of writing, their Church St house was being converted into a boutique hotel.

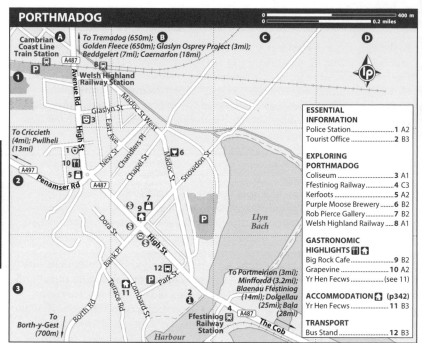

SNOWDONIA & THE LLŶN

PORTHMADOG

To Tremadog (650m); Golden Fleece (650m); Glaslyn Osprey Project (3mi); Beddgelert (7mi); Caernarfon (18mi)

Cambrian Coast Line Train Station

Welsh Highland Railway Station

Glaslyn St

Madoc St West

To Criccieth (4mi); Pwllheli (13mi)

High St

East Ave

New St

Chandlers Pl

Chapel St

Madoc St

Snowdon St

Penamser Rd

Dora St

Bank Pl

High St

Park St

Terrace Rd

Lombard St

Borth Rd

To Borth-y-Gest (700m)

Ffestiniog Railway Station

To Portmeirion (3mi); Minffordd (3.2mi); Blaenau Ffestiniog (14mi); Dolgellau (25mi); Bala (28mi)

The Cob

Harbour

Llyn Bach

ESSENTIAL INFORMATION
Police Station..........................1 A2
Tourist Office 2 B3

EXPLORING PORTHMADOG
Coliseum 3 A1
Ffestiniog Railway................4 C3
Kerfoots 5 A2
Purple Moose Brewery 6 B2
Rob Pierce Gallery................7 B2
Welsh Highland Railway 8 A1

GASTRONOMIC HIGHLIGHTS
Big Rock Cafe 9 B2
Grapevine 10 A2
Yr Hen Fecws ....(see 11)

ACCOMMODATION (p342)
Yr Hen Fecws 11 B3

TRANSPORT
Bus Stand 12 B3

Pubs don't get much more atmospheric or fun than the **Golden Fleece** (☎ 512421; www.goldenfleeceinn.com; Market Sq; mains £4-12) on Tremadog's main square. It's an inviting and friendly old inn with hop flowers hanging from the ceilings, real ales, decent pub grub, an open fire for cold nights and a sunny courtyard for balmy days. This is a great spot to sample a pint of the local microbrewery ale from the Purple Moose Brewery. A roster of live music and jam sessions entertains the troops, although the punters can be pretty entertaining themselves.

❧ PORTMEIRION // ITALY MEETS DISNEY ON THE WELSH COAST
Set on its own tranquil peninsula reaching into the estuary, **Portmeirion village** (☎ 01766-70000; www.portmeirion-village.com; adult/ child £8/4; ⏱ 9.30am-5.30pm) is an oddball, gingerbread collection of buildings with a heavy Italian influence, masterminded by the Welsh architect Sir Clough Williams-Ellis. Starting in 1926, Clough collected bits and pieces from disintegrating stately mansions to create this weird and wonderful seaside utopia over the course of 50 years. When it was deemed to be finished in 1976, Clough had reached the ripe old age of 90 and had designed and built many of the structures himself. Today all the buildings are listed and the whole site is a Conservation Area.

It's really more like an amusement park or a stage set than an actual village and, indeed, it formed the ideally surreal set for the cult TV series, *The Prisoner*, which was filmed here from 1966 to 1967; it still draws fans of the show in droves with *Prisoner* conventions held annually in April. More recently the village was the setting for the hugely popular TV series, *Cold Feet*. The giant plaster of Paris Buddha, just off the piazza, also featured in the 1958 film, *The Inn of the Sixth Happiness*, starring Ingrid Bergman.

A documentary on Williams-Ellis and Portmeirion screens on the hour in a building just above the central piazza. Clough's lifelong concern was with the whimsical and intriguing nature of architecture, his raison d'être to demonstrate how a naturally beautiful site could be developed without defiling it. His life's work now stands as a testament to beauty, something he described as 'that strange necessity'. He died in 1978, having campaigned for the environment throughout his life. He was a founding member of the Council for the Protection of Rural Wales in 1928 and served as its president for 20 years.

Most of the kooky cottages or scaled-down mansions scattered about the site are available for holiday lets, while other buildings contain cafes, restaurants and gift shops. Portmeirion pottery (the famously florid pottery designed by Susan, Sir Clough's daughter) is available, even though these days it's made in Stoke-on-Trent (England).

Portmeirion is about 2 miles east of Porthmadog. It's an easy enough walk, but Williams bus 99B has services at 9.55am and 1.05pm, Monday to Saturday (10 minutes).

❧ BORTH-Y-GEST // TUCKED AWAY SEASIDE VILLAGE WITH STRIKING VIEWS

The best views over the estuary are from Terrace Rd, which becomes Garth Rd above the harbour. At its end a path heads down to Borth-y-Gest, a pretty horseshoe of candy coloured houses overlooking a sandy bay. At the other

end of the crescent the path continues around the cliffs; if you look carefully you should be able to spot Harlech Castle in the distance.

❧ GLASLYN OSPREY PROJECT // TRAIN A TELESCOPE ON A RAPTOR FAMILY

This **RSPB project** (www.rspb.org.uk; ☺ 10am-6pm Apr-Aug) was founded after a pair of ospreys, regular visitors to Wales from Africa, first nested near Porthmadog in 2004. A round-the-clock protection scheme now operates during the breeding season while a public viewing site is open at Pont Croesor with telescopes and live footage from the nest-cams. The project is on the B4410, off the A498 northeast of Tremadog.

❧ LOCAL BUSINESSES // WAVING THE FLAG FOR INDEPENDENT ENTERPRISE

Although the High St (Stryd Fawr) has an extravagant number of charity shops and more than a few boarded up businesses, Porthmadog is proud of its status as a bastion for independent, local enterprises – including **Kerfoots** (☎ 512256; www.kerfoots.com; 138-145 High St), a department store founded in 1874, and the **Coliseum** (☎ 512108; High St), a classic, old-fashioned picture house.

One of approximately 30 micro-breweries across Wales, **Purple Moose** (☎ 515571; www.purplemoose.co.uk; Madoc St; ☺ 9am-5pm Mon-Fri) has grown from humble beginnings to employ four people and supply pubs across North Wales. Its award-winning tipples include Snowdonia Ale, Madog's Ale, Glaslyn Ale and Dark Side of the Moose. You can buy these and associated memorabilia from the brewery shop. Tours are given on request, if they're not too busy.

⚘ ROB PIERCY GALLERY // TAKE THE LANDSCAPE HOME WITH YOU

This small commercial **gallery** (☎ 513833; www.robpiercy.com; Snowdon St; ☺ 10am-5pm Mon-Sat) showcases the work of Piercy, a local artist and member of the Watercolour Society of Wales, who specialises in mountain landscapes.

⚘ EATERIES // IF YOU'RE BASED HERE, YOU'LL NEED TO EAT

Porthmadog isn't known for its restaurants but there are a few decent cafes scattered about. **Big Rock Cafe** (Y Graig Fawr; ☎ 512098; 71 High St; ☺ breakfast & lunch Mon-Sat) is a cool place serving excellent coffee by Welsh standards, as well as soup, sandwiches and homemade sweets. No-frills **Grapevine** (☎ 514230; www .grapevinebistrorestaurant.co.uk; 152 High St; mains £7-13; ☺ 8am-9pm Mon & Wed-Sat, to 5pm Tue, 11am-4pm Sun) offers cooked breakfasts, snack lunches (including delicious, fresh, filled baguettes) and simple cooked meals in the evening.

Another good, more upmarket, daytime option is **Yr Hen Fecws** (p342), or try the **Golden Fleece** (p342) in Tremadog.

TRANSPORT

BIKE // Lôn Las Cymru passes through Porthmadog, heading west to Criccieth and south to Harlech.

BUS // Bus route 1B heads to Blaenau Ffestiniog (31 minutes); 3 to Tremadog (four minutes), Criccieth (13 minutes), Llanystumdwy (23 minutes), and Pwllheli (41 minutes); and X32 to Aberystwyth (2¼ hours), Machynlleth (1½ hours), Dolgellau (1½ hours), Caernarfon (43 minutes) and Bangor (1¼ hours). Snowdon Sherpa bus S97 goes to Beddgelert 25 minutes) and Pen-y-Pass (45 minutes).

COACH // A National Express (www.national express.com) coach runs between Pwllheli (£7, 30 minutes) and London (£31, 10 hours) daily, via Caernarfon (£6.80, 35 minutes), Llandudno (£7.30, 1½ hour) and Birmingham (£24, 6½ hours).

PARKING // The main car park is off Madoc St and there are more spaces on Park St (50p per hour, over four hours £5.30, free 6pm to 8pm).

TRAIN // Porthmadog is on the Cambrian Coast Line, with direct trains to Machynlleth (£11, 1¾ hours), Fairbourne (£6.20, 58 minutes), Barmouth (£5.40, 48 minutes), Harlech (£3, 22 minutes) and Pwllheli (£3.90, 22 minutes). See also the Ffestiniog & Welsh Highland Railways (p244) for steamy services to Blaenau Ffestiniog, the Snowdon trailheads and Caernarfon.

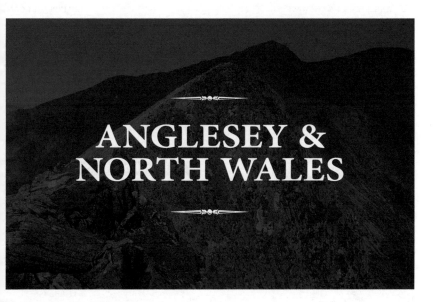

ANGLESEY & NORTH WALES

3 PERFECT DAYS

❧ DAY 1 // ESSENTIAL ANGLESEY

Start with a hearty breakfast at Beaumaris' Townhouse (p343) before taking a spin over the top of the island, stopping for coffee at Ann's Pantry in Moelfre (p255) and enjoying the sea air in Church Bay (p259). Continue the loop for lunch, stopping for gastropub fare at the White Eagle (p255), before heading inland. After browsing the Kyffin Williams collection at Oriel Ynys Môn (p260), head back to Beaumaris for a slap-up dinner and a stroll along the pier.

❧ DAY 2 // ESCAPE THE CROWDS

The north coast has its brash and busy pockets but there are plenty of places to escape to. Set out from Llandudno's Escape B&B (p344) for the West Shore and a crowd-free walk (p269). In Conwy, the crowds are swamping the castle but the birdlife is your sole companion as you explore the Conwy estuary mapped by Whinward House (p344). Late afternoon could include an excursion to Bangor to watch the boats bobbing in the harbour from the Victorian Pier (p262).

❧ DAY 3 // HIDDEN GEMS

Begin the day exploring lesser-known northeast Wales by cleansing your soul with a visit to St Winefride's Well (p274). Then try a bracing stroll through the Clwydian Range (p273), tackling Moel Famau if you're feeling energetic. Lunch awaits in Llangollen with Gales Wine Bar (p277) an ideal spot to slake a post-walk thirst. Finally, head for Ruthin to explore a quintessential Welsh market town, plus dinner and art-inspired rooms at manorhaus (p278).

ANGLESEY & NORTH WALES

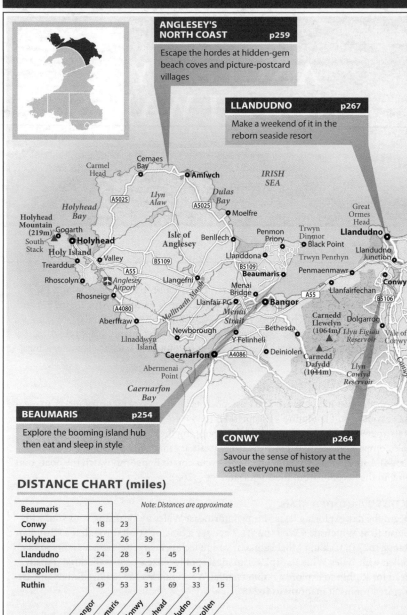

ANGLESEY'S NORTH COAST p259

Escape the hordes at hidden-gem beach coves and picture-postcard villages

LLANDUDNO p267

Make a weekend of it in the reborn seaside resort

BEAUMARIS p254

Explore the booming island hub then eat and sleep in style

CONWY p264

Savour the sense of history at the castle everyone must see

DISTANCE CHART (miles)

Note: Distances are approximate

	Bangor	Beaumaris	Conwy	Holyhead	Llandudno	Llangollen
Beaumaris	6					
Conwy	18	23				
Holyhead	25	26	39			
Llandudno	24	28	5	45		
Llangollen	54	59	49	75	51	
Ruthin	49	53	31	69	33	15

GETTING AROUND

Make the A55 your best friend – it will take you from the English–Welsh border to Holyhead docks for ferries to Ireland. The key train line, Arriva's North Coast Line, runs parallel to the A55 but also has the better of the sea views, while Virgin Trains' speedy new Pendolino trains connect Bangor, Holyhead and Llandudno Junction to London on the West Coast Main Line. Heading further inland, Arriva offers regular bus services. For more details and information on travel passes, see p362 and p366.

HOLYWELL   p274

If cleanliness is next to godliness, then take the waters here

RUTHIN   p278

Go native in this up-and-coming market town with lots of local colour

LLANGOLLEN   p272

Catch the male voice choir in rehearsal at Llangollen's Hand Hotel

PONTCYSYLLTE AQUEDUCT   p275

Take a ride across Wales' latest World Heritage site near Llangollen

ANGLESEY & NORTH WALES

ANGLESEY & NORTH WALES GETTING STARTED

MAKING THE MOST OF YOUR TIME

Some consider North Wales the poorer cousin of the south. They're wrong. The ancient island enclave of Anglesey and the towns of the north coast, plus the burgeoning heartland of northeast Wales, punch well above their weight. Highlights include medieval castles, rejuvenated seaside towns, superb coastal hiking, cosy boltholes and crowd-free beach coves. Best of all, it feels authentically Welsh: you'll hear the language on the street, see the Celtic legacy in the landscape and soak up the cultural pride in galleries, museums and attractions. For a grass-roots cultural experience, ignore the nay-sayers and go north, young man.

TOP TRAILS

☙ SLOW FOOD
Savour the flavour of traditional local produce by exploring Anglesey's food trail. Save room to stock up at Sarah's Delicatessen (p256) and the Deri Môn Smokery (p255).

☙ ROMANS & DRUIDS
Anglesey marks the Druids' last stand against the Romans, so where you find an ancient site associated with one, you'll find the hand of the other. Start by establishing the facts at the History Gallery at Oriel Ynys Môn (p260).

☙ LAND OF SONG
Follow your ears for a note-perfect tour of Welsh musical genres. Start with a folk night in Holyhead (p259), catch the Male Voice Choir practising in Llandudno and finish on a high note at the International Musical Eisteddfod in Llangollen (p277).

☙ WORLD HERITAGE
Two Unesco-listed sites are in the north. Follow the heritage trail from the Pontcysyllte Aqueduct and Canal (p274) to the castles of Conwy (p264) and Beaumaris (p254).

☙ LITERARY GIANTS
Pick up a secondhand copy of George Borrows' *Wild Wales* and follow in his footsteps around Llangollen, then head over to Llandudno to pick up the trail of Lewis Carroll of *Alice's Adventures in Wonderland* fame (p267).

GETTING AWAY FROM IT ALL

* **Clwydian Range AONB** Hike through the pristine landscape of the Clwydians and tackle the summit of Moel Famau (p273).

* **St Winefride's Well** Take a moment to soak up the spiritual atmosphere at this holy site (p274).

* **West Shore, Llandudno** Sunny day and the pier packed? No problem. Head across to the west shore for an empty beach, sunset views and a walk only the locals know about (p269).

* **North Coast, Anglesey** Leave the crowds behind by exploring the North Anglesey Heritage Coast, stopping for a picnic and a paddle between Cemaes and Church Bay (p259).

ADVANCE PLANNING

* **Victorian Extravaganza** (www.victorian-extravaganza.co.uk) Book your B&B well in advance if you're planning to join this festival, staged on bank-holiday weekend in early May.

* **A55** The main dual carriageway through North Wales and over the bridge to Anglesey is renowned for traffic jams in peak season. Turn off at the next junction and take the B roads. No rush.

* **Rain** North Wales has high rainfall, so pack waterproof gear no matter how clear the sky looks.

TOP CAFE CULTURE

* **RED BOAT ICE CREAM PARLOUR** Retro-design parlour offering yummy and authentic Italian gelato with a Welsh twist in Beaumaris (p256).

* **HARBOURFRONT BISTRO** With harbour views and great espresso, this is Holyhead's new favourite hangout (p258).

* **KYFFIN** Bangor's bastion of all things fair-trade and vegetarian is cool, calm and very green (p263).

* **NINETEEN** Llandudno's finest latte served in relaxed coffee-shop surroundings (p271).

* **LEONARDO'S** Grab a take-away latte and a muffin to go from Ruthin's superb local deli (p278).

RESOURCES

* **Visit Anglesey** (www.visitanglesey.co.uk) The council's tourism website

* **Anglesey Attractions** (www.angleseyattractions.co.uk) Ideas for days out on the island

* **North Wales Tourism** (www.borderlands.co.uk) Official tourism guide to North Wales

* **Visit Llandudno** (www.visitllandudno.org.uk) The official guide to the resort

* **Traveline Cymru** (www.traveline-cymru.info) Public transport information

THE ISLE OF ANGLESEY (YNYS MÔN)

At 276 sq miles, the Isle of Anglesey is the largest island in England and Wales. It's a popular destination for visitors with miles of inspiring coastline, hidden beaches, chocolate-box villages and Wales' greatest concentration of ancient sites (check out the Neolithic burial mound Bryn Celli Ddhu, 2 miles west of Llanfair PG on the A4080). The new A55 expressway also means that getting round the island by car is now much easier.

Fertile farming land attracted early settlers, while the island was holy to the Celts and it was the last outpost of Wales to fall to the Romans around AD 60. Given its outpost status and singular character, Anglesey stakes a fair claim to being the Welsh heartland. Gerald of Wales quoted the ancient name for the island 'Môn mam Cymru' (Mother of Wales) at the end of the 12th century.

The industrial age arrived in 1826 when Thomas Telford established the first permanent link to the mainland. His iconic 174m Menai Suspension Bridge across the Menai Strait has a 30m-high central span, allowing the passage of tall ships. It was joined in 1850 by Robert Stephenson's Britannia Bridge to carry the newly laid railway.

Beaumaris is the most convenient base on the island with the best range of infrastructure. Off-the-beaten-track highlights include Cemaes Bay rock pools for crabbing and Church Bay for its idyllic beach.

The two official tourist offices are at Llanfair PG and Holyhead. Menai Bridge is the island's hub for bus services with regular local connections across the region.

BEAUMARIS (BIWMARES)

☎ 01248 / pop 2000

The attractive visitor hub of the island, Beaumaris boasts a winning combination of an attractive waterfront location, a romantic castle lording it over a pretty collection of Georgian buildings and a burgeoning number of boutiques, deli-cafes and galleries. Sailing and walking lure a new generation of Anglesey converts to its smart hotels and chic eateries, while a major new project to extend the pier and introduce fast-track water-taxi services across the Menai Strait keeps the town moving with the times.

ESSENTIAL INFORMATION

EMERGENCIES // Gwynedd Hospital (☎ 384384; ◷ 24hr) Back over the Menai Bridge in Bangor **North Wales Police** (☎ 0845 6071002) **TOURIST OFFICES //** Tourist office (☎ 810040; Castle St) This unofficial tourist office is run by volunteers in the town hall and has erratic opening hours.

EXPLORING BEAUMARIS

❦ **BEAUMARIS CASTLE //** **QUITE POSSIBLY THE PERFECT CASTLE** It's a history teacher's fantasy castle with its 13th-century classic proportions and perfect symmetry. It was the last hurrah of Edward I's building program, and it retains its wow factor – even for those who aren't history buffs.

Run by Cadw (the Welsh historic monuments agency) and listed as a World Heritage site, **Beaumaris Castle** (☎ 810361; www.cadw.wales.gov.uk; adult/child £3.60/3.20; ◷ 9.30am-6pm Jul-Aug, 9.30am-5pm

TOP FIVE

HIDDEN GEMS FOR FOOD LOVERS

Anglesey is well known for its abundance of great local produce. Recently, the restaurant scene has caught up, using this regional wealth to superb effect in the preparation of fine food with a proudly local flavour. You can also go straight to the supplier and stock up on the best local produce at the **Deri Môn Smokery & Shop** (☎ 01248 410536; www.derimon smokery.co.uk; Dulas Bay; ⊗ 9am-5pm Mon-Sat), where a local food champion smokes fish, poultry, meat and cheese in a rustic, traditional farmhouse smokery. It's a real experience. Here are some of our favourite places to eat:

Ann's Pantry (☎ 01248 410386; www.annspantry.co.uk; Moelfre; snacks £2-8; ⊗ 9am-5pm, dinner Thu-Sat) With a delightful garden setting, a funky, beach hut–chic interior, great homemade food and fair-trade drinks, it's little wonder that Ann's Pantry was voted Bistro of the Year at the Anglesey Tourism Awards 2010.

Lobster Pot (☎ 01407 730241; www.lobster-pot.net; Church Bay; mains £13-27; ⊗ noon-1.30pm & 6-8.30pm) Local institution for fresh seafood in a delightful location; call ahead for bookings.

Ship Inn (☎ 01248 852568; Red Wharf Bay; mains £10-17; ⊗ lunch & dinner) Hearty pub grub and local ales served with appetite-whetting bay views.

White Eagle (☎ 01407 860267; Rhoscolyn; mains £8-20; ⊗ lunch & dinner Mon-Fri, all day Sat & Sun & holidays) Busy gastropub with a huge suntrap decking area and gardens for kids to explore.

Wavecrest Café (☎ 01407 730650; Church Bay; snacks £5-8; ⊗ 10.30am-5pm Thu-Mon) Cosy, relaxed cafe with great snack lunches (try the homemade fish pie) and creamy afternoon teas.

Apr-Jun & Sep-Oct, 9.30am-4pm Mon-Sat, 11am-4pm Sun Nov-Mar) is a bit of stunner. So what if it's an unfinished masterpiece of military architecture? The money ran out before completion but the four successive lines of fortifications and concentric 'walls within walls' make it the most technically perfect castle in Great Britain.

The overall effect may seem more fairy tale than horror story, but the massive gates with their murder holes (used to pour boiling oil on invaders), hint at its dark past. There is a great walk along the top of part of the inner wall, from where you get a super view of the castle layout and the breathtaking scenery that surrounds it. Look out for the old latrines for a sense of the living castle community and the arrow slits in the wall for picking off unwelcome visitors.

🐧 PUFFIN ISLAND CRUISES // HOP ABOARD FOR A NATURE LOVER'S DREAM

Off Anglesey's east coast, Puffin Island is a hotbed of bird and marine life. It has been designated a Special Protection Area (SPA). The cliffs are alive with puffins, cormorants and kittiwakes, while a colony of playful Atlantic seals, porpoise and dolphins also call the tiny, 28-hectare island home.

The best way to get up close to the wildlife is to take a one-hour cruise with Beaumaris-based cruise operator **Puffin Island Cruises** (☎ 810746; www.beaumaris marine.com; adult/child £7/5; ⊗ Apr-Oct). The (weather-dependent) trips aboard the vessel *Cerismar Two* take in spectacular views across the Menai Strait to the Snowdonia range and promise encounters with 12 species of sea birds in their

ANGLESEY & NORTH WALES

natural habitat. Buy your tickets from the kiosk on Beaumaris Pier.

✤ BEAUMARIS COURTHOUSE & GAOL // A MACABRE TAKE ON OLD ANGLESEY

Atmospheric and eerie, a visit to the town's **Courthouse & Gaol** (☎ 810921; combined ticket adult/child £6/4.50; ◷ 10.30am-5pm Apr-Sep) speaks of the bad old days before shiny, happy Beaumaris turned into a Georgian gem. The courthouse, nearly 400 years old, retraces the prisoner's grim journey to the dock, while the Victorian gaol contains the last-surviving treadwheel in Britain (a punishment for hard-labour prisoners). It's a forbidding witness to the harshness of Victorian law and order.

GASTRONOMIC HIGHLIGHTS

✤ COURTS ££

☎ 810565; www.courtyardcuisine.com; Regent House, Church St; mains £9-21; ◷ 11.30am-3pm & 6-9pm Wed-Mon

Chi-chi Courts retains an air of quiet sophistication with quality brasserie fare in stylish, contemporary surroundings. The menu plays to local strengths and European influences with lots of fresh fish, locally reared meat, pasta and vegetarian options. Lunch offers lighter options and children are well catered for.

✤ LOFT AT THE YE OLDE BULLS HEAD INN £££

☎ 810329; www.bullsheadinn.co.uk; Castle St; 3 courses £39.50; ◷ lunch & dinner Tue-Sat

Dinner at the Loft is the full fine-dining experience compared to the hotel's more pedestrian Brasserie restaurant. Peruse the menu over aperitifs in the lounge before climbing the stairs for elegant decor, a refined ambience and lovingly crafted food, focussing on seasonal Anglesey produce. The roast loin of Ogwen Val-ley lamb is succulent and flavoursome, as is the extensive wine list. Impeccable service and an atmosphere of gentle calm complete the winning formula.

✤ RED BOAT ICE CREAM PARLOUR £

☎ 810022; www.redboatgelato.com; 34 Castle St; ◷ 10am-6pm

The latest opening on Beaumaris' burgeoning foodie scene, Red Boat is a stylish gelato parlour, using authentic Italian recipes to prepare the tastiest frozen ice cream this side of Florence. Try the exotic strawberry, mascarpone and balsamic vinegar, or the local-flavour *bara brith*, for an unusual seaside scoop. Stay in to settle back on diner-style seats and soak up an espresso boost.

✤ SARAH'S DELICATESSEN & COFFEE HOUSE £

☎ 811534; 11 Church St; ◷ 9am-5pm Mon-Sat

You want to sample something deliciously local? Well, you're in the right place. This excellent little deli champions the best of Anglesey and Welsh produce; its shelves are positively groaning under the weight of ales, cheese, meat and more. The spin-off cosy coffee shop next door has great coffee and yummy deserts served up from a curb-side spot ideal for people-watching.

TRANSPORT

BUS // Buses stop on Church St. **Arriva** (www .arrivabus.co.uk) runs bus services 53, 57 and 58 to Bangor (30 minutes, half-hourly Monday to Saturday) for onwards connections.

PARKING // Parking is at a premium in Beaumaris. Head for free spaces by the library for a secure spot.

HOLYHEAD (CAERGYBI)

☎ 01407 / pop 13,000

In the heyday of the mail coaches, Holyhead was the vital terminus of the London road, which was created by the Tudor Acts of Union in 1801 and completed in 1826 by Thomas Telford. It has been a hub for onward travel to Ireland by boat since its historic golden age, but the rise of cheap flights reduced the demand for ferries and the town fell on hard times. Today, the first shoots of regeneration are now brightening the grey-moribund town centre. The Celtic Gateway bridge, linking the train station to the main thoroughfare, Market St, invites visitors to 'Pass this way with a pure heart', while major plans to overhaul the harbour were at planning stage at the time of writing.

Holyhead is on Holy Island (Ynys Gybi), a 7-mile stretch of land divided from the west coast of Anglesey by a narrow channel. It's 'Holy' because this was the domain of St Cybi, a well-travelled monk thought to have lived in the 6th century.

ESSENTIAL INFORMATION

TOURIST OFFICES // Tourist office
(☎ 762622; ◷ 9.30am-5.30pm daily Apr-Sep, Mon-Wed & Fri & Sat Oct-Mar) Located in Ferry Terminal 1.

EXPLORING HOLYHEAD

♥ HOLYHEAD MARITIME MUSEUM // SOAK UP THE MARITIME HERITAGE OF THE PORT
Small but lovingly restored, this little **museum** (☎ 769745; www.holyheadmaritime museum.co.uk; Newry Beach; adult/child £3.50/2; ◷ 10am-4pm Apr-Oct) is housed in what is believed to be the oldest lifeboat house in Wales (c 1858). It's a family-friendly visit with model ships, photographs and exhibits on Holyhead's maritime history from Roman times onwards. Don't be put off by the small-scale exterior – it's an atmospheric place to get a feel for Holyhead's seafaring heyday.

THE DRUIDS

Mysterious and magical, the druidic mystique is assisted by a lack of evidence – they wrote nothing down about their beliefs. It is known that they had charge of Celtic religion and ritual, and were educators and healers as well as political advisors, and so were vastly influential. However, the main sources of information about this spiritual aristocracy are Roman scholars, whose accounts are seen through an adversarial glass. The Romans are coloured as a civilising force, and the Celts and druids as bloodthirsty and keen on human sacrifice.

Resistance to the Romans was powered by druidic influence in Britain. Anglesey was a major seat of druidic learning because of its strategic placement between Wales, Ireland and France, and was the last place to fall to the Romans. According to the Roman historian Tacitus, when the Romans attacked Anglesey in AD 61, they were terrified by the resident wild women and holy fanatics who greeted them with howls and prayers, and found the altars there covered in the blood of prisoners. The conquerors did all they could to impress their culture on the locals, but the result was inevitably a mix of new and old beliefs.

Druidism became a fashionable interest in the 18th century, and the Welsh poetic tradition is believed to stem from the druids. In 1820 Edward Williams created druidic ceremonies to be performed during the annual Eisteddfod, which accounts for many of the long beards and solemn ceremonies still in evidence at this festival of poetry and literature today.

ANGLESEY & NORTH WALES

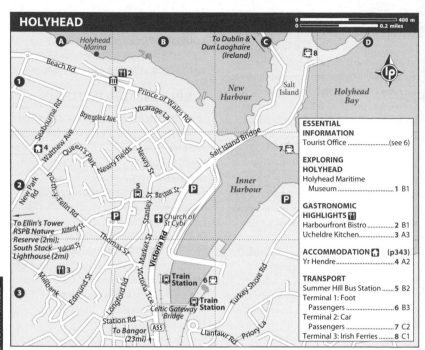

HOLYHEAD

ESSENTIAL INFORMATION	
Tourist Office	(see 6)

EXPLORING HOLYHEAD		
Holyhead Maritime Museum	1	B1

GASTRONOMIC HIGHLIGHTS		
Harbourfront Bistro	2	B1
Ucheldre Kitchen	3	A3

ACCOMMODATION	(p343)	
Yr Hendre	4	A2

TRANSPORT		
Summer Hill Bus Station	5	B2
Terminal 1: Foot Passengers	6	B3
Terminal 2: Car Passengers	7	C2
Terminal 3: Irish Ferries	8	C1

❦ **SOUTH STACK LIGHTHOUSE //**
GET UP CLOSE WITH NATURE AT ITS
MOST RAW

The walk between **South Stack Lighthouse** (☎ 763207; www.trinityhouse.co.uk; tours adult/child £4.25/2.25; ☷ 10.30am-5pm Apr-Sep) and **Ellin's Tower RSPB Nature Reserve** (☎ 764973; www.rspb.org.uk/wales; Plas Nico; admission free; ☷ 11am-5pm Apr-Sep) has a very exposed but gloriously end-of-the-earth feel. There are waves crashing dramatically around the base of the cliffs and birds nesting overhead. The trail down to the lighthouse from the main road is not for the faint hearted with 400 slippery steps and a rickety, old bridge.

South Stack is still a working lighthouse, closely linked with nearby RAF Valley Mountain Rescue. A visit here includes a lighthouse tour; you can buy tickets at the office by the car park. The nature reserve has a live TV feed to seabird colonies of choughs, fulmars, kittiwakes, guillemots, razorbills, gulls and, from about mid-April to July, puffins. Staff of the Royal Society for the Protection of Birds (RSPB) are on site to discuss the wildlife and you can hire binoculars for £2.

To get here follow the South Stack road 2 miles west of Holyhead along rural, gorse-strewn lanes. There's free parking opposite Hut Circle, an iron-age site.

GASTRONOMIC HIGHLIGHTS

❦ **HARBOURFRONT BISTRO ££**

☎ 763433; Newry Beach; mains £9-15; ☷ lunch noon-2.15pm daily, dinner 6-9pm Thu-Sat

For good food and marina views, this cosy little bistro adjoining the Holyhead Maritime Museum is hard to beat. The chef serves up a menu of tasty home-made food and daily specials, plus coffee and pastries outside meal times. The seaview decking area is a relaxed spot to watch the ships approaching the harbour on summer evenings.

♥ UCHELDRE KITCHEN £

☎ 763361; www.ucheldre.org; Millbank; ☺ 10am-4.30pm Mon-Sat, 2-4.30pm Sun

Attached to Holyhead's excellent arts hub, the Ucheldre Arts Centre is a re-laxed, friendly cafe for lunches and cof-fee. It offers lunch specials (around £4.50) daily, except Sunday, and homemade, hearty snacks. Time your lunch well and you could catch one of the com-munity arts events or folk-music jams in the studio next door, then browse the impressive Welsh literature collection in the shop.

TRANSPORT

BUS // The bus station is on Summer Hill. **Arriva** (www.arrivabus.co.uk) bus 4/X4 runs to Bangor (1½ hours, half-hourly Monday to Saturday); bus 44 (five daily) runs on Sunday.

FERRY // Holyhead's Terminal 1 is connected to the train station for foot passengers, Terminal 2 is the hub for car passengers, Terminal 3 is reserved for Irish Ferries. A free shuttle-bus service runs between terminals for foot passen-gers. There are two ferry services to Dublin (p359). **Irish Ferries** (☎ 08717 300400; www.irishferries.com) has two daily slow ferries (3¼ hours) and two fast services (one hour 50 minutes). **Stena Line** (☎ 08705 421126; www.stenaline.co.uk) has four daily services to Dublin for car passengers (3¼ hours) and two daily services to Dun Laoghaire for foot passengers (one hour 10 minutes).

TRAIN // Holyhead's train station has direct services to London Euston with **Virgin Trains** (www.virgintrains.co.uk) on the West Coast Main Line, and to Chester (via Bangor) with **Arriva Trains** (www.arrivatrainswales.co.uk).

ANGLESEY & NORTH WALES

THE ISLE OF ANGLESEY COASTAL PATH

Anglesey is a big drawcard for walkers thanks to the **Isle of Anglesey Coastal Path** (www.angleseycoastalpath.co.uk), a 125-mile coastal walking path with clear, yellow waymarking and spectacular views. The full trail, a 12-day walk appealing to all ability ranges and reaching a maximum altitude of just 219m, passes through a changing landscape of coastal heath, salt marsh, beaches and even a National Nature Reserve.

The official trailhead is at St Cybi's Church in Holyhead but the 12 stages can easily be tackled as individual day hikes, ranging from seven to 13 miles per day. Some of the stages, particularly the far northern legs from Cemaes Bay to Church Bay, make for bracing strolls against a dramatic backdrop of wild, wind-swept scenery.

A great, introductory day walk from Beaumaris takes in the ancient monastic site of Penmon Priory; Penmon Point with views across to Puffin Island; and Llanddona, a Blue Flag beach for a refreshing dip.

Alternatively, Moelfre is one of the prettiest harbour villages on the east coast. It's home to Ann's Pantry (p255) and the **Seawatch Centre** (☎ 01248 410277; admission free; ☺ 11am-5pm Tue-Sat, 1-5pm Sun Apr-Sep), where a statue of local coxswain, Richard Evans, who won the first Royal National Lifeboat Institute (RNLI) gold medal in 1959, overlooks the sea.

Walkers should equip themselves with a copy of the OS Explorer Maps 262 (west coast) and 263 (east coast) before setting out.

Anglesey Walking Holidays (☎ 01248 713611; www.angleseywalkingholidays.com; per person from £395) offers self-guided walking packages, including accommodation, luggage transfers and transport between trailheads.

MORE ANGLESEY HIGHLIGHTS

❦ LLANFAIRPWLLGWYNGY-
LLGOGERYCHWYRNDROBWLL-
LLANTYSILIOGOGOGOCH
(LLANFAIR PG) // VERY BIG NAME,
VERY SMALL PLACE
The small town with the absurdly famous multi-syllable moniker is an unlikely hot spot for visitors. The consonant-mangling name, which means St Mary's Church in the Hollow of the White Hazel near a Rapid Whirlpool and the Church of St Tysilio near the Red Cave, was dreamt up in the 19th century to get the tourists in. And it worked. Today the coach parties are all jostling for a photo opportunity on the train station platform by the sign.

But they're all missing the point. Far more interesting is the **Oriel Tŷ Gor-saf** (☎ 01248 717876; Station Rd; ❧ 9am-5pm Mon-Sat), a gallery showcasing Welsh and international glass artists in the converted station building next door. And the **Marquess of Anglesey's Column** (☎ 01248 714393; adult/child £1.50/75p; ❧ 9am-5pm) just down the road, which commemorates Wellington's right-hand man at the 1815 Battle of Waterloo, Henry William Paget. Climb the 115 steps up to the base to enjoy great views across the island.

Also check out the Llanfair PG **tourist office** (☎ 01248 713177; ❧ 9.30am-5.30pm Mon-Sat, 10am-4pm Sun) across the car park from the train station, to stock up on information, maps and souvenirs.

❦ MENAI HERITAGE EXPERIENCE
// MARVEL AT THE WONDER OF
ENGINEERING HERITAGE
Anglesey is synonymous with the twin iconic bridges that connect the island to the Welsh mainland. This small, volunteer-run **museum** (☎ 01248 715046; www.menaibridges.co.uk; Menai Bridge; adult/child £3/ free; ❧ 10am-4pm Sun-Thu Apr-Oct) is a good way to learn more about the feat of Victorian engineering and explore the ecology of the Menai Straits. And don't groan. It's not a stuffy affair. The friendly volunteers regularly arrange talks, tours and family activities to show off some of their deserved local pride.

❦ ORIEL YNYS MÔN // VISIT THE
FATHER OF ANGLESEY'S ART SCENE
This lively **arts centre** (☎ 01248 724444; kyffinwilliams.info; Llangefni; ❧ 10.30am-5pm), home to a mix of galleries, is the lynch-pin of Anglesey's visual-arts scene. The art space hosts a program of exhibitions, the History Gallery explores Anglesey's past and its pivotal role in the Roman invasion and there's a great little coffee shop, **Blas Mwy** (mains £5-10), plus a children's discovery area for rainy days and bored kids. But the main draw is the Oriel Kyffin Williams, featuring 400-odd works by Wales' most celebrated artist. His grey-slate portraits really bring out the sense of living Welsh culture. In the great man's own words: 'I believe that some of my best work has been of the many interesting faces I have painted'.

❦ PLAS NEWYDD // EXPLORE A
CLASSIC STATELY HOME
If you only visit one National Trust (NT) property in North Wales, make it **Plas Newydd** (☎ 01248 715272; www.nationaltrust. org.uk; Llanfair PG; adult/child £7.80/3.90; ❧ house & garden noon-5pm Sat-Wed). The 18th-century Gothic masterpiece was home to the first Marquess of Anglesey, who commanded the cavalry during the 1815 Battle of Waterloo. The house contains the largest permanent collection of Rex Whistler works, including an enormous, fantastical dreamscape of Mt Snowdon.

But don't confuse this stately property with the Llangollen's Plas Newydd (p273). They're not the same place.

THE NORTH COAST & NORTHEAST WALES

· · · · · ·

Wales' windswept north coast and rural northeast are packed with great places to visit, from castles and walled towns to luxury seaside escapes and sacred holy sites.

Bangor is a handsome university town along the coast with a youthful spark (at least during term time). Beyond is Conwy, an extraordinary walled city that has one of Wales' World Heritage–listed castles. Llandudno is a stately Victorian resort busily maintaining its popularity into the 21st century. Further east, Llangollen is a hotbed of North Wales culture and Ruthin is emerging as a hot spot for the best of local food and shopping. Overall, it's definitely worth exploring the lesser-travelled inland roads for a true taste of the north and an escape from the high-season crowds.

BANGOR

☎ 01248 / pop 12,000

Bangor, one of the campus centres of the University of Wales, feels more university city than visitor hot spot with its large student body swelling the population in term time and dominating the landscape of Upper Bangor. St Deiniol established the first settlement with a monastery here in AD 525, but Bangor's glory days have long since faded. The town has been hit hard by economic problems in recent years and the new, but rather bland, Deiniol Shopping Centre now makes for a somewhat soulless heart of the town. The handsome clock tower, also on High St, is now overshadowed by a huge Debenhams store. Bangor does, however, remain a major transport hub with a raft of onward connections to Anglesey and Snowdonia.

The lack of a cultural life has been a major bugbear for Bangor in recent years but plans for a new £35m arts centre at the university are fuelling hopes for something of a renaissance. The university's new Arts and Innovation Centre will stage theatre productions, films, music, circus, dance and other performing arts shows upon completion in 2012. The plans include a 500-seat theatre, studio space and an outdoor amphitheatre.

ESSENTIAL INFORMATION

EMERGENCIES // Gwynedd Hospital (☎ 384384; ⊙ 24hr) Two miles southwest of the city centre. **North Wales Police** (☎ 0845 6071001)
TOURIST OFFICES // Tourist office (☎ 352786; Deiniol Rd; ⊙ 9.30am-1pm & 2-4.30pm Mon-Fri Apr-Oct) It's a bit hit and miss but the staff can advise on handling the dearth of local accommodation.

EXPLORING BANGOR

❦ BANGOR CATHEDRAL // A SAINTLY OASIS OF CALM
Also known as the Cathedral Church of St Deiniol, this ancient cathedral occupies one of the oldest ecclesiastical sites in Britain. More recently, Aled Jones (choirboy turned TV and radio presenter) trained his adolescent vocal chords here.

Bangor Cathedral (☎ 33983; www.churchinwales.org.uk; admission free) is dedicated to St Deiniol, who founded a community here in AD 525 and who was consecrated as bishop in AD 546. The cathedral's earliest remains are a 12th-century stone

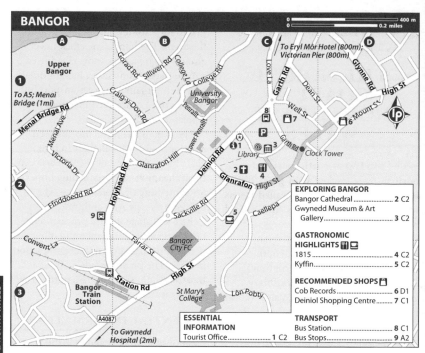

BANGOR

EXPLORING BANGOR
Bangor Cathedral 2 C2
Gwynedd Museum & Art
Gallery 3 C2

GASTRONOMIC
HIGHLIGHTS
1815 .... 4 C2
Kyffin 5 C2

RECOMMENDED SHOPS
Cob Records 6 D1
Deiniol Shopping Centre 7 C1

ESSENTIAL
INFORMATION
Tourist Office 1 C2

TRANSPORT
Bus Station 8 C1
Bus Stops 9 A2

building with responsibility for damage blamed on King John, whose men burned the city and cathedral in 1211. Further ravages took place at the turn of the 15th century, during the Glyndŵr rebellion (p284), and two centuries later Cromwell's men used the cathedral as stables.

Much of the architecture seen today is thanks to the sensitive reconstruction by the eminent Victorian architect Sir George Gilbert Scott between 1870 and 1880. The highlight of a visit is a late-15th-century, almost life-sized, oak carving of Christ, seated and shackled in the moments before his crucifixion.

It has a small shop and an exhibition about the history of the cathedral. A stroll in the adjoining bible gardens makes for a delightfully tranquil counterpoint to the city's bawdy pub scene.

👻 GWYNEDD MUSEUM & ART GALLERY // EXPLORE NORTH WALES CULTURE AND LIFE

This small **museum** (☎ 353368; Ffordd Gwynedd; admission free; 🕙 12.30-4.30pm Tue-Fri, 10.30am-4.30pm Sat) is split between the downstairs gallery with modern works of art and the upstairs rooms given over to a more traditional museum format. While a bit hard going at times, the most interesting section of the latter traces the evolution of the Welsh identity and the movement to preserve the Welsh culture from the 18th century to the present day.

👻 VICTORIAN PIER // A PERFECT NORTH WALES VIEW

Built in 1896, the **Victorian pier** (adult/child 25p/10p; 🕙 8am-6pm Mon-Sat, 10am-5pm Sun), with its fanciful oriental kiosks, is a lovely place for a stroll, stretching 450m out into the Menai Strait – it feels like it's

ANGLESEY & NORTH WALES ACCOMMODATION

North Wales is home to some superb, hidden-gem boltholes that offer special places to stay. Read more in the dedicated accommodation chapter (p321). These places are popular year-round, so book ahead and try to make a weekend of it. While a good base from which to explore, they are often best savoured as an escape in their own right. So don't worry if the weather is a let down, there's plenty to keep you cosily occupied inside without even venturing out the front door. We've listed some of our favourites.

★ **Whinward House** (p344) Traditional, welcoming B&B in Conwy.

★ **Osborne House** (p344) Cool design and hedonism are the order of the day in Llandudno.

★ **Quay Hotel & Spa** (p345) Dine in style in Deganwy, with a World Heritage–listed view.

★ **Cornerstones B&B** (p345) Get-away-from-it-all bolthole in the centre of lively Llangollen.

★ **manorhaus** (p345) Ruthin's art-led hotel boasts a private cinema for a post-prandial screening.

almost touching the beaches of Anglesey. In the distance, catch the sun glinting off Thomas Telford's handsome Menai Suspension Bridge.

GASTRONOMIC HIGHLIGHTS

🍽 **1815** £

☎ 355969; 2 Waterloo Pl; breakfast £6, mains around £7; ⏰ 8.30am-6pm Mon-Thu & Sun, to 10pm Fri & Sat

Fresh local produce, lovingly presented, and a strong Mediterranean influence over the menu are the key themes of this lively, friendly cafe-bar, bringing a touch of Euro-cool cafe culture to North Wales. By day it's a buzzy place for coffee and snack lunches. By night it takes on more of a wine-bar vibe with chilled vino and tasty tapas plates (choose three tasty tapas for £8).

🍽 **KYFFIN** ££

☎ 355161; 129 High St; lunch mains around £5, evening menu £13; ⏰ 9am-9pm Mon-Sat

A hidden-gem, fair-trade, vegetarian and vegan cafe with jazz music, a cosy lounge and antique-shop fittings, plus a deli counter for organic goodies, Kyffin is a true gem at the less salubrious end of main street. The owners now offer evening meals at weekends and have introduced world cinema nights with a set menu prepared to match the film. All this and by far the best coffee in Bangor – brilliant!

RECOMMENDED SHOPS

🛍 **COB RECORDS // A TREASURE TROVE FOR WELSH MUSIC FANS**

☎ 353020; www.cobrecordsbangor.com; 320 High St; ⏰ 9.30am-5.30pm Mon-Sat

If you know your Cate le Bon from your Cerys Matthews, then you'll be in your element browsing the racks at Cob Records. An old-school independent record shop, this place has everything for vinyl junkies and serious collectors. In addition to its other treasures, it also has a section dedicated to Welsh music so you can lose yourself in the latest Cool Cymru releases.

TRANSPORT

BUS // The bus station is behind the Deiniol Shopping Centre with some buses also stopping just outside the station. **Arriva** (www.arrivabus.co.uk) bus 4/X4/44 runs to Holyhead (one hour 10 minutes, half-hourly Monday to Saturday, two-hourly Sunday); bus 5/X5 runs to Caernarfon (30 minutes, every 15 minutes Monday to Saturday, hourly Sunday); bus 53/57/58 runs to Beaumaris (30 minutes, every 35 minutes Monday to Saturday, two-hourly Sunday) and bus X32 TrawsCambria runs to Aberystwyth (three hours, six daily Monday to Saturday, two on Sunday).

PARKING // Try the short-stay car park by the tourist office (£1.50 per two hours).

TRAIN // Bangor's train station has direct services to London Euston with **Virgin Trains** (www.virgin trains.co.uk) on the West Coast Main Line, and to Holyhead with **Arriva Trains** (www.arrivatrainswales.co.uk).

CONWY

☎ 01492 / pop 4000

Conwy Castle, the Unesco-designated cultural treasure, dominates the town of Conwy both physically and spiritually. Conwy is the most complete walled town in Britain and the castle is an essential visit for fans of Welsh heritage – as is the stroll around the castle walls. It's a highly evocative insight into the era of Edward I, when the monarch planted an iron ring of fortifications around the coast to keep the Welsh in check. Even today, the castle dominates the approach to town with a sense of pomp and ceremony, while with three bridges spanning the river (Thomas Telford's now-pedestrianised 1826 suspension bridge, Robert Stephenson's 1848 steel railway bridge and the newer road-crossing bridge) add a sense of a theatrical flourish.

More recently, a project to regenerate the rundown Conwy Quay has finally been completed, sprucing up the waterfront no end. However, there's still more work to do to refresh the town centre, and there are better eating and sleeping options in nearby Llandudno, which makes it a better base to stay than Conwy.

ESSENTIAL INFORMATION

TOURIST OFFICES // Tourist office
(☎ 592248; Castle Sq; ☼ 9.30am-6pm daily Jul-Aug, 9.30am-5pm daily Jun, Sep-Oct, 9.30am-4pm Mon-Sat, 11am-4pm Sun Nov-Mar) A rather small and often-swamped tourist office next to the Cadw desk in the castle visitors centre.

EXPLORING CONWY

♥ CONWY CASTLE // VISIT ONE OF THE GREAT CASTLES OF WALES
Some say Conwy is *the* most drop-your-crossbow stunning of all Edward I's Welsh fortresses, built between 1277 and 1307. It was certainly the most costly to build at around £15,000 and today it remains one of the finest surviving medieval fortifications in Britain. No wonder Unesco snapped it up for the World Heritage list in 1986.

Rising from a rocky outcrop with commanding views across the estuary and Snowdonia National Park, **Conwy Castle** (Cadw; ☎ 592358; www.cadw.wales.gov.uk; adult/child £4.60/4.10; ☼ 9am-5pm Apr-Oct, 9.30am-4pm Mon-Sat, 11am-4pm Sun Nov-Mar) may well look like a fairy-tale construction. But don't be fooled. With two barbicans (fortified gateways), eight fierce, slightly tapered towers of coarse dark stone and a great bow-shaped hall all within the elongated complex, it's very, very solid indeed. After the Civil War in the 17th century, the castle fell into some disrepair and the Council of State ordered it to be partially pulled down. But today it lives on, a slightly more tumbledown sister to its Unesco partner at Caernarfon (p232), and a must-visit for anyone with an interest in Welsh history.

Exploring the castle's nooks and crannies makes for a superb, living-history visit, but best of all, head to the battlements for panoramic views and an overview of Conwy's majestic complexity.

Pick up a new **joint ticket** (adult/child £6.85/5.85) for Conwy Castle and Plas Mawr (below) from the Cadw desk within the castle visitor centre.

☙ **HISTORIC PROPERTIES // A TOUR OF CONWY'S HISTORIC BUILDINGS**
For a small town, Conwy really packs in the historical interest. All within a short stroll of each other, Conwy's three key properties encapsulate the town's rich heritage and its continuing role in the Welsh art scene. Explore all three to get a feel for the town's importance to North Wales. **Plas Mawr** (☎ 580167; High St; adult/child £4.90/4.50; ⏲ 9.30am-5pm Tue-Sun Apr-Sep, to 4pm Oct) is the UK's finest surviving Elizabethan town house. It was completed in 1585 for the Welsh merchant and courtier Robert Wynn, and the lavish decoration is testament to his social standing. Rugged, whitewashed outer walls give way to a lavish interior:

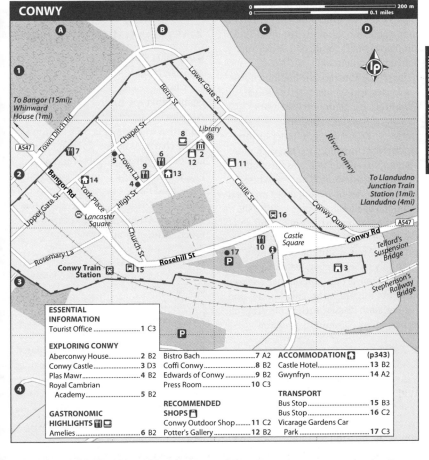

CONWY

ANGLESEY & NORTH WALES

the painted plasterwork is extraordinarily vivid, while the decorated ceilings and friezes dance with colour and life. A free audio tour of the house describes the restoration and the life of the Tudor gentry.

The nearby timber-and-plaster **Aberconwy House** (NT; ☎ 592246; www.nationaltrust.org.uk; Castle St; adult/child £3/1.50; ☉ 11am-5pm Wed-Mon mid-Feb & Mar-Oct, 11am-5pm daily Jul-Aug) is the town's oldest medieval merchant's house, dating from around 1300. Over the years it has been a coffee house, a temperance hotel, a bakery and antique shop, but it remains surprisingly well preserved. An audiovisual presentation shows daily life from different periods of history. Check out the National Trust shop downstairs for a good choice of souvenirs and gifts.

By way of contrast, the building housing Wales' top art institute, the **Royal Cambrian Academy** (☎ 593413; www.rcaconwy.org; Crown Lane; admission free; ☉ 11am-5pm Tue-Sat, 1-4.30pm Sun) is another historic landmark. The gallery focuses on a more contemporary side to Wales through its burgeoning art scene. The twin white-walled galleries host a full program of exhibitions by members, plus visiting shows from the National Museum Cardiff and elsewhere. The academy also hosts the excellent Annual Summer Exhibition from July to September, featuring the cream of fine art in Wales under one roof. Look out too for the art club for kids and regular adult classes, such as life drawing, as part of the community program.

❦ A WALK ALONG THE RIVER CONWY // FRESH AIR AND SEA VIEWS ON A CIRCULAR ROUTE

With all that history, it's easy to forget that Conwy benefits from a superb natural location. One of the best ways to appreciate the simple country pleasures of Conwy life is by taking a stroll along the quayside and the beach towards the marina, hugging the headland with views across the River Conwy en route. Handily, the owners of Whinward House (p344) produce a very useful walking map of Conwy to illustrate some of the best walking trails. It's a short and leisurely stroll with fine views of boats bobbing gently in the water, birdlife fluttering around and wildflowers peeking through the grassy banks. Perfect for a sunset stretch of the legs before heading back to the B&B for a sundowner in the garden. Better still, the hordes are still queuing to get into the castle. Ahh, bliss.

GASTRONOMIC HIGHLIGHTS

❦ AMELIES ££
☎ 583142; 10 High St; mains £10-17; ☉ 11am-2pm & 6-9pm Tue-Sat
Named after the Audrey Tautou film, Amelies is a smart, French-style bistro with a soupcon of la belle Tautou's Gallic charm. It boasts wooden floors and flower-decorated tables and offers hearty lunches and dinners. The menu has a good range of options from fish to steak, while vegetarian choices and the inclusion of homemade cakes are a nice touch. Audrey would love it.

❦ BISTRO BACH £££
☎ 596326; Chapel St; mains £15-21; ☉ 6.30am-9pm Mon-Sat
For modern Welsh food in an intimate bistro setting, the recently renamed Bistro Bach remains the smartest option for dinner in town. Think well-prepared local beef, lamb and other traditional recipes served with a healthy modernist twist. The red-brick cottage in a secluded courtyard makes for an attractive setting, while service remains quietly assured despite the change of name.

☙ COFFI CONWY £
☎ 596436; 2 High St; snacks £2-6; ⏱ 10.30am-4.30pm Mon-Sat; 🛜

A cosy little cafe for simple snacks and fresh-brewed, fair-trade coffee, Coffi Conwy is a decent pit stop on the walking circuit around the walls. Browse the newspapers over a sandwich lunch, log on for free wi-fi or simply pull up a window seat for a spot of people-watching. Very homely.

☙ EDWARDS OF CONWY £
☎ 592443; www.edwardsofconwy.co.uk; 18 High St; ⏱ 9am-5pm Mon-Sat

To stock up on some of the best local produce, try Edwards, an award-winning butcher-cum-deli. It offers superb meat, savoury pies and local cheeses – all top-notch quality and served with a smile.

☙ PRESS ROOM £
☎ 592242; 3 Rosehill St; mains £4.50-8.50; ⏱ 10.30am-4.30pm

Located right next to the castle entrance, this arty-style cafe has funky artworks on the walls, a menu of tasty fare and a shady terrace for an al-fresco lunch. The owners run a **craft shop** (⏱ 10.30am-4.30pm Mon-Fri, 10.30am-5pm Sat & Sun) next door for souvenirs with a design and craft-led motif.

RECOMMENDED SHOPS

☙ CONWY OUTDOOR SHOP
☎ 593390; 9 Castle St; ⏱ 9am-5.30pm Mon-Sat

A useful, friendly store with a good range of practical kit for indulging in some outdoors adventures and plenty of practical advice for making the best of the local activities.

☙ THE POTTER'S GALLERY
☎ 593590; www.northwalespotters.co.uk; 1 High St; ⏱ 10am-5pm Thu-Tue

Run by a cooperative of North Wales–based potters and designers, this gallery acts as information centre about the art scene across the region. It also showcases the latest ceramic works from the members. Ask in the shop about how to find a local pottery class to brush up your own pot-throwing skills.

TRANSPORT

BUS // Most buses stop by the train station. **Arriva** (www.arrivabus.co.uk) runs bus 5 to Caernarfon (40 minutes, half-hourly Monday to Saturday, hourly Sunday) and bus 19 to Llandudno (30 minutes, half-hourly Monday to Saturday, hourly Sunday) via Llandudno Junction (five minutes) for train connections. But Arriva bus 19 stops on Castle St for Llanrwst (1¾ hours, hourly Monday to Saturday).

PARKING // For the easiest parking, head for the spaces by the castle in the vicarage gardens short-stay car park (£2 per three hours).

TRAIN // Conwy's train station is a request stop on the North Coast Line of **Arriva Trains** (www.arriva trainswales.co.uk) . Nearby Llandudno Junction station has direct services to London Euston with **Virgin Trains** (www.virgintrains.co.uk) on the West Coast Main Line – take bus 19 to the station.

LLANDUDNO

☎ 01492 / **pop 15,000**

Llandudno is a master of reinvention. Developed as an upmarket Victorian holiday town, it still retains much of its 19th-century grandeur today, yet continues to find new fans with its booming boutique accommodation, upmarket dining, big-name retail outlets and Welsh art and performance. No wonder the American travel writer Bill Bryson was moved to describe Llandudno as his 'favourite seaside resort'. Praise indeed.

The town straddles its own peninsula, with Llandudno Bay and North Shore Beach to the northeast and Conwy Bay and West Shore Beach to the southwest. The twin humps of the ancient mountains, the Great Orme and Little Orme, loom over the graceful Victorian wedding-cake architecture of the seafront buildings that line the sweeping prom for a full mile. Parc Llandudno, a major retail park, marks the eastern fringe of town, while the nearby Venue Cymru attracts big-name stars to the seaside town. A project to regenerate the rather forlorn-looking train station is yet to get the green light.

ESSENTIAL INFORMATION

EMERGENCIES // Llandudno Hospital
(☎ 860066; ⊗ 24hr) One mile south of the town centre.

TOURIST OFFICES // Tourist office
(☎ 577577; www.visitllandudno.org.uk; Mostyn St; ⊗ 9am-5.30pm Mon-Sat & 9.30am-4.30pm Sun Apr-Oct, 9am-5pm Mon-Sat Nov-Mar) The new tourist office shares a building with the library and is backed by the Victoria Shopping Centre.

EXPLORING LLANDUDNO

♥ **GREAT ORME COUNTRY PARK & NATURE RESERVE // EXPLORE THE NATURAL BEAUTY OF THE MAJESTIC MOUNTAIN**
The sheer scale of the Great Orme, designated a Site of Special Scientific Interest

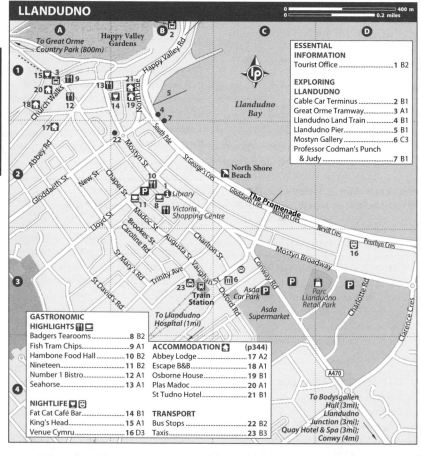

LLANDUDNO

0 — 400 m
0 — 0.2 miles

Llandudno Bay

Happy Valley Gardens

To Great Orme Country Park (800m)

North Shore Beach

The Promenade

Library
Victoria Shopping Centre

Train Station

Asda Car Park

Asda Supermarket

Parc Llandudno Retail Park

To Llandudno Hospital (1mi)

To Bodysgallen Hall (3mi); Llandudno Junction (3mi); Quay Hotel & Spa (3mi); Conwy (4mi)

A470

ANGLESEY & NORTH WALES

(SSSI), is impressive. From the promenade, it appears a gentle giant looming benevolently over the sunshine-lit town. But take some time to explore further and you'll find the Orme (Y Gogarth; named after a Norse word for worm or sea serpent) was instrumental to Llandudno's rapid development.

Close up, the rough terrain is home to several Neolithic sites, a cornucopia of flowers, butterflies and sea birds, three waymarked summit trails (of which the Haulfre Gardens Trail is the easiest stroll to negotiate) and some of the most, jaw-dropping, imagination-firing views in North Wales across the Snowdonia National Park (p210) and over to the Isle of Man. There's even a herd of around 150 Kashmir mountain goats roaming free – the original pair were donated by Queen Victoria). Pick up maps and inspiration from the **Great Orme Visitor Centre** (☎ 874151; www. coney.gov.uk/countryside; ☺ 9.30am-5pm mid-Mar–Oct), which also has picnic tables, a cafe and a gift shop.

To get the summit, you have two options. The **Great Orme Tramway** (☎ 879306; www.greatormetramway.com; Church Walks; adult/child return £5.60/3.80; ☺ 10am-6pm mid-Mar–Oct) hauls you up the steep incline in a lovingly restored Victorian tram-car – much as it has been doing for over 100 years. It's one of only three cable-operated trams in the world (the other two are to be found in equally glamorous Lisbon and San Francisco). Otherwise, The **cable car** (☎ 877205; adult/child return £6.50/4.50; ☺ 10am-5pm mid-Mar–Oct), the longest in Britain, runs from the Happy Valley Gardens above the pier (subject to the somewhat changeable weather, of course) and completes the journey to the summit in just 18 minutes with superb seaviews en route.

The summit is also home to the **Great Orme Mines** (☎ 870447; www.greatormemines. info; adult/child £6/4; ☺ 10am-5pm Mar-Oct), the oldest Bronze Age copper mine in the world that's open to visitors (the *Guinness Book of Records* confirms this). Take the self-guided tour to explore 4 miles of 3500-year-old tunnels and learn how our ancient ancestors turned rock into metal at the smelting site.

🍲 SEASIDE ATTRACTIONS //
A RETURN TO CHILDHOODS BY THE SEASIDE

For a step-back-in-time, kiss-me-quick take on the genteel resort town, head for Llandudno's **Victorian pier** (☎ 876258; ☺ 9am-6pm). At 670m, it's the longest pier in Wales and extends into the sea with amusements, candyfloss and slot machines. High art it isn't but the kids will love it. The pier was first opened 1878 and its main use was as a disembarkation point for passengers from the Isle of Man steamers. Those are long gone and high-kitsch is now the order of the day.

After strolling down the pier, the **Llandudno Land Train** (☎ 878228; ☺ Apr-Oct) offers a leisurely chug across town to the west shore, which is a quieter and more windswept counterpoint to the glitz of the north shore. This beach is particularly good for a sea-air walk and a moment of peace away from the crowds during the day tripper–packed high season.

Take the train back to the north shore to catch **Professor Codman's Punch & Judy** (☺ noon, 2pm & 4pm Apr-Sep) show by the pier. In 2010 the Codman family, who established Llandudno's Punch and Judy theatre in 1860, celebrated 150 years of performances still using the original theatre and puppets. During that time, they have entertained such visiting dignitaries as Queen Victoria,

Queen Alexandra and the Duke of Westminster. Show times are weekends and school holidays (weather permitting).

❦ MOSTYN GALLERY // EXPLORE NORTH WALES' BURGEONING ART SCENE

After a three-year renovation, this **gallery** (☎ 879201; www.mostyn.org; 12 Vaughan St; admission free; ◷ 10am-5pm Mon-Sat) has finally reopened to establish itself as North Wales' premier arts space. Call in to explore the shop or grab a coffee upstairs even if you're not a fan of modern art.

❦ VICTORIAN EXTRAVAGANZA // STEP BACK IN TIME TO A MORE GENTEEL AGE

Lesser known is Llandudno's connection to the Liddell family, whose daughter was Lewis Carroll's model for the main character of *Alice's Adventures in Wonderland*. Their summer holiday house is today the St Tudno Hotel. For a more in-your-face

INTERVIEW: JACQUELINE MILLBAND CODMAN

How important is Punch and Judy to Llandudno and its history? We're part of its history and the Codman family is one of the oldest in town. My great-grandfather, Richard Codman, started a Punch and Judy show outside the Empire Hotel in 1860. He moved to the Promenade in 1864 and went on to perform for Queen Victoria.

The family recently celebrated 150 years of Mr Punch in Llandudno. How have you seen the resort change over the years? It's very much a year-round place these days, always bustling and definitely moving with the times. But it also retains its genteel Victorian ambience. A lot of European Union money was invested in updating the Promenade in 2000 and lots of smart new places opened up. It's not new, though. Llandudno always did cater for top-end clientele with private jazz clubs and cafes in its post-war heyday.

Who does Llandudno appeal to, and what would you recommend for them to see and do? It's perfect for young families. I advise people to take a picnic to Happy Valley, or head to west shore to feed the swans on the boating pool. Older people often come back after 40-odd years to relive their childhood holidays. For them, walking around the Great Orme is good for sea views, and taking the Great Orme Tramway is perfect for nostalgia.

What are your favourite hidden-gem corners of Llandudno? I don't get out as much as I used to but The Seahorse is still superb for fresh fish and Fish Tram Chips remains perennially popular for a simple but good-value supper. Personally, I rather like Fortes, a cafe on Mostyn St for coffee or a snack lunch.

What makes Llandudno so special as a place to visit and live? Unlike some resorts on the North Wales coast, Llandudno is definitely not rough and ready. We work hard to maintain the Victorian ambience of the town and to preserve its natural beauty, with the bay sandwiched between two mountains. I can honestly say that much of the Promenade and many of the hotels along the seafront haven't changed much since I was a girl growing up in Llandudno in the 1950s. We're also very lucky that we're so close to the mountains of Snowdonia. My tip for visitors is, after a couple of days exploring the resort itself, take the train down to Betws-y-Coed. From Llandudno, you're just 20 minutes from the seaside into the heart of the Snowdonia National Park.

Jacqueline Millband Codman is head of the Codman family who have staged Punch and Judy shows in Llandudno for 150 years.

celebration of Llandudno's heritage, the dress-up-fest **Victorian Extravaganza** (www.victorian-extravaganza.co.uk), held over the first of the two May bank-holiday weekends, is the social event of the year with parades, events, funfairs – and grossly over-inflated prices for a place to stay.

GASTRONOMIC HIGHLIGHTS

☙ BADGERS TEAROOMS £
☎ 871649; Victoria Shopping Centre, Mostyn St; ⏲ 10am-4.30pm Mon-Fri, 9.30am-5pm Sat, 10.30am-4pm Sun

Badgers is something of a local institution. It's a traditional tearoom, best known for its creamy afternoon teas and gooey cakes, but it's the Victorian attire of the staff that really adds a frisson of genteel nostalgia to the eat-in experience. Expect starched tablecloths and sometimes even starchier sandwiches, but revel in the step-back-in-time ambience.

☙ FISH TRAM CHIPS £
☎ 872673; Old Rd; ⏲ 9am-5pm Mon-Sat, noon-2pm & 5-7pm Mon-Sat

Another local institution, this is where the locals go for one of the tastiest and best-value fish suppers in North Wales – it's just £6.95 for the cod special, including mushy peas and a pot of tea. Fish Tram Chips is a pretty low-frills place but it's big on tasty, fresh fish and homemade side dishes with views across to the Great Orme Tramway station. Probably the best bargain in the resort and great chips. Don't miss it.

☙ HAMBONE FOOD HALL £
☎ 860084; Lloyd St; ⏲ 9.30am-5.30pm Mon-Sat

The best deli in Llandudno, the Hambone has a huge range of freshly made sandwiches to eat in or take away. The menu takes in delicious hot food with an international twist and a selection of speciality coffees, plus cakes and pastries. Watch out for the lunchtime queue snaking out the door, though. If the sun is out, choose a take-away option and enjoy an al-fresco picnic on the nearby promenade.

☙ NINETEEN £
☎ 873333; 19 Lloyd St; ⏲ 9am-5pm Mon-Sat; 🛜

This is a great, chilled-out little coffee shop for smoothies, juices and a caffeine-boost pit stop. Settle in among big comfy sofas and soak up the jazz-music background. It has free wi-fi and newspapers to browse over your latte. If only the service were a little sharper, this could be a contender for the coolest cafe in North Wales.

☙ NUMBER 1 BISTRO £££
☎ 875424; Old Rd; early-evening set menu 2/3 courses £18/22; ⏲ 5.30-9.30pm Mon-Sat

There's a touch of la belle France about this stylish, dark-red bistro with wood tables, a long-standing favourite on the town's dining scene. The menu includes some interesting twists on the standard bistro fare with venison and ostrich, plus lots of fresh fish. Best of all, however, is the early-evening set menu – it's cracking value but only available until 6.30pm each evening.

☙ THE SEAHORSE £££
☎ 875315; www.the-seahorse.co.uk; 7 Church Walks; set menu Tue-Fri £21; ⏲ 5pm-late Tue-Sat

Lots of ocean-fresh fish are the name of the game at this well-regarded restaurant, formerly known as Richard's Bistro. It's a split-level affair with the more intimate cellar room better suited to informal dining and the street-level restaurant the domain of a good-value set menu (except weekends). Expect friendly service and a genuine enthusiasm for local food.

ANGLESEY & NORTH WALES

NIGHTLIFE

Upper Mostyn St is the place to head to get a taste for Llandudno's nightlife with a group of fashion-conscious bars lining the strip.

♥ FAT CAT CAFE BAR

☎ 871844; 149 Upper Mostyn St

The local outpost of Wales' Fat Cat chain serves up designer beers and pub food in a contemporary, student-friendly cafe-bar setting.

♥ KING'S HEAD

☎ 877993; Old Rd

For a quieter pint, the King's Head, overlooking the tramway station (p268), is a traditional Victorian pub with real ales and decent bar meals.

♥ VENUE CYMRU

☎ 872000; www.venuecymru.co.uk; The Promenade; ⏲ box office 9.30am-8.30pm Mon-Sat, noon-4pm Sun, plus prior to performances

Having undergone a major expansion program, Venue Cymru is now one of North Wales' leading event and performance venues. The program covers all bases from rock gigs to high-brow classical performances via shows for young children. Catch a pre-show dinner at the venue's Y Review (☎ 873641; 2-course menu £15; ⏲ 5.30pm-show start) to avoid those troublesome, mid-performance tummy rumbles.

TRANSPORT

BUS // Buses stop on the corner of Upper Mostyn St and Gloddaeth St. **Arriva** (www.arrivabus.co.uk) runs bus 5 to Caernarfon (1¾ hours, half-hourly Monday to Saturday, hourly Sunday) and bus 19/19A to Llanrwst (30 minutes, half-hourly Monday to Saturday, hourly Sunday).

PARKING // Parking on the promenade is at a premium. Head for the large number of spaces within the

Parc Llandudno complex and its accompanying Asda supermarket.

TRAIN // Llandudno's train station is three blocks south of Mostyn St; taxis wait by the station. **Arriva Trains** (www.arrivatrainswales.co.uk) runs services to Holyhead and nearby Llandudno Junction station on the North Coast Line. The latter station connects to direct services to London Euston with **Virgin Trains** (www.virgintrains.co.uk) on the West Coast Main Line. Arriva also runs services to Blaenau Ffestiniog via Betws-y-Coed on the Conwy Valley Line.

LLANGOLLEN

☎ 01978 / pop 3500

Llangollen, huddled in the fertile Vale of Llangollen around the banks of the tumbling River Dee, has long been a scenic gem of North Wales. The engineer Thomas Telford certainly thought so, and he helped to put the town on the map by adapting the London to Holyhead stagecoach route to the present-day A5 and the routing the Llangollen Canal through it.

Llangollen was a traditionally seen as a day-trip destination but its appeal has evolved rapidly in recent years with a slew of smart new places to eat, a burgeoning walking and outdoors scene and a growing reputation for its cultural appeal with two major arts festivals now attracting a large number of new visitors to the town.

ESSENTIAL INFORMATION

EMERGENCIES // Wrexham Maelor Hospital (☎ 291100; www.newalesnhstrust.org.uk; ⏲ 24hr) Eleven miles away in Wrexham.

TOURIST OFFICES // Tourist office (☎ 860828; the Chapel, Castle St; ⏲ 9am-5.30pm Apr-Oct, 9.30am-5pm Nov-Mar) The staff are helpful and professional at this tourist office, housed in an old chapel along with the library upstairs. As well as offering information, it houses regular art exhibitions, a gift shop and sells tickets for local arts events.

A WALK IN THE CLWYDIAN RANGE

Designated an Area of Outstanding National Beauty (AONB), the 62-sq-mile Clwydian Range stretches from Prestatyn in the north to Nant y Garth near Llandegla in the south. The highest point is atop Moel Famau (554m) and is marked by the ruined Jubilee Tower, which was built in 1810 for the 50th jubilee of King George III. The original monument, a 35m obelisk, was the first Egyptian-style monument to be built in Britain. The summit offers a spectacular view across the northwest from Liverpool to the Cheshire Plains.

Most walkers tend to rush past the Clwydian Range in their haste to get to Snowdonia, making it a lesser-known but nonetheless-stunning area for family walking and more strenuous hiking. It boasts waymarked paths and easy access from rambling hubs, such as Mold, Ruthin or Prestatyn with some of the day walks criss-crossing the Offa's Dyke Path (p195). The trailhead for many of the most popular day walks is the **Loggerheads Country Park Centre** (10am-4.30pm Sat, Sun & school holidays, 10am-4pm at other times), which is on the A494 Mold to Ruthin Rd (car park £5 per day).

A popular day walk is the 10-mile circular route from Loggerheads via Moel Famau and along the Clwydian Way (allow five to six hours). Take a copy of OS Explorer Map 265. For a shorter and more geologically diverse walk, Bryn Alun is a moderate, 4-mile circular walk (allow 2½ hours) through a landscape dominated by the largest limestone pavement in North Wales. The trailhead is at Pistyll Gwyn car park. But do take care on the slippy limestone in wet conditions.

More from www.clwydianrangeaonb.co.uk.

EXPLORING LLANGOLLEN

❧ **EXPLORE ANCIENT SITES //**
REVEL IN THE SENSE OF HISTORY
COMING ALIVE
Llangollen is the base for exploring two of North Wales' best-known ancient sites, both of which can be reached by an engaging if, at times, strenuous walk from the centre of town. To the north of Llangollen, **Dinas Brân** marks the remnants of an Iron Age fort and the tumbledown ruins of a castle whose history is shrouded in mystery. The reward for yomping along the wildflower-strewn footpath is a fantastic panorama across North Wales from the hilltop site, some 229m above the Dee Valley. Don't expect any heritage interpretation or a gift shop – just delicious silence.

For more of a guided visit, the dignified ruins of **Valle Crucis Abbey** (Cadw; ☎ 860326; www.cadw.wales.gov.uk; adult/ child £2.60/2.25; 10am-5pm Apr-Oct) evoke the lives of Wales' Cistercian monks. Founded in 1201 by Madog ap Gruffydd, ruler of Northern Powys, its serene setting and largely Gothic form predates its more famous sibling at Tintern (p77). A visit is brought to life at the Summerhouse Interpretation Centre, which includes an animated tour of the 13th-century abbey – complete with a virtual reality monk. Take a picnic for an alfresco lunch by the ancient fishpond.

Valle Crucis Abbey is 2 miles from Llangollen on the A542.

❧ **PLAS NEWYDD // THE ULTIMATE**
HISTORIC-ROMANTIC HIDEAWAY
The 18th-century home of the Ladies of Llangollen (p277), **Plas Newydd** (☎ 861314; Hill St; adult/child £3.50/2.50; 10am-5pm Apr-Oct) is an atmospheric step back in time. Lady Eleanor Butler and

Miss Sarah Ponsonby transformed the house into their own private romantic hybrid of Gothic and Tudor styles, complete with stained-glass windows, carved-oak panels and formal gardens. Highlights of the visit include exploring the tranquil grounds, an audio tour (included in the admission) and a regular program of arts events staged in the gardens. Don't confuse this place with the stately home of the same name on Anglesey (p260).

❦ BOAT TRIPS AROUND LLANGOLLEN // FOLLOW THE CANAL TO CRUISE WALES' LATEST UNESCO SITE

The 46-mile Llangollen Canal's place in history is assured by the involvement of the great civil engineer Thomas Telford (1757–1834), who designed an elegant curving weir, the Horseshoe Falls, to collect water for the canal from the River Dee. Today the towpaths and canal locks are back in use again thanks to the 45-minute, horse-drawn boat excursions from Llangollen Wharf by the **Horse Draw Boat Centre** (☎ 860702; Wharf Hill; www.horsedrawnboats.co.uk; adult/child £5/2.50; ☼ 11am-4.30pm Apr-Oct). The company also offers two-hour return trips by motorised narrowboat (adult/child £10/8, at 12.15pm and 2pm April to October). Note: only the horse-drawn narrowboats are wheelchair accessible.

The village of Trevor, 4 miles east along the canal, is home to Telford's masterpiece and Wales' latest addition to the Unesco World Heritage list. The

---

∼ WORTH A TRIP ∼

Flintshire is home to a religious site that makes the market town of **Holywell** unique as Wales' answer to Lourdes. It has been a revered site of pilgrimage and religious healing for body and soul for over 1300 years.

Take the A55 expressway to junction 32, and follow the A5026 through Holywell to **St Winefride's Well** (☎ 01352 713054; www.stwinefrideswell.com; adult/child 80p/20p; ☼ 9am-5pm Apr-Sep, 9am-4pm Oct-Mar), one of the seven wonders of Wales. There's free car parking opposite.

Named after the 7th-century Welsh woman venerated as a saint, St Winefride's Well marks the site of her gruesome death and resurrection from the dead by her uncle, St Bueno. Curative bathing in the holy waters started in the 12th century.

Henry V made the pilgrimage there in 1416 to take the curative waters after his victory at Agincourt and Princess Victoria visited in 1828.

Modern-day pilgrims still take the waters today (by arrangement with the custodian), bathing in the holy well at designated times before visiting the adjoining Museum of the Pilgrimage, attending one of the pilgrims' masses or stocking up on vials of holy water in the shop. The site is packed in June for the National Catholic Pilgrimage.

There's even accommodation just up the road courtesy of the Bridgettine Sisters at **St Winefride's Guesthouse** (☎ 01352 714073; www.bridgettine.org; 20 New Rd; s/d £29/50, per person half-board £37; ℗), where the simple but cosy rooms offer an evening of quiet contemplation after enjoying a home-cooked meal.

More from www.holywell-town.gov.uk.

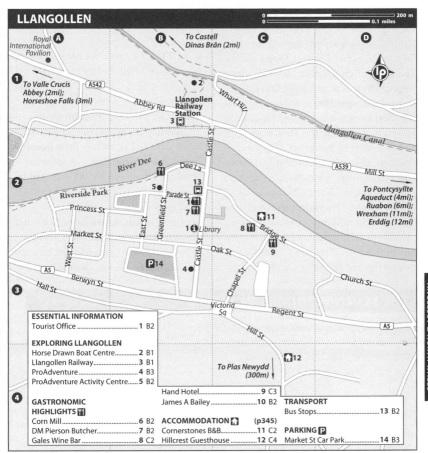

LLANGOLLEN

ESSENTIAL INFORMATION
Tourist Office **1** B2

EXPLORING LLANGOLLEN
Horse Drawn Boat Centre **2** B1
Llangollen Railway **3** B1
ProAdventure **4** B3
ProAdventure Activity Centre **5** B2

GASTRONOMIC HIGHLIGHTS
Corn Mill **6** B2
DM Pierson Butcher **7** B2
Gales Wine Bar **8** C2

Hand Hotel **9** C3
James A Bailey **10** B2

ACCOMMODATION   (p345)
Cornerstones B&B **11** C2
Hillcrest Guesthouse **12** C4

TRANSPORT
Bus Stops **13** B2

PARKING
Market St Car Park **14** B3

ANGLESEY & NORTH WALES

Pontcysyllte Aqueduct was completed in 1805 in order to carry the canal over the Dee. The aqueduct is probably the most spectacular piece of engineering on the entire UK canal system. It soars 126ft above the river, and this makes it definitely the tallest navigable aqueduct in the world. Fun 45-minute **narrow-boat trips** (☎ 01691 690322; www.canaltrip.co.uk; adult/child £4.50/3.50; ☻ daily May-Aug, Sat & Sun Apr & Sep-Oct) run across the aqueduct. It's an odd experience – the effect is like being suspended in mid-air. Buy tickets at the canal-side shop.

AngloWelsh Waterway Holidays (☎ 0117 3041122; www.anglowelsh.co.uk; Mon-Fri/Sat & Sun £99/120, ☻ bookings 8.30am-5.30pm Mon-Fri, 9am-4pm Sat, 10am-4pm Sun), based at Trevor, arranges self-drive day cruises by narrowboat for up to 10 people.

♥ LLANGOLLEN RAILWAY //
HERITAGE AND NOSTALGIA FROM THE AGE OF STEAM

Trainspotters beware: a trip on the Llangollen's heritage railway is not just about recording engine numbers. The 7.5-mile jaunt through the Dee Valley via Berwyn (near Horseshoe Falls) and Carrog on the former Ruabon to Barmouth Line is a superb day out for rail fans, families and heritage lovers alike. The **Llangollen Railway** (☎ 860979; www. llangollen-railway.co.uk; adult/child return £11/5.50; ☺ daily Apr-Oct, special services Nov-Mar) is probably best known today for its regular program of Thomas the Tank Engine and Ivor the Engine theme days for children, although train-driving courses and murder-mystery excursions are also popular options. The railway recently celebrated the 175th anniversary of the Great Western Railway and the 35th anniversary of the reopening of the line by rail enthusiasts. Plans are now afoot to extend the line to Corwen with a longer track and a new station due for completion in 2013.

♥ **ACTIVE LLANGOLLEN // TIME TO GET SOME ADRENALIN PUMPING**
Llangollen has long since shaken off its blue-rinse image, reinventing the Dee Valley as a hub for adventure sports. The leading exponents of these activity-based days and courses is **ProAdventure** (☎ 860605; www.proadventure.co.uk; 36 Castle St; white-water rafting per day £90, rock climbing per day £45; ☺ 10am-6pm, to 5pm Sun), which runs an outdoor shop in town and also manages the **ProAdventure Activity Centre** (☎ 861912; www.llangollenclimbing.co.uk; Parade St; ☺ 6pm-10pm Mon-Fri, 10am-9pm Sat, 10am-5pm Sun). The latter is home to the Llangol-

THE SEVEN WONDERS OF WALES

Pistyll Rhaeadr and Wrexham steeple,
Snowdon's mountain without its people,
Overton yew trees, St Winefride's wells,
Llangollen bridge and Gresford bells

The anonymous 18th-century English traveller who penned this piece of doggerel, the *Seven Wonders of Wales,* did a major service for the cause of the lesser-explored northeast of Wales. Unlike the *Seven Wonders of the World,* all the Welsh marvels cited remain in good condition and no less than six of them are to be found in the northeast – ideal for a list-ticking long weekend.

Start with Pistyll Rhaeadr, the water-cascading falls cut into the Berwyn Mountains before heading over to Llangollen, where Cornerstones (p345) not only makes a good base to stay, but also offers a vantage point on that medieval, multiple-arched bridge recorded in verse. St Giles' church in Wrexham, marked by a faded stone explaining, 'This steeple was completed in 1506', boasts superb views of the Dee Valley if you climb the steeple (well, more of a tower actually). Look hard enough and you may even spot some of those waxed-lyrical yew trees in Overton, near Wrexham. Meanwhile, Gresford industrial-sized bells are ringing out from atop a winding stone-spiral staircase with gusty chimes. You can't miss them.

To finish the wonder-inspired odyssey, St Winefride's Well (p274) marks a spiritual conclusion to proceedings and a chance to wash away your fatigue with the well's curative waters. Better still, you can end the journey secure in the knowledge that there's more to northeast Wales than just shopping centres and motorways. And, besides, six out of seven ain't bad.

THE LADIES OF LLANGOLLEN

Lady Eleanor Butler and Miss Sarah Ponsonby, the 'Ladies of Llangollen', lived in Plas Newydd from 1780 to 1829 with their maid, Mary Carryl. They had fallen in love in Ireland but their aristocratic Anglo-Irish families discouraged the relationship. In a desperate bid to be allowed to live together the women eloped to Wales, disguised as men, and set up home in Llangollen to devote themselves to 'friendship, celibacy and the knitting of stockings'.

Their romantic friendship became well known yet respected, and they were visited by many national figures of the day, including the Duke of Wellington, William Wordsworth and Sir Walter Scott. Wordsworth was even suitably moved to pen the following words: 'Sisters in love, a love allowed to climb, even on this earth above the reach of time'.

The ladies' relationship with their maid, Mary, was also close. Mary managed to buy the freehold of Plas Newydd and left it to the 'sisters' when she died. They erected a large monument to her in the graveyard at St Collen's Parish Church in Llangollen, where they are also buried. Lady Eleanor died in 1829; Sarah Ponsonby was reunited with her soul mate just two years later.

len Climbing Centre with a dedicated indoor climbing wall (classes from £15 per hour).

FESTIVALS & EVENTS

Llangollen Comedy Festival (www.llancomedy.com) This recently launched festival is also now staged at the Royal International Pavilion each June.

International Musical Eisteddfod (www.llangollen2010.co.uk) Staged at the Royal International Pavilion each July, this multicultural affair with traditional choirs, fringe stages, family-friendly shows and stalls, and big-name evening concert galas, is staged in the spirit of building peace through music.

Llangollen Fringe Festival (www.llangollenfringe.co.uk) Staged in the town hall each July, this has grown into a mini-me version of the famous Edinburgh Fringe Festival.

GASTRONOMIC HIGHLIGHTS

✿ THE CORN MILL ££

☎ 869555; Dee Lane; mains £9-17; ☽ noon-9pm
With its summer-breeze riverside location, stripped floorboards and exposed, thick stone walls, the Corn Mill has rapidly become the town's favourite gastropub. The watermill still turns at the heart of this converted mill while the outdoor decking area is perfect for a chilled-out sundowner. Food wise, it's hearty pub fare with a twist, plus some decent vegetarian options.

✿ GALES WINE BAR ££

☎ 860089; www.galesofllangollen.co.uk; 18 Bridge St; mains £8-16; ☽ noon-2pm & 6-9.30pm Mon-Sat
With over 30 years as a wine bar and a 100-strong wine list that spans the globe, this wood-lined eatery is a smart and sophisticated option. The menu changes daily with dishes based around lamb, beef and fish; it features a good selection of steaks and daily specials, all of which are best enjoyed with a good glass of wine. The owners also run a **Wine Shop** (☽ 10am-5.30pm Mon-Sat, 10am-4pm Sun) next door to take home your favourite fruity vintage from last night's dinner.

❤ HAND HOTEL £

☎ 860303; www.hand-hotel-llangollen.com; Bridge St; lunches around £8

A historic old hotel with glorious river views, the Hand is best known for its excellent Sunday lunches, a pile-it-high affair with various roast meats and vegetables served from a series of hot plates. It's very good value and very, very filling. The hotel also hosts the Llangollen Male Voice Choir each Friday evening and you can catch them in the bar after practice around 9pm for a pint and an impromptu sing along.

To stock up on some of the best local produce, try **DM Pierson Butcher** (☎ 860650; Castle St) for great organic meat. Just next door, the deli **James**

A Bailey (☎ 860617; Castle St) offers laver bread (boiled seaweed mixed with oatmeal), Welsh cakes and Welsh wines among other treats – try a Welsh Oggie (a meat, potato and onion pasty). Mmm, filling!

TRANSPORT

BUS // Buses stop on Market St. **Arriva** (www.arriva bus.co.uk) runs bus service 5A to Wrexham (30 minutes, half-hourly Monday to Saturday, hourly Sunday) and X94 to Barmouth (one hour, two-hourly Monday to Saturday, five daily on Sunday).

PARKING // Parking is at a premium in Llangollen, especially on a sunny day. Best to head for the short-stay car park on Market St (£1 per hour).

TRAIN // The nearest mainline station is at Ruabon, 6 miles east on Arriva Trains' Holyhead–Cardiff line.

ANGLESEY & NORTH WALES

∼ WORTH A TRIP ∼

Follow the A494 to the sturdy market town of **Ruthin**, Denbighshire, for history, honey buns and haute couture. No, really.

Ruthin, built around the clock tower on St Peter's Sq, feels on the up these days. Offa's Dyke National Trail (p195) passes through the nearby **Clwydian Range AONB** (p273) and the town is packed with history: the 15th-century **Nantclwyd y Dre** (☎ 01824 709822; adult/child £3.60/2.50; ☷ 10am-5pm Fri-Sun Apr-Sep) is the oldest timber-framed building in Wales. The **Ruthin Craft Centre** (☎ 01824 704774; www.ruthincraftcentre. org.uk; Park Rd; admission free; ☷ 10am-5.30pm; ℗) is the town's new arts hub with galleries, events and a decent cafe.

But what sets Ruthin apart is the way local independent shops are showcasing local produce and enterprise. Shops to look out for include the following:

Cerrig & the Green Lady (☎ 01824 705118; St Peter's Sq; ☷ 10am-5.30pm Mon-Sat) Selling quality local smellies made from natural ingredients.

Leonardo's (☎ 01824-707161; www.leonardosdeli.co.uk; 4 Well St; ☷ 9.30am-5.30pm Mon-Sat) A mouth-watering deli for local cheeses, preserves and award-winning savoury pies.

Ruthin Book Shop (☎ 01824 703840; 3 Upper Clwyd St; ☷ 10am-1pm & 1.30-5pm Tue-Sat) A fabulously traditional place for maps and local history.

Spavens (☎ 01824 707726; 6 Clwyd St; ☷ 10am-5.30pm Mon-Sat) A gloriously retro sweet shop for sweets straight out of childhood.

Park in the pay-and-display car park opposite county offices on Market St (three hours £1), and if you're making a weekend of it, base yourself at the town's art-themed boutique hotel, manorhaus (p345). More from **Visit Ruthin** (www.visitruthin.com).

AROUND LLANGOLLEN

❦ ERDDIG HALL & GARDENS //
A GREAT FAMILY DAY OUT

For a glimpse into the life of the British upper class in the 18th and 19th century, and perhaps the best insight in the UK into the 'upstairs-downstairs' relationship that existed between masters and their servants, this stately house and gardens make for a highly worthwhile visit. **Erddig** (NT; ☎ 01978 355314; www.nationaltrust.org.uk; adult/child/family £9.35/4.68/23.40, grounds only £6.10/3.05/15.25; ☺ house noon-5pm Sat-Thu Jul-Aug, Sat-Wed Mar-Jun & Sep-Oct, noon-4pm Sat & Sun Nov-Dec, garden 11am-6pm Sat-Thu Jul-Aug, Sat-Wed Mar-Jun & Sep-Oct, 11am-4pm daily Nov-Mar) was the Yorke family's ancestral home for over two centuries (until 1973).

Today the property is managed by the National Trust, which has added a decent cafe and a gift shop. The house and out-buildings trace the historical element of the Yorke family's story while the country estate includes a walled garden, restored in Victorian style, rare fruit trees, a canal and the National Ivy Collection. Best of all, however, Erddig now hosts a huge program of family-friendly activities, school-holiday events and themed days out, ranging from autumnal apple days to Easter egg trails and a Christmas fair.

Erddig is about 12 miles northeast of Llangollen in the village of Rhostyllen, signposted off the A483.

BACKGROUND

☙ HISTORY
The history of Wales features ancient civilisations and contemporary characters, but most of all, it's a roller-coaster ride of conflict and eventual emancipation (p281).

☙ CULTURE
Know your Owen Sheers from your Cate Le Bon? The cultural life of Wales has never been in ruder health or more celebrated (p290).

☙ ICONS OF WALES
What is the essence of Welsh identity in the 21st century? The Welsh icons – music, rugby and sport, castles and architecture – reveal all (p295).

☙ OUTDOOR ACTIVITIES
Walkers, hikers, bikers, golfers. They all love Wales. Join in with the slew of activities for all ages and explore the great outdoors Welsh style (p301).

☙ THE NATURAL ENVIRONMENT
For a small country, Wales is hugely diverse. Brush up on the geology that shaped a nation, its fauna and flora, and its burgeoning green awareness (p306).

☙ MYTHS & LEGENDS
The landscape and history of Wales is steeped in folk legends. But what do the key figures reveal of the national psyche (p311)?

☙ FOOD & DRINK
The food revolution in Wales continues apace. Tickle your tastebuds with the best of local produce, Michelin stars and farmers markets (p316).

HISTORY

EARLY HISTORY

Little is known about Wales' early history, but rare discoveries date the earliest human habitation back to 250,000 BC. The first Homo sapiens, people who are physically identical to us today, came to Wales between the Palaeolithic period and the end of the Bronze Age around 2000 BC. Today sites like the Palaeolithic cave at Minchin Hole and the Neolithic oval cairns of Sweyne's Howe on Rhossili Down are a rich source of clues about Welsh ancestors, with animal bones, basic tools and early weapons offering hints to their lifestyle.

It was much later, around 600 BC, that the first wave of Celtic warriors arrived on Wales' shores from central Europe and with them the Druids, the poets and priests who would change the course of Welsh history forever. The Celts had a defining role in Wales, making enormous technical and artistic advances and introducing a new language, social hierarchy and belief system. The Druids were revered as much for their knowledge as their divine power. They initiated the oral tradition of storytelling and songwriting that is celebrated to this day. They are most closely associated with sites on Anglesey, such as Caer y Twr and Llyn Cerrig Bach.

> *'The Druids initiated the oral tradition of storytelling and songwriting that is celebrated to this day'*

The most famous clue to early history is the red-ochre-stained skeleton of the Red Lady of Paviland Cave, the earliest known formal human burial in Britain. Found in a wave-washed cave in Gower's Rhossili Bay, it is today exhibited in the Origins gallery at the National Museum Cardiff.

THE ROMANS

When the Romans conquered Britain in the years after AD 43, the Celts had occupied Wales for almost six centuries and put up staunch resistance. So, when the Romans invaded in the mid–1st century AD they put up staunch resistance. Mona (Anglesey) was the centre of Druidic power and the site of a raging battle in AD 60. After the Druids' last stand on Anglesey, the Romans took control of Wales but they never really conquered it. Instead, the Celts managed to live alongside the Romans, adopting and adapting to the new cultural force.

BACKGROUND

» 250,000 BC	» 2000 BC	» 600 BC
The earliest human inhabitants of Wales have been traced to this period by rare archaeological finds.	The arrival of the first Homo sapiens; this is an era marked by a major evolutionary jump, with the first cave art, music and stone-crafted tools.	The Celtic people begin to settle in Wales, bringing with them the mystic faith healers, the Druids, who would shape traditional Welsh culture.

WALES IS BORN

Wales' isolated position meant that it missed out on the heaving battles that spread across Europe in the wake of the fall of the Roman Empire in the 5th century. A number of separate kingdoms arose across Wales and a British leader, possibly the myth-infused King Arthur, proved victorious against Saxon invaders, inspiring romantic fables in the process.

Among the visiting missionaries spreading Christianity and founding basic churches in the 6th century, Dewi Sant (St David; see p283) became a key figure, establishing his eponymous town as a centre of religion and learning. During that time the written word also graduated from biblical purposes to literature, and the poems of Taliesin and Aneirin, from the late 6th and early 7th centuries, are the earliest surviving examples of Welsh literature. A distinct Welsh language had emerged and Cymry, a word describing the land and its people, was established – Welsh identity was born.

EARLY WELSH RULERS

Territorial scuffles continued between the disparate kingdoms. A present-day reminder of this unstable period is Offa's Dyke, the 8th-century fortification to mark the boundary between the Welsh on one side and the Saxons (the Kingdom of Mercia, under King Offa), on the other. Today the fortification forms the Offa's Dyke Path National Trail.

During the 9th and 10th centuries savage coastal attacks in the south by Danish and Norse pirates forced the small kingdoms of Wales to cooperate. Rhodri Mawr (Rhodri the Great), a charismatic leader, managed to unite most of the kingdoms, only to see them split among his sons. His grandson, Hywel Da (Hywel the Good), reunified the country and then went on to consolidate its laws, decreeing communal agricultural practices and affording women and children greater rights than other legal systems of the time.

Ironically, as Wales was becoming a recognisable entity, it was forced to acknowledge the authority of the Anglo-Saxon king of England in return for an alliance against the marauding Vikings.

THE NORMANS

When the Normans claimed England in 1066, William the Conqueror set up feudal barons, the marcher lords, along the Welsh border to secure his kingdom. Under sustained attack, the Welsh were pushed back and it was not until Llewellyn ap Gruffydd

» AD 60	» 5TH CENTURY	» 6TH CENTURY
The Druids' last stand on Anglesey unleashes the brute force of the Roman army, but the Romans fall short of total conquest.	As the Romans pull out of Britain and the empire starts to crumble, a number of disparate Welsh kingdoms emerge.	St David is born, going on to establish a sacred place of worship in Pembrokeshire and becoming the patron saint of Wales.

WHO WAS ST DAVID?   *NONA REES*

St David (Dewi Sant) is the only truly native patron saint of his country in the British Isles. He was born in the 6th century on a cliff top near present-day St Davids (p157). The site is marked by St Non's chapel (dedicated to his mother) and a spring of holy water.

Like many young men of noble birth, David was educated by monks and went on to found churches across South and East Wales. In company with Saints Teilo and Padarn he made a pilgrimage to the Holy Land, eventually returning to West Wales. Fellow churchmen acclaimed his spiritual stature when he preached at the Synod of Brefi (Ceredigion). The ground rose under him and a dove, representing the Holy Spirit, landed on his shoulder. He performed many miracles of healing.

David established his monastery beside Pembrokeshire's River Alyn, where the cathedral now stands. His claim to the site was disputed by Boia, a local chieftain, whose scheming wife made her maidens dance naked in the river to tempt the monks. But David and his fellow monks led a spartan life dedicated to manual labour, care for the poor and prayer. He subdued the appetites of the flesh by standing up to his neck in cold water and reciting the psalms.

David died on Tuesday 1 March, in the late 6th century. In 1123, Pope Callistus II recognised his sainthood and he has since become a focus for Welsh identity.
Nona Rees is the author of St David of Dewisland

(Llewellyn the Last) that a true Welsh leader emerged. He adopted the title 'Prince of Wales' and by 1267 had forced England's Henry III to recognise him as such. But Llewellyn's triumph was short-lived and by 1277 he had lost much of what he had achieved.

Edward I fought to control the Welsh upstart and eventually killed both Llewellyn and his brother Dafydd. He then set up his 'Iron Ring' of castles to prevent further Welsh revolt. Of these, Caernarfon is the ultimate expression of military and royal authority, and it was here that his infant son, Edward II, was crowned Prince of Wales, a title bestowed, to this day, on the eldest son of the reigning monarch.

Curiously, against this troubled backdrop Welsh storytelling and literature flourished. In 1176 Rhys ap Gruffydd (Lord Rhys), one of Wales' great leaders, convened the first bardic tournament – Wales' original eisteddfod (see p14) – for a seat of honour in his house. The 13th-century Black Book of Carmarthen, the oldest surviving Welsh-language manuscript, also dates from this period and is today held at the National Library of Wales in Aberystwyth.

BACKGROUND

» 8TH CENTURY

The construction of Offa's Dyke Path marks the division between the land of the Welsh and English kings, a de-facto border to this day.

» 1066

The Normans invade Wales and a prolonged period of Welsh resistance begins with warring factions on both sides of the borders vying for land.

» 13TH CENTURY

Llewellyn ap Gruffydd emerges as unifying Welsh leader but is trounced by Edward I, who builds a ring of castles to suppress the Welsh uprising.

OWAIN GLYNDŴR

Anti-English feeling was rife throughout Wales by 1400 and Owain ap Gruffydd (better known as Owain Glyndŵr), a descendant of the royal house of Powys, became the uprising's unlikely leader, declaring himself Prince of Wales and attacking neighbouring marcher lords.

Henry IV reacted harshly and passed a series of penal laws imposing severe restrictions on the Welsh. This only increased support for the rebellion and by 1404 Glyndŵr controlled most of Wales, capturing Harlech and Aberystwyth and summoning a parliament at Machynlleth. But Glyndŵr met his match in Prince Henry, son of Henry IV and hero of the Battle of Agincourt. After a series of defeats, his allies deserted him and after 1406 Glyndŵr fades into myth-shrouded obscurity.

THE ACTS OF UNION

By the later part of the 15th century the Welsh and English had learnt to coexist uneasily. The Welsh saw Henry Tudor as a prophesied ruler who would restore their fortunes and lead them to victory over their age-old enemy. After years of exile in Brittany, Henry defeated Richard III in the Battle of Bosworth Field in 1485 and ascended the throne. This began the Tudor dynasty, which would reign until the death of Elizabeth I in 1603.

But it was Henry VIII who brought real change with the Tudor Acts of Union in 1536 and 1543 to establish English sovereignty over the country. Although the Welsh became equal citizens and were granted parliamentary representation, Welsh law was abolished and English was declared the official language of law and administration. The glory years of the Cistercian abbeys as centres of learning also came to an end when Henry VIII declared the independence of the Church of England in 1534 and dissolved the abbeys in 1536.

BACKGROUND

THE LANDSKER LINE

The so-called Landsker Line, which runs roughly along the present-day A40 through Pembrokeshire, is considered something of a cultural divide between Welsh and English heartlands. The line was originally created by a series of strongholds built by the Normans after their invasion of West Wales in the 11th century. The *landsker*, the Norse word for frontier, marked the edge of their conquered lands. The south of what is now Pembrokeshire became anglicised, leaving the north a bastion of Welsh identity.

» 1400	» 1536 & 1543	» 1588
Welsh nationalist hero Owain Glyndŵr leads the Welsh in rebellion, declaring a parliament in Machynlleth, but his rebellion is short-lived and victory fleeting.	The Tudor Acts of Union introduced by Henry VIII unite Wales and England, granting equal rights and parliamentary representation, but make English the main language.	The first complete translation of the Bible into Welsh helps the cause of Protestantism and serves to prop up the neglected Welsh language.

ROMANTIC WALES

Towards the end of the 18th century the influence of the Romantic revival made the wild landscapes of Wales fashionable with genteel travellers. The works of landscape painters such as Richard Wilson did much to popularise the rugged mountains and ruined castles, and the rediscovery of Celtic and Druidic traditions fuelled a growing cultural revival and sense of Welsh identity.

Scholars were increasingly concerned about the need to preserve the culture and heritage of their country and efforts were made to collect and publish literature. Edward Williams (Iolo Morganwg to use his bardic name) went on to revive ancient bardic competitions and held the first 'modern' eisteddfod in Carmarthen in 1819.

INDUSTRIALISATION

The iron industry had been growing steadily across Wales since the mid-18th century with an explosion of ironworks around Merthyr Tydfil. English industrialists took control and constructed roads, canals and tramways, changing the face of the valleys forever. Major engineering developments from this period include Thomas Telford's spectacular Pontcysyllte Aqueduct and his graceful suspension bridge at Conwy.

As the Industrial Revolution gathered pace, workers were increasingly dissatisfied with the appalling conditions and low rates of pay. Trade unions emerged and the first half of the 19th century was characterised by calls for a universal right to vote. In 1839 the Chartist Riots broke out in towns such as Newport when a petition of more than one million signatures was rejected by Westminster. Between 1839 and 1843 the Rebecca Riots ravaged the rural southwest. The name 'Rebecca' refers to a biblical verse in Genesis – the 'Daughters of Rebecca' (men dressed in women's clothes)

TWM SIÔN CATTI

All Welsh children read stories of the Welsh folk hero Thomas Jones, better known as Twm Siôn Catti, who was born in 1530 and turned outlaw at the age of 18 to save his mother from starvation. His banditry developed into a Robin Hood–style crusade to redistribute regional wealth. A master of disguise with a sense of humour, he relied on trickery rather than violence, retreating when necessary to a secret hideout near the River Tywi. He was never caught and in later life bought himself a royal pardon and went straight, writing poetry (winning a prize at the Llandaff eisteddfod) and even serving as mayor of Brecon.

BACKGROUND

» 1759–82	» 1819	» 1839
With the Industrial Revolution gripping the South Wales valleys, Dowlais and Merthyr Tydfil ironworks start production and Bethesda's slate quarry opens for business.	The first modern eisteddfod is held in Carmarthen against a backdrop of a Welsh cultural revival inspired by the Romantic period of art and literature.	The Chartist Riots across South Wales indicate the growing discontent among workers about the conditions of the burgeoning Industrial Revolution .

would act out a pantomime and tear down the turnpike tollgates on the order of 'Mother Rebecca'.

In 1847 the Commission on Education published a damning report, known as *The Treason of the Blue Books,* on the state of education in Wales. It questioned Welsh morality and blamed the influences of nonconformity and the Welsh language for allegedly lax morals. The introduction of the 'Welsh Not', a ban on speaking Welsh in schools, created a tide of anger.

THE DEPRESSION

By the second half of the 19th century, coal had superseded iron and the sheer number of migrants from England threatened the fabric of Welsh society. In 1867 industrial workers and small tenant farmers were given the right to vote, and elections in 1868 were a turning point for Wales. Henry Richard was elected as Liberal MP for Merthyr Tydfil, and brought ideas of land reform and native language to parliament for the first time.

> *'the sheer number of migrants from England threatened to weaken the fabric of Welsh society'*

The Secret Ballot Act of 1872 and the Reform Act of 1884 broadened suffrage and gave a voice to the rising tide of resentment over the hardships of the valleys and the payment of tithes (taxes) to the church. In 1900 Merthyr Tydfil returned Keir Hardie as Wales' first Labour MP.

National sentiment grew and education improved substantially. During WWI, Wales boomed and living standards rose as Welsh coal and agriculture fed the economy. A quarter of a million people were employed in Wales' coal industry in the 1920s; the results of this industrialisation can be seen at the former mining town of Blaenavon, today a Unesco World Heritage site.

Between the world wars the country suffered the results of economic depression and thousands were driven to emigrate in search of employment. The Labour Party weathered the storm and, as the 20th century progressed, became the political force of the nation. In 1925 six young champions of Welsh nationalism founded Plaid Cenedlaethol Cymru (the Welsh Nationalist Party; later shortened to Plaid Cymru) in Pwllheli and began the slow campaign for self-government.

POSTWAR WALES

The postwar years were not kind to Wales. The coal industry went into steep decline, forcing the closure of mines and a bitter struggle as unemployment levels rose to twice

» 1847	» 1868 & 1900	» 1916
The Commission on Education introduces the 'Welsh Not', a ban on speaking Welsh in schools that fuels the Welsh-language struggle for more than a century.	Political strength builds with Henry Richard elected as Liberal MP for Merthyr Tydfil in 1868 and Keir Hardie voted in as Wales' first Labour MP in Merthyr Tydfil in 1900.	Welsh Liberal MP David Lloyd George becomes British prime minister in an alliance with the Conservative Party, having built a reputation for championing the needy.

BACKGROUND

the UK average. The Welsh language was suffering and national pride was at an all-time low.

The final blow came in 1957 when the North Wales village of Capel Celyn, near Bala, and the surrounding valley were flooded to provide water for the city of Liverpool, despite vigorous campaigning across Wales. There were too few Welsh MPs in the House of Commons to oppose the project and resentment still lingers over the issue even today, intensified in dry summers by the appearance of the chapel, school and farms above the waters of Llyn Celyn.

The 1960s became a decade of protest in Wales and Plaid Cymru gained ground. Welsh pop began to flourish and Welsh publishing houses and record labels were

DAVID LLOYD GEORGE (1863–1945)

David Lloyd George began his career as the champion of Welsh populist democracy and a critic of society and its institutions. A talented and witty orator, in 1890 he won his first seat as Liberal MP for Caernarfon Boroughs and, at 27, became the youngest member of the House of Commons.

As Chancellor of the Exchequer he launched a broad but controversial program of social reform, including the introduction of old-age pensions, a 1909 budget that taxed the wealthy to fund services for the poor, and the 1911 National Insurance Act to provide health and unemployment insurance. Elected prime minister in 1916 after a divisive alliance with the Conservatives, Lloyd George went on to become an energetic war leader. He excelled at a time when strong leadership was needed, dismissing red tape and forcing his opinion when necessary.

Postwar industrial unrest and economic reconstruction dogged the country, however, and he eventually agreed to Irish independence to end civil war, a solution the Conservative alliance never forgave. Accusations of corruption, financial greed and the selling of honours began to ruin his reputation. Radicals, Welsh nationalists and campaigners for women's rights all felt betrayed. In 1922 the Conservatives staged a party revolt and broke up the shaky coalition. Lloyd George resigned immediately.

His popularity faded, the Liberal Party was in disarray, political allies had abandoned him, and both the Welsh and the British working class felt thoroughly deceived. Lloyd George's political career had reached a sad anticlimax.

He died in 1945 at Llanystumdwy, where there is now a small museum devoted to his life (see p243).

» 1925	» 1955 & 1959	» 1962
Plaid Cenedlaethol Cymru (Welsh Nationalist Party) is formed, initiating the struggle for Welsh self-governance and laying the foundations for modern-day Plaid Cymru.	Cardiff is declared the Welsh capital in 1955 and Wales finally gets its very own official flag in 1959.	Cymdeithas yr Iaith Gymraeg (the Welsh Language Society) is founded to campaign for legal status for the language and for Welsh-speaking radio and TV.

set up. In 1962 Cymdeithas yr Iaith Gymraeg (the Welsh Language Society) was founded.

Support for Plaid Cymru soared and further electoral successes by the party in the 1970s started people thinking about a measure of Welsh self-government. Besides, with only a shaky parliamentary majority, the governing Labour Party was doing all it could to maintain Welsh support. In 1976 the Welsh Development Agency (WDA) was established to foster new business opportunities across Wales in the face of the decline in traditional industry.

Margaret Thatcher's Conservative Party initiated a sweeping program of privatisation during the 1980s, leading to severe cuts in the coal, manufacturing and steel industries. Agriculture, too, was in a state of disarray and unemployment began to soar. Welsh living standards lagged far behind the rest of Britain, and with the collapse of the UK Miners' Strike (1984–85) Welsh morale hit an all-time low.

Something good did come out of the eighties, however, when in 1982 the Conservative government was forced to come good on election promises and establish S4C (Sianel Pedwar Cymru), the Welsh-language TV channel (see p15). Support and enthusiasm for the Welsh language increased, night courses popped up all over the country, Welsh-speaking nurseries and schools opened, university courses were established and the number of Welsh speakers started to stabilise at around 20% of the population.

DEVOLUTION

The 1997 general election brought Tony Blair's 'New Labour' to power and the devolution process got off the ground once again. In September of that year a referendum on the establishment of the National (Welsh) Assembly scraped through by the narrowest of margins.

The Assembly got off to a shaky start, however. Alun Michael, First Secretary in the new Assembly, was quickly ousted by a vote of no confidence and was replaced by the populist Assembly Member (AM) Rhodri Morgan. Lacking the powers granted to the Scottish Parliament, the Assembly was always going to have a hard time convincing the world, including Wales, of its merit. But as the Assembly settled down, Wales played host to the world's rugby elite in its sparkling new Millennium Stadium, and Welsh rock bands started making headlines under the 'Cool Cymru' banner, Welsh pride soared and the quest for national identity was firmly back on the agenda.

BACKGROUND

» 1976	» 1980S	» 1982
The Welsh Development Agency (WDA) is established to try to stem the industrial decline across Wales and move towards a new era of economic expansion.	Margaret Thatcher's government leads a sweeping program of privatisation, devastating Wales' coal and steel industries, and sending unemployment skywards.	The Welsh-language movement forces the opening of S4C (Sianel Pedwar Cymru), the Welsh Channel Four; Welsh speakers stabilise at about 20% of the population.

WALES TODAY

From the turn of the millennium, Wales surged ahead with new confidence. The unveiling of the new National Assembly building in Cardiff Bay and the ratification of the Government of Wales Bill helped the new seat of government to become part of the fabric of daily Welsh life. In November 2004, Wales Millennium Centre opened as a new permanent home for, among others, the Welsh National Opera. The move marked the culmination of Cardiff's regeneration, which can be traced back to the mid-1980s and the establishment of the Cardiff Bay Development Corporation. National pride was soaring with glory on the sports field, in the arts and in politics.

But what of the future? A new age of economic austerity, a new Conservative-Liberal coalition government in May 2010 and the threat of severe cuts to public services raise more questions than answers. In the early days of the new administration a promise to introduce a referendum on further Welsh devolution was announced, but no timescale for doing so was outlined. For the newly elected First Minister, the Rt Hon Carwyn Jones AM, it means both a new era for Wales and a new set of challenges.

» 1999

The first National (Welsh) Assembly is elected with the members sitting in a new building in Cardiff Bay and MP Rhodri Morgan taking the hot seat as First Minister.

» 2007

The Government of Wales Bill heralds the largest transfer of power from Westminster to Wales since the founding of the National Assembly.

» 2010

Rhodri Morgan retires, and Carwyn Jones is elected First Minister as a new political coalition in Westminster warns of the austerity measures to come.

CULTURE

· · · · · · ·

Wales, and its arts scene, has changed – really changed. Historically Wales has struggled to overcome negative stereotypes about its lack of sophistication. But, post millennium, Welsh pride and Wales' international standing have both been buoyed by the success of pop and rock stars, actors and film-makers, writers and thinkers. Devolution has also contributed to this positive enforcement with the National Assembly government funding more arts projects. Today Wales is reaffirming its identity through the arts but also examining the shifting sands of modern life.

The resurgence of the Welsh language goes hand in hand with the growth of the arts scene. Strongholds for the language in the Swansea Valley, northwest Wales (especially around Caernarfon) and Anglesey have produced their own creative projects, while BBC Radio Cymru and broadcaster S4C (Sianel Pedwar Cymru) champion Welsh-language programming.

LITERATURE

Wales has an incredibly rich literary history, with storytelling firmly embedded in the national psyche. From 2000-year-old bardic poetry to the Welsh-inspired 'sprung-rhythm' of English poet Gerard Manley Hopkins, latter-day Welsh writers have had a store of impressive works to refer to. However, it is primarily 20th-century writing that brought Welsh literature to a worldwide audience. A milestone was the 1915 publication of the controversial *My People,* by Caradoc Evans (1883–1945), in which the author exposes the dark side of Welsh life with stories of 'little villages hidden in valleys and reeking with malice'. Up until then, writers had pursued more established nostalgic themes.

> *'Wales has an incredibly rich literary history, with storytelling firmly embedded in the national psyche'*

In an international sense, however, it was the bad-boy genius of Welsh literature, Dylan Thomas (1914–53), who was Wales' most notable export. His reputation for hard drinking almost overshadows the impact of his literary works, yet fans insist he remains much misunderstood. Thomas is acclaimed for writing half a dozen of the greatest poems in the English language, including such timeless works as *Fern Hill* and *Do Not Go Gentle into That Good Night.* He is probably best known, however, for his comic play for voices, *Under Milk Wood,* describing a day in the life of an insular Welsh community.

Welsh literature also matured with home-grown heroes taking on the clichés of valley life and developing more realistic, socially rooted works. Among the leading figures, poet and painter David Jones (1895–1974) began the trend with his epic of war, *In Parenthesis,* published in 1937. Kate Roberts (1891–1985) explored the experiences of working men and women in rural Wales, often evoking qualities of a time since past with *Feet in Chains.* The elegant *On the Black Hill,* by Bruce Chatwin (1940–89), also evokes the joys and hardships of small-town life, exploring Welsh spirit and cross-border antipathy through the lives of torpid twin-brother farmers.

BACKGROUND

In terms of poetry, the loss of the referendum for devolution in March 1979 was a catharsis for modern Welsh literature. Like the investiture of Prince Charles as the Prince of Wales in July 1969, it heralded a flood of political and engaged writing and poetry, most notably the left-wing historian Gwyn Alf Williams' re-evaluation of Welsh history in his masterpiece *When Was Wales?*

This renaissance of Welsh poetry among a younger generation of poets, such as Menna Elfyn, Myrddin ap Dafydd, Ifor ap Glyn and Iwan Llwyd, took poetry out of the chapel, study and lecture room to be performed in pubs, clubs and cloisters. This led to a series of poetry tours, making Welsh-language poetry once again a popular medium of protest and performance. Boosted by the establishment of S4C and BBC Radio Cymru (the Welsh-language TV and radio stations) during the 1980s, a generation of professional Welsh-language writers have for the first time enabled Welsh poetry, drama and prose to have a life outside the traditional amateur and academic enclaves. Recent years have also seen an increasing crossover between Welsh and English poetry and literature with poets and musicians, such as Twm Morys and Gwyneth Glyn, establishing new audiences with their blend of words and music.

The most recent contemporary novels from Wales take an irreverent look at youth culture. Lewis Davies' critically acclaimed debut novel *Work, Sex & Rugby* is a hideously funny weekend odyssey of nights on the pull and days on the dole in the South Wales valleys. Niall Griffiths has garnered critical plaudits for his gritty, dark take on Welsh life with *Grits* and *Sheepshagger*. The Chandler-esque crime caper *Aberystwyth Mon Amour*, by Malcolm Pryce, delivers deadpan the most absurd of events to great comedic effect.

THE POETRY OF RS THOMAS

One of Wales' most passionate and most reclusive modern writers, the priest-turned-poet RS Thomas (1913–2000), was an outspoken critic of the so-called Welsh 'cultural suicide' and a staunch supporter of unpopular causes. Nominated for the Nobel Prize in Literature in 1996, his uncompromising work has a pure, sparse style, which he used to explore his profound spirituality and the natural world.

RS Thomas was also more politically controversial than any other Welsh writer, becoming the Welsh conscience and campaigning fervently on behalf of indigenous language and culture. His unflinching support of Welsh issues did not always extend to his compatriots, however, with him proclaiming at one point that they were 'an impotent people/sick with inbreeding/worrying the carcass of an old song'. In the late 1980s and early 1990s he was at the centre of a highly public row when he publicly praised the arsonists who firebombed English-owned holiday homes in Wales. He claimed that English speakers were destroying the country and asked 'What is one death against the death of the whole Welsh nation?' His inflammatory views were picked up by the rock band Manic Street Preachers, who quoted his work on their album *This is My Truth, Tell Me Yours*.

You can follow sites closely associated with Thomas around the Llŷn Peninsula, including the Aberdaron church where he was the local vicar from 1967 to 1978 (p240).

BACKGROUND

Fans of Welsh literature congregate at the Hay Festival of literature and the arts (p92) and the National Eisteddfod of Wales (p296). A full program of readings, events, festivals and spoken-word evenings is organised by **Academi** (www.academi.org), the national society that promotes the writers and literature of Wales.

CINEMA & TELEVISION

The first genuinely Welsh film was Karl Francis' *Above Us the Earth* in 1977. Based on the true story of a colliery closure, it featured an amateur cast in real valley locations. It marked a break from the stereotypes of Welsh life as depicted in early films, such as John Ford's *How Green Was My Valley* (1941), and the tendency to use non-Welsh actors and few, if any, Welsh locations. In recent years, a fledgling film industry has emerged in Wales with a growth in film workshops, a Welsh media agency and BAFTA (British Academy of Film and Television Arts) awards.

One of the most successful recent releases is *The Edge of Love* (2008), the biopic about the life and loves of Dylan Thomas, which stared Keira Knightley, Sienna Miller and Matthew Rhys in the role of Thomas. The film was nominated for awards at Edinburgh Film Festival and the British Independent Spirit Awards. Another cult success is a low-budget documentary about life in a Mid-Wales village. *Sleep Furiously* (2008), described as an elegy for the landscape and population of Trefeurig, Ceredigion, beat a slew of big-budget films to claim the Guardian First Film Award for 2009. The film was directed by Gideon Koppel, who himself was brought up in Trefeurig – where his family sought refuge from Nazi Germany – and was funded by the Film Agency for Wales.

Meanwhile, the Welsh-language TV channel S4C (see p15) has been instrumental in supporting emerging talent and promoting Welsh culture to the outside world. A fantastic success story for S4C was the Welsh-language docudrama *Solomon a Gaenor*, nominated for an Oscar for Best Foreign Language Film in 1999. Another S4C production *Eldra*, a coming-of-age tale about a young Romany girl growing up in a slate-

DON'T MISS...

FILM LOCATIONS

* **Robin Hood (2010)** // For the latest take on the Robin Hood legend, director Ridley Scott and lead man Russell Crowe filmed at Pembrokeshire's Freshwater West.

* **28 Weeks Later (2007)** // For this zombie-horror sequel starring Robert Carlyle, London's Wembley Stadium was, in fact, Cardiff's Millennium Stadium.

* **The Hitchhikers' Guide to the Galaxy (2005)** // Recognise the desolate landscape of the distant planet Vogon? Yes, it's the Trefil Quarry near Tredegar, of course!

* **Die Another Day (2002)** // Pierce Brosnan and Halle Berry in Korea? Err, no. Actually it's Penbryn on the Ceredigion coast.

* **An American Werewolf in London (1981)** // Except the werewolf-haunted village wasn't actually in London. It was Crickadarn, near Builth Wells.

quarrying community in North Wales, won the 2003 Spirit of Moondance award at the Sundance Film Festival.

S4C and BBC Wales have also provided a springboard for small-screen success, challenging preconceptions and fuelling independent production. One BAFTA award-winning production was the hard-hitting documentary *Ar y Stry* (Streetlife), which follows the lives of homeless heroin addicts. More recently the revival of BBC TV series *Doctor Who,* set in Cardiff, and its spin-off series, *Torchwood,* have introduced sci-fi fans to Cardiff as the centre of alien activity. Both are filmed extensively around Cardiff Bay, and *Doctor Who* has won several BAFTAs.

Wales' oldest claim to celluloid fame, however, is not an actor or a film, but a location. The stunning landscape of Snowdonia has provided the backdrop for a slew of films, including *The Inn of the Sixth Happiness* (1958) and, more recently, *Tomb Raider II* (2003). The 1960s TV classic *The Prisoner* was filmed on location around Portmeirion and the original remains far more evocative than the recent American remake. Pembrokeshire, too, has become a film-location hub.

For more information about Welsh film, visit the website of the **Film Agency for Wales** (www.filmagencywales.com).

VISUAL ARTS

Wales was first recognised by the arts world as a fashionable place for landscape painters, particularly at the end of the 18th century, when the French Revolution effectively closed Europe to British artists. The rugged mountains and undulating valleys around Dolgellau made it a popular retreat, while rolling hills inspired artists such as Richard Wilson and, later, Turner, who painted both the Wye Valley and Valle Crucis. Ceri Richards (1903–71), heavily influenced by Matisse, is one of the leading lights of the 20th-century art movement. His work is on permanent view at the Glynn Vivian Art Gallery in Swansea. But best known of all contemporary artists is Sir Kyffin Williams (1918–2006), whose trademark is thickly layered oil on canvas mark. Williams returned to the Welsh landscape for his inspiration and his starkly striking portraits capture perfectly the essence of Welsh life. His work is collected at the Oriel Ynys Môn in Llangefni, Anglesey.

Wales has a long tradition of visual arts and currently has more energy, inspiration and experimentation in this area than at any time in its history. Wales' leading international art prize is the Artes Mundi (Arts of the World) award. The prize brings together outstanding artists from around the world who stimulate thinking about the human condition and humanity. Its aim is to give a platform to contemporary artists who are established in their own countries but have received little critical recognition in the UK. In 2010, Israeli artist Yael Bartana won the 4th Artes Mundi Prize, beating shortlisted artists from Albania, Bulgaria, Kyrgyzstan, Peru, Russia and Taiwan to the £40,000 prize. The prize, one of the UK's biggest arts prizes, is awarded on a biannual basis. The shortlisted entrants are displayed at National Museum Wales in Cardiff.

For more information on art in Wales visit the website of the **Arts Council of Wales** (www.artswales.org.uk).

BACKGROUND

THEATRE & DANCE

Theatre is thriving in Wales with 20 major theatre companies and many smaller community and educational groups. A number of Hollywood stars, including Charlie Chaplin, Christian Bale and Catherine Zeta-Jones, first trod the boards at regional theatres in Wales. Wales' leading English-language professional company is the **Clwyd Theatr Cymru** (www.clwyd-theatr-cymru.co.uk), based in northeast Wales and attracting top-name performers such as Sir Anthony Hopkins, after whom one of the theatre's auditoriums is now named.

Cardiff's acclaimed theatrical organisation, **Sherman Cymru** (www.shermancymru.co.uk), produces a wide range of productions each year, including theatre for young people and inventive adaptations of classic dramas. The highly acclaimed **Music Theatre Wales** (www.musictheatrewales.org.uk), a pioneering force in contemporary opera, has a growing international reputation and tours annually across Europe. Experimental theatre companies include the **Fiction Factory** (www.fictionfactoryfilms.com), geared to original work with a Welsh voice, and **Green Ginger** (www.greenginger.net), which produces absurdist street shows. Dance lovers should look out for **Earthfall** (www.earthfall.org.uk), Wales' leading dance-theatre company and one of the most sought-after companies across Europe.

> *'Charlie Chaplin, Christian Bale and Catherine Zeta-Jones first trod the boards at regional theatres in Wales'*

The highest-profile theatre and dance performances on the Welsh stage are today found at the Wales Millennium Centre in Cardiff Bay; the newly revamped Chapter Arts Centre in Cardiff is an important venue for more fringe events.

For more, visit the website of the **Arts Council of Wales** (www.artswales.org.uk).

ICONS OF WALES

· · · · · · ·

Post devolution and post Cool Cymru, debate in Wales – from the art centres of Cardiff to the back rooms of pubs in Caernarfon – often centres on one theme: identity. What is the identity of Wales in the 21st century? What are the defining elements of Welsh culture? And, while the leek and the daffodil are the national symbols, what are the true icons of Wales?

To be Welsh today is a complex blend of historical association, ingrained defiance and Celtic spirit. For clues, head to the Gwynedd Museum & Art Gallery (p262) in Bangor, where in a dusty upstairs room, a tucked-away exhibition offers a definition. The language is one defining characteristic of Welsh culture. The wonderful, sing-song lilt, littered with an incomprehensible mix of double *l*'s and consecutive consonants, has helped to strengthen Wales' identity as a separate nation to the UK. The devolved Welsh government has doubtless helped this with the insistence on bilingual translation. The mountains, too, play a crucial role, while the mythology of the Welsh dragon is also important. But three icons of contemporary Welsh culture stand out: music, rugby and castles. We explore all three here in turn.

MUSIC

According to a Welsh proverb, 'to be born Welsh is to be born with music in your blood and poetry in your soul'. Tom Jones has it. Duffy has it. And Katherine Jenkins definitely has it when she holds the audience in her hand during *Hen Wlad Fy Nhadau* (Land of My Fathers). And she can sing, too. Hence, Wales is officially known as the land of song. But where does this close association between Wales and music actually originate?

There are references to the Celts as a musical race as early as the 1st century BC when ancient scholars wrote of bards (poets who sing songs of eulogy and satire) and Druids (philosophers or theologians who are held in extreme honour). There are traditional Welsh songs with harp accompaniment from the early 19th century and unaccompanied folks songs that tell a story in the form of verse. The revival of the eisteddfod in the second half of the 19th century brought together four distinct threads of Welsh cultural life, namely the mythology of the bards, the musical tradition, the influence of the chapel, and the social aspect of coming together in song.

'rock music changed the staid image of Wales as a nation of melodious harpists and male voice choirs forever'

Today, the diversity of music in Wales is huge, yet united by a common factor – music remains at the heart of this nation. In just the last few years the Cory Band from the Rhondda Valley has won the European Brass Band Championships. The Green Man Festival held each summer in the Brecon Beacons has managed to combine an environmental conscience and an anticorporate agenda with headline sets by the likes of Billy Bragg and the Flaming Lips. And the Welsh National Opera has gone from strength to strength since launching the career of opera singer Bryn Terfel, plucked from a North Wales sheep farm to become a national champion for the Welsh voice.

BACKGROUND

THE EISTEDDFOD

The eisteddfod (*ey-steth-vot;* plural eisteddfodau, *ey-steth-vuh-dye;* literally a gathering or session), a uniquely Welsh celebration, is the descendant of ancient tournaments in which poets and musicians competed for a seat of honour in the households of noblemen. The first is believed to have been held in 1176 at Rhys ap Gruffydd's castle in Cardigan. Eisteddfodau grew less frequent and less lively following the Tudor Acts of Union in the mid-16th century, but in the late 18th century Edward Williams (better known by his bardic name of Iolo Morganwg) reinvented the eisteddfod as a modern Welsh festival.

The **National Eisteddfod of Wales** (www.eisteddfod.org.uk) was first held in 1861 and has since become Europe's largest cultural shindig. It's a quintessentially Welsh event and has become a barometer of contemporary Welsh culture with aspiring bands and emerging artists often making their debut there. The whole event takes place in Welsh, but larger events are simultaneously translated and there's loads of help on hand for non-Welsh speakers. The festival is held during the first week of August, alternately in North and South Wales.

Each July in Llangollen the **International Musical Eisteddfod** (www.international -eisteddfod.co.uk) kicks off for a week of unrivalled action. Acts from over 40 countries compete with folk tunes, choral harmony and recitals. Competitions take place daily and famous names take to the stage for gala concerts every night.

The third national event is the roving **Urdd National Eisteddfod** (www.urdd.org), a festival of performing and visual arts for children. This is Europe's largest youth festival, and brings together roughly 15,000 performers chosen from all over Wales.

It is traditional folk and the emerging nu-folk that is the keeper of the flame of traditional Welsh music. Catch a live session at local pubs, folk clubs or smaller festivals, and look out for bands such as Hin-Deg, Calenning and Mabsant, which blend traditional and contemporary Welsh sounds with international influences. Welsh folk music even has a permanent home at TŷSiamas (National Centre for Welsh Folk Music; p212) in Dolgellau. Events at the centre are an ideal way to keep abreast of new acts and influences.

But it was rock music that really put Wales on the map. The late 1990s marked the high tide of the Cool Cymru movement with a series of Welsh groups, including Manic Street Preachers, Catatonia and Super Furry Animals, making headlines for their innovative sounds, clever lyrics, rabble-rousing rock sound and poignant ballads packed with pathos. They changed the staid image of Wales as a nation of melodious harpists and male voice choirs forever.

Today, the Welsh music scene may not be as hyped as it once was, but its true substance has come to the fore with an important network of artists, labels and agencies. Pop has a new star in the multi-award-winning singer Duffy, who released the album *Rockferry* to global and critical acclaim, and won a Grammy award in 2009. If you visit Wales in the spring, look out for the Duffydil, a specially grown variant of the daffodil named in her honour. The Welsh metal scene, meanwhile, has Bullet For My Valentine, a group who regularly headline metal festivals around the world, and Funeral for a Friend, who can often be found gracing the metal stage at the Reading Festival.

There is even a Welsh hip-hop scene, thanks in part to the rise of comic rappers Goldie Lookin' Chain from Newport. Those with a more sophisticated hip-hop style should take a look at Akira the Don, the political and electronic rapper from Anglesey, who is signed to the same label as Eminem and 50 Cent.

For more, see www.walesonline.co.uk/showbiz-and-lifestyle/music-in-wales.

RUGBY & SPORT

The Welsh and rugby go hand in hand. Wales is known as one of the world's biggest exponents of the sport, hosting the rugby union World Cup in 1999. The national side has recently restored Welsh pride after a lengthy period spent in the wilderness, culminating in grand-slam successes at the 2005 and 2008 Six Nations tournaments. Tickets for international matches are guaranteed to sell out, while recent success on the pitch has elevated the team's star players, such as Shane Williams, Stephen Jones and Gethin Jenkins, into national sporting heroes. Fans of the Welsh national team are known for their fanatical support and are famous for their vocal backing of the team. The national rugby (and football) teams play their home fixtures at Cardiff's Millennium Stadium (p47), which has become the iconic home for Welsh sport.

Rugby union is equally well supported at club level, with four teams representing different regions of South Wales. The Cardiff Blues, Newport Gwent Dragons, Scarlets (Llanelli) and Ospreys (Swansea) compete in the Magners League, against teams from Scotland, Ireland and Italy. Ospreys' championship victory in 2007 represents the last time a Welsh side won the competition, but they, along with the Cardiff Blues, have been among the league's most competitive teams in recent years. The 15-man 'union' variety of the sport has proved the most popular variant, but its alternative 13-man rugby league counterpart has enjoyed the biggest resurgence in Wales since the founding of the Wrexham-based Crusaders in 2005. The rugby season takes place between September and Easter; more information from the **Welsh Rugby Union** (www.wru.co.uk) website.

MALE VOICE CHOIRS

Born out of the Temperance Movement in the mid-19th century, the male voice choir *(cor meibion)* became an institution in the coal-mining towns of the southern valleys. With the collapse of the former coal-mining communities, the choirs struggled to keep numbers up and some even allowed women to join their ranks.

But they have enjoyed a renaissance of late with younger people signing up to their local choir to flex their vocal chords. The latest incarnation made their name as winners of a BBC TV reality show, *Last Choir Standing*. Only Men Aloud!, an 18-strong Cardiff-based choir of part-timers, beat off stiff competition from fellow Welsh finalists, Ysgol Glanaethwy from Bangor, to take the title. They went on to sign a multi-million-pound, five-record contract and record an album.

Local choirs still practise in the back rooms of pubs and church halls each week. Most are happy to have visitors sit in on rehearsals. One of the best can be found each Monday evening at the Greyhound Hotel in Builth Wells (p190).

While the rugby team has enjoyed something of a purple patch in recent years, Wales' national football (soccer) team have endured mixed fortunes. The so-called Dragons narrowly missed out on qualification to the Euro 2004 tournament, a blow the squad struggled to recover from over the following years. However, a new crop of promising young players, mentored by captain and fan favourite Craig Bellamy, has given fresh optimism to football supporters hoping to see Wales take part in their first international tournament in over 50 years. Wales can also take pride in producing one of the finest footballers of the last 20 years, with Ryan Giggs holding a number of Premier League records and having the honour of being the most decorated player in English footballing history.

The top two clubs of the **Welsh Premier League** (www.welsh-premier.com), Cardiff City and Swansea City, are also enjoying equally promising times and their best seasons in years. Both the Bluebirds and the Swans (as they are respectively known) have recently moved to newly built stadiums and have aspirations of becoming a force in the Premier League. The **League of Wales** (www.welshleague.org.uk), meanwhile, is the home of regional football across the country, with both professional and semi-professional clubs competing to be crowned the champions of Wales. The league, undergoing a revamp for the 2010/11 season, brings an excellent standard of football to clubs across the country, and gives Welsh teams an opportunity to qualify for high-profile European competitions. Bangor City has developed a reputation as a cup team, winning the Welsh Cup three times in the last decade.

The importance of sport to the people of Wales has led to a great number of athletes enjoying success on an individual basis. Joe Calzaghe's domination in the boxing ring – he retired in 2009 as an undefeated super middleweight boxing champion of the world – led to him becoming (in 2007) the first Welshman to win the coveted BBC Sports Personality of the Year in over 40 years. His stint on the popular TV dancing show, *Strictly Come Dancing,* was a less glorious affair. Still, Calzaghe's legacy has led to a new batch of young Welsh boxers striving to follow in his footsteps, most notably Nathan Cleverly, the current European light-heavyweight champion. With the 2012

BACKGROUND

MORE SPORTING FIRSTS

While the winter sports of rugby and football (soccer) are widely regarded as the country's most popular games, cricket fills the void left in many Welsh sports fans' calendars during the summer months. Glamorgan County Cricket Club is Wales' county team, playing the majority of their home matches at Cardiff's SWALEC Stadium. The venue was also chosen as one of the five venues to host matches for the England cricket side's winning 2009 Ashes series. The decision was a coup for Welsh cricket, paving the way for further Ashes matches in Cardiff; more from www.glamorgancricket.com.

Golf, too, has fixed the eyes of the sporting world on Wales with the 2010 Ryder Cup held at the Celtic Manor resort in Newport. The 28th biennial competition brought the cream of the golfing fraternity to South Wales, as Colin Montgomerie's European team battled to wrestle the cup back from the USA. It is hoped that top Welsh golfers, such as Ian Woosnam, will play an active part in boosting the profile of Welsh golf following the success of the tournament.

London Olympics looming large, Wales' top sportsmen and women will be hoping to bring home the medals in what is sure to be a successful games. Cyclists Nicole Cooke and Geraint Thomas, swimmer David Davies and rower Tom James will be hoping to match their gold medal exploits from the Beijing games, while a generation of promising young athletes from Wales look set to emulate their success.

More on Welsh sport from www.walesonline.co.uk/sports.

CASTLES & ARCHITECTURE

Castles are Wales' most famous historical and architectural attraction and the country is covered with them – 'The magnificent badge of our subjection', as the writer Thomas Pennant put it. They are a living-history statement on Wales' past and a symbol of its complex social heritage. The most impressive castles are those built by Edward I in North Wales. Among them, Caernarfon Castle (p233), built between 1283 and 1330, has retained all of its original strength and beauty, and Harlech Castle (p218) is a great example of a perfectly concentric castle, whereby one line of defence is enclosed by another. Conwy Castle (p264) is considered to be one of the greatest fortresses of medieval Europe, and the medieval city walls are among the most complete in the world.

Cardiff, meanwhile, boasts two rather different castles. Cardiff Castle (p42) holds medieval-style events throughout the year, and Castell Coch (p63), designed by William Burges, is a Victorian dandy with a love-it-or-hate-it repro-Gothic motif. It is often referred to as a romantic folly as the interiors of the castle are wonderfully ornate.

The equivalent of the National Trust in Wales is **Cadw** (www.cadw.wales.org.uk), the division within the National Assembly government charged with the protection, conservation and promotion of the historic environment.

Apart from castles, Welsh architecture is most commonly associated with the country's industrial heritage and its contemporary, post-millennium transformation. Among the former, Blaenavon's ironworks, quarries and workers' houses (p105) received Unesco World Heritage status at the turn of the millennium. And the town was

BACKGROUND

DON'T MISS...

A CASTLE FOR EVERY OCCASION

- ★ **Carreg Cennen Castle** // For breathtaking, year-round views. This limestone crag rises majestically above the rolling hills of Carmarthenshire (p115).

- ★ **Powis Castle** // For stunning, flower-strewn gardens. This mecca for horticulture fans boasts Italianate terraces, herbaceous borders and exotic plants (p199).

- ★ **Bodelwyddan Castle** // For spooks and ghouls. Shadowy figures haunt the castle, gardens and even the tearooms (www.bodelwyddan-castle.co.uk).

- ★ **Beaumaris Castle** // For fiendish fun. This 13th-century castle has the last word in castle defences: murder holes to drop boiling oil on attackers – ouch (p254)!

- ★ **Caerphilly Castle** // For a family day out. Britain's largest medieval fortress runs a huge program of family events, including the annual Big Cheese festival (p64).

recently joined on the Unesco World Heritage list by the Pontcysyllte Aqueduct in Llangollen (p275).

Isolated from the fickle fashions of urban England, much of rural Wales developed regionally distinctive building forms. These used locally available materials to create buildings that answered local needs. They are best exhibited in the rural cottages and farms that vary from county to county (and in some cases from village to village). Look out for locally distinctive traditions such as slate roofs grouted with cement washes in Pembrokeshire, ancient oak-framed buildings in Montgomeryshire, and humble earth-walled thatched cottages in Ceredigion and Carmarthenshire.

For a taste of modern architecture, there are numerous new and exciting buildings to explore. The Senedd (p49), the National Assembly debating chamber in Cardiff Bay completed in 2005 by the Richard Rogers Partnership, is a stunning mix of slate and Welsh Oak, designed with the ideas of openness and transparency in mind – hence the prevalence of glass in the design. Also in Cardiff, the Millennium Stadium (p47), built in 1999 to a striking architectural design of stacked Welsh slate topped with a bronzed-steel shell, holds global sporting events and huge pop concerts. During the 2012 Olympics it will be hosting some of the big football matches. Outside the capital, Sir Norman Foster's Great Glasshouse at the National Botanic Garden of Wales (p132) embodies simple beauty – and was even used as a location for *Doctor Who*. Praise indeed!

> '*Castles are a living-history statement on Wales' past and a symbol of its complex social heritage*'

Most recently, 12 of the nation's newest buildings were shortlisted for an internationally renowned award, affirming Wales as a home of world-class architecture. Projects like Hafod Eryri (p226) on the summit of Snowdon, the grass-roofed Oriel y Parc (p160) in St Davids, and Cardiff's landmark library in the Hayes have all been praised for the quality of their design and their contribution to the local environment by the Royal Institute of British Architects (RIBA). The latest winners of the award will join the likes of the Ruthin Craft Centre (p278) in Denbighshire and Penderyn Distillery (p102) in Brecon as part of an elite list of buildings across the UK and Europe to be given top recognition. Unusually, two of the buildings on the 2010 list were private homes, both designed by Hyde + Hyde Architects, a relatively new firm with offices in Cardiff and Swansea.

OUTDOOR ACTIVITIES

· · · · · · ·

Looking for the great outdoors? Simple. Head for Wales. There are elements of beauty in every nook and cranny of its changeable landscape, and the terrain lends itself to all manner of activities, from relaxing to rigorous. Wales really packs a lot into a small space. The landscape is stunning, access is easy and there's always a cosy pub with a warm fire nearby when you need to dry out – and you will.

But remember: the great Welsh outdoors is not only about active options or adrenalin thrills. One of the greatest joys of a trip to Wales is exploring the pristine beaches. From secluded coves for soul-searchers to expanses of sand for wannabe castle architects, there's a beach for everyone along Wales' 750-mile coastline. The Marine Conservation Society's **Good Beach Guide** (www.goodbeachguide.co.uk) sets the UK's highest benchmark for bathing-water quality, only recommending beaches with an excellent rating. In 2010, over 80 beaches across Wales made the grade; more than half of them were also accorded prestigious Blue Flag status, highlighting their place among the best in the world. Pembrokeshire boasts the highest number of Blue Flag beaches, with 13, followed by the Isle of Anglesey with seven.

Whatever your plans, start with a look at www.adventure.visitwales.com.

WALKING

Whether you're an ambler or a rambler, Wales is a walker's dream. There are some 25,500 miles of footpaths, bridleways and byways – all public rights of way – granting walkers access to the Welsh countryside. But be aware: the red flags deter the public from using rights of way crossing land owned by the Ministry of Defence during manoeuvres or firing exercises, and in the interests of preservation access to national parks and other protected areas is limited to designated walking trails.

For challenging walks, head for Snowdonia National Park, home to the highest mountain in England and Wales, impressive peaks and dramatic valleys, or for the craggy terrain of the Brecon Beacons, where, in the western end of the park, you can walk for days in total isolation. Outside the national parks there are many trails and paths across myriad surfaces and landscapes.

One of the growing activities for walkers is geocaching, a kind of treasure hunt with the advantages of satellite navigation GPS units, combined with all the resources of the internet. There are now some 4000 geocaches in Wales and it's a free activity; for more information visit www.geocachingwales.com.

BACKGROUND

FIVE OF THE BEST COASTAL PATHS

★ Carmarthen Bay Coastal & Estuaries Way: 55 miles, Amroth to Gower

★ Ceredigion Coastal Path: 70 miles, Ynyslas to Cardigan

★ Glamorgan Heritage Coast Path: 14 miles, Newton Burrows to Gileston

★ Llŷn Coastal Path: 95 miles, Caernarfon to Porthmadog

★ Pembrokeshire Coast Path National Trail: 186 miles, Poppit Sands to Amroth

Walking can be enjoyed year-round, but be prepared for crowds in July and August, short days in winter and rain at any time. Guard against the fickle Welsh weather with decent, warm clothing, footwear and waterproofs, even on short walks. A map, compass, first-aid kit, food and water are musts for more adventurous hikes. It's advisable to let someone know your intended route and planned return time and to check the weather forecast with the **Met Office** (www.metoffice.gov.uk/loutdoor/mountainsafety) or the local tourist information centre before setting off.

For more information, visit www.walking.visitwales.com; the Events section includes details of numerous walking festivals taking place throughout Wales, generally between June and October.

CYCLING

Cyclists in Wales are thoroughly spoiled with official trails, traffic-free routes and quiet back roads taking them ever closer to the breathtaking landscapes. Indeed, the traffic-free section of the **National Cycle Network** (NCN; www.sustrans.org.uk) North Wales Coastal Route (5), running along the seaside promenade from Colwyn Bay to Prestatyn, is said to be one of the best in the UK for cyclists of all abilities.

Take your own bike or rent one from many outlets across the country. Be aware it's best to stick to tracks marked as bridleways on Ordnance Survey maps and cycling lanes (sandy-red sections of pavement stamped with the bicycle motif). Avoid footpaths that haven't been split to incorporate cycling lanes. With the exception of July and August when tourism peaks, the unnumbered roads and lanes are quiet and supremely cyclist friendly.

For mountain biking, Wales offers some of the best facilities in the world – it boasts no less than six purpose-built centres throughout the country. The centres offer a mix-

---

BACKGROUND

CYCLING IN WALES

Two of Wales' most popular long-distance rides come under the auspices of the **National Cycle Network** (NCN; www.sustrans.org.uk), a charity that coordinates over 12,000 miles of cycling and walking paths throughout the UK:

Lôn Las Cymru (Greenways of Wales/Welsh National Route; NCN routes 8 and 42) The more demanding of the two. The 254-mile route runs from Holyhead, through to Hay-on-Wye, then on to Cardiff via Brecon or Chepstow via Abergavenny. Encompassing three mountain ranges – Snowdonia, the Brecon Beacons and the Cambrian Mountains – there's a fair amount of uphill, low-gear huffing and puffing to endure along the way. That said, each peak promises fantastic views and plenty of downhill, free-wheeling delights.

Lôn Geltaidd (Celtic Trail; NCN routes 4 and 47) A 337-mile route snaking from Fishguard through the West Wales hills, the Pembrokeshire Coast, the former coalfields of South Wales and ending at Chepstow Castle. The glorious, ever-changing landscape provides a superb backdrop.

Choose to tackle the routes in their entirety, or pick and mix parts in tandem with your pedalling power and scenery wish list. Both routes incorporate sections of traffic-free cycling and circular rides of varying length and physical demand. End points are linked with the rail network so you can make your way back to the start by train.

FIVE OF THE BEST REGIONAL ROUTES

- ★ Cambrian Way: 275 miles, Cardiff to Conwy
- ★ Dyfi Valley Way: 108 miles, Aberdyfi to Borth
- ★ Taff Trail (p39): 68 miles, Brecon to Cardiff
- ★ Usk Valley Walk: 48 miles, Newport to Brecon
- ★ Wye Valley Walk (p73): 136 miles, Chepstow to Plylimon, Hafren Forest

ture of routes to suit all abilities, and all have one trail designed especially for families. Coed-y-Brenin Forest Park near Dolgellau is the premier centre, boasting the rockiest, most technically advanced trails and a dual slalom course.

For more information, check out www.cycling.visitwales.com. For a description of each of the six mountain-biking centres and an overview of the top mountain-bike bases around Wales, see www.mbwales.com.

WATER SPORTS

Whether you want to tour along glassy inland lakes and rivers, surf or paddle on sheltered bays, or take a thrilling ride down a white-water river, you'll find somewhere in Wales just waiting to be discovered. Most paddle sports are easy to pick up, and centres across the country have lessons for beginners and improvers alike, many of which can be combined with weekend breaks.

For canoeing and sea kayaking, head to Pembrokeshire or Anglesey to explore coves and sea caves while paddling the flat waters below the towering cliffs. Inland, Llyn Tegid (Bala Lake) and Llyn Gwynant in North Wales are worth exploring, while slow-moving rivers include the Teifi, near Cardigan, and North Wales' River Dee. Powerful tidal currents create huge standing waves between the Pembrokeshire coast and off-shore islands, making this national park (the only coastal park in Britain), one of the UK's finest sea-kayaking areas. Freshwater Bay, featured in the final Harry Potter film and the 2010 version of *Robin Hood,* and Newgale beach are favourite kayaking spots. The **Welsh Canoeing Association** (www.canoewales.com/paddling-in-wales.aspx) lists the waterways that permit kayaking and canoeing.

An incredible variety of sea life and a seabed littered with shipwrecks make diving in Wales an exciting prospect. Pembrokeshire, again, is the diving hot spot, and is the access point for the Smalls, a group of rocks famous for marine life, including a large colony of seals and pods of dolphins. Visibility here can reach up to 25m, although diving is restricted by the weather and tides. In North Wales, plump for Bardsey Island, the Skerries or the Menai Straits. Be aware that tidal currents rage dangerously at many of Wales' best dive sites, so always seek advice locally before taking the plunge. For a list of diving schools and operators, see www.visitwales.co.uk/things-to-do-in-wales/active-outdoor-activities-sports-and-adventure/diving-in-wales.

Surrounded by sea on three sides and netting some of the highest tidal ranges in the world – the Severn Estuary has the second-biggest tidal range anywhere – Wales has no shortage of surfing opportunities. Popular beaches can become crowded between

BACKGROUND

April and September but with a little effort, you're sure to find your own space. Sea temperatures are often warmer than you might imagine thanks to the North Atlantic Drift, but you'll always need a wetsuit, and possibly boots, a hood and gloves in winter.

The Gower Peninsula is home to the Welsh surfing industry, cramming in a wide choice of breaks and plenty of postsurf activity. Hot spots include Caswell Bay, the Mumbles, Langland Bay, Oxwich Bay and Llangennith. The best breaks in Pembrokeshire are to be found at Tenby South Beach, Manorbier, Freshwater West and West Dale Bay. St Davids' immense Whitesands Bay is good for beginners, although it's often busy. You'll find surf schools at most surf beaches. For more information, check the **Welsh Surfing Federation Surf School** (www.wsfsurfschool.co.uk) website.

There's great potential for windsurfing all around Wales' coast and on many inland lakes. Many surf beaches are also suitable for windsurfing and have gear hire and lessons available. Rhosneigr, on the Isle of Anglesey, is particularly growing as a centre for windsurfing and other water sports. Check out www.ukwindsurfing.com.

Belying Wales' substantial rainfall and mountainous terrain, opportunities for white-water rafting are limited. One of the few Welsh rivers with big and fairly predictable summertime white water (grade three to four) is the dam-released Tryweryn near Bala. Moderate rapids (grade two to four) are found on the River Usk and between Corwen and Llangollen on the River Dee.

For more information about water sports, visit www.waleswatersports.co.uk.

OTHER ACTIVITIES

According to the Cambrian Cave Registry's Database of the Caves of Wales, the country offers some 1400 caves, and hence can accommodate cavers at every level. South Wales harbours the largest cave area, stretching from Crickhowell to Carreg Cennen Castle. Caves are also found in North Wales, on the Gower Peninsula and in Pembrokeshire. Highlights for the more experienced caver include the UK's second-longest cave, Ogof Draenen, and the deepest, Ogof Ffynnon Ddu. Porth-yr-Ogof in the Brecon Beacons and Paviland Cave on the Gower Peninsula are better suited to beginners. For more information, contact the **British Caving Association** (www.british-caving.org.uk).

Wales also has some of the best climbing sites in the UK. There's a peak in Snowdonia or a cliff on the coast tailored to your requirements, whether you're an accomplished climber or a nervous novice. It's hardest to get a foothold during summer when rock faces are particularly crowded. In winter, ice-climbing is popular in Snowdonia. But climbing isn't a walk in the park. Equip yourself for emergencies, check the **Met Office** (www.metoffice.gov.uk/loutdoor/mountainsafety) weather forecast and seek advice from local climbing shops, climbers' cafes and tourist-information points before making your ascent.

To get a feel for the rock face, have a trial climb at the ProAdventure Activity Centre in Llangollen (p276) or sign up for a course at the Plas y Brenin National Mountain Centre (p226) in Capel Curig. For more information, contact the **British Mountaineering Council** (www.thebmc.co.uk).

Wales' abundant rivers and lakes, long and winding coastline, and numerous fisheries offer many opportunities for game, sea and coarse fishing. Many types of species are found in waters in and around Wales: brown trout are among the catches on the

Rivers Usk, Teifi, Wye, Dee, Seiont and Taff in spring. Reel in Welsh shy sewin (sea trout) on the banks of the River Towy, Teifi, Rheidol, Dyfi, Mawddach and Conwy in spring and summer. Chances of salmon improve in autumn in the River Usk. During the winter months, catch grayling in the Rivers Wye, Dee and upper Severn.

To angle for sea fish, you don't necessarily need to charter a boat; cast off from any number of spots along the rocky coastline. For advice on likely catches at various locations throughout the year and a comprehensive list of fisheries, see the **Environment Agency** (www.environment–agency.gov.uk/fish) website. This is your first port of call for information on important fishing regulations too, such as how to obtain a fishing licence. For more information on fishing in Wales, visit www.fishing.visitwales.com.

Wales has much to offer the equestrian set, too, thanks to its mix of sandy beaches, rolling hills and dense forest. The horseback vantage point is best exploited in Mid-Wales and the national parks. Riding schools catering for all levels of proficiency are found throughout the country. You can hire a horse or bring your own steed (guest horses are offered B&B at some riding centres); check out www.ridingwales.com.

But the biggest growth activity in Wales is golf. In October 2010, the 38th Ryder Cup teed off at Newport's Celtic Manor Resort – the historic occasion marked the first time the competition has been played in Wales. The Ryder Cup is a team-based golf contest fought out between top American and European players, with golfers playing in pairs to what is known as 'match-pay rules'. The golf resort's Twenty Ten Course was built exclusively for the competition and the event has left a huge legacy for Wales, both in terms of golfing facilities and the wider regeneration of the Newport area, plus countless new academies, clubs and training facilities to encourage young people to try golf.

Today, Wales is one of few countries in the world whose golf courses (200 of them) can be categorised under the headings links, moorland, mountain, parkland and woodland. Choices for professional players include Royal Porthcawl and Royal St David's. For a less testing round, try Cradoc in the picturesque Brecon Beacons, Cardigan's clifftop course, or the windswept Nefyn & District course on the Llŷn Peninsula. For more information, see www.golfasitshouldbe.com.

DON'T MISS...

TOP PLACES TO PLAY A ROUND

- ★ **West Monmouthshire Golf Club** // The highest golf course in Britain as recognised by the Guinness Book of Records.

- ★ **Llanymynech Golf Club** // Has 15 holes in Wales and three in England. On the fourth, tee off in Wales, putt in England and return to Wales three holes later.

- ★ **Machynys Peninsula Golf & Country Club** // Designed by Gary Nicklaus, son of golf legend Jack.

- ★ **Dewstow Golf Club** // The Park Course has the UK's only par 6 hole – a monster 690yd.

- ★ **Tenby** // Wales' oldest golf club – established in 1888.

THE NATURAL ENVIRONMENT

They say that good things come in small parcels. Well, perhaps that's an apt idiom for Wales, which boasts one marine nature reserve, more than 60 nature reserves, no less than 1000 SSSIs (Sites of Special Scientific Interest) and at least six additional categories of protected land. No other country in Europe is as densely packed with nature conservation sites.

Beneath the impressive packaging of craggy peaks, rugged coastlines and patchwork fields, Wales' natural environment is simply a gift that keeps on giving. The Welsh people are fiercely protective of the historic, cultural and economic treasures that adorn the diverse Welsh landscape. Thankfully, the National Assembly is now equally passionate about the country's sustainable development, and has written into the statute books that they have 'a statutory duty [to have due regard to sustainable development in all their work] and have to report on it annually'.

> *'Welsh people are fiercely protective of the historic, cultural and economic treasures that adorn the landscape'*

Such ecofriendly attitudes predate contemporary environmental awareness, however. This visionary zeal for greener lifestyles can be traced back many centuries to the era of St David (p283) himself. The patron saint of Wales had great respect for nature and relied on the land for his simple, healthy diet. He taught his followers the importance of living in harmony with the natural environment. More recently, the Centre for Alternative Technology (CAT; p203) in Machynlleth, Mid-Wales, has become the epicentre of the environmental movement in Wales. Founded in 1974 to test alternative technologies, the centre has gone from strength to strength as an ecologically driven laboratory and information resource. It recently unveiled the new Wales Institute for Sustainable Education (WISE), a major new centre of green learning to bolster its already impressive array of courses.

GEOLOGY

Wales can claim one of the richest and most diverse geological heritages in the world; and it is geology, more than anything else, that has helped shape the destiny of Wales in modern times. Since the 17th century, geologists have pondered the mysteries of Wales' rippled rocks, puzzling fossils and ice-moulded valleys. In contrast with Wales' relatively young evolutionary age of just 200 million years, some of the oldest rocks in the world lie exposed at St Davids Head on the Pembrokeshire coast. The fossilised marine life augmenting Snowdon's summit reveals the area's underwater history. Snowdonia's peaks and valleys are remnants of a continental collision that occurred some 520 million years ago, swallowing the ancient Iapetus Ocean that divided Britain. Before melting away into dark, dramatic lakes such as Llyn Ldwal near Capel Curig, the Ice Age chiselled steep slopes into the valleys.

BACKGROUND

The flat-topped Brecon Beacons in South Wales are the product of extreme, rock-shattering temperatures. The mountains were eroded to form the red-sandstone moorland and the porous limestone cliffs were perforated with waterfalls, creating massive cave systems. Rich deposits of coal south of the Brecon Beacons and the slate mountains of Snowdonia altered the face of Wales, sparking an industrial revolution that attracted hordes of fortune-hungry workers.

But the natural wonder of Wales is not solely related to geological history. Two of the world's 64 geoparks, scenic locations of special geoscientific significance, are today found in Wales. For a more contemporary take on natural beauty, visit Fforest Fawr (p88) in the western half of the Brecon Beacons National Park or Geo Môn in Anglesey.

FAUNA

Offering opportunities for unexpected encounters, Wales is less of a wonderland and more of a wild card when it comes to wildlife. Atlantic grey seals headline the fascinating coastal wildlife, delivering around 1000 fluffy white pups on southwest Wales' Pembrokeshire shore in late September and early October. Twitchers, meanwhile, head for Pembrokeshire's offshore islands (p155), a haven for seabirds from April to mid-August. Grassholm Island, in particular, has one of the world's largest gannet colonies, with 34,000 pairs nesting there during breeding season (April to September). Colonies of guillemots, razorbills, storm petrels, kittiwakes and puffins crowd the rock faces of Skomer and Skokholm Islands. Nearby Ramsey Island plays host to 30% of the world's Manx shearwater population and, together with Bardsey Island, boasts a few pairs of rare choughs. The biggest success story for wildlife fans in recent years has been the reintroduction of red kites to the southern Cambrian Mountains of Mid-Wales (see p308).

Elsewhere, otters are re-establishing themselves along the River Teifi and in the border area of northern Powys, but salmon, sea trout and brown trout populations are diminishing. Pine martens and polecats – staples of Welsh wildlife – are found almost everywhere.

BACKGROUND

DON'T MISS...

NATURAL WONDERS

★ **Dan-yr-Ogof //** A wonderland of stalactites, stalagmites and secret chambers that forms part of a 10-mile complex of caves (p103).

★ **Porthcawl //** The dune system on the Glamorgan coast is the largest in Europe, rising to a height of over 61m.

★ **Llyn Tegid (Bala Lake) //** Home to the elusive *qwynaid,* a unique species of fish that was trapped under the lake's tranquil waters after the last ice age (p220).

★ **St Cadoc's Church //** This Abergavenny church is home to large communities of lesser horseshoe bats between March and October.

★ **Dee Valley //** Marvel at the power of the white-water rapids thundering through the Dee Valley near Llangollen (p272).

RED KITE COUNTRY

Doggedly fighting its way back from the verge of extinction, the majestic red kite (*Milvus milvus*) is now a common sight in Mid-Wales. This aerobatic bird with its 2m-long wing-span was once common across the UK and was even afforded royal protection in the Middle Ages. However, in the 16th century it was declared vermin and mercilessly hunted until only a few pairs remained.

The red kites owe their reprieve in part to a 100-year-long campaign in the Tywi and Cothi Valleys of Mid-Wales, the longest-running protection scheme for any bird in the world. Despite persistent threats from egg-hunters and poison intended for crows and foxes, more than 300 pairs of red kites navigate the Welsh sky.

An ecotourism initiative, the Kite Country Project was launched in 1994 to encourage visitors to see the red kite in action without disturbing or endangering the species. It runs five designated information points throughout Mid-Wales, where visitors can watch kites being fed at close range.

More information from the **Welsh Kite Trust** (www.welshkitetrust.org).

FLORA

Following years of industrialisation, just 12% of the Welsh countryside remains covered by woodland, characterised mostly by non-native Sitka spruce, a fast-growing crop shirked by most wildlife. For an impression of how the Welsh landscape looked before indigenous oak forests gave way to agriculture, shipbuilding, charcoal burning and mining, visit one of the five sites managed by Forestry Commission Wales, such as the Coed y Brenin Visitor Centre near Dolgellau (p216). Erosion caused by cultivation and overgrazing has damaged habitats and prevented native species from rooting and reseeding. Native ash is the exception, and it's especially common along rivers and in woods on the Gower Peninsula and in Brecon Beacons; several types of orchid flower in its shade, together with common dog violets, from March to May.

Away from grazing animals, alpine-arctic plants breed in mountainous regions, although hikers and climbers can cause irreparable damage to purple saxifrage and moss campion nestling between the rocks on higher slopes. Rare cotton grass sprouts from inland bogs and soggy peat lands in midsummer, among bog pimpernel and thriving myrtle. Butterworth, one of Britain's few insectivorous plants, traps insects in wet grassland at Cwm Cadlan near Penderyn, in southwest Wales. Evening primrose, sea bindweed and marram grass may be spotted on the coast between the sand dunes. Thrift and samphire grace the Gower Peninsula.

PROTECTED SPECIES

Animals once on the endangered list, such as bottlenose dolphins, Risso's dolphins, minke whales and lesser horseshoe bats are no longer officially endangered per se, but they each are subject to a National Biodiversity Action Plan. Indeed, one of only two semi-resident bottlenose dolphin populations in the UK can today be found in Cardigan Bay near Aberystwyth. Sightings occur all year round, although numbers

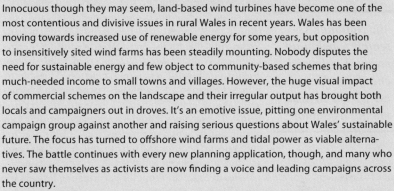

ALTERNATIVE ENERGY

Innocuous though they may seem, land-based wind turbines have become one of the most contentious and divisive issues in rural Wales in recent years. Wales has been moving towards increased use of renewable energy for some years, but opposition to insensitively sited wind farms has been steadily mounting. Nobody disputes the need for sustainable energy and few object to community-based schemes that bring much-needed income to small towns and villages. However, the huge visual impact of commercial schemes on the landscape and their irregular output has brought both locals and campaigners out in droves. It's an emotive issue, pitting one environmental campaign group against another and raising serious questions about Wales' sustainable future. The focus has turned to offshore wind farms and tidal power as viable alternatives. The battle continues with every new planning application, though, and many who never saw themselves as activists are now finding a voice and leading campaigns across the country.

More recently, controversy has surrounded the proposal to build the UK's next nuclear power plant on Anglesey by 2020. Wylfa, the existing nuclear plant on the island, was decommissioned in December 2010. Wylfa Mark II would be one of the first of the new generation of new-build nuclear power stations, but the UK government still needs to give its permission before work can actually start.

The island's council estimates that the development could bring £8 billion into the local economy. But environmental NGO Greenpeace maintains that nuclear power is 'eye-wateringly expensive' and there is 'no solution to dealing with nuclear waste'.

increase throughout the summer, peaking in late September and October. Common and Risso's dolphins are found further out to sea, along with minke whales.

A vestige of the last ice age, the Snowdon lily has survived on the slopes of Snowdon for over 10,000 years, yet warmer climates and overgrazing have drastically reduced its number. It could be mistaken for a grass before its white flowers emerge between May and mid-June. Also on the critical list is the distinctive shrub Ley's whitebeam, which flowers in late May and early June in the Taff Valley. The fen orchid, rare throughout Europe, is protected in the Kenfig National Nature Reserve near Port Talbot.

NEW ENVIRONMENTAL CHALLENGES

When it comes to environmental issues, Wales is determined to infuse the world with the green glow of envy. But environmental focus may be sharper in Wales in part because Wales' crucial tourism industry is so closely associated with the country's natural environment. Dogged in this endeavour, the National Assembly sought and received independence from the rest of the UK on environmental legislation.

The 'One Wales: One Planet' manifesto lays down challenges to be achieved by 2025, among them a minimum 80% reduction in carbon-based energy reliance and an electricity supply derived entirely from renewable sources. Bolstering its ambition to eliminate waste production by 2050, Wales already recycles and composts more than 40% of its rubbish.

BACKGROUND

The current threats to the countryside are largely rooted in agricultural practice. The curse of having the highest density of sheep in the EU has proven to be a major source of overgrazing and soil erosion. Pesticide, slurry and silage residues have contaminated waters and a decline in the number of full-time farmers is endangering Welsh rural life. Increasingly, farmers consider the protection of Wales' image as a clean, green, rural idyll preferable to traditional agricultural practices. This shift in mindset began in 1999 with agri-environment schemes and was accelerated by the 2001 foot-and-mouth epidemic. The schemes remunerate farmers who adopt environmentally sensitive practices, respect historical and cultural land features and offer the public greater countryside access. When existing schemes are replaced with the Glastir New Sustainable Land Management Scheme for Wales in 2012, the remit for participating farmers will extend to tackling climate change. Glastir incorporates a tree-planting program aimed at expanding woodland by 1000 sq km in 20 years. It will also firm up commitments to soil quality and the management of biodiversity, soil carbon and water.

> 'the National Assembly sought and received independence from the rest of the UK on environmental legislation'

BACKGROUND

MYTHS & LEGENDS

· · · · · ·

Wales inspires legends and mythology. The lyrical nature of the language, the era-spanning history and, most of all, the fairytale landscape all help to shape a full cast of characters. Of these, the grand peaks, wild passes, ancient cairns, cromlechs (burial chambers), menhirs (standing stones), ruined fortresses and ancient abbeys are often the leading men. The mysteries surrounding these natural features have been embellished by generations of storytellers, musicians and poets into folk tales, and been relied upon to enrich the lives of the nation's many close-knit communities. Today, these tales form the centrepiece of eisteddfodau (p296), the modern-day celebration of Welsh literature and culture.

But it's not just the landscape that makes people tell tales; the country's dramatic history evoked stories of giants, saints, fairies, kings, mythological beasts and supernatural events. From the times of the Celts and their Druid priests to Roman occupation and Saxon struggles, to the arrival of Christianity in the 5th and 6th centuries AD, professional storytellers had reams of material with which to entertain their god-and-death-fearing, oft-invaded, sometime-suppressed and just occasionally victorious audience. During the 9th century, *Historia Brittonum,* the first collection of folk legends, emerged. Nennius, thought to be a monk from Bangor, compiled the collection of folk tales, featuring mysterious lakes, stones and the ever-present, heroic King Arthur.

Few of the popular Welsh stories, however, were written down by Welsh speakers in their own language; hence many of these tales, derived from myths of the Celtic gods, were lost or adapted to fit other cultures. Two remarkable 14th-century compendiums contain the few stories that have survived: *The White Book of Rhydderch* and *The Red Book of Hergest.* By the 15th century, with the addition of specifically Welsh heroes to the cast of characters – seen as leading the resistance against the English conquerors – the source material was richer than ever. The translation of these books from Welsh into English, the *Mabinogion (Tales of Hero's Youth),* provides us today with an insight into Welsh mythology and the magical, sometimes terrifying, pagan Celtic world. It remains the key source of Welsh folk legends and, while many of the tales have evolved over time, the definitive insight beyond the swirling mists of Welsh folklore. Here we explore three of its most popular folk legends.

THE LADY OF THE LAKE & OTHER WATERY TALES

Llyn y Fan Fach, a small, dark lake in the Black Mountains of eastern Carmarthenshire, is the backdrop for one of the best known of Wales' many Lady-of-the-Lake stories. The tale depicts a farm boy who marries a beautiful fairy-woman from the lake, promising him prosperity and respect in return for his pledge not to strike her three times or reveal her origin. While the lake-born lady keeps her promise, her successful husband proves disloyal to his roots and values, and eventually reneges on his end of the bargain. His wife and his livestock return to the lake, leaving him heartbroken. For more on this legend, see the boxed text on p136.

Many other Welsh legends, notably those about floods and submerged cities, probably have some basis in fact. The most prolific is that of Cardigan Bay, once a dry, fertile region called Cantref Gwaelod (The Lowland Hundred) if legend is to be believed. The keeper of the dikes, named Seithenyn, got drunk one night and forgot to shut the sluice gates, allowing the sea to swallow 16 cities. It's said the submerged church bells can still be heard ringing today; a similar tale is told about Llangorse Lake near Brecon.

Menhirs (standing stones) are a popular feature in such folk tales. Said to have been thrown by giants or saints, their strange markings signal finger-grip points. Allegedly, the stones wander about in search of water to quench their thirsts. For example, on Christmas morning, Samson's stone, otherwise found near Kenfig, South Wales, heads for the River Sker, while the Fish Stone near Crickhowell takes a Midsummer Eve's dip in the River Usk. Of Wales' many burial chambers, St Lythan's chamber, 5 miles southwest of Cardiff, has a capstone that is said to spin around three times every Midsummer's Eve. Others are said to be the resting places of giants, or deposited by the devil. There's a semblance of truth in the notion that those with the nerve to disturb these mounds may encounter misfortune or disaster. Tomen yr Ellyllon, located in North Wales and known as Mound of the Goblins, was alleged to be haunted by a gold-armoured horseman. When excavated in 1833, a man's skeleton swaddled in a 3500-year-old gold cape was discovered.

THE RED DRAGON

One of the first mythical beasts in British heraldry, the red dragon is a powerful symbol in ancient legends. It was apparently used on the banners of British soldiers on their way to Rome in the 4th century, and was then adopted by Welsh kings in the 5th century to demonstrate their authority after the Roman withdrawal.

The Anglo-Saxon King Harold, and Cadwaladr, the 7th-century king of Gwynedd, liked it so much they used it for their standards in battle, forever associating the symbol with Wales. In the 14th century Welsh archers used the red dragon as their emblem, and Owain Glyndŵr used it as a standard in his revolt against the English crown.

A century later, quarter-Welsh Henry Tudor (later King Henry VII) made the dragon part of the Welsh flag, though it was only in 1959 that Queen Elizabeth II commanded that the red dragon, on a green-and-white field, be recognised as the official flag of Wales.

To bring the dragon legend up to date, a new public-art dragon sculpture could soon be built on the Wales–England border. The proposed bronze sculpture, Waking the Dragon, would be the tallest public artwork in the UK. Nicknamed 'The Dragon of the North' (a reference to Antony Gormley's Angel of the North near Newcastle), it will sit on a gleaming 130ft concrete and glass tower and have a wingspan of 170ft. The proposed site next to the A5 at Chirk would include a state-of-the-art cultural centre along with a 100-seat cafe-bar, a 125-seat restaurant and a museum. Project organisers hope the dragon, a symbol of North Wales heritage and culture, will be dominating the skyline by August 2011.

KING ARTHUR

King Arthur has inspired more legends, folk tales and curiosities, and given his name to more features of the landscape in Wales, than any other historical figure. He is present in the oldest surviving Welsh manuscript, the 12th-century *Llyfr Du Caerfyrddin* (The Black Book of Carmarthen; on display at the National Library of Wales in Aberystwyth). His true identity, however, remains unknown because he is so closely interwoven with the legends, folk tales and curiosities he inspired; he's taken on the guise of a giant with superhuman strength, a dwarf king who rode a goat and a Celtic god associated with the Great Bear constellation (Arth Fawr in Welsh). Most likely, however, he was a 5th- or 6th-century cavalry leader, who led early Britons against Saxon invaders. But, by the 9th century, Arthur was famous as a fighter throughout the British Isles. In the centuries that followed, other writers – most recently and perhaps most famously the Victorian poet Alfred Lord Tennyson – climbed on the bandwagon, weaving in love stories, Christian symbolism and medieval pageantry to create the romance that surrounds Arthur today.

Tintagel in Cornwall has the strongest claim to being Arthur's birthplace, Cadbury Castle in Somerset contends it is the site of Camelot (his court), and Glastonbury Abbey his burial place. However, Wales makes many fervent claims of its own on the Arthurian legend. The 12th-century historian and novelist Geoffrey of Monmouth asserted King Arthur's first court, swarming with scholars, astrologers, philosophers, fine knights and ladies, was held at Caerleon near Newport in Gwent. This site had previously served as a Roman headquarters for the 6000-strong 2nd Augustan Legion. The remains of its grand amphitheatre are visible today (p67). Of the other key sites linked with the legend, Wales proffers two candidates for Camlan, Arthur's final battle ground: Camlan Hill in Cwm Cerist, North Wales, and Maes Camlan in Mid-Wales. Bardsey Island, off the tip of the Llŷn Peninsula, is a contender for Avalon, the blessed 'island of apples' where Merlin took King Arthur to die. Most stories culminate in Arthur and followers retreating to a cave, sleeping in mythical cold storage until the Once and Future King is called upon again to defend Britain.

Many sites in Wales have used natural features or curiosities to suit the Arthurian legends, notably the Preseli Hills of northern Pembrokeshire (p170), the source of the bluestone megaliths that form the inner circle of Stonehenge in England, and home to scores of Neolithic monuments bearing Arthur's name. A massive burial chamber on the Gower Peninsula's Cefn Bryn (p126), near Reynoldston, has a 25-tonne capstone well known as Arthur's Stone. The Holy Grail, the vessel with supernatural qualities used by Christ at the Last Supper and sought obsessively by King Arthur and his knights, is said to hide in Llangollen's Castell Dinas Brân (p273).

MERLIN THE MAGICIAN

This great Welsh wizard is probably modelled upon Myrddin Emrys (Ambrosius), a 6th-century holy man. He is thought to have been born around the time of the warrior Vortigern, who led the Roman British against the Saxons in Carmarthen, whose

DON'T MISS...

LEGENDARY SITES

* ★ **Cader Idris** // Spend a night on the mountain in southern Snowdonia and, according to legend, you'll wake up either blind, mad or a poet. Dare you (p214)!

* ★ **Snowdon** // Arthur slew Rita Gawr, a giant notorious for killing kings and making coats from their beards, atop the mountain. No giants today, just lots of hikers (p226).

* ★ **Snowdonia lakes** // Llyn Tegid (Bala Lake) is closely associated with the story of Teggie, Wales' answer to the Loch Ness Monster, while Gwernan Lake is home to the Green Man of Gwernan, who announces his hunger for fresh blood with the mantra, 'The hour is come but not the man' (p220).

* ★ **St Winefride's Well** // The holy well in Holywell, North Wales, is said to have sprung up when its namesake's decapitated head hit the ground. Pilgrims still take the waters today (p274).

Welsh name Caerfyrddin means Merlin's City. Myrddin, who apparently inherited wizardry from his magical, but evil, father became famous in the 10th-century for his prophecies. The most potent of these concerned two dragons, one red, one white, revealed by Myrddin to be lurking in a cave near Beddgelert, Snowdonia (p228), where King Vortigern tried and failed to build a castle. Myrddin told the king the fighting dragons symbolised the battle between the Britons and Saxons, and was lauded when the Welsh red dragon won the battle.

It was probably Geoffrey of Monmouth who changed Myrddin's name to Merlin and presented him as the wise, wizardly advisor to Arthur's father King Uther Pendragon. One of Merlin's seminal acts was to disguise Uther as Duke Gorlois, allowing him to spend the night with the duke's wife, Ygerna, who duly conceived Arthur. Merlin also predicted that Uther's true heir would draw a sword from a stone and acquired the sword Excalibur from a Lady of the Lake. And it was Merlin who advised Uther to establish a fellowship of knights (actually making the Round Table at which those knights would eventually sit), and then ensured the remaining knights found safety in the Scilly Isles after he predicted Uther's demise. These stories would become essential ingredients in the highly romanticised Arthurian legend that developed in the following centuries, most notably in the hands of the French poet Chrétien de Troyes in the 12th century, and in the English-language *Morte d'Arthur,* written by Sir Thomas Malory in the 15th century.

Merlin's own end appears to have come courtesy of the Lady of the Lake (of Excalibur fame). She trapped the wizard in a cave on Bryn Myrddin (Merlin's Hill), east of Carmarthenshire, where wind-carried groans and clanking chains are part of local lore even today. Alternative versions insist that Merlin isn't dead but held in a trance in Brittany or in a glasshouse on Bardsey Island. Such tales still hold a powerful grip on the Welsh imagination even today, especially in Carmarthenshire, the spiritual home of the Merlin legend. When 'Merlin's Tree', a 17th-century oak rooted inconveniently in Carmarthen's Priory St, was removed in 1978, the town didn't fall as Merlin predicted. But it was flooded in 1987 when the River Tywi burst its banks. Cinematically, too, Merlin still retains strong links with Wales and Carmarthenshire to this day. The popular BBC TV series, *Merlin,* and the 1998 film also bearing his name, were both filmed in and around the region, serving to maintain interest in the legend for new generations of visitors to Wales.

FOOD & DRINK

· · · · · · ·

A quiet revolution has been taking place across the kitchens of Wales. Boosted by the abundance of fresh, local produce and a new generation of young masterchefs with an innovative, modern take on traditional Welsh recipes, the food scene is now buzzing. The last decade has witnessed a huge increase in the number of local farmers markets and food festivals, focusing attention on organic produce and encouraging people to support local suppliers. These have made the public aware that good produce has to be paid for, and while it is more expensive than supermarkets, the quality is far higher. For example, the Riverside Real Food Market (p53) on Cardiff's Fitzhamon Embankment offers an embarrassment of riches each Sunday morning, and Abergavenny, the Mid-Wales town regarded by many as the spiritual home of the Welsh food movement, is home to Wales' biggest annual food festival in mid-September (p86).

> *'smell the new sense of pride in the Welsh food experience wafting out from under the kitchen door'*

At the same time there has been a huge increase in the number of restaurants in Wales that make a point of sourcing and using seasonal food from local suppliers. Organic cheeses, succulent meats, vegetables pulled fresh from the ground and fantastic fish are all making their way onto menus across the country. There are now many seriously good local restaurants and country-house hotels with fine-dining experiences. The biggest trend in recent years, however, has been the rise of the gastropub and the restaurant with rooms, both in towns and rural locations. Such places offer informal surroundings yet high-quality fare with a savvy local twist. In fact, you can almost smell the new sense of pride in the Welsh food experience wafting out from under the kitchen door.

WELSH SPECIALITIES

Traditionally, Welsh food was based on what could be grown locally and cheaply. This meant that oats, root vegetables, dairy products, honey and meat featured highly in most recipes. Food was functional and needed to satisfy the needs of labourers on the farm or workers down the mine. It was hearty and wholesome but not exactly haute cuisine. The food revolution in Wales has changed that, but traditional staples, such as Welsh lamb, Welsh Black beef, sewin (wild sea trout), Penclawdd cockles, Conwy mussels, laver bread and farmhouse cheeses, still have their place in the kitchens of any decent eating place in Wales – albeit the recipes may come with a more contemporary twist.

These days there's a simple rule: when in Wales, play to its strengths. Most menus will feature Welsh lamb or Welsh Black beef and you rarely go wrong with these. On the coast try some sewin or cockles. The most traditional Welsh dish remains *cawl,* the hearty, one-pot meal of bacon, lamb, cabbage, swede and potato. It's one of those warm, cosy dishes that you long for when you're walking in the hills. Another traditional favourite is Welsh rarebit, a kind of sophisticated cheese on toast, generously

LOCAL FOOD HEROES

The bon-viveur restaurant critic Michael Winner is famously a sucker for a well-baked brownie. Should he find himself on the Gower Peninsula, he would doubtless be in brownie heaven with a visit to the HQ of **Gower Cottage Brownies** (www.gowercottagebrownies. co.uk). Kate Jenkins founded a family catering business, Crumbles Catering, from her Gower cottage kitchen and her home-baked teatime treats soon became a runaway success. Awarded silver in the Online Retailer of the Year category at the latest True Taste of Wales awards, the company is a prime example of a small local business harnessing the power of the internet to punch well above its weight. It probably also helps that her brownies are described by BBC *Good Food* magazine as 'The best brownies we have ever tasted.'

Another True Taste award nominee is Aberystwyth-based **Tropical Forest Products** (www.tropicalforest.com), the company behind Welsh Heather Honey. Today the company produces speciality honeys from around 1000 hives throughout the Welsh countryside, although the founders first started the business during a Voluntary Service Overseas placement in Zambia to help forest-dwelling wild honey collectors improve their yield. Village beekeepers from Zambia, Cameroon and Ethiopia now make a living by exporting honey to Tropical Forest.

drizzled with a secret ingredient tasting suspiciously like beer. For breakfast, try laver bread, not bread at all, but boiled seaweed mixed with oatmeal and served with bacon or cockles.

A top tip is to finish your meal with some great Welsh cheese, notably Caws Cenarth, Celtic Blue or Pearl Las. The real cheese cognoscenti head to the award-winning Blaenavon Cheddar Co, located in the industrial town of Blaenavon, where the handmade cheeses are matured down the mineshaft of the Big Pit: National Coal Museum. Also worth a look is Ultracomida, a small, independent chain of delis. The main branch is in the coastal town of Aberystwyth (p184), but there's a smaller outpost in Narberth. With its blend of Spanish, French and Welsh produce, it is a food lover's idea of nirvana.

LOCAL TIPPLES

Village life in Wales traditionally revolved around the local pub. It was part of the social fabric of the community and a focal point of village life. The new breed of Welsh drinking den, however, offers a far more modern spin on the traditional cocktail hours, bar food and live music de rigueur in urban Wales. Pubs are closing across the UK as their community element is eroded, but the traditional boozer still lives on in Wales with some fine historic examples to be found in Swansea and Cardiff – see regional chapters for details. Meanwhile a new generation of local microbreweries are creating an artisan range of tasty real ales, supplying local bars and selling direct to the consumer via their websites.

Among the places to look out for, Cardiff's Zerodegrees (p53) is a specialist microbrewery with a great selection of artisan beers with a flavoursome twist. Across town, the Brewery Quarter, located on the site of the old Brains Brewery dating from 1713,

BACKGROUND

has a slew of modern bars for a drop of Brains Gold. In North Wales, the town of Porthmadog, located on the fringes of the Snowdonia National Park, is home to the Purple Moose Brewery (p247), one of Wales' most successful microbreweries, supplying pubs from Anglesey to Harlech. The Snowdonia Ale was voted CAMRA Champion Beer of Wales 2009, while the Dark Side of the Moose, a hoppy and fruity brew for winter, was named the Gold Medal winner at the International Beer Challenge 2009.

Welsh whisky is also enjoying a renaissance with the Penderyn Distillery (p102), located in the southern reaches of the Brecon Beacons National Park, boasting a new high-tech visitors centre. The independently owned distillery released its first whisky in 2004 and remains, unlike Scottish and Irish whisky, a single-distilled malt.

WELSH AWARD WINNERS

The defining characteristic of the Welsh food scene in recent years is the huge number of awards and critical plaudits it has garnered. In 2010 the number of Michelin-starred restaurants in Wales quadrupled overnight with three new restaurants awarded a prestigious star. They are the Walnut Tree (p87) in Llandewi Skirrid, Abergavenny, Monmouthshire; Tyddyn Llan (p222) in Llandrillo, Denbighshire; and Ynyshir Hall (p186) in Machynlleth, Powys. The triumvirate joined the Crown at Whitebrook (p78) in Monmouthshire, which retained its star under executive chef James Sommerin from Newport. Tyddyn Llan owner and chef Bryan Webb won his first star, having previously had his restaurant voted Welsh Restaurant of the Year three times by the *Good Food Guide*. For more on Wales' top chefs, see p17.

Tyddyn Llan was also awarded the coveted title of the *Good Food Guide* readers' restaurant of the year. It gained a score of seven out of 10 by the judges for its cooking, the joint highest score awarded to a Welsh restaurant. Among the other highly rated

BACKGROUND

THE WELSH NIGELLA

Wales has its fair share of celebrity chefs and TV-cookery-show regulars: cookery school proprietor Angela Gray, *Food Wales* author Colin Pressdee and *Great British Menu* stalwart Stephen Terry among them. But a new champion of Welsh cuisine recently emerged: the Welsh wife of a former vicar who cooks in Jimmy Choos and landed a £20,000 cookery book deal. Elisa Beynon entered a competition with supermarket group Waitrose, impressing judges including Nigel Slater of the *Observer* newspaper and seeing off competition from 2500 aspiring food writers. Her debut book, *The Vicar's Wife's Cookbook* (Fourth Estate), has sold like hot cakes with its no-nonsense recipes, such as cheap and cheery chickpea curry.

Beynon, who was born in Trelewis and whose grandfather was a butcher in the Rhondda Valley, now lives in London with her husband Nigel and two children. She started out as a self-confessed 'hopeless cook', but after marrying then-vicar Nigel in 1993 she bought a cauldron and set about impressing his friends with vast suppers and tapas dinners for 80. Since landing her book deal, daytime TV has beckoned and she is being described as the next Nigella Lawson for her 'yummy mummy' sense of style.

DON'T MISS...

TRUE TASTE WINNERS

Every year the **True Taste** (www.walesthetruetaste.co.uk) awards highlight Wales' real food heroes. Some recent winners:

- ★ **Blas ar Fwyd //** The True Taste Champion was awarded to Deiniol ap Dafydd, owner of the Llanrwst-based deli (www.blasarfwyd.com).
- ★ **Pembrokeshire Fish Week //** The Food Tourism Destination award went to the annual summer celebration of all things fishy (www.pembrokeshirefishweek.com).
- ★ **Hawarden Estate Farm Shop //** The Retailer of the Year award was picked up by this produce-heavy farm shop in northeast Wales (www.hawardenestate.co.uk).
- ★ **Gentle Jane Tearoom //** Winner of the Eating Out in Wales (tearooms) award was this delightful boutique guesthouse and tearoom, handily located for exploring Hay-on-Wye (www.gentlejane.co.uk).
- ★ **Primrose Organic Centre //** The Healthy Eating award went to this Brecon-based pioneer of sustainable food production for its mixed-leaf salad pack (www.primroseearthcentre.co.uk).

restaurants were the Crown at Whitebrook, the Hardwick (p87) in Abergavenny, the Chandlery in Newport and the Foxhunter (p87) in Nant-y-derry. The Hardwick also received the *Good Pub Guide*'s County Dining Award 2010, while the overall award went to another Welsh pub, the Bear Hotel (p95), in Crickhowell, Powys. The historic pub, sandwiched between the Black Mountains and the Brecon Beacons, was named Wales' best inn in the *Good Pub Guide* 2010.

> '*In 2010 the number of Michelin-starred restaurants quadrupled overnight with three new restaurants awarded a star*'

Finally, a pub in the Brecon Beacons won the title of Great British Pub of the Year in 2009. The Pen-y-Cae Inn, Powys, beat hundreds of pubs to take top prize at the event, organised by industry magazine the *Morning Advertiser*. The pub's owner and chef Anthony Christopher also walked away with the Best Gastropub title and Best Pub in Wales. The Great British Pub Awards attract hundreds of entries from pubs throughout Wales and England. Other Welsh winners included the Commercial Inn in Risca near Newport (Best Community Pub in Wales), the Red Lion at Llangadog, Carmarthenshire (Best Freehouse in Wales) and the Carne Park Hotel in Abercynon in the Cynon Valley (Best Entertainment Pub in Wales).

BACKGROUND

FOOD & DRINK GLOSSARY

THE BASICS

brecwast brekooast breakfast
cinio kinyo dinner
cinio canol dydd kinyo kanol deedd lunch
cyllell kuhllell knife
fforc phork fork
llwy llooee spoon

STAPLES

bara bara bread
cawl kaool soup
caws kaoos cheese
halen halen salt
llefrith llevrith milk
siwgr shoogoor sugar

DRINKS

coffi kophee coffee
coffi gyda llefrith kophee guhda llevrith coffee with milk
cwrw kooroo beer
dŵr door water
gwin gooeen wine
seidr say·duhr cider
sudd seedd juice
sudd oren seedh o·ren orange juice
te te tea

FISH & SEAFOOD

brithyll brithill trout
corgimychiaid korgeemycheeaid prawns
eog eog salmon
penllwyd penllooeed sewin
pysgodyn puhsgodin fish
tiwna tioona tuna

MEAT

cig keeg meat
cig oen keeg oeen lamb
cig eidion keeg e·eedyon beef
cig moch keeg moch bacon
cyw iâr kioo yar chicken
hwyaden hooeeaden duck
porc pork pork
selsig selseeg sausage

VEGETABLES

blodfresychen blodvresuhchen cauliflower
ffa pob pha pob beans
llysiau llushayaee vegetables
madarchen madarchen mushroom
moronen moronen carrot
nionyn neeonin onion
pys pis peas
taten taten potato

FRUIT

afal aval apple
banana banana banana
eirinen wlanog e·eereenen goolanog peach
ffrwyth phrooeeth fruit
grawnwinen graoonooinen grape
mefus mevis strawberry
oren oren orange

DESSERTS

bisgeden bisgeden biscuit
crymbl kruhmbl crumble
hufen iâ heeven ee·'a ice cream
iogwrt yogoort yoghurt
pwdinau poodinau desserts
tarten ffrwyth tarten phrooeeth fruit pie
teisen te·eesen cake

BACKGROUND

ACCOMMODATION

FINDING ACCOMMODATION

Wales has been attracting tourists in the modern sense for 350 years, so it's fair to say that the country is well prepared for visitors. **VisitWales** (www.visitwales.com), the national tourist board, operates a grading system based on facilities and quality of service. Participating establishments usually display their star-rating (from one to five), although some excellent places don't join the scheme, as it costs to do so. Tourist offices rarely mention good nonparticipating places, or may simply dismiss them as 'not approved'. In practice, there's variability within each classification, and a one-star guesthouse might be better than the three-star hotel around the block.

Bed and breakfast (B&B) accommodation in private homes is plentiful, and is often the only option in smaller towns and villages. Some of the finest and most family-friendly B&Bs are in rural farmhouses, used to the muddy boots and large appetites of walkers, cyclists and climbers. Guesthouses, which are often just large converted houses with half a dozen rooms, are an extension of the

BOOK YOUR STAY ONLINE

For more accommodation reviews and recommendations by Lonely Planet authors, check out the online booking service at www.lonelyplanet.com/hotels. You'll find the true, insider low-down on the best places to stay. Reviews are thorough and independent. Best of all, you can book online.

B&B idea. In general they're less personal and more like small hotels, but without the same level of service.

Both B&Bs and guesthouses usually have, as a minimum, central heating, TV, tea-and-coffee-making facilities and a wash basin in the bedrooms. They range from boutique establishments with chic decor, en suites and every gadget imaginable to basic places with shared bathroom facilities. Likewise, the standard of breakfast varies enormously, although the norm is a full Welsh fry-up – bacon and eggs (and often mushrooms, tomatoes and baked beans) on toast – with cereals, yoghurts and fruit also provided.

The term 'hotel' is used with abandon in Wales, and may refer to anything from a pub to a castle. In general, hotels tend to have a reception desk, room service and other extras such as a licensed bar. The very best hotels are magnificent places, often with restaurants to match. In rural areas you'll find country-house hotels set in vast grounds, and castles complete with crenulated battlements, grand staircases, oak panelling and the obligatory rows of stags' heads. A new breed of boutique hotel has emerged, offering individually styled designer rooms, clublike bars, top-quality restaurants and a range of spa treatments.

A variation is the restaurant with rooms, where the main focus is on the gourmet cuisine; the attached rooms sometimes come comparatively cheaply.

Such places usually offer dinner, bed and breakfast (DB&B) rates.

Many pubs offer accommodation, though they vary widely in quality. Staying in a pub or inn can be good fun as it places you at the hub of the community, but they can be noisy and aren't always ideal for solo women travellers. Many of the better pubs are former coaching inns (places where horse and coach passengers would stop on long journeys), offering what Brits like to call an 'olde-worlde atmosphere'.

For longer stays, self-contained weekly rentals are popular. Options include traditional stone farmhouses, tiny quaint cottages, gracious manor houses and seaside hideaways. For something special, the **National Trust** (NT; ☎ 0844 800 2070; www.nationaltrustcottages.co.uk) has rural properties that are let as holiday

ONLINE RESOURCES

Brecon Beacons Holiday Cottages (www.breconcottages.com)
Camping & Caravanning Club (www.campingandcaravanningclub.co.uk)
Coastal Cottages of Pembrokeshire (www.coastalcottages.co.uk)
Forestry Commission (www.forestholidays.co.uk) Forestry campsites.
Freedom Days (www.freedom-days.co.uk)
Great Little Places (www.wales.little-places.co.uk) Atmospheric accommodation.
Home Base Holidays (www.homebase-hols.com) Home swaps.
Homelink (www.homelink.org.uk) Home swaps.
Hostels Wales (www.hostelswales.com)
Quality Cottages (www.qualitycottages.co.uk)
Rural Retreats (www.ruralretreats.co.uk) Holiday cottages.
Snowdonia Tourist Services (www.sts-holidays.co.uk) Holiday cottages.
Stay in Wales (www.stayinwales.co.uk)
UK Campsite (www.ukcampsite.co.uk)
Venue Masters (www.venuemasters.co.uk) University accommodation.
VisitWales (www.visitwales.com) Official tourism organisation.
Wales Directory (www.walesdirectory.co.uk)
Wales Holidays (www.wales-holidays.co.uk) Holiday cottages.
Wales in Style (www.walesinstyle.com) Atmospheric accommodation.
Welsh Rarebits (www.rarebits.co.uk) Atmospheric accommodation.
Youth Hostel Association (www.yha.org.uk)

cottages. Similarly splendid rentals are offered by the **Landmark Trust** (☎ 01628-825925; www.landmarktrust.co.uk), an architectural charity that rescues unique old buildings and supports the work by renting them out.

Hostels in Wales are generally basic, institutional affairs with bunk beds in dormitories. However, they're often spectacularly located and very handy for long-distance walkers.

Free camping is rarely possible in Wales but there are plenty of camp sites around the country, concentrated in the national parks and along the coast. Most camping grounds have reasonable facilities, though quality can vary widely and some can be tricky to reach without your own transport. Price structures vary widely but will often include a per person charge, an additional charge for a vehicle or a powered site, and sometimes a minimum site charge at busy times regardless of how many people are staying. See p335 for some top picks.

PRICES & BOOKING

Wales is a popular 'weekender' destination for people throughout Britain. Consequently prices shoot up and availability plummets on Friday and Saturday nights, regardless of the season, especially in popular beauty spots such as Pembrokeshire and Snowdonia. In business-orientated establishments in Cardiff, prices sometimes drop over the weekend, depending on what's on in the city. If there's a big rugby game scheduled, you won't get a room in the city or its surrounds for love or money.

It is essential to book ahead for Easter and Christmas, when it seems everyone's dreaming of a white Welsh one. Otherwise, the high season runs from mid-May to mid-September, with

PRICE GUIDE

We've categorised the listings in this chapter according to the following scale, based on the cheapest double on offer in high (but not necessarily peak) season. Unless otherwise stated, prices include private bathrooms.

£	below £60
££	£60 to £100
£££	over £100

the absolute peak (especially in seaside towns) between July and August. Prices are generally cheaper for longer stays and advance bookings.

Outside the peak season, room rates are often reduced and special offers may be available – it's always worth enquiring. Some establishments, especially hostels and camping grounds, shut up shop completely from November until Easter.

Most tourist offices will book accommodation for you for a small fee. Almost all B&Bs charge between £60 and £100 for a double room; in many places it's hard to find anything cheaper or more expensive.

CARDIFF

CENTRAL CARDIFF

❦ BARCELÓ CARDIFF ANGEL HOTEL ££

Map p44; ☎ 029-2064 9200; www.barcelo-hotels. co.uk; Castle St; r from £71; 🖳 🛜

Across the street from the castle, this lavish Victorian confection was founded in 1883 by the third marquis of Bute. The rooms don't quite live up to the promise of the sparkling chandeliers and painted ceilings of the atrium, but cheap advance-purchase rates compensate for any scuffed edges.

❤ NOSDA BUDGET HOTEL £

Map p44; ☎ 029-2037 8866; www.nosda.co.uk; 53-59 Despenser St; dm/tw from £19/43; P 🖵 🛜

You won't find a better budget bed closer to the city centre than at this stylishly refurbished hostel right across the river from the Millennium Stadium. It's family-friendly, and it has an in-house bar, restaurant and gym.

❤ PARC HOTEL £££

Map p44; ☎ 0871 376 9011; www.thistle.com/theparchotel; Park Pl; r from £99; 🖵 🛜

A smart contemporary hotel located right at the heart of the main shopping area, with tasteful rooms, good facilities and helpful staff.

❤ PARK PLAZA £££

Map p44; ☎ 029-2011 1111; www.parkplazacardiff.com; Greyfriars Rd; r from £109; 🖵 🛜 🖳

Luxurious without being remotely stuffy, the Plaza has all the five-star facilities you'd expect from a business-orientated hotel. For something more offbeat, it offers *Doctor Who* breaks complete with remote-controlled Daleks.

❤ RIVER HOUSE BACKPACKERS £

Map p44; ☎ 029-2039 9810; www.riverhousebackpackers.com; 59 Fitzhamon Embankment; dm/r from £18/35; 🖵 🛜

Professionally run by a young brother and sister team, the River House has a well-equipped kitchen, small garden and TV lounge. Free breakfast (cereal and toast) and pizza nights are a nice touch, but the private rooms are very dormlike.

CARDIFF BAY

❤ JOLYONS BOUTIQUE HOTEL ££

Map p48; ☎ 029-2048 8775; www.jolyons.co.uk; 5 Bute Cres; r £65-140; 🛜

A touch of Georgian elegance in the heart of Cardiff Bay, Jolyons has six in-

dividually designed rooms combining antique furniture with contemporary colours and crisp cotton sheets.

❤ ST DAVID'S HOTEL & SPA £££

Map p48; ☎ 029-2045 4045; www.thestdavidshotel.com; Havannah St; r from £99; 🖵 🛜 🖳

A glittering, glassy tower topped with a sail-like flourish, St David's epitomises Cardiff Bay's transformation from wasteland to stylish place-to-be. Every room has a private balcony with a harbour view.

CATHEDRAL ROAD AREA

❤ BEAUFORT GUEST HOUSE ££

Map p54; ☎ 029-2023 7003; www.beauforthousecardiff.co.uk; 65 Cathedral Rd; s/d from £55/79; 🛜

Despite having had a thorough refurbishment, the Beaufort retains a Victorian atmosphere, with period-style furniture, gilt mirrors, heavy drapes and even a portrait of the old queen herself.

❤ LINCOLN HOUSE ££

Map p54; ☎ 029-2039 5558; www.lincolnhotel.co.uk; 118 Cathedral Rd; s/d from £65/85; P 🛜

At the top end of the guesthouse scale, Lincoln House is a large Victorian property with a guest lounge and bar. For added romance, book the four-poster room.

❤ SACO HOUSE ££

Map p54; ☎ 0845 122 0405; www.sacoapartments.co.uk; 74-76 Cathedral Rd; apt from £82; P

This Victorian town house has been given a contemporary makeover and converted into serviced apartments, complete with comfortable lounges and fitted kitchens. The two-bedroom apartments are good value for families with kids and there's an extra sofa bed in the lounge. They're set up for longer visits but a two-day stay is the minimum.

❦ TOWN HOUSE ££

Map p54; ☎ 029-2023 9399; www.thetownhouse cardiff.co.uk; 70 Cathedral Rd; s/d from £50/70; Ⓟ 🛜

Succinctly named, this is yet another elegant Victorian town house with a welcoming owner. It retains lots of period features, including tiled hallway, original fireplaces and stained glass.

GRANGETOWN

❦ TŶ ROSA £

off Map p36; ☎ 0845 643 9962; www.tyrosa.com; 118 Clive St; s/d from £42/49; 🛜

Half an hour's walk from either Central Cardiff or the bay, this wonderful gay-friendly B&B is noted for its sumptuous breakfasts and affable hosts. The thoughtfully equipped rooms are split between the main house and a less impressive annex across the road. Some share bathrooms.

TOP FIVE

B&Bs

* ★ Tŷ Rosa, Cardiff (above)
* ★ Tides Reach Guest House, Mumbles (p330)
* ★ Fronlas, Llandeilo (p332)
* ★ Maelgwyn House, Harlech (p339)
* ★ Whinward House, Conwy (p344)

AROUND NEWPORT

❦ OLD RECTORY // CHRISTCHURCH ££

Map p61; ☎ 01633-430700; www.the-oldrectory. co.uk; s/d £50/75; Ⓟ 🛜

Handy for Caerleon and Newport with the distinct advantage of not actually being in Newport, the Old Rectory offers a warm welcome and three luxurious rooms with views over the estuary to England.

❦ WEST USK LIGHTHOUSE // ST BRIDES WENTLOOG £££

Map p61; ☎ 01633-810126; www.westusk lighthouse.co.uk; St Brides Wentloog; s/d from £75/120; Ⓟ 🛜

Quirky doesn't even begin to describe this restored 19th-century lighthouse offering views over the Severn Estuary. It's a little worn around the edges but filled with endearingly eccentric details, such as a full-size Dalek in the lobby. It's at the end of a potholed private road off the B4239, southwest of Newport.

SOUTHEAST WALES & BRECON BEACONS

MONMOUTHSHIRE

❦ CASTLE VIEW HOTEL // CHEPSTOW ££

Map p75; ☎ 01291-620349; www.hotelchepstow. co.uk; 16 Bridge St; s/d from £55/77

The 300-year-old Castle View has intriguing historic details, including 18th-century wall paintings and hand-painted glass in the back door. Most rooms are small and the floors are creaky, but there's plenty of atmosphere.

❦ ABBEY HOTEL // TINTERN ££

☎ 01291-680020; www.tinternabbeyhotel.co.uk; Monmouth Rd; s/d from £55/75; Ⓟ 🛜

Wake up to arguably Wales' most picturesque sight, with the crumbling ruins of

ACCOMMODATION

Tintern Abbey directly across the road. Luxury rooms have spa baths and are much more spacious than the standard rooms.

❦ PARVA FARMHOUSE //
TINTERN ££
☎ 01291-689411; www.parvafarmhouse.co.uk; s/d from £47/68

This cosy 17th-century farmhouse has low oak-beamed ceilings, leather Chesterfield sofas and a wood-burning stove in the lounge, and a garden with beautiful views across the valley. The bedrooms are chintzy and appealingly old-fashioned; one has a four-poster.

❦ BELL AT SKENFRITH //
SKENFRITH £££
☎ 01600-750235; www.skenfrith.co.uk; r £110-220; ℗ ⌂

Another picturesque village getaway, the Bell has an acclaimed restaurant and elegant rooms, all named after fishing flies. Some have four-posters but all marry an antique feel with contemporary comfort.

❦ GENTLE JANE // GROSMONT ££
☎ 01981-241655; www.gentlejane.com; s/d £65/90

At the heart of a tiny village this genteel tearoom and B&B offers three classy rooms with creamy marble bathrooms and contemporary furnishings. One has an ancient staircase leading to its en suite.

❦ ANGEL HOTEL //
ABERGAVENNY ££
Map p84; ☎ 01873-857121; www.angelhotelabergavenny.com; 15 Cross St; s/d from £69/89; ℗ ⌂

Abergavenny's top hotel is housed in a fine Georgian building that was once a famous coaching inn. Seemingly in the middle of a never-ending refurbishment, the completed communal areas downstairs feel sleek and sophisticated. Those rooms that have been finished have de-

signer Villeroy & Boch bathrooms, and there's one with a four-poster bed.

❦ GUEST HOUSE //
ABERGAVENNY ££
Map p84; ☎ 01873-854823; www.theguesthouseabergavenny.co.uk; 2 Oxford St; s/d from £35/65; ⌂

This family-friendly B&B with cheerful, flouncy rooms (not all en suite) has a mini-menagerie of pigs, rabbits, chickens and a parrot that can match the gregarious owners in colourful language. It's certainly not lacking in character.

❦ HIGHFIELD HOUSE //
ABERGAVENNY ££
Map p84; ☎ 01873-852371; www.highfieldabergavenny.co.uk; 6 Belmont Rd; s/d £45/68; ℗

A handsome Victorian villa set in attractive gardens, not far from the town centre, peaceful Highfield has three comfortable guest bedrooms. Front-facing rooms have views over Sugar Loaf Mountain.

❦ MULBERRY HOUSE //
ABERGAVENNY £
Map p84; ☎ 01873-855959; www.mulberrycentre.com; Pen-y-Pound; dm/d £27/54; ℗ ▯ ⌂

Housed in an old convent (and reputedly haunted by a nun), Mulberry House is a joint venture between an educational facility and the YHA. It's popular with school groups but the family room will give you all the privacy you need.

BRECON BEACONS NATIONAL PARK

❦ SKIRRID INN // LLANFIHANGEL
CRUCORNEY ££
☎ 01873-890258; www.skirridmountaininn.co.uk; r £90

Those with a taste for the macabre and ghostly will love this place. Wales' oldest inn (dating prior to 1110) once doubled as a court and over 180 people were hung here. Just so you don't forget, a noose dangles from the well-worn hanging beam directly outside the doors to the bedrooms, which, incidentally, are very nice.

☙ LLANTHONY PRIORY HOTEL // LLANTHONY ££

☎ 01873-890487; www.llanthonyprioryhotel.co.uk; r £80

Seemingly growing out of the priory ruins, and incorporating some of the original medieval buildings, the Priory Hotel is wonderfully atmospheric, with four-poster beds, stone spiral staircases and rooms squeezed into turrets; there are only five rooms and no en suites.

☙ BEAR // HAY-ON-WYE ££

Map p92; ☎ 01497-821302; www.thebearhay.co.uk; Bear St; s/d £33/72; Ⓟ 🛜

Homely and rustic with exposed stone walls and original beams, plus a liberal sprinkling of books, this former coaching inn (1590) is an excellent choice. It only has four rooms, of which two are en suite.

☙ OLD BLACK LION // HAY-ON-WYE ££

Map p92; ☎ 01497-820841; www.oldblacklion. co.uk; Lion St; s/d £53/90; Ⓟ

As traditional and atmospheric as they come, this inn looks 17th-century but parts of it date from the 13th; expect low ceilings and uneven floors. The accumulated weight of centuries of hospitality is cheerfully carried by the current staff.

☙ START // HAY-ON-WYE ££

Map p92; ☎ 01497-821391; www.the-start.net; Bridge St; s/d £45/70; Ⓟ 🛜

Peacefully set on the fringes of town, this little place boasts an unbeatable riverside setting, homely rooms in a renovated 18th-century house and a flagstone-floored breakfast room. The owner can advise on local activities and walks.

☙ BEAR HOTEL // CRICKHOWELL ££

☎ 01873-810408; www.bearhotel.co.uk; Beaufort St; s/d from £73/90; Ⓟ 🛜

The Bear is a local institution, a fine old coaching inn with a range of chintzy, old-fashioned rooms, the more expensive ones with four-posters and Jacuzzis. Some renovated rooms have a fresher look.

☙ DRAGON INN // CRICKHOWELL ££

☎ 01873-810362; www.dragoncrickhowell.co.uk; 47 High St; s/d from £45/65; Ⓟ 🛜

Though set in an 18th-century listed building, the pretty-in-pink Dragon has a modern feel. The 15 bedrooms, while not super flash, boast crisp, clean design with pine furniture and bold colours.

☙ GWYN DERI // CRICKHOWELL ££

☎ 01873-812494; www.gwynderibedandbreakfast. co.uk; Mill St; s/d £40/60; Ⓟ 🛜

The friendly couple who run this homely B&B keep the modern rooms immaculately clean. Bonuses include iPod docks, fresh fruit in the rooms and an excellent breakfast selection.

☙ TŶ GWYN // CRICKHOWELL ££

☎ 01873-811625; www.tygwyn.com; Brecon Rd; s/d from £40/64; Ⓟ 🖳

Once the home of Regency architect John Nash, Tŷ Gwyn is a lovely old Georgian house with four spacious en suite rooms. It's only two minutes' walk from the town centre.

☙ OLD RECTORY // LLANGATTOCK ££

☎ 01873-810373; www.rectoryhotel.co.uk; s/d from £45/75; Ⓟ 🛜

Surprisingly grand for the price, this partly 16th-century stone mansion was once the home of poet Henry Vaughan. Now it has its own golf course and a clubby atmosphere pervades the

HOSTELS

The concept of flashpacking hasn't yet taken hold in Wales and the vast majority of hostels and bunkhouses run the risk of triggering repressed memories of school camps and scout dens. On the upside, many of them are spectacularly located and well set up for walkers, with drying rooms and places for muddy boots. Only the very best hostels have been given full reviews within this chapter.

Britain's **Youth Hostel Association** (YHA; www.yha.org.uk) operates hostels throughout the national parks that may come in handy for filling overnight gaps in your walking or cycling itinerary. Many of the more remote ones close from November to Easter. A dorm bed costs from £14 unless otherwise stated below.

BRECON BEACONS NATIONAL PARK
Brecon (☎ 0845 371 9506; Groesffordd) Victorian farmhouse, 2 miles east of Brecon.
Danywenallt (☎ 0845 371 9548; Talybont-on-Usk; dm from £18) Converted farmhouse nestling beneath the dam of Talybont Reservoir, halfway between Brecon and Crickhowell.
Llwyn-y-Celyn (☎ 0845 371 9029; dm from £18) An 18th-century farmhouse in 6 hectares of woodland, 6 miles south of Brecon on the A470.
Llanddeusant (☎ 0845 371 9750; Old Red Lion; dm from £12) Former inn nestled in the western fringes of Black Mountain.

PEMBROKESHIRE COAST NATIONAL PARK
Broad Haven (☎ 0845 371 9008) Purpose-built hostel close to the beach; only open weekends and school holidays.
St Davids (☎ 0845 371 9141; Llaethdy, Whitesands Bay) Former farmhouse tucked beneath Carn Llidi, 2 miles northwest of town, with snug dorms in the cow sheds.
Pwll Deri (☎ 0845 371 9536; Castell Mawr, Trefasser) Perched atop a 120m-high cliff overlooking the sea.
Newport (☎ 0845 371 9543; Lower St Mary's St) Converted Victorian school.
Poppit Sands (☎ 0845 371 9037) Tucked into a hillside overlooking the beach.

MID-WALES
Borth (☎ 0845 371 9724; dm from £10) Beachside Edwardian, 7 miles north of Aberystwyth on the B4572.

SNOWDONIA NATIONAL PARK
Kings (☎ 0845 371 9327) Remote country-house hostel set in woods, southwest of Dolgellau.
Betws-y-Coed (☎ 01690-710796; Swallow Falls; dm from £16) Part of a bustling traveller hub with camping and a pub.
Capel Curig (☎ 0845 371 9110; dm from £16) Great views across to the Snowdon Horseshoe.
Pen-y-Pass (☎ 0845 371 9534; dm from £16) Superbly situated on the slopes of Snowdon, 5.5 miles up the A4086 from Llanberis.
Bryn Gwynant (☎ 0845 371 9108; Nantgwynant; dm from £10) Victorian mansion overlooking the lake, 4 miles east of Beddgelert.
Snowdon Ranger (☎ 0845 371 9659; dm from £12) On the A4085, 5 miles north of Beddgelert, at the trailhead for the Snowdon Ranger Path up Snowdon, this former inn is full of character and has its own adjoining lakeside beach.
Llanberis (☎ 0845 371 9645; dm from £18) Former quarry manager's house on the slopes above the town.

downstairs bar and restaurant. Rooms are chic and comfortable.

❧ GLIFFAES HOTEL // NEAR TRETOWER £££

☎ 01874-730371; www.gliffaeshotel.com; s/d from £89/99; Ⓟ 📶

This Victorian mansion makes quite an impression with its Romanesque towers rising through its thickly wooded grounds on the banks of the Usk. Standard doubles start from £160, but the considerably cheaper 'small doubles' have the same facilities. It's about 4 miles northwest of Crickhowell, off the A40.

❧ PETERSTONE COURT // LLANHAMLACH £££

off Map p99; ☎ 01874-665387; www.peterstone -court.com; r £120-220; Ⓟ 📶 🖥

An elegant Georgian manor house overlooking the River Usk, Peterstone enjoys views across the valley to the peaks of Cribyn and Pen-y-Fan. Despite the country-house setting the atmosphere is relaxed. The bedrooms are large, mixing antiques with modern designer furniture and crisp linen. Llanhamlach is 3 miles southeast of Brecon, just off the A40.

❧ BRIDGE CAFE B&B // BRECON £

Map p99; ☎ 01874-622024; www.bridgecafe.co.uk; 7 Bridge St; s/d from £30/50

Owned by keen mountain-bikers and hill walkers who can advise on local activities, the Bridge has three plain but comfortable bedrooms with down-filled duvets and crisp cotton sheets.

❧ CANTRE SELYF // BRECON ££

Map p99; ☎ 01874-622904; www.cantreselyf.co.uk; 5 Lion St; s/d from £56/72; Ⓟ 📶

This elegant 17th-century town house, right in the middle of Brecon, has atmospheric period decor and furnishings,

including plaster mouldings, original fireplaces and cast-iron bedsteads.

❧ CASTLE OF BRECON HOTEL // BRECON ££

Map p99; ☎ 01874-624611; www.breconcastle. co.uk; Castle Sq; s/d from £65/75; Ⓟ

Built into the ruined walls of Brecknock Castle, this grand old hotel had been getting a bit creaky but an ongoing renovation has been leaving a trail of comfortable, refurbished rooms. The welcome remains as warm as ever.

❧ FELIN FACH GRIFFIN // FELINFACH £££

off Map p99; ☎ 01874-620111; www.felinfachgrif fin.co.uk; s/d from £85/120; Ⓟ

There are no chintz or floral patterns here, just neutral decor with a splash of colour to set off antique four-poster beds equipped with goose-down pillows and duvets. The Griffin is 5 miles northeast of Brecon, just off the A470.

SWANSEA, THE GOWER & CARMARTHENSHIRE

SWANSEA

❧ DRAGON HOTEL // CITY CENTRE ££

Map p116; ☎ 01792-657141; www.dragon-hotel. co.uk; The Kingsway; r £69-129; Ⓟ 🖥

This 1960s city centre hotel has been given an expensive upgrade, with dragonred carpets, orange backlighting and well-turned-out bedrooms. It also has a good-sized gym and a pool.

❧ MORGANS // CITY CENTRE ££

Map p116; ☎ 01792-484848; www.morganshotel. co.uk; Somerset Pl; r £65-250; Ⓟ

The city's first boutique hotel, set in the gorgeous red-brick and Portland stone former Ports Authority building, Morgans combines historic elegance with contemporary design and a high pamper factor – Egyptian cotton bed linen, suede curtains, big bathrobes, flat-screen TVs. An annexe across the road has lower ceilings but similar standards.

❧ LEONARDO'S GUEST HOUSE // WATERFRONT £

Map p116; ☎01792-470163; www.leonardos guesthouse.co.uk; 380 Oystermouth Rd; s/d from £23/40; ☜

Leonardo's is the best in the long strip of budget seafront guesthouses on Oystermouth Rd, with small rooms in bright, sunny colours. Five of the nine bedrooms enjoy views over Swansea Bay and some have en suites.

❧ CHRISTMAS PIE B&B // UPLANDS ££

Map p116; ☎01792-480266; www.christmaspie.co.uk; 2 Mirador Cres; s/d £48/75; ℗

The name suggests something warm and comforting, and this suburban villa does not disappoint – three tastefully decorated en suite bedrooms, fresh fruit and an out-of-the-ordinary, vegetarian-friendly breakfast selection.

❧ CRESCENT GUEST HOUSE // UPLANDS ££

Map p116; ☎01792-465782; www.crescentguest house.co.uk; 132 Eaton Cres; r £65-70; ☜

The Crescent has a great location, perched on a slope with great views across the rooftops to Swansea Bay. The bedrooms are immaculate, with an antique feel, in keeping with the house, without being chintzy.

❧ MIRADOR TOWN HOUSE // UPLANDS ££

Map p116; ☎01792-466976; www.themirador.co.uk; 14 Mirador Cres; s/d from £59/69

Kooky in the extreme, all seven B&B rooms are elaborately themed – Roman, Mediterranean, African, Spanish, Egyptian, Oriental, French – with murals on the walls and sometimes the ceilings as well.

❧ PATRICKS WITH ROOMS // MUMBLES £££

☎01792-360199; www.patrickswithrooms.com; 638 Mumbles Rd; d £115-170

Patricks has 16 individually styled designer bedrooms in bold contemporary colours, with art on the walls, fluffy robes and, in some of the rooms, roll-top baths and sea views.

❧ TIDES REACH GUEST HOUSE // MUMBLES ££

☎01792-404877; www.tidesreachguesthouse.com; 388 Mumbles Rd; s/d from £50/75; ▢ ☜

Delicious eco-conscious breakfasts and stacks of local information are served with a smile at this smart waterfront guesthouse. Some rooms have sea views; our favourite is suite-like room 9, where the dormer windows open out to create a virtual deck from within the sloping roof.

GOWER PENINSULA

❧ MAES-YR-HAF // PARKMILL £££

☎01792-371000; www.maes-yr-haf.com; s/d £95/125; ℗ ☜

A boutique restaurant with smallish rooms above, boasting a stylish, contemporary feel. The rooms are a treat for gadget fans, with iPod docking stations and PlayStations that double as DVD players.

❧ PARC-LE-BREOS HOUSE // PARKMILL ££

☎01792-371636; www.parc-le-breos.co.uk; s/d £45/70; ℗ ☜

Set in its own private estate north of the main road, Parc-le-Breos offers en suite B&B accommodation in a Victorian hunting lodge. The majestic lounge and dining room downstairs have log fires in winter.

❦ CULVER HOUSE // PORT EYNON ££
☎ 01792-390755; www.culverhousehotel.co.uk; apt from £90; 🖳 🛜

A welcome change from B&Bs, this 19th-century house offers eight modern self-contained apartments with TVs that double as computers, dishwashers, laundry facilities and continental breakfasts delivered daily to your fridge.

❦ PORT EYNON YHA // PORT EYNON £
☎ 0845 371 9135; www.yha.org.uk; Old Lifeboat House; dm from £18

Worth special mention for its spectacular location, this former lifeboat station is as close as you could come to the sea without sleeping on the beach itself. It's cosier than your average youth hostel, with an attractive lounge with sea views, well stocked with board games.

❦ FAIRYHILL // REYNOLDSTON £££
☎ 01792-390139; www.fairyhill.net; s/d from £155/175; 🅿 🛜

An 18th-century country house set in extensive grounds, Fairyhill lives up to its name in terms of its location, aesthetics and holistic treatments. Dinner-inclusive rates are available for the acclaimed on-site restaurant.

❦ KING ARTHUR HOTEL // REYNOLDSTON ££
☎ 01792-390775; www.kingarthurhotel.co.uk; Higher Green; s/d from £55/65; 🅿

Downstairs there's a lovely, old-fashioned, wood-panelled bar with open fires that serves real ales and good pub grub. The bedrooms above are less atmospheric but clean and comfortable. For true romance, ask for stone-walled 18th-century Guinevere's Cottage (self-catering or B&B).

❦ KING'S HEAD // LLANGENNITH ££
☎ 01792-386212; www.kingsheadgower.co.uk; r from £85; 🅿 🛜

Up the hill behind the pub of the same name, these two stone blocks have been simply but stylishly fitted out with modern bathrooms, pale stone tiles and crimson duvet covers.

CARMARTHENSHIRE

❦ BOAT HOUSE // LAUGHARNE ££
☎ 01994-427263; www.theboathousebnb.co.uk; 1 Gosport St; s/d from £40/70; 🖳 🛜

Friendly, homely and tastefully decorated, this is the smartest B&B in town, with four superior rooms. The building was formerly the Corporation Arms pub, where Dylan Thomas told stories in exchange for free drinks. The great home-cooked breakfasts would assuage even Thomas' legendary hangovers.

❦ HURST HOUSE // LAUGHARNE £££
☎ 01994-427417; www.hurst-house.co.uk; East Marsh; r from £175; 🅿 🛜 🖳

Having had a £5 million makeover, you would expect this converted Georgian farm on the salt-marsh flats south of Laugharne to be luxurious. And it is. Rooms have big beds, bold colours and roll-top baths, and there's massage therapy on tap and a convivial, clubbish lounge bar and restaurant.

TOP **FIVE**

BOUTIQUE HOTELS

★ Morgans, Swansea (p329)

★ New White Lion, Llandovery (p332)

★ Ffynnon, Dolgellau (p339)

★ Venetia, Abersoch (p342)

★ Escape B&B, Llandudno (p344)

ACCOMMODATION

❦ KEEPERS COTTAGE //
LAUGHARNE ££
☎ 01994-427404; www.keepers-cottage.com; s/d £50/70; Ⓟ ☞

Sitting on the top of the hill by the main approach to town, this pretty cottage has simply decorated but very comfortable rooms. Complimentary bottled water and glasses of wine are a nice touch.

❦ FRONLAS // LLANDEILO ££
☎ 01558-824733; www.fronlas.com; 7 Thomas St; s/d from £80/95; Ⓟ ☞

A Victorian town house given a chic makeover, Fronlas has three rooms dressed in fresh tones, designer wallpaper and travertine marble tiles. A similarly well-attired guest lounge has an honesty bar and a DVD library.

❦ PLOUGH INN // RHOSMAEN ££
☎ 01558-823431; www.ploughrhosmaen.com; s/d from £60/80; Ⓟ ☞

On the A40, just north of Llandeilo, this baby-blue inn offers hip, contemporary rooms, some with countryside views. The standard rooms are spacious enough but the corner-hogging executives have cat-swinging space and then some.

❦ DROVERS B&B // LLANDOVERY ££
☎ 01550-721115; www.droversllandovery.co.uk; 9 Market Sq; s/d from £45/65; Ⓟ ☞

This attractive Georgian house on the town's main square has a comfortably old-fashioned feel with its ancient stone hearth, antique furniture and simply decorated bedrooms. You can take breakfast in front of a roaring fire in winter.

❦ NEW WHITE LION //
LLANDOVERY £££
☎ 01550-720685; www.newwhitelion.co.uk; 43 Stone St; s/d from £70/100; Ⓟ ☞

With its exterior an inviting chocolate-milkshake colour and its opulent interiors just shy of over-the-top, this boutique hotel is a stylish proposition indeed. There are only seven rooms, so book ahead.

PEMBROKESHIRE

SOUTH PEMBROKESHIRE

❦ CANASTON OAKS // NARBETH ££
☎ 01437-541254; www.canastonoaks.co.uk; Canaston Bridge; s/d from £70/95; ▯

Set amid 81 hectares of working farm, this luxurious B&B has four en suite rooms positioned around a Celtic cross–shaped garden. Earl Grey tea and Welsh cakes on arrival, and a Welsh dresser groaning under the weight of homemade muesli and fresh fruit for breakfast, testify to the warmth of the hospitality.

❦ ST BRIDES SPA HOTEL //
SAUNDERSFOOT £££
☎ 01834-812304; www.stbridesspahotel.com; St Bride's Hill; s/d from £135/150; Ⓟ ▣

Pembrokeshire's premier spa hotel offers the chance to relax after a massage in the infinity-edge pool overlooking the beach, before dining in the candle-lit Cliff restaurant (mains £17 to £22). The bedrooms are stylish and modern, in colours that evoke the seaside.

❦ BAY HOUSE // TENBY ££
Map p145; ☎ 01834-849015; www.bayhousetenby.co.uk; 5 Picton Rd; r from £70

A stylish, modern take on the seaside B&B, Bay House offers a relaxed, friendly atmosphere, airy rooms with flat-screen TVs and DVDs, and an emphasis on local, organic produce.

❦ IVY BANK // TENBY ££
Map p145; ☎ 01834-842311; www.ivybanktenby.co.uk; Harding St; r from £60

Swagged curtains, tasselled lamp shades and busy-patterned wallpapers are the

ACCOMMODATION

order of the day in this traditional – and very comfortable – Victorian B&B, close to the train station.

❦ LINDHOLME HOUSE // TENBY ££

Map p145; ☎ 01834-843368; www.lindholmehouse. co.uk; 27 Victoria St; s/d £30/60

A traditional B&B with friendly owners and fry-up breakfasts, salmon-hued Lindholme is a little chintzy but clean, comfy and central.

❦ MYRTLE HOUSE // TENBY ££

Map p145; ☎ 01834-842508; St Mary's St; s/d £40/64

A great location a few metres from the steps down to Castle Beach; rooms that are tastefully decorated and spacious, great breakfasts and a friendly, helpful owner make this late-Georgian house an attractive place to stay.

❦ SOUTHCLIFF HOTEL // TENBY ££

Map p145; ☎ 01834-842410; www.southcliffhotel. com; Victoria St; r from £72

Tenby has dozens of these tall, pastel-painted, Victorian B&B guesthouses. This pale-green version is one of the best, offering nine scrupulously clean, spacious rooms and a warm welcome.

❦ MANORBIER YHA // MANORBIER £

☎ 0845 371 9031; www.yha.org.uk; dm/d from £16/31; [P]

Looking like a cross between a space station and a motorway diner, this futuristic ex–Ministry of Defence building is 1.5 miles east of the village centre, close to the beach at Skrinkle Haven. It's a terrific, remote spot and the facilities are good.

❦ ST GOVAN'S COUNTRY INN // BOSHERSTON ££

☎ 01646-661643; www.stgovanscountryinn.web eden.co.uk; s/d £45/80

This friendly village pub in sleepy Bosherston has simple, bright B&B accommodation above a convivial bar decorated with hair-raising photos of rock climbs on the local sea cliffs.

❦ OLD POINT HOUSE // ANGLE ££

☎ 01646-641205; Angle Point; r £70-80; [P]

The rooms are basic and overpriced, but this 15th-century cottage pub, partly built with shipwreck timbers, has plenty of character and is a handy stop for Coast Path walkers.

❦ BEECH HOUSE // PEMBROKE £

Map p151; ☎ 01646-683740; www.beechhousepem broke.com; 78 Main St; s/d £19/37

Wearing a garland of ivy, this simple place at the western end of the main street has spick-and-span rooms with period Georgian features. It's handy to the train station and family friendly.

❦ HIGH NOON GUEST HOUSE // PEMBROKE £

Map p151; ☎ 01646-683736; www.highnoon.co.uk; Lower Lamphey Rd; s/d £25/50; [P] [≋]

Handy to Pembroke train station, and offering good value rather than atmosphere, this modern house has decent, though smallish, rooms with a pleasant garden terrace out back. The single rooms share bathrooms.

❦ PENFRO // PEMBROKE ££

Map p151; ☎ 01646-682753; www.penfro.co.uk; 111 Main St; d £65-85

Austerely elegant from the outside, this large Georgian town house is a delight inside, retaining many of its original 18th-century features, including 250-year-old glass, Georgian wood panelling, moulded plaster ceilings and period fireplaces. Rooms are not en suite, as the owner has chosen not to destroy original features.

ACCOMMODATION

☙ TREGENNA // PEMBROKE ££

off Map p151; ☎ 01646-621525; www.tregennapembroke.co.uk; 7 Upper Lamphey Rd; s/d £40/60; Ⓟ 🛜

When the treats in the room include a sewing kit, shaving kit, mini toothbrush and toothpaste, bottled water and Welsh cakes, you know you're somewhere special. It's a newly built house, so everything's modern, shiny and crisp.

☙ MARLOES SANDS YHA // MARLOES £

☎ 0845 371 9333; www.yha.org.uk; Runwayskiln; dm/d from £16/32; ☽ Easter-Oct; Ⓟ

Housed in a group of National Trust–owned farm buildings near the Coast Path above Marloes Sands, a mixture of dorms and private rooms is offered.

☙ COLLEGE GUEST HOUSE // HAVERFORDWEST ££

☎ 01437-763710; www.collegeguesthouse.com; 93 Hill St; s/d from £50/70; 🖳 🛜

Set in a spacious Georgian town house in the town centre, the College offers eight homely rooms with high ceilings and remodelled bathrooms. There's a free car park directly across the road.

NORTH PEMBROKESHIRE

☙ ALANDALE // ST DAVIDS ££

Map p159; ☎ 01437-720404; www.stdavids.co.uk/guesthouse/alandale.htm; 43 Nun St; s/d £36/80; 🖳 🛜

A neat terraced house built in the 1880s for coastguard officers, Alandale has a bright, cheerful atmosphere – ask for one of the rooms at the back, which are quieter and have sweeping countryside views.

☙ GROVE // ST DAVIDS ££

Map p159; ☎ 01437-720341; www.grovestdavids.com; High St; r/ste £95/110; Ⓟ 🛜

Offering upmarket pub accommodation, the Grove's rooms have been given a fresh, up-to-the-moment look in a recent refurbishment. Expect a bit of noise from the drinkers downstairs – pack earplugs or join in.

☙ RAMSEY HOUSE // ST DAVIDS £££

Map p159; ☎ 01437-720321; www.ramseyhouse.co.uk; Lower Moor; r £100; Ⓟ 🛜

The young owners have fashioned a fresh-looking B&B from their new house on the outskirts of town, which is still only a short stroll from the centre. The six rooms are all different but it's the kind of place where the chandeliers match the wallpaper.

☙ Y GLENNYDD // ST DAVIDS ££

Map p159; ☎ 01437-720576; www.yglennydd.co.uk; 51 Nun St; s/d £40/65; 🛜

Mixing maritime memorabilia and antique oak furniture, this 10-room guesthouse has a traditional bordering on old-fashioned feel, with smallish, unfussy bedrooms and a cosy lounge bar.

☙ OLD SCHOOL HOSTEL // TREFIN £

☎ 01348-831800; www.theoldschoolhostel.co.uk; Ffordd-yr-Afon; dm/s/d £13/20/30; 🖳 🛜

We don't mean Old School in the hip-hop sense – this actually *is* an old school building. If we were actually speaking 'street', this place would definitely be New School: it's one of a new breed of independent, brightly painted, personably run backpackers, and it's really handy to the Coast Path.

☙ MANOR TOWN HOUSE // FISHGUARD ££

Map p167; ☎ 01348-873260; www.manortownhouse.com; Main St; s/d from £45/70; 🛜

This graceful Georgian house has a lovely garden terrace where you can sit and gaze over the harbour. The young owners are charm personified and there's a generally upmarket ambience, although the decor doesn't always hit the spot.

ACCOMMODATION

❤ PENTOWER // FISHGUARD ££
Map p167; ☎01348-874462; www.pentower.co.uk;
Tower Hill; s/d £45/75; Ⓟ

Built by Sir Evan Jones, the architect who designed the harbour, this rambling home is perched on a hill at the edge of town, overlooking his creation. Rooms are spacious and romantic.

❤ CNAPAN // NEWPORT ££
☎01239-820575; www.cnapan.co.uk; East St; s/d £52/84; ⬤

Light-filled rooms and a flower-filled garden are offered at this listed Georgian town house above a popular restaurant. If you're man enough for the floral wallpaper, ask for room 4: it's bigger.

❤ GOLDEN LION HOTEL // NEWPORT ££
☎01239-820321; www.goldenlionpembrokeshire. co.uk; East St; s/d £60/85; Ⓟ ⬤

Sunny decor, golden pine furniture and colourful flower arrangements make for a warm atmosphere in this appealing country inn. It also has a snug traditional bar with a log fire, serving real ales, and a good restaurant (mains £10 to £20).

HAPPY CAMPING

Scattered all around the country, these are some of our favourite spots to pitch a tent. Unless otherwise stated, the site prices quoted are for two people with a small tent and car.

Monnow Bridge (☎01600-714004; Drybridge St; sites £11) Just across the Monnow Bridge from Monmouth town centre, this tiny site has a quiet riverside location.

Riverside (☎01873-810397; www.riversidecaravanscrickhowell.co.uk; New Rd; sites £10; ⦾ Mar-Oct) Well kept and very central, next to the Crickhowell bridge, but it can get crowded in high summer; no under 18s.

Hillend (☎01792-386204; Llangennith; sites around £20; ⦾ Easter-Oct) As close to Rhossili Bay as you can get. The on-site Eddy's Restaurant has brilliant views, and rustles up breakfast for under a fiver and dinner for £6 to £8.

Nicholaston Farm (☎01792-37109; www.nicholastonfarm.co.uk; Penmaen; sites £11-13; ⦾ Apr-Oct) A working farm that's a short walk from Tor Bay and Three Cliffs Bay.

Trevayne Farm (☎01834-813402; www.camping-pembrokeshire.co.uk; Monkstone, Saundersfoot; sites £8-12) Large clifftop field site on the Pembrokeshire Coast Path.

Caerfai Bay (☎01437-720274; www.caerfaibay.co.uk; sites £12) A 15-minute walk south of St Davids, this large site has good facilities and great coastal views across St Brides Bay.

fforest (☎01239-615286; www.coldatnight.co.uk; near Cardigan; d per week from £335) On the edge of Teifi Marshes Nature Reserve, fforest challenges the notion that camping means roughing it. Stay in large tents, tipis or geodesic domes.

Wyeside (☎01597-810183; www.wyesidecamping.co.uk; Llangurig Rd, Rhayader, Powys; sites £15) A short walk from the centre of Rhayader, this relaxed, grassy site has river views and lots of trees.

Beddgelert Forest (☎01766-890288; www.forestholidays.co.uk; sites £8-23) Well equipped and well situated, a mile west of Beddgelert on the A4085 Caernarfon road.

Swallow Falls (☎01690-710796; www.swallowfallshotel.co.uk; Betws-y-Coed; sites £12) Part of the Swallow Falls complex, which includes a pub and YHA.

Wern Isaf Farm (☎01978-860632; www.wernisaf.co.uk; Wern Rd; sites £18) A simple but welcoming family-run farm site close to Llangollen with views of Dinas Brân.

Kingsbridge (☎01248-490636; www.kingsbridgecaravanpark.co.uk; near Beaumaris, Anglesey; sites £15-19) A well-equipped site with a range of family facilities, it's also a haven for local wildlife and wildflowers.

ACCOMMODATION

☙ **LLYS MEDDYG // NEWPORT £££**
☎ 01239-820008; www.llysmeddyg.com; East St; r
£100-150; 💻 📶

This converted doctor's residence takes
contemporary big-city cool and plonks it
firmly by the seaside. Bedrooms are large
and bright, the lounge boasts leather
sofas and a period fireplace, and there's a
secluded garden at the back.

MID-WALES

CEREDIGION

☙ **LLETY TEIFI // CARDIGAN ££**
Map p179; ☎ 01239-615566; www.llety.co.uk;
Pendre; s/d from £45/70; 🅿 📶

New and stylish, this is Cardigan's
first boutique B&B and easily its best.
Breakfast is served at the much less hip
place next door belonging to the owner's
mother-in-law.

☙ **BODALWYN // ABERYSTWYTH ££**
Map p182; ☎ 01970-612578; www.bodalwyn.co.uk;
Queen's Ave; s/d from £45/65; 📶

Simultaneously upmarket and homely,
this handsome Edwardian B&B offers
tasteful rooms and a hearty cooked
breakfast (with vegetarian options). Ask
for room 3, with the bay window.

☙ **GWESTY CYMRU //**
ABERYSTWYTH ££
Wales Hotel; Map p182; ☎ 01970-612252; www.
gwestycymru.com; 19 Marine Tce; s/d from £65/85; 📶

A real gem, the Wales Hotel is a characterful boutique property with a strong
sense of Welsh identity right on the waterfront. Local slate features throughout,
paired with rich aubergine carpets.

☙ **YNYSHIR HALL // EGLWYSFACH £££**
☎ 01654-781209; www.ynyshirhall.co.uk;
r £160-395; 🅿 📶

With a 15th-century core, stately Ynyshir
was once owned by Queen Victoria and

has hosted Hollywood royalty (Richard
Gere stayed in the Vermeer room). It's
quietly opulent without being stuffy
and one of the drawing rooms is now a
Michelin-starred restaurant.

POWYS

☙ **ARDWYN HOUSE // LLANWRTYD**
WELLS ££
☎ 01591-610768; www.ardwynhouse.co.uk; Station
Rd; s/d £49/70; 🅿 📶

The young owners have been busy restoring the art-nouveau grandeur of this once
derelict house. Some rooms have claw-foot
baths and rural views, and there is oak
parquet flooring, period wallpaper and a
guest lounge with a pool table and bar.

☙ **CARLTON RIVERSIDE //**
LLANWRTYD WELLS ££
☎ 01591-610248; www.carltonriverside.com; Irfon
Cres; s £50-60, d £75-100

This upscale restaurant with rooms has a
boutique feel and a mantelpiece that positively groans under the strain of its foodie
awards. The rooms are modern, simple
and tasteful. It's well catered to bon
vivants with late breakfasts and checkouts;
ask about all-inclusive foodie breaks.

☙ **GREYHOUND HOTEL // BUILTH**
WELLS ££
☎ 01982-553255; www.thegreyhoundhotel.co.uk; 3
Garth Rd; s/d £55/80; 🅿 📶

Currently being spruced up from the top
down, this friendly local pub will soon
have a complete set of up-to-the-minute
rooms. It's at the northwest end of town
by the Wesley Methodist Church.

☙ **WOODLANDS // BUILTH WELLS £**
☎ 01982-552354; woodlandsbandb@hotmail.co.uk;
Hay Rd; s/d £35/55; 🅿

A traditional Edwardian house, this
place is set up a driveway off the A470,

half a mile east of the township. The four rooms, all en suite, offer simple home comforts at a budget price.

❧ COTTAGE // LLANDRINDOD WELLS £
Map p191; ☎ 01597-825435; www.thecottage bandb.co.uk; Spa Rd; s/d £38/58
This large, appealing Edwardian house, set in a flower-adorned garden, has comfortable rooms with heavy wooden furniture and lots of original features. Not all are en suite and the only TV is in the guest lounge.

❧ METROPOLE HOTEL // LLANDRINDOD WELLS £££
Map p191; ☎ 01597-823700; www.metropole.co.uk; Temple St; s/d from £94/120; ℗ 🛜 🏊
Dating from the town's Victorian heyday, this grand turreted inn has spacious, updated rooms and an excellent leisure complex with a swimming pool, sauna and gym.

❧ BRYNAFON WORKHOUSE // RHAYADER ££
☎ 01597-810735; www.brynafon.co.uk; South St; s/d from £46/72; ℗ 🛜
Rest assured, you won't be enduring any Dickensian treatment at this former workhouse. There's an attractive range of rooms, some with four-poster beds, some with exposed beams, but all with leafy outlooks over the River Wye and Elan Valley.

❧ OLD VICARAGE // NORTON £££
☎ 01544-260038; www.oldvicarage-nortonrads. co.uk; s/d from £78/104; ℗
A real treat in the lesser-known Welsh Marches region, this three-room gay-friendly boutique B&B features Victorian fittings, all rescued and recycled from auctions and scrapyards. It boasts an

almost womblike ambience of opulent, rich colours and perfect calm, the latter only interrupted by the chiming of antique clocks.

❧ FLEECE HOUSE // KNIGHTON ££
☎ 01547-520168; www.fleecehouse.co.uk; Market St; s/d from £45/60; ℗
Another coaching inn, this one 18th-century and situated at the top of the Narrows, Fleece House has cosy rooms with cheery quilted features. With simple facilities, it's a good base for tired walkers.

❧ HORSE & JOCKEY INN // KNIGHTON ££
☎ 01547-520062; www.thehorseandjockeyinn. co.uk; Station Rd; s/d £45/70
This former 14th-century coaching inn is still in the eating-drinking-sleeping game. The five upmarket en suite rooms have flat-screen TVs, modern fittings, ancient exposed stone walls and flash bathrooms.

❧ HIGHGATE // NEWTOWN ££
☎ 01686-623763; www.highgatebandb.co.uk; Betws Cedewain; s/d £45/75; ℗ 🛜
Fields still surround this heritage-listed half-timbered farmhouse (1651), making it a particularly bucolic retreat. The decor is understated, keeping the focus on the original oak beams and other period features. From Newtown, cross the bridge at the end of the main street, turn right, veer left at All Saints Church and continue for 2.5 miles.

❧ OLD VICARAGE DOLFOR // NEWTOWN ££
☎ 01686-629051; www.theoldvicaragedolfor.co.uk; Dolfor; s/d £65/95; ℗ 🛜
Another rural property, this one 4 miles south of Newtown by the busy A483, the Old Vicarage is tastefully decorated,

with wallpaper and claw-foot bathtubs in keeping with its Victorian vintage.

❦ ROYAL OAK HOTEL //
WELSHPOOL ££

☎01938-552217; www.royaloakhotel.info; The Cross; s/d from £60/80; ☎

By far the smartest place in Welshpool, this historic hotel sits at the very centre of town. Rooms are divided into standard (with older-style bathrooms), contemporary (colourful feature walls and new bathrooms) and classic (boutique meets antique).

❦ PLAS LLWYNGWERN //
MACHYNLLETH £

off Map p202; ☎01654-703970; www.plas-llwyngwern.com; Pantperthog; s/d from £35/55; ℗

A welcoming place located just 300 metres north of the Centre for Alternative Technology, this grand house (1750) has substantial grounds for children to run wild in. Most of the spacious bedrooms share bathrooms and the eccentric decor is encapsulated by a carpet portrait of the late Queen Mother.

❦ WYNNSTAY HOTEL //
MACHYNLLETH ££

Map p202; ☎01654-702941; www.wynnstay-hotel.com; Maengwyn St; s/d from £59/90; ℗ ☎

This erstwhile Georgian coaching inn (1780) remains the best all-rounder in town, with charming older-style rooms, one with a four-poster bed, and creaky, uneven floors. Downstairs is given over to a rustic bar-eatery.

❦ ECO RETREATS //
DYFI FOREST £££

☎01654-781375; www.ecoretreats.co.uk; d for 2 nights midweek/weekend tipi £305/339, yurt £315/359

For the ultimate get-away-from-it-all break with a green conscience, Eco Retreats offers 21ft-diameter Native American tipis and an 18ft Mongolian yurt. It's a low-tech experience, with wood burners, compost toilets and outdoor showers. Prices include tickets to the Centre for Alternative Technology (p203), reiki and a meditation session (subtract £65 for accommodation only).

STAYING IN HISTORIC BUILDINGS   *DR GREG STEVENSON*

Historic buildings make enjoyable day trips, but staying in them is an entirely more satisfying experience. If you are looking for accommodation with a difference, try the following:

Elan Valley Trust (www.elanvalley.org.uk) Has the best-preserved long house in Wales (Llannerch y Cawr), as well as the wonderfully isolated farmhouse of Tynllidiart.

Landmark Trust (www.landmarktrust.org.uk) Lets a tower in Caernarfon castle, a Victorian fort in Pembrokeshire and what is probably Britain's fanciest chicken shed at Leighton.

National Trust Cottages (www.nationaltrustcottages.co.uk) Lets Abermydyr, a Georgian estate cottage near Aberaeron designed by no less an architect than John Nash, as well as the Old Rectory at Rhossili, which is the only building above what is consistently voted as Wales' finest beach.

Portmeirion (www.portmeirion-village.com) Provides the opportunity to stay in Clough's architectural masterpiece in either self-catering cottages, the waterfront hotel or the boutique-chic Castell Deudraeth.

Under the Thatch (www.underthethatch.co.uk) Specialises in traditional thatched cottages but also lets a converted Edwardian railway carriage by the sea at Aberporth and traditional Romany caravans.

Architectural historian Dr Greg Stevenson runs the website www.underthethatch.co.uk

ACCOMMODATION

SNOWDONIA & THE LLŶN

SNOWDONIA NATIONAL PARK

❦ BRYN MAIR HOUSE //
DOLGELLAU ££

Map p212; ☎ 01341-422640; www.brynmairbedandbreakfast.co.uk; Love Lane; r £85-90; Ⓟ 🛜

Right next to Ffynnon on the wistfully monikered Love Lane, this is another impressive stone house with three comfortable B&B rooms. They're all kitted out with DVDs and iPod docks and some have sublime mountain views.

❦ FFYNNON // DOLGELLAU £££

Map p212; ☎ 01341-421774; www.ffynnontownhouse.com; Love Lane; s/d from £85/125; Ⓟ 🛜

With a keen eye for contemporary design and a super-friendly welcome, this first-rate boutique guesthouse feels both homely and stylish. French antiques are mixed in with modern chandeliers, clawfoot tubs and electronic gadgets, and there's a children's play area.

❦ Y MEIRIONNYDD // DOLGELLAU ££

Map p212; ☎ 01341-422554; www.themeirionnydd.com; Smithfield Sq; s/d £55/75; 🛜

The owners have been steadily restoring this listed Georgian town house. The bedrooms are now fully refurbished, with a hip new look complementing the roughly hewn stone walls.

❦ PENMAENUCHAF HALL //
PENMAENPOOL £££

☎ 01341-422129; www.penhall.co.uk; s/d from £95/150; Ⓟ

With imposing furnishings and elaborate gardens, this stately country-house hotel is the former pile of Bolton cotton magnate, James Leigh. The 14 rooms have a lavish old-world air but also CD players and satellite TV.

❦ RICHMOND HOUSE //
BARMOUTH ££

☎ 01341-281366; www.barmouthbedandbreakfast.co.uk; High St; s/d £55/70; Ⓟ 🖥 🛜

This handsome town house has big, contemporary rooms and an attractive garden area for summer lounging on chunky wooden furniture. Thoughtful touches include in-room DVD players and free biscuits.

❦ CASTLE COTTAGE // HARLECH £££

☎ 01766-780479; www.castlecottageharlech.co.uk; Ffordd Pen Llech; s/d from £80/120; Ⓟ 🛜

An excellent restaurant with rooms, offering spacious bedrooms in a contemporary style with exposed beams, in-room DVD players and a bowl of fresh fruit for each guest.

❦ MAELGWYN HOUSE // HARLECH ££

☎ 01766-780087; www.maelgwynharlech.co.uk; Ffordd Isaf; r £70-95; Ⓟ 🛜

A model B&B, Maelgwyn has interesting hosts, delicious breakfasts and a small set of elegant rooms stocked with DVD players, tea-making facilities and Ferrero Rocher chocolates. Full marks.

❦ ABERCELYN COUNTRY HOUSE //
BALA ££

☎ 01678-521109; www.abercelyn.co.uk; Llanycil; s/d £60/90; Ⓟ 🛜

Located on the A494, 1 mile from the centre of Bala, this former rectory (1729) is not the easiest to spot but it's worth the effort. Stylish rooms, a homely atmosphere, excellent breakfasts and a lovely setting in gardens with a gurgling brook make this a great option.

❦ BALA BACKPACKERS // BALA £

☎ 01678-521700; www.bala-backpackers.co.uk; 32 Tegid St; dm/tw from £15/45

A leap up in comfort from most of Wales' hostels, the main building has brightly painted dorms with a maximum of four single beds (it's a bunk-free zone) and newly renovated kitchen and bathrooms. Across the road in a separate building are four smartly decorated twins, some with en suites.

❦ TYDDYN LLAN // LLANDRILLO ££

☎ 01490-440264; www.tyddynllan.co.uk; r £70-140, dinner B&B £115-185; Ⓟ

For a rural escape with a foodie twist, Tyddyn Llan is hard to beat. An elegant property set among gardens in the tranquil Vale of Edeyrnion, it's a cosy bolt-hole for an off-season retreat or a flower-garlanded base for exploring North Wales in bloom. The 12 rooms each boast their own individual style, some frou-frou romantic, some shabby-chic modern. The main draw, however, is the restaurant with its new Michelin star and menu of locally sourced, seasonal fare. A real treat.

❦ AFON GWYN // BETWS-Y-COED ££

off Map p224; ☎ 01690-710442; www.guest-house-betws-y-coed.com; Coed-y-Celyn, A470; r £80-109; Ⓟ

Down in the valley, this old stone house has been skilfully converted into a grand boutique guesthouse. The decor is faultlessly tasteful, with hushed tones, white-wooden panelling, glittering chandeliers, and bathrooms bedecked in Italian tiles and marble. While all the rooms are spacious, the Alice Suite is massive.

❦ MAES-Y-GARTH // BETWS-Y-COED ££

Map p224; ☎ 01690-710441; www.maes-y-garth.co.uk; Lon Muriau, off A470; r £66-70; Ⓟ ⓦ

Just across the river and a field from the township, this completely ordinary-looking newly built home has earned itself a legion of B&B fans. Inside you'll

find a warm welcome and three quietly stylish guest rooms.

❦ TY GWYN HOTEL // BETWS-Y-COED £

Map p224; ☎ 01690-710383; www.tygwynhotel.co.uk; A5; r £52-120; Ⓟ ⓦ

Since 1636 this ex-coaching house has been welcoming guests. Its venerable age is borne out by misshapen rooms, low ceilings and exposed beams. Predictably, not all rooms have en suites.

❦ PEN-Y-GWYRD // NANT GWYNANT £

☎ 01286-870211; www.pyg.co.uk; r with/without bathroom £48/40; ☙ Jan-Oct

Eccentric but full of atmosphere, Pen-y-Gwyrd was used as a training base by the 1953 Everest team, and memorabilia from their stay includes their signatures on the dining-room ceiling. At the time of research the hotel was closed for renovations. You'll find it 5 miles southeast of Llanberis, at the junction of the A498 and A4086.

❦ PLAS TAN Y GRAIG // BEDDGELERT ££

☎ 01766-890310; www.plastanygraig.co.uk; s/d £49/78; ⓦ

This bright, friendly place is the best B&B in the heart of the village. It has seven uncluttered rooms, five with bathrooms, and a lounge full of maps and books.

❦ TANRONNEN INN // BEDDGELERT £££

☎ 01766-890347; www.tanronnen.co.uk; s/d £55/100; Ⓟ ⓦ

Following a recent refit, this traditional coaching inn has smart, albeit slightly formal rooms at the top end of the scale. It's right at the heart of the village and bar meals are available.

⚘ DOLAFON // LLANBERIS ££

☎ 01286-870993; www.dolafon.com; High St; s/d from £30/60; ℗

Set back from the road, this imposing 19th-century house offers a series of traditional rooms, most of them with en suites. The hearty breakfast includes vegetarian options and is served in the oriental-wallpapered specialty tearoom downstairs.

⚘ GLYN AFON // LLANBERIS ££

☎ 01286-872528; www.glyn-afon.co.uk; 72 High St; s/d £38/60; ℗

The recently refurbished rooms have no frills but are warm and homely at this midrange guesthouse. A hearty breakfast is assured and all dietary needs are catered for.

WEST OF SNOWDONIA

⚘ BLACK BOY INN // CAERNARFON ££

Map p234; ☎ 01286-673604; www.black-boy-inn.com; Northgate St; s/d £65/95; ℗ 🛜

Dating from 1522, the creaky but atmospheric rooms at this traditional inn have original wooden beams and panelling but a modern sensibility. It's said to be haunted.

⚘ CAER MENAI // CAERNARFON ££

Map p234; ☎ 01286-672612; www.caermenai.co.uk; 15 Church St; s/d from £40/60; 🖳 🛜

A former county school (1894), this elegant building is the biggest and brightest on the street. New owners are in the process of updating the seven en suite rooms; number 7 has sunset sea views.

⚘ TOTTERS // CAERNARFON £

Map p234; ☎ 01286-672963; www.totters.co.uk; 2 High St; dm/d/tr £15/45/60

Modern, clean and very welcoming, this excellent independent hostel is the best-value place to stay in town by a country mile. In addition to traveller-friendly facilities, the 14th-century arched basement hosts a long table that gives a sense of history to guests' free breakfasts. In addition to dorms, there's a two-bed attic apartment.

⚘ VICTORIA HOUSE // CAERNARFON ££

Map p234; ☎ 01286-678263; www.thevictoriahouse.co.uk; 15 Church St; r £50-70; 🛜

Victoria House is an exceptional four-bedroom guesthouse with a homely feel, spacious modern rooms and some nice touches, such as an impressive selection of free toiletries and a DVD on the town's history in each room.

⚘ SHIP HOTEL // ABERDARON ££

☎ 01758-760204; www.theshiphotelaberdaron.co.uk; r from £79

Renovations were rumbling on at this pub-hotel when we visited. The rooms were comfortable before, so we can only presume they'll be even better. Some have sea views.

⚘ TŶ NEWYDD // ABERDARON ££

☎ 01758-760207; www.gwesty-tynewydd.co.uk; s/d from £60/95

Right on the beach, this friendly hotel has fully refurbished, light-drenched, spacious rooms and some truly wonderful sea views. The terrace off the pub restaurant seems designed with afternoon gin and tonics in mind.

⚘ EGRYN // ABERSOCH ££

☎ 01758-712332; www.egryn.com; Lôn Sarn Bach; s/d from £55/80; ℗ 🛜

With tones as muted as Venetia's (p342) are bright, this Edwardian house has eight comfortable, modern rooms with marbled en suites and sea views from the front.

☙ VENETIA // ABERSOCH £££
☎ 01758-713354; www.venetiawales.com; Lôn Sarn Bach; r £108-148; Ⓟ

No sinking old Venetian palazzo, just five beautifully styled rooms above an excellent Italian restaurant, decked out with designer lighting and modern art. Cinque has a TV above its bathtub.

☙ PLAS BODEGROES // PWLLHELI £
☎ 01758-612363; www.bodegroes.co.uk; A497; s £50, d £55-88; Ⓟ ⓦ

Set in a stately 1780 manor house with immaculately coiffured gardens, this restaurant with rooms is a romantic option. The emphasis is on the eating, which perhaps explains why the comfortable rooms are so reasonably priced.

☙ BRON EIFION // CRICCIETH £££
☎ 01766-522385; www.broneifion.co.uk; s/d from £95/130; Ⓟ ⓦ

The former palace of a slate magnate, with fabulously formal gardens, grand old Bron Eifion has been refurbished with flat-screen TVs sitting alongside faux-gothic carvings and wooden panels. The hotel is half a mile from Criccieth, off the A497 towards Pwllheli.

☙ SEASPRAY GUEST HOUSE // CRICCIETH ££
☎ 01766-522373; www.seasprayguesthouse.co.uk; 4 Marine Tce; s/d from £40/60

A narrow lemon slice in a block of pastel four-storey town houses lining the waterfront, this old-fashioned B&B has a set of well-kept rooms, some with unimpeded sea views.

☙ YR HEN FECWS // PORTHMADOG £
Map p246; ☎ 01766-514625; www.henfecws.com; 16 Lombard St; s/d £43/55; Ⓟ

Stylishly restored, this stone cottage has seven simply decorated en suite rooms with exposed-slate walls and fireplaces.

Add £6 per person for breakfast at the excellent cafe below.

☙ GOLDEN FLEECE // TREMADOG £
off Map p246; ☎ 01766-512421; www.goldenflee ceinn.com; Market Sq; s/d £25/40; ⓦ

Above a very special pub, these budget rooms are much more comfortable and atmospheric than you'd expect for the price. Be prepared for noise until closing, or just join the party.

☙ HOTEL PORTMEIRION & CASTELL DEUDRAETH // PORTMEIRION £££
☎ 01766-70000; www.portmeirion-village.com; r £170-300

You can live the fantasy and stay within the famous fairytale village itself. The original Hotel Portmeirion (1926) has classic, elegant rooms and a dining room designed by Sir Terence Conran. Up the drive, storybook Castell Deudraeth is, perversely, a more modern alternative. Better still, there are 17 whimsical self-catering cottages on site, hired out according to a complex series of rates for weekly, weekend or midweek stays.

ANGLESEY & NORTH WALES

ISLE OF ANGLESEY

☙ CLEIFIOG B&B // BEAUMARIS ££
☎ 01248-811507; www.cleifiogbandb.co.uk; Townsend; s/d from £60/90

A charmingly dotty little gem, this artistic town house oozes character and history, and boasts superb views of the Menai Strait. Of the three rooms, all stylishly designed, Tapestry is the largest and features the original 18th-century panelling. Breakfast is served *en famille* in the downstairs parlour and, afterwards, you ask the owner about her latest needlework creations. Quirky but cool.

❤ THE TOWNHOUSE //
BEAUMARIS £££

☎ 01248-810329; www.bullsheadinn.co.uk; Castle St; s/d/ste £80/120/155; 🛜

From the team that brought you Beaumaris' stately Ye Olde Bulls Head, this funky, new little-sister property, located just across the road, provides quite a contrast. While the Bulls Head is historic and elegant, Townhouse is contemporary, high tech and design driven. The rooms are highly individual: Clementine, for example, is a Sixties pastiche of Austin Powers proportions, while Pearl is more neutral and minimalist. Breakfast and drinks are back across the road at its big sister. Groovy.

❤ YR HENDRE // HOLYHEAD ££

Map p258; ☎ 01407-762929; www.yr-hendre.net; Porth-y-Felin Rd; s/d £45/65; 🅿 🖳

A local institution, Yr Hendre remains the best place to stay in Holyhead. Professionally managed but homely, it's a welcome change from the town's recent proliferation of budget chain hotels. Rooms are elegant, some with sea views. The breakfast buffet is hearty, picnic lunches are available and pick-ups from the station and ferry are included as part of the service. No credit cards accepted.

❤ DERI ISAF // DULAS BAY ££

☎ 01248-410536; www.angleseyfarms.com/deri. htm; Dulas; s/d £36/72; 🅿

A member of a well-regarded group of farmstead B&Bs, this gloriously ramshackle Victorian country house is a real home from home. It's owned by a local farming family and, as such, the three rooms are rustic but cosy, while the gutbusting breakfast features fresh farm produce and smoked meats from the adjoining Deri Môn Smokery (p255). It's a quiet spot but the views of Dulas Bay are stunning and there's a nice touch: binoculars on the breakfast table for some mid-muesli birdwatching.

NORTH COAST & NORTHEAST WALES

❤ ERYL MÔR HOTEL //
BANGOR ££

off Map p262; ☎ 01248-353789; www.erylmorhotel. com; 2 Upper Garth Rd; s/d/f £48/75/80; 🅿 🖳

Bangor isn't exactly blessed with accommodation options but this place, while a bit stuck in the past, is the best of the bunch, notably for the superb views across the Menai Strait. The rooms are comfortable if a little dated, while the restaurant serves up simple food with decent fish mains (around £10).

❤ CASTLE HOTEL // CONWY £££

Map p265; ☎ 01492-582800; www.castlewales. co.uk; High St; s/d/ste £89/140/170; 🅿

A wind of change has been blowing through this stately old coaching inn, modernising rooms with contemporary flourishes and loosening the tie on the once stuffy ambience. The new-look rooms feature a purple and gold decor and Bose sound systems, while higher-priced rooms boast castle views and free-standing baths. Head downstairs for quality bar snacks or more formal dining.

❤ GWYNFRYN // CONWY ££

Map p265; ☎ 01492-576733; www.gwynfrynbandb. co.uk; 4 York Pl; s/d £60/80; 🛜

Gwynfryn is a great little family B&B in a refurbished, five-bedroom Victorian property just off the main square. The owners have added some nice, thoughtful touches to the rooms, such as small fridges and a DVD library, while breakfast is served in the conservatory. No children under 12.

☙ WHINWARD HOUSE // CONWY ££
off Map p265; ☎ 01492-573275; www.whinward-house.thefoxgroup.co.uk; s/d £60/70; Ⓟ 🛜

This three-room B&B, located just outside Conwy's city walls, is a cosy, homely affair. Rooms – one a warming deep red, another more floral, all en suite – feature modern touches, while more traditional is the hearty breakfast, served around a communal parlour table. A conservatory and outside decking area for summer nights, the latter with a maritime theme, add to the overall appeal. But book ahead. It's popular.

☙ ABBEY LODGE // LLANDUDNO ££
Map p268; ☎ 01492-878042; 14 Abbey Rd; s/d £45/75; Ⓟ 🛜

The owners of this well-run Victorian-style guesthouse pay close attention to detail. Hence, homely touches like the local-interest books in each of the four immaculate rooms, and marble bathrooms. They take their green policy seriously and keep the garden pristine for a summer-evening mooching.

☙ BODYSGALLEN HALL // LLANDUDNO £££
off Map p268; ☎ 01492-584466; www.bodysgallen.com; s/d hotel £145/165, cottage £150/215; Ⓟ 🛜

Three miles south of Llandudno on the A470, this stately country-house hotel and spa maintains a genteel ambience with manicured gardens and panoramic views across to Conwy Castle. The rooms, split between the Main Hall and the more secluded Cottage Suites in the grounds, are traditional with a nod to mod cons, while the fine-dining restaurant, open to nonguests, offers a decent Sunday lunch (£27 per person).

☙ ESCAPE B&B // LLANDUDNO ££
Map p268; ☎ 01492-877776; www.escapebandb.co.uk; 48 Church Walks; r £85-135; Ⓟ 🛜

Escape brought a style revolution to Llandudno with its boutique-chic ambience and magazine-spread design. It recently upped the ante again, with the rooms given a major, design-led makeover to include a host of energy-saving and trendsetting features. Even if you're not a *Wallpaper** subscriber, you'll still love the honesty-bar lounge, the DVD library, the tasty breakfasts and the atmosphere of indulgence. Unique.

☙ OSBORNE HOUSE // LLANDUDNO £££
Map p268; ☎ 01492-860330; www.osbornehouse.com; 17 North Pde; ste £150-190; Ⓟ 🖥

All marble, antique furniture and flouncy drapes, the lavish Osborne House takes a more classical approach to aesthetics, but the results are no less impressive. The best suites are on the 1st floor with Victorian-style sitting rooms and sea views. The stylish in-house restaurant serves an excellent three-course set menu (£18.50). Guests have use of spa facilities at nearby sister property, the Empire Hotel.

☙ PLAS MADOC // LLANDUDNO ££
Map p268; ☎ 01492-876514; www.plasmadocguesthouse.co.uk; 60 Church Walks; s/d £40/60; Ⓟ

At this formerly fully vegetarian, vegan and gluten-free guesthouse, the new owners have widened the remit to nonvegetarian guests, but maintained the soya milk and free-range eggs tradition for those who request it. The five cosy rooms are light and airy with lots of homely touches. No children under 10 years.

♥ ST TUDNO HOTEL //
LLANDUDNO ££
Map p268; ☎ 01492-874411; www.st-tudno.co.uk;
16 North Pde; s/d from £75/85; 🖻

This Victorian hotel on the seafront, a
stylish, boutique option with 18 individual
rooms, is closely linked to the story
of *Alice's Adventures in Wonderland* (see
p267) – check out the Alice suite. The
in-house restaurant oozes genteel sophistication
and offers a hearty Sunday lunch
(£18.50 for three courses), while the pool
and garden are nice extra touches.

♥ QUAY HOTEL & SPA //
DEGANWY £££
off Map p268; ☎ 01492-564100; www.quayhotel.
co.uk; Deganwy Quay, Deganwy; r from £175-285;
🅿 📶

High-end suites, a popular day spa and
fine dining, the latter with superb views
of Conwy Castle illuminated by night,
are the big draw at this stylish, quayside
property. It can feel a bit corporate during
the weekend but lets its hair down
at weekends with regular promotional
offers.

♥ THE KINMEL ARMS // ST GEORGE,
ABERGELE £££
☎ 01745-832207; www.thekinmelarms.co.uk; St
George; r from £135-175; 🅿 📶

The country village pub has gone gourmet.
The Kinmel Arms, located some
20 minutes drive east of Conwy, is a
rural enclave of fine food, real ales and,
now, four boutique, Alpine-style chalets.
The four units are totally self-contained
with high-end features and lots of rustic
touches. The only downside is, after a
fine dinner in the pub, the breakfast in
your fridge (included in the price) feels a
bit of a letdown.

♥ CORNERSTONES B&B //
LLANGOLLEN ££
Map p275; ☎ 01978-861569; www.cornerstones
-guesthouse.co.uk; 15 Bridge St; r £80-100; 🅿 📶

Still the best place in town, this converted
16th-century house, all sloping
floorboards and oak beams, has charm
and history. And then some. The River
Room is the cosiest of the five rooms
with the gentle lapping of the River Dee
to send you off to sleep, while The Suite
has more space and sofa beds for groups
or families. Come prepared – there's a
wine chiller in each room.

♥ HILLCREST GUESTHOUSE //
LLANGOLLEN £
off Map p275; ☎ 01978-860208; www.hillcrest
-guesthouse.com; Hill St; r from £50

Hillcrest is a traditional little B&B,
tucked away from town on the way to
Plas Newydd. Pet friendly and charmingly
traditional, it's a simple but homely
place that gets consistently good reports
from visitors for its cosy rooms, hearty
breakfast and warm welcome. On a chilly
day, settle down by the open fire in the
residents lounge with a good book. Bliss.

♥ MANORHAUS // RUTHIN ££
☎ 01824-704830; www.manorhaus.com; Well St; d
£85-150, per person half board £135-200; 📶

Borrowing from the German 'art hotel'
concept, this rambling period property
(as such, not suited to children or people
with access needs) offers eight artistically
styled rooms, each one showcasing the
works of different local and national artists.
It has a reservable steam room and a
private cinema for up to eight people but
dining is the real highlight. Don't miss
the excellent, local-produce-heavy dinner
(two/three courses £23.50/29.50).

ACCOMMODATION

DIRECTORY

BUSINESS HOURS

Wales follows the general UK conventions when it comes to opening hours, but as Great Britain moves closer to a 24-hour society, hours are extending and Sundays are no longer a day of rest.

Where reviews in this book do not list business hours, it is because they adhere to the standard hours we have identified following.

Business hours are generally 9am to 5.30pm weekdays. Banks are open from 9.30am to 5pm Monday to Friday and 9.30am to 1pm Saturday (main branches). Post offices open from 9am to 6pm Monday to Friday and 9am to 12.30pm Saturday.

Shops generally open from 9am to 5.30pm or 6pm Monday to Saturday, with an increasing number of shops also opening on Sundays from 11am to 4pm. Late-night shopping (to 8pm) is usually on Thursday or Friday nights.

Cafes tend to open from 9am to 5pm Monday to Saturday, while restaurants generally open from noon to 2pm and also 6pm to 10pm. Pubs and bars usually open at around 11am and close at 11pm (10.30pm on Sunday). Many bars in larger towns have a late licence and stay open until 2am from Thursday to Saturday.

Some businesses in small country towns still have a weekly early-closing day – it's different in each region, but is usually Tuesday, Wednesday or Thursday. However, not all shops honour it. Early closing is more common in winter.

If someone tells you a place (eg a shop, cafe or restaurant) opens daily, they nearly always mean 'daily except Sunday'.

CHILDREN

Wales is very family friendly, but, as ever when travelling with children, a bit of planning and research will help to make for a smoother ride.

Most hotels and B&Bs offer a warm welcome to families and can rustle up a baby cot or heat a bottle, but to avoid any hassle upon check-in it's best to confirm this when you book. Most cafes and midrange restaurants are very tolerant of children and can provide high chairs. Some will also warm up baby food or offer a child's portion at a reduced price. Many pubs have children's menus and gardens with playgrounds.

Baby-changing facilities are available in most supermarkets and at bigger train stations, motorway service stations and major attractions. Some trains also offer separate family carriages, where you needn't cringe when your tots enjoy themselves at high volume. If you're hiring a car and need a baby or booster seat, you need to specify this at the time of booking.

Preschool children usually get into museums and other sights for free, and those aged up to about 16 get in for one-half to two-thirds of the adult price.

A good idea is to pick up a copy (from any tourist office) of Visit Wales' free brochure *Wales: View,* which gives plenty of helpful tips and ideas for family holidays and activities.

Wales presents no major health risks for children, other than cold, wet mountains and the occasional hot, sunny beach. For more suggestions for keeping children healthy and entertained while on the road, pick up Lonely Planet's *Travel with Children* and talk to fellow travellers with kids for the best up-to-the-minute advice.

See also p24.

CUSTOMS REGULATIONS

Goods brought in and out of countries within the EU incur no additional taxes provided duty has been paid somewhere within the EU and the goods are strictly for personal consumption only. Duty-free shopping is available only if you're leaving the EU.

Travellers arriving in the UK from other EU countries can bring in up to 3200 cigarettes (only 200 cigarettes if arriving from the Czech Republic, Estonia, Hungary, Latvia, Lithuania, Poland, Slovakia or Slovenia), 400 cigarillos, 200 cigars, 3kg of smoking tobacco, 10L of spirits, 20L of fortified wine, 90L of wine and 110L of beer, provided the goods are for personal use only.

For travellers arriving from outside the EU the duty-free allowance for adults is a maximum of 200 cigarettes *or* 100 cigarillos *or* 50 cigars *or* 250g of tobacco; 2L of still table wine; 1L of spirits *or* 2L of

PRACTICALITIES

* ★ Wales uses the metric system for weights and measures. However, speed and distance are measured in miles, and pubs still pull pints.
* ★ Wales uses the PAL video system.
* ★ Electricity supply is 240V AC, 50Hz. Wales uses a three-pin square plug.
* ★ The popular *Western Mail* is Wales' only national English-language daily newspaper.
* ★ For the low-down on what's happening around the country, try the magazines *Cambria, Planet* or *Golwg* (Vision), the latter only available in Welsh.
* ★ Tune in to BBC Radio Wales (103.9FM) for English-language news and features, or BBC Radio Cymru (a range of frequencies between 103.5FM and 105FM) for the Welsh-language version.
* ★ S4C (Sianel Pedwar Cymru) is the national Welsh-language television broadcaster.

fortified wine, sparkling wine or liqueurs; 60mL of perfume; 250mL of eau de toilette; and £145 worth of all other goods (including gifts and souvenirs). Anything over this limit must be declared to customs officers. People under 17 do not get the alcohol and tobacco allowances.

For details of prohibited and restricted goods (such as meat, milk and other animal products), and quarantine regulations, see the website of **HM Customs & Excise** (www.hmrc.gov.uk).

DANGERS & ANNOYANCES

In general you'll receive a warm welcome all across Wales. The country is, overall, a pretty safe place to travel, but use your common sense when it comes to hitchhiking or walking alone in city centres at night. Traffic issues and car theft are not major concerns.

The obvious things to guard are your passport, travel documents, tickets and money. Don't leave valuables lying around in your hotel or B&B room and never leave valuables in a car, especially overnight, even in more rural locations. Look for secure parking near tourist offices and national-park visitor centres. Otherwise, while you're discovering the countryside, someone else may be exploring the contents of your glove compartment. Report thefts to the police and always ask for a statement otherwise your travel insurance company won't pay out on claims.

If you do encounter a problem, it could be inspired by alcohol. Binge drinking remains a social curse in Wales. If you're unlucky enough to encounter a brawl outside a bar or club at closing time, just give it a wide berth. Wales is increasingly cosmopolitan, but outside the main cities the population is still overwhelmingly white, and although racists are a small, uneducated minority, there have been some unpleasant incidents.

In Wales never assume that just because it's midsummer it will be warm and dry. General wetness aside, it's even more important to treat outdoor adventures in areas such as Brecon Beacons and Snowdonia National Parks with respect. Mist can drop with startling suddenness, leaving you dangerously chilled and disoriented. Never venture onto the heights without checking the weather forecast and without being sensibly clad and equipped, and always make sure someone knows where you're heading. Check mountain area forecasts in advance at the website of the **Met Office** (www.metoffice.gov.uk/loutdoor/mountainsafety).

DISCOUNT CARDS

There are several passes available to travellers that offer good value for people keen on castles, stately homes, ruined abbeys and other properties owned by Wales' two heritage trusts, Cadw (pronounced *ka*-doo; Welsh for 'to keep') and the Welsh arm of the UK-wide National Trust (NT).

Membership of one, or both, of the trusts is well worth considering, especially if you're going to be in Wales for a couple of weeks or more. Both organisations care for hundreds of spectacular sites and membership allows you to visit them for free. You can join at any staffed Cadw or NT site, by post or phone, or online. **Cadw** (☎ 0800 074 3121; www.cadw.wales.gov. uk; Freepost CF1142/9, Cardiff CF24 5GZ) One year's membership costs £34 for individuals and £57 for a family (two adults plus all children under 16). Wheelchair users and the visually impaired, together with assisting companions, are admitted free to all Cadw monuments.

National Trust (NT; ☎ 0844 800 1895; www.na
tionaltrust.org.uk; PO Box 39, Warrington WA5 7WD) One
year's membership costs £48.50 for individuals and £84.50
for a family (two adults plus all children or grandchildren
under 18). Children under five get in free at NT properties.

The **Great British Heritage Pass** (www
.britishheritagepass.com) gives free access
to almost 600 properties under the
care of Cadw, NT (and NT Scotland),
Historic Scotland and English Heritage. A 4-/7-/15-/30-day adult pass costs
£40.50/58.50/76.50/103.50 irrespective of
age, but it's available only to non-British
citizens. You can buy the pass online, and
in the UK at many international airports
and seaports and selected tourist offices.

It's also worth noting that students
carrying valid NUS (National Union of
Students) cards and people carrying a
valid **16–25 Railcard** (www.16-25railcard.
co.uk) can get discounted entrance to
many attractions across Wales.

Travellers aged 60 and over can get
50% off standard National Express bus
fares with **Routesixty** (www.nationalexpress.
com/coach/offers/routesixty.cfm; no card required)
and 30% off most rail fares with a **Senior
Railcard** (www.senior-railcard.co.uk; 1-year card
£26).Many attractions have lower admission prices for those aged over 60 or 65
(sometimes 55 for women); it's always
worth asking even if it's not posted.

If you plan to do a lot of travelling by
bus or train, there are some good-value
travel passes (see p362 and p366 respectively). Most local bus operators also
offer day and family passes.

FOOD & DRINK

The Food & Drink section on p316 has
more detailed information about eating
in Wales, while some highlights of the
burgeoning eat-local movement are presented on p16.

PRICE GUIDE

Listings for Gastronomic Highlights
throughout this book are categorised according to the following scale, based on
the cost of a main course at dinner.

£	below £8
££	£8 to £16
£££	over £16

WHERE TO EAT & DRINK

There has never been a better time to eat
out in Wales, with four Michelin-starred
chefs now working in the country, plus
a host of food festivals, farmers markets
and amazing hidden-gem delis and restaurants dotted across the entire country.
The days when you would drive into
town and find nothing more wholesome
than the local greasy spoon are – on the
whole – long gone. So put in a little effort
and you'll find places in which to sample
the very best of local food.

Pub grub remains the most convenient
and affordable option with most pubs
serving food between noon and 2pm,
and 5pm and 9pm. It can be hit-and-
miss sometimes, but mostly you get a
perfectly reasonable lunch or dinner. An
increasing number of places are championing local produce and bringing the
concept of the gastropub to Wales. The
trend for talented chefs to abandon their
urban stomping grounds, wind down a
peg or two and get closer to their ingredients is making waves in rural Wales,
and could turn your quick pit-stop lunch
into a long, lingering affair.

In larger towns and cities you'll find
switched-on bistros and restaurants serving up anything from decent to superbly
inspired food. An increasingly popular
extension of the restaurant business is
the concept of the restaurant with rooms,
whereby fine dining and a cosy bed are

generally only a staircase apart. Most of these places combine gourmet food with a small number of lovingly decorated rooms. The best bit of the restaurant-with-rooms experience? You can linger as long as you like over that final, post-prandial brandy.

For most restaurants you'll need to book ahead, particularly at the weekend, and a 10% to 15% tip is expected on top of the bill. In smaller towns, the only food available on Sunday may be the popular roast dinner served at pubs and hotel restaurants.

Continental-style cafe society is blooming all over Wales, though aesthetics vary between towns from the more twee tea-and-cake teashops to the hip hang-out coffee shops for loafers who are young, underemployed and looking for free wi-fi connections. Most places across Wales can serve up both a decent, European-style frothy coffee and an old-fashioned bacon sandwich, dripping in brown sauce. That is, of course, the best of both worlds.

Also worth looking out for is the new generation of wholefood cafes that has sprouted up in recent years, particularly around Mid-Wales and West Wales, as alternative lifestylers order in the tofu and set up shop.

When it comes to drinking in Wales, the local pub is still the social hub of the community – despite increasing concerns about the number of pubs closing in rural locations. You can buy alcohol at most supermarkets and at off-licences (liquor stores), but you'll miss out on a great part of Welsh culture if you never make it through the swinging doors and onto the sticky carpet of the village local. Welsh pubs vary enormously, from cosy watering holes with big fires and an inviting atmosphere to tough inner-city bars where solo women travellers may feel decidedly ill at ease.

Sadly, the curse of the nondescript chain bar with little character and poor beer has spread into many Welsh towns, offering cheap drinks and two-for-one meals. But it's well worth seeking out the older and more atmospheric places to get a real sense of local culture.

VEGETARIANS & VEGANS

Happily, vegetarianism has also taken off in a big way in Wales; practically every eating place, including pubs, has at least one token vegetarian dish, though don't expect it to always be inspired. Things are decidedly easier in larger towns as well as in Mid-Wales and West Wales, where alternative lifestyles continue to blossom. Many cafes in these areas are strictly vegetarian and even vegans should be able to find a decent meal. In addition to the listings throughout this book, check out www.happycow.net/europe/wales for more suggestions.

GAY & LESBIAN TRAVELLERS

In general, Wales is tolerant of homosexuality. Certainly, it's possible for people to acknowledge their homosexuality in a way that would have been unthinkable 20 years ago or more. But tolerance only goes so far, as a glance at any tabloid newspaper will confirm, and the macho image of rugby-playing Welshmen still prevails in smaller – and smaller-minded – communities.

Cardiff and Swansea both have active gay and lesbian scenes, and there are small above-the-parapet gay communities in Newport and in the university towns of Aberystwyth and Bangor, although overt displays of affection may not be wise beyond acknowledged venues. The latter two University of Wales campuses also have limited but regular social events for gay and lesbian students (and visitors), and have lesbian/gay/bisexual student officers who can be contacted for information and help.

Wales' biggest gay/lesbian/bisexual bash is the extravagant **Cardiff Mardi Gras** (www.cardiffmardigras.co.uk) held in late August or early September.

For more information try the following websites.

Diva (www.divamag.co.uk) British lesbian magazine.
Gay Times (www.gaytimes.co.uk) British gay periodical.
Gay Wales (www.gaywales.co.uk) The best Wales-specific resource, with news, events, listings and helplines.
Lesbian & Gay Switchboard (☎ 020-7837 7324; www.llgs.org.uk; ☒ 10am-11pm) London resource that can help with most enquiries.
Pink UK (www.pinkuk.com) UK-wide gay and lesbian resource.

HOLIDAYS

Most banks and businesses and a few museums and attractions are closed on public holidays. A 'bank holiday' is a weekday closure of major businesses and tends to fall on the first or last Monday of particular months. The term is used colloquially for public holidays that are not officially bank holidays.

Wales' official public holidays are:
New Year's Day 1 January
Good Friday March/April
Easter Monday March/April
May Day Bank Holiday First Monday in May
Spring Bank Holiday Last Monday in May
Summer Bank Holiday Last Monday in August
Christmas Day 25 December
Boxing Day/St Stephen's Day 26 December

If New Year's Day, Christmas Day or Boxing Day falls on a weekend, the following Monday is also a bank holiday. Most museums and attractions in Wales close on Christmas and Boxing Day but stay open for the other holidays. Exceptions are those that normally close on Sunday. Some smaller museums close on Monday and/or Tuesday.

Peak holiday times in Wales coincide with the school holidays, notably Christmas and New Year, Easter, six weeks in July and August and two mid-term breaks of a week each (one in February and one in October). During these times it's essential to book transport and accommodation in advance, and be prepared for larger crowds at the major attractions. In particular, for B&B accommodation during the August school holidays start looking for vacancies a good six months in advance. You'll be amazed just how fast things get booked up.

For information on festivals and events, see p10.

INSURANCE

However you're travelling, make sure you take out a comprehensive travel insurance policy that covers you for medical expenses, luggage theft or loss, and cancellation of (or delays in) your travel arrangements. When choosing a policy, check whether the insurance company will make payments directly to providers or reimburse you later for overseas health expenditures.

The National Health Service (NHS) provides free treatment across the UK, including Wales, and foreign nationals are entitled to register with a local doctor if staying in the UK for an extended period. EU nationals carrying the European Health Insurance Card (EHIC) may receive free treatment. However, the UK notified all European member states in 2008 that their citizens will be expected to show an EHIC in order to access necessary hospital treatment without charge. If overseas visitors are not able to do this, they will be liable for NHS charges. Any prescriptions issued will still be chargeable unless the patient is covered by one of the NHS exemptions. For more details of the scheme and how to apply for an EHIC card, visit www.nhs.uk/NHSEngland/Healthcareabroad/EHIC.

Paying for your flight tickets with a credit card often provides limited travel-accident insurance (ie it covers accidental death, loss of limbs or permanent total disablement). You may be able to reclaim the payment if the operator doesn't deliver the service, but this should not be relied on instead of a full travel-insurance policy.

Finally, it's a good idea to photocopy all your important documents (including your travel insurance policy) before you leave home. Leave one copy with someone at home and keep another with you, separate from the originals. If something does go wrong, you'll be glad you did.

For information on car insurance, see p362.

INTERNET ACCESS

If you're travelling in Wales with a laptop, or a handheld wireless device such as an iPhone, then getting online has never been easier. Many upmarket hotels, and plenty of midrange B&Bs, now offer in-room internet access via an ethernet connection or wi-fi. Increasingly, it's free to guests (sometimes password protected).

If the hotel insists on making a charge, there is an ever-increasing number of wi-fi hot spots around Wales where you can access the internet with a wi-fi-enabled laptop for free, including McDonald's restaurants, Starbucks coffee shops, and anywhere within 50m of blue-topped BT internet payphones. Search for wi-fi hot spots on www.jiwire.com.

If you don't have a laptop, the best places to check email and surf the internet are public libraries – almost every town and village in Wales has at least a couple of computer terminals devoted to the internet, and they are mostly free to use.

Internet cafes are also common in cities and larger towns, and generally charge £2 to £5 per hour. Always check the minimum charge, though, before you settle in – it's sometimes not worth the 10 minutes it takes to check your emails.

Many of the larger tourist offices across the country have internet access as well.

LEGAL MATTERS

If you are a victim of petty crime, head to the nearest police station to file a crime report. You will need this for your insurance claim. It's a good idea to take some identification with you, such as a passport.

Police have the power to detain anyone suspected of having committed an offence punishable by imprisonment (including drugs offences) for up to six hours. They can search you, take photographs and fingerprints, and question you. You are legally required to provide your correct name and address – not doing so, or giving false details, is an offence – but you are not obliged to answer any other questions.

After six hours, the police must either formally charge you or let you go. If you are detained and/or arrested, you have the right to inform a lawyer and one other person, though you have no right to actually see the lawyer or make a telephone call. If you don't know a lawyer, the police will inform the duty solicitor for you.

In the wake of September 11, the UK parliament passed the Anti-Terrorism, Crime and Security Act 2001. The legislation makes it possible for the government to detain foreigners suspected of terrorist activities, without trial. Since the London Underground and bus bombings in July 2005, further laws have been introduced.

Possession of a small amount of cannabis is an offence punishable by a fine, but possession of a larger amount of cannabis, or any amount of harder drugs, is much more serious, with a sentence of up to 14 years in prison. Police have the right to search anyone they suspect of possessing drugs.

You're allowed to have a maximum blood alcohol level of 35mg/100mL when driving. Traffic offences (illegal parking, speeding etc) often incur a fine, which you're usually given 30 to 60 days to pay. Speeding incurs a £60 fine and two penalty points if you hold a UK licence.

MAPS

Two useful countrywide maps, updated annually by **Visit Wales** (www.visitwales. co.uk), are available at nearly every tourist office. The *Wales Tourist Map* presents all major roads and major sights, national parks, towns with tourist offices (and a list of those open in winter), several town plans, and suggested car tours. The free *Wales Bus, Rail and Tourist Map and Guide* manages to map just about every bus and train route in Wales that has more than three services per week, plus the essentials of bus, train and ferry connections into Wales, as well as tables of frequencies and information numbers. Both maps will come in very handy on the ground.

Free regional transport booklets, with complete maps and timetables, are also available at tourist offices, and train stations stock free timetables provided by each train operator.

For motoring, there is a huge array of maps available. You can pick up a decent road map, such as the *AA Road Atlas Great Britain and Ireland,* at just about any motorway service station you stop at on the way through Wales. Also look for the OS Routemaster series at 1:250,000, while A to Z publishes 1:200,000 *North Wales* and *South Wales* road maps, with useful detailed town indexes.

For walkers and cyclists, it's essential to have a good map before setting off on any trip. Most tourist offices and local bookshops stock maps produced by the UK's national mapping agency, the **Ordnance Survey** (OS; www.ordnancesurvey. co.uk), which cover their regions, including the useful 1:50,000 Landranger series and the excruciatingly detailed 1:25,000 Explorer series. OS Pathfinder Walking Guides cover short walks in popular areas, and Outdoor Leisure maps cover the national parks, both at 1:25,000.

Maps can be ordered online at the OS website or from www.amazon.co.uk.

MONEY

The currency in Wales is the pound sterling (£) and Wales boasts the same major banks as the rest of the UK. There are 1p, 2p, 5p, 10p, 20p, 50p, £1 and £2 coins and £5, £10, £20 and £50 notes.

Most banks and larger post offices can change foreign currency; US dollars and euros are the easiest currencies to change. For exchange rates, see the inside front cover of this book.

Nearly all banks in Wales have ATMs linked to international systems such as

Cirrus, Maestro or Plus. However, an increasing number of ATMs, especially the ones you find in small shops and at service stations, will make a charge for withdrawal (at least £1.50). It's best to avoid these and simply seek out a regular ATM that offers free withdrawals.

Various cards, including Visa, MasterCard, American Express (Amex) and Diners Club, are widely accepted in Wales, although some smaller businesses and B&Bs may prefer payment in cash. If your credit card is lost or stolen, contact the relevant provider.

Amex (☎ 01273-696933)
Diners Club (☎ 0870 190 0011)
MasterCard (☎ 0800 964767)
Visa (☎ 0800 891725)

POST

Mail sent within the UK can go either 1st or 2nd class. First-class mail is faster (normally next-day delivery) and more expensive (from 39p for a letter up to 100g) than 2nd-class mail (from 30p); rates depend on the size and weight of the letter or packet.

Airmail postcards to European countries/rest of the world cost from 56p/62p, airmail letters (up to 60g) to European countries/rest of the world start from £1.05/£1.82, and airmail small packets (up to 60g) to European countries/rest of the world start from £1.21/£1.68. An airmail letter generally takes five days to get to the USA or Canada and a week to Australia or New Zealand.

For more information, see the **Post Office** (www.postoffice.co.uk) website.

If you don't have a permanent address in Wales, mail can be sent to poste restante in the town or city where you're staying. Amex offices hold cardholders' mail for free.

TELEPHONE

The UK uses the GSM 900/1800 mobile phone network, which covers the rest of Europe, Australia and New Zealand, but isn't compatible with the North American GSM 1900 (though some North Americans have GSM 1900/900 phones that work in the UK). If you have a GSM phone, check with your service provider about using it in the UK, and beware of calls being routed internationally (very expensive for a 'local' call).

You can also rent a mobile phone – ask at a local tourist office for details – or buy a 'pay-as-you-go' UK SIM card for as little as £10.

To dial a UK number from overseas, dial your country's international access code, then 44 (the country code for the UK), then the local number *without* the initial 0.

For useful numbers and codes see the inside front cover of this book.

TIME

All of the UK is on GMT/UTC in winter and GMT/UTC plus one hour during summer. Clocks are set forward by an hour on the last Sunday in March and set back on the last Sunday in October.

TOILETS

Public toilets can be a hit-and-miss affair, depending on how much the local council spends on their upkeep, but they are almost always of the sit-down variety and equipped with toilet paper. In major towns and cities, the public toilets are generally clean and free to use. Likewise, toilets at train stations and motorway service stations are regularly maintained and fine on the whole.

For a more luxurious loo off the beaten track, you can always stop off at a local cafe, a village pub or a rural coffee shop to use the facilities. You will be expected to buy a coffee or drink while you're there, but it's a chance to sit down and plan your route at the same time.

If you're particularly concerned about public conveniences, do some advance research at www.loo.co.uk.

TOURIST INFORMATION

You're in luck. Wales is blessed with a network of superb, government-funded tourist offices in just about every major town and city you could hope to visit, and they are staffed with friendly, knowledgeable staff. Make the tourist office your friend. It will serve you well.

Having said that, there are, of course, a few exceptions. Some of the smaller tourist offices can be less impressive; local councils are closing them down in some areas (especially around Mid-Wales); and ones attached to major tourist attractions can be murderously busy during school holidays.

Tourist offices can provide maps and brochures, and often also feature books on Welsh culture, food and mythology, OS maps for walkers, and even local art exhibitions. Staff speak English, often Welsh, and sometimes have a basic grasp of other main European languages. For specialist outdoors information, towns in and around Wales' three national parks also often boast a tourist office run by the park (which can be attached to the regular town tourist office).

Many tourist offices make local hotel and B&B reservations, sometimes for a small fee. Under the auspices of the Book-A-Bed-Ahead (BABA) scheme, you pay a £2 fee and a 10% deposit, which is then deducted from the cost of your accommodation. Some tourist offices now have limited currency-exchange services and internet access, the latter especially in more rural areas.

Visit Wales is the department for tourism within the National (Welsh) Assembly. The **Visit Wales Contact Centre** (☎ 08708-300306; info@visitwales.co.uk; 9am-5pm Mon-Fri) is your first port of call for information on holidays and short breaks in Wales.

Details of tourist offices appear in Essential Information sections at the beginning of each major city, town or area listing. For a list of web resources offering regional tourist information, see p9.

TRAVELLERS WITH DISABILITIES

For many disabled travellers, Wales is a strange mix of user-friendliness and unfriendliness. Most new buildings are wheelchair accessible, so large new hotels and modern tourist attractions are usually fine. However, most B&Bs and guesthouses have been converted from hard-to-adapt older buildings. This means that travellers with mobility problems may pay more for accommodation than their able-bodied fellows.

It's a similar story with public transport. Newer buses sometimes have steps that lower for easier access, as do trains, but it's always wise to check before setting out. Most tourist offices, tourist attractions and public buildings reserve parking spaces for the disabled near the entrance. Most tourist offices in Wales are wheelchair accessible, have counter sections at wheelchair height and provide information on accessibility in their particular area.

Many ticket offices and banks are fitted with hearing loops to assist the hearing impaired; look for the ear logo.

Visit Wales (www.visitwales.co.uk) publishes useful information on accommodation for people with disabilities in its *Where to Stay* guide, which is available at tourist offices and online.

The **National Trust** (NT; www.nationaltrust. org.uk) has its own *Access Guide* (downloadable as a PDF file) and offers free admission at all sites for companions of the disabled. **Cadw** (www.cadw.wales.gov.uk), the Welsh historic monument agency, allows wheelchair users and the visually impaired (and their companions) free entry to all monuments under its auspices.

For more information contact the following organisations:

Disability Wales (☎ 029-2088 7352; www. disabilitywales.org) The national association of disability groups in Wales is a good source of information.

Royal Association for Disability & Rehabilitation (Radar; ☎ 020-7250 3222; www.radar. org.uk) Radar publishes *Where to Stay* (formerly *Holidays in Britain and Ireland*), an annually updated guide to accessible accommodation in the UK and Ireland.

Royal National Institute for the Blind (RNIB; ☎ 0303-123 9999; www.rnib.org.uk) RNIB's holiday service provides information for the visually impaired. It also produces a guidebook of hotels recommended by visually impaired people, which is available in large print and Braille, and on tape and disc.

Shopmobility (☎ 0845-644 2446; www.shopmo bilityuk.org) UK-wide scheme under which wheelchairs and electric scooters are available in some towns at central points for access to shopping areas. The scheme is run as a charity in Cardiff; in other Welsh towns (including Swansea, Newport, Merthyr Tydfil and Wrexham) it's council-run, with modest rental fees.

Tourism for All (☎ 0845-124 9971; www.tourism forall.org.uk) A UK-based group that provides tips and information for travellers with disabilities.

VISAS

No visas are required if you arrive in Wales from within the UK. If you arrive

directly from any other country, British regulations apply.

At present, citizens of Australia, Canada, New Zealand, South Africa and the USA are given 'leave to enter' the UK at their point of arrival for up to six months, but are prohibited from working. If you're a citizen of the EU, you don't need a visa to enter the country and may live and work freely. However, visa regulations are always subject to change, so check with your local British embassy, high commission or consulate before leaving home. For more information, visit www.ukvisas.gov.uk.

To extend your stay in the UK, contact the **Home Office, Immigration & Nationality Directorate** (☎ 0870 606 7766; www.ind.homeoffice.gov.uk; Lunar House, 40 Wellesley Rd, Croydon, London CR9 2BY) *before* your existing permit expires. You'll need to send your passport with your application.

WOMEN TRAVELLERS

Women travellers shouldn't encounter any problems in Wales, though they should use common sense in larger cities, especially at night. There's nothing to stop women going into pubs alone, although not everyone likes doing this. It may cause a few curious glances or a brief conversation but in general it's very rarely a problem.

In the unlikely event you fall victim to an attack, Rape Crisis Centres can offer support. There are two in Wales:

New Pathways Rape & Sexual Abuse Support Service (☎ 01685 379310; www.new pathways.co.uk; Willow House, 57-58 Lower Thomas St, Merthyr Tydfil CF47 0DA)

Rape & Sexual Abuse Support Centre North Wales (☎ 01286 669266; PO Box 87, Caernarfon, Gwynedd LL55 9AA)

TRANSPORT

ARRIVAL & DEPARTURE

AIR

Although Cardiff has an international airport, most overseas visitors fly into London. Five international airports service the UK's capital but Heathrow is by far the biggest, serving most of the world's major airlines. It's also the closest to Wales. Manchester is handy for North Wales, while Bristol and Birmingham are also close to the Welsh border.

THINGS CHANGE...

The information in this chapter is particularly vulnerable to change. Check directly with the airline or a travel agent to make sure you understand how a fare (and ticket you may buy) works and be aware of the security requirements for international travel. Shop carefully. The details given in this chapter should be regarded as pointers and are not a substitute for your own careful, up-to-date research.

AIRLINES

Many of the airlines directly servicing Wales are budget operators, which means you might get a good deal if you're coming from one of the handful of destinations that they fly from. The following airlines fly directly into Wales:

Aer Lingus (code EI; www.aerlingus.com) Flights from Cork and Dublin.

bmibaby (code WW; www.bmibaby.com) Bargain flights from Edinburgh, Jersey, Munich, Murcia and Geneva.

Eastern Airways (code T3; www.easternairways. com) Flights from Newcastle.

flybe (code BE; www.flybe.com) Budget flights from Newcastle, Glasgow, Edinburgh, Jersey, Belfast and Paris.

KLM (code KL; www.klm.com) Flights from Amsterdam.

Manx2 (code NM; www.manx2.com) Small aircraft flying to Anglesey from Cardiff and the Isle of Man.

AIRPORTS
England
London Heathrow (code LHR; ☎ 0844 335 1801; www.heathrowairport.com) The UK's major hub welcoming flights from all over the world.

Manchester (code MAN; ☎ 08712 710 711; www.manchesterairport.co.uk) Flights from all over Europe and the Middle East, as well as some destinations in Africa, Asia, North America and Central America.

Bristol (code BRS; ☎ 0871 334 4344; www.bristolairport.co.uk) Serves a variety of UK domestic and European routes, as well as New York, Cancún (Mexico) and some African destinations.

Birmingham International (code BHX; ☎ 0844 576 6000; www.birminghamairport.co.uk) Flights from all over the world, but mainly Europe, New York and Dubai.

Wales

Cardiff (code CWL; ☎ 01446-711111; www.tbicardiffairport.com) Flights to Anglesey and UK destinations including Newcastle, Glasgow, Edinburgh, Belfast and Jersey. European destinations include Cork, Dublin, Paris, Amsterdam, Munich, Geneva and Murcia; charter flights service holiday destinations in summer.

Anglesey (code VLY; www.angleseyairport.com) Flights to Cardiff and the Isle of Man.

BUS

Compared to trains, buses are slower, (usually) cheaper and serve a greater variety of destinations. Cheapest of all are the local bus services zipping across the English border from towns such as Gloucester, Hereford and Ludlow.

ONLINE TICKETS

Cheap Flights (www.cheapflights.com)
Ebookers (www.ebookers.com)
Expedia (www.expedia.com)
Flight Centre (www.flightcentre.com)
Kayak (www.kayak.com)
Last Minute (www.lastminute.com)
Mobissimo (www.mobissimo.com)
Orbitz (www.orbitz.com)
Priceline (www.priceline.com)
STA Travel (www.statravel.com)
Travelocity (www.travelocity.com)

Coaches cover longer distances, with **National Express** (☎ 08717 81 81 78; www.nationalexpress.co.uk) operating frequent services between most major cities in the UK. From London's **Victoria Coach Station** (☎ 020-7824 0000; 164 Buckingham Palace Rd, SW1) buses head to Chepstow (£22, three hours), Cardiff (£22, 3¼ hours), Merthyr Tydfil (£24, 4¼ hours), Swansea (£26, five hours), Carmarthen (£26, 5¾ hours), Tenby (£30, 6½ hours), Pembroke (£30, seven hours), Aberystwyth (£33, seven hours), Newtown (£30, 5½ hours), Welshpool (£30, five hours), Caernarfon (£31, 10½ hours), Pwllheli (£31, 10½ hours) and Porthmadog (£31, 10 hours).

There are nine daily coaches between Bristol and Cardiff (£8, 1¼ hours), via Newport. From Birmingham there are services to Monmouth (£20, 1½ hours), Abergavenny (£12, three hours), Brecon (£27, 4¼ hours), Aberystwyth (£27, four hours), Newtown (£10, 2½ hours), Welshpool (£9.40, 2¼ hours), Caernarfon (£24, six hours), Pwllheli (£24, seven hours), Porthmadog (£24, 6½ hours) and Bangor (£27, 5¼ hours).

A daily coach heads from Edinburgh to Wrexham (£40, 12 hours), via Newcastle, Leeds and Manchester. Two daily buses head between Manchester and Llandudno (£15, four hours), via Liverpool and Prestatyn.

Megabus (www.megabus.com) has one-way fares from London to Cardiff (via Newport) from as little as £1 if you book really, really early.

Travelling by bus from Europe can be a slow, painful process and with so many cheap flights available it isn't always cost effective either. You can book a bus ticket right through to Wales via London with **Eurolines** (www.eurolines.com), Europe's largest international bus network.

CAR & MOTORCYCLE

From London, getting to Wales is a simple matter of heading west on the M4 motorway (which passes Heathrow airport) and sitting on it until you cross the impressive bridge over the River Severn.

SEA

Until the **Severn Link** (www.severnlink.com) to Swansea from Ilfracombe in Devon gets the go ahead, all direct ferry crossings to Wales are from Ireland. There are four routes: Dublin and Dun Laoghaire to Holyhead (1¼ to 3¼ hours); Rosslare to Pembroke Dock (four hours); Rosslare to Fishguard (two to 3½ hours); and Cork to Swansea (10 hours).

Fares vary considerably (depending on the season, day, time and length of stay) and some return fares don't cost much more than a one-way ticket. Typical one-way fares start from £25 for a foot passenger and from £69 for a car and driver. Bikes can be transported for around £5.

It's worth keeping an eye out for promotional fares that can reduce the cost considerably. International Student Identity Card (ISIC) holders and Hostelling International (HI) members qualify for a discount on the normal fare.

The following companies operate ferries between Ireland and Wales:

Fastnet Line (☎ 0844 576 8831; www.fastnetline.com) Ferry services from Swansea to Cork.

Irish Ferries (☎ 08717 300 400; www.irishferries.com) Ferry and fast-boat services from Dublin to Holyhead, and ferry services from Rosslare to Pembroke Dock.

Stena Line (☎ 08447 70 70 70; www.stenaline.co.uk) Ferry services from Dublin to Holyhead and fast-boat services from Dun Laoghaire to Holyhead and Rosslare to Fishguard.

FERRIES TO ENGLAND

There's a wide array of ferry services to England from Continental Europe, including services from Denmark to Harwich; from the Netherlands to Newcastle, Hull and Harwich; from Belgium to Hull and Ramsgate; from Spain to Plymouth and Portsmouth; and from France to Dover, Newhaven, Portsmouth, Poole,

TRANSPORT

CLIMATE CHANGE & TRAVEL

Every form of transport that relies on carbon-based fuel generates CO_2, the main cause of human-induced climate change. Modern travel is dependent on aeroplanes and while they might use less fuel per kilometre per person than most cars, they travel much greater distances. It's not just CO_2 emissions from aircraft that are the problem. The altitude at which aircraft emit gases (including CO_2) and particles contributes significantly to their total climate change impact. The Intergovernmental Panel on Climate Change believes aviation is responsible for 4.9% of climate change – double the effect of its CO_2 emissions alone.

Lonely Planet regards travel as a global benefit. We encourage the use of more climate-friendly travel modes where possible and, together with other concerned partners across many industries, we support the carbon offset scheme run by ClimateCare. Websites such as climatecare.org use 'carbon calculators' that allow people to offset the greenhouse gases they are responsible for with contributions to portfolios of climate-friendly initiatives throughout the developing world. Lonely Planet offsets the carbon footprint of all staff and author travel.

TRANSPORT

Weymouth and Plymouth. For details check out www.directferries.co.uk or www.ferrybooker.com.

All of these port towns are linked into the train network, allowing you to get to Wales with two or three connecting trains.

TRAIN

Fast-train services run to Cardiff from Bristol (one hour), Birmingham (two hours) and London's Paddington station (2¾ hours). Direct trains from London Paddington also stop in Newport (2½ hours) and Swansea (three hours). Other direct services head from London's Euston station to Bangor and Holyhead on the **Virgin Trains** (www.virgintrains.co.uk) West Coast Main Line.

Shrewsbury has trains to Abergavenny (1¼ hours) and is the English terminus for the **Heart of Wales Line** (www.heart-of -wales.co.uk), which cuts diagonally across Mid-Wales to Swansea (four hours) via Knighton (52 minutes), Llandrindod Wells (1½ hours), Llanwrtyd Wells (two hours), Llandovery (2¾ hours) and Llandeilo (three hours).

The **Cambrian Line** (www.thecambrianline. co.uk) from Birmingham to Aberystwyth (three hours) passes through Shrewsbury, as well as Welshpool (1½ hours), Newtown (1¾ hours) and Machynlleth (2¼ hours). From Chester there are trains to Bangor (one hour) and Holyhead (1¾ hours).

Trains in the UK are privatised and expensive in comparison to the rest of Europe. The fare structure is bewildering, but in general the cheapest tickets are those bought well in advance of the date of travel. Timetables and fares are available from **National Rail** (☎ 08457 48 49 50; www.nationalrail.co.uk) and good deals can often be found by booking online

through the National Rail–accredited **thetrainline.com** (www.thetrainline.com).

All rail connections from Continental Europe to Wales pass through the Channel Tunnel to London. The high-speed passenger service **Eurostar** (☎ in the UK 08705 186 186, in France 0892 35 35 39; www. eurostar.com) links London (St Pancras International) with Paris (Gare du Nord) or Brussels. Like National Rail, the fare structure is baffling but, in short, it pays to book early. Cheaper rail connections can be had by crossing the Channel by ferry.

GETTING AROUND

When people talk of the north-south divide in Wales, it's not just about language – part of it is physical. The barrier created by the Cambrian Mountains, Brecon Beacons and Snowdonia means that it's quicker to duck in and out of England to get from the Welshest bits of the north to the capital. The same is true by train: there's a network of lines that slowly zigzag their way through the country but the faster trains head through Bristol and Birmingham. That said, both roads and rail lines are extremely scenic. In Wales that old adage about the journey outweighing the destination is aptly demonstrated.

Wales is one of those destinations where Brits come to get back to nature, so it's extremely well set up for walkers and cyclists. With a flexible schedule and a modicum of patience it's quite possible to explore the country by public transport. However, it's worth considering hiring a car for at least part of your trip, especially if you're on a limited time frame and you're not averse to losing yourself in the sort of narrow country lanes that require pulling over when a car approaches from the other direction.

Buses are nearly always the cheapest way to get around but you'll generally get to places quicker by train. For information on services your best bet is the local tourist office, where you'll be able to pick up maps and timetables. For up-to-date information on public transport throughout Wales, check with **Traveline** (☎ 0871 200 22 33; www.traveline-cymru.info). Unfortunately, the website doesn't list prices but the **Arriva Trains Wales** (www.arrivetrainswales.co.uk) website does, as does the **National Express** (www.nationalexpress.co.uk) website.

BICYCLE

Rural Wales is a great place for cycling enthusiasts: traffic on back roads is limited; there are loads of multiuse trails and three long-distance cycling routes as part of Sustrans' **National Cycle Network** (NCN; www.sustrans.org.uk); and distances are generally short. For long-distance travel around Wales, though, the hilly and often mountainous terrain is mostly for experienced tourers.

In the larger towns and cities, there are few bike lanes and the usual problems with inconsiderate motorists. Bike theft can also be a major problem in urban areas; try to keep your bike in a secure area (many guesthouses and hotels offer secure bicycle storage).

Bikes can be taken on most trains, although there is limited space for them. On most services it's worth making a reservation for your bike at least 24 hours in advance; there is a small charge for this on some routes, but on others bikes are carried free as long as there is space available (and if there's not, you're stuck). Timetables usually have an 'R' symbol above each service on which a reservation is necessary.

Arriva Trains Wales (www.arrivatrains wales.co.uk), which operates most rail services in Wales, publishes an annual guide called *Cycling by Train*. It's also available for download from the website.

For more information on cycling around Wales, see p302.

HIRE

All large towns have bicycle shops where you can buy a bike on arrival; you may even be able to negotiate a deal for the shop to buy the bike back later.

Most sizeable or tourist towns in Wales have at least one shop where you can hire bikes for between £12 and £25 per day for a tourer and between £25 and £50 for a full-suspension mountain bike. Many hire outfits will require you to make a deposit of about £50 for a tourer and up to £100 for a top-of-the-line mean machine.

BUS

Wales' bus services are operated by dozens of private bus companies around the country, but information for them all is centralised within **Traveline Cymru** (☎ 0870 608 2608; www.traveline-cymru.org.uk), where you'll find route and timetable information. Buses are generally reasonably priced and efficient, although some have limited services (or don't run) on the weekends. Generally you'll need to hail the bus with an outstretched arm and pay the driver on board. Some buses, particularly in the cities, don't give change, so it pays to carry coins. Most fares within a region will be less than £5, while those within a city are generally less than £2.

Coaches are mainly run by **National Express** (☎ 08717 81 81 78; www.nationalexpress.co.uk), and for these you'll need to book and pay in advance. We've separated

TRANSPORT

them out from the regular bus services within the regional chapters.

Long-distance bus services are thin on the ground. These are the principal cross-regional routes, all of which operate at least Monday to Saturday throughout the year:

National Express 409 London, Birmingham, Shrewsbury, Welshpool, Newtown, Aberystwyth
X32 Bangor, Caernarfon, Dolgellau, Machynlleth, Aberystwyth
X40 Cardiff, Swansea, Carmarthen, Aberystwyth
X50 Cardigan, Aberaeron, Aberystwyth
X94 Wrexham, Llangollen, Bala, Dolgellau, Barmouth
704 Brecon, Builth Wells, Llandrindod Wells, Newtown

Apart from National Express, these are the biggest bus operators in Wales:
Arriva Cymru (☎ 0871 200 22 33; www.arriva bus.co.uk) Services in North and West Wales.
First Cymru (☎ 01792-582233; www.firstcymru. co.uk) Services in Swansea and southwest Wales.
Stagecoach (☎ 01633-485118; www.stagecoach bus.com/southwales) Services in southeast Wales.

BUS PASSES
Apart from the combined bus and rail Flexipasses (see p366), there are lots of regional and local one-day and one-week passes, but many are only worthwhile if you're planning to do a lot of travelling.

For example, the FirstWeek South & West Wales pass (adult/child £19/12) gives unlimited travel for seven days on all First bus services in South and West Wales. The FirstDay Swansea Bay pass (adult/child £4.25/2.75) gives unlimited travel for a day (on the day of purchase only) on First and Pullman buses in Swansea and the Gower Peninsula. You can buy these passes in Swansea bus station, or from the driver on any First bus.

The Snowdon Sherpa Day Ticket (adult/child £4/2) covers all of the buses zipping around Snowdonia National Park, while the Red Rover (adult/child £5.40/2.70) is valid for one day on buses 1 to 99 in Gwynedd and the Isle of Anglesey in northwest Wales, including the Snowdon Sherpas. Again, you can buy these tickets from the driver; for full details, ask at a tourist office.

If you are planning to travel throughout the United Kingdom, National Express has a variety of passes and discount cards, including options for senior travellers. More information is available online at www.nationalexpress.com.

NATIONAL PARK BUS SERVICES
Each of Wales' national park authorities runs or organises dedicated bus services aimed at walkers and cyclists travelling around the parks. Many routes include transport for bicycles. These services are described in more detail in the regional chapters.

CAR & MOTORCYCLE
If you want to see the more remote regions of Wales or cram in as much as possible in a short time, travelling by car or motorcycle is the easiest way to go. There are very few tolls (only on a couple of remote private roads) but petrol is expensive – about £1.20 per litre at the time of research.

Getting around North or South Wales is easy, but elsewhere roads are considerably slower, especially in the mountains and through Mid-Wales. To get from the northeast to the southeast, it's quickest to go via England. Rural roads are often single-track affairs with passing places only at intervals, and they can be treacherous in winter. In built-up areas be sure to check the parking restrictions as traffic wardens and clampers can be merciless.

Wales can be a dream for motorcyclists, with good-quality winding roads and stunning scenery. Just make sure your wet-weather gear is up to scratch.

If you're bringing your own vehicle from abroad, make sure you check that your insurance will cover you in the UK; third-party insurance is a minimum requirement. If you're renting a car, check the fine print – policies can vary widely and the cheapest hire rates often include an excess (for which you are liable in the event of an accident) of up to £800.

AUTOMOBILE ASSOCIATIONS

The main motoring organisations provide services such as 24-hour breakdown assistance, maps and touring information – usually for an annual fee of around £30. Others are more like clubs.

Auto-Cycle Union (☎ 01788-566400; www.acu.org.uk)

Automobile Association (AA; ☎ 0161 333 0004; www.theaa.co.uk)

Bike Tours UK (☎ 0115 846 2993; www.biketours-uk.com) For information on motorcycle touring.

Environmental Transport Association (☎ 0800 212 810; www.eta.co.uk)

Royal Automobile Club (RAC; ☎ 0800 82 82 82; www.rac.co.uk)

HIRE

Hire cars are expensive in the UK and you'll often get a better rate by taking advantage of package deals booked in advance. The best deals can generally be found on the internet. To hire a car, drivers must usually be between 23 and 65 years of age – outside these limits special conditions or insurance requirements may apply. You will also need a credit card to make an advance booking and act as a deposit.

For a compact car, expect to pay in the region of £140 a week (including insurance etc). Most cars are manual; automatic cars are available but they're generally more expensive to hire. If you need a baby chair or booster seat, specify this at the time of booking.

TRANSPORT

DISTANCE CHART (miles)

Note: Distances are approximate

	Llangollen	Holyhead	Caernarfon	Betws-y-Coed	Porthmadog	Machynlleth	Aberystwyth	Fishguard	St Davids	Tenby	Swansea	Brecon	Abergavenny	Chepstow
Holyhead	75													
Caernarfon	55	28												
Betws-y-Coed	32	43	23											
Porthmadog	50	47	20	24										
Machynlleth	51	83	56	47	40									
Aberystwyth	69	101	74	65	58	17								
Fishguard	124	155	128	119	113	72	55							
St Davids	140	171	144	135	128	88	71	16						
Tenby	140	172	144	134	129	88	70	33	34					
Swansea	130	170	143	134	127	86	70	65	72	53				
Brecon	90	145	118	109	102	61	61	86	93	74	43			
Abergavenny	106	161	134	125	118	77	76	106	113	96	48	19		
Chepstow	136	184	157	156	141	101	99	131	138	118	67	42	22	
Cardiff	132	187	160	159	114	104	104	105	112	92	42	41	32	28

TRANSPORT

Some agencies in Wales:

Alamo (☎ 0871 384 1081; www.alamo.co.uk)

Avis (☎ 0844 581 0147; www.avis.co.uk)

Budget (☎ 0844 544 3407; www.budget.co.uk)

Europcar (☎ 0871 384 9847; www.europcar.co.uk)

Hertz (☎ 0870 844 8844; www.hertz.co.uk)

Holiday Autos (☎ 0871 472 5229; www.holiday autos.co.uk)

ROAD RULES

A copy of the Highway Code can be bought in most bookshops or read online at www.direct.gov.uk/en/travelandtransport/highwaycode.

The most basic rules:

★ Drive on the left, overtake to the right.

★ When entering a roundabout, give way to the right.

★ Safety belts must be worn by the driver and all passengers.

★ Motorcyclists and their passengers must wear helmets.

★ The legal alcohol limit is 80mg of alcohol per 100mL of blood or 35mg on the breath.

★ It is illegal to use a mobile phone while driving a car unless you have a hands-free kit installed.

TAXI

You'll usually find a taxi rank outside the train station in bigger towns. The best place to find the local taxi phone number is in the local pub. In rural areas a 5-mile ride will cost around £12.

SPEED LIMITS

★ 30mph (48km/h) in built-up areas

★ 60mph (96km/h) on main roads

★ 70mph (112km/h) on motorways and dual carriageways

TRAIN

Like in the rest of the UK, the Welsh rail network has been privatised; almost all train services in Wales are run by **Arriva** (www.arrivatrainswales.co.uk), except for the London (Paddington)–Cardiff–Swansea route (operated by First Great Western) and the London (Euston)–Chester–Holyhead route (Virgin Trains).

National Rail (☎ 08457 48 49 50; www.na tionalrail.co.uk) provides centralised timetable information for all train operators in the UK, and allows you to buy tickets and make reservations by phone using a credit card. You can buy tickets online through www.thetrainline.com, though you'll need a UK address to register with the site.

To a large extent, trains along Wales' north and south coasts were built to link the English rail network with seaports at Swansea, Pembroke Dock, Fishguard and Holyhead. But there are some fine rail journeys across the middle of the country and a staggering number of 'heritage' railways (mainly steam and narrow-gauge), survivors of an earlier era. Some of these are an integral part of the network, especially the **Ffestiniog & Welsh Highland Railways** (www.festrail. co.uk), heading from Porthmadog (on the Cambrian Coast Line) to Blaenau Ffestiniog and Caernarfon respectively.

Wales' most beautiful railway journeys fan out from Shrewsbury in England: the **Heart of Wales Line** (www.heart-of-wales. co.uk) through southern Mid-Wales and the **Cambrian Line** (www.thecambrianline. co.uk) across northern Mid-Wales to Aberystwyth and its spectacular branch line up the coast and along the Llŷn. Another gem is the **Conwy Valley Line** (www.conwy. gov.uk/cvr) down through Snowdonia. Each trip is worth the fare just for the scenery and the hypnotic, clickety-clack pace.

TRAIN ROUTES

CLASSES & COSTS

There are two classes of rail travel in the UK: 1st class and what is referred to as 'standard' class. First class costs about 50% more than standard and, except on very crowded trains, simply isn't worth the extra money.

You can roll up to a station and buy a standard single (one-way) or return ticket, but this is often the dearest way to go. Each train company sets its own fares and has its own discounts, and passengers can only use tickets on services operated by the company that issued the ticket.

You might find that the same journey will have a different fare depending on whether you buy it at the station, over the phone or on the internet. The system is so bizarre that in some cases two singles are cheaper than a return ticket, and even a one-way journey can be cheaper if you split it into two (ie if you're going from A to C, it can be cheaper to buy a single from A to B, and another single from B to C; go figure). If you have the time, it's worth playing around with the various combinations on www.thetrainline.com.

The least expensive fares have advance-purchase and minimum-stay requirements, as well as limited availability. Children under five travel free; those aged between five and 15 pay half-price for most tickets. When travelling with children, it is almost always worth buying a Family & Friends Railcard (see p366).

Main fare classifications:

Advance Has limited availability so must be booked well in advance; can only be used on the specific trains booked.

Anytime Buy any time, travel any time.

Off-peak Buy any time, travel outside peak hours.

RAILCARDS

Railcards are valid for one year and entitle the holder to discounts of up to 30% on most rail (and some ferry) fares in the UK. Most train stations have application forms or you can apply online at www.railcard.co.uk; note that processing for some cards can take up to two weeks. Railcards are accepted by all train companies.

16-25 Railcard (£26) For those aged between 16 and 25, or a full-time UK student of any age.

Disabled Persons Railcard (£18) Applies to its holder and one person accompanying them.

Family & Friends Railcard (£26) A great bargain – it allows discounts for up to four adults travelling together (only one needs to hold a card and you'll need one child in tow), and a 60% discount on children's fares.

Senior Railcard (£26) For anyone aged over 60.

TRAIN PASSES

BritRail passes (available only to non-Brits and bought overseas) are not cost effective for a holiday in Wales. The following local passes, both available through National Rail, will be more useful. They allow unlimited one-day rail travel on weekdays after 9am and on all weekends and holidays.

Cambrian Coaster Day Ranger (£8.60) Pwllheli, Criccieth, Porthmadog, Harlech, Barmouth, Fairbourne, Machynlleth, Aberystwyth

Heart of Wales Circular Day Rover (£28) Circular trip in either direction: Cardiff, Shrewsbury, Knighton, Llandrindod Wells, Llanwrtyd Wells, Llandovery, Llandeilo, Swansea, Cardiff

TRAVEL PASSES

If you're planning a whirlwind tour of Wales by public transport, getting a **Flexipass** (www.walesflexipass.co.uk) is a good idea. Passes allow free travel in Wales and adjacent areas of England, on all rail routes and nearly all intercity bus routes.

The passes also get you discounts at Youth Hostels Association (YHA) hostels in Wales; free or discounted travel on heritage railways; and discounts on various sights and activities.

The passes on offer include the following:

4 in 8 Day All Wales Pass Eight days of bus travel plus four days of train travel (within that period) throughout Wales (£78).

Freedom of South Wales Flexi Rover Eight days of bus travel plus any four days of train travel (within the eight-day period) in South Wales (£54).

North & Mid-Wales Flexi Rover (£54) As above, but for North and Mid-Wales.

Passes are 50% cheaper for those aged between five and 15, and a third cheaper for those aged 16 to 25, Disabled Persons and Senior Railcard holders. Passes can be bought online, at most staffed train stations and at rail-accredited travel agencies in Wales.

LANGUAGE

You can get by almost anywhere in Wales these days without speaking Welsh. Nevertheless, anyone who's serious about getting to grips with Welsh culture will find it fun trying to speak basic Welsh.

The Welsh language belongs to the Celtic branch of the Indo-European language family. Closely related to Breton and Cornish, and more distantly to Irish, Scottish and Manx, it's the strongest Celtic language both in terms of numbers of speakers (estimated at over 700,000 in Wales) and place in society.

For more Welsh than we've included here, pick up a copy of Lonely Planet's *British Language & Culture* phrasebook.

PRONUNCIATION

All letters in Welsh are pronounced and the stress is usually on the second-last syllable. Letters are pronounced as in English, except for those listed below.

VOWELS

Vowels can be long or short. Those marked with a circumflex (eg ê) are long; those with a grave accent (eg è) short.

a	short as in 'map'; long as in 'farm'
e	short as in 'pen'; long as in 'there'
i	short as in 'bit'; long as in 'sleep'
o	short as in 'box'; long as in 'bore'
u	as i (short and long)
w	short as the 'oo' in 'book'; long as the 'oo' in 'spook'
y	as i (short or long); sometimes as the 'a' in 'about', especially in common one-syllable words like *y*, *yr*, *fy*, *dy* and *yn*

In words of one syllable, vowels followed by two consonants are short – eg *corff* (body). If a one-syllable word ends in **p**, **t**, **c**, **m** or **ng**, the vowel is short – eg *llong* (ship). If it ends in **b**, **d**, **g**, **f**, **dd**, **ff**, **th**, **ch**, or **s**, the vowel is long – eg *bad* (boat) – as is any vowel at the end of a one-syllable word, such as *pla* (plague).

In words of more than one syllable, all unstressed vowels are short, such as in the first and final vowels of *cariadon* (lovers). Stressed vowels can be long or short and in general follow the rules for vowels in monosyllables.

Welsh also has several vowel sound combinations.

ae/ai/au	as the 'y' in 'my'
aw	as the 'ow' in 'cow'
ei/eu/ey	as the 'ay' in 'day'
ew	as a short 'e' followed by 'oo'
iw/uw/yw	as the 'ew' in 'few'
oe/oi	as 'oy' in 'boy'
ow	as the 'ow' in 'tow'
wy	sometimes as 'uey' (as in 'chop suey'); sometimes as the 'wi' in 'wing' (especially after g)

CONSONANTS

The combinations ch, dd, ff, ng, ll, ph, rh and th count as single consonants.

c	always as 'k'
ch	as the 'ch' in Scottish loch
dd	as the 'th' in 'this'
ff	as the 'f' in 'fork'
g	always as the 'g' in 'garden', not as in 'gentle'
ng	as the 'ng' in 'sing'
ll	as 'hl' (put the tongue in the position for 'l' and breathe out)
ph	as 'f'
r	rolled, as in Spanish or Italian
rh	pronounced as 'hr'
s	always as in 'so', never as in 'rose'
si	as the 'sh' in 'shop'
th	always as the 'th' in 'thin'

CONVERSATION & ESSENTIALS

Hello.
  Sut mae. sit mai
Good morning.
  Bore da. bo·re dah
Good afternoon.
  Prynhawn da. pruhn·hown dah
Good evening.
  Noswaith dda. nos·waith thah
Goodnight.
  Nos da. nohs dah
See you (later).
  Wela i chi (wedyn). we·lah ee khee (we·din)

PLACE NAMES

Welsh place names are often based on words that describe a landmark or a feature of the countryside.

bach	bahkh	small
bro	broh	vale
bryn	brin	hill
caer	kair	fort
capel	ka·pl	chapel
carreg	kar·eg	stone
clwn	kloon	meadow
coed	koyd	wood/forest
cwm	koom	valley
dinas	dee·nas	hill fortress
eglwys	eglueys	church
fach	vahkh	small
fawr	vowr	big
ffordd	forth	road
glan	glahn	shore
glyn	glin	valley
isa	issa	lower
llan	hlan	church/enclosure
llyn	hlin	lake
maes	mais	field
mawr	mowr	big
mynydd	muhneeth	mountain
nant	nahnt	valley/stream
ogof	o·gov	cave
pen	pen	head/top/end
plas	plahs	hall/mansion
pont	pont	bridge
rhos	hros	moor/marsh
twr	toor	tower
tŷ	tee	house
uchaf	ikhav	upper
ynys	uh·nis	island/holm

Goodbye.
  Hwyl fawr. hueyl vowr
Please.
  Os gwelwch in dda. os gwe·lookh uhn thah
Thank you (very much).
  Diolch (in fawr iawn). dee·olkh (uhn vowr yown)
You're welcome.
  Croeso. kroy·soh
Excuse me.
  Esgusodwch fi. es·gi·so·dookh vee
Sorry./Excuse me./Forgive me.
  Mae'n ddrwg gyda fi. main throog guh·da vee
Don't mention it.
  Peidiwch â sôn. pay·dyookh ah sohn

YES & NO

How you say 'yes' and 'no' in Welsh depends on the verb used in the question. So, rather than simply 'yes', you might answer 'I do' (Ydw) or 'It is' (Ydy). Below are just a few examples.

Yes./No.	Ie./Nage.	yeh/*nah*·geh (general use when the question doesn't start with a verb)
I do./I am.	Ydw.	uh·*doo*
I don't./I'm not.	Nac ydw.	nak uh·*doo*
It is.	Ydy.	uh·*dee*
It isn't.	Nac ydy.	nak uh·*dee*
There is.	Oes.	oys
There isn't.	Nac oes.	nak oys

How are you?
  Sut ydych chi?　　sit *uh*·deekh khee
(Very) well.
  (Da) iawn.　　(dah) yown
What's your name?
  Beth yw eich enw chi?　　beth yu uhkh *e*·noo khee
My name's...
  Fy enw i yw...　　vuh *e*·noo ee yu...
Where are you from?
  O ble ydych chi'n dod?　　oh ble *uh*·deekh kheen dohd
I'm from...
  Dw i'n dod o...　　doo een dohd oh...

LANGUAGE DIFFICULTIES

I don't understand.
  Dw i ddim in deall.　　doo ee thim uhn *deh*·ahl
How do you say...?
  Sut mae dweud...?　　sit mai dwayd...
What's this called in Welsh?
  Beth yw hwn yn Gymraeg?　　beth yu hoon uhn *guhm*·raig

DAYS & MONTHS

Monday	*Dydd Llun*	deeth hleen
Tuesday	*Dydd Mawrth*	deeth mowrrth
Wednesday	*Dydd Mercher*	deeth merr·kherr
Thursday	*Dydd Iau*	deeth yigh
Friday	*Dydd Gwener*	deeth *gwe*·ner
Saturday	*Dydd Sadwrn*	deeth *sa*·doorn
Sunday	*Dydd Sul*	deeth seel

January	*Ionawr*	*yo*·nowr
February	*Chwefror*	khwev·rohr
March	*Mawrth*	mowrth
April	*Ebrill*	ehb·rihl
May	*Mai*	mai
June	*Mehefin*	me·*he*·vin
July	*Gorffennaf*	gor·*fe*·nahv
August	*Awst*	owst
September	*Medi*	me·dee
October	*Hydref*	huhd·rev
November	*Tachwedd*	tahkh·weth
December	*Rhagfyr*	hrag·vir

EATING OUT

A table for..., please.
  Bwrdd i... os gwelwch　　boordh ee... os *gwe*·lookh
  yn dda.　　uhn thah
Can I see the menu, please?
  Ga i weld y fwydlen,　　gah ee weld uh *voo*·eed·len
  os gwelwch yn dda?　　os *gwe*·lookh uhn thah
Are you serving food?
  Ydych chi'n gweini　　uh·deekh kheen *gway*·nee
  bwyd?　　bweed
What's the special of the day?
  Beth yw pryd arbennig　　beth yu preed ar·*be*·nig
  y dydd?　　uh deeth
May I have...?
  Ga i...　　gah ee...
I'd like a (half) pint of...
  Ga i (hanner o) beint o...　　gah ee (*ha*·ner oh) baynt oh...
Cheers!
  Iechyd Da!　　ye·khid dah
The bill, please.
  Y bil, os gwelwch yn dda.　　uh bil os *gwe*·lookh uhn thah

NUMBERS

0	*dim*	dim
1	*un*	een
2	*dau/dwy*	dy/duey (m/f)
3	*tri/tair*	tree/tair (m/f)
4	*pedwar/pedair*	ped·wahr/ped·air (m/f)
5	*pump*	pimp
6	*chwech*	khwekh
7	*saith*	saith
8	*wyth*	ueyth
9	*naw*	now
10	*deg*	dehg

GLOSSARY

For additional Welsh words and roots, see the Language chapter (p367). See also the Food & Drink Glossary (p320).

ap – prefix in a Welsh name meaning 'son of' (Welsh)

bridleway – path that can be used by walkers, horse riders and cyclists

Cadw – Welsh historic monuments agency (Welsh)
castell – castle (Welsh)
cromlech – burial chamber (Welsh)
Cymraeg – Welsh language (Welsh); also Gymraeg
Cymru – Wales (Welsh)

dolmen – chambered tomb

eisteddfod – literally a gathering or session; festival in which competitions are held in music, poetry, drama and the fine arts; plural eisteddfodau (Welsh)

hiraeth – sense of longing for the green, green grass of home (Welsh)

Landsker Line – boundary between Welsh-speaking and English-speaking areas in southwest Wales

Mabinogion – key source of Welsh folk legends
menhir – standing stone
merthyr – burial place of a saint (Welsh)

newydd – new (Welsh)

ogham – ancient Celtic script
oriel – gallery (Welsh)
OS – Ordnance Survey

Plaid Cymru – Party of Wales; originally Plaid Cenedlaethol Cymru (Welsh Nationalist Party)

S4C – Sianel Pedwar Cymru; national Welsh-language TV broadcaster
Sustrans – sustainable transport charity encouraging people to walk, cycle and use public transport

tre – town (Welsh)

BEHIND THE SCENES

THIS BOOK

This 4th edition of Lonely Planet's *Wales* guide was researched and written by Peter Dragicevich and David Atkinson. The previous edition was written by David Atkinson and Neil Wilson; the 2nd edition by Abigail Hole and Etain O'Carroll; and the 1st edition by John King. This guidebook was commissioned in Lonely Planet's London office, and produced by the following people:

Commissioning Editor Clifton Wilkinson
Coordinating Editors Gabrielle Stefanos, Simon Williamson
Coordinating Cartographer Andrew Smith
Coordinating Layout Designer Lauren Egan
Senior Editor Helen Christinis
Managing Editor Imogen Bannister
Managing Cartographers Alison Lyall, Herman So
Managing Layout Designers Indra Kilfoyle, Celia Wood
Assisting Editors Andrew Bain, Victoria Harrison, Helen Yeates
Assisting Cartographers Anita Banh, Julie Dodkins, Mark Griffiths, David Kemp
Cover Research Marika Mercer, lonelyplanetimages.com

THE LONELY PLANET STORY

Fresh from an epic journey across Europe, Asia and Australia in 1972, Tony and Maureen Wheeler sat at their kitchen table stapling together notes. The first Lonely Planet guidebook, *Across Asia on the Cheap*, was born.

Travellers snapped up the guides. Inspired by their success, the Wheelers began publishing books to Southeast Asia, India and beyond. Demand was prodigious, and the Wheelers expanded the business rapidly to keep up. Over the years, Lonely Planet extended its coverage to every country and into the virtual world via lonelyplanet.com and the Thorn Tree message board.

As Lonely Planet became a globally loved brand, Tony and Maureen received several offers for the company. But it wasn't until 2007 that they found a partner whom they trusted to remain true to the company's principles of travelling widely, treading lightly and giving sustainably. In October of that year, BBC Worldwide acquired a 75% share in the company, pledging to uphold Lonely Planet's commitment to independent travel, trustworthy advice and editorial independence.

Today, Lonely Planet has offices in Melbourne, London and Oakland, with over 500 staff members and 300 authors. Tony and Maureen are still actively involved with Lonely Planet. They're travelling more often than ever, and they're devoting their spare time to charitable projects. And the company is still driven by the philosophy of *Across Asia on the Cheap*: 'All you've got to do is decide to go and the hardest part is over. So go!'

SEND US YOUR FEEDBACK

We love to hear from travellers – your comments keep us on our toes and help make our books better. Our well-travelled team reads every word on what you loved or loathed about this book. Although we cannot reply individually to postal submissions, we always guarantee that your feedback goes straight to the appropriate authors, in time for the next edition. Each person who sends us information is thanked in the next edition – and the most useful submissions are rewarded with a free book.

To send us your updates – and find out about Lonely Planet events, newsletters and travel news – visit our award-winning website: **lonelyplanet.com/contact**.

Note: We may edit, reproduce and incorporate your comments in Lonely Planet products such as guidebooks, websites and digital products, so let us know if you don't want your comments reproduced or your name acknowledged. For a copy of our privacy policy visit lonelyplanet.com/privacy.

Internal Image Research Aude Vauconsant, lonelyplanetimages.com
Language Content Laura Crawford, Branislava Vladisavljevic

Thanks to Daniel Corbett, Trent Paton, Sally Schafer, Glenn van der Knjiff

THANKS

PETER DRAGICEVICH

Special thanks to Kerri Tyler for joining me for the Bala research. Also, thanks to Becky Ohlsen for use of her words on the Offa's Dyke and Glyndŵr's Way paths, and to David Atkinson and Neil Wilson whose work on the last edition formed the foundation of this book. The most entertaining nights on the road were provided by the crew at the Golden Fleece in Tremadog and the Nefyn boys in Cardiff: *lechyd da!*

DAVID ATKINSON

Diolch yn fawr to Visit Wales for their advice and assistance, especially to Ceri Jones for acting as a North Wales sounding board. Thanks also to Melanie Salisbury for her valuable input and Pip Cockeram for Anglesey tips.

OUR READERS

Many thanks to the travellers who used the last edition and wrote to us with helpful hints, useful advice and interesting anecdotes:

Daniel Alton, Wendy Barker, Martin Barlow, Kirrily Bateup, Rosemary Baxter, Don Beer, Christine Black, Ann Bowyer, Mark & Alexandra Bransby, Andrew Burton, Keith Butler, Gillon Campbell, Jane Charles, Chris Clements, Ed Cortis, Vanessa Cox, Jenni Croot, Sherrie Daley, Angela Dellebeke, Carol Duffy, William Duncan, Erwin Elands, Michael Fredericks, Jeri Gertz, Rebecca Giglia, Galina Hale, Andrew Hall, Alana Hamilton, Frederik Hansen, Gavin Harris, Anthony Hasselbach, Rosanna Hong, Helen Jewell, DS Jones, Gary Jones, Rob Laird, Roy Laverick, Emilie Lawson, Philip Leighton, Anthony Loomes, Ruth Male, Janet McGarry, Colleen McLaughlin, Jubran Moe, Tom Morgan, Diana Mortlock, John Newton, Rose O'Brien, Dennis Oliver, Martin

Oliver, David Paull, Jenny Platt, Ingrid
Pos, Charles Prothero, Ronit Ridberg,
Greer Rochford, Melissa Romeyn,
Zbigniew Sas, Ron Scott, Paul Scourfield,
Tania Sissaguian, Morgan Sleeper, Marge
Snijder, Jonathan Standing, Pamela
Stokes, Erick Strauss, Maria Symonds,
Liesbeth Tangelder-Schouten, Paul
Tennant, Mark Timperley, Nicole Travis,
Lars Udsholt, Jillis Van Nes, Ernest Van
Pomeren, Annette Vickers, Ian Walters,
Lucy Wilkins, Heather Williams,
Llywelyn Williams, Jo Winston.

ACKNOWLEDGMENTS

All images are the copyright of the photographers unless otherwise indicated.
Many of the images in this guide are
available for licensing from Lonely Planet Images: www.lonelyplanetimages.com.

**Many thanks to the following for the
use of their content:**
Iwan Llwd, Becky Ohlsen, Nona Rees,
Dr Greg Stevenson.

INDEX

INDEX

INDEX

INDEX

MAP LEGEND

Note Not all symbols displayed below appear in this guide.

ROUTES

Tollway	Tunnel
Freeway	Pedestrian Mall
Primary Road	Steps
Secondary Road	Walking Track
Tertiary Road	Walking Path
Lane	Walking Tour
Unsealed Road	Walking Tour Detour
Under Construction	Pedestrian Overpass

TRANSPORT

Ferry Route & Terminal	Train Line & Station
Metro Line & Station	Underground Rail Line
Monorail & Stop	Tram Line & Stop
Bus Route & Stop	Cable Car, Funicular

AREA FEATURES

Airport	Land
Beach	Mall, Plaza
Building	Market
Campus	Park
Cemetery, Christian	Sportsground
Cemetery, Other	Urban

HYDROGRAPHY

River, Creek	
Canal	
Water	
Swamp	
Lake (Dry)	

BOUNDARIES

International	
State, Provincial	
Suburb	
City Wall	
Cliff	

SYMBOLS IN THE KEY

Essential Information
- Tourist Office
- Police Station

Exploring
- Beach
- Buddhist
- Castle, Fort
- Christian
- Diving, Snorkelling
- Garden
- Hindu
- Islamic
- Jewish
- Monument
- Museum, Gallery
- Place of Interest
- Snow Skiing
- Swimming Pool
- Ruin
- Tomb
- Winery, Vineyard
- Zoo, Bird Sanctuary

Gastronomic Highlights
- Eating
- Cafe

Nightlife
- Drinking
- Entertainment

Recommended Shops
- Shopping

Accommodation
- Sleeping
- Camping

Transport
- Airport, Airfield
- Cycling, Bicycle Path
- Border Crossing
- Bus Station
- Ferry
- General Transport
- Train Station
- Taxi Rank

Parking
- Parking

OTHER MAP SYMBOLS

Information
- Bank, ATM
- Embassy, Consulate
- Hospital, Medical
- Internet Facilities
- Post Office
- Telephone

Geographic
- Cave
- Lighthouse
- Lookout
- Mountain, Volcano
- National Park
- Picnic Area

LONELY PLANET OFFICES

AUSTRALIA
Head Office
Locked Bag 1, Footscray, Victoria 3011
☎ 03 8379 8000, fax 03 8379 8111

USA
150 Linden St, Oakland, CA 94607
☎ 510 250 6400, toll free 800 275 8555
fax 510 893 8572

UK
2nd fl, 186 City Road, London EC1V 2NT
☎ 020 7106 2100, fax 020 7106 2101

CONTACT
talk2us@lonelyplanet.com
lonelyplanet.com/contact

Published by Lonely Planet Publications Pty Ltd
ABN 36 005 607 983
© Lonely Planet 2011
© photographers as indicated 2011
Cover photograph Harlech Castle, Chris Warren/
Corbis. **Internal title page photograph** Mt
Snowdon, Grant Dixon/Lonely Planet Images. Many
of the images in this guide are available for licensing
from Lonely Planet Images: lonelyplanetimages.com.

MIX
Paper from
responsible sources
FSC
www.fsc.org
FSC™ C021741

Although the authors and Lonely Planet have taken all reasonable care in preparing this book, we make no warranty about the
accuracy or completeness of its content and, to the maximum extent permitted, disclaim all liability arising from its use.